ISBN 978-1-365-89417-6

90000

The Bonsai Book
A Reference for Bonsai Plants & Aesthetics

Contents

1 Introduction   **1**
- 1.1 Bonsai 1
  - 1.1.1 History 2
  - 1.1.2 Cultivation and care 5
  - 1.1.3 Aesthetics 6
  - 1.1.4 Display 7
  - 1.1.5 Bonsai styles 9
  - 1.1.6 Size classifications 11
  - 1.1.7 Indoor bonsai 11
  - 1.1.8 See also 11
  - 1.1.9 References 11
  - 1.1.10 External links 13
- 1.2 Penjing 13
  - 1.2.1 History 14
  - 1.2.2 Penjing aesthetics 16
  - 1.2.3 Styles 17
  - 1.2.4 Maintenance and care 18
  - 1.2.5 See also 18
  - 1.2.6 Notes 19
  - 1.2.7 References 19
  - 1.2.8 External links 20

2 Bonsai Aesthetics   **21**
- 2.1 Bonsai aesthetics 21
  - 2.1.1 Bonsai styles 21
  - 2.1.2 General aesthetic principles 22
  - 2.1.3 General aesthetic guidelines 23
  - 2.1.4 Concrete aesthetic guidelines 24
  - 2.1.5 See also 24
  - 2.1.6 External links 25

		2.1.7	References	25
	2.2	Bonsai cultivation and care		25
		2.2.1	Sources of bonsai material	26
		2.2.2	Styling techniques	27
		2.2.3	Care	29
		2.2.4	See also	31
		2.2.5	References	31
		2.2.6	External links	32
	2.3	Bonsai styles		32
		2.3.1	Concept of styles	32
		2.3.2	Catalog of styles	35
		2.3.3	Common styles	35
		2.3.4	See also	35
		2.3.5	References	35

3 Plants Used in Bonsai (in Alphabetical Order)   37

	3.1	Acer buergerianum		37
		3.1.1	Description	37
		3.1.2	Cultivation	37
		3.1.3	References	38
		3.1.4	External links	38
	3.2	Acer campestre		38
		3.2.1	Description	38
		3.2.2	Distribution	39
		3.2.3	Ecology	39
		3.2.4	Cultivation	39
		3.2.5	*Bonsai*	39
		3.2.6	References	41
		3.2.7	Further reading	41
		3.2.8	External links	41
	3.3	Acer circinatum		41
		3.3.1	References	42
	3.4	Acer ginnala		43
		3.4.1	Description	43
		3.4.2	Taxonomy	43
		3.4.3	Cultivation and uses	43
		3.4.4	Cultivars	43
		3.4.5	References	43
		3.4.6	External links	44

CONTENTS

3.5	Acer monspessulanum	44
	3.5.1 Description	44
	3.5.2 Cultivation	44
	3.5.3 References	44
	3.5.4 External links	44
3.6	Acer palmatum	45
	3.6.1 Description	45
	3.6.2 Cultivation and uses	45
	3.6.3 References	49
	3.6.4 External links	49
3.7	Acer rubrum	49
	3.7.1 Description	50
	3.7.2 Distribution and habitat	51
	3.7.3 Ecology	52
	3.7.4 Cultivation	54
	3.7.5 Other uses	56
	3.7.6 See also	56
	3.7.7 References	56
	3.7.8 External links	57
3.8	Adenium	57
	3.8.1 Cultivation and uses	57
	3.8.2 Classification	57
	3.8.3 Common names	58
	3.8.4 References	58
	3.8.5 External links	58
3.9	Adenium arabicum	58
	3.9.1 References	58
3.10	Aesculus hippocastanum	58
	3.10.1 Description	58
	3.10.2 Etymology	58
	3.10.3 Distribution and habitat	59
	3.10.4 Uses	59
	3.10.5 Medical uses	60
	3.10.6 Other chemicals	60
	3.10.7 Anne Frank Tree	60
	3.10.8 Bonsai	60
	3.10.9 Diseases	60
	3.10.10 Gallery	61

3.10.11 See also 61

3.10.12 References 61

3.10.13 External links 62

3.11 Aesculus indica 62

    3.11.1 Description 62

    3.11.2 Distribution 62

    3.11.3 Uses 63

    3.11.4 References 63

    3.11.5 External links 63

3.12 Afrocarpus falcatus 63

    3.12.1 Description 63

    3.12.2 Biology 63

    3.12.3 Uses 64

    3.12.4 Conservation 64

    3.12.5 Gallery 64

    3.12.6 External links 64

    3.12.7 References 65

3.13 Alnus cordata 65

    3.13.1 Use 65

    3.13.2 Bonsai 66

    3.13.3 References 66

    3.13.4 External links 66

3.14 Alnus glutinosa 66

    3.14.1 Description 66

    3.14.2 Taxonomy 67

    3.14.3 Distribution and habitat 67

    3.14.4 Ecological relationships 68

    3.14.5 Cultivation and uses 68

    3.14.6 Health 69

    3.14.7 Details of Alder structure and galls 70

    3.14.8 References 71

    3.14.9 External links 72

3.15 Azalea 72

    3.15.1 Cultivation 72

    3.15.2 Classification 73

    3.15.3 Disease 73

    3.15.4 Cultural significance and symbolism 73

    3.15.5 Azalea festivals 73

CONTENTS

- 3.15.6 See also 74
- 3.15.7 References 74
- 3.15.8 External links 75
- 3.16 Berberis 75
  - 3.16.1 Description 75
  - 3.16.2 Ecology 75
  - 3.16.3 Cultivation 76
  - 3.16.4 Culinary uses 76
  - 3.16.5 Traditional medicine 76
  - 3.16.6 Other uses 76
  - 3.16.7 Gallery 76
  - 3.16.8 References 77
  - 3.16.9 External links 78
- 3.17 Birch 78
  - 3.17.1 Description 78
  - 3.17.2 Taxonomy 79
  - 3.17.3 Ecology 81
  - 3.17.4 Uses 81
  - 3.17.5 Culture 83
  - 3.17.6 See also 83
  - 3.17.7 References 83
  - 3.17.8 Sources 84
  - 3.17.9 External links 84
- 3.18 Bougainvillea glabra 84
  - 3.18.1 Description 84
  - 3.18.2 Cultivation 85
  - 3.18.3 References 85
- 3.19 Buxus 85
  - 3.19.1 Selected species 86
  - 3.19.2 Uses 88
  - 3.19.3 See also 88
  - 3.19.4 References 88
  - 3.19.5 External links 89
- 3.20 Camellia japonica 89
  - 3.20.1 Description 89
  - 3.20.2 Taxonomy 89
  - 3.20.3 History 90
  - 3.20.4 Cultivars 92

3.20.5 Cultivation 95

3.20.6 In culture and art 95

3.20.7 See also 95

3.20.8 References 95

3.20.9 External links 97

3.21 Camellia sasanqua 97

3.21.1 History and uses 97

3.21.2 See also 98

3.21.3 Citations and references 98

3.22 Carissa 98

3.22.1 Description 98

3.22.2 Fruit 99

3.22.3 Horticulture 99

3.22.4 Species 99

3.22.5 References 99

3.23 Carissa macrocarpa 99

3.23.1 Distribution 100

3.23.2 Horticultural aspects 100

3.23.3 Environmental requirements 101

3.23.4 References 101

3.23.5 External links 101

3.24 Carmona (plant) 101

3.24.1 References 101

3.24.2 External links 101

3.25 Carmona retusa 102

3.25.1 Description 102

3.25.2 Distribution and habitat 102

3.25.3 Uses 102

3.25.4 References 102

3.25.5 Sources 102

3.26 Carpinus orientalis 102

3.26.1 Description 103

3.26.2 References 103

3.27 Casuarina equisetifolia 103

3.27.1 Taxonomy 103

3.27.2 Description 103

3.27.3 Distribution and habitat 104

3.27.4 Uses 104

3.28 Cedrus 105

- 3.27.5 References 104
- 3.28.1 Description 105
- 3.28.2 Taxonomy 106
- 3.28.3 Ecology 106
- 3.28.4 Uses 106
- 3.28.5 Etymology 107
- 3.28.6 See also 107
- 3.28.7 References 107
- 3.28.8 External links 108

3.29 Cedrus atlantica 108

- 3.29.1 Description 108
- 3.29.2 Ecology 108
- 3.29.3 Cultivation and uses 108
- 3.29.4 References 109
- 3.29.5 External links 110

3.30 Cedrus libani 110

- 3.30.1 Description 110
- 3.30.2 Taxonomy 110
- 3.30.3 Distribution and habitat 111
- 3.30.4 History and symbolism 111
- 3.30.5 Uses 112
- 3.30.6 Ecology and conservation 112
- 3.30.7 Diseases and pests 112
- 3.30.8 See also 113
- 3.30.9 References 113
- 3.30.10 Bibliography 113
- 3.30.11 External links 114

3.31 Celtis 114

- 3.31.1 Description 114
- 3.31.2 Selected species 115
- 3.31.3 Uses and ecology 116
- 3.31.4 Gallery 117
- 3.31.5 Footnotes 117
- 3.31.6 References 117

3.32 Chaenomeles 118

- 3.32.1 Common names 118
- 3.32.2 Species and hybrids 118

	3.32.3 See also	119
	3.32.4 References and external links	119
	3.32.5 External links	119
3.33	Chamaecyparis obtusa	119
	3.33.1 Spreading and uses	119
	3.33.2 Chemistry	120
	3.33.3 Images	120
	3.33.4 References	121
	3.33.5 External links	121
3.34	Chamaecyparis pisifera	121
	3.34.1 Uses	121
	3.34.2 References	122
	3.34.3 External links	122
3.35	Cherry blossom	122
	3.35.1 Flower viewing	124
	3.35.2 Symbolism	125
	3.35.3 Varieties and blooming	125
	3.35.4 By country	126
	3.35.5 Culinary use	131
	3.35.6 See also	131
	3.35.7 References	131
	3.35.8 External links	133
3.36	Citrus	134
	3.36.1 History	134
	3.36.2 Taxonomy	134
	3.36.3 Description	135
	3.36.4 Cultivation	135
	3.36.5 Uses	138
	3.36.6 Sweet and sour	139
	3.36.7 Fossil record	139
	3.36.8 List of citrus fruits	139
	3.36.9 See also	143
	3.36.10 Footnotes	144
	3.36.11 References	145
	3.36.12 Further reading	145
	3.36.13 External links	145
3.37	Cornus	146
	3.37.1 Common name "dogwood"	147

	3.37.2	Characteristics	147
	3.37.3	Uses	148
	3.37.4	Classification	148
	3.37.5	Cultural references	150
	3.37.6	Etymology	150
	3.37.7	Notes	150
	3.37.8	References	151
	3.37.9	External links	151
3.38	Cycas revoluta		152
	3.38.1	Names	152
	3.38.2	Description	152
	3.38.3	Cultivation and uses	152
	3.38.4	Chemistry	153
	3.38.5	Toxicity	153
	3.38.6	References	153
	3.38.7	External links	154
3.39	Ebenopsis ebano		155
	3.39.1	Description	155
	3.39.2	Habitat and range	156
	3.39.3	Uses	156
	3.39.4	Ecology	156
	3.39.5	References	156
	3.39.6	External links	156
3.40	Ficus aurea		156
	3.40.1	Description	157
	3.40.2	Taxonomy	157
	3.40.3	Reproduction and growth	158
	3.40.4	Distribution	159
	3.40.5	Ecology	159
	3.40.6	Uses	160
	3.40.7	References	160
	3.40.8	External links	162
3.41	Ficus benjamina		162
	3.41.1	Cultivation	162
	3.41.2	Destructive roots	163
	3.41.3	Allergic Reactions	163
	3.41.4	Gallery	163
	3.41.5	References	164

- 3.41.6 Bibliography 164
- 3.42 Ficus coronata 164
  - 3.42.1 Taxonomy 164
  - 3.42.2 Description 164
  - 3.42.3 Distribution and habitat 164
  - 3.42.4 Ecology 164
  - 3.42.5 Uses 165
  - 3.42.6 References 165
  - 3.42.7 External links 165
- 3.43 Ficus microcarpa 165
  - 3.43.1 Taxonomy 165
  - 3.43.2 Distribution and habitat 166
  - 3.43.3 Ecology 166
  - 3.43.4 Cultivation 166
  - 3.43.5 References 166
  - 3.43.6 External links 167
- 3.44 Ficus neriifolia 167
  - 3.44.1 Description 167
  - 3.44.2 Taxonomy 167
  - 3.44.3 Distribution and habitat 167
  - 3.44.4 Ecology 168
  - 3.44.5 Uses 168
  - 3.44.6 References 168
- 3.45 Ficus obliqua 168
  - 3.45.1 Taxonomy 168
  - 3.45.2 Description 169
  - 3.45.3 Distribution and habitat 169
  - 3.45.4 Ecology 170
  - 3.45.5 Uses 171
  - 3.45.6 References 171
- 3.46 Ficus platypoda 173
  - 3.46.1 Taxonomy 173
  - 3.46.2 Description 173
  - 3.46.3 Distribution and habitat 173
  - 3.46.4 Ecology 173
  - 3.46.5 Uses 173
  - 3.46.6 References 174
- 3.47 Ficus retusa 174

- 3.47.1 Description 174
- 3.47.2 Notes 174
- 3.47.3 External links 174

3.48 Ficus rubiginosa 174

- 3.48.1 Taxonomy 175
- 3.48.2 Description 175
- 3.48.3 Distribution and habitat 176
- 3.48.4 Ecology 176
- 3.48.5 Cultivation 177
- 3.48.6 Notes 178
- 3.48.7 References 178
- 3.48.8 External links 180

3.49 Forsythia 180

- 3.49.1 Description 180
- 3.49.2 Species 180
- 3.49.3 Garden history 181
- 3.49.4 Cultivation and uses 181
- 3.49.5 Gallery 182
- 3.49.6 See also 182
- 3.49.7 References 182
- 3.49.8 External links 183

3.50 Fraxinus hubeiensis 183

- 3.50.1 References 183

3.51 Fuchsia 183

- 3.51.1 Taxonomy 183
- 3.51.2 Description 183
- 3.51.3 Species 184
- 3.51.4 Cultivation 188
- 3.51.5 Cultivars 188
- 3.51.6 Pests and diseases 188
- 3.51.7 Pronunciation and spelling 189
- 3.51.8 History 189
- 3.51.9 References 190
- 3.51.10 External links 191

3.52 Ginkgo biloba 191

- 3.52.1 Taxonomy and naming 192
- 3.52.2 Uses 192
- 3.52.3 Side effects 193

- 3.52.4 Cultivation 194
- 3.52.5 Palaeontology 195
- 3.52.6 Description 196
- 3.52.7 Branches 196
- 3.52.8 Leaves 197
- 3.52.9 Reproduction 197
- 3.52.10 Distribution and habitat 199
- 3.52.11 History 199
- 3.52.12 1000-year-old ginkgo at Tsurugaoka Hachimangū 200
- 3.52.13 See also 200
- 3.52.14 References 200
- 3.52.15 Bibliography 203
- 3.52.16 External links 203
- 3.53 Halleria lucida 203
  - 3.53.1 Appearance 203
  - 3.53.2 Distribution 203
  - 3.53.3 Growing *Halleria lucida* 203
  - 3.53.4 Gallery 204
  - 3.53.5 References 205
  - 3.53.6 External links 205
- 3.54 History of bonsai 205
  - 3.54.1 History 205
  - 3.54.2 See also 210
  - 3.54.3 References 210
- 3.55 Ilex mitis 212
  - 3.55.1 Appearance 212
  - 3.55.2 Distribution 213
  - 3.55.3 Growing *Ilex mitis* 213
  - 3.55.4 Pictures 213
  - 3.55.5 References 213
  - 3.55.6 External links 213
- 3.56 Ilex vomitoria 213
  - 3.56.1 Description 214
  - 3.56.2 Habitat and range 214
  - 3.56.3 Ecology 214
  - 3.56.4 Cultivation and uses 214
  - 3.56.5 See also 214
  - 3.56.6 References 215

- 3.57 Jabuticaba ... 215
  - 3.57.1 Description ... 215
  - 3.57.2 Cultural aspects ... 216
  - 3.57.3 References ... 216
  - 3.57.4 External links ... 217
- 3.58 Juniperus californica ... 217
  - 3.58.1 Distribution ... 217
  - 3.58.2 Description ... 217
  - 3.58.3 Uses ... 217
  - 3.58.4 References ... 218
  - 3.58.5 External links ... 218
- 3.59 Juniperus chinensis ... 218
  - 3.59.1 Growth ... 218
  - 3.59.2 Cultivation and uses ... 218
  - 3.59.3 References ... 219
  - 3.59.4 Further reading ... 219
- 3.60 Juniperus procumbens ... 219
  - 3.60.1 Cultivation and uses ... 220
  - 3.60.2 References ... 220
  - 3.60.3 External links ... 220
- 3.61 Juniperus squamata ... 220
  - 3.61.1 Cultivation and uses ... 220
  - 3.61.2 References and external links ... 221
- 3.62 Juniperus virginiana ... 221
  - 3.62.1 Description ... 221
  - 3.62.2 Ecology ... 222
  - 3.62.3 Uses ... 222
  - 3.62.4 Allergen ... 223
  - 3.62.5 See also ... 223
  - 3.62.6 References ... 223
  - 3.62.7 External links ... 224
- 3.63 Malus ... 224
  - 3.63.1 Description ... 224
  - 3.63.2 Cultivation ... 225
  - 3.63.3 Uses ... 226
  - 3.63.4 Species ... 226
  - 3.63.5 Cultivars ... 227
  - 3.63.6 References ... 227

- 3.63.7 External links 227
- 3.64 Olive 227
  - 3.64.1 Description 228
  - 3.64.2 Taxonomy 228
  - 3.64.3 History 229
  - 3.64.4 Symbolic connotations 229
  - 3.64.5 Oldest known olive trees 231
  - 3.64.6 Uses 232
  - 3.64.7 Cultivation 234
  - 3.64.8 Global production 237
  - 3.64.9 Nutrition 238
  - 3.64.10 Allergenic potential 238
  - 3.64.11 Image gallery 238
  - 3.64.12 See also 239
  - 3.64.13 References 239
  - 3.64.14 External links 241
- 3.65 Pemphis 242
  - 3.65.1 Habitat 242
  - 3.65.2 Range and distribution 242
  - 3.65.3 Uses 242
  - 3.65.4 Species 242
  - 3.65.5 See also 242
  - 3.65.6 References 243
- 3.66 Pemphis acidula 243
  - 3.66.1 Distribution and habitat 243
  - 3.66.2 Uses 243
  - 3.66.3 Leaves, flowers and fruits 243
  - 3.66.4 See also 243
  - 3.66.5 References 243
  - 3.66.6 External links 244
- 3.67 Pinus clausa 244
  - 3.67.1 Distribution 244
  - 3.67.2 Description 244
  - 3.67.3 Uses 244
  - 3.67.4 References 244
  - 3.67.5 External links 244
- 3.68 Pinus mugo 244
  - 3.68.1 Distribution 244

- 3.68.2 Subspecies 244
- 3.68.3 Uses 245
- 3.68.4 Invasive species 245
- 3.68.5 Gallery 245
- 3.68.6 References 246
- 3.68.7 Sources 246
- 3.68.8 External links 246
- 3.69 Pinus parviflora 246
  - 3.69.1 Gallery 246
  - 3.69.2 References 247
- 3.70 Pinus ponderosa 247
  - 3.70.1 Description 247
  - 3.70.2 Ecology and distribution 248
  - 3.70.3 Taxonomy 248
  - 3.70.4 See also 250
  - 3.70.5 References 250
  - 3.70.6 External links 252
- 3.71 Pinus rigida 252
  - 3.71.1 Distribution 252
  - 3.71.2 Description 252
  - 3.71.3 Uses 252
  - 3.71.4 Gallery 253
  - 3.71.5 References 253
  - 3.71.6 External links 253
- 3.72 Pinus strobus 253
  - 3.72.1 Distribution 253
  - 3.72.2 Description 254
  - 3.72.3 Mortality and disease 255
  - 3.72.4 Historical uses 256
  - 3.72.5 Contemporary uses 257
  - 3.72.6 Symbolism 258
  - 3.72.7 See also 258
  - 3.72.8 References 258
  - 3.72.9 External links 259
- 3.73 Pinus thunbergii 259
  - 3.73.1 Description 259
  - 3.73.2 Ecology 259
  - 3.73.3 Uses 259

Contents

- 3.73.4 Images ... 259
- 3.73.5 Notes ... 260
- 3.73.6 References ... 260
- 3.73.7 External links ... 260
- 3.74 Pinus virginiana ... 260
  - 3.74.1 Introduction ... 260
  - 3.74.2 Description ... 261
  - 3.74.3 Taxonomy ... 261
  - 3.74.4 Distribution and habitat ... 261
  - 3.74.5 Ethnobotany ... 261
  - 3.74.6 Etymology ... 261
  - 3.74.7 Uses ... 261
  - 3.74.8 Conservation ... 261
  - 3.74.9 Gallery ... 262
  - 3.74.10 References ... 262
  - 3.74.11 External links ... 262
- 3.75 Podocarpus costalis ... 262
  - 3.75.1 References ... 262
- 3.76 Podocarpus latifolius ... 263
  - 3.76.1 Appearance ... 263
  - 3.76.2 Distribution ... 264
  - 3.76.3 Human usage ... 264
  - 3.76.4 References ... 264
  - 3.76.5 External links ... 264
- 3.77 Pomegranate ... 264
  - 3.77.1 Etymology ... 265
  - 3.77.2 Description ... 265
  - 3.77.3 Cultivation ... 265
  - 3.77.4 Cultural history ... 266
  - 3.77.5 Nutrition ... 268
  - 3.77.6 Research ... 268
  - 3.77.7 Symbolism ... 269
  - 3.77.8 Gallery ... 273
  - 3.77.9 References ... 273
  - 3.77.10 Further reading ... 275
  - 3.77.11 External links ... 275
- 3.78 Portulacaria afra ... 276
  - 3.78.1 Description ... 276

	3.78.2 Distribution and habitat	276
	3.78.3 Cultivation and uses	276
	3.78.4 References	277
3.79	Portulacaria pygmaea	277
	3.79.1 Description	277
	3.79.2 References	277
3.80	Prunus serrulata	277
	3.80.1 Description	277
	3.80.2 Cultivation	277
	3.80.3 References	278
	3.80.4 Further reading	278
	3.80.5 Gallery	278
	3.80.6 External links	279
3.81	Pseudocydonia	279
	3.81.1 Uses	280
	3.81.2 See also	280
	3.81.3 References	280
3.82	Quince	280
	3.82.1 Description	280
	3.82.2 Taxonomy	281
	3.82.3 Distribution and habitat	281
	3.82.4 Pests and diseases	281
	3.82.5 Cultivation	282
	3.82.6 Cultivars	282
	3.82.7 Production	282
	3.82.8 Uses	282
	3.82.9 Cultural associations	283
	3.82.10 See also	283
	3.82.11 References	283
	3.82.12 External links	284
3.83	Rapanea melanophloeos	284
	3.83.1 Distribution	284
	3.83.2 Description	284
	3.83.3 Cultivation	284
	3.83.4 Gallery	285
	3.83.5 References	285
	3.83.6 External links	285
3.84	Rhaphiolepis indica	286

- 3.84.1 References . . . 286
- 3.85 Robinia pseudoacacia . . . 286
  - 3.85.1 History and naming . . . 286
  - 3.85.2 Distribution and invasive habit . . . 286
  - 3.85.3 Description . . . 287
  - 3.85.4 Reproduction and dispersal . . . 289
  - 3.85.5 Ecology . . . 289
  - 3.85.6 Pests . . . 290
  - 3.85.7 Uses . . . 290
  - 3.85.8 Toxicity . . . 292
  - 3.85.9 Flavonoids content . . . 292
  - 3.85.10 See also . . . 292
  - 3.85.11 References . . . 292
  - 3.85.12 External links . . . 293
- 3.86 Rosemary . . . 293
  - 3.86.1 Taxonomy . . . 293
  - 3.86.2 Description . . . 293
  - 3.86.3 Mythology . . . 294
  - 3.86.4 Usage . . . 294
  - 3.86.5 See also . . . 297
  - 3.86.6 References . . . 297
  - 3.86.7 External links . . . 297
- 3.87 Schefflera . . . 297
  - 3.87.1 Taxonomy . . . 298
  - 3.87.2 References . . . 298
  - 3.87.3 Further reading . . . 299
  - 3.87.4 External links . . . 299
- 3.88 Serissa . . . 299
  - 3.88.1 Notes . . . 299
  - 3.88.2 External links . . . 299
- 3.89 Syringa vulgaris . . . 299
  - 3.89.1 Description . . . 299
  - 3.89.2 Taxonomy and naming . . . 300
  - 3.89.3 Garden history . . . 300
  - 3.89.4 Cultivation . . . 300
  - 3.89.5 Gallery . . . 300
  - 3.89.6 References . . . 301
  - 3.89.7 External links . . . 302

CONTENTS

- 3.90 Taxodium ascendens ... 302
  - 3.90.1 Description ... 302
  - 3.90.2 Distribution ... 302
  - 3.90.3 Habitat ... 302
  - 3.90.4 References ... 302
  - 3.90.5 External links ... 303
- 3.91 Taxodium distichum ... 303
  - 3.91.1 Description ... 303
  - 3.91.2 Taxonomy ... 303
  - 3.91.3 Habitat ... 304
  - 3.91.4 Reproduction and early growth ... 305
  - 3.91.5 Ecology ... 306
  - 3.91.6 Conservation ... 307
  - 3.91.7 Cultivation and uses ... 307
  - 3.91.8 References ... 308
  - 3.91.9 External links ... 309
  - 3.91.10 See also ... 309
- 3.92 Taxus baccata ... 309
  - 3.92.1 Taxonomy and naming ... 309
  - 3.92.2 Description ... 309
  - 3.92.3 Longevity ... 310
  - 3.92.4 Significant trees ... 310
  - 3.92.5 Allergenic potential ... 311
  - 3.92.6 Toxicity ... 311
  - 3.92.7 Uses and traditions ... 311
  - 3.92.8 Conservation ... 314
  - 3.92.9 See also ... 314
  - 3.92.10 Notes ... 314
  - 3.92.11 References ... 316
  - 3.92.12 External links ... 316
- 3.93 Taxus chinensis ... 316
  - 3.93.1 References ... 317
- 3.94 Taxus cuspidata ... 317
  - 3.94.1 Uses ... 317
  - 3.94.2 Toxicity ... 317
  - 3.94.3 References ... 317
  - 3.94.4 Further reading ... 317
- 3.95 Taxus × media ... 317

	3.95.1	Taxonomy and common naming	317
	3.95.2	Description	318
	3.95.3	Toxicity	318
	3.95.4	Varieties (Cultivars)	318
	3.95.5	See also	318
	3.95.6	References	318
3.96	Tetraclinis	318
	3.96.1	Uses and symbolism	319
	3.96.2	Fossil record	319
	3.96.3	Gallery	319
	3.96.4	References	319
3.97	Ulmus alata	320
	3.97.1	Description	320
	3.97.2	Pests and diseases	320
	3.97.3	Cultivation	320
	3.97.4	Notable trees	320
	3.97.5	Cultivars	321
	3.97.6	Other uses	321
	3.97.7	Accessions	321
	3.97.8	Nurseries	321
	3.97.9	References	321
3.98	Ulmus crassifolia	322
	3.98.1	Description	322
	3.98.2	Pests and diseases	322
	3.98.3	Cultivation	322
	3.98.4	Notable trees	322
	3.98.5	Cultivars	323
	3.98.6	Hybrids	323
	3.98.7	Accessions	323
	3.98.8	Nurseries	323
	3.98.9	References	323
	3.98.10	External links	324
3.99	Ulmus parvifolia	324
	3.99.1	Description	324
	3.99.2	Wood and timber	324
	3.99.3	Taxonomy	325
	3.99.4	Pests and diseases	325
	3.99.5	Cultivation	325

- 3.99.6 Cultivars ... 325
- 3.99.7 Accessions ... 326
- 3.99.8 Nurseries ... 327
- 3.99.9 References ... 327
- 3.99.10 External links ... 327
- 3.100 Ulmus parvifolia 'Catlin' ... 327
  - 3.100.1 Description ... 328
  - 3.100.2 Cultivation ... 328
  - 3.100.3 Accessions ... 328
  - 3.100.4 Nurseries ... 328
  - 3.100.5 References ... 328
  - 3.100.6 External links ... 328
- 3.101 Wisteria floribunda ... 328
  - 3.101.1 *Wisteria floribunda* cultivars ... 329
  - 3.101.2 External links ... 329
  - 3.101.3 References ... 329
- 3.102 Wisteria sinensis ... 329
  - 3.102.1 Gallery ... 330
  - 3.102.2 References ... 330
  - 3.102.3 Further reading ... 330
  - 3.102.4 External links ... 331
- 3.103 Zelkova serrata ... 331
  - 3.103.1 Description ... 331
  - 3.103.2 Cultivation ... 332
  - 3.103.3 Threats ... 332
  - 3.103.4 Cultivation and uses ... 332
  - 3.103.5 Suppliers ... 333
  - 3.103.6 Gallery ... 333
  - 3.103.7 References ... 333
  - 3.103.8 External links ... 333
- 3.104 Zoysia 'Emerald' ... 334
  - 3.104.1 Adaptation and characteristics ... 334
  - 3.104.2 Care and maintenance ... 334
  - 3.104.3 References ... 334

4 Text and image sources, contributors, and licenses ... **335**
- 4.1 Text ... 335
- 4.2 Images ... 353
- 4.3 Content license ... 381

Chapter 1

Introduction

1.1 Bonsai

For other uses, see Bonsai (disambiguation).
Not to be confused with Banzai (disambiguation).
Bonsai (盆栽, "tray planting" ◀) pronunciation)[*][1] is

Acer buergerianum

Bonsai at the Omiya Bonsai Art Museum

Bonsai at the National Bonsai & Penjing Museum at the United States National Arboretum

Japanese white pine from the National Bonsai & Penjing Museum at the United States National Arboretum.

a Japanese art form using trees grown in containers. Similar practices exist in other cultures, including the Chinese tradition of *penjing* from which the art originated, and the miniature living landscapes of Vietnamese *hòn non bộ*. The Japanese tradition dates back over a thousand years. "Bonsai" is a Japanese pronunciation of the earlier Chinese term *penzai*. The word *bonsai* is often used in English as an umbrella term for all miniature trees in containers or pots.

The purposes of bonsai are primarily contemplation (for the viewer) and the pleasant exercise of effort and ingenuity (for the grower).*[2] By contrast with other plant cultivation practices, bonsai is not intended for production of food or for medicine. Instead, bonsai practice focuses on long-term cultivation and shaping of one or more small trees growing in a container.

A bonsai is created beginning with a specimen of source material. This may be a cutting, seedling, or small tree of a species suitable for bonsai development. Bonsai can be created from nearly any perennial woody-stemmed tree or shrub species*[3] that produces true branches and can be cultivated to remain small through pot confinement with crown and root pruning. Some species are popular as bonsai material because they have characteristics, such as small leaves or needles, that make them appropriate for the compact visual scope of bonsai.

The source specimen is shaped to be relatively small and to meet the aesthetic standards of bonsai. When the candidate bonsai nears its planned final size it is planted in a display pot, usually one designed for bonsai display in one of a few accepted shapes and proportions. From that point forward, its growth is restricted by the pot environment. Throughout the year, the bonsai is shaped to limit growth, redistribute foliar vigor to areas requiring further development, and meet the artist's detailed design.

The practice of bonsai is sometimes confused with dwarfing, but dwarfing generally refers to research, discovery, or creation of plant cultivars that are permanent, genetic miniatures of existing species. Bonsai does not require genetically dwarfed trees, but rather depends on growing small trees from regular stock and seeds. Bonsai uses cultivation techniques like pruning, root reduction, potting, defoliation, and grafting to produce small trees that mimic the shape and style of mature, full-size trees.

1.1.1 History

Main article: History of bonsai

Early versions

The Japanese art of bonsai originated from the Chinese practice of penjing.*[6] From the 6th century onward, Imperial embassy personnel and Buddhist students from Japan visited and returned from mainland China. They brought back many Chinese ideas and goods, including container plantings.*[7] Over time, these container plantings

The earliest illustration of a penjing is found in the Qianling Mausoleum murals at the Tang-dynasty tomb of Crown Prince Zhanghuai, dating to 706.[4]*[5]*

began to appear in Japanese writings and representative art.

In the medieval period, recognizable bonsai were portrayed in handscroll paintings like the *Ippen shonin eden* (1299).*[8] The 1195 scroll *Saigyo Monogatari Emaki* was the earliest known to depict dwarfed potted trees in Japan. Wooden tray and dish-like pots with dwarf landscapes on modern-looking wooden shelves also appear in the 1309 *Kasuga-gongen-genki* scroll. In 1351, dwarf trees displayed on short poles were portrayed in the *Boki Ekotoba* scroll.*[9] Several other scrolls and paintings also included depictions of these kinds of trees.

A close relationship between Japan's Zen Buddhism and the potted trees began to shape bonsai reputation and esthetics. In this period, Chinese Chan Buddhist monks taught at Japan's monasteries. One of the monks' activities was to introduce political leaders to various arts of miniature landscapes as admirable accomplishments for men of taste and learning.*[10]*[11] Potted landscape arrangements up to this period included miniature figurines after the Chinese fashion. Japanese artists came to consider these items unnecessary, simplifying their creations in the spirit of Zen Buddhism.*[12]

Hachi-no-ki

Chinese Penjing specimen with decorated and relatively deep ("bowl"-style) container

Around the 14th century, the term for dwarf potted trees was "the bowl's tree" (鉢の木 *hachi no ki*).*[13] This indicated use of a fairly deep pot, rather than the shallow pot denoted by the eventual term *bonsai*. *Hachi no Ki (The Potted Trees)* is also the title of a Noh play by Zeami Motokiyo (1363–1444), based on a story c. 1383 about an impoverished samurai who burns his last three potted trees as firewood to warm a traveling monk. The monk is a disguised official who later rewards the samurai for his actions. In later centuries, woodblock prints by several artists depicted this popular drama. There was even a fabric design of the same name. Through these and other popular media, bonsai became known to a broad Japanese population.

Bonsai cultivation reached a high level of expertise in this period. Bonsai dating to the 17th century have survived to the present. One of the oldest-known living bonsai trees, considered one of the National Treasures of Japan, can be seen in the Tokyo Imperial Palace collection.*[14] A five-needle pine (*Pinus pentaphylla* var. *negishi*) known as Sandai-Shogun-No Matsu is documented as having been cared for by Tokugawa Iemitsu.*[14]*[15] The tree is thought to be at least 500 years old and was trained as a bonsai by, at latest, the year 1610.*[14]

By the end of the 18th century, bonsai cultivation in Japan was becoming widespread and began to interest the general public. In the Tenmei era (1781–88), an exhibit of traditional dwarf potted pines began to be held every year in Kyoto. Connoisseurs from five provinces and neighboring areas would bring one or two plants each to the show in order to submit them to visitors for ranking.*[16]

Classical period

Depicting foliage in the Manual of the Mustard Seed Garden

In Japan after 1800, bonsai began to move from being the esoteric practice of a few specialists to becoming a widely popular art form and hobby. In Itami, Hyōgo (near Osaka), Japanese scholars of Chinese arts gathered in the early 19th century to discuss recent styles in the art of miniature trees. Many terms and concepts adopted by this group were derived from *Kai-shi-en Gaden*, the Japanese version of *Jieziyuan Huazhuan* (Manual of the Mustard Seed Garden).*[17]*[18]*[19]*[20] The Japanese version of potted trees, which had been previously called "bunjin ueki", "bunjin hachiue", or other terms, were renamed "bonsai" (the Japanese pronunciation of the Chinese term penzai). This word connoted a shallow container, not a deeper bowl style. The term "bonsai", however, would not become broadly used in describing Japan's dwarf potted trees for nearly a century.

The popularity of bonsai began to grow outside the limited scope of scholars and the nobility. On October 13, 1868, the Meiji Emperor moved to his new capital in Tokyo. Bonsai were displayed both inside and outside Meiji Palace, and those placed in the grand setting of the Imperial Palace had to be "Giant Bonsai," large enough to fill the grand space.*[21]*[22]*[23] The Meiji Emperor encouraged interest in bonsai, which broadened its importance and appeal to his government's professional staff.*[24]*[25]

New books, magazines, and public exhibitions made bonsai more accessible to the Japanese populace. An Artistic Bonsai Concours was held in Tokyo in 1892, followed by publication of a three-volume commemorative picture book. This event demonstrated a new tendency to see bonsai as an independent art form.*[26] In 1903, the Tokyo association Jurakukai held showings of bonsai and ikebana at two Japanese-style restaurants. Three years later, *Bonsai Gaho* (1906 to c. 1913), became the first monthly magazine on the subject.*[27] It was followed by *Toyo Engei* and *Hana* in 1907.*[28] The initial issue of *Bonsai* magazine was published in 1921 by Norio Kobayashi (1889–1972), and this influential periodical would run for 518 consecutive issues.

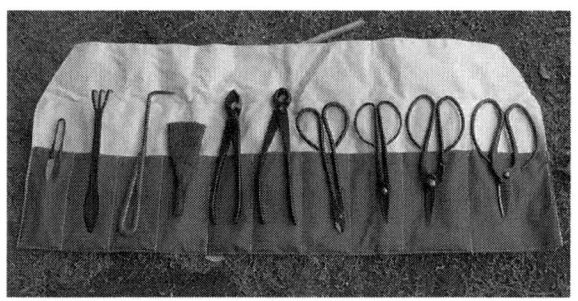

Modern bonsai tools (left to right): leaf trimmer; rake with spatula; root hook; coir brush; concave cutter; knob cutter; wire cutter; small, medium and large shears

Bonsai shaping aesthetics, techniques, and tools became increasingly sophisticated as bonsai's popularity grew in Japan. In 1910, shaping with wire rather than the older string, rope, and burlap techniques, appeared in the Sanyu-en Bonsai-Dan (History of Bonsai in the Sanyu nursery). Zinc-galvanized steel wire was initially used. Expensive copper wire was used only for selected trees that had real potential.*[29]*[30] In the 1920s and 1930s, Toolsmith Masakuni I (1880–1950) helped design and produce the first steel tools specifically made for the developing requirements of bonsai styling.*[31] These included the concave cutter, a branch cutter designed to leave a shallow indentation on the trunk when a branch was removed. Properly treated, this indentation would fill over with live tree tissue and bark over time, greatly reducing or eliminating the usual pruning scar.

Prior to World War II, international interest in bonsai was fueled by increased trade in trees and the appearance of books in popular foreign languages. By 1914, the first national annual bonsai show was held (an event repeated annually through 1933) in Tokyo's Hibiya Park.*[32]*[33] Another great annual public exhibition of trees began in 1927 at the Asahi Newspaper Hall in Tokyo.*[34] Beginning in 1934, the prestigious Kokufu-ten annual exhibitions were held in Tokyo's Ueno Park.*[35] The first major book on the subject in English was published in the Japanese capital: *Dwarf Trees (Bonsai)* by Shinobu Nozaki (1895–1968).*[36]

By 1940, about 300 bonsai dealers worked in Tokyo. Some 150 species of trees were being cultivated, and thousands of specimens annually were shipped to Europe and America. The first bonsai nurseries and clubs in the Americas were started by first and second-generation Japanese immigrants. Though this progress to international markets and enthusiasts was interrupted by the war, bonsai had by the 1940s become an art form of international interest and involvement.

Modern bonsai

Following World War II, a number of trends made the Japanese tradition of bonsai increasingly accessible to Western and world audiences. One key trend was the increase in the number, scope, and prominence of bonsai exhibitions. For example, the Kokufu-ten bonsai displays reappeared in 1947 after a four-year cancellation and became annual affairs. These displays continue to this day, and are by invitation only for eight days in February.*[35] In October 1964, a great exhibition was held in Hibya Park by the private Kokufu Bonsai Association, reorganized into the Nippon Bonsai Association, to mark the Tokyo Olympics.

A large display of bonsai and suiseki was held as part of Expo '70, and formal discussion was made of an international association of enthusiasts. In 1975, the first Gafu-ten (Elegant-Style Exhibit) of *shohin* bonsai (13–25 cm (5–10 in) tall) was held. So was the first Sakufu-ten (Creative Bonsai Exhibit), the only event in which professional bonsai growers exhibit traditional trees under their own names rather than under the name of the owner.

The First World Bonsai Convention was held in Osaka during the World Bonsai and Suiseki Exhibition in 1980.*[37] Nine years later, the first World Bonsai Convention was held in Omiya and the World Bonsai Friendship Federation (WBFF) was inaugurated. These conventions attracted several hundreds of participants from dozens of countries and have since been held every four years at different locations around the globe: 1993, Orlando, Florida; 1997, Seoul, Korea; 2001, Munich, Germany; 2005, Washington, D.C.; 2009, San Juan, Puerto Rico.*[37]*[38] Currently, Japan continues to host regular exhibitions with the world's largest numbers of bonsai specimens and the highest recognized specimen quality.

Another key trend was the increase in books on bonsai and related arts, now being published for the first time in English and other languages for audiences outside Japan. In 1952,

1.1. BONSAI

Yuji Yoshimura, son of a leader in the Japanese bonsai community, collaborated with German diplomat and author Alfred Koehn to give bonsai demonstrations. Koehn had been an enthusiast before the war, and his 1937 book *Japanese Tray Landscapes* had been published in English in Peking. Yoshimura's 1957 book *The Art of Bonsai*, written in English with his student Giovanna M. Halford, went on to be called the "classic Japanese bonsai bible for westerners" with over thirty printings.*[39]

Multi-species saikei named Roan Mountain *contains Shimpaku juniper and Zakura azalea.*

The related art of saikei was introduced to English-speaking audiences in 1963 in Kawamoto and Kurihara's book *Bonsai-Saikei*. This book described tray landscapes made with younger plant material than was traditionally used in bonsai, providing an alternative to the use of large, older plants, few of which had escaped war damage.

A third trend was the increasing availability of expert bonsai training, at first only in Japan and then more widely. In 1967 the first group of Westerners studied at an Ōmiya nursery. Returning to the U.S., these people established the American Bonsai Society. Other groups and individuals from outside Asia then visited and studied at the various Japanese nurseries, occasionally even apprenticing under the masters. These visitors brought back to their local clubs the latest techniques and styles, which were then further disseminated. Japanese teachers also traveled widely, bringing hands-on bonsai expertise to all six continents*[40]

The final trend supporting world involvement in bonsai is the widening availability of specialized bonsai plant stock, soil components, tools, pots, and other accessory items. Bonsai nurseries in Japan advertise and ship specimen bonsai worldwide. Most countries have local nurseries providing plant stock as well. Japanese bonsai soil components, such as Akadama clay, are available worldwide, and suppliers also provide similar local materials in many locations. Specialized bonsai tools are widely available from Japanese and Chinese sources. Potters around the globe provide material to hobbyists and specialists in many countries.*[41]

Bonsai has now reached a worldwide audience. There are over twelve hundred books on bonsai and the related arts in at least twenty-six languages available in over ninety countries and territories.*[42]*[43] A few dozen magazines in over thirteen languages are in print. Several score of club newsletters are available on-line, and there are at least that many discussion forums and blogs.*[44] There are at least a hundred thousand enthusiasts in some fifteen hundred clubs and associations worldwide, as well as over five million unassociated hobbyists.*[45] Plant material from every location is being trained into bonsai and displayed at local, regional, national, and international conventions and exhibitions for enthusiasts and the general public.

1.1.2 Cultivation and care

Main article: Bonsai cultivation and care

Bonsai cultivation and care requires techniques and tools that are specialized to support the growth and long-term maintenance of trees in small containers.

Material sources

All bonsai start with a specimen of source material, a plant that the grower wishes to train into bonsai form. Bonsai practice is an unusual form of plant cultivation in that growth from seeds is rarely used to obtain source material. To display the characteristic aged appearance of a bonsai within a reasonable time, the source plant is often mature or at least partially grown when the bonsai creator begins work. Sources of bonsai material include:

- *Propagation* from a source tree through cuttings or layering.
- *Nursery stock* directly from a nursery, or from a garden centre or similar resale establishment.
- *Commercial bonsai growers*, which, in general, sell mature specimens that display bonsai aesthetic qualities already.
- *Collecting* suitable bonsai material in its original wild situation, successfully moving it, and replanting it in a container for development as bonsai. These trees are called yamadori and are often the most expensive and prized of all Bonsai.

Techniques

The practice of bonsai development incorporates a number of techniques either unique to bonsai or, if used in other

This juniper makes extensive use of both jin (deadwood branches) and shari (trunk deadwood).

forms of cultivation, applied in unusual ways that are particularly suitable to the bonsai domain. These techniques include:

- *Leaf trimming*, the selective removal of leaves (for most varieties of deciduous tree) or needles (for coniferous trees and some others) from a bonsai's trunk and branches.

- *Pruning* the trunk, branches, and roots of the candidate tree.

- *Wiring* branches and trunks allows the bonsai designer to create the desired general form and make detailed branch and leaf placements.

- *Clamping* using mechanical devices for shaping trunks and branches.

- *Grafting* new growing material (typically a bud, branch, or root) into a prepared area on the trunk or under the bark of the tree.

- *Defoliation*, which can provide short-term dwarfing of foliage for certain deciduous species.

- *Deadwood bonsai techniques* such as *jin* and *shari* simulate age and maturity in a bonsai.

Care

Small trees grown in containers, like bonsai, require specialized care. Unlike houseplants and other subjects of container gardening, tree species in the wild, in general, grow roots up to several meters long and root structures encompassing several thousand liters of soil. In contrast, a typical bonsai container is under 25 centimeters in its largest dimension and 2 to 10 liters in volume. Branch and leaf (or needle) growth in trees is also of a larger scale in nature. Wild trees typically grow 5 meters or taller when mature, whereas the largest bonsai rarely exceed 1 meter and most specimens are significantly smaller. These size differences affect maturation, transpiration, nutrition, pest resistance, and many other aspects of tree biology. Maintaining the long-term health of a tree in a container requires some specialized care techniques:

- *Watering* must be regular and must relate to the bonsai species' requirement for dry, moist, or wet soil.

- *Repotting* must occur at intervals dictated by the vigor and age of each tree.

- *Tools* have been developed for the specialized requirements of maintaining bonsai.

- *Soil composition and fertilization* must be specialized to the needs of each bonsai tree, although bonsai soil is almost always a loose, fast-draining mix of components.*[46]

- *Location and overwintering* are species-dependent when the bonsai is kept outdoors as different species require different light conditions. Few of the traditional bonsai species can survive inside a typical house, due to the usually dry indoor climate.*[47]

1.1.3 Aesthetics

Main article: Bonsai aesthetics

Bonsai aesthetics are the aesthetic goals characterizing the Japanese tradition of growing an artistically shaped miniature tree in a container. Many Japanese cultural characteristics, in particular the influence of Zen Buddhism and the expression of Wabi-sabi,*[48] inform the bonsai tradition in Japan. Established art forms that share some aesthetic principles with bonsai include penjing and saikei. A number of other cultures around the globe have adopted the Japanese aesthetic approach to bonsai, and, while some variations have begun to appear, most hew closely to the rules and design philosophies of the Japanese tradition.

1.1. BONSAI

Over centuries of practice, the Japanese bonsai aesthetic has encoded some important techniques and design guidelines. Like the aesthetic rules that govern, for example, Western common practice period music, bonsai's guidelines help practitioners work within an established tradition with some assurance of success. Simply following the guidelines alone will not guarantee a successful result. Nevertheless, these design rules can rarely be broken without reducing the impact of the bonsai specimen. Some key principles in bonsai aesthetics include:

- *Miniaturization*: By definition, a bonsai is a tree kept small enough to be container-grown while otherwise fostered to have a mature appearance.

- *Proportion among elements*: The most prized proportions mimic those of a full-grown tree as closely as possible. Small trees with large leaves or needles are out of proportion and are avoided, as is a thin trunk with thick branches.

- *Asymmetry*: Bonsai aesthetics discourage strict radial or bilateral symmetry in branch and root placement.

- *No trace of the artist*: The designer's touch must not be apparent to the viewer. If a branch is removed in shaping the tree, the scar will be concealed. Likewise, wiring should be removed or at least concealed when the bonsai is shown, and must leave no permanent marks on the branch or bark.*[49]

- *Poignancy*: Many of the formal rules of bonsai help the grower create a tree that expresses Wabi-sabi, or portrays an aspect of *mono no aware*.

1.1.4 Display

A bonsai display presents one or more bonsai specimens in a way that allows a viewer to see all the important features of the bonsai from the most advantageous position. That position emphasizes the bonsai's defined "front", which is designed into all bonsai. It places the bonsai at a height that allows the viewer to imagine the bonsai as a full-size tree seen from a distance, siting the bonsai neither so low that the viewer appears to be hovering in the sky above it nor so high that the viewer appears to be looking up at the tree from beneath the ground. Noted bonsai writer Peter Adams recommends that bonsai be shown as if "in an art gallery: at the right height; in isolation; against a plain background, devoid of all redundancies such as labels and vulgar little accessories." *[50]

For outdoor displays, there are few aesthetic rules. Many outdoor displays are semi-permanent, with the bonsai trees

Bonsai displayed on an outdoor bench - note automated watering apparatus

A Seiju elm bonsai on display with a shitakusa of miniature hosta and a hanging scroll.

in place for weeks or months at a time. To avoid damaging the trees, therefore, an outdoor display must not impede the amount of sunlight needed for the trees on display, must support watering, and may also have to block excessive wind or precipitation.*[51] As a result of these practical constraints, outdoor displays are often rustic in style, with simple wood or stone components. A common design is the bench, sometimes with sections at different heights to suit different sizes of bonsai, along which bonsai are placed in a line. Where space allows, outdoor bonsai specimens are spaced far enough apart that the viewer can concentrate on one at a time. When the trees are too close to each other, aesthetic discord between adjacent trees of different sizes or styles can confuse the viewer, a problem addressed by exhibition displays.

Exhibition displays allow many bonsai to be displayed in a temporary exhibition format, typically indoors, as would be seen in a bonsai design competition. To allow many trees to be located close together, exhibition displays often use a sequence of small alcoves, each containing one pot and its bonsai contents. The walls or dividers between the alcoves make it easier to view only one bonsai at a time. The back of the alcove is a neutral color and pattern to avoid distracting the viewer's eye. The bonsai pot is almost always placed on a formal stand, of a size and design selected to complement the bonsai and its pot.*[52]

Indoors, a formal bonsai display is arranged to represent a landscape, and traditionally consists of the featured bonsai tree in an appropriate pot atop a wooden stand, along with a shitakusa (companion plant) representing the foreground, and a hanging scroll representing the background. These three elements are chosen to complement each other and evoke a particular season, and are composed asymmetrically to mimic nature.*[53] When displayed inside a traditional Japanese home, a formal bonsai display will often be placed within the home's tokonoma or formal display alcove. An indoor display is usually very temporary, lasting a day or two, as most bonsai are intolerant of indoor conditions and lose vigor rapidly within the house.

Containers

Assorted bonsai pots

A variety of informal containers may house the bonsai during its development, and even trees that have been formally planted in a bonsai pot may be returned to growing boxes from time to time. A large growing box can house several bonsai and provide a great volume of soil per tree to encourage root growth. A training box will have a single specimen, and a smaller volume of soil that helps condition the bonsai to the eventual size and shape of the formal bonsai container. There are no aesthetic guidelines for these development containers, and they may be of any material, size, and shape that suit the grower.

Completed trees are grown in formal bonsai containers. These containers are usually ceramic pots, which come in a variety of shapes and colors and may be glazed or unglazed. Unlike many common plant containers, bonsai pots have drainage holes in the bottom surface to complement fast-draining bonsai soil, allowing excess water to escape the pot. Growers cover the holes with a screening to prevent soil from falling out and to hinder pests from entering the pots from below. Pots usually have vertical sides, so that the tree's root mass can easily be removed for inspection, pruning, and replanting, although this is a practical consideration and other container shapes are acceptable.

There are alternatives to the conventional ceramic pot. Multi-tree bonsai may be created atop a fairly flat slab of rock, with the soil mounded above the rock surface and the trees planted within the raised soil. In recent times, bonsai creators have also begun to fabricate rock-like slabs from raw materials including concrete*[54] and glass-reinforced plastic.*[55] Such constructed surfaces can be made much lighter than solid rock, can include depressions or pockets for additional soil, and can be designed for drainage of water, all characteristics difficult to achieve with solid rock slabs. Other unconventional containers can also be used, but in formal bonsai display and competitions in Japan, the ceramic bonsai pot is the most common container.

For bonsai being shown formally in their completed state, pot shape, color, and size are chosen to complement the tree as a picture frame is chosen to complement a painting. In general, containers with straight sides and sharp corners are used for formally shaped plants, while oval or round containers are used for plants with informal designs. Many aesthetic guidelines affect the selection of pot finish and color. For example, evergreen bonsai are often placed in unglazed pots, while deciduous trees usually appear in glazed pots. Pots are also distinguished by their size. The overall design of the bonsai tree, the thickness of its trunk, and its height are considered when determining the size of a suitable pot.

Some pots are highly collectible, like ancient Chinese or Japanese pots made in regions with experienced pot makers such as Tokoname, Japan or Yixing, China. Today many potters worldwide produce pots for bonsai.*[41]

1.1. BONSAI

1.1.5 Bonsai styles

Main article: Bonsai styles

The Japanese tradition describes bonsai tree designs

Formal upright style Bald cypress

Informal upright style Juniper

using a set of commonly understood, named styles.*[56] The most common styles include formal upright, informal upright, slanting, semi-cascade, cascade, raft, literati, and group/forest. Less common forms include windswept, weeping, split-trunk, and driftwood styles.*[2]*[57] These terms are not mutually exclusive, and a single bonsai specimen can exhibit more than one style characteristic. When a bonsai specimen falls into multiple style categories, the common practice is to describe it by the dominant or most striking characteristic.

A frequently used set of styles describes the orientation of the bonsai tree's main trunk. Different terms are used for a tree with its apex directly over the center of the trunk's entry into the soil, slightly to the side of that center, deeply inclined to one side, and inclined below the point at which the trunk of the bonsai enters the soil.*[58]

- **Formal upright** or *chokkan* (直幹) style trees are characterized by a straight, upright, tapering trunk. Branches progress regularly from the thickest and broadest at the bottom to the finest and shortest at the top.*[59]

- **Informal upright** or *moyogi* (模様木) trees incorporate visible curves in trunk and branches, but the apex of the informal upright is located directly above the trunk's entry into the soil line.*[60]

- **Slant-style** or *shakan* (斜幹) bonsai possess straight trunks like those of bonsai grown in the formal upright style. However, the slant style trunk emerges from the soil at an angle, and the apex of the bonsai will be located to the left or right of the root base.*[61]

- **Cascade-style** or *kengai* (懸崖) specimens are modeled after trees that grow over water or down the sides of mountains. The apex (tip of the tree) in the **semi-cascade-style** or *han kengai* (半懸崖) bonsai extend just at or beneath the lip of the bonsai pot; the apex of a (full) cascade style falls below the base of the pot.*[62]

A number of styles describe the trunk shape and bark finish. For example, the deadwood bonsai styles identify trees with prominent dead branches or trunk scarring.*[63]

- **Shari** or *sharimiki* (舎利幹) style involves portraying a tree in its struggle to live while a significant part of its trunk is bare of bark.*[64]

Although most bonsai trees are planted directly into the soil, there are styles describing trees planted on rock.*[65]

Slant-style conifer

Cascade style conifer

Forest style Black Hills Spruce

mens with multiple trunks.*[66]

- **Forest (or group)** or *yose ue* (寄せ植え) style comprises a planting of several or many trees of one species, typically an odd number, in a bonsai pot.*[67]

- **Multi-trunk** styles like *sokan* and *sankan* have all the trunks growing out of one spot with one root system, so the bonsai is actually a single tree.

- **Raft-style** or *ikadabuki* (筏吹き) bonsai mimic a natural phenomenon that occurs when a tree topples onto its side, for example, from erosion or another natural force. Branches along the top side of the trunk continue to grow as a group of new trunks.

Other styles

A few styles do not fit into the preceding categories. These include:

- **Literati** or *bunjin-gi* (文人木) style is characterized by a generally bare trunk line, with branches reduced to a minimum, and foliage placed toward the top of a long, often contorted trunk.

- **Broom** or *hokidachi* (箒立ち) style is employed for trees with fine branching, like elms. The trunk is straight and branches out in all directions about ⅓ of the way up the entire height of the tree. The branches and leaves form a ball-shaped crown.*[68]

- **Windswept** or *fukinagashi* (吹き流し) style describes a tree that appears to be affected by strong winds blowing continuously from one direction, as might shape a tree atop a mountain ridge or on an exposed shoreline.*[69]

- **Root-over-rock** or *sekijoju* (石上樹) is a style in which the roots of the tree are wrapped around a rock, entering the soil at the base of the rock.

- **Growing-in-a-rock** or *ishizuke* or *ishitsuki* (石付) style means the roots of the tree are growing in soil contained within the cracks and holes of the rock.

While the majority of bonsai specimens feature a single tree, there are well-established style categories for speci-

1.1.6 Size classifications

Japanese bonsai exhibitions and catalogs frequently refer to the size of individual bonsai specimens by assigning them to size classes (see table below). Not all sources agree on the exact sizes or names for these size ranges, but the concept of the ranges is well-established and useful to both the cultivation and the aesthetic understanding of the trees. A photograph of a bonsai may not give the viewer an accurate impression of the tree's real size, so printed documents may complement a photograph by naming the bonsai's size class. The size class implies the height and weight of the tree in its container.

In the very largest size ranges, a recognized Japanese practice is to name the trees "two-handed", "four-handed", and so on, based on the number of men required to move the tree and pot. These trees will have dozens of branches and can closely simulate a full-size tree. The very largest size, called "imperial", is named after the enormous potted trees of Japan's Imperial Palace.*[70]

At the other end of the size spectrum, there are a number of specific techniques and styles associated solely with the smallest common sizes, *mame* and *shito*. These techniques take advantage of the bonsai's minute dimensions and compensate for the limited number of branches and leaves that can appear on a tree this small.

1.1.7 Indoor bonsai

Main article: Indoor bonsai

The Japanese tradition of bonsai does not include indoor bonsai, and bonsai appearing at Japanese exhibitions or in catalogs have been grown outdoors for their entire lives. In less-traditional settings, including climates more severe than Japan's, indoor bonsai may appear in the form of potted trees cultivated for the indoor environment.*[72]

Traditionally, bonsai are temperate climate trees grown outdoors in containers.*[73] Kept in the artificial environment of a home, these trees weaken and die. But a number of tropical and sub-tropical tree species will survive and grow indoors. Some of these tropical and sub-tropical species are suited to bonsai aesthetics and can be shaped much as traditional outdoor bonsai are.

1.1.8 See also

- Bonsai aesthetics – aesthetics of Japanese tradition in bonsai
- Bonsai cultivation and care – cultivation and care of small, container-grown trees
- Bonsai styles – conventional styles in the Japanese tradition
- Huntington Library
- List of bonsai on stamps
- List of species used in bonsai
- Mambonsai – pop culture twist on bonsai
- Micro landschaft - more general miniature gardening and aquatics

1.1.9 References

[1] Gustafson, Herbert L. (1995). *Miniature Bonsai*. Sterling Publishing Company, Inc. p. 9. ISBN 0-8069-0982-X.

[2] Chan, Peter (1987). *Bonsai Masterclass*. Sterling Publishing Co., Inc. ISBN 0-8069-6763-3.

[3] Owen, Gordon (1990). *The Bonsai Identifier*. Quintet Publishing Ltd. p. 11. ISBN 0-88665-833-0.

[4] Taylor, Patrick (2008). *The Oxford companion to the garden* (2nd ed.). Oxford: Oxford University Press. p. 53. ISBN 978-0-19-955197-2.

[5] Hu, Yunhua (1987). *Chinese penjing: Miniature trees and landscapes*. Portland: Timber Press. p. 128. ISBN 978-0-88192-083-3.

[6] Keswick, Maggie; Oberlander, Judy; Wai, Joe (1991). *In a Chinese Garden: The Art and Architecture of the Dr. Sun Yat-Sen Classical Chinese Garden*. Vancouver: Raincoast Book Dist Ltd. p. 59. ISBN 978-0-9694573-0-5.

[7] Yoshimura, Yuji (1991). "Modern Bonsai, Development Of The Art Of Bonsai From An Historical Perspective, Part 2". *International Bonsai* (4): 37.

[8] Kobayashi, Konio (2011). *Bonsai*. Tokyo: PIE International Inc. p. 15. ISBN 978-4-7562-4094-1.

[9] "Japanese Paintings: to 1600". Magical Miniature Landscapes. Retrieved 2010-04-07.

[10] Covello, Vincent T. & Yuji Yoshimura (1984). *The Japanese Art of Stone Appreciation, Suiseki and Its Use with Bonsai*. Charles E. Tuttle. p. 20.

[11] Nippon Bonsai Association. *Classic Bonsai of Japan*. p. 144.

[12] Redding, Myron. "Art of the Mud Man". Art of Bonsai. Retrieved 2010-04-07.

[13] "Hachi-No-Ki". Magical Miniature Landscapes. Retrieved 2016-08-10.

[14] Naka, John Yoshio (1982). *Bonsai Techniques II*. Bonsai Institute of California. p. 258.

[15] "Oldest Bonsai trees". Bonsai Empire. Retrieved 2013-11-11.

[16] Nippon Bonsai Association. *Classic Bonsai of Japan*. pp. 151–152.

[17] Covello, Vincent T. & Yuji Yoshimura (1984). *The Japanese Art of Stone Appreciation, Suiseki and Its Use with Bonsai*. Charles E. Tuttle. p. 25.

[18] Koreshoff. *Bonsai: Its Art, Science, History and Philosophy*. pp. 7–8.

[19] Naka, John (1989). "Bunjin-Gi or Bunjin Bonsai". *Bonsai in California*. **23**: 48.

[20] Dalby, Liza, ed. (1984). *All-Japan: The Catalogue of Everything Japanese*. Quarto Marketing, Inc. p. 44.

[21] Yamada, Tomio (2005). "Fundamentals of Wiring Bonsai". *International Bonsai* (4): 10–11.

[22] Hill, Warren (2000). "Reflections on Japan". *NBF Bulletin*. **XI**: 5.

[23] Yamanaka, Kazuki. "The Shimpaku Juniper: Its Secret History, Chapter II. First Shimpaku: Ishizuchi Shimpaku". World Bonsai Friendship Federation. Archived from the original on February 22, 2008. Retrieved 2011-09-29.

[24] Nozaki. *Dwarf Trees (Bonsai)*. p. 24.

[25] Itoh, Yoshimi (1969). "Bonsai Origins". *ABS Bonsai Journal*. **3** (1): 3.

[26] Nippon Bonsai Association. *Classic Bonsai of Japan*. p. 153.

[27] "Bonsai and Other Magical Miniature Landscape Specialty Magazines, Part 1". Magical Miniature Landscapes. Retrieved 2016-09-13.

[28] Kobayashi, Konio (2011). *Bonsai*. Tokyo: PIE International Inc. p. 16. ISBN 978-4-7562-4094-1.

[29] "The Books on Bonsai and Related Arts, 1900 - 1949". Magical Miniature Landscapes. Retrieved 2016-09-13.

[30] Yamada, Tomio (2005). "Fundamentals of Wiring Bonsai". *International Bonsai* (4): 10.

[31] "Kyuzo Murata, the Father of Modern Bonsai in Japan, Part 1". Magical Miniature Landscapes. Retrieved 2016-09-16.

[32] Terry, Thomas Philip, F.R.G.S. *Terry's Japanese Empire*. Houghton Mifflin Company. p. 168. Retrieved 2010-04-07.

[33] Pessy, Christian & Rémy Samson (1992). *Bonsai Basics, A Step-by-Step Guide to Growing, Training & General Care*. Sterling Publishing Co., Inc. p. 17.

[34] Koreshoff. *Bonsai: Its Art, Science, History and Philosophy*. p. 10.

[35] "Kokufu Bonsai Ten Shows, Part 1". Magical Miniature Landscapes. Retrieved 2016-09-16.

[36] Nozaki. *Dwarf Trees (Bonsai)*. pp. 6, 96.

[37] "Bonsai Book of Days for April". Magical Miniature Landscapes. Retrieved 2016-09-13.

[38] "The Conventions, Symposia, Demos, Workshops, and Exhibitions, Part 6". Magical Miniature Landscapes. Retrieved 2016-09-13.

[39] "Yuji Yoshimura, the Father of Popular Bonsai in the Non-Oriental World". Magical Miniature Landscapes. Retrieved 2016-09-13.

[40] "Saburō Katō, International Bridge-builder, His Heritage and Legacy, Part 1". Magical Miniature Landscapes. Retrieved 2016-09-13.

[41] "About Bonsai Pots and Potters". Magical Miniature Landscapes. Retrieved 2016-09-13.

[42] "The Imperial Bonsai Collection, Part 1". Magical Miniature Landscapes. Retrieved 2016-09-13.

[43] "The Nations -- When Did Bonsai Come to the Various Countries and Territories?". Magical Miniature Landscapes. Retrieved 2016-09-13.

[44] "Club Newsletter On-Line". Magical Miniature Landscapes. Retrieved 2016-09-13.

[45] "How Many Bonsai Enthusiasts Are There?". Magical Miniature Landscapes. Retrieved 2016-09-13.

[46] "It's All In The Soil by Mike Smith, published in "Norfolk Bonsai" (Spring 2007) by Norfolk Bonsai Association". Norfolkbonsai.co.uk. Archived from the original on 2007-09-30.

[47] "Indoor Bonsai Tree". Bonsaidojo.net. December 25, 2013. Archived from the original on December 5, 2015.

[48] Chan. *Bonsai Masterclass*. pp. 12–14.

[49] Chan. *Bonsai Masterclass*. p. 14.

[50] Adams, Peter D. (1981). *The Art of Bonsai*. Ward Lock Ltd. p. 134. ISBN 978-0-8317-0947-1.

[51] Norman, Ken (2005). *Growing Bonsai: A Practical Encyclopedia*. Lorenz Books. pp. 176–177. ISBN 978-0-7548-1572-3.

[52] Adams, Peter D. *The Art of Bonsai*. Color plates facing pp. 89, 134.

[53] Andy Rutledge, "Bonsai Display 101", *The Art of Bonsai Project*. Accessed 18 July 2009.

[54] Lewis, Colin (2001). *The Art of Bonsai Design*. Sterling Publishing Company, Inc.: New York. pp. 44–51. ISBN 0-8069-7137-1.

[55] Adams, Peter D. *The Art of Bonsai*. Color plates following p. 88; p. 134.

[56] "Japanese Styles of Bonsai". Magical Miniature Landscapes. Retrieved 2016-09-13.

[57] D'Cruz, Mark. "Ma-Ke Bonsai Care Guide - Bonsai Styles". Ma-Ke Bonsai. Retrieved 2012-12-24.

[58] Koreshoff. *Bonsai: Its Art, Science, History and Philosophy*. p. 153.

[59] Zane, Thomas L. (2003). "Formal Upright Style Bonsai," *Intermediate Bonsai*; retrieved 2012-12-20.

[60] Zane, "Informal Upright Style Bonsai"; retrieved 2012-12-20.

[61] Zane, "Stanting Style Bonsai"; retrieved 2012-12-20.

[62] Zane, "Semi-Cascade Style Bonsai"; "Cascade Style Bonsai"; retrieved 2012-12-20.

[63] Naka, John Yoshio (1973). *Bonsai Techniques I*. Bonsai Institute of California. pp. 123–124. ISBN 0-930422-31-7.

[64] "Sharimiki Bonsai". Bonsaiempire.com. Retrieved 2009-11-21.

[65] Masakuni Kawasumi II; Masakuni Kawasumi III (2005). *The Secret Techniques of Bonsai: A guide to starting, raising, and shaping bonsai*. Kodansha International. pp. 86–91. ISBN 978-4-7700-2943-0.

[66] Yuji Yoshimura & Barbara M. Halford (1957). *The Art of Bonsai: Creation, Care and Enjoyment*. Tuttle Publishing, North Clarendon VT USA. pp. 65–66. ISBN 0-8048-2091-0.

[67] Zane, "Forest Style Bonsai"; retrieved 2012-12-20.

[68] Zane, "Broom Style Bonsai"; retrieved 2012-12-20.

[69] Koreshoff. *Bonsai: Its Art, Science, History and Philosophy*. pp. 178–185.

[70] Gustafson. *Miniature Bonsai*. p. 17.

[71] Gustafson. *Miniature Bonsai*. p. 18.

[72] Lesniewicz, Paul (1996). *Bonsai in Your Home*. Sterling Publishing Company. ISBN 0-8069-0781-9.

[73] Indoor Bonsai, online article from the Montreal Botanical Garden

1.1.10 External links

- National Bonsai & Penjing Museum - U.S. National Arboretum, Washington, DC
- The Art of Bonsai Project - galleries to show bonsai variations
- A guide to growing miniature trees - Website dedicated to techniques for growing bonsai

1.2 Penjing

Penjing (Chinese: 盆景; pinyin: *pénjǐng*; literally: "**tray scenery**"), also known as **penzai** (Chinese: 盆栽; pinyin: *pénzāi*; literally: "tray plant"), tray landscape, potted scenery, potted landscape, or miniature trees and rockery, is the ancient Chinese art of depicting artistically formed trees, other plants, and landscapes in miniature.

Penjing generally fall into one of three categories:[1]

- **Shùmù pénjǐng** (樹木盆景): Tree penjing that focuses on the depiction of one or more trees and optionally other plants in a container, with the composition's dominant elements shaped by the creator through trimming, pruning, and wiring.
- **Shānshuǐ pénjǐng** (山水盆景): Landscape penjing that depicts a miniature landscape by carefully selecting and shaping rocks, which are usually placed in a container in contact with water. Small live plants are placed within the composition to complete the depiction.
- **Shuǐhàn pénjǐng** (水旱盆景): A water and land penjing style that effectively combines the first two, including miniature trees and optionally miniature figures and structures to portray a landscape in detail.

Similar practices exist in other cultures, including the Japanese traditions of *bonsai* and *saikei*, as well as the miniature living landscapes of Vietnamese *hòn non bộ*. Generally speaking, tree *penjing* specimens differ from *bonsai* by allowing a wider range of tree shapes (more "wild-looking") and by planting them in bright-colored and creatively shaped pots. In contrast, *bonsai* are more simplified in shape (more "refined" in appearance) with larger-in-proportion trunks, and are planted in unobtrusive, low-sided containers with simple lines and muted colors.

While *saikei* depicts living landscapes in containers, like water and land *penjing*, it does not use miniatures to decorate the living landscape. *Hòn non bộ* focuses on depicting landscapes of islands and mountains, usually in contact with water, and decorated with live trees and other plants. Like water and land *penjing*, *hòn non bộ* specimens can feature miniature figures, vehicles, and structures. Distinctions among these traditional forms have been blurred by some practitioners outside of Asia, as enthusiasts explore the potential of local plant and pot materials without strict adherence to traditional styling and display guidelines.

1.2.1 History

Penjing at the Rock and Penjing Museum in Wuhan, China

Classical Chinese gardens often contain arrangements of miniature trees and rockeries known as penjing. These creations of carefully pruned trees and rocks are small-scale renditions of natural landscapes. They are often referred to as living sculptures or as three-dimensional poetry. Their artistic composition captures the spirit of nature and distinguishes them from ordinary potted plants.

Origin of the components

The container known as the *pen* originated in Neolithic China in the Yangshao culture as an earthenware shallow dish with a foot. It was later one of the vessels manufactured in bronze for use in court ceremonies and religious rituals during the Shang dynasty and Zhou dynasty.*[2]

When foreign trade introduced into China new herbal aromatics in the 2nd century BC, a unique incense burner was designed.*[3] The *boshanlu* stemmed cup was topped by a perforated lid in the shape of one of the sacred mountains/islands, such as Mount Penglai – focus of a strong contemporary belief – often with the images of mythical persons and beasts throughout the hillsides. Smaller versions of the *pen* dish were sometimes used as bottom pieces either to catch hot embers or to be filled with water to represent the ocean out of which the sacred mountains/islands arose. Originally made out of bronze, ceramic, or talc stone, some later versions were believed to be actual interestingly-shaped stones which occasionally were partly covered with moss and lichens to further heighten the miniature representation.*[4]

Since at least the 1st century AD, Daoist mysticism has included the recreating of magical sites in miniature to focus and increase the properties found in the full-size sites. The various schools of Buddhism introduced from India after the mid-2nd century included the meditative *dhyana* sect, whose translations of Sanscrit texts sometimes used Daoist terminology to convey non-physical concepts. Also, floral altar decorations were introduced and floral designs started to become a dominant force in Chinese art. Five centuries later the Chán school of Buddhism was established, in which renewed Indian *dhyana* Buddhist teachings were merged with native Chinese Daoism. Chán maintained its more active, vital spirit even as other Buddhist sects were becoming more rigidly formalized.*[5]

Earliest versions

While there were legends dating from at least the 3rd and 4th centuries of Daoist persons said to have had the power to shrink whole landscapes down to small vessel size,*[6] written descriptions of miniature landscapes are not known until Tang Dynasty times. As the information at that point shows a somewhat developed craft, (then called "punsai")*[7] the making of dwarfed tree landscapes had to have been taking place for a while, either in China or possibly based on a form brought in from outside.*[4]

The earliest-known graphic dates from 706 and is found in a wall mural on a corridor leading to the tomb of Prince Zhang Huai at the Qianling Mausoleum site.*[8]*[9] Excavated in 1972, the frescoes show two maid servants carrying penjing with miniature rockeries and fruit trees.*[9]

The first highly prized trees are believed to have been collected in the wild and were full of twists, knots, and deformities. These were seen as sacred, of no practical profane value for timber or other ordinary purpose. These naturally dwarfed plants were held to be endowed with special concentrated energies due to age and origin away from human influence. The viewpoint of Chán Buddhism would continue to impact the creation of miniature landscapes. Smaller and younger plants which could be collected closer to civilization but still bore a resemblance to the rugged old treasures from the mountains would also have been chosen. Horticultural techniques to increase the appearance of age by emphasizing trunk, root, and branch size, texture, and shapes would eventually be employed with these specimens.*[10]

From Tang times onward, various poets and essayists

1.2. PENJING

Tang Dynasty prince Zhang Huai tomb mural (AD 706), with tray of pebbles and miniature fruit trees

praised dwarf potted landscapes. A decorative tree guild from around 1276 is known to have supplied dwarf specimens for use in Suzhou restaurants in the province of Jiangsu.*[11]

In Japan

Although imperial embassy personnel and Buddhist students from Japan had returned from the mainland with miniature landscape souvenirs since the 6th century, the oldest known depiction of a dwarfed tray landscape in Japan dates from 1309. The fifth of the twenty-scroll *Kasuga-gongen-genki* masterpiece depicts the household of a wealthy Japanese individual who has an outdoors slatted-workbench holding a shallow wooden tray and ceramic dish of Chinese origin with dwarf trees, grasses, and stones.*[12] By this time Chán Buddhism had been developed in Japan as Zen. Its influence of "beauty in severe austerity" led native Japanese dwarf potted landscapes to be distilled into single, ideal trees being representatives of the universe. What is termed bonsai derives from this.

Middle years

Depiction of the Ming imperial court ladies tending or standing beside penjing

Since at least the 16th century, shops of the name "Garden of Dragon Flowers", to the southwest of Shanghai, were engaged in cultivating miniature trees in containers. (These would continue to the present day.) Meanwhile, Suzhou was still considered at century's end to be the source of the finest exponents of the art of penjing.*[13]*[14]

The earliest-known English observation of penjing in China/Macau dates from 1637.*[15]

During the end of the 18th century, Yangzhou in central Jiangsu province boasted landscape penjing that contained water and soil.*[16]

19th century

In 1806, a very old dwarf tree from Canton (now Guangzhou) was gifted to Sir Joseph Banks and eventually presented to Queen Charlotte for Her Majesty's inspection.*[17] This tree and most others seen by Westerners in southeast China probably originated at the celebrated Fa Ti gardens near Canton.*[18]

By the first half of the 19th century, according to various Western accounts, air layering was the primary propagation method for penjing, which were then generally between one and two feet in height after two to twenty years of work. Elms were the main specimens used, along with pines, junipers, cypresses, and bamboos; plums were the favored fruit trees, along with peaches and oranges. The branches could be bent and shaped using various forms of bamboo scaffolding, twisted lead strips, and iron or brass wire to hold them in place; they could be also be cut, burnt, or grafted. The bark was sometimes lacerated at places or smeared with sugary substance to induce termites ("white ants") to roughen it or even to eat the similarly sweetened heartwood. Rocks with moss or lichens were also a frequent feature of these compositions.*[19]

The earliest known photograph from China which included penjing was made c.1868 by John Thomson.*[20] He was particularly delighted by the collection in the garden of the Hoi Tong Monastery on Henan Island near Guangzhou.*[21] A collection of dwarf trees and plants from China was also exhibited that year in Brooklyn, New York.*[22] In America, laws such as the Chinese Exclusion Act led to Japanese bonsai becoming more familiar to Americans. This led to the prevalence of knowledge of the Japanese forms of dwarf potted trees for the next several decades and prior to Chinese forms.*[23]

Near the end of the 19th century, the Lingnan or Cantonese school of "Clip and Grow" styling was developed at a monastery in southeast China. Fast-growing tropical trees and shrubs could be more easily and quickly shaped using these techniques.*[24]

20th century

Established in 1954, the Longhua nursery in Shanghai included the teaching of classical theory and all aspects of the practice of penjing, a process which could take student-gardeners ten years.*[25]

As late as the early 1960s, it is reported that some 60 characteristic regional forms of penjing could be distinguished by the expert eye.*[26] A few of these forms dated back to at least the 16th century.*[27]

During the upheaval of the Great Proletarian Cultural Revolution (May 1966-April 1969), one relatively small effect was that many collections of penjing in Mainland China, especially around Beijing, were damaged or neglected because they were seen as a bourgeois pastime. After their trees were gone, some Chinese penjing masters, men in their sixties and seventies, were forced to do something considered socially redemptive—many were sent to fields to plant rice. However, in other areas of China, especially in eastern and southern China, penjing were collected for safe keeping.*[28]*[29]*[30]

Wu Yee-sun (1905–2005), third generation penjing master and grandson of a Lingnan school founder, held the first exhibition of artistic pot plants jointly with Mr. Liu Fei Yat in Hong Kong in 1968. This was a display of traditional aristocratic penjing which had survived the 1949 Chinese Communist Revolution by leaving/being protected from Mainland China. The two editions of Wu's Chinese/English book, *Man Lung Garden Artistic Pot Plants*, helped develop interest in this older form of what the West only knew as the later-refined Japanese art of bonsai.*[30]

The Yuk Sui Yuen Penzai Exhibition was held in Canton in 1978. This was the first public show in ten years with approximately 250 penjing from private collections displayed in a public park. Antique pots were also shown.*[31] The Shanghai Botanical Garden opened that year and permanently displays 3,000 penjing.*[32] The First National Penjing Show was held the following year in Beijing with over 1,100 exhibits from 13 provinces, towns, and autonomies.*[33]

One division of the Hangzhou Flower Nursery by 1981 specialized in penjing, including over fifteen hundred once abandoned older specimens being maintained and in the initial stages of being retrained. The art of penjing would again become vastly popular in China, in part due to stability returning to most people's lives and the significantly improved economic conditions; growth would be most pronounced particularly in coastal provinces of Jiangsu, Zhejiang, Fujian, Guangdong as well as Shanghai. There would be increasing numbers of good public and private collections, the latter with anywhere from several hundred to several thousand pieces.

By the end of 1981, the China Flower and Penjing Association was formed, and seven years later the China Penjing Artists Association was likewise established.*[32]

The Hong Kong Baptist University opened the Man Lung Garden in 2000 to promote the Chinese heritage of penjing. Temporarily located on the University's Shaw Campus, in February 2005 a permanent site was set up at the Kam Shing Road Entrance of its Ho Sin Hang Campus.*[34]

1.2.2 Penjing aesthetics

Using artificially dwarfed trees and shrubs, these arrangements are created in special trays or pots which are placed on ornately carved wooden stands. Often, rocks, miniature ceramic structures (like buildings and bridges), and figurines are added to give the proper scales as part of the natural scenery. These miniatures add to the symbolism of a

A specimen in the Landscape Penjing (shanshui penjing) style

penjing specimen, by providing a social or historical context in which to interpret the overall penjing design.*[29]

These miniature landscapes include trees which are frequently over a hundred years old. Like the plants in the Chinese garden, they have been carefully selected and tended so that they develop into twisted and gnarled shapes reminiscent of their full-size counterparts in the wild. Like the chinese gardens, these miniature landscapes are designed to convey landscapes experienced from various viewpoints - a close-up view, a medium-range view or a panorama.

As an art form, penjing is an extension of the garden, since it enables an artist to recreate parts of the natural landscape in miniature. Penjing is often used indoors as part of a garden's overall design, since it reiterates the landscape features found outside. Penjing pots grace pavilions, private studies or living rooms, and public buildings. They are either free-standing elements within the gardens or are placed on furniture such as a table or bookshelf. Sometimes a lattice display stand is built which adds particular prominence to the penjing specimen and exemplifies the interplay between architecture and nature.

Penjing seeks to capture the essence and spirit of nature through contrasts. Philosophically, it is influenced by the principles of Taoism, specifically the concept of Yin and Yang: the idea of the universe as governed by two primal forces, opposing but complementary. Some of the contrasting concepts used in penjing include portrayal of "dominance and subordination, emptiness (void) and substance, denseness and sparseness, highness and lowness, largeness and smallness, life and death, dynamics and statics, roughness and meticulousness, firmness and gentleness, lightness and darkness, straightness and curviness, verticality and horizontality[,] and lightness and heaviness." *[1]

Design inspiration is not limited to observation or representation of nature, but is also influenced by Chinese poetry, calligraphy, and other visual arts. Common penjing designs include evocation of dragons and the strokes of well-omened characters. At its highest level, the artistic value of penjing is on par with that of poetry, calligraphy, brush painting and garden art.*[35]

1.2.3 Styles

Bamboo penjing in Chengdu, China

Penjing in the US National Bonsai and Penjing Museum

Styles of the traditional **Penjing** in China are mainly classified by the most representative (dominant) plants used, and named after the regions of their origin. Since different plants require different techniques to handle, different styles thus formed. There are more than a dozen styles of traditional **Penjing**:

Anhui Style Anhui Penjing (徽派盆景) is most famous for its utilization of ume.

Beijing Style Beijing Penjing (京派盆景) reflects its artistic origin from the ancient traditional Chinese

Ginkgo penjing

architecture in Beijing. The branches are often horizontal and the crowns of the trees are often in hemisphere or in the form of traditional folding fan.

Guangdong (or Lingnan) Style Guangdong Style Penjing (粤派盆景) is also called Lingnan ("South of the (Nan)ling Range") penjing (嶺南派盆景), because Guangdong is located south of the Nanling mountain range. The main characteristic of this style is its natural appeal and the appeal of easy and smooth.

Guangxi Style Guangxi Penjing (桂派盆景) reflect the beautiful natural landscape such as that of Guilin. This style utilizes different type of stones considerably more frequent than other styles.

Fujian Style Fujian Penjing (閩派盆景) specializes in utilization of banyan.

Hubei Style Hubei Penjing (湖北盆景) enphasizes on the producing the sense of dynamic feelings by the static plants and rocks, and thus also called Dynamic Penjing (☒☒盆景).

Jiangsu Style Like the culinary art of the **Jiangsu cuisine**, the art of **Jiangsu Penjing** (☒派盆景) is also complicated, with the crowns of the trees often being shaped like clouds.

Sichuan Style Sichuan Penjing (川派盆景) tends to be well-knit, simple and unsophisticated.

Shanghai Style Shanghai Penjing (海派盆景) has influenced the Japanese bonsai, but at the same time, has kept its original artistic origin, which is from the traditional Chinese painting.

Taiwan Style Taiwan Penjing (台灣盆景) is a cross of Japanese bonsai and traditional **Chinese Penjing**.

Xuzhou Style Xuzhou Penjing (徐州盆景) is a branch of **Jiangsu style**, but it is distinct enough to be listed separately for hundreds of years for its utilization of fruit trees.

Yangzhou Style Yangzhou Penjing (揚派盆景) is also called northern Jiangsu style (☒北派),[36] it is distinct from **Jiangsu style** The three twists of tree trunks is the most distinctive characteristic of this style.

Yunnan Style Yunnan Penjing (云南盆景) benefits from the extreme climatic and biodiversity of Yunnan region, between the Himalayas and the tropics. A permanent display of Yunnan style penjing is visible at Daguan Park, Kunming.

Zhejiang Style Zhejiang Penjing (浙派盆景) specializes in utilization of pine and cypress, often have three to five plants in one tray.

Zhongzhou Style Zhongzhou Penjing (中州盆景) specializes in utilizing Tamarix.

1.2.4 Maintenance and care

Main article: Bonsai cultivation and care

The maintenance and care of penjing trees are similar to that of the bonsai.

1.2.5 See also

- Chinese garden
- Gongshi - Chinese scholar's rock
- Bonsai - Japanese art of growing trees in trays
- Saikei - Japanese living tray landscapes
- Bonkei - Japanese dry tray landscapes
- List of organic gardening and farming topics
- National Bonsai Foundation

1.2.6 Notes

[1] Zhao Qingquan (2012). *Penjing: The Chinese Art of Bonsai*. Shanghai Press and Publishing Development Company. p. 11.

[2] "pen, the origins of the shallow tray". Pyramid Dancer. Retrieved 2009-10-09.

[3] Laufer, Berthold (1909). *Chinese Pottery of the Han Dynasty*. E.J. Brill, Ltd.

[4] Stein, Rolf A. (1990). *The World in Miniature*. Stanford University Press. p. 41.

[5] Fitzgerald, C.P. (1985). *China, A Short Cultural History*. Westview Press. p. 283.

[6] "Fei Jiang-Fang". Pyramid Dancer. Retrieved 2009-10-09.

[7] "Penjing and its predecessor Punsai history". Bonsaiempire.com. Retrieved 2009-11-21.

[8] Hu, Yunhua (1987). *Chinese penjing: Miniature trees and landscapes*. Portland: Timber Press. p. 128. ISBN 978-0-88192-083-3.

[9] "Dwarf Potted Trees in Paintings, Scrolls and Woodblock Prints". Pyramid Dancer. Retrieved 2009-10-09.

[10] Stein, p. 104

[11] Gernet, Jacques (1962). *Daily Life in China on the Eve of the Mongol Invasion 1250-1276*. The Macmillan Company. p. 193.

[12] "Dwarf Potted Trees in Paintings, Scrolls and Woodblock Prints". Pyramid Dancer. Retrieved 2009-10-09.

[13] Hrdlickovi, V.aZ. (1989). "The Garden of the Dragon Flowers". *Bonsai Magazine*. 28 (3): 20.

[14] Clunas, Craig (1996). *Fruitful Sites, Garden Culture in Ming Dynasty China*. Duke University Press. p. 100.

[15] Peter Mundy. "Peter Mundy's 'Smalle Trees' observation". Pyramid Dancer. Retrieved 2009-10-09.

[16] Zhao, Qingquan (1997). *Penjing: Worlds of Wonderment*. Venus Communications, LLC;. p. 41.

[17] "A Chronology of Dwarf Potted Trees in England". Pyramid Dancer. Retrieved 2009-10-09.

[18] "'Dwarf Trees' from Dr. Clarke Abel's Book". Pyramid Dancer. Retrieved 2009-10-09.

[19] "'Dwarf Trees' from John Livingstone's Letters to the Horticultural Society". Pyramid Dancer. Retrieved 2009-10-09.

[20] "Earliest Known Photograph of Dwarfed Potted Trees in China". Pyramid Dancer. Retrieved 2009-10-06.

[21] Thomson, John (1874), *Illustrations of China and Its People: A Series of Two Hundred Photographs with Letterpress Descriptive of the Places and People Represented*, Vol. I, London: Sampson Low, Marston, Low, & Searle, "Honam Temple, Canton".

[22] "Dwarf Plants from Brooklyn Daily Eagle". Pyramid Dancer. Retrieved 2009-10-06.

[23] Iriye, Akira (ed.) (1975). *Mutual Images, Essays in American-Japanese Relations,*. Harvard University Press.

[24] Wu, Yee-Sun (1969). *Man Lung Garden Artistic Pot Plants*. Wing-Lung Bank Ltd. p. 63.

[25] Richardson, S.D. (1966). *Forestry in Communist China*. The Johns Hopkins Press. p. 75.

[26] Richardson, S.D. (1966). *Forestry in Communist China*. The Johns Hopkins Press. p. 155.

[27] Albert, Karen (1992). "Chinese Penjing Artist Visits America". *Bonsai Magazine*. 31 (4): 13.

[28] Davis, Rosalie H. (August 1987). "A Gift From the East". *Horticulture*: 51.

[29] Fukumoto, David W. (1981). "China: Stepping Back Into Bonsai's Past". *ABS Bonsai Journal*. 15 (3): 70.

[30] Fukumoto, David W. (2002). "Yee-Sun Wu: The Spirit of Man Lung Penjing!". *Bonsai Magazine*. 41 (4): 33.

[31] Koreshoff, Deborah R. (1984). *Bonsai: Its Art, Science, History and Philosophy*. Timber Press, Inc. p. 6. ISBN 0-88192-389-3.

[32] Su, Prof. Xuehen. "The Organization and Activity of Penjing in China". *World Bonsai Friendship Federation*. Retrieved 2004-05-31.

[33] Hu, Yun-hua (1993). "Bonsai in China". In Ted T. Tsukiyama ed. *Bonsai of the World, Book I*. Japan: World Bonsai Friendship Federation. pp. 82, 83.

[34] "HKBU's unique Penjing garden opens to public". Hong Kong Baptist University. Retrieved 2009-10-09.

[35] Hu Yunhua, *Penjing: The Chinese Art of Miniature Gardens*. (Beaverton, Oregon: Timber Press in cooperation with the American Horticultural Society, 1982) p.7.

[36] " 盆景雅舍 PenjingYashe". 盆景雅舍. Retrieved 2010-09-08.

1.2.7 References

- Zhao, Qingquan. Penjing: Worlds of Wonderment. Venus Communications, LLC.

- Chen Lifang and Yu Sianglin, The Garden Art of China. (Portland, Oregon: Timber Press, 1986) p. 149.

1.2.8 External links

- The Art of Bonsai Project
- Bonsai Art
- Magical Miniature Landscapes - comprehensive history of bonsai and related arts
- 盆景雅舍 PenjingYashe
- National Bonsai Foundation / National Bonsai & Penjing Museum, Washington, DC

Chapter 2

Bonsai Aesthetics

2.1 Bonsai aesthetics

A bald cypress in the formal upright style.

Bonsai aesthetics are the aesthetic goals and characteristics of the Japanese tradition in the art of growing a miniature tree in a container. Many Japanese cultural characteristics, particularly the influence of Zen Buddhism and the expression of *wabi* or *sabi*,[1] inform the bonsai tradition in that culture. As well, a lengthy catalog of conventional tree shapes and styles helps provide cohesion to the Japanese styling tradition. A number of other cultures around the globe have adopted the Japanese approach to bonsai, and while some variations have begun to appear, most hew closely to the rules and design philosophies of the Japanese tradition.

The aesthetics of *penjing*, a Chinese form of container-grown tree, are distinct from those of bonsai and are discussed elsewhere. The aesthetics of *saikei*, Japanese multi-tree landscapes in a container, are also distinct and are not described in this article.

A Japanese Black Pine in an informal style.

Over centuries of practice, the Japanese bonsai aesthetic has encoded some important methods and aesthetic guidelines. Like the type of aesthetic rules that govern, for example, Western common practice period music, bonsai's guidelines help practitioners work within an established tradition with some assurance of success. Guidelines alone do not guarantee a successful result. Nevertheless, these design rules can rarely be broken without reducing the impact of the bonsai specimen.

2.1.1 Bonsai styles

Main article: Bonsai styles

A key design practice in bonsai is a set of commonly understood, named styles that describe canonical tree and setting designs. These well-known styles provide a convenient shorthand means for communicating about existing bonsai and for designing new ones. Bonsai styles describe a num-

John Naka's famous bonsai Goshin, *showing some deadwood effects.*

ber of basic attributes of a bonsai, such as the angle and straightness of its trunk, its branch configuration, and the number of trees in the bonsai container.

The system of styles serves many purposes, some practical, some aesthetic.*[2]*:3-1 In their simplest and most common application, styles provide a form of shorthand description for bonsai specimens. Predefined styles also aid the designer in making a development plan for a pre-bonsai tree. The untrained specimen may have characteristics that suggest or rule out certain styles. The designer can evaluate the pre-bonsai specimen against the catalog of accepted styles to determine what branches to remove or reshape, what foliage to remove or encourage, and what detailed shaping to apply to trunk and branches.

As with all aesthetic rules or guidelines, the various accepted styles will guide a bonsai designer, but are not completely deterministic. The species of the bonsai, the age of the tree when it began bonsai training, the tree's pre-existing shape and structure, even the bonsai artist's training and preferences, strongly affect the shape of the resulting bonsai. These competing influences ensure that the style system acts mostly as a creative aid, not a dominating constraint, in producing a finished bonsai.

A Blue Atlas Cedar (Cedrus libani var. atlantica) bonsai on display at the National Bonsai & Penjing Museum at the United States National Arboretum.

2.1.2 General aesthetic principles

The main aim of bonsai aesthetic practices is to create miniature trees with an air of age in their overall shapes, proportions, and details. The quintessential bonsai is a single, dwarfed tree in a small container. It has the appearance of a mature tree, but not of a completely natural one. Instead, a designer or artist has manipulated the shape and surfaces of the tree to enhance or exaggerate the tree's apparent age, and also to give it a defined "front" from which it is meant to be viewed. Anyone questioning the effect of the bonsai designer's work can test the quality of the design by viewing it from the rear, where exactly the same trunk and branches will generally look awkward, cluttered, or otherwise unattractive.

No trace of the artist

At the same time, the designer's touch must not be apparent to the viewer. If a branch is removed in shaping the tree, the scar will be placed at the "back" of the tree where it cannot be seen. Alternatively, the tree will not be shown until the scar has been covered by years of bark growing over it, or a stub of the branch will remain to be cleaned and shaped into looking like it was broken by wind or lightning. Similarly, wiring should be removed or at least concealed when the bonsai is shown, and must leave no permanent marks on

2.1. BONSAI AESTHETICS

the branch or bark.*[3]

Visual balance

Other guidelines address the balance of visual weight among the trunk, roots, foliage, and branches. The extensive catalog of recognized tree styles form part of this set of guidelines. The term "balance" here may refer to either:

- **static** visual balance, where careful application of symmetry leads to a stable and restful shape (like the formal upright, or *Chokkan*, style), or
- **dynamic** visual balance, which may arise from an asymmetric shape or one that implies instability and movement (like the cascade, or *Kengai*, style).

The trunk, roots, foliage, and branches are manipulated through a variety of techniques to meet the designer's goals of visual balance. Negative spaces (the "empty space" between solid elements like branches or foliage) are also shaped and proportioned to appear in balance. In almost all designs, the viewer can see completely through the tree's negative spaces to the background behind it. In this combination of positive and negative shapes, bonsai aesthetics overlap to a certain extent with the aesthetics of sculpture.

Proportion among elements

Another general guideline touches on the proportion of the bonsai's various elements. The most prized proportions mimic those of a full-grown tree as closely as possible. Slender branches with heavy leaves or needles that are out of proportion are avoided, as is a thin trunk with thick branches. One of the few exceptions to this guideline is that flowers and fruit (on trees that produce them) are not considered to be flawed if they appear too large for the tree.

Flexibility of the rules

One or more of the accepted rules of bonsai form can be bent or broken for a particular tree without destroying its fundamental aesthetic and artistic impact. In fact, going beyond the prescribed rules allows aesthetic growth in the bonsai art, as seen in many of the masterpieces created by Masahiko Kimura*[4] and Kunio Kobayashi.*[5]

2.1.3 General aesthetic guidelines

The following characteristics are desirable in many Japanese bonsai and other styles of container-grown trees, whatever the style:

Gravitas

This is the trait which all of the remaining points of aesthetics seek to create. It is a sense of physical weight, the illusion of mass, the appearance of maturity or advanced age, and the elusive quality of dignity. Many of the formal rules of bonsai help the grower create a tree that expresses *wabi* or *sabi*, or portrays an aspect of *mono no aware*.

Miniaturization

By definition, a bonsai is a tree which is kept small enough to be container-grown while otherwise fostered to have a mature appearance. Bonsai can be classified according to size. *Mame* are ideally less than 10 cm (4 inches) tall and can be held in the palm of the hand. *Shohin* are about 25 cm (10 inches) tall, while other bonsai are larger and can not be easily moved.*[6] For both practical and aesthetic reasons, the guidelines outlined here are generally most effective and most often applied to larger bonsai, while the smallest specimens of bonsai may adhere to no rules other than "miniature tree" and "grown in a container".

Lignification

This refers to enhancing the "woody-ness" of a bonsai's trunk and branches so that they have a mature appearance. This typically means the bark surface is encouraged to become rough and dark-colored. In some cases this aesthetic technique will vary, as in a birch tree bonsai attaining the white colour and exfoliating bark of a mature specimen.

Asymmetry

Bonsai aesthetics discourage strict symmetry in branch and root placement.*[7] Radial symmetry is nearly always broken by the requirement for a clear "front", which exposes the tree's trunk and major branches. The left, right, and back sides will have more branches than the front. Left-right (bilateral) symmetry across the trunk is also discouraged, and designers work to alternate branches among the left, right, and back parts of the tree without ever placing two branches at the same height or extending two branches the same distance away from the trunk.

Leaf Reduction

Leaf reduction is related to the general miniaturization described above but is something which varies over the life cycle of a particular bonsai. For example, a bonsai's leaves might be allowed to attain full size for many years in order to encourage vigor and growth of trunk, roots, and branches.

It is usually desirable to attain a degree of leaf reduction prior to exhibiting a bonsai. Leaf reduction may be encouraged by pruning and is sometimes achieved by the total defoliation of a bonsai during one part of its growing season. Conifer needles are more difficult to reduce than other sorts of foliage.

Nebari

Also known as "buttressing", *nebari* is the visible spread of roots above the growing medium at the base of a bonsai. Nebari help a bonsai seem grounded and well-anchored and make it look mature, akin to a full-sized tree.*[6]

Ramification

Ramification is the splitting of branches and twigs into smaller ones. It is encouraged by pruning and may be integrated with practices that promote leaf reduction.

Deadwood

Bonsai artists sometimes create or emphasize the appearance of dead wood on a bonsai tree, reflecting the occasional presence of dead branches or snags on full-sized trees. Two specific styles of deadwood are *jin* and *shari*. The presence of deadwood is not as common as most of the other points mentioned here, but can be used very effectively on selected tree species and bonsai styles.*[6] See deadwood techniques for more details.

Curvature

Trunk and branch curvature or contortion is an optional goal. Bonsai can achieve a sense of age while remaining straight and upright, but many bonsai rely upon curvature of the trunk to build the illusion of weight and age. Curvature of the trunk that occurs between the roots and the lowest branch is known as *tachiagari*.*[6] Branches are also curved and recurved to help them fit the designer's requirement for "positive space", and to separate small branches so that they do not cross or collide.

2.1.4 Concrete aesthetic guidelines

To support the general goals and principles of bonsai aesthetics, a number of detailed heuristics are taught in the bonsai tradition and documented in its literature (somewhat similar to the bonsai styles).*[8] Example guidelines include:*[9]

- The tree will appear in a formal container, relatively small compared to the tree.

- Except for the tree(s) and optional patches of moss, no other vegetation should appear in a bonsai container.

- Except for the soil, allowed vegetation, and optionally natural-looking rocks, no other object should appear in a bonsai container.

- The tree will have a distinct "front" from which it is intended to be viewed.

- The trunk should taper significantly from base to top.

- The tree's rootage should be exposed at the base of the trunk and should flare wider than the trunk as it enters the ground.

- No visible root should cross another.

- Branches should begin about one-third of the way up the trunk, and be continuous from there to the tip of the trunk (this guideline is specifically broken for the literati, or *Bunjin-gi*, style).

- Branch size should diminish from the base to the top of the tree.

- No major tree branch should cross the trunk when viewed from the tree's "front".

- Branch ramification, particularly in deciduous trees, should increase towards the tip of each branch.

- Branch shape should reflect the weight of age, particularly in conifers, and branches may be shaped to tend downwards toward the tip in support of this practice.

- The trunk may be a straight vertical shape or may be contorted in different directions over its length, but in styles where the tip of the tree is above the container, the tip should tilt slightly forward at the top (toward the viewer).

- Foliage (leaves or needles) should be small and to scale with the tree and its branches.

- All trees in a multi-tree bonsai planting should be of the same species.

2.1.5 See also

- Bonsai

- Bonsai styles - conventional styles in the Japanese tradition

- Deadwood Bonsai Techniques

- Bonsai cultivation and care
- Penjing
- Mambonsai
- Saikei
- Topiary
- List of species used in bonsai
- List of bonsai on stamps

2.1.6 External links

- The Art of Bonsai Project
- Bonsai tree care tips infographics

2.1.7 References

[1] Chan, Peter (1987). *Bonsai Masterclass.* Sterling Publishing Co., Inc. pp. 12–14. ISBN 0-8069-6763-3.

[2] "Intermediate Bonsai: A Course Syllabus" (PDF). Bonsaiempire.com. Retrieved 2010-07-25.

[3] Chan, Peter (1987). *Bonsai Masterclass.* Sterling Publishing Co., Inc. p. 14. ISBN 0-8069-6763-3.

[4] A visit to Masahiko Kimura's garden Archived December 25, 2008, at the Wayback Machine.

[5] "about KUNIO KOBAYASHI". *kunio-kobayashi.com.*

[6] Bonsai Terms Archived December 6, 2006, at the Wayback Machine.

[7] Douthitt, Jack (2001). *Bonsai: The Art of Living Sculpture.* Rizzoli International Publications, Inc. ISBN 0-8478-2320-2.

[8] Somewhat similar to the bonsai styles Archived November 30, 2009, at the Wayback Machine.

[9] Adams, Peter D. (1981). *The Art of Bonsai.* Ward Lock Ltd. ISBN 978-0-7063-7116-1.

2.2 Bonsai cultivation and care

Bonsai cultivation and care involves the long-term cultivation of small trees in containers, called *bonsai* in the Japanese tradition of this art form. Similar practices exist in other Japanese art forms and in other cultures, including *saikei* (Japanese), *penjing* (Chinese), and *hòn non bộ* (Vietnamese). Trees are difficult to cultivate in containers, which restrict root growth, nutrition uptake, and resources

A Trident Maple bonsai from the National Bonsai & Penjing Museum at the United States National Arboretum.

for transpiration (primarily soil moisture). In addition to the root constraints of containers, bonsai trunks, branches, and foliage are extensively shaped and manipulated to meet aesthetic goals. Specialized tools and techniques are used to protect the health and vigor of the subject tree. Over time, the artistic manipulation of small trees in containers has led to a number of cultivation and care approaches that successfully meet the practical and the artistic requirements of bonsai and similar traditions.

The term *bonsai* is generally used in English as an umbrella term for all miniature trees in containers or pots. In this article *bonsai* should be understood to include any container-grown tree that is regularly styled or shaped, not just one being maintained in the Japanese bonsai tradition.

Bonsai can be created from nearly any perennial woody-stemmed tree or shrub species[1] which produces true branches and remains small through pot confinement with crown and root pruning. Some species are popular as bonsai material because they have characteristics, such as small leaves or needles, that make them appropriate for the compact visual scope of bonsai. Bonsai cultivation techniques are different from other tree cultivation techniques in allowing mature (though miniature) trees to grow in small containers, to survive with extremely restricted root and canopy structures, and to support comprehensive, repeated styling manipulations.

2.2.1 Sources of bonsai material

All bonsai start with a specimen of source material, a plant that the grower wishes to train into bonsai form. Bonsai practice is an unusual form of plant cultivation in that growth from seeds is rarely used to obtain source material. To display the characteristic aged appearance of a bonsai within a reasonable time, the source plant is often partially grown or mature stock. A specimen may be selected specifically for bonsai aesthetic characteristics it already possesses, such as great natural age for a specimen collected in the wild, or a tapered, scar-free trunk from a nursery specimen. Alternatively, it may be selected for non-aesthetic reasons, such as known hardiness for the grower's local climate or low cost (as in the case of collected materials).

Propagation

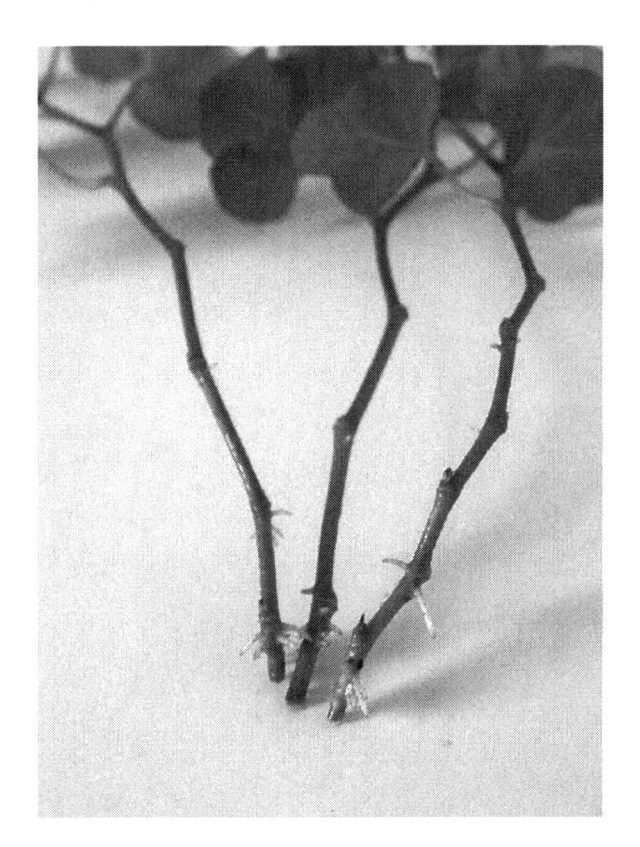

Plant cuttings can be rooted and grown as potential bonsai.

While any form of plant propagation could generate bonsai material, a few techniques are favored because they can quickly produce a relatively mature trunk with well-placed branches.

Cuttings. In taking a cutting, part of a growing plant is cut off and placed in a growing medium to develop roots. If the part that is cut off is fairly thick, like a mature branch, it can be grown into an aged-looking bonsai more quickly than can a seed. Unfortunately, thinner and younger cuttings tend to strike roots more easily than thicker or more mature ones.*[2] In bonsai propagation, cuttings usually provide source material to be grown for some time before training.

Layering. Layering is a technique in which rooting is encouraged from part of a plant, usually a branch, while it is still attached to the parent plant. After rooting, the branch is removed from the parent and grown as an independent entity. For bonsai, both ground layering and air layering can create a potential bonsai, by transforming a mature branch into the trunk of a new tree.*[3] The point at which rooting is encouraged can be close to the location of side branches, so the resulting rooted tree can immediately have a thick trunk and low branches, characteristics that complement bonsai aesthetics.

Commercial bonsai growers

Commercial bonsai growers may use any of the other means of obtaining starter bonsai material, from seed propagation to collecting expeditions, but they generally sell mature specimens that display bonsai aesthetic qualities already. The grower trains the source specimens to a greater or lesser extent before sale, and the trees may be ready for display as soon as they are bought. Those who purchase commercially grown bonsai face some challenges, however, particularly of buying from another country. If the purchaser's local climate does not closely match the climate in which the bonsai was created, the plant will have difficulties surviving and thriving. As well, importing living plant material from a foreign source is often closely controlled by import regulations and may require a license or other special import arrangement on the buyer's part. If a local commercial bonsai grower does not exist, buying from a distant one may be unsatisfactory.

Nursery stock

A plant nursery is an agricultural operation where (non-bonsai) plants are propagated and grown to usable size. Nursery stock may be available directly from the nursery, or may be sold in a garden centre or similar resale establishment. Nursery stock is usually young but fully viable, and is often potted with sufficient soil to allow plants to survive a season or two before being transplanted into a more permanent location. Because the nursery tree is already pot-conditioned, it can be worked on as a bonsai immediately. The large number of plants that can be viewed in a single visit to a nursery or garden centre allows the buyer to identify plants with better-than-average bonsai characteristics. According to Peter Adams, a nursery visit "offers the opportunity to choose an instant trunk" ."[3] One issue with nursery stock is that many specimens are shaped into popular forms, such as the standard or half-standard forms, with several feet of clear trunk rising from the roots. Without branches low on the trunk, it is difficult for a source specimen to be trained as bonsai.

Collecting

Collecting bonsai consists of finding suitable bonsai material in its original wild situation, successfully moving it, and replanting it in a container for development as bonsai. Collecting may involve wild materials from naturally treed areas, or cultivated specimens found growing in yards and gardens.*[4] For example, mature landscape plants being discarded from a building site can provide excellent material for bonsai. Hedgerow trees, grown for many years but continually trimmed to hedge height, provide heavy, gnarled trunks for bonsai collectors. In locations close to a tree line (the line beyond which trees do not grow, whether due to altitude, temperature, soil moisture, or other conditions), aged and naturally dwarfed survivors can be found.

The main benefit of collecting bonsai specimens is that collected materials can be mature, and will display the natural marks and forms of age, which makes them more suitable for bonsai development than the young plants obtained through nurseries. Low cost is another potential benefit, with a tree harvest license often being more economical than purchase of nursery trees. Some of the difficulties of collecting include finding suitable specimens, getting permission to remove them, and the challenges of keeping a mature tree alive while transplanting it to a bonsai pot.

2.2.2 Styling techniques

Bonsai are carefully styled to maintain miniaturization, to suggest age, and to meet the artist's aesthetic goals. Tree styling also occurs in a larger scale in other practices like topiary and niwaki. In bonsai, however, the artist has close control over every feature of the tree, because it is small and (in its container) easily moved and worked on. The greater scale of full-sized trees means that styling them may be restricted to pruning and shaping the exterior volume once per growing season, never pruning within the canopy nor bending and forming individual branches. In contrast, in a bonsai being prepared for display, each leaf or needle may be subject to decision regarding pruning or retention, and every branch and twig may be formed and wired into place each year. Given these differences in scope and purpose, bonsai styling uses a number of styling techniques either

This juniper makes extensive use of both jin (deadwood branches) and shari (trunk deadwood).

unique to bonsai or (if used in other forms of plant cultivation) applied in ways particularly suitable to meet the goals of bonsai development.

Leaf trimming

This technique involves selective removal of leaves (for most varieties of deciduous tree) or needles (for coniferous trees and some others) from a bonsai's branches. A common aesthetic technique in bonsai design is to expose the tree's branches below groups of leaves or needles (sometimes called "pads") by removing downward-growing material. In many species, particularly coniferous ones, this means that leaves or needles projecting below their branches must be trimmed off. For some coniferous varieties, such as spruce, branches carry needles from the trunk to the tip and many of these needles may be trimmed to expose the branch shape and bark. Needle and bud trimming can also be used in coniferous trees to force back-budding on old wood, which may not occur naturally in many conifers.*[3] Along with pruning, leaf trimming is the most common activity used for bonsai development and maintenance, and the one that occurs most frequently during the year.

Pruning

The small size of the tree and some dwarfing of foliage result from pruning the trunk, branches, and roots. Pruning is often the first step in transforming a collected plant specimen into a candidate for bonsai. The top part of the trunk may be removed to make the tree more compact. Major and minor branches that conflict with the designer's plan will be removed completely, and others may be shortened to fit within the planned design. Pruning later in the bonsai's life is generally less severe, and may be done for purposes like increasing branch ramification or encouraging growth of non-pruned branches. Although pruning is an important and common bonsai practice, it must be done with care, as improper pruning can weaken or kill trees.*[5] Careful pruning throughout the tree's life is necessary, however, to maintain a bonsai's basic design, which can otherwise disappear behind the uncontrolled natural growth of branches and leaves.

Wiring

Extensive wiring can be seen on this bonsai specimen.

Wrapping copper or aluminium wire around branches and trunks allows the bonsai designer to create the desired general form and make detailed branch and leaf placements. When wire is used on new branches or shoots, it holds the branches in place until they lignify (convert into wood). The time required is usually 6–9 months or one growing season for deciduous trees, but can be several years for conifers like pines and spruce, which maintain their branch flexibility through multiple growing seasons. Wires are also used to connect a branch to another object (e.g., another branch, the pot itself) so that tightening the wire applies force to the branch. Some species do not lignify strongly, and some specimens' branches are too stiff or brittle to be bent easily. These cases are not conducive to wiring, and shaping them is accomplished primarily through pruning.

Clamping

For larger specimens, or species with stiffer wood, bonsai artists also use mechanical devices for shaping trunks and branches. The most common are screw-based clamps, which can straighten or bend a part of the bonsai using much greater force than wiring can supply. To prevent damage to the tree, the clamps are tightened a little at a time and make their changes over a period of months or years.

Grafting

In this technique, new growing material (typically a bud, branch, or root) is introduced to a prepared area under the bark of the tree. There are two major purposes for grafting in bonsai. First, a number of favorite species do not thrive as bonsai on their natural root stock and their trunks are often grafted onto hardier root stock. Examples include Japanese red maple and Japanese black pine.*[3] Second, grafting allows the bonsai artist to add branches (and sometimes roots) where they are needed to improve or complete a bonsai design.*[6]*[7] There are many applicable grafting techniques, none unique to bonsai, including branch grafting, bud grafting, thread grafting, and others.

Defoliation

Short-term dwarfing of foliage can be accomplished in certain deciduous bonsai by partial or total defoliation of the plant partway through the growing season. Not all species can survive this technique. In defoliating a healthy tree of a suitable species, most or all of the leaves are removed by clipping partway along each leaf's petiole (the thin stem that connects a leaf to its branch). Petioles later dry up and drop off or are manually removed once dry. The tree responds by producing a fresh crop of leaves. The new leaves are generally much smaller than those from the first crop, sometimes as small as half the length and width. If the bonsai is shown at this time, the smaller leaves contribute greatly to the bonsai aesthetic of dwarfing. This change in leaf size is usually not permanent, and the leaves of the following spring will often be the normal size. Defoliation weakens the tree and should not be performed in two consecutive years.*[8]

Deadwood

Main article: Deadwood bonsai techniques

Bonsai growers create or shape dead wood using techniques such as *jin* and *shari* to simulate age and maturity in a bonsai. Jin is the term used when the bark from an entire branch is removed to create the impression of a snag of deadwood.

Shari denotes stripping bark from areas of the trunk to simulate natural scarring from a broken limb or lightning strike. In addition to stripping bark, deadwood techniques may also involve the use of tools to scar the deadwood or to raise its grain, and the application of chemicals (usually lime sulfur) to bleach and preserve the exposed deadwood.

2.2.3 Care

Small trees grown in containers, like bonsai, require specialized care. Unlike most houseplants, flowering shrubs, and other subjects of container gardening, tree species in the wild generally grow individual roots up to several meters long and root structures encompassing hundreds or thousands of liters of soil. In contrast, a typical bonsai container allows a fraction of a meter for root extension, and holds 2 to 10 liters of soil and root mass. Branch and leaf (or needle) growth in trees is also large-scale in nature. Wild trees typically grow 5 meters or taller when mature, while the largest bonsai rarely exceed 1 meter and most specimens are significantly smaller. These size differences affect maturation, transpiration, nutrition, pest resistance, and many other aspects of tree biology. Maintaining the long-term health of a tree in a container requires a number of specialized care techniques.

Growing environment

Most bonsai species are trees and shrubs that must by nature grow outdoors. They require temperature, humidity, and sunlight conditions approximating their native climate year round. The skill of the grower can help bonsai from outside the local hardiness zone survive and even thrive, but doing so takes careful watering, shielding of selected bonsai from excessive sunlight or wind, and possibly protection from winter conditions (e.g., through the use of cold frames or winter greenhouses).*[9]

Common bonsai species (particularly those from the Japanese tradition) are temperate climate trees from hardiness zones 7 to 9, and require moderate temperatures, moderate humidity, and full sun in summer with a dormancy period in winter that may need be near freezing. They do not thrive indoors, where the light is generally too dim, and humidity often too low, for them to grow properly. Only during their dormant period can they safely be brought indoors, and even then the plants require cold temperatures, reduced watering, and lighting that approximates the number of hours the sun is visible. Raising the temperature or providing more hours of light than available from natural daylight can cause the bonsai to break dormancy, which often weakens or kills it.

Even for bonsai specimens that are native to the grower's location, outdoor cultivation requires specific cultivation practices to ensure successful long-term survival of the bonsai. The trees used in bonsai are constrained by the need to grow in a relatively small pot. This state greatly reduces the volume of roots and soil normally available to a freely grown tree, and brings the roots much closer to the surface of the soil than would occur in the wild. Trees in bonsai pots have much less access to water and to nutrients than they do natively, and physically confining roots changes their growth pattern and indirectly the growth pattern of the tree above the soil.

The grower has some control over the following environmental variables, and by controlling them effectively for individual specimens can ensure the health of native species grown as bonsai, and can cultivate some non-native species successfully.

- *Watering*: Different species of tree have roots with different tolerances for soil moisture. Some species tolerate continual wetness, while others are prone to rotting if the soil remains wet for long periods. A standard bonsai practice is to grow trees in a soil mixture that drains rapidly, so that roots are not allowed to be wet for long. To compensate for the relatively low water retention of the bonsai soil, water is applied frequently. The tree absorbs sufficient moisture for its needs while the water is passing through the soil, then the soil dries enough to reduce the chance of rotting. It is the grower's responsibility to ensure that watering occurs frequently enough to satisfy the bonsai with high watering requirements, while not waterlogging trees that use little water or have roots prone to rotting.

- *Soil volume*: Giving a bonsai a relatively large soil volume encourages the growth of roots, then corresponding growth of the rest of the tree. With a large amount of soil, the tree trunk extends in length and increases in diameter, existing branches increase in size and new branches appear, and the foliage expands in volume. The grower can move an outdoor bonsai from a pot to a training box or to open ground to stimulate this sort of growth. Replacing the tree in a bonsai pot will slow or halt the tree's growth, and may lead to die-back if the volume of foliage is too great for the limited root system to support. Managing the tree's available soil volume allows the grower to manage the overall size of the bonsai, and to increase vigor and growth when new branches are required for a planned styling.

- *Temperature*: Bonsai roots in pots are exposed to much greater variation in temperature than tree roots deep in the soil. For bonsai from native species, local temperatures do not generally harm the tree. But for bonsai from warmer native climates, the grower can increase the likelihood of successful cultivation either by insulating the tree from local winter conditions, or by actively increasing the bonsai temperature during the cold season. For trees from climates slightly warmer than the local one, bonsai pots can be partially buried in the ground and can be covered with an insulating layer of mulch. For trees from significantly warmer climates, warmer temperatures can be maintained in a cold frame or greenhouse, so that a relatively tender tree is not exposed to temperatures lower than it can bear. This approach may also artificially extend the bonsai's growing season, affecting watering and fertilization schedules.

- *Sunlight*: Trees generally require a good deal of sun, and most bonsai need direct sunlight during the growing season to thrive. Some shade-tolerant species of bonsai cannot thrive with too much direct sunlight, however, and it is the grower's role to site the bonsai specimens to provide the correct lighting for each type. Most bonsai will be located in an area that gets several hours of direct daylight. Shade-tolerant bonsai can be placed behind barriers (walls, buildings), sited on shaded benches or stands, or shaded by netting to reduce the impact of direct sunlight.

Repotting

Bonsai are repotted and root-pruned at intervals dictated by the vigor and age of each tree. In the case of deciduous trees, this is done as the tree is leaving its dormant period, generally around springtime. Bonsai are often repotted while in development, and less often as they become more mature. This prevents them from becoming pot-bound and encourages the growth of new feeder roots, allowing the tree to absorb moisture more efficiently.

Specimens meant to be developed into bonsai are often placed in "growing boxes", which have a much larger volume of soil per plant than a bonsai pot does. These large boxes allow the roots to grow freely, increasing the vigor of the tree and helping the trunk and branches grow thicker. After using a grow box, the tree may be replanted in a more compact "training box" that helps to create a smaller, denser root mass which can be more easily moved into a final presentation pot.

Tools

Special tools are available for the maintenance of bonsai. The most common tool is the concave cutter (5th from left in picture), a tool designed to prune flush, without leaving a stub. Other tools include branch bending jacks, wire pliers

An uprooted bonsai, ready for repotting

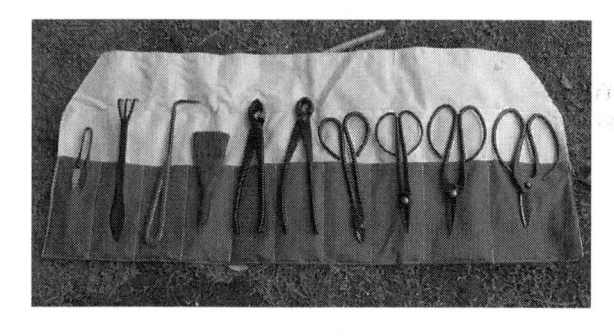

Set of bonsai tools (left to right): leaf trimmer; rake with spatula; root hook; coir brush; concave cutter; knob cutter; wire cutter; small, medium and large shears

and shears of different proportions for performing detail and rough shaping.

Soil and fertilization

Bonsai soil is usually a loose, fast-draining mix of components,*[10] often a base mixture of coarse sand or gravel, fired clay pellets, or expanded shale combined with an organic component such as peat or bark. The inorganic com-

Akadama soil

ponents provide mechanical support for bonsai roots, and —in the case of fired clay materials—also serve to retain moisture. The organic components retain moisture and may release small amounts of nutrients as they decay.

In Japan, bonsai soil mixes based on volcanic clays are common. The volcanic clay has been fired at some point in time to create porous, water-retaining pellets. Varieties such as akadama, or "red ball" soil, and kanuma, a type of yellow pumice used for azaleas and other calcifuges, are used by many bonsai growers. Similar fired clay soil components are extracted or manufactured in other countries around the world, and other soil components like diatomaceous earth can fill a similar purpose in bonsai cultivation.

Opinions about fertilizers and fertilization techniques vary widely among practitioners. Some promote the use of organic fertilizers to augment an essentially inorganic soil mix, while others will use chemical fertilizers freely. Many follow the general rule of little and often, where a dilute fertilizer solution or a small amount of dry fertilizer are applied relatively frequently during the tree's growing season. The flushing effect of regular watering moves unmetabolized fertilizer out of the soil, preventing the potentially toxic build-up of fertilizer ingredients.

Pest management

The common pests afflicting bonsai include insects both above and beneath the soil, and infections, usually fungal. A tree grown as a bonsai is subject to the pests that affect the same species full-grown, and also to pests common to other potted plants.*[11] Most pests are species-specific, so a detailed understanding of the specific bonsai species is necessary for identifying and treating most pests. The same materials and techniques used for other affected plants can be applied to the bonsai, with some relatively minor variation. Pesticide chemicals are usually diluted more for bonsai than for a larger plant, as a regular-strength application may overwhelm the smaller bonsai's biological processes.

Location

Outdoors Bonsai are sometimes marketed or promoted as house plants, but few of the traditional bonsai species can thrive or even survive inside a typical house. Most bonsai are located out of doors. The best guideline to identifying a suitable growing environment for a bonsai is its native hardiness. If the bonsai grower can closely replicate the full year's temperatures, relative humidity, and sunlight, the bonsai should do well. In practice, this means that trees from a hardiness zone closely matching the grower's location will generally be the easiest to grow, and others will require more work or will not be viable at all.*[12]

Indoors Main article: Indoor bonsai

Tropical and Mediterranean species typically require consistent temperatures close to room temperature, and with correct lighting and humidity many species can be kept indoors all year. Those from cooler climates may benefit from a winter dormancy period, but temperatures need not be dropped as far as for the temperate climate plants and a north-facing windowsill or open window may provide the right conditions for a few winter months.*[13]

2.2.4 See also

- Bonsai
- Indoor bonsai
- Bonsai aesthetics
- Penjing – Chinese precursor to bonsai
- Saikei – tray gardens using live trees

2.2.5 References

[1] Owen, Gordon (1990). *The Bonsai Identifier*. Quintet Publishing Ltd. p. 11. ISBN 0-88665-833-0.

[2] Chan, Peter (1987). *Bonsai Masterclass*. Sterling Publishing Co., Inc. ISBN 0-8069-6763-3.

[3] Adams, Peter D. (1981). *The Art of Bonsai*. Ward Lock Ltd. pp. 71–74. ISBN 978-0-7063-7116-1.

[4] Treasure, Martin (2002). *Bonsai Life Histories*. Firefly Books Ltd. pp. 12–14. ISBN 1-55209-615-7.

[5] Lewis, Colin (2003). *The Bonsai Handbook*. Advanced Marketing Ltd. ISBN 1-903938-30-9.

[6] "Grafting as a Bonsai Tool". Bonsaikc.com. Retrieved 2009-04-28.

[7] "Root Grafts for Bonsai". Evergreengardenworks.com. Retrieved 2009-04-28.

[8] Norman, Ken (2005). *Growing Bonsai: A Practical Encyclopedia*. Lorenz Books. ISBN 978-0-7548-1572-3.

[9] Chan, Peter (1987). *Bonsai Masterclass*. Sterling Publishing Co., Inc. p. 24. ISBN 0-8069-6763-3.

[10] "It's All In The Soil by Mike Smith, published in "Norfolk Bonsai" (Spring 2007) by Norfolk Bonsai Association". Norfolkbonsai.co.uk. Archived from the original on 2007-09-30.

[11] Prescott, David (2001). *The Bonsai Handbook*. New Holland Publishers Ltd. p. 62. ISBN 978-1-85974-708-7.

[12] Pike, Dave (1989). *Indoor Bonsai*. The Crowood Press. ISBN 978-1-85223-254-2.

[13] Lesniewicz, Paul (1996). *Bonsai in Your Home*. Sterling Publishing Company. ISBN 0-8069-0781-9.

2.2.6 External links

- Bonsai cultivation and care at DMOZ

2.3 Bonsai styles

Bonsai is a Japanese art form using miniature trees grown in containers. Similar practices exist in other cultures, including the Chinese tradition of *penjing* from which the art originated, and the miniature living landscapes of Vietnamese *hòn non bộ*, but this article describes the Japanese tradition.

The Japanese art of bonsai dates back over a thousand years, and has evolved its own unique aesthetics and terminology. A key design practice in bonsai is a set of commonly understood, named styles that describe canonical tree and setting designs. These well-known styles provide a convenient shorthand means for communicating about existing bonsai and for designing new ones.

2.3.1 Concept of styles

Styles can be grouped based on different criteria, such as the trunk orientation or the number of trunks in the bonsai specimen.[*][1][*]:63–66 Some of the major style groupings include:

Formal upright style Bald cypress

Informal upright style Juniper

- **Trunk orientation.** A frequently used set of styles describe the orientation of the bonsai tree's main trunk. Different terms are used for a tree with its apex

2.3. BONSAI STYLES

Semi-cascade style mountain pine (Pinus mugo)

Cascade style conifer

Forest style Black Hills Spruce

Slant style Hinoki cypress

Driftwood style Sierra juniper (Juniperus occidentalis var. australis)

directly over the center of the trunk's entry into the soil (these are the upright styles, including *chokkan* and *moyogi*), slightly to the side of that center (e.g., *sho-shakan*), deeply inclined to one side (e.g., *chu-shakan* and *dai-shakan*), and inclined below the point at which the trunk of the bonsai enters the soil (the cascade or *kengai* styles).*[2]*:153

- **Trunk and bark surface.** A number of styles de-

Twin-trunk style smoothleaf elm (Ulmus minor)

scribe the trunk shape and bark finish. For example, a bonsai with a twisted trunk is *nebikan* (also *nejikan* (ねじ幹)), and one with a vertical split or hollows is *sabakan*. The deadwood bonsai styles identify trees with prominent dead branches or trunk scarring.*[3]*:123–124

- **Trunk and root placement.** Although most bonsai trees are planted directly into the soil, there are styles describing trees planted on rock. For example, the root-over rock style is *deshojo* (出猩々), and the style in which trees are rooted wholly within (atop or on the sides of) a large rock is *ishizuki*.*[4]*:86–91

- **Multiple trunks.** While the majority of bonsai specimens feature a single tree, there are well-established style categories for specimens with multiple trunks. Within these styles, a bonsai can be classified by number of trunks alone (e.g., *sokan* for a double trunk from a single root, *soju* for two separate trees, *sambon-yose* for three trees, and so on). The configuration of the trunks can also be described by specific styles, including raft (*ikadabuji* or *ikadabuki*) and sinuous (*netsunagari*) styles for multiple trees growing from a connected root, and the general term *yose-ue* for multiple unconnected trees in large number.*[1]*:65–66

These terms are not mutually exclusive, and a single bonsai specimen can exhibit more than one style characteristic. When a bonsai specimen falls into multiple style categories, the common practice is to describe it by the dominant or most striking characteristic. For example, an informal upright tree with prominent areas of missing bark and trunk scarring will be described as a *sharimiki* rather than a *moyogi*.

Purposes

The system of styles serves many purposes, some practical, some aesthetic.*[5]*:3–13 In their simplest and most common application, styles provide a form of shorthand description for bonsai specimens. The brief style term appears in catalog descriptions, usually with a species identifier, and thereby compactly describes the subject bonsai. Style names can also be used to group comparable specimens in bonsai viewing and competition. Even considering the styles simply as descriptive labels, the system still simplifies bonsai teaching and learning, and provides widely understood terms for public communications about bonsai.

Predefined styles also aid the designer in making a development plan for a pre-bonsai tree. The untrained specimen may have characteristics that suggest or rule out certain styles. For example, a crooked trunk makes a tree unsuitable for the formal upright style,*[6]*:132 and suggests to the designer that the tree may be trained better as an informal upright or a slanted style instead. A damaged or highly asymmetrical tree may not appear suitable for bonsai development, yet may be adapted to an uncommon style like windswept or raft, which both work for trees that have branches only on one side of the trunk. Some tree species are not suitable for some styles: a bonsai artist working with a deciduous tree will not produce bonsai in the cascade style, for example. The designer can evaluate the pre-bonsai specimen against the catalog of accepted styles to determine what branches to remove or reshape, what foliage to remove or encourage, and what detailed shaping to apply to trunk and branches.

Although the styles will guide a bonsai designer, they are not completely deterministic. A review of actual bonsai from competition catalogs will reveal that even highly regarded specimens rarely meet every rule laid out for their style. The species of the bonsai, the age of the tree when it began bonsai training, the tree's pre-existing shape and structure, even the bonsai artist's training and preferences, strongly affect the shape of the resulting bonsai. These competing influences ensure that the style system acts mostly as a creative aid, not a dominating constraint, in producing a finished bonsai.

2.3.2 Catalog of styles

2.3.3 Common styles

- Upright or *chokkan* style

- Informal upright style or *moyogi* style

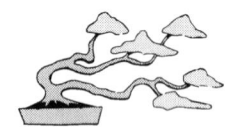

- Slanted or *shakan* style

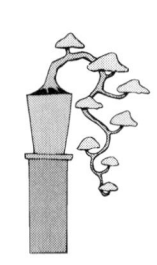

- Cascade or *kengai* style

- Semi-cascade or *han kengai* style

- Broom or *hokidachi* style

- Multi-trunk or *sokan* style (twin-trunk style in this example)

- Literati or *bunjin-gi* style

2.3.4 See also

- Bonsai aesthetics - aesthetics of Japanese bonsai
- Bonsai cultivation and care - cultivation and care of small, container-grown trees
- Deadwood bonsai techniques - description of deadwood techniques and effects in small trees
- Penjing – Chinese precursor to bonsai
- Saikei – tray gardens using bonsai
- Indoor bonsai - cultivation and care of trees grown indoors in containers

2.3.5 References

[1] Yuji Yoshimura and Barbara M. Halford (1957). *The Art of Bonsai: Creation, Care and Enjoyment*. Tuttle Publishing, North Clarendon VT USA. ISBN 0-8048-2091-0.

[2] Koreshoff, Deborah R. (1984). *Bonsai: Its Art, Science, History and Philosophy*. Timber Press, Inc. ISBN 0-88192-389-3.

[3] Naka, John Yoshio (1973). *Bonsai Techniques I*. Bonsai Institute of California. ISBN 0-930422-31-7.

[4] Masakuni Kawasumi II with Masakuni Kawasumi III (2005). *The Secret Techniques of Bonsai: A guide to starting, raising, and shaping bonsai*. Kodansha International. ISBN 978-4-7700-2943-0.

[5] "Intermediate Bonsai: A Course Syllabus" (PDF). Bonsaiempire.com. Retrieved 2010-07-25.

[6] Amy Liang (2005). *The Living Art of Bonsai: Principles and Techniques of Cultivation and Propagation*. Sterling Publishing Co., Inc.: New York. ISBN 1-4027-1901-9.

[7] "Types of Bonsai Trees - The 5 Most Common Styles". *BonsaiDojo - Bonsai Tree Care Guide*.

[8] *Handbook on Bonsai: Special Techniques*. Brooklyn Botanic Garden: Brooklyn, New York. 1966. pp. 24–31.

[9] "bunjingi". Phoenixbonsai.com. Retrieved 2009-04-28.

Chapter 3

Plants Used in Bonsai (in Alphabetical Order)

3.1 Acer buergerianum

Acer buergerianum (**trident maple**; Chinese: 三角枫 *san jiao feng*) is a species of maple native to eastern China (from Shandong west to southeastern Gansu, south to Guangdong and Taiwan, and southwest to Sichuan) and Japan.*[2]*[3]

3.1.1 Description

It is a small to medium-sized deciduous tree reaching a height of 5–20 m with a trunk up to 50 cm diameter. The leaves are in opposite pairs, 2.5–8 cm long (excluding the 2–5 cm petiole) and 3.5–6.5 cm broad, hard, glossy dark green above, paler below, usually with three lobes; on mature trees the lobes forward-pointing and with smooth margins, on young trees with more spreading lobes and serrated margins. The flowers are produced in spring, yellow-green, in pendulous corymbs; they are small, with five greenish sepals and five yellow-white petals about 2 mm long, and eight stamens. The fruit is a samara with two winged seeds, each seed 4–7 mm diameter, with a 15 mm wing; the wings are forward-pointing and often overlapping each other.*[2]*[4]*[5]

The species is variable, and a number of varieties have been described:*[2]

- *Acer buergerianum* var. *buergerianum*. Hubei, Hunan, Jiangsu, Jiangxi, Shandong, Zhejiang.

- *Acer buergerianum* var. *jiujiangense* Z.X.Yu. Jiangxi.

- *Acer buergerianum* var. *horizontale* F.P.Metcalf. Southern Zhejiang.

- *Acer buergerianum* var. *formosanum* (Hayata ex Koidzumi) Sasaki. Taiwan (endemic).

- *Acer buergerianum* var. *kaiscianense* (Pampanini) W.P.Fang. Gansu, Hubei, Shaanxi.

- *Acer buergerianum* var. *yentangense* W.P.Fang & M.Y.Fang. Zhejiang.

A few trees have consistently unlobed leaves; these were first described as a variety *A. trifidium* var. *integrifolium* Makino (*A. trifidium* is an old synonym of *A. buergerianum*), but are now not distinguished from the species.*[6] Occasional unlobed leaves also occur on most trees with otherwise normal three-lobed leaves.*[7]

3.1.2 Cultivation

It is widely grown in temperate regions as an ornamental tree. It was introduced very early to Japan, where its name translates as "China maple".*[5]*[8] More recently, it was introduced to Europe and North America in 1896, and is now occasionally grown in parks and large gardens there.*[7] Mature examples may be seen at Westonbirt Arboretum in England, the Esveld Aceretum in Boskoop, Netherlands, Arnold Arboretum in Boston, Massachusetts and many other locations.*[4]

Bonsai

Trident maple is a popular choice for the art of bonsai and responds well to techniques that create leaf reduction and ramification,*[4] is suitable for many style and sizes of bonsai.*[9]

Cultivars

Several interesting cultivars have been developed, many of these bear Japanese names. Notable cultivars include 'Goshiki Kaede' (striking pink and green variegation), 'Kifu Nishiki' (roundish, almost un-lobed leaves), 'Mino Yatsubusa' (dwarf with long, narrow leaves) 'Mitsubato Kaede'

Trident maple bonsai

(distinctive cork-like trunk) and 'Naruto' (strongly incurved leaf surface).*[4]

3.1.3 References

[1] The Plant List, *Acer buergerianum* Miq.

[2] Flora of China (draft): Aceraceae

[3] Germplasm Resources Information Network: *Acer buergerianum*

[4] van Gelderen, C.J. & van Gelderen, D.M. (1999). *Maples for Gardens: A Color Encyclopedia*

[5] Rushforth, K. (1999). *Trees of Britain and Europe*. Collins ISBN 0-00-220013-9.

[6] Makino Herbarium, Tokyo: *Acer trifidium*

[7] Mitchell, A. F. (1974). *A Field Guide to the Trees of Britain and Northern Europe.* Collins ISBN 0-00-212035-6

[8] Kanon tree book: *Acer buergerianum* (in Japanese; google translation)

[9] D'Cruz, Mark. "Ma-Ke Bonsai Care Guide for Acer buergerianum". Ma-Ke Bonsai. Retrieved 2011-07-05.

3.1.4 External links

- line drawing, Manual of Vascular Plants of the Lower Yangtze Valley China Illustration fig. 219

3.2 Acer campestre

Acer campestre, known as the **field maple**,*[2] is a flowering plant species in the soapberry and lychee family Sapindaceae. It is native to much of Europe, the British Isles, southwest Asia from Turkey to the Caucasus, and north Africa in the Atlas Mountains. It has been widely planted, and is introduced outside its native range in Europe and areas of USA and Western Australia with suitable climate.

3.2.1 Description

It is a deciduous tree reaching 15–25 m (49–82 ft) tall, with a trunk up to 1 m (3 ft 3 in) in diameter, with finely fissured, often somewhat corky bark. The shoots are brown, with dark brown winter buds. The leaves are in opposite pairs, 5–16 cm (2.0–6.3 in) long (including the 3–9 cm (1.2–3.5 in) petiole) and 5–10 cm (2.0–3.9 in) broad, with five blunt, rounded lobes with a smooth margin. Usually monoecious, the flowers are produced in spring at the same time as the leaves open, yellow-green, in erect clusters 4–6 cm (1.6–2.4 in) across, and are insect-pollinated. The fruit is a samara with two winged achenes aligned at 180°, each achene is 8–10 mm (0.31–0.39 in) wide, flat, with a 2 cm (0.79 in) wing.*[3]*[4]

The two varieties, not accepted as distinct by all authorities, are:*[3]*[5]

- *A. c.* var. *campestre* - downy fruit
- *A. c.* var. *leiocarpum* (Opiz) Wallr. (syn. *A. c.* subsp. *leiocarpum*) - hairless fruit

The closely related *Acer miyabei* replaces it in eastern Asia.*[3]

-  Field maple flowers
-  Field maple in autumn, France
-  Field maple, Germany

-  Field maple, Spain
-  Leaves and inflorescence
-  Leaves and fruits
-  Trunk

Maple field tree, Weinsberg

3.2.2 Distribution

The native range of field maple includes much of Europe, including Denmark, Poland and Belarus, England north to southern Scotland (where it is the only native maple), southwest Asia from Turkey to the Caucasus, and north Africa in the Atlas Mountains.*[3]*[4]*[5]*[6]*[7]*[8]*[9] In many areas, the original native range is obscured by widespread planting and introductions.*[10] In North America it is known as **hedge maple***[11]*[12] and in Australia, it is sometimes called **common maple.***[13] In Nottinghamshire, England it was known locally as **dog oak**.*[14]

3.2.3 Ecology

Field maple is an intermediate species in the ecological succession of disturbed areas; it typically is not among the first trees to colonise a freshly disturbed area, but instead seeds in under the existing vegetation. It is very shade-tolerant during the initial stages of its life, but it has higher light requirements during its seed-bearing years. It exhibits rapid growth initially, but is eventually overtaken and replaced by other trees as the forest matures. It is most commonly found on neutral to alkaline soils, but more rarely on acidic soil.*[9]

Diseases include a leaf spot fungus *Didymosporina aceris*, a mildew *Uncinula bicornis*, a canker *Nectria galligena*, and verticillium wilt *Verticillium alboatrum*. The leaves are also sometimes damaged by gall mites in the genus *Aceria*, and the aphid *Periphyllus villosus*.*[15]

3.2.4 Cultivation

The field maple is widely grown as an ornamental tree in parks and large gardens. The wood is white, hard and strong, and used for furniture, flooring, wood turning and musical instruments,*[16] though the small size of the tree and its relatively slow growth make it an unimportant wood.*[3]

It is locally naturalised in parts of the United States*[11] and more rarely in New Zealand.*[17] The hybrid maple *Acer × zoeschense* has *A. campestre* as one of its parents.*[4]

The tree has gained the Royal Horticultural Society's Award of Garden Merit.*[18]

Cultivars

Over 30 cultivars of *Acer campestre* are known, selected for their foliage or habit, or occasionally both; several have been lost to cultivation.*[19]

3.2.5 *Bonsai*

A. campestre (and the similar *A. monspessulanum*) are popular among *bonsai* enthusiasts. The dwarf cultivar 'Microphyllum' is especially useful in this regard. *A. campestre*

Maple field illustration

Leaf

- Field maple leaf
- Leaves and flowers
- Field maple, Germany
- Leaves
- Foliage in spring
- Field maple leaf
- Field maple, Hesse, Germany

bonsai have an appearance distinct from those selected from some other maples such as *A. palmatum* with more frilly, translucent, leaves. The shrubby habit and smallish leaves of *A. campestre* respond well to techniques encouraging ramification and leaf reduction.*[20]*[21]

-  Field maple leaf
- 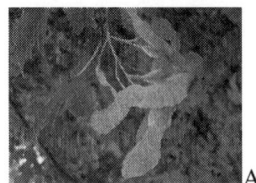 Acer campestre
-  Field maple

3.2.6 References

[1] Stevens, P. F. (2001 onwards). Angiosperm Phylogeny Website Version 9, June 2008 [and more or less continuously updated since].

[2] "BSBI List 2007". Botanical Society of Britain and Ireland.

[3] Rushforth, K. (1999). *Trees of Britain and Europe.* Collins ISBN 0-00-220013-9.

[4] Mitchell, A. F. (1974). *A Field Guide to the Trees of Britain and Northern Europe.* Collins ISBN 0-00-212035-6

[5] Euro+Med Plantbase Project: *Acer campestre*

[6] "*Acer campestre*". Flora Europaea. Retrieved August 29, 2007.

[7] Flora of NW Europe: *Acer campestre*

[8] Den virtuella floran: *Acer campestre* distribution map

[9] Nagy, L. & Ducci, F. (2004). "Acer campestre - Field maple" (PDF). *EUFORGEN Technical guidelines for genetic conservation and use*: 6 p.

[10] "Online atlas of the British and Irish flora, *Acer campestre (Field maple)*". Biological Records Centre and Botanical Society of Britain and Ireland.

[11] "*Acer campestre*". USDA Plants Profile. Retrieved August 29, 2007.

[12] "*Acer campestre*". Ohio State University. Retrieved August 29, 2007.

[13] Department of Agriculture, Western Australia: Pests and Diseases Image Library

[14] Wright, Joseph. *The English dialect dictionary.* **6**. London: Oxford University Press. p. 109.

[15] Field maple images and diseases

[16] "Field maple_Woodland Trust".

[17] *Trans. and Proc. Roy. Soc. New Zealand* 36: 203-225 Plants naturalised in the County of Ashburton

[18] RHS Plant Selector Acer campestre AGM / RHS Gardening

[19] van Gelderen, C.J.; van Gelderen, D.M. (1999). Maples for Gardens: A Color Encyclopedia.

[20] "*A. campestre*". Bonsai Club International. Archived from the original on November 11, 2006. Retrieved November 26, 2006.

[21] D'Cruz, Mark. "Ma-Ke Bonsai Care Guide for Acer campestre". Ma-Ke Bonsai. Retrieved April 15, 2011.

3.2.7 Further reading

- Chybicki, Igor J.; Waldon-Rudzionek, Barbara; Meyza, Katarzyna (December 2014). "Population at the edge: increased divergence but not inbreeding towards northern range limit in Acer campestre". *Tree Genetics and Genomes*. **10** (6): 1739–1753. doi:10.1007/s11295-014-0793-2.

3.2.8 External links

- *Abies campestre* - distribution map, genetic conservation units and related resources. European Forest Genetic Resources Programme (EUFORGEN)

3.3 Acer circinatum

Acer circinatum (**vine maple**) is a species of maple native to western North America, from southwest British Columbia to northern California, usually within 300 kilometres (190 mi) of the Pacific Ocean coast, found along the Columbia Gorge and Coastal Forest.[3][4] It belongs to the *Palmatum* group of maple trees native to East Asia with its closest relatives being the *Acer japonicum* (Fullmoon Maple) and *Acer pseudosieboldianum* (Korean Maple). It can be difficult to distinguish from these species in cultivation. It is the only member of the *Palmatum* group that resides outside of Asia.

It most commonly grows as a large shrub growing to around 5 to 8 metres (16 to 26 ft) tall, but it will occasionally form a small to medium-sized tree, exceptionally to 18 metres (59 ft) tall. The shoots are slender and hairless. It typically grows in the under story below much taller forest trees, but can sometimes be found in open ground, and occurs at altitudes from sea level up to 1,500 metres (4,900 ft).*[3]*[4]

The leaves are opposite, and palmately lobed with 7 to 11 lobes, almost circular in outline, 3 to 14 centimetres (1.2 to 5.5 in) long and broad, and thinly hairy on the underside; the lobes are pointed and with coarsely toothed margins. The leaves turn bright yellow to orange-red in fall. The flowers are small, 6 to 9 millimetres (0.24 to 0.35 in) in diameter, with a dark red calyx and five short greenish-yellow petals; they are produced in open corymbs of 4 to 20 together in spring. The fruit is a two-seeded samara, each seed 8 to 10 millimetres (0.31 to 0.39 in) in diameter, with a lateral wing 2 to 4 centimetres (0.79 to 1.57 in) long.*[3]*[4]*[5]

Vine maple trees can bend over easily. Sometimes, this can cause the top of the tree to grow into the ground and send out a new root system, creating a natural arch. This characteristic makes it the only maple capable of layering.

It is occasionally cultivated outside its native range as an ornamental tree, from Juneau, Alaska*[6] and Ottawa, Ontario*[7] to Huntsville, Alabama,*[8] and also in northwestern Europe.*[9]

Flower with reddish calyx and five short petals

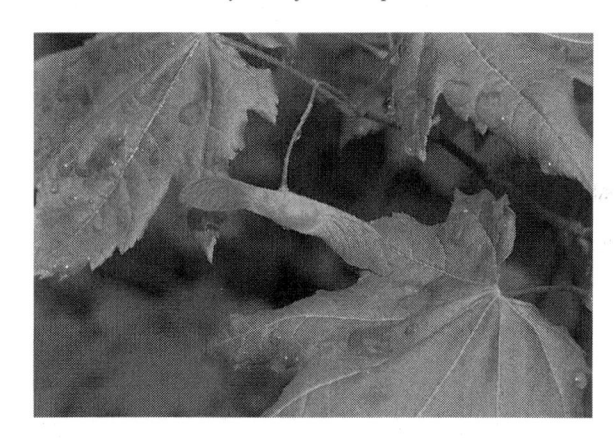

3.3.1 References

[1] Stevens, P. F. (2001 onwards). Angiosperm Phylogeny Website. Version 9, June 2008 [and more or less continuously updated since]. http://www.mobot.org/MOBOT/research/APweb/.

[2] The Plant List, *Acer circinatum* Pursh

[3] Plants of British Columbia: *Acer circinatum*

[4] Jepson Flora: *Acer circinatum*

[5] Ashley, A. & Ashley, P. (1990). *The Canadian Plant Sourcebook*. Cheriton Graphics, Ottawa, Ontario, Canada.

[6] Downtown Juneau Tree Guide

[7] Buckley, A. R. (1980). *Trees and Shrubs of the Dominion Arboretum*. Research Branch, Agriculture Canada, Ottawa.

[8] University of Alabama, Huntsville: Oregon Vine Maple at UAH Arboretum Archived February 24, 2007, at the Wayback Machine.

[9] Rushforth, K. (1999). *Trees of Britain and Europe*. Collins ISBN 0-00-220013-9.

The fruit is borne in pairs. With wings nearly 180 degrees apart, it is initially green, later becoming reddish (shown) to brown.

Autumn foliage of Acer circinatum

3.4 Acer ginnala

Acer ginnala (**Amur maple**) is a plant species with woody stems native to northeastern Asia from easternmost Mongolia east to Korea and Japan, and north to the Russian Far East in the Amur River valley. It is a small maple with deciduous leaves that is sometimes grown as a garden subject or boulevard tree.

3.4.1 Description

Acer ginnala is a deciduous spreading shrub or small tree growing to 3–10 m tall, with a short trunk up to 20–40 cm diameter and slender branches. The bark is thin, dull gray-brown, and smooth at first but becoming shallowly fissured on old plants. The leaves are opposite and simple, 4–10 cm long and 3-6 wide, deeply palmately lobed with three or five lobes, of which two small basal lobes (sometimes absent) and three larger apical lobes; the lobes are coarsely and irregularly toothed, and the upper leaf surface glossy. The leaves turn brilliant orange to red in autumn, and are on slender, often pink-tinged, petioles 3–5 cm long. The flowers are yellow-green, 5–8 mm diameter, produced in spreading panicles in spring as the leaves open. The fruit is a paired reddish samara, 8–10 mm long with a 1.5–2 cm wing, maturing in late summer to early autumn.*[2]

3.4.2 Taxonomy

Amur maple is closely related to *Acer tataricum* (Tatar maple), and some botanists treat it as a subspecies *A. tataricum* subsp. *ginnala* (Maxim.) Wesm.*[3] The glossy, deeply lobed leaves of *A. ginnala* distinguish it from *A. tataricum*, which has matte, unlobed or only shallowly lobed leaves.*[2]

3.4.3 Cultivation and uses

Acer ginnala is grown as an ornamental plant in northern regions of Europe and North America. It is the most cold-tolerant maple, hardy to zone 2. It is naturalised in parts of North America. Planted on exceptional sites facing south west with consistent moisture and light loamy soils, this tree can grow 3 to 4 feet per year making it a fast grower. It is often planted as a shrub along borders.*[4]

In the UK it has gained the Royal Horticultural Society's Award of Garden Merit.*[5]

It is also valued in Japan and elsewhere as a species suitable for bonsai. It is a nonnative invasive species in parts of northern America.*[6]

3.4.4 Cultivars

Due to its vigor and fall colors of yellows and bright reds, the size being a small tree of 20 feet wide by 20 feet tall on average, it suits many for smaller landscapes and for planting under power lines. Cultivars have emerged for those wanting these attributes.

- Flame (Fiery red autumn foliage, very strong vigor)

3.4.5 References

[1] Stevens, P. F. (2001 onwards). Angiosperm Phylogeny Website. Version 9, June 2008 [and more or less continuously updated since

[2] Rushforth, K. (1999). *Trees of Britain and Europe*. Collins ISBN 0-00-220013-9.

[3] "Acer tataricum *subsp*. ginnala". *Germplasm Resources Information Network (GRIN)*. Agricultural Research Service (ARS), United States Department of Agriculture (USDA).

[4] "*Acer ginnala*". Natural Resources Conservation Service PLANTS Database. USDA.

[5] "Acer tataricum subsp. ginnala" . *rhs.org.uk*.

[6] Randall John *The Encyclopedia of Intrusive Plants* Brooklyn Botanic Garden, Janet Marinelli, Brooklyn Botanic

- Xu, Tingzhi; Chen, Yousheng; de Jong, Piet C.; Oterdoom, Herman John; Chang, Chin-Sung. *Flora of China*. Missouri Botanical Garden. 11 http://www.efloras.org/florataxon.aspx?flora_id=2&taxon_id=250084170 – via eFloras.org. Missing or empty |title= (help)

3.4.6 External links

- Media related to Acer ginnala at Wikimedia Commons
- Data related to Acer ginnala at Wikispecies
- Winter ID pictures

3.5 Acer monspessulanum

Acer monspessulanum (**Montpellier maple**) is a species of maple native to the Mediterranean region from Morocco and Portugal in the west, to Turkey, Syria, Lebanon, and Israel in the east, and north to the Jura Mountains in France and the Eifel in Germany.*[2]*[3]*[4]

3.5.1 Description

Acer monspessulanum is a medium-sized deciduous tree or densely branched shrub that grows to a height of 10–15 m (rarely to 20 m).*[5] The trunk is up to 75 cm diameter, with smooth, dark grey bark on young trees, becoming finely fissured on old trees. Among similar maples is most easily distinguished by its small three-lobed leaves, 3–6 cm long and 3–7 cm wide, glossy dark green, sometimes a bit leathery, and with a smooth margin, with a 2–5 cm petiole. The leaves fall very late in autumn, typically in November. The flowers are produced in spring, in pendulous, yellow to white corymbs 2–3 cm long. The samaras are 2–3 cm long with rounded nutlets.*[3]*[4]

Flowers and young leaves in spring

Subspecies

It is variable, and a number of subspecies and varieties have been described, but few are widely accepted as distinct. The most widely accepted as distinct is *Acer monspessulanum* subsp. *microphyllum* (Boiss.) Bornmueller, from Turkey and Lebanon, with smaller leaves not over 3 cm broad.*[3]

The species can be mistaken for *Acer campestre* (field maple), another maple native to Europe, from which it is best distinguished by the clear sap in the leaves (milk-white in field maple), and the much narrower angle between the samara wings.*[3]*[4]

3.5.2 Cultivation

Among maples not endemic to Japan, *A. monspessulanum* (and the similar *A. campestre*) are popular among bonsai enthusiasts.*[6] In both cases, the smallish leaves and shrubby habit of the maple respond well to techniques to encourage leaf reduction and ramification.*[7] These bonsai have an appearance distinct from those created from maples such as *Acer palmatum* whose leaves are more frilly and translucent.

Otherwise, *Acer monspessulanum* is rarely seen in cultivation outside of arboreta. In the United States, a mature specimen may be seen at Arnold Arboretum in Boston, Massachusetts. A specimen can also be found in the arboretum of the Montreal Botanical Gardens.

3.5.3 References

[1] Stevens, P. F. (2001 onwards). Angiosperm Phylogeny Website. Version 9, June 2008 [and more or less continuously updated since]. http://www.mobot.org/MOBOT/research/APweb/.

[2] Flora Europaea: *Acer monspessulanum*

[3] Rushforth, K. D. (1999). *Trees of Britain and Europe*. ISBN 0-00-220013-9.

[4] van Gelderen, C.J. & van Gelderen, D.M. (1999). *Maples for Gardens: A Color Encyclopedia*.

[5] (French)Fleurs de France: *Acer monspessulanum*

[6] Bonsai Club International: *Acer monspessulanum* Archived November 11, 2006, at the Wayback Machine.

[7] Bonsai Club International: *Acer campestre* Archived November 11, 2006, at the Wayback Machine.

3.5.4 External links

- *Acer monspessulanum* - genetic conservation units and related resources. European Forest Genetic Resources Programme (EUFORGEN)

3.6 Acer palmatum

"Momiji" redirects here. For other uses, see Momiji (disambiguation).

Acer palmatum, commonly known as **palmate maple**,[3] **Japanese maple**[4] or **smooth Japanese-maple**[5] (Japanese: *irohamomiji*, イロハモミジ, or *momiji*, 紅葉), is a species of woody plant native to Japan, China, Korea, eastern Mongolia, and southeast Russia.[6] Many different cultivars of this maple have been selected and they are grown worldwide for their large variety of attractive forms, leaf shapes, and spectacular colors.[7]

3.6.1 Description

Acer palmatum is a deciduous shrub or small tree reaching heights of 6 to 10 m (20 to 33 ft), rarely 16 metres (52 ft), often growing as an understory plant in shady woodlands. It may have multiple trunks joining close to the ground. In habit, it is often shaped like a hemisphere (especially when younger) or takes on a dome-like form, especially when mature.[8] The leaves are 4–12 cm long and wide, palmately lobed with five, seven, or nine acutely pointed lobes. The flowers are produced in small cymes, the individual flowers with five red or purple sepals and five whitish petals. The fruit is a pair of winged samaras, each samara 2–3 cm long with a 6–8 mm seed. The seeds of *Acer palmatum* and similar species require stratification in order to germinate.[8][9]

Even in nature, *Acer palmatum* displays considerable genetic variation, with seedlings from the same parent tree typically showing differences in such traits as leaf size, shape, and color. Overall form of the tree can vary from upright to weeping.[8]

Colored leaves of a Japanese maple at the Nison-in temple in Kyoto

Three subspecies are recognised:[8][9]

- *Acer palmatum* subsp. *palmatum*. Leaves small, 4–7 cm wide, with five or seven lobes and double-serrate margins; seed wings 10–15 mm. Lower altitudes throughout central and southern Japan (not Hokkaido).

- *Acer palmatum* subsp. *amoenum* (Carrière) H.Hara. Leaves larger, 6–12 cm wide, with seven or nine lobes and single-serrate margins; seed wings 20–25 mm. Higher altitudes throughout Japan and South Korea.

- *Acer palmatum* subsp. *matsumurae* Koidz. Leaves larger, 6–12 cm wide, with seven (rarely five or nine) lobes and double-serrate margins; seed wings 15–25 mm. Higher altitudes throughout Japan.

3.6.2 Cultivation and uses

This Japanese maple shows a dome-like shape.

Acer palmatum has been cultivated in Japan for centuries and in temperate areas around the world since the 1800s.[8] The first specimen of the tree reached England in 1820.

When Swedish doctor-botanist Carl Peter Thunberg traveled in Japan late in the eighteenth century, he secreted out drawings of a small tree that would eventually become synonymous with the high art of oriental gardens.[10] He gave it the species name *palmatum* after the hand-like shape of its leaves, similar to the centuries-old Japanese names *kaede* and *momiji*, references to the 'hands' of frogs[11] and babies, respectively.

For centuries Japanese horticulturalists have developed cultivars from maples found in Japan and nearby Korea and China. They are a popular choice for bonsai[12] enthusiasts and have long been a subject in art.

Numerous cultivars are currently available commercially and are a popular item at garden centres and other retail stores in Europe and North America. Red-leafed cultivars are the most popular, followed by cascading green shrubs with deeply dissected leaves.*[8]

Preparations from the branches and leaves are used as a treatment in traditional Chinese medicine.*[13]

Growing conditions

Fall maples in Nara, Japan

Acer palmatum includes hundreds of named cultivars with a variety forms, colors, leaf types, sizes, and preferred growing conditions. Heights of mature specimens range from 0.5 m to 25 m, depending on type. Some tolerate sun, but most prefer part shade, especially in hotter climates. Almost all are adaptable and blend well with companion plants. The trees are particularly suitable for borders and ornamental paths because the root systems are compact and not invasive. Many varieties of *Acer palmatum* are successfully grown in containers.*[14] Trees are prone to die during periods of drought and prefer consistent water conditions; more established trees are less prone to drought. Trees should be mulched with a thick layer of bark. Well-drained soil is essential as they will not survive in soggy waterlogged soil. Trees do not require or appreciate heavy fertilization and should only be lightly fertilized, preferably using slow-release fertilizer with a 3 to 1 ratio of nitrogen to phosphorus respectively. Nitrogen lawn fertilizer should be avoided in the immediate vicinity of these trees as excessive nitrogen can cause overly vigorous growth that is prone to pathogens.

Pruning

See also: Bonsai

If space is not a constraint, no pruning is necessary except to remove any dead branches. Trees naturally self-prune foliage that doesn't receive enough light, such as internal branches which are overly shaded by its own canopy. Some growers prefer to shape their trees artistically or to thin out interior branches to better expose the graceful main branches. The form of the tree, especially without leaves in winter, can be of great interest and can be pruned to highlight this feature. Trees heal readily after pruning without needing aftercare. This species should not be pruned like a hedge, but instead methodically shaped by carefully choosing individual branches to remove. They can also be pruned just to maintain a smaller size to suit a particular location. *Acer palmatum* can also be used as espalier.

Cultivars

Over 1,000 cultivars have been chosen for particular characteristics, which are propagated by asexual reproduction most often by grafting, but some cultivars can also be propagated by budding, cuttings, tissue culture, or layering. Some cultivars are not in cultivation in the Western world or have been lost over the generations, but many new cultivars are developed each decade.*[8] Cultivars are chosen for phenotypical aspects such as leaf shape and size (shallowly to deeply lobed, some also palmately compound), leaf color (ranging from chartreuse through dark green or from red to dark purple, others variegated with various patterns of white and pink), bark texture and color, and growth pattern. Most cultivars are less vigorous and smaller than is typical for the species, but are more interesting than the relatively mundane species. Cultivars come in a large variety of forms including upright, broom, weeping, cascading, dwarf, and shrub. Most cultivars are artificially selected from seedlings of open-pollinated plants, purposeful breeding is not common, and less often from grafts of witch's brooms.

In Japan, *iromomiji* is used as an accent tree in Japanese gardens, providing gentle shade next to the house in the summer and beautiful colors in autumn. Many cultivars have characteristics that come into prominence during different

3.6. ACER PALMATUM

Example of leaf variation among various cultivars of Acer palmatum

seasons, including the color of new or mature leaves, extraordinary autumn color, color and shape of samaras, or even bark that becomes more brightly colored during the winter. Some cultivars can scarcely be distinguished from others unless labeled. In some cases, identical cultivars go by different names, while in other cases, different cultivars may be given the same name.

Example cultivars A selection of notable or popular cultivars, with brief notes about characteristics that apply during at least one season, includes the following.*[8] agm indicates the cultivar has gained the Royal Horticultural Society's Award of Garden Merit.

112+ year old bonsai example, from the Brooklyn Botanic Garden.

- 'Aka shigitatsu sawa'; pinkish-white leaves with green veins

- 'Ao ba jo'; a dwarf with bronze-green summer foliage
- Atropurpureum; wine-red, including new branches
- 'Bloodgood'agm;*[15] an improved cultivar of 'Atropurpureum'
- 'Burgundy Lace'agm*[16]
- 'Butterfly'; small leaves with white borders
- 'Chitose-Yama'agm*[17]
- 'Crimson Queen' *(see under 'Dissectum')*
- 'Dissectum'; lace-like leaves, drooping habit
- 'Dissectum Atropurpureum'
- var. *dissectum* 'Garnet'agm*[18]
- var. *dissectum* 'Inaba-shidare'agm*[19]
- var. *dissectum* 'Crimson Queen'agm*[20]
- var. *dissectum* 'Seiryu';agm*[21] a green, tree-like shrub with finely dissected leaves
- 'Emperor 1'
- 'Garnet' *(see under 'Dissectum atropurpureum')*
- 'Golden Pond'; greenish-yellow summer foliage
- 'Goshiki koto hime'; a delicate, variegated dwarf
- 'Higasa yama'; crinkled leaves variegated with yellow
- 'Hogyuko'; rich green leaves, turning orange in autumn
- 'Hupp's Dwarf'; a small, dense shrub with miniature leaves
- 'Inaba-shidare' *(see under 'Dissectum atropurpureum')*
- 'Issai nishiki kawazu'; very rough, rigid bark
- 'Kagiri nishiki'; similar to 'Butterfly' but more pinkish tones
- 'Karasu gawa'; slow-growing variegate with brilliant pink and white
- 'Katsura'agm;*[22] yellow-green leaves tipped with orange
- 'Koto no ito'; light green, thread-like leaves
- 'Little Princess'; a sparsely branched dwarf with irregular habit
- 'Mama'; a bushy dwarf with extremely variable foliage
- 'Masu murasaki'; a shrubby tree with purple leaves

- 'Mizu kuguri'; orange-tinted new growth and very wide habit

- 'Nigrum';agm*[23] deep purple leaves turning to crimson

- 'Nishiki gawa'; pinetree-like bark desirable for bonsai

- 'Nomura nishiki'; dark purple, lace-like leaves

- 'Ojishi'; tiny dwarf, grows only a few centimetres per year

- 'Orange Dream';agm*[24] leaves yellow in spring, greenish in summer, orange-yellow in autumn. Bark bright green.

- 'Osakazuki';agm*[25] tree-like shrub with spectacular autumn colour

- 'Peaches and Cream'; similar to 'Aka shigitatsu sawa'

- 'Pink Filigree'; finely dissected, brownish-pink leaves

- 'Red Filigree Lace'; delicate, finely dissected, dark purple

- 'Red Pygmy'agm*[26]

- 'Sango kaku';agm*[27] Coral-bark maple (formerly 'Senkaki'); with pinkish-red bark

- 'Seiryu' *(see under 'Dissectum atropurpureum')*

- 'Shaina'; a dwarf sport from 'Bloodgood'

- 'Shindeshojo'

- 'Shikage ori nishiki'; vase-shaped shrub with dull purple foliage

- 'Shishigashira'

- 'Skeeter's Broom'; derived from a 'Bloodgood' witch's broom

- 'Tamukeyama'; finely dissected, dark purple, cascading habit

- 'Trompenburg';agm*[28] slender, upright grower, convex lobes, purple leaves

- 'Tsuma gaki'; yellow leaves with reddish-purple borders

- 'Yuba e'; upright tree with scarlet variegation

Red-foliaged plants such as this are sold under names such as 'Atropurpureum' and 'Bloodgood'.

In addition to the cultivars described above, a number of cultivar groups have been naturally selected over time to such an extent that seedlings often resemble the parent. Many of these are sold under the same name as the cultivars, or even propagated by grafting, so there is often much ambiguity in distinguishing them.*[8] In particular, a number of dark-red *Acer palmatum* are sold with the names "Atropurpureum" and "Bloodgood." Many different cultivars with delicate lace-like foliage are sold under names such as "Dissectum", "Filigree" and "Laceleaf." .*[8]

Similar species

The term "Japanese maple" is also sometimes used to describe other species usually within series *Palmata* that are similar to *A. palmatum* and are native to China, Korea or Japan including:

- *Acer duplicatoserratum* (syn. *A. palmatum* var. *pubescens* Li)

- *Acer japonicum*—Downy Japanese maple

- *Acer pseudosieboldianum*—Korean maple

- *Acer shirasawanum*—Fullmoon maple

- *Acer sieboldianum*—Siebold's maple

- *Acer buergerianum*—Trident maple

Given that these maples are phenotypically variable within each species, and may hybridise with one another, distinguishing between them may be a matter of gradient speciation. In commercial propagation, *A. palmatum* is often used as rootstock for many of these other species.*[8]

3.6.3 References

[1] Stevens, P. F. (2001 onwards). Angiosperm Phylogeny Website. Version 9, June 2008 [and more or less continuously updated since]. http://www.mobot.org/MOBOT/research/APweb/.

[2] The Plant List, *Acer palmatum* Thunb.

[3] *English Names for Korean Native Plants* (PDF). Pocheon: Korea National Arboretum. 2015. p. 334. ISBN 978-89-97450-98-5. Retrieved 25 January 2016 – via Korea Forest Service.

[4] "*Acer palmatum*". Natural Resources Conservation Service PLANTS Database. USDA. Retrieved 6 January 2016.

[5] "BSBI List 2007" (xls). Botanical Society of Britain and Ireland. Archived from the original on 2015-01-25. Retrieved 2014-10-17.

[6] Germplasm Resources Information Network: *Acer palmatum*

[7] Philips, Roger (1979). *Trees of North America and Europe*. New York: Random House. ISBN 0-394-50259-0.

[8] van Gelderen, C.J. & van Gelderen, D.M. (1999). *Maples for Gardens: A Colour Encyclopedia*.

[9] Rushforth, K. (1999). *Trees of Britain and Europe*. Collins ISBN 0-00-220013-9.

[10] Japanese Red Maple - arborday.org Archived April 25, 2010, at the Wayback Machine.

[11] (Japanese) Etymology of 楓. The word *kaede* derives from *kaeru te* "frog hand" and went through the intermediary form *kaende*.

[12] D'Cruz, Mark. "Acer palmatum Bonsai Care Guide". Ma-Ke Bonsai. Retrieved 2010-11-26.

[13] School of Chinese Medicine database Archived March 3, 2016, at the Wayback Machine.

[14] Vertrees, J.D. (1987) *Japanese Maples*. Timber Press, Inc. ISBN 0-88192-048-7

[15] "RHS Plant Selector - *Acer palmatum* 'Bloodgood'".

[16] "RHS Plant Selector - *Acer palmatum* 'Burgundy Lace'". Retrieved 10 June 2013.

[17] "RHS Plant Selector - *Acer palmatum* 'Chitose-Yama'". Retrieved 10 June 2013.

[18] "RHS Plant Selector - *Acer palmatum* var. *dissectum* 'Garnet'". Retrieved 10 June 2013.

[19] "RHS Plant Selector - *Acer palmatum* var. *dissectum* 'Inabashidare'". Retrieved 10 June 2013.

[20] "RHS Plant Selector - *Acer palmatum* var. *dissectum* 'Crimson Queen'". Retrieved 10 June 2013.

[21] "RHS Plant Selector - *Acer palmatum* 'Seiryu'". Retrieved 10 June 2013.

[22] "RHS Plant Selector - *Acer palmatum* 'Katsura'". Retrieved 10 June 2013.

[23] "RHS Plant Selector - *Acer palmatum* 'Nigrum'". Retrieved 10 June 2013.

[24] *Acer palmatum 'Orange Dream' (P):Japanese maple 'Orange Dream'* at the Royal Horticultural Society site. Retrieved 6 Apr 2017.

[25] "RHS Plant Selector - *Acer palmatum* 'Osakazuki'". Retrieved 10 June 2013.

[26] "RHS Plant Selector - *Acer palmatum* 'Red Pygmy'". Retrieved 10 June 2013.

[27] "RHS Plant Selector - *Acer palmatum* 'Sango-kaku'". Retrieved 10 June 2013.

[28] "RHS Plant Selector - *Acer palmatum* 'Trompenburg'". Retrieved 10 June 2013.

3.6.4 External links

- RHS: *Acer palmatum* cultivation
- photo of herbarium specimen at Missouri Botanical Garden, collected in Japan
- Shoot: *Acer palmatum 'Orange Dream'*

3.7 Acer rubrum

Acer rubrum (**red maple**, also known as **swamp**, **water** or **soft maple**) is one of the most common and widespread deciduous trees of eastern and central North America. The U.S. Forest service recognizes it as the most abundant native tree in eastern North America.*[4] The red maple ranges from southeastern Manitoba around the Lake of the Woods on the border with Ontario and Minnesota, east to Newfoundland, south to Florida, and southwest to eastern Texas. Many of its features, especially its leaves, are quite variable in form. At maturity it often attains a height of around 15 m (50 ft). Its flowers, petioles, twigs and seeds are all red to varying degrees. Among these features, however, it is best known for its brilliant deep scarlet foliage in autumn.

Over most of its range, red maple is adaptable to a very wide range of site conditions, perhaps more so than any other tree in eastern North America. It can be found growing in swamps, on poor dry soils, and most anywhere in between. It grows well from sea level to about 900 m (3,000 ft). Due to its attractive fall foliage and pleasing form, it is often used as a shade tree for landscapes. It is used commercially on a small scale for maple syrup production as well as for its medium to high quality lumber. It is also the State Tree of Rhode Island. The red maple can be considered weedy or invasive.*[5] It is taking over forests in the eastern US, replacing traditional mainstays like oaks, as well as hickories and pines.*[6]

3.7.1 Description

Typical fall foliage in red maple country.

Red Maple leaf from specimen in northern Florida

Though *A. rubrum* is usually easy to identify, it is highly changeable in morphological characteristics. It is a medium to large sized tree, reaching heights of 18 to 27 metres (60 to 90 ft) and exceptionally over 35 metres (115 feet). The leaves are usually 9 to 11 centimetres (3 ½ to 4 ¼ in) long on a full grown tree. The trunk diameter can range from 46 to 76 cm (18 to 30 in), depending on the growing conditions.*[7] Its spread is about 12 m (40 ft). A 10-year-old sapling will stand about 6 m (20 ft) tall. In forests, the bark will remain free of branches until some distance up the tree. Individuals grown in the open are shorter and thicker with a more rounded crown.*[8] Generally speaking, however, the crown is irregularly ovoid with ascending whip-like curved shoots. The bark is a pale grey and smooth when the individual is young. As the tree grows the bark becomes darker and cracks into slightly raised long plates.*[9] The largest known living red maple is located near Armada, Michigan, at a height of 38.1 m (125 ft) and a bole circumference, at breast height, of 4.95 m (16 ft 3 in).*[7]

The leaves of the red maple offer the easiest way to distinguish it from its relatives. As with nearly all North American maple trees, they are deciduous and arranged oppositely on the twig. They are typically 5–10 cm (2–4 in) long and wide with 3-5 palmate lobes with a serrated margin. The sinuses are typically narrow, but the leaves can exhibit considerable variation.*[8] When 5 lobes are present, the three at the terminal end are larger than the other two near the base. In contrast, the leaves of the related silver maple, *A. saccharinum*, are much more deeply lobed, more sharply toothed and characteristically have 5 lobes. The upper side of *A. rubrum*'s leaf is light green and the underside is whitish and can be either glaucous or hairy. The leaf stalks are usually red and are up to 10 cm (4 in) long. Furthermore, the leaves can turn a brilliant red in autumn, but can also become yellow or orange on some individuals.

The twigs of the red maple are reddish in color and somewhat shiny with small lenticels. Dwarf shoots are present on many branches. The buds are usually blunt and greenish to reddish in color, generally with several loose scales. The lateral buds are slightly stalked, and in addition there may be collateral buds present as well. The buds form in fall and winter and are often visible from a distance due to their reddish tint. The leaf scars on the twig are V-shaped and contain 3 bundle scars.*[8]

The flowers are generally unisexual, with male and female flowers appearing in separate sessile clusters, though they are sometimes also bisexual. They appear in spring from April to May (though as early as late January in the southern part of its range), usually coming before the leaves. The tree itself is considered Polygamodioecious, meaning some individuals are male, some female, and some monoecious.*[7] Under the proper conditions, the tree can sometimes switch from male to female, male to hermaphroditic, and hermaphroditic to female*[10] The red maple will begin blooming when it is about 8 years old,

Immature foliage of Acer rubrum (Red Maple)

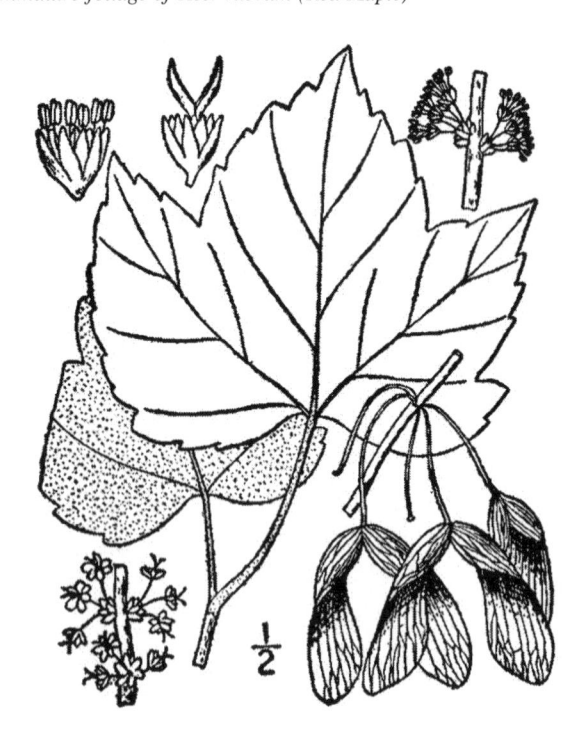

Drawing showing male and female flower, leaf and samara

but it significantly varies between tree to tree: some trees may begin flowering when they are 4 years old. The flowers are red with 5 small petals and a 5-lobed calyx borne in hanging clusters, usually at the twig tips. They are lineal to oblong in shape and are pubescent. The pistillate flowers have one pistil formed from two fused carpels with a glabrous superior ovary and two long styles that protrude beyond the perianth. The staminate flowers contain between 4 and 12 stamens, often with 8.[*][11]

The fruit is a samara 15 to 25 millimeters ($^5/_8$ to 1 in) long that grows in pairs with somewhat divergent wings at an angle of 50 to 60 degrees. They are borne on long slender stems and are variable in color from light brown to reddish.[*][8] They ripen from April through early June, before even the leaf development is altogether complete. After they reach maturity, the seeds are dispersed for a 1 to 2 week period from April through July.[*][7]

3.7.2 Distribution and habitat

A. rubrum is one of the most abundant and widespread trees in eastern North America. It can be found from the south of Newfoundland, Nova Scotia and southern Quebec to the south west of Ontario, extreme southeastern Manitoba and northern Minnesota; south to Wisconsin, Illinois, Missouri, eastern Oklahoma, and eastern Texas in its western range; and east to Florida. It has the largest continuous range along the North American Atlantic Coast of any tree that occurs in Florida. In total it ranges 2,600 km (1,600 mi) from north to south.[*][7] The species is native to all regions of the United States east of the 95th meridian. The tree's range ends where the −40 °C (−40 °F) mean minimum isotherm begins, namely in southeastern Canada. *A. rubrum* is not present in the Prairie Peninsula of the northern Midwest, the coastal prairie in southern Louisiana and southeastern Texas and the swamp prairie of the Florida Everglades.[*][7] The absence of red maple in the Prairie Peninsula is perhaps due to the specie's intolerance of fire.[*][12]

In several other locations, the tree is absent from large areas but still present in a few specific habitats. An example is the Bluegrass region of Kentucky, where red maple is not found in the dominant open plains, but is present along streams.[*][13] Here the red maple is not present in the bottom land forests of the Grain Belt, despite the fact it is common in similar habitats and species associations both to the north and south of this area.[*][7]

A. rubrum does very well in a wide range of soil types, with varying textures, moisture, pH, and elevation, probably more so than any other forest tree in North America. *A. rubrum*'s high pH tolerance means that it can grow in a variety of places, and it is widespread along the eastern United States.[*][14] It grows on glaciated as well as unglaciated soils derived from the following rocks: granite, gneiss, schist, sandstone, shale, slate, conglomerate, quartzite, and limestone. Chlorosis can occur on very alkaline soils, though otherwise its pH tolerance is quite high. Moist mineral soil is best for germination of seeds.*[12]

The red maple can grow in a variety of moist and dry biomes, from dry ridges and sunny, southwest-facing slopes to peat bogs and swamps. While many types of tree prefer a south or north facing aspect, the red maple does not appear to have a preference.*[7] Its ideal conditions are in moderately well-drained, moist sites at low or intermediate elevations. However, it is nonetheless common in mountainous areas on relatively dry ridges, as well as on both the south and west sides of upper slopes. Furthermore, it is common in swampy areas, along the banks of slow moving streams, as well as on poorly drained flats and depressions. In northern Michigan and New England, the tree is found on the tops of ridges, sandy or rocky upland and otherwise dry soils, as well as in nearly pure stands on moist soils and the edges of swamps. In the far south of its range, it is almost exclusively associated with swamps.*[7] Additionally, Red maple is one of the most drought-tolerant species of maple in the Carolinas.*[15]

Red maple is far more abundant today than when Europeans first arrived in North America, where along with its cousin Silver Maple, it may have comprised a mere 5% of forest area and was confined mostly to riparian zones.*[7] The density of the tree in many of these areas has increased 6 to 7 fold and this trend seems to be continuing, much of it due to human factors, especially suppression of wildfires which would kill shallow-rooted pioneer species like red maple, but leave mainline forest trees like oaks and hickories untouched.

Additionally, conservation efforts of the red maple have caused a major increase in the population of white-tailed deer since the mid-20th century. Deer will readily consume acorns, but leave maple seeds untouched, thus reducing the ability of oaks to regenerate compared to maples.*[16] Because it can grow on a variety of substrates, has a high pH tolerance, and grows in both shade and sun, *A. rubrum* can be called a "super-generalist," and it is predicted to replace historically dominant tree species in the eastern United States such as oaks, hickorys and pines.*[17] Extensive use of red maple in landscaping has also contributed to the surge in the species' numbers as volunteer seedlings proliferate. Finally, disease epidemics have greatly reduced the population of elms and chestnuts in the forests of the US. While mainline forest trees continue to dominate mesic sites with rich soil, more marginal areas are increasingly being dominated by red maple.*[18]

3.7.3 Ecology

Red maple seldom lives longer than a comparatively brief 150 years.*[7] It reaches maturity in 70 to 80 years. Its ability to thrive in a large number of habitats is largely due to its ability to produce roots to suit its site from a young age. In wet locations, red maple seedlings produce short taproots with long and developed lateral roots, while on dry sites, they develop long taproots with significantly shorter laterals. The roots are primarily horizontal, however, forming in the upper 25 cm (9.8 in) of the ground. Mature trees have woody roots up to 25 m (82 ft) long. They are very tolerant of flooding, with one study showing that 60 days of flooding caused no leaf damage. At the same time, they are tolerant of drought due to their ability to stop growing under dry conditions by then producing a second growth flush when conditions later improve, even if growth has stopped for 2 weeks.*[7]

Samaras from a specimen in Milford, New Hampshire

A. rubrum is one of the first plants to flower in spring. A crop of seeds is generally produced every year with a bumper crop often occurring every second year. A single tree between 5 and 20 cm (2.0 and 7.9 in) in diameter can produce between 12,000 and 91,000 seeds in a season. A tree 30 cm (0.98 ft) in diameter was shown to produce nearly a million seeds.*[7] Red maple produces one of the smallest seeds of any of the maples.*[15] Fertilization has also been shown to significantly increase the seed yield for up to two years after application. The seeds are epigeal and tend to germinate in early summer soon after they are released, assuming a small amount of light, moisture, and sufficient temperatures are present. If the seeds are densely shaded, then germination commonly does not occur until the next spring. Most seedlings do not survive in closed forest canopy situations. However, one- to four-year-old seedlings are common under dense canopy and though they eventually die if no light reaches them, they serve as a reservoir, waiting to fill any open area of the canopy above. Trees growing in a Zone 9 or 10 area such as Florida will usually die from cold damage if transferred up north, Canada, Maine, Vermont, New Hampshire and New York, even if the southern trees were planted with northern red maples. Due to their wide range, genetically the trees have adapted to the climatic differences.

Female flowers

Male flowers

Red maple is able to increase its numbers significantly when associate trees are damaged by disease, cutting, or fire. One study found that 6 years after clearcutting a 3.4 hectares (8.4 acres) Oak-Hickory forest containing no red maples, the plot contained more than 2,200 red maple seedlings per hectare (900 per acre) taller than 1.4 m (4.6 ft).*[7] One of its associates, the black cherry (*Prunus serotina*), contains benzoic acid, which has been shown to be a potential allelopathic inhibitor of red maple growth. Red maple is one of the first species to start stem elongation. In one study, stem elongation was one-half completed in 1 week, after which growth slowed and was 90% completed within only 54 days. In good light and moisture conditions, the seedlings can grow 30 cm (0.98 ft) in their first year and up to 60 cm (2.0 ft) each year for the next few years making it a fast grower.*[7]

The red maple is a used as a food source by several forms of wildlife. Elk and white-tailed deer in particular use the current season's growth of red maple as an important source of winter food. Several Lepidoptera (butterflies and moths) utilize the leaves as food; see List of Lepidoptera that feed on maples.

Due to *A. rubrum*'s very wide range, there is significant variation in hardiness, size, form, time of flushing, onset of dormancy, and other traits. Generally speaking, individuals from the north flush the earliest, have the most reddish fall color, set their buds the earliest and take the least winter injury. Seedlings are tallest in the north-central and east-central part of the range. In Florida, at the extreme south of the red maple's range, it is limited exclusively to swamp-lands. The fruits also vary geographically with northern individuals in areas with brief, frost-free periods producing fruits that are shorter and heavier than their southern counterparts. As a result of the variation there is much genetic potential for breeding programs with a goal of producing red maples for cultivation. This is especially useful for making urban cultivars that require resistance from verticillium wilt, air pollution, and drought.*[7]

Acer × freemanii 'Jeffersred' in Toronto

Red maple frequently hybridizes with Silver Maple; the

hybrid, known as Freeman's Maple *Acer x freemanii*, is intermediate between the parents.

Allergenic potential

The allergenic potential of red maples varies widely based on the cultivar.

The following cultivars are completely male and are highly allergenic, with an OPALS allergy scale rating of 8 or higher:[19]

- 'Autumn Flame' ('Flame')
- 'Autumn Spire'
- 'Columnare' ('Pyramidale')
- 'Firedance' ('Landsburg')
- 'Karpick'
- 'Northwood'
- 'October Brilliance'
- 'Sun Valley'
- 'Tiliford'

The following cultivars have an OPALS allergy scale rating of 3 or lower; they are completely female trees, and have low potential for causing allergies:[19]

- 'Autumn Glory'
- 'Bowhall'
- 'Davey Red'
- 'Doric'
- 'Embers'
- 'Festival'
- 'October Glory'
- 'Red Skin'
- 'Red Sunset' ('Franksred')

Toxicity

The leaves of red maple, especially when dead or wilted, are extremely toxic to horses. The toxin is unknown, but believed to be an oxidant because it damages red blood cells, causing acute oxidative hemolysis that inhibits the transport of oxygen. This not only decreases oxygen delivery to all tissues, but also leads to the production of methemoglobin, which can further damage the kidneys. The ingestion of 700 grams (1.5 pounds) of leaves is considered toxic and 1.4 kilograms (3 pounds) is lethal. Symptoms occur within one or two days after ingestion and can include depression, lethargy, increased rate and depth of breathing, increased heart rate, jaundice, dark brown urine, colic, laminitis, coma, and death. Treatment is limited and can include the use of methylene blue or mineral oil and activated carbon in order to stop further absorption of the toxin into the stomach, as well as blood transfusions, fluid support, diuretics, and anti-oxidants such as Vitamin C. About 50% to 75% of affected horses die or are euthanized as a result.[16]

3.7.4 Cultivation

Red maple's rapid growth, ease of transplanting, attractive form, and value for wildlife (in the eastern US) has made it one of the most extensively planted trees. In parts of the Pacific Northwest, it is one of the most common introduced trees. Its popularity in cultivation stems from its vigorous habit, its attractive and early red flowers, and most importantly, its flaming red fall foliage. The tree was introduced into the United Kingdom in 1656 and shortly thereafter entered cultivation. There it is frequently found in many parks and gardens, as well as occasionally in churchyards.[9]

Mature bark, at Hemingway, South Carolina

Red maple is a good choice of a tree for urban areas when there is ample room for its root system. Forming an association with Arbuscular Mycorrhizal Fungi can help A. rubrum grow along city streets.*[20] It is more tolerant of pollution and road salt than Sugar Maples, although the tree's fall foliage is not as vibrant in this environment. Like several other maples, its low root system can be invasive and it makes a poor choice for plantings near paving. It attracts squirrels, who eat its buds in the early spring, although squirrels prefer the larger buds of the silver maple.*[21]

Red Maple make vibrant and colorful bonsai, and have year around attractive features for display.*[22]

Specimen showing variation of autumn leaf coloration

Cultivars

Numerous cultivars have been selected, often for intensity of fall color, with 'October Glory' and 'Red Sunset' among the most popular. Toward its southern limit, 'Fireburst', 'Florida Flame', and 'Gulf Ember' are preferred. Many cultivars of the Freeman maple are also grown widely. Below is a partial list of cultivars:*[23]*[24]

- **'Armstrong'** – Columnar to fastigate in shape with silvery bark and modest orange to red fall foliage

- **'Autumn Blaze'** – Rounded oval form with leaves that resemble the silver maple. The fall color is orange red and persists longer than usual

- **'Autumn Flame'** – A fast grower with exceptional bright red fall color developing early. The leaves are also smaller than the species.

- **'Autumn Radiance'** – Dense oval crown with an orange-red fall color

- **'Autumn Spire'** – Broad columnar crown; red fall color; very hardy

- **'Bowhall'** – Conical to upright in form with a yellow-red fall color

- **'Burgundy Bell'** – Compact rounded uniform shape with long lasting, burgundy fall leaves

- **'Columnare'** – An old cultivar growing to 20 metres (66 feet) with a narrow columnar to pyramidal form with dark green leaves turning orange and deep red in fall

- **'Gerling'** – A compact, slow growing selection, this individual only reaches 10 metres (33 feet) and has orange-red fall foliage

- **'Northwood'** – Branches are at a 45 degree angle to the trunk, forming a rounded oval crown. Though the foliage is deep green in summer, its orange-red fall color is not as impressive as other cultivars.

- **'October Brilliance'** – This selection is slow to leaf in spring, but has a tight crown and deep red fall color

- **'October Glory'** – Has a rounded oval crown with late developing intense red fall foliage. Along with 'Red Sunset', it is the most popular selection due to the dependable fall color and vigorous growth. This cultivar has gained the Royal Horticultural Society's Award of Garden Merit.*[25]

- **'Redpointe'** – Superior in alkaline soil, strong central leader, red fall color

- **'Red Sunset'** – The other very popular choice, this selection does well in heat due to its drought tolerance and has an upright habit. It has very attractive orange-red fall color and is also a rapid and vigorous grower.

- **'Scarlet Sentinel'** – A columnar to oval selection with 5-lobed leaves resembling the silver maple. The fall color is yellow-orange to orange-red and the tree is a fast grower.

- **'Schlesingeri'** – A tree with a broad crown and early, long lasting fall color that a deep red to reddish purple. Growth is also quite rapid.

- **'Shade King'** – This fast growing cultivar has an upright-oval form with deep green summer leaves that turn red to orange in fall.

- **'V.J. Drake'** – This selection is notable because the edges of the leaves first turn a deep red before the color progresses into the center.

3.7.5 Other uses

A bottle of maple syrup

In the lumber industry *Acer rubrum* is considered a soft maple. The wood is close grained and as such it is similar to that of *A. saccharum*, but its texture is softer, less dense, and has a poorer figure and machining qualities. High grades of wood from the red maple can nonetheless be substituted for hard maple, particularly when it comes to making furniture. As a soft maple, the wood tends to shrink more during the drying process than with the hard maples.

Red maple is also used for the production of maple syrup, though the hard maples *Acer saccharum* (sugar maple) and *Acer nigrum* (black maple) are more commonly utilized. One study compared the sap and syrup from the sugar maple with those of the red maple, as well as those of the *Acer saccharinum* (silver maple), *Acer negundo* (boxelder), and *Acer platanoides* (Norway maple), and all were found to be equal in sweetness, flavor, and quality. However, the buds of red maple and other soft maples emerge much earlier in the spring than the sugar maple, and after sprouting chemical makeup of the sap changes, imparting an undesirable flavor to the syrup. This being the case, red maple can only be tapped for syrup before the buds emerge, making the season very short.*[7]

Red maple is a medium quality firewood,*[26] possessing high heat energy, nominally 5.4 MJ/m^3 (18.7 million BTU (mbtu) per cord), than other hardwoods such as Ash: 7 MJ/m^3 (24 mbtu/cord), Oak: 7 MJ/m^3 (24 mbtu/cord), or Birch: 5.8 MJ/m^3 (20 mbtu/cord).

3.7.6 See also

- List of plants poisonous to equines
- List of foods made from maple

3.7.7 References

[1] NatureServe (2006). "*Acer rubrum*". *NatureServe Explorer: An online encyclopedia of life, Version 6.1.* Arlington, Virginia.

[2] Stevens, P. F. (2001 onwards). Angiosperm Phylogeny Website. Version 9, June 2008 [and more or less continuously updated since]. http://www.mobot.org/MOBOT/research/APweb/.

[3] The Plant List, *Acer rubrum* L.

[4] Nix, Steve. "Ten Most Common Trees in the United States". About.com Forestry. Retrieved 8 October 2016.

[5] "Plants Profile for Acer rubrum". United States Department of Agriculture. Retrieved 30 March 2015.

[6] "Eastern Forests Change Color As Red Maples Proliferate". New York Times. Retrieved 30 March 2015.

[7] Walters, R. S.; Yawney, H. W. (1990). "*Acer rubrum*". In Burns, Russell M.; Honkala, Barbara H. *Hardwoods. Silvics of North America*. Washington, D.C.: United States Forest Service (USFS), United States Department of Agriculture (USDA). **2**. Retrieved 9 May 2007 – via Northeastern Area State and Private Forestry (www.na.fs.fed.us).

[8] Seiler, John R.; Jensen, Edward C.; Peterson, John A. "Acer rubrum Fact Sheet". *Virginia Tech Dendrology Tree Fact Sheets*. Virginia Tech. Archived from the original on 2 June 2007. Retrieved 9 May 2007.

[9] Mitchell, A. F. (1974). *Trees of Britain & Northern Europe*. London: Harper Collins Publishers. p. 347. ISBN 0-00-219213-6.

[10] Primack, R.B.; McCall, C. (1986). "Gender Variation in Red Maple Populations (Acer rubrum; Aceraceae): A Seven-Year Study of a "Polygamodioecious" Species.". *American Journal of Botany*. **73** (9): 1239–1248.

[11] Goertz, D. "Acer rubrum plant description". Northern Ontario Plant Database. Retrieved 10 May 2007.

[12] Walters, Russell S; Yawney, Harry W. "Acer rubrum L.".

[13] Campbell, J (1985). "The Land of Cane and Clover". University of Kentucky: 25.

[14] 18(2), 177–184., Jared; McCarthy, Brian (2011). "Diminished Soil Quality in an Old-Growth, Mixed Mesophytic Forest Following Chronic Acid Deposition Diminished Soil Quality in an Old-growth, Mixed Mesophytic Forest Following Chronic Acid Deposition". *Northeast Naturalist*. **18** (2): 177–184.

[15] Miller, J.H., & Miller, K.V. (1999). *Forest plants of the southeast and their wildlife uses*. Champaign, IL: Kings Time Printing.

[16] Goetz, R. J. "Red Maple Toxicity". *Indiana Plants Poisonous to Livestock and Pets*. Purdue University. Archived from the original on May 5, 2007. Retrieved 9 May 2007.

[17] Abrams, M.D. (1998). "The Red Maple Paradox: what explains the widespread expansion of red maple in eastern forests?". *BioScience*. **48** (5): 355–364.

[18] Abrams, Marc D (May 1998). "The Red Maple Paradox". *BioScience*. **48** (5): 335–364. doi:10.2307/1313374. JSTOR 1313374.

[19] Ogren, Thomas (2015). *The Allergy-Fighting Garden*. Berkeley, CA: Ten Speed Press. pp. 54–55. ISBN 978-1-60774-491-7.

[20] Appleton, Bonnie; Koci, Joel (2003). "Mycorrhizal Fungal Inoculation of Established Street Trees". *Journal of Arboriculture*. **29** (2): 107–110.

[21] Reichard, Timothy A. (October 1976). "Spring Food Habits and Feeding Behavior of Fox Squirrels and Red Squirrels". *American Midland Naturalist*. American Midland Naturalist, Vol. 96, No. 2. **96** (2): 443–450. doi:10.2307/2424082. JSTOR 2424082.

[22] D'Cruz, Mark. "Acer Rubrum Bonsai Care Guide". Ma-Ke Bonsai. Retrieved 2010-10-20.

[23] Evans, E. "Select Acer rubrum Cultivars". North Carolina State University.

[24] Gilman, E. F.; Watson, Dennis G. "Acer rubrum 'Gerling'". University of Florida.

[25] "RHS Plant Selector Acer rubrum 'October Glory' AGM / RHS Gardening". Apps.rhs.org.uk. Retrieved 2012-11-09.

[26] Michael Kuhns and Tom Schmidt (n.d.). "Heating With Wood: Species Characteristics and Volumes". UtahState University Cooperative Extension.

3.7.8 External links

- NRCS: United States Department of Agriculture Plants Profile and map: *Acer rubrum*
- *Acer rubrum* images from Vanderbilt University
- Portrait of the Earth, Winter ID photos

3.8 Adenium

Adenium is a genus of flowering plants in the Apocynum family, Apocynaceae, first described as a genus in 1819. It is native to Africa and the Arabian Peninsula.[3]

3.8.1 Cultivation and uses

Adenium obesum is grown as a houseplant in temperate regions. Numerous hybrids have been developed. Adeniums are appreciated for their colorful flowers, but also for their unusual, thick caudices. They can be grown for many years in a pot and are commonly used for bonsai.

Because seed-grown plants are not genetically identical to the mother plant, desirable varieties are commonly propagated by grafting. Genetically identical plants can also be propagated by cutting. However, cutting-grown plants do not tend to develop a desirable thick caudex as quickly as seed-grown plants.

The sap of *Adenium boehmianum*, *A. multiflorum*, and *A. obesum* contains toxic cardiac glycosides and is used as arrow poison throughout Africa for hunting large game.[4]

3.8.2 Classification

The genus *Adenium* has been held to contain as many as twelve species. These are considered by other authors to be subspecies or varieties. A late-20th-century classification by Plazier recognizes five species.[5]

Species[3]

1. *Adenium arabicum* Balf.f. = *A. obesum*
2. *Adenium boehmianum* Schinz - (Namibia, Angola)
3. *Adenium multiflorum* Klotzsch. (Southern Africa, from Zambia south)
4. *Adenium obesum* (Forssk.) Roem. & Schult. - widespread from Senegal to Somalia, and also Arabian Peninsula
5. *Adenium oleifolium* Stapf - South Africa, Botswana, Namibia
6. *Adenium swazicum* Stapf (Eastern South Africa)[5][6]

Formerly placed here

- *Pachypodium namaquanum* (Wyley ex Harv.) Welw. (as *A. namaquanum* Wyley ex Harv.)[6]

3.8.3 Common names

Adenium obesum is also known as the Desert Rose. In the Philippines, due to its resemblance to the related genus *Plumeria*, and the fact that it was introduced to the Philippines from Bangkok, Thailand, the plant is also called as *Bangkok kalachuchi*.

Due to its resemblance to a miniature Frangipani tree and its popularity in Bonsai, it is also sometimes known as Japanese Frangipani.

This plant has a flower boom in the month of October till December.

3.8.4 References

[1] "Genus: *Adenium* Roem. & Schult.". *Germplasm Resources Information Network*. United States Department of Agriculture. 2003-03-14. Retrieved 2010-06-26.

[2] "World Checklist of Selected Plant Species".

[3] Kew World Checklist of Selected Plant Families

[4] Schmelzer, G.H.; A. Gurib-Fakim (2008). *Medicinal Plants*. Plant Resources of Tropical Africa. pp. 43–49. ISBN 978-90-5782-204-9.

[5] Stoffel Petrus Bester (June 2004). "Adenium multiflorum Klotzsch". *South African National Biodiversity Institute's plant information website*.

[6] "GRIN Species Records of *Adenium*". *Germplasm Resources Information Network*. United States Department of Agriculture. Retrieved 2010-06-26.

3.8.5 External links

3.9 Adenium arabicum

Adenium arabicum is a species of plant commonly used for bonsai and cultivated for its leaves, growth form and flowering characteristics.

The leaves of this species have a broad surface. Leaves also tend to be large and somewhat leathery in appearance. Growth form is squat and fat, with a definite caudex and without much differentiation between trunk and branches. Skin is purple to dark brown color. Flowers range from pink to reddish pink.

3.9.1 References

3.10 Aesculus hippocastanum

"Horse-chestnut" redirects here. For other uses, see Horse chestnut (disambiguation).

Aesculus hippocastanum is a species of flowering plant in the soapberry and lychee family Sapindaceae. It is a large deciduous, synoecious[1] tree, commonly known as **horse-chestnut**[2] or **conker tree**.

3.10.1 Description

Aesculus hippocastanum is a large tree, growing to about 39 metres (128 ft) tall[3]:371 with a domed crown of stout branches; on old trees the outer branches often pendulous with curled-up tips. The leaves are opposite and palmately compound, with 5–7 leaflets; each leaflet is 13–30 cm long, making the whole leaf up to 60 cm across, with a 7–20 cm petiole. The leaf scars left on twigs after the leaves have fallen have a distinctive horseshoe shape, complete with seven "nails". The flowers are usually white with a yellow to pink blotch at the base of the petals;[3] they are produced in spring in erect panicles 10–30 cm tall with about 20–50 flowers on each panicle. Usually only 1–5 fruit develop on each panicle; the shell is a green, spiky capsule containing one (rarely two or three) nut-like seeds called conkers or horse-chestnuts. Each conker is 2–4 cm diameter, glossy nut-brown with a whitish scar at the base.[4]

3.10.2 Etymology

The common name "horse-chestnut" (often unhyphenated) is reported as having originated from the erroneous belief

Inflorescence

that the tree was a kind of chestnut (though in fact only distantly related), together with the observation that the fruit is most likely to be toxic to horses.*[5]

3.10.3 Distribution and habitat

Aesculus hippocastanum is native to a small area in the Pindus Mountains mixed forests and Balkan mixed forests of South East Europe.*[6] However, it can be found in many parts of Europe as far north as Gästrikland in Sweden, as well as in many parks and cities in the United States and Canada.

3.10.4 Uses

It is widely cultivated in streets and parks throughout the temperate world, and has been particularly successful in places like Ireland, the United Kingdom and New Zealand, where they are commonly found in parks, streets and avenues. Cultivation for its spectacular spring flowers is successful in a wide range of temperate climatic conditions provided summers are not too hot, with trees being grown as far north as Edmonton, Alberta, Canada,*[7] the Faroe Islands,*[8] Reykjavík, Iceland and Harstad, Norway.

In Britain and Ireland, the seeds are used for the popular children's game conkers. During the First World War, there was a campaign to ask for everyone (including children) to collect horse-chestnuts and donate them to the government. The conkers were used as a source of starch for fermentation using the *Clostridium acetobutylicum* method devised by Chaim Weizmann to produce acetone for use as a solvent for the production of cordite, which was then used in military armaments. Weizmann's process could use any source of starch, but the government chose to ask for conkers to avoid causing starvation by depleting food sources. But conkers were found to be a poor source, and the factory only produced acetone for three months; however, they were collected again in World War II for the same reason.*[9]

A selection of fresh conkers from a horse-chestnut

The seeds, especially those that are young and fresh, are slightly poisonous, containing alkaloid saponins and glucosides. Although not dangerous to touch, they cause sickness when eaten; consumed by horses, they can cause tremors and lack of coordination.*[10]

Though the seeds are said to repel spiders there is little evidence to support these claims. The presence of saponin may repel insects but it is not clear whether this is effective on spiders.*[11]

Horse-chestnuts have been threatened by the leaf-mining moth *Cameraria ohridella*, whose larvae feed on horse chestnut leaves. The moth was described from Macedonia where the species was discovered in 1984 but took 18 years to reach Britain.*[12]

The flower is the symbol of the city of Kiev, capital of Ukraine.*[13] Although the horse-chestnut is sometimes known as the buckeye, this name is generally reserved for the New World members of the *Aesculus* genus.

In Germany, horse-chestnuts are often found in beer gardens, particularly in Bavaria. Prior to the advent of mechanical refrigeration, brewers would dig cellars for lagering. To further protect the cellars from the summer heat, they would plant chestnut trees, which have spreading, dense canopies but shallow roots which would not intrude on the caverns. The practice of serving beer at these sites evolved into the modern beer garden.*[14]

3.10.5 Medical uses

The seed extract standardized to around 20 percent aescin (escin) is used for its venotonic effect, vascular protection, anti-inflammatory and free radical scavenging properties.*[15]*[16] Primary indication is chronic venous insufficiency.*[16]*[17] A recent Cochrane Review found the evidence suggests that Horse Chestnut Seed Extract is an efficacious and safe short-term treatment for chronic venous insufficiency, but definitive randomized controlled trials are required to confirm the efficacy.*[18]

Aescin reduces fluid leaks to surrounding tissue by reducing both the number and size of membrane pores in the veins.

Safety in medical use

Two preparations are considered; whole horsechestnut extract (whole HCE) and purified β-aescin. Historically, whole HCE has been used both for oral and IV routes (as of year 2001). The rate of adverse effects are low, in a large German study, 0.6%, consisting mainly of gastrointestinal symptoms. Dizziness, headache and itching have been reported. One serious safety issue is rare cases of acute anaphylactic reactions, presumably in a context of whole HCE. Purified β-aescin would be expected to have a better safety profile.

Another is the risk of acute renal failure, "when patients, who had undergone cardiac surgery were given high doses of horse chestnut extract i.v. for postoperative oedema. The phenomenon was dose dependent as no alteration in renal function was recorded with 340 μg kg−1, mild renal function impairment developed with 360 μg kg−1 and acute renal failure with 510 μg kg−1".*[19] This almost certainly took place in a context of whole HCE.

Three clinical trials were since performed to assess the effects of aescin on renal function. A total of 83 subjects were studied; 18 healthy volunteers given 10 or 20 mg iv. for 6 days, 40 in-patients with normal renal function given 10 mg iv. two times per day (except two children given 0.2 mg/kg), 12 patients with cerebral oedema and normal renal function given a massive iv. dose on the day of surgery (49.2 ± 19.3 mg) and 15.4 ± 9.4 mg daily for the following 10 days and 13 patients with impaired renal function due to glomerulonephritis or pyelonephritis, who were given 20–25 mg iv. daily for 6 days. "In all studies renal function was monitored daily resorting to the usual tests of renal function: BUN, serum creatinine, creatinine clearance, urinalysis. In a selected number of cases paraaminohippurate and labelled EDTA clearance were also measured. No signs of development of renal impairment in the patients with normal renal function or of worsening of renal function in the patients with renal impairment were recorded." It is concluded that aescin has excellent tolerability in a clinical setting.*[20]

Raw Horse Chestnut seed, leaf, bark and flower are toxic due to the presence of esculin and should not be ingested. Horse chestnut seed is classified by the FDA as an unsafe herb.*[16] The glycoside and saponin constituents are considered toxic.*[16]

Aesculus hippocastanum is used in Bach flower remedies. When the buds are used it is referred to as "chestnut bud" and when the flowers are used it is referred to as "white chestnut".

3.10.6 Other chemicals

Quercetin 3,4'-diglucoside, a flavonol glycoside can also be found in horse chestnut seeds.*[21] Leucocyanidin, leucodelphinidin and procyanidin A2 can also be found in horse chestnut.

3.10.7 Anne Frank Tree

A famous specimen of the horse-chestnut was the Anne Frank Tree in the centre of Amsterdam, which she mentioned in her diary and which survived until August 2010, when a heavy wind blew it over.*[22]*[23] Eleven young specimens, sprouted from seeds from this tree, were transported to the United States. After a long quarantine in Indianapolis, each tree was shipped off to a new home at a notable museum or institution in the United States, such as the 9/11 Memorial Park, Central H.S. in Little Rock, and two Holocaust Centers. One of them was planted outdoors in March 2013 in front of the Children's Museum of Indianapolis, where they were originally quarantined.

3.10.8 Bonsai

The horse-chestnut is a favourite subject for bonsai.*[24]

3.10.9 Diseases

- Bleeding canker. Half of all horse-chestnuts in Great Britain are now showing symptoms to some degree of this potentially lethal bacterial infection.*[25]*[26]

3.10. AESCULUS HIPPOCASTANUM

- Guignardia leaf blotch, caused by the fungus *Guignardia aesculi*

- Wood rotting fungi, e.g. such as Armillaria and Ganoderma

- Horse-chestnut scale, caused by the insect *Pulvinaria regalis*

- Horse-chestnut leaf miner, *Cameraria ohridella*, a leaf mining moth.*[27] also affecting large numbers of UK trees.*[26]

- Phytophthora bleeding canker, a fungal infection.*[28]

3.10.10 Gallery

- Horse-chestnut planted as a feature tree in a park

- Leaves and trunk

- Foliage and flowers

- Close-up of flowers

- Trunk

- Germination on lawn

3.10.11 See also

- Trees portal

3.10.12 References

Notes

[1] https://bioweb.uwlax.edu/bio203/s2013/phillips_reb2/reproduction.htm

[2] "BSBI List 2007". Botanical Society of Britain and Ireland. Archived from the original (xls) on 2015-01-25. Retrieved 2014-10-17.

[3] Stace, C. A. (2010). *New Flora of the British Isles* (Third ed.). Cambridge, U.K.: Cambridge University Press. ISBN 9780521707725.

[4] Rushforth, K. (1999). *Trees of Britain and Europe*. Collins ISBN 0-00-220013-9.

[5] Lack, H. Walter. "The Discovery and Rediscovery of the Horse Chestnut" (PDF). *Arnoldia*. **61** (4).

[6] Euro+Med Plantbase Project: *Aesculus hippocastanum* Archived September 28, 2007, at the Wayback Machine.

[7] Edmonton

[8] Højgaard, A., Jóhansen, J., & Ødum, S. (1989). A century of tree planting on the Faroe Islands. *Ann. Soc. Sci. Faeroensis* Supplementum 14.

[9] "Conkers - collected for use in two world wars". *Making history*. BBC. Retrieved 27 September 2014.

[10] Lewis, Lon D. (1995). *Feeding and care of the horse*. Wiley-Blackwell. ISBN 9780683049671. Retrieved 2011-10-21.

[11] Edwards, Jon (2010). "Spiders vs conkers: the definitive guide". Royal Society of Chemistry. Retrieved 2013-09-09.

[12] Lees, D.C.; Lopez-Vaamonde, C.; Augustin, S. 2009. Taxon page for Cameraria ohridella Deschka & Dimic 1986. In: EOLspecies, http://www.eol.org/pages/306084. First Created: 2009-06-22T13:47:37Z. Last Updated: 2009-08-10T12:57:23Z.

[13] Kiev

[14] Schäffer, Albert (2012-05-21). "120 Minuten sind nicht genug" [120 minutes aren't enough]. *Frankfurter Allgemeine Zeitung* (in German). Retrieved 2016-10-11.

[15] Diehm C, Trampisch HJ, Lange S, Schmidt C. Comparison of leg compression stocking and oral horse-chestnut seed extract therapy in patients with chronic venous insufficiency. Lancet. 1996;347:292–4.

[16] Horse Chestnut, Memorial Sloan-Kettering Cancer Center

[17] http://nccih.nih.gov/health/horsechestnut NCCIH.nih.gov Horse Chestnut page

[18] Pittler MH, Ernst E. (2012). "Horse chestnut seed extract for chronic venous insufficiency". *Cochrane Database Syst Rev.* **11**: CD003230. doi:10.1002/14651858.CD003230.pub4. PMID 23152216.

[19] Supplementary drugs and other substances: Aesculus. In: Martindale. The Complete Drug Reference, 32nd edn. Pharmaceutical Press, 1999: 1543–4.

[20] Sirtori CR (September 2001). "Aescin: pharmacology, pharmacokinetics and therapeutic profile". *Pharmacol. Res.* **44** (3): 183–193. doi:10.1006/phrs.2001.0847. PMID 11529685.

[21] Quercetin-3,4'-diglukosid, ein Flavonolglykosid des Roßkastaniensamens. Wagner J, Naturwissenschaften, 1961, Volume 48, Issue 2, page 54, doi:10.1007/BF00603428

[22] Sterling, Toby (24 August 2010). "Anne Frank's 'beautiful' tree felled by Amsterdam storm". *The Scotsman*. Retrieved 24 August 2010.

[23] Gray-Block, Aaron (23 August 2010). "Anne Frank tree falls over in heavy wind, rain". *Reuters*. Archived from the original on 24 August 2010. Retrieved 24 August 2010.

[24] D'Cruz, Mark. "Ma-Ke Bonsai Care Guide for Aesculus hippocastanum". Ma-Ke Bonsai. Retrieved 2011-07-05.

[25] "Extent of the bleeding canker of horse chestnut problem". UK Forestry Commission. Retrieved 2010-01-09.

[26] http://www.suffolkcoastal.gov.uk/yourdistrict/trees/chestnuts/default.htm

[27] "Other common pest and disease problems of horse chestnut". UK Forestry Commission. Retrieved 2010-01-09.

[28] "Bleeding Canker". Royal Horticultural Society. 11 November 2009. Archived from the original on 16 January 2010. Retrieved 2010-01-09.

3.10.13 External links

- NCCIH.nih.gov Horse Chestnut page
- NIH.gov Horse Chestnut page
- Taxon page for Cameraria ohridella Deschka & Dimic 1986
- Eichhorn, Markus (October 2010). "The Conker Tree (Horse Chestnut)". *Test Tube*. Brady Haran for the University of Nottingham.

3.11 Aesculus indica

Aesculus indica, the **Indian horse-chestnut**[*][1] or **Himalayan horse chestnut**, is a plant species in the Sapindaceae family.

3.11.1 Description

Aesculus indica is an attractive tree growing to about 30 meters (100 feet) with a spread of about 12 meters (39 feet). It is hardy to −15°C (5°F), USDA zones 7-9.[*][2] It is in flower from June to July, and the seeds ripen in October. The flowers are hermaphroditic and with plentiful white blossoms during May and June pollinated by bees. Its large leaves 10–20 cm long by 2–6 cm wide are also ornamental and the mature tree forms a beautiful round canopy.

3.11.2 Distribution

It is common along the Himalayan Lowlands, between Kashmir and Western Nepal at elevations between 900 and

3,000 metres.*[3] In the British Isles it is popular in many parks and estates where it was introduced in the mid-19th century. It is also found in many parts of the USA.*[2] The commercial collection of its seeds for flour production seems to have impacted on the natural distribution of this species.

3.11.3 Uses

Its leaves are used as cattle fodder in parts of Northern India. Its seeds are dried and ground into a bitter flour, called *tattawakher*. The bitterness is caused by saponins, which are rinsed out by thoroughly washing the flour during its preparation. The flour is often mixed with wheat flour to make chapatis*[4] and also to make a halwa (Indian sweetmeat) and sometimes is served as a *dalia*, (a type of porridge or gruel) during fasting periods.

It is used in traditional Indian medicine, for the treatment of some skin diseases, rheumatism, as an astringent, acrid and narcotic, and in the relief of headaches.*[4]

Its large leaves and flowers make it suitable for use as large-sized bonsai.*[5]

3.11.4 References

[1] "BSBI List 2007" (xls). Botanical Society of Britain and Ireland. Archived from the original on 2015-02-25. Retrieved 2014-10-17.

[2] Aesculus indica Fact Sheet ST-63 http://hort.ufl.edu/database/documents/pdf/tree_fact_sheets/aesinda.pdf

[3] Indian Journal of Traditional Knowledge. Vol. 8(2), April 2009, pp. 285-286. Ethnobotany of Indian horse chestnut (Aesculus indica) in Mandi district, http://nopr.niscair.res.in/bitstream/123456789/3963/1/IJTK%208(2)%20285-286.pdf

[4] Plants and people of Nepal, By N. P. Manandhar, Sanjay Manandhar, Pg. 76

[5] D'Cruz, Mark. "Ma-Ke Bonsai Care Guide for Aesculus indica". Ma-Ke Bonsai. Retrieved 2010-12-02.

3.11.5 External links

Media related to Aesculus indica at Wikimedia Commons

3.12 Afrocarpus falcatus

Afrocarpus falcatus (syn. *Podocarpus falcatus*) is a species of tree in the family Podocarpaceae. It is native to the montane forests of southern Africa, where it is distributed in Malawi, Mozambique, South Africa, and Swaziland.*[1] Common names include **common yellowwood**, **bastard yellowwood**, **outeniqua yellowwood**,*[2] **African fern pine**, **weeping yew**,*[3] Afrikaans: *outeniekwageelhout*, *kalander*, Sotho: *mogôbagôba*, Xhosa: *umkhoba* and Zulu: *umsonti*.*[4] It is widespread, in some areas abundant, and not considered threatened,*[1] but it is a protected tree in South Africa.*[4] It is grown as an ornamental tree, especially in South Africa, and occasionally abroad.*[3]

3.12.1 Description

This is an evergreen conifer often growing up to about 45 meters tall, but known to reach 60 m.*[3] At higher elevations and in exposed, coastal habitat it rarely exceeds 25 m tall.*[1] The trunk can be 2 to 3 m wide, and is gray-brown to reddish. It is smooth and ridged on young stems, but increasingly flaky on older trunks.*[5] The leaves are arranged in spirals on the branches. They are small and narrow, up to 4.5 cm long by about 6 mm wide. They are green to yellowish, hairless, and leathery and somewhat waxy in texture. It is a dioecious species, with male and female structures on separate plants. The male cone is brown with spiralling scales and measures 5 to 15 mm long by 3 mm wide. It grows from the leaf axils. The female cone has one scale bearing one seed about 1 to 2 cm long. The gray-green seed is drupe-like with a woody coat covered in a fleshy, resinous skin.*[3]

Some of the largest individuals occur in the Knysna-Amatole montane forests, where some specimens are over 1,000 years old.*[1]

3.12.2 Biology

Female trees bear their fruit irregularly, only every few years. The fleshy epimatium of the strobilus (or "cone") covers all of the seed, and ripens to a yellow colour, when it acquires a soft, jelly-like consistency. The main agents of seed dispersal are fruit bats, which eat the fleshy covering but discard the hard, woody seed.*[3] Many birds feed on the fruits, such as Cape parrot, purple-crested turaco, Knysna turaco, Ross's turaco, African olive pigeon, African green pigeon, and eastern bronze-naped pigeon.*[5] Animals that feed on the seeds include colobus monkeys, bushpigs, hornbills, turacos, and rodents. These may not be effective seed dispersal agents, because it appears that seeds that have gone through animal guts do not germinate well.*[3]

The tree has been found to host arbuscular mycorrhizae.*[3]

It may grow as a solitary tree, in small clusters, or in wide monotypic stands. It is associated with African juniper (*Ju-*

niperus procera).*[3]

3.12.3 Uses

The wood, often called podo or yellowwood, is good for construction, particularly shipbuilding. It is also made into plywood and used to make many products, including furniture, boxes, vats, toys, farm implements, musical instruments, and railroad ties. It is used in the construction of houses. It is also used as firewood.*[3] Some examples of South African yellowwood antique woodworking were created with the wood of this tree.*[5] The wood is useful, but not very durable, as it is susceptible to blue stain fungus, powderpost beetles, longhorn beetles, and termites.*[3]

The seed is edible, but resinous. The bark and seeds have been used in traditional African medicine. The tree is cultivated as an ornamental and a windbreak, and to prevent erosion. It has been used as a Christmas tree.*[3]

3.12.4 Conservation

The species has been vulnerable to logging, a practice which likely claimed many large, ancient specimens. In parts of South Africa logging has ceased, but in other regions the situation is not known. In general, it is not considered a current threat.*[1]

3.12.5 Gallery

In Cape Town

Bark texture

Foliage and bark

3.12.6 External links

- PlantzAfrica
- Biodiversity Explorer
- Images on iSpot
- SA Forestry Magazine

The Big Tree

3.12.7 References

[1] Farjon, A. 2013. *Afrocarpus falcatus.* In: IUCN 2013. IUCN Red List of Threatened Species. Version 2013.1. Downloaded on 31 August 2013.

[2] *Afrocarpus falcatus.* Germplasm Resources Information Network (GRIN).

[3] *Afrocarpus falcatus* (Thunb.) C.N.Page. Plant Resources of Tropical Africa (PROTA).

[4] Protected Trees. Department of Water Affairs and Forestry, Republic of South Africa. 3 May 2013.

[5] Klapwijk, Nick (November 2002). "Podocarpus falcatus". *plantzafrica.com.* Pretoria National Botanical Garden. Retrieved 27 October 2014.

3.13 Alnus cordata

Alnus cordata *tree*

Alnus cordata (**Italian alder***[1]*[2]) is a tree or shrub species belonging to the family of Betulaceae and native to southern Apennine Mountains (Campania, Basilicata and Calabria, mainly on western mountain sides) and north-eastern mountains of Corsica.*[3] It has been introduced in Sicily and Sardinia and more recently in Central-North Italy,*[4]*[5]*[6] other European countries (France, Belgium, Spain, Azores, United Kingdom)*[7] and extra-European countries (Chile, New Zealand),*[4] where it has become naturalised.

It is a medium-sized tree growing up to 25 m tall*[8] (exceptionally to 28 m), with a trunk up to 70–100 cm diameter. The leaves are deciduous but with a very long season in leaf, from April to December in the Northern Hemisphere; they are alternate, cordate (heart-shaped), rich glossy green, 5–12 cm long, with a finely serrated margin.

Italian Alder mature female (seed) catkins

The slender cylindrical male catkins are pendulous, reddish and up to 10 cm long;*[8] pollination is in early spring, before the leaves emerge. The female catkins are ovoid, when mature in autumn 2–3 cm long and 1.5–2 cm broad, dark green to brown, hard, woody, and superficially similar to some conifer cones. The small winged seeds disperse through the winter, leaving the old woody, blackish 'cones' on the tree for up to a year after.

Alnus cordata has gained The Royal Horticultural Society's Award of Garden Merit.*[9]

3.13.1 Use

Like other alders, it is able to improve soil fertility through symbiotic nitrogen fixation with the bacteria Actinomyces alni (Frankia alni).*[10] It thrives on much drier soils than most other alders, and grows rapidly even under very unfavourable circumstances, which renders it extremely valuable for landscape planting on difficult sites such as mining spoil heaps and heavily compacted urban sites. It is commonly grown as a windbreak.

The tree also produces valuable reddish-orange wood. It breaks down rapidly when exposed to air, but is durable when immersed in water. The timber is used for turning and carving, for moulding, furniture, panelling and plywood.*[10]

3.13.2 Bonsai

The Italian Alder makes a medium to large bonsai, a quick grower it responds well to pruning with branches ramifying well and leaf size reducing quite rapidly.*[11]

3.13.3 References

[1] Kew World Checklist of Selected Plant Families

[2] "BSBI List 2007" (xls). Botanical Society of Britain and Ireland. Archived from the original on 2015-01-25. Retrieved 2014-10-17.

[3] Gamisans, J. (1983). L'Aulne à feuilles en coeur *Alnus cordata* (Loisel.) Loisel. dans son milieu naturel en Corse. ENGREF, Ecole nationale du génie rural, des eaux et des forêts, Nancy (FRA).

[4] Caudullo, G., Mauri, A., 2016. *Alnus cordata* in Europe: distribution, habitat, usage and threats. In: San-Miguel-Ayanz, J., de Rigo, D., Caudullo, G., Houston Durrant, T., Mauri, A. (Eds.), European Atlas of Forest Tree Species. Publications Office of the European Union, Luxembourg, pp. e015443+

[5] Camarda, I. (1982). Note su alberi e arbusti della Sardegna. Bollettino della Società sarda di scienze naturali, Vol. 21: 323-331

[6] Salvatore Cambria, Flora e Vegetazione della Sicilia: Alnus cordata (Loisel.) Duby. Accessed on July 2016

[7] Shaw, K., Wilson, B. & Roy, S. 2014. *Alnus cordata*. The IUCN Red List of Threatened Species 2014: e.T194657A2356349. . Downloaded on 15 July 2016

[8] Rushforth, Keith (1986) [1980]. *Bäume* [*Pocket Guide to Trees*] (in German) (2nd ed.). Bern: Hallwag AG. p. 91. ISBN 3-444-70130-6.

[9] "Alnus cordata AGM". The Royal Horticultural Society. Retrieved 25 August 2012.

[10] Ducci, F.; Tani, A. (2009). "Italian alder - *Alnus cordata*" (PDF). *EUFORGEN Technical guidelines for conservation and use*.

[11] D'Cruz, Mark. "Ma-Ke Bonsai Care Guide for Alnus cordata". Ma-Ke Bonsai. Retrieved 2011-07-05.

3.13.4 External links

- *Alnus cordata* - distribution map, genetic conservation units and related resources. European Forest Genetic Resources Programme (EUFORGEN)

3.14 Alnus glutinosa

Alnus glutinosa, the **common alder**, **black alder**, **European alder** or just **alder**, is a species of tree in the family Betulaceae, native to most of Europe, southwest Asia and northern Africa. It thrives in wet locations where its association with the bacterium *Frankia alni* enables it to grow in poor quality soils. It is a medium size, short-lived tree growing to a height of up to 30 metres (100 ft). It has short-stalked rounded leaves and separate male and female flower in the form of catkins. The small, rounded fruits are cone-like and the seeds are dispersed by wind and water.

The common alder provides food and shelter to wildlife, with a number of insects, lichens and fungi being completely dependent on the tree. It is a pioneer species, colonising vacant land and forming mixed forests as other trees appear in its wake. Eventually common alder dies out of woodlands because the seedlings need more light than is available on the forest floor. Its more usual habitat is forest edges, swamps and riverside corridors. The timber has been used in underwater foundations and for manufacture into paper and fibreboard, for smoking foods, for joinery, turnery and carving. Products of the tree have been used in ethnobotany, providing folk remedies for various ailments, and research has shown that extracts of the seeds are active against pathogenic bacteria.

3.14.1 Description

Alnus glutinosa is a tree that thrives in moist soils, and grows under favourable circumstances to a height of 20 to 30 metres (66 to 98 ft) and exceptionally up to 37 metres (121 ft).*[4] Young trees have an upright habit of growth with a main axial stem but older trees develop an arched crown with crooked branches. The base of the trunk produces adventitious roots which grow down to the soil and may appear to be propping the trunk up. The bark of young trees is smooth, glossy and greenish-brown while in older trees it is dark grey and fissured. The branches are smooth and somewhat sticky, being scattered with resinous warts. The buds are purplish-brown and have short stalks. Both male

Foliage

Male inflorescence (left) and mature cones (right)

and female catkins form in the autumn and remain dormant during the winter.*[5]

The leaves of the common alder are short-stalked, rounded, up to 10 cm (4 in) long with a slightly wedge-shaped base and a wavy, serrated margin. They have a glossy dark green upper surface and paler green underside with rusty-brown hairs in the angles of the veins. As with some other trees growing near water, the common alder keeps its leaves longer than do trees in drier situations, and the leaves remain green late into the autumn. As the Latin name *glutinosa* implies, the buds and young leaves are sticky with a resinous gum.*[5]*[6]*[7]

The species is monoecious and the flowers are wind-pollinated; the slender cylindrical male catkins are pendulous, reddish in colour and 5 to 10 cm (2 to 4 in) long; the female flowers are upright, broad and green, with short stalks. During the autumn they become dark brown to black in colour, hard, somewhat woody, and superficially similar to small conifer cones. They last through the winter and the small winged seeds are mostly scattered the following spring. The seeds are flattened reddish-brown nuts edged with webbing filled with pockets of air. This enables them to float for about a month which allows the seed to disperse widely.*[5]*[6]*[7]

Unlike some other species of tree, common alders do not produce shade leaves. The respiration rate of shaded foliage is the same as well-lit leaves but the rate of assimilation is lower. This means that as a tree in woodland grows taller, the lower branches die and soon decay, leaving a small crown and unbranched trunk.*[8]

3.14.2 Taxonomy

Alnus glutinosa was first described by Carl Linnaeus in 1753, as one of two varieties of alder (the other being *A. incana*), which he regarded as a single species *Betula alnus*.*[9] In 1785, Jean-Baptiste Lamarck treated it as a full species under the name *Betula glutinosa*.*[10] Its present scientific name is due to Joseph Gaertner, who in 1791 accepted the separation of alders from birches, and transferred the species to *Alnus*.*[2] The epithet *glutinosa* means "sticky", referring particularly to the young shoots.*[11]

Within the genus *Alnus*, the common alder is placed in subgenus *Alnus* as part of a closely related group of species including the grey alder, *Alnus incana*,*[12] with which it hybridizes to form the hybrid *A.* × *hybrida*.*[13]

3.14.3 Distribution and habitat

The common alder is native to almost the whole of continental Europe (except for both the extreme north and south) as well as the United Kingdom and Ireland. In Asia its range includes Turkey, Iran and Kazakhstan, and in Africa it is found in Tunisia, Algeria and Morocco. It is naturalised in the Azores.*[14] It has been introduced, either by accident or by intent, to Canada, the United States, Chile, South Africa, Australia and New Zealand. Its natural habitat is in moist ground near rivers, ponds and lakes but it can also grow in drier locations and sometimes occurs in mixed woodland and on forest edges. It tolerates a range of soil types and grows best at a pH of between 5.5 and 7.2. Because of its association with the nitrogen-fixing bacterium *Frankia alni*, it can grow in nutrient-poor soils where few other trees thrive.*[15]

Nodules on the roots caused by the bacterium Frankia alni

Galls on the leaves caused by the mite Eriophyes inangulis

3.14.4 Ecological relationships

The common alder is most noted for its symbiotic relationship with the bacterium *Frankia alni*, which forms nodules on the tree's roots. This bacterium absorbs nitrogen from the air and fixes it in a form available to the tree. In return, the bacterium receives carbon products produced by the tree through photosynthesis. This relationship, which improves the fertility of the soil, has established the common alder as an important pioneer species in ecological succession.*[16]

The common alder is susceptible to *Phytophthora alni*, a recently evolved species of oomycete plant pathogen probably of hybrid origin. This is the causal agent of phytophthora disease of alder which is causing extensive mortality of the trees in some parts of Europe.*[17] The symptoms of this infection include the death of roots and of patches of bark, dark spots near the base of the trunk, yellowing of leaves and in subsequent years, the death of branches and sometimes the whole tree.*[15] *Taphrina alni* is a fungal plant pathogen that causes alder tongue gall, a chemically induced distortion of female catkins. The gall develops on the maturing fruits and produces spores which are carried by the wind to other trees. This gall is believed to be harmless to the tree.*[18] Another, also harmless, gall is caused by a midge, *Eriophyes inangulis*, which sucks sap from the leaves forming pustules.*[19]

The common alder is important to wildlife all year round and the seeds are a useful winter food for birds. Deer, sheep, hares and rabbits feed on the tree and it provides shelter for livestock in winter.*[15] It shades the water of rivers and streams, moderating the water temperature, and this benefits fish which also find safety among its exposed roots in times of flood. The common alder is the foodplant of the larvae of a number of different butterflies and moths*[20] and is associated with over 140 species of plant-eating insect.*[19] The tree is also a host to a variety of mosses and lichens which particularly flourish in the humid moist environment of streamside trees. Some common lichens found growing on the trunk and branches include tree lungwort (*Lobaria pulmonaria*), *Menneguzzia terebrata* and *Stenocybe pullatula*, the last of which is restricted to alders.*[19] Some 47 species of mycorrhizal fungi have been found growing in symbiosis with the common alder, both partners benefiting from an exchange of nutrients. As well as several species of *Naucoria*, these symbionts include *Russula alnetorum*, the milkcaps *Lactarius obscuratus* and *Lactarius cyathula*, and the alder roll-rim *Paxillus filamentosus*, all of which grow nowhere else except in association with alders. In spring, the catkin cup *Ciboria amentacea* grows on fallen alder catkins.*[19]

As an introduced species, the common alder can affect the ecology of its new locality. It is a fast-growing tree and can quickly form dense woods where little light reaches the ground, and this may inhibit the growth of native plants. The presence of the nitrogen-fixing bacteria and the annual accumulation of leaf litter from the trees also alters the nutrient status of the soil. It also increases the availability of phosphorus in the ground, and the tree's dense network of roots can cause increased sedimentation in pools and waterways. It spreads easily by wind-borne seed, may be dispersed to a certain extent by birds and the woody fruits can float away from the parent tree. When the tree is felled, regrowth occurs from the stump, and logs and fallen branches can take root.*[15] *A. glutinosa* is classed as an environmental weed in New Zealand.*[21]

3.14.5 Cultivation and uses

The common alder is used as a pioneer species and to stabilise river banks, to assist in flood control, to purify water in waterlogged soils and to moderate the temperature and nutrient status of water bodies. It can be grown by itself or in mixed species plantations, and the nitrogen-rich leaves falling to the ground enrich the soil and increase the pro-

Infrutescence and Achenes

duction of such trees as walnut, Douglas fir and poplar on poor quality soils. Although the tree can live for up to 160 years, it is best felled for timber at 60 to 70 years before heart rot sets in.*[8]

On marshy ground it is important as coppice-wood, being cut near the base to encourage the production of straight poles. It is capable of enduring clipping as well as marine climatic conditions and may be cultivated as a fast-growing windbreak. In woodland natural regeneration is not possible as the seeds need sufficient nutrients, water and light to germinate. Such conditions are rarely found at the forest floor and as the forest matures, the alder trees in it die out.*[22]*[23] The species is cultivated as a specimen tree in parks and gardens, and the cultivar 'Imperialis' has gained the Royal Horticultural Society's Award of Garden Merit.*[24]

Timber

The wood is soft, white when first cut, turning to pale red; the knots are attractively mottled. The timber is not used where strength is required in the construction industry, but is used for paper-making, the manufacture of fibreboard and the production of energy.*[8] Under water the wood is very durable and is used for deep foundations of buildings. The piles beneath the Rialto in Venice, and the foundations of several medieval cathedrals are made of alder. The Roman architect Vitruvius mentioned that the timber was used in the construction of the causeways across the Ravenna marshes.*[25] The wood is used in joinery, both as solid timber and as veneer, where its grain and colour are appreciated, and it takes dye well. As the wood is soft, flexible and somewhat light, it can be easily worked as well as split. It is valued in turnery and carving, in making furniture, window frames, clogs, toys, blocks, pencils and bowls.*[5]

Tanning and dyeing

The bark of the common alder has long been used in tanning and dyeing. The bark and twigs contain 16 to 20% tannic acid but their usefulness in tanning is limited by the strong accompanying colour they produce.*[26] Depending on the mordant and the methods used, various shades of brown, fawn, and yellowish-orange hues can be imparted to wool, cotton and silk. Alder bark can also used with iron sulphate to create a black dye which can substitute for the use of sumach or galls.*[27] The Laplanders are said to chew the bark and use their saliva to dye leather. The shoots of the common alder produce a yellowish or cinnamon-coloured dye if cut early in the year. Other parts of the tree are also used in dyeing; the catkins can yield a green colour and the fresh-cut wood a pinkish-fawn colour.*[26]

Other uses

It is also the traditional wood that is burnt to produce smoked fish and other smoked foods, though in some areas other woods are now more often used. It supplies high quality charcoal.*[5]

The leaves of this tree are sticky and if they are spread on the floor of a room, their adhesive surface is said to trap fleas.*[26]

Chemical constituents of *Alnus glutinosa* include hirsutanonol, oregonin, genkwanin,*[28] rhododendrin {3-(4-hydroxyphenyl)-1-methylpropyl-β-D-glucopyranoside} and glutinic acid (2,3-pentadienedioic acid).*[29]

3.14.6 Health

Pollen from the common alder, along with that from birch and hazel, is one of the main sources of tree pollen allergy. As the pollen is often present in the atmosphere at the same time as that of birch, hazel, hornbeam and oak, and they have similar physicochemical properties, it is difficult to separate out their individual effects. In central Europe, these tree pollens are the second most common cause of allergic conditions after grass pollen.*[30]

The bark of common alder has traditionally been used as an astringent, a cathartic, a hemostatic, a febrifuge, a tonic and a restorative (a substance able to restore normal health). A decoction of the bark has been used to treat swelling, inflammation and rheumatism, as an emetic, and to treat pharyngitis and sore throat.*[29] Ground up bark has been used as an ingredient in toothpaste, and the inner bark can be boiled in vinegar to provide a skin wash for treating dermatitis, lice and scabies. The leaves have been used to reduce breast discomfort in nursing mothers and folk remedies advocate the use of the leaves against various forms of cancer.*[22] Alpine farmers are said to use the leaves to alleviate rheumatism by placing a heated bag full of leaves on the affected areas. Alder leaves are consumed by cows, sheep, goats and horses though pigs refuse to eat them. According to some people, consumption of alder leaves causes blackening of the tongue and is harmful to horses.*[26]

In a research study, extracts from the seeds of the common alder have been found to be active against all the eight pathogenic bacteria against which they were tested, which included *Escherichia coli* and methicillin-resistant *Staphylococcus aureus* (MRSA). The only extract to have significant antioxidant activity was that extracted in methanol. All extracts were of low toxicity to brine shrimps. These results suggest that the seeds could be further investigated for use in the development of possible anti-MRSA drugs.*[31]

3.14.7 Details of Alder structure and galls

- Details

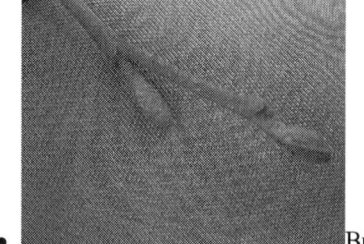

- Buds

-  Bark

-  Alder Tongue Gall fungus, *Taphrina alni*

-  Detail - Alder Tongue Gall

- Alder carr in Germany

- Trees in winter, Germany

- Black alder in Ås, Norway

Black alder defies harsh conditions in the Swedish archipelago

3.14.8 References

[1] Participants of the FFI; IUCN SSC Central Asian regional tree Red Listing workshop, Bishkek, Kyrgyzstan (11–13 July 2006) (2007). "*Alnus glutinosa*". *IUCN Red List of Threatened Species. Version 2014.2*. International Union for Conservation of Nature. Retrieved 8 October 2014.

[2] "*Alnus glutinosa*". *The International Plant Names Index*. Retrieved 2014-08-31.

[3] "*Alnus glutinosa*". *World Checklist of Selected Plant Families*. Royal Botanic Gardens, Kew. Retrieved 2014-08-31.

[4] "Spitzenbäume". Land Brandenburg. Archived from the original on 2016-03-03. Retrieved 2009-01-19.

[5] Vedel, Helge; Lange, Johan (1960). *Trees and Bushes in Woods and Hedgerows*. Methuen. pp. 143–145. ISBN 978-0-416-61780-1.

[6] Trees for Life Species Profile: *Alnus glutinosa*

[7] Flora of NW Europe: *Alnus glutinosa*

[8] Claessens, Hugues; Oosterbaan, Anne; Savill, Peter; Rondeux, Jacques (2010). "A review of the characteristics of black alder (*Alnus glutinosa* (L.) Gaertn.) and their implications for silvicultural practices". *Forestry*. **83** (2): 163–175. doi:10.1093/forestry/cpp038.

[9] "*Betula alnus* var. *glutinosa*". *The International Plant Names Index*. Retrieved 2014-08-31.

[10] "*Betula glutinosa*". *The International Plant Names Index*. Retrieved 2014-08-31.

[11] Coombes, Allen J. (1994). *Dictionary of Plant Names*. London: Hamlyn Books. p. 8. ISBN 978-0-600-58187-1.

[12] Chen, Zhiduan & Li, Jianhua (2004). "Phylogenetics and Biogeography of *Alnus* (Betulaceae) Inferred from Sequences of Nuclear Ribosomal DNA ITS Region". *International Journal of Plant Sciences*. **165**: 325–335. doi:10.1086/382795.

[13] Stace, Clive (2010). *New Flora of the British Isles* (3rd ed.). Cambridge, UK: Cambridge University Press. p. 296. ISBN 978-0-521-70772-5.

[14] "*Alnus glutinosa*". *Flora Europaea*. Royal Botanic Garden Edinburgh. Retrieved 2014-08-09.

[15] "*Alnus glutinosa* (tree)". *Global Invasive Species Database*. IUCN SSC Invasive Species Specialist Group. 2010-08-27. Retrieved 2014-08-04.

[16] Schwencke, J.; Caru, M. (2001). "Advances in actinorhizal symbiosis: Host plant-*Frankia* interactions, biology, and application in arid land reclamation: A review". *Arid Land Research and Management*. **15** (4): 285–327. doi:10.1080/153249801753127615.

[17] Phytophthora Disease of Alder

[18] Ellis, Hewett A. (2001). *Cecidology*. Vol.16, No.1. p. 24.

[19] Featherstone, Alan Watson (2012-11-26). "Common or black alder". Trees for life. Retrieved 2014-08-07.

[20] Carter, David James; Hargreaves, Brian (1986). *A field guide to caterpillars of butterflies and moths in Britain and Europe*. Collins. ISBN 978-0-00-219080-0.

[21] Clayson, Howell (May 2008). *Consolidated list of environmental weeds in New Zealand*. Wellington: Department of Conservation. ISBN 978-0-478-14412-3.

[22] "*Alnus glutinosa* - (L.)Gaertn.". Plants For A Future. 2012. Retrieved 2014-08-05.

[23] Kajba, D. & Gračan, J. (2003). "*Alnus glutinosa*" (PDF). *EUFORGEN Technical guidelines for genetic conservation and use for black alder*: 4 p.

[24] "*Alnus glutinosa* Imperialis". Royal Horticultural Society. Retrieved 2014-08-06.

[25] Paterson, J. M. "The Alder Tree". *A Tree in Your Pocket*. Retrieved 2014-08-03.

[26] Grieve, M. "Alder, Common". *Botanical.com: A Modern Herbal*. Retrieved 2014-08-05.

[27] Adrosko, Rita J. (2012). *Natural Dyes and Home Dyeing*. Courier Dover Publications. pp. 41–42. ISBN 978-0-486-15609-5.

[28] O'Rourke, Ciara; Sarker, Satyajit D.; Stewart, Fiona; Byres, Maureen; Delazar, Abbas; Kumarasamy, Yashodharan; Nahar, Lutfun. "Hirsutanonol, oregonin and genkwanin from the seeds of *Alnus glutinosa* (Betulaceae)". *Biochemical Systematics and Ecology*. **33** (7): 749–752. doi:10.1016/j.bse.2004.10.005. ISSN 0305-1978.

[29] Sati, Sushil Chandra; Sati, Nitin; Sati, O. P. (2011). "Bioactive constituents and medicinal importance of genus *Alnus*". *Pharmacognosy Review*. **5** (10): 174–183. doi:10.4103/0973-7847.91115. PMC 3263052. PMID 22279375.

[30] "Erle: Schwarzerle, *Alnus glutinosa*". Alles zur Allergologie (in German). Retrieved 2014-08-05.

[31] Middleton, P.; Stewart, F.; Al-Qahtani, S.; Egan, P.; O'Rourke, C.; Abdulrahman, A.; Byres, M.; Middleton, M.; Kumarasamy, Y.; Shoeb, M.; Nahar, L.; Delazar, A.; Sarker, S. D. (2005). "Antioxidant, Antibacterial Activities and General Toxicity of *Alnus glutinosa*, *Fraxinus excelsior* and *Papaver rhoeas*". *Iranian Journal of Pharmaceutical Research*. **4** (2): 101–103.

3.14.9 External links

- *Alnus glutinosa* - distribution map, genetic conservation units and related resources. European Forest Genetic Resources Programme (EUFORGEN)

3.15 Azalea

For other uses, see Azalea (disambiguation).

Azaleas /əˈzeɪliə/ are flowering shrubs in the genus

Rhododendron *'Hinodegiri'*

Rhododendron, particularly the former sections *Tsutsuji* (evergreen) and *Pentanthera* (deciduous). Azaleas bloom in spring, their flowers often lasting several weeks. Shade tolerant, they prefer living near or under trees. They are part of the family Ericaceae.

Fifty-year-old azalea

3.15.1 Cultivation

Plant enthusiasts have selectively bred azaleas for hundreds of years. This human selection has produced over 10,000 different cultivars which are propagated by cuttings. Azalea seeds can also be collected and germinated.

Azaleas are generally slow-growing and do best in well-drained acidic soil (4.5–6.0 pH).[1] Fertilizer needs are low; some species need regular pruning.

Azaleas are native to several continents including Asia, Europe and North America. They are planted abundantly as ornamentals in the southeastern USA, southern Asia, and parts of southwest Europe.

A George Taber *azalea*

According to azalea historian Fred Galle, in the United States, *Azalea indica* (in this case, the group of plants called Southern indicas) was first introduced to the outdoor landscape in the 1830s at the rice plantation Magnolia-on-the-Ashley in Charleston, South Carolina. Magnolia's owner John Grimke Drayton imported the plants for use in his estate garden from Philadelphia, where they were grown only in greenhouses. With encouragement from Charles Sprague Sargent from Harvard's Arnold Arboretum, Magnolia Gardens was opened to the public in 1871, following the American Civil War. Magnolia is one of the oldest public gardens in America. Since the late nineteenth century, in late March and early April, thousands visit to see the azaleas bloom in their full glory.

3.15.2 Classification

Native American Azaleas

R. occidentale flowers are larger than other azaleas and are usually white with a splotch of yellow, though sometimes are yellow. Can grow to 8 feet.*[2]

R. arborescens are native to the east coast of North America and can be found growing wild from Alabama to Pennsylvania in wooded, higher altitude areas. Plants grow up to 20 feet high and flowers are white and fragrant.*[2]

The Flame Azalea, R. Native to the mountain regions of Pennsylvania to Georgia and Kentucky. Flowers do not smell but bloom in every shade from pale yellow to crimson red. Flowers bloom in the late spring. A good variety for drier soils and shady areas. Foliage turns bright yellow in the Fall.*[2]

3.15.3 Disease

Main article: List of azalea diseases

Azalea leafy gall can be particularly destructive to azalea leaves during the early spring. Hand picking infected leaves is the recommended method of control.

They can also be subject to phytophthora root rot in moist, hot conditions.*[3]

3.15.4 Cultural significance and symbolism

In Chinese culture, the azalea is known as "thinking of home bush" (sixiang shu) and is immortalized in the poetry of Du Fu.

The azalea is also one of the symbols of the city of São Paulo, in Brazil.*[4]

In addition to being renowned for its beauty, the azalea is also highly toxic—it contains andromedotoxins in both its leaves and nectar, including honey from the nectar.*[5] Azaleas and rhododendrons were once so infamous for their toxicity that to receive a bouquet of their flowers in a black vase was a well-known death threat.*[6]

Azaleas in New Jersey

3.15.5 Azalea festivals

Azalea Festival at Nezu Jinja

Japan

Motoyama, Kochi also has a flower festival in which the blooming of Tsutsuji is celebrated and Tatebayashi, Gunma is famous for its Azalea Hill Park, Tsutsuji-ga-oka. Nezu Shrine in Bunkyo, Tokyo, holds a Tsutsuji Matsuri from early April until early May. Higashi Village has hosted an azalea festival each year since 1976. The village's 50,000 azalea plants draw an estimated 60,000 to 80,000 visitors each year.

Korea

Sobaeksan, one of the 12 well-known Sobaek Mountains, lying on the border between Chungbuk Province and

Azalea in Korea

Gyeongbuk has a royal azalea (*Rhododendron schlippenbachii*) festival held on May every year. Sobaeksan has an azalea colony dotted around Biro mountaintop, Gukmang and Yonwha early in May. When royal azaleas have turned pink in the end of May, it looks like Sobaeksan wears a pink Jeogori (Korean traditional jacket).*[7]

Hong Kong

The Ma On Shan Azalea Festival is held in Ma On Shan, where six native species (*Rhododendron championae, Rhododendron farrerae, Rhododendron hongkongense, Rhododendron moulmainense, Rhododendron simiarum* and *Rhododendron simsii* *[8]) are found in the area. The festival has been held since 2004; it includes activities such as exhibitions, photo contests and carnivals.*[9]

United States

Many cities in the United States have festivals in the spring celebrating the blooms of the azalea, including Summerville, South Carolina; Hamilton, NJ; Mobile, Alabama; Jasper, Texas; Tyler, Texas; Norfolk, Virginia;*[10] Wilmington, North Carolina (North Carolina Azalea Festival);*[11] Valdosta, Georgia;*[12] Palatka,

Azalea, a member of the genus Rhododendron

Florida (Florida Azalea Festival);*[13] Pickens, South Carolina;*[14] Muskogee, Oklahoma; Brookings, Oregon; and Nixa, Missouri.

The Azalea Trail is a designated path, planted with azaleas in private gardens, through Mobile, Alabama.*[15] The Azalea Trail Run is an annual road running event held there in late March. Mobile, Alabama is also home to the Azalea Trail Maids, fifty women chosen to serve as ambassadors of the city while wearing antebellum dresses, who originally participated in a three-day festival, but now operate throughout the year.

3.15.6 See also

- List of Award of Garden Merit rhododendrons
- List of plants poisonous to equines

3.15.7 References

[1] Clemson University Factsheet

[2] *New Illustrated Encyclopedia of Gardening: Volume Two.* New York, USA: Greystone Press. 1964. pp. 145, 146.

[3] Benson, D.M. "Azalea Diseases in the Landscape" . *Plant pathology extension NCSU*. North Carolina State University. Retrieved 27 January 2011.

[4] Municipal law of the city of São Paulo nr. 14472 of 2007.

[5] "University of Pennsylvania's Poisonous Plants Home Page" . Archived from the original on 2012-03-17.

[6] "Stopping to Smell the Rhododendron | Natural Selections" . *selections.rockefeller.edu*. Retrieved 2016-11-02.

[7] Department of Culture & Tourism, Danyang-gun County Office

[8] "Native Azaleas in Hong Kong" (PDF).

[9] "Ma On Shan Azalea".

[10] Norfolk NATO Azalea Festival Website

[11] North Carolina Azalea Festival Website

[12] Valdosta, Georgia, Spring Celebration at Callaway Gardens in Pine Mountain, GA, Azalea Festival Website

[13] Palatka, Florida, Azalea Festival Website

[14] Pickens' Azalea Festival Website

[15] "City of Mobile, Azalea Trail Maps".

3.15.8 External links

- "Azalea". *Encyclopædia Britannica* (11th ed.). 1911.
- Azalea Society of America
- American Rhododendron Society: What is an Azalea?
- Azalea Collection of the U.S. National Arboretum
- Azalea Collection of Botany garten Pruhonice CZ

3.16 Berberis

"Calafate" redirects here. For the Patagonian town, see El Calafate.

Berberis (/ˈbɜːrbərɪs/), commonly known as **barberry**,[1] is a large genus of deciduous and evergreen shrubs from 1–5 m (3.3–16.4 ft) tall found throughout the temperate and subtropical regions of the world (apart from Australia). Species diversity is greatest in South America, Africa and Asia; Europe and North America have native species as well. The most well-known *Berberis* species is the European barberry, *Berberis vulgaris*, which is common in Europe, North Africa, the Middle East, and central Asia. Many of the species have spines on the shoots and along the margins of the leaves.[2][3]

3.16.1 Description

The genus *Berberis* has dimorphic shoots: long shoots which form the structure of the plant, and short shoots only 1–2 mm (0.039–0.079 in) long. The leaves on long shoots are non-photosynthetic, developed into one to three or more spines[4]:96 3–30 mm (0.12–1.18 in) long. The bud in the axil of each thorn-leaf then develops a short shoot with several normal, photosynthetic leaves. These leaves are 1–10 cm (0.39–3.94 in) long, simple, and either entire, or with spiny margins. Only on young seedlings do leaves develop on the long shoots, with the adult foliage style developing after the young plant is 1–2 years old.

Many deciduous species, such as *Berberis thunbergii or B. vulgaris*, are noted for their attractive pink or red autumn color. In some evergreen species from China, such as *B. candidula or B. verruculosa*, the leaves are brilliant white beneath, a feature valued horticulturally. Some horticultural variants of *B. thunbergii* have dark red to violet foliage.

The flowers are produced singly or in racemes of up to 20 on a single flower-head. They are yellow or orange, 3–6 mm (0.12–0.24 in) long, with six sepals and six petals in alternating whorls of three, the sepals usually colored like the petals. The fruit is a small berry 5–15 mm (0.20–0.59 in) long, ripening red or dark blue, often with a pink or violet waxy surface bloom; in some species, they may be long and narrow, but are spherical in other species.

Some authors regard the compound-leaved species as a separate genus, *Mahonia*. There are no consistent differences between the two groups other than the compound leaves, and studies suggest that the simple-leaved group is very likely polyphyletic.[2][5][6][7]

3.16.2 Ecology

Berberis species are used as food plants by the larvae of some Lepidoptera species, including the moths Barberry Carpet Moth (*Pareulype berberata*), and Mottled Pug (*Eupithecia exiguata*).

Berberis vulgaris (European barberry) and *Berberis canadensis* (American barberry) serve as alternate host species of the wheat rust fungus *(Puccinia graminis)*, a grass-infecting rust fungus that is a serious fungal disease of wheat and related grains. For this reason, cultivation of *B. vulgaris* is prohibited in many areas, and imports to the United States are forbidden. The North American *B. canadensis*, native to Appalachia and the Midwest United States, was nearly eradicated for this reason, and is now rarely seen extant, with the most remaining occurrences in the Virginia mountains.

Some *Berberis* species have become invasive when planted outside of their native ranges, including *B. glaucocarpa* and *B. darwinii* in New Zealand (where it is now banned from sale and propagation), and green-leaved *B. thunbergii* in much of the eastern United States.

3.16.3 Cultivation

Several species of *Berberis* are popular garden shrubs, grown for such features as ornamental leaves, yellow flowers, or red or blue-black berries. Numerous cultivars and hybrids have been selected for garden use. Low-growing *Berberis* plants are also commonly planted as pedestrian barriers. Taller-growing species are valued for crime prevention; being very dense, viciously spiny shrubs, they make very effective barriers impenetrable to burglars. For this reason they are often planted below potentially vulnerable windows, and used as hedges.

Species in cultivation include:-

- *B. darwinii*
- *B. dictyophylla*
- *B. julianae*
- *B. thunbergii*
- *B. verruculosa*

The following hybrid selections have gained the Royal Horticultural Society's Award of Garden Merit:-

- *B.* 'Georgei'[8]
- *B.* x *lologensis* 'Apricot Queen'[9]
- *B.* x *media* 'Red Jewel'[10]
- *B.* x *ottawensis* f. *purpurea* 'Superba'[11]
- *B.* x *stenophylla* 'Corallina Compacta'[12]
- *B.* x *stenophylla* Lindl (golden barberry)[13]

3.16.4 Culinary uses

Berberis vulgaris grows in the wild in much of Europe and West Asia. It produces large crops of edible berries, rich in vitamin C, but with a sharp acid flavour. In Europe for many centuries the berries were used for culinary purposes in ways comparable to how citrus peel might be used. Today in Europe they are very infrequently used. The country in which they are used the most, is Iran where they are referred to as "Zereshk" (زرشک) in Persian. The berries are common in Iranian (Persian) cuisine such as in rice pilafs (known as "Zereshk Polo") and as a flavouring for poultry meat. Due to their inherent sour flavor, they are sometimes cooked with sugar before being added to Persian rice. Iranian markets sell Zereshk dried. In Russia they are sometimes used in jams (especially the mixed berry ones) and extract from them is a common flavouring for soft drinks and candies/sweets.

Berberis microphylla and *B. darwinii* (both known as *calafate* and *michay*) are two species found in *Patagonia* in Argentina and Chile. Their edible purple fruits are used for jams and infusions. The calafate and michay are symbols of *Patagonia*.

3.16.5 Traditional medicine

The dried fruit of *Berberis vulgaris* is used in herbal medicine.[14] The chemical constituents include isoquinolone alkaloids, especially berberine. One study reports that it is superior to metformin in treating polycystic ovary syndrome.[15]

3.16.6 Other uses

Historically, yellow dye was extracted from the stem, root, and bark.[16]

3.16.7 Gallery

- *Berberis aggregata*, fruits.

- *Berberis aristata*, from the Himalayas

- *Berberis hybrid*, with three-spined thorn (modified long shoot leaf) with leafy short shoot. Each thorn is 20 mm (0.79 in) long.

Berberis hybrid, flower detail (flowers 7 mm (0.28 in) diameter).

Berberis hybrid, fruit.

Berberis thunbergii, shrub.

Berberis valdiviana, flowers, from Chile (cultivated at Birmingham Botanical Gardens)

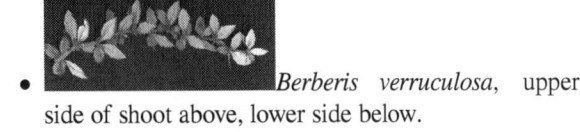

Berberis verruculosa, upper side of shoot above, lower side below.

Berberis vulgaris, flowers and foliage, cultivated in Denmark

3.16.8 References

[1] *English Names for Korean Native Plants* (PDF). Pocheon: Korea National Arboretum. 2015. p. 371. ISBN 978-89-97450-98-5. Retrieved 26 January 2017 – via Korea Forest Service.

[2] Flora of North America, vol 3

[3] Flora of China Vol. 19 Page 715 小檗属 xiao bo shu *Berberis* Linnaeus, Sp. Pl. 1: 330. 1753.

[4] Stace, C. A. (2010). *New Flora of the British Isles* (Third ed.). Cambridge, U.K.: Cambridge University Press. ISBN 9780521707725.

[5] Loconte, H., & J. R. Estes. 1989. Phylogenetic systematics of Berberidaceae and Ranunculales (Magnoliidae). Systematic Botany 14:565-579.

[6] Marroquín, Jorge S., & Joseph E. Laferrière. 1997. Transfer of specific and infraspecific taxa from *Mahonia* to *Berberis*. Journal of the Arizona-Nevada Academy of Science 30(1):53-55.

[7] Laferrière, Joseph E. 1997. Transfer of specific and infraspecific taxa from *Mahonia* to *Berberis*. Bot. Zhurn. 82(9):96-99.

[8] "RHS Plant Selector Berberis 'Georgei' AGM / RHS Gardening". Apps.rhs.org.uk. Retrieved 2013-04-07.

[9] "RHS Plant Selector Berberis × lologensis 'Apricot Queen' AGM / RHS Gardening". Apps.rhs.org.uk. Retrieved 2013-04-07.

[10] "RHS Plant Selector Berberis × media 'Red Jewel' AGM / RHS Gardening". Apps.rhs.org.uk. Retrieved 2013-04-07.

[11] "RHS Plant Selector Berberis × ottawensis f. purpurea 'Superba' / RHS Gardening". Apps.rhs.org.uk. Retrieved 2013-04-07.

[12] "RHS Plant Selector Berberis × stenophylla 'Corallina Compacta' AGM / RHS Gardening". Apps.rhs.org.uk. Retrieved 2013-04-07.

[13] "RHS Plant Selector Berberis × stenophylla Lindl. AGM / RHS Gardening". Apps.rhs.org.uk. Retrieved 2013-04-07.

[14] See e.g. "Barberry" @ Alternative Medicine @ University of Maryland Medical Center

[15] "Berberine Compared to Metformin in Women with PCOS - Natural Medicine Journal: The Official Journal of the American Association of Naturopathic Physicians". Natural Medicine Journal. Retrieved 2013-04-07.

[16] C. Tomlinson (1866). *Tomlinson's Cyclopaedia of Useful Arts*. London: Virtue & Co. Vol I, page 97.

- Murrills, Angela (2005-11-24). "Best Eating: Check, please". Straight.com. Retrieved 2007-05-02.

- Wilkinson, Bobbie; Tom Wilkinson (2004-08-15). "It's an Adventure in Persian Cuisine at Darya Kabob". The Washington Post. Retrieved 2007-05-02.

- Arellano, Gustavo (2004-03-18). "Naan & Kabob". Orange County Weekly. Retrieved 2007-05-02.

- Royal New Zealand Institute of horticulture. *Berberis glaucocarpa*

3.16.9 External links

- Platt, Karen, "Gold Fever" descriptions of golden or yellow leaved Berberis http://www.karenplatt.co.uk

3.17 Birch

For other uses, see Birch (disambiguation).

A **birch** is a thin-leaved deciduous hardwood tree of the genus ***Betula*** (/ˈbɛtjʊlə/),[2] in the family Betulaceae, which also includes alders, hazels, and hornbeams. It is closely related to the beech-oak family Fagaceae. The genus *Betula* contains 30 to 60 known taxa of which 11 are on the IUCN 2011 Green List of Threatened Species. They are a typically rather short-lived pioneer species widespread in the Northern Hemisphere, particularly in northern temperate and boreal climates.[3]

3.17.1 Description

Birch species are generally small to medium-sized trees or shrubs, mostly of northern temperate and boreal climates. The simple leaves are alternate, singly or doubly serrate, feather-veined, petiolate and stipulate. They often appear in pairs, but these pairs are really borne on spur-like, two-leaved, lateral branchlets.[4] The fruit is a small samara, although the wings may be obscure in some species. They differ from the alders (*Alnus*, other genus in the family) in that the female catkins are not woody and disintegrate at maturity, falling apart to release the seeds, unlike the woody, cone-like female alder catkins.

The bark of all birches is characteristically marked with long, horizontal lenticels, and often separates into thin, papery plates, especially upon the paper birch. Its decided color gives the common names gray, white, black, silver and yellow birch to different species.

The buds form early and are full grown by midsummer, all are lateral, no terminal bud is formed; the branch is prolonged by the upper lateral bud. The wood of all the species is close-grained with satiny texture, and capable of taking a fine polish; its fuel value is fair.

The front and rear sides of a piece of birch bark

Flower and fruit

The flowers are monoecious, opening with or before the leaves and borne once fully grown these leaves are usually 3–6 millimetres (0.12–0.24 in) long on three-flowered clusters in the axils of the scales of drooping or erect catkins or aments. Staminate aments are pendulous, clustered or solitary in the axils of the last leaves of the branch of the year or near the ends of the short lateral branchlets of the year. They form in early autumn and remain rigid during the winter. The scales of the staminate aments when mature are broadly ovate, rounded, yellow or orange color below the middle, dark chestnut brown at apex. Each scale bears two bractlets and three sterile flowers, each flower consisting of a sessile, membranaceous, usually two-lobed, calyx. Each calyx bears four short filaments with one-celled anthers or strictly, two filaments divided into two branches, each bearing a half-anther. Anther cells open longitudinally. The pistillate aments are erect or pendulous, solitary; terminal on the two-leaved lateral spur-like branchlets of the year. The pistillate scales are oblong-ovate, three-lobed, pale yellow green often tinged with red, becoming brown at maturity. These scales bear two or three fertile flowers, each flower consisting of a naked ovary. The ovary is compressed, two-celled, and crowned with two slender styles; the ovule is solitary. Each scale bear a single small, winged nut that is oval, with two persistent stigmas at the apex.

3.17.2 Taxonomy

Subdivision

Main article: List of Betula species

Betula species are organised into five subgenera.

Birch leaves

Birches native to Europe and Asia include

1. *Betula albosinensis*—Chinese red birch (northern + central China)
2. *Betula alnoides*—alder-leaf birch (China, Himalayas, northern Indochina)
3. *Betula ashburneri* (Bhutan, Tibet, Sichuan, Yunnan Provinces in China)
4. *Betula baschkirica* (eastern European Russia)
5. *Betula bomiensis* (Tibet)
6. *Betula browicziana* (Turkey and Georgia)
7. *Betula calcicola* (Sichuan + Yunnan Provinces in China)
8. *Betula celtiberica* (Spain)
9. *Betula chichibuensis* (Chichibu region of Japan)*[5]
10. *Betula chinensis*—Chinese dwarf birch (China, Korea)
11. *Betula coriaceifolia* (Uzbekistan)
12. *Betula corylifolia* (Honshu Island in Japan)
13. *Betula costata* (northeastern China, Korea, Primorye region of Russia)
14. *Betula cylindrostachya* (Himalayas, southern China, Myanmar)
15. *Betula dahurica* (eastern Siberia, Russian Far East, northeastern China, Mongolia, Korea, Japan)
16. *Betula delavayi* - (Tibet, southern China)
17. *Betula ermanii*—Erman's birch (eastern Siberia, Russian Far East, northeastern China, Korea, Japan)
18. *Betula falcata* (Tajikistan)
19. *Betula fargesii* (Chongqing + Hubei Provinces in China)
20. *Betula fruticosa* (eastern Siberia, Russian Far East, northeastern China, Mongolia, Korea, Japan)
21. *Betula globispica* (Honshu Island in Japan)
22. *Betula gmelinii* (Siberia, Mongolia, northeastern China, Korea, Hokkaido Island in Japan)
23. *Betula grossa*—Japanese cherry birch (Japan)
24. *Betula gynoterminalis* (Yunnan Province in China)
25. *Betula honanensis* - (Henan Province in China)
26. *Betula humilis* or Betula kamtschatica —*Kamchatka birch* platyphylla (*northern + central Europe, Siberia, Kazakhstan, Xinjiana, Mongolia, Korea*)
27. *Betula insignis* - (southern China)
28. *Betula karagandensis* (Kazakhstan)
29. *Betula klokovii* (Ukraine)
30. *Betula kotulae* (Ukraine)
31. *Betula litvinovii* (Turkey, Iran, Caucasus)
32. *Betula luminifera* (China)
33. *Betula maximowiczii*—monarch birch (Japan, Kuril Islands)
34. *Betula medwediewii*—Caucasian birch (Turkey, Iran, Caucasus)

35. *Betula megrelica* (Republic of Georgia)

36. *Betula microphylla* (Siberia, Mongolia, Xinjiang, Kazakhstan, Kyrgyzstan, Uzbekistan)

37. *Betula nana*—dwarf birch (northern + central Europe, Russia, Siberia, Greenland, Northwest Territories of Canada))

38. *Betula pendula*—silver birch (widespread in Europe and northern Asia; Morocco; naturalized in New Zealand and scattered locations in US + Canada)

39. *Betula platyphylla* (*Betula pendula* var. *platyphylla*) —Siberian silver birch (Siberia, Russian Far East, Manchuria, Korea, Japan, Alaska, western Canada)

40. *Betula potamophila* (Tajikistan)

41. *Betula potaninii* (southern China)

42. *Betula psammophila* (Kazakhstan)

43. *Betula pubescens*—downy birch, also known as white, European white or hairy birch (Europe, Siberia, Greenland, Newfoundland; naturalized in scattered locations in US)

44. *Betula raddeana* (Caucasus)

45. *Betula saksarensis* (Khakassiya region of Siberia)

46. *Betula saviczii* (Kazakhstan)

47. *Betula schmidtii* (northeastern China, Korea, Japan, Primorye region of Russia)

48. *Betula sunanensis* (Gansu Province of China)

49. *Betula szechuanica* (*Betula pendula* var. *szechuanica*) —Sichuan birch (Tibet, southern China)

50. *Betula tianshanica* (Kazakhstan, Kyrgyzstan, Tajikistan, Uzbekistan, Xinjiang, Mongolia)

51. *Betula utilis*—Himalayan birch (Afghanistan, Central Asia, China, China, Tibet, Himalayas)

52. *Betula wuyiensis* (Fujian Province of China)

53. *Betula zinserlingii* (Kyrgyzstan)

Note: many American texts have B. pendula *and* B. pubescens *confused, though they are distinct species with different chromosome numbers.*

Birches native to North America include

1. *Betula alleghaniensis*—yellow birch (*B. lutea*) (eastern Canada, Great Lakes, Northeastern US, Appalachians)

2. *Betula cordifolia*—mountain paper birch (eastern Canada, Great Lakes, Northeastern US)

3. *Betula glandulosa*—American dwarf birch (Siberia, Mongolia, Russian Far East, Alaska, Canada, Greenland, mountains of western US and New England, Adirondacks)

4. *Betula lenta*—sweet birch, cherry birch, or black birch (Quebec, Ontario, eastern US)

5. *Betula michauxii*—Newfoundland dwarf birch (Newfoundland, Labrador, Quebec, Nova Scotia)

6. *Betula minor*—dwarf white birch (eastern Canada, mountains of northern New England and Adirondacks)

7. *Betula nana*—dwarf birch or bog birch (also in northern Europe and Asia)

8. *Betula neoalaskana*—Alaska paper birch also known as Alaska Birch or Resin Birch (Alaska and northern Canada)

9. *Betula nigra*—river birch or black birch (eastern US)

10. *Betula occidentalis*—water birch or red birch (*B. fontinalis*) (Alaska, Yukon, Northwest Territories, western Canada, western US)

11. *Betula papyrifera*—paper birch, canoe birch or American white birch (Alaska, most of Canada, northern US)

12. *Betula populifolia*—gray birch (eastern Canada, northeastern US)

13. *Betula pumila*—swamp birch (Alaska, Canada, northern US)

14. *Betula uber*-Virginia round-leaf birch (southwestern Virginia)

Etymology

The common name *birch* comes from Old English *birce*, *bierce*, from Proto-Germanic **berk-jōn* (cf. German *Birke*, West Frisian *bjirk*), an adjectival formation from **berkōn* (cf. Dutch *berk*, Low German *Bark*, Danish *birk*, Norwegian *bjørk*), itself from the Proto-Indo-European root **bʰerHǵ- ~ bʰrHǵ-*, which also gave Lithuanian *béržas*, Latvian *Bērzs*, Russian *beréza*, Ukrainian *beréza*, Albanian *bredh* 'fir', Ossetian *bærz(æ)*, Sanskrit *bhurja*, Polish *brzoza*, Latin *fraxinus* 'ash (tree)'. This root is presumably derived from **bʰreh₁ǵ-* 'to shine', in reference to the birch's white bark. The Proto-Germanic rune *berkanan* is named after the birch.

The generic name *betula* is from Latin, which is a diminutive borrowed from Gaulish *betua* (cf. Old Irish *bethe*, Welsh *bedw*).

3.17.3 Ecology

Birch trees near stream in Hankasalmi, Finland

A stand of birch trees

Birch tree in autumn

Birches often form even-aged stands on light, well-drained, particularly acidic soils. They are regarded as pioneer species, rapidly colonising open ground especially in secondary successional sequences following a disturbance or fire. Birches are early tree species to become established in primary successions, and can become a threat to heathland if the seedlings and saplings are not suppressed by grazing or periodic burning. Birches are generally lowland species, but some species, such as *Betula nana*, have a montane distribution. In the British Isles, there is some difference between the environments of *Betula pendula* and *Betula pubescens*, and some hybridization, though both are "opportunists in steady-state woodland systems". Mycorrhizal fungi, including sheathing (ecto)mycorrhizas, are found in some cases to be beneficial to tree growth.*[6]

Birch foliage is used as a food plant by the larvae of a large number of lepidopteran (butterflies and moths) species.

3.17.4 Uses

Birch plywood

Because of the hardness of birch, it is easier to shape it with power tools, as it is quite difficult to work it with hand tools.*[7]

- Birch wood is fine-grained and pale in colour, often with an attractive satin-like sheen. Ripple figuring may occur, increasing the value of the timber for veneer and furniture-making. The highly decorative Masur (or Karelian) birch, from *Betula verrucosa* var. *carelica*, has ripple textures combined with attractive dark streaks and lines.

- Birch plywood is made from laminations of birch veneer. It is light but strong, and has many other good properties. It's among the strongest and dimensionally most stable plywoods, although it is unsuitable for exterior use. Birch plywood is used to make longboards (skateboard), giving it a strong yet flexible ride. It is

- also used (often in very thin grades with many laminations) for making model aircraft.

- Extracts of birch are used for flavoring or leather oil, and in cosmetics such as soap or shampoo. In the past, commercial oil of wintergreen (methyl salicylate) was made from the sweet birch (*Betula lenta*).

- Birch-tar or Russian oil extracted from birch bark is thermoplastic and waterproof; it was used as a glue on, for example, arrows, and also for medicinal purposes.*[8]

- Fragrant twigs of silver birch are used in saunas to relax the muscles.

- Birch is also associated with the feast of Pentecost in Central and Eastern Europe and Siberia, where its branches are used as decoration for churches and homes on this day.

- Birch leaves are used to make a diuretic tea and extracts for dyes and cosmetics.

- Ground birch bark, fermented in sea water, is used for seasoning the woolen, hemp or linen sails and hemp rope of traditional Norwegian boats.

- Birch twigs bound in a bundle, also called birch, were used for birching, a form of corporal punishment.

- Many Native Americans in the United States prized the birch for its bark, which because of its light weight, flexibility, and the ease with which it could be stripped from fallen trees, was often used for the construction of strong, waterproof but lightweight canoes, bowls, and wigwams.

- The Hughes H-4 Hercules was made mostly of birch wood, despite its better-known moniker, "The Spruce Goose".

- Birch plywood was specified by the BBC as the only wood that can be used in making the cabinets of the long-lived LS3/5A loudspeaker.*[9]

- Birch is used as firewood because of its high calorific value per unit weight and unit volume. It burns well, without popping, even when frozen and freshly hewn. The bark will burn very well even when wet because of the oils it contains. With care, it can be split into very thin sheets that will ignite from even the smallest of sparks.

- Birch sap is a traditional drink in Northern Europe, Siberia, and Northern China. The sap is also bottled and sold commercially. Birch sap can be used to make birch syrup, which is used like maple syrup for pancakes and waffles. Birch wood can be used to smoke foods.

- Birch seeds are used as leaf litter in miniature terrain models.*[10]

- Birch oil is used in the manufacture of Russia leather, a water-resistant leather.

Cultivation

White-barked birches in particular are cultivated as ornamental trees, largely for their appearance in winter. The Himalayan birch, *Betula utilis*, especially the variety or subspecies *jacquemontii*, is among the most widely planted for this purpose. It has been cultivated since the 1870s, and many cultivars are available, including 'Doorenbos', 'Grayswood Ghost' and 'Silver Shadow'; 'Knightshayes' has a slightly weeping habit. Other species with ornamental white bark include *Betula ermanii*, *Betula papyrifera*, *Betula pendula* and *Betula raddeana*.*[11]

Medical

- Birch bark is high in betulin and betulinic acid, phytochemicals which have potential as pharmaceuticals, and other chemicals which show promise as industrial lubricants.

- Birch buds are used in folk medicine.*[12]

- Birch bark can be soaked until moist in water, and then formed into a cast for a broken arm.*[13]

- The inner bark of birch can be ingested safely.

- In northern latitudes, birch is considered to be the most important allergenic tree pollen, with an estimated 15–20% of hay fever sufferers sensitive to birch pollen grains. The major allergen is a protein called Bet v I.

Paper

See also: Birch bark document
Wood pulp made from birch gives relatively long and slender fibres for a hardwood. The thin walls cause the fibre to collapse upon drying, giving a paper with low bulk and low opacity. The birch fibres are, however, easily fibrillated and give about 75% of the tensile strength of softwood.*[14] The low opacity makes it suitable for making glassine.

In India, the birch (Sanskrit: भूर्ज, *bhurja*) holds great historical significance in the culture of North India, where the thin bark coming off in winter was extensively used as writing paper. Birch paper (Sanskrit: भूर्ज पत्र, *bhurja patra*) is exceptionally durable and was the material used for many ancient Indian texts.*[15]*[16] The Roman period Vindolanda tablets also use birch as a material on which to

A birch bark inscription excavated from Novgorod, circa 1240–1260

write and birch bark was used widely in ancient Russia as note paper (*beresta*) and for decorative purposes and even making footwear.

Tonewood

Baltic birch is among the most sought-after wood in the manufacture of speaker cabinets. Birch has a natural resonance that peaks in the high and low frequencies, which are also the hardest for speakers to reproduce. This resonance compensates for the roll-off of low and high frequencies in the speakers, and evens the tone. Birch is known for having "natural EQ".

Drums are often made from birch. Prior to the 1970s, it was one of the most popular drum woods. Because of the need for greater volume and midrange clarity, drums were made almost entirely from maple until recently, when advances in live sound reinforcement and drum microphones have allowed the use of birch in high-volume situations. Birch drums have a natural boost in the high and low frequencies, which allows the drums to sound fuller.

Birch wood is sometimes used as a tonewood for semi-acoustic and acoustic guitar bodies, and occasionally for solid-body guitar bodies. It is also a common material used in mallets for keyboard percussion.

3.17.5 Culture

Birches have spiritual importance in several religions, both modern and historical. In Celtic cultures, the birch symbolises growth, renewal, stability, initiation and adaptability because it is highly adaptive and able to sustain harsh conditions with casual indifference. Proof of this adaptability is seen in its easy and eager ability to repopulate areas damaged by forest fires or clearings. Birches are also associated with the *Tír na nÓg*, the land of the dead and the *Sidhe*, in Gaelic folklore, and as such frequently appear in Scottish, Irish, and English folksongs and ballads in association with death, or fairies, or returning from the grave. The leaves of the silver birch tree are used in the festival of St George, held in Novosej and other villages in Albania.*[17]

The birch is New Hampshire's state tree and the national tree of Finland and Russia. The Ornäs birch is the national tree of Sweden. The Czech word for the month of March, Březen, is derived from the Czech word bříza meaning birch, as birch trees flower in March under local conditions. The silver birch tree is of special importance to the Swedish city of Umeå. In 1888, the Umeå city fire spread all over the city and nearly burnt it down to the ground, but some birches, supposedly, halted the spread of the fire. To protect the city against future fires, it was decided to plant silver birch trees all over the city. Umeå later adopted the unofficial name of "City of the Birches (*Björkarnas stad*)". Also, the ice hockey team of Umeå is called *Björklöven*, translated to English "The Birch Leaves".

"Swinging" birch trees was a common game for American children in the nineteenth century. American poet Lucy Larcom's "Swinging on a Birch Tree" celebrates the game.*[18] The poem inspired Robert Frost, who pays homage to the act of climbing birch trees his more famous poem, "Birches".*[19] Frost once told "it was almost sacrilegious climbing a birch tree till it bent, till it gave and swooped to the ground, but that's what boys did in those days".*[20]

3.17.6 See also

- Birch bark manuscript
- Birch beer
- Taxonomy of Betula

3.17.7 References

[1] http://apps.kew.org/wcsp/synonomy.do?name_id=21065

[2] *Sunset Western Garden Book,* 1995:606–607

[3] Ashburner, K. & McAllister, H.A. (2013). The genus *Betula*: a taxonomic revision of birches: 1-431. Royal Botanic Gardens, Kew.

[4] Keeler, Harriet L. (1900). *Our Native Trees and How to Identify Them*. New York: Charles Scriber's Sons. pp. 295–297.

[5] Kinver, Mark (30 September 2015). "UK team germinates critically endangered Japanese birch". *BBC News*. BBC. Retrieved 30 September 2015.

[6] *Birches*. (A Symposium, Royal Botanic Garden, Edinburgh 24–26 September 1982. Proceedings of the Royal Society of Edinburgh, 85B, 1–11, 1984.

[7] "Birch". Wood Magazine. Retrieved December 1, 2013.

[8] "Birch Tar – How to collect it". Archived from the original on February 27, 2008.

[9] Prakel, David (August 1979). "BBC's Home Service", *Hi-Fi Answers*, pp67–9 (Courtesy link)

[10] Joyce, Daniel. "Birch Seed Leaves". reapermini.com.

[11] Bartlett, Paul (2015). "White-barked birches". *The Plantsman (New Series)*. **14** (3): 146–151.

[12] White Birch – American Cancer Society (cancer.org)

[13] William Arthur Clark (January 1, 1937). "History of Fracture Treatment Up to the Sixteenth Century". *The Journal of Bone & Joint Surgery*. Needham, MA, USA: The Journal of Bone & Joint Surgery, Inc. **19** (1): 61–62. Another method cited was that of splints made of birch bark soaked in water until quite soft. They were then carefully fitted to the limb and tied with bark thongs. On drying, they became stiff and firm. There is no record of the use of extension, but, nevertheless, very few crippled and deformed Indians were to be seen.

[14] Nanko, Hiroki; Button, Alan; Hillman, Dave (2005). *The World of Market Pulp*. USA: WOMP, LLC. pp. 192–195. ISBN 0-615-13013-5.

[15] Sanjukta Gupta, "Lakṣmī Tantra: A Pāñcarātra Text", Brill Archive, 1972, ISBN 90-04-03419-6. Snippet:... *the text recommends that the bark of the Himalayan birch tree (bhurja-patra) should be used for scribbling mantras ...*

[16] Amalananda Ghosh, "An Encyclopaedia of Indian Archaeology", BRILL, 1990, ISBN 90-04-09264-1. Snippet:... *Bhurja-patra, the inner bark on the birch tree grown in the Himalayan region, was a very common writing material ...*

[17] "Traditional celebrations in Novosej". RASP. Retrieved August 28, 2013.

[18] Pfleger, Pat. "Our Young Folks: Swinging on a Birch-Tree, by Lucy Larcom & Winslow Homer (1867)". *Merry Coz*.

[19] Fagan, Deirdre J. (2007). *Critical Companion to Robert Frost: A Literary Reference to His Life and Work*. Infobase Publishing. p. 42. ISBN 978-1-4381-0854-4. Retrieved 10 November 2013.

[20] Parini, Jay (1999). *Robert Frost: A Life*. New York: Halt. p. 22. ISBN 0-8050-3181-2.

3.17.8 Sources

- Flora of North America: *Betula*
- Flora of China: *Betula*
- Grimshaw, John (2009). *New Trees, Recent introductions to cultivation*. Kew Publishing, RBG Kew. pp. 163–174.
- Chisholm, Hugh, ed. (1911). "Birch". *Encyclopædia Britannica*. **3** (11th ed.). Cambridge University Press.

3.17.9 External links

- Tree Family Betulaceae Diagnostic photos of many species, Morton Arboretum specimens
- Eichhorn, Markus (July 2010). "The Birch Tree". *Test Tube*. Brady Haran for the University of Nottingham.

3.18 Bougainvillea glabra

***Bougainvillea glabra*, lesser bougainvillea** or **paperflower**,[2] is the most common species of bougainvillea used for bonsai.[3]

3.18.1 Description

Bougainvillea glabra

It is an evergreen, climbing shrub with thorny stems. It usually grows 10–12 ft (3.0–3.7 m) tall, occasionally up to 30 ft (9 m). Tiny white flowers usually appear in clusters surrounded by colorful papery bracts, hence the name paperflower. The leaves are dark green, variable in shape, up to 4 in (10 cm) long.[4] The flowers are about 0.4 cm in diameter (the pink petal-like structures are not petals, but bracts.)[5]

3.18.2 Cultivation

B. glabra is heat and drought tolerant and frost sensitive. It is easily propagated by cuttings.*[4] It needs full sunlight, warm weather and well drained soil to flower well.

- Vine
- Flowers
- *Bougainvillea glabra* with yellow bracts

3.18.3 References

[1] Germplasm Resources Information Network (GRIN), *Taxon:* Bougainvillea glabra *Choisy*, United States Department of Agriculture, Agricultural Research Service, Beltsville Area, retrieved 2014-01-30

[2] Common names for Lesser Bougainvillea (*Bougainvillea glabra*)—Encyclopedia of Life

[3] "Bougainvillea bonsai" (PDF). Archived March 9, 2014, at the Wayback Machine. (96 KB)

[4] *Bougainvillea glabra* - University of Arizona Pima County Cooperative Extension

[5] Bougainvillea glabra. "Bougainvillea glabra". *Flower View*.

3.19 Buxus

For the asteroid, see 8852 Buxus.
"Boxtree" redirects here. For the publisher, see Macmillan Publishers.

"Boxwood" redirects here. For other uses, see Boxwood (disambiguation).

Buxus is a genus of about 70 species in the fam-

Buxus sempervirens

Buxus sinica *foliage*

Buxus henryi *foliage*

ily Buxaceae. Common names include **box** (majority of

Buxus wallichiana *foliage and seed capsules*

Buxus sempervirens *bark*

Buxus sempervirens *bark closeup*

English-speaking countries) or **boxwood** (North America).*[1]

The boxes are native to western and southern Europe, southwest, southern and eastern Asia, Africa, Madagascar, northernmost South America, Central America, Mexico and the Caribbean, with the majority of species being tropical or subtropical; only the European and some Asian species are frost-tolerant. Centres of diversity occur in Cuba (about 30 species), China (17 species) and Madagascar (9 species).

They are slow-growing evergreen shrubs and small trees, growing to 2–12 m (rarely 15 m) tall. The leaves are opposite, rounded to lanceolate, and leathery; they are small in most species, typically 1.5–5 cm long and 0.3-2.5 cm broad, but up to 11 cm long and 5 cm broad in *B. macrocarpa*. The flowers are small and yellow-green, monoecious with both sexes present on a plant. The fruit is a small capsule 0.5-1.5 cm long (to 3 cm in *B. macrocarpa*), containing several small seeds.

The genus splits into three genetically distinct sections, each section in a different region, with the Eurasian species in one section, the African (except northwest Africa) and Madagascan species in the second, and the American species in the third. The African and American sections are genetically closer to each other than to the Eurasian section.*[2]

3.19.1 Selected species

Europe, northwest Africa, Asia

- *Buxus austro-yunnanensis* (Yunnan box; southwest China)

- *Buxus balearica* (Balearic box; Balearic Islands, southern Spain, northwest Africa)

- *Buxus bodinieri* (China)

- *Buxus cephalantha* (China)

- *Buxus cochinchinensis* (Malaysia)

- *Buxus colchica* (Georgian box; western Caucasus; considered also a syn. of *B. sempervirens*)

- *Buxus hainanensis* (Hainan box; China: Hainan)

- *Buxus harlandii* (Harland's box; southern China)

- *Buxus hebecarpa* (China)

3.19. BUXUS

- *Buxus henryi* (Henry's box; China)
- *Buxus hyrcana* (Caspian box; Alborz, eastern Caucasus; considered also a syn. of *B. sempervirens*)
- *Buxus ichangensis* (China)
- *Buxus latistyla* (China)
- *Buxus linearifolia* (China)
- *Buxus megistophylla* (China)
- *Buxus microphylla* (Japanese box; Korea, China; long cultivated in Japan)
- *Buxus mollicula* (China)
- *Buxus myrica* (China)
- *Buxus papillosa* (western Himalaya)
- *Buxus pubiramea* (China)
- *Buxus rivularis* (Philippines)
- *Buxus rolfei* (Borneo)
- *Buxus rugulosa* (China, eastern Himalaya)
- *Buxus rupicola* (Malaysia)
- *Buxus sempervirens* (Common box or European box; western and southern Europe, except far southwest)
- *Buxus sinica* (Chinese box; China, Korea, Japan)
- *Buxus stenophylla* (China)
- *Buxus wallichiana* (Himalayan box; Himalaya)

Africa, Madagascar

- *Buxus acuminata* (Africa: Zaire; syn. *Notobuxus acuminata*)
- *Buxus calcarea* (Madagascar endemic)
- *Buxus capuronii* (Madagascar endemic)
- *Buxus hildebrantii* (eastern Africa: Somalia, Ethiopia)
- *Buxus humbertii* (Humbert's box; Madagascar endemic)
- *Buxus itremoensis* (Madagascar endemic)
- *Buxus lisowskii* (Congo)
- *Buxus macowanii* (Cape box; eastern and northern South Africa)
- *Buxus macrocarpa* (Madagascar endemic)
- *Buxus madagascarica* (Madagascan box; Madagascar, Comoros)
- *Buxus monticola* (Madagascar endemic)
- *Buxus moratii* (Madagascar, Comoros)
- *Buxus natalensis* (Natal box; eastern South Africa; syn. *Notobuxus natalensis*)
- *Buxus obtusifolia* (eastern Africa; syn. *Notobuxus obtusifolia*)
- *Buxus rabenantoandroi* (Madagascar endemic; syn. *B. angustifolia* GE Schatz & Lowry *non* Mill.)

Americas

- *Buxus aneura* (Cuba)
- *Buxus bartletii* (Central America)
- *Buxus brevipes* (Cuba)
- *Buxus citrifolia* (Venezuela)
- *Buxus crassifolia* (Cuba)
- *Buxus ekmanii* (Cuba)
- *Buxus excisa* (Cuba)
- *Buxus heterophylla* (Cuba)
- *Buxus imbricata* (Cuba)
- *Buxus lancifolia* (Mexico)
- *Buxus macrophylla* (Central America)
- *Buxus mexicana* (Mexico)
- *Buxus muelleriana* (Cuba)
- *Buxus olivacea* (Cuba)
- *Buxus pilosula* (Cuba)
- *Buxus portoricensis* (Puerto Rico)
- *Buxus pubescens* (Mexico)
- *Buxus rheedioides* (Cuba)
- *Buxus vahlii* (Vahl's box or smooth box; Puerto Rico; syn. *B. laevigata*)

3.19.2 Uses

Cultivation

Box plants are commonly grown as hedges and for topiary.

In Great Britain and Mainland Europe box is subject to damage from caterpillars of *Diaphania perspectalis* which can devastate a box hedge within a short time. This is a recently introduced species first noticed in Europe in 2007 and in the UK in 2008 but spreading. There were 3 UK reports of infestation in 2011, 20 in 2014 and 150 in the first half of 2015.*[3]

Wood carving

Main article: Gothic boxwood miniature
Owing to its fine grain it is a good wood for fine wood

The white pieces are made of boxwood. The black piece is ebonized, not ebony.

carving, although this is limited by the small sizes available. It is also resistant to splitting and chipping, and thus useful for decorative or storage boxes. Formerly, it was used for wooden combs. As a timber or wood for carving it is "boxwood" in all varieties of English.

Owing to the relatively high density of the wood (it is one of the few woods that are denser than water), boxwood is often used for chess pieces, unstained boxwood for the white pieces and stained ('ebonized') boxwood for the black pieces, in lieu of ebony.*[4]

The extremely fine endgrain of box makes it suitable for woodblock printing and woodcut blocks, for which it was the usual material in Europe. In the 16th century, boxwood was used to create intricate decorative carvings; as of 2016, the largest collection of these carvings is at the Art Gallery of Ontario in Toronto.*[5]

High quality wooden spoons have usually been carved from box, with beech being the usual cheaper substitute.

Boxwood was once called dudgeon, and was used for the handles of dirks, and daggers, with the result that such a knife was known as a dudgeon. Although one "in high dudgeon" is indignant and enraged, and while the image of a dagger held high, ready to plunge into an enemy, has a certain appeal, lexicographers have no real evidence as to the origin of the phrase.

Musical instruments

Due to its high density and resistance to chipping, boxwood is a relatively economical material, and has been used to make parts for various stringed instruments since antiquity.*[6] It is mostly used to make tailpieces, chin rests and tuning pegs, but may be used for a variety of other parts as well. Other woods used for this purpose are rosewood and ebony.

Boxwood was a common material for the manufacture of recorders in the eighteenth century, and a large number of mid- to high-end instruments made today are produced from one or other species of boxwood. Boxwood was once a popular wood for other woodwind instruments, and was among the traditional woods for Great Highland bagpipes before tastes turned to imported dense tropical woods such as cocuswood, ebony, and African blackwood.*[7]

Historical

General Thomas F. Meagher decorated the hats of the men of the Irish Brigade with boxwood during the American Civil War, as he could find no shamrock.*[8]

3.19.3 See also

- Boxwood blight
- Cydalima perspectalis - box tree moth

3.19.4 References

[1] Only the wood as a material is "boxwood" in British English

[2] von Balthazar, M.; Endress, P. K.; Qiu, Y.-L. (2000). "Phylogenetic relationships in Buxaceae based on nuclear internal transcribed spacers and plastid *ndhF* sequences". *International Journal of Plant Science*. **161** (5): 785–792. doi:10.1086/314302.

[3] Invasive caterpillar 'could spread in UK'

[4] "Chess Piece Materials". The Chess ZoneDiaphania perspectalis.

[5] "Inner Space: In Small Wonders, the AGO's strangest possessions take centre stage". *Toronto Star*, NOvember 13, 2016. Page E1. Murray White.

[6] See Theocritus Idyll 24.110, where Heracles is taught to play a boxwood lyre.

[7] Joshua Dickson (9 October 2009). *The Highland bagpipe: music, history, tradition*. Ashgate Publishing, Ltd. pp. 50–. ISBN 978-0-7546-6669-1. Retrieved 29 April 2011.

[8] "Illustrations of the Irish Brigade at Fredericksburg". *Irish in the American Civil War*. Damian Shiels. November 27, 2011. Retrieved January 12, 2017.

3.19.5 External links

- Box / Royal Horticultural Society
- American Boxwood Society
- Revision of the genus Buxus in Madagascar (pdf file)

3.20 Camellia japonica

Camellia japonica, known as **common camellia**[1] or **Japanese camellia**, is one of the best known species of the genus *Camellia*. Sometimes called the **Rose of winter**,[2] it belongs to the Theaceae family. It is the official state flower of Alabama. There are thousands of cultivars of *C. japonica* in cultivation, with many different colors and forms of flowers.

In the wild, it is found in mainland China (Shandong, east Zhejiang), Taiwan, southern Korea and southern Japan.[3] It grows in forests, at altitudes of around 300–1,100 metres (980–3,610 ft).[4]

3.20.1 Description

Camellia japonica is a flowering tree or shrub, usually 1.5–6 metres (4.9–19.7 ft) tall, but occasionally up to 11 metres (36 ft) tall. Some cultivated varieties achieve a size of 72m^2 or more. The youngest branches are purplish-brown, becoming grayish-brown as they age. The alternately arranged leathery leaves are dark green on the top side, paler on the underside, usually 5–11 centimetres (2.0–4.3 in) long by 2.5–6 centimetres (1.0–2.4 in) wide with a stalk (petiole) about 5–10 millimetres (0.2–0.4 in) long. The base of the leaf is pointed (cuneate), the margins are very finely toothed (serrulate) and the tip somewhat pointed.[4]

In the wild, flowering is between January and March. The flowers appear along the branches, particularly towards the ends, and have very short stems. They occur either alone or in pairs, and are 6–10 centimetres (2.4–3.9 in) across. There are about nine greenish bracteoles and sepals. Flowers of the wild species have six or seven rose or white petals, each 3–4.5 centimetres (1.2–1.8 in) long by 1.5–2.5 centimetres (0.6–1.0 in) wide; the innermost petals are joined at the base for up to a third of their length. (Cultivated forms often have more petals.) The numerous stamens are 2.5–3.5 centimetres (1.0–1.4 in) long, the outer whorl being joined at the base for up to 2.5 centimetres (1.0 in). The three-lobed style is about 3 centimetres (1.2 in) long.[4]

A bud of a Japanese camellia

The fruit consists of a globe-shaped capsule with three compartments (locules), each with one or two large brown seeds with a diameter of 1–2 centimetres (0.4–0.8 in). Fruiting occurs in September to October in the wild.[4]

C. japonica leaves are eaten by the caterpillars of some Lepidoptera, such as The Engrailed (*Ectropis crepuscularia*). The Japanese white eye bird (*Zosterops japonica*) pollinates *Camellia japonica*.[5]

3.20.2 Taxonomy

The genus *Camellia* was named after a Jesuit priest and botanist named Georg Kamel.[6] The specific epithet *japonica* was given to the species by Carl Linnaeus in 1753 because Engelbert Kaempfer was the first to give a description of the plant while in Japan.[7]

Two varieties are distinguished in the *Flora of China*: *C. japonica* var. *japonica* and *C. japonica* var. *rusticana*[4][8]

Camellia japonica var. japonica

C. japonica var. *japonica* is the form named by Linnaeus, and naturally occurs in forests at altitudes of 300–1,100 metres (980–3,610 ft) in Shandong, eastern Zhejiang in mainland China and in Taiwan, south Japan, and South Korea.

The leaf has a glabrous stem (petiole) about 1 centimetre (0.4 in) long. The bracteoles and sepals are velvety (velutinous). It flowers between January–March, and from September–October.*[8] It is grown as a garden plant in the form of many cultivars throughout the world.

Camellia japonica var. rusticana

C. japonica var. rusticana in the wild, Aizu area, Fukushima pref., Japan

Camellia japonica var. *rusticana* (Honda) T. L. Ming naturally occurs in forests in Zhejiang (island of Zhoushan Qundao) in mainland China*[8] and in Honshu, Japan. The leaf has a shorter petiole, about 5 millimetres (0.2 in) long, with fine hairs (pubescent) at the base. The bracteoles and sepals are smooth (glabrous) on the outside. The color of the flowers ranges from red through rose to pink, flowering in April to May. This variety is regarded by some botanical authorities to be a separate species: *Camellia rusticana*.*[9]

In Japan it is known by the common name "yuki-tsubaki" (snow camellia) as it naturally occurs in areas of heavy snowfall at altitudes ranging from 1,100 metres (3,500 ft) down to 120 metres (400 ft) on sloping land under deciduous beech trees in the mountain regions to the north of the main island of Honshu and facing the East Sea. In December heavy drifts of snow come in from the north, covering the plants to a depth of up to 2.4 metres (8 ft). The bushes remain covered by snow from December till the end of March when the snow melts in early Spring and the camellias start flowering.*[10]

Cultivars of *C. japonica* var. *rusticana* include: 'Nishiki-kirin', 'Nishiki-no-mine', 'Toyo-no-hikari' and 'Otome'.

3.20.3 History

China

A bonsai specimen of C. japonica

Camellia japonica has appeared in paintings and porcelain in China since the 11th century. Early paintings of the plant are usually of the single red flowering type. However, a single white flowering plant is shown in the scroll of the *Four Magpies* of the Song Dynasty.*[7]

Australia

Camellia japonica *'Aspasia Macarthur'*

The first records of camellias in Australia pertain to a

consignment to Alexander Macleay of Sydney that arrived in 1826 and were planted in Sydney at Elizabeth Bay House.*[11]

In 1838 six *C. japonica* plants were imported by the botanist, horticulturist and agriculturist William Macarthur. During the years that followed he brought in several hundred varieties and grew them at Camden Park Estate.*[12] For many years Macarthur's nursery was one of the main sources of supply to the colony in Australia of ornamental plants, as well as fruit trees and vines.*[11]

In 1845, William Macarthur wrote to the London nurseryman Conrad Loddiges, acknowledging receipt of camellias and mentioning: "I have raised four or five hundred seedlings of camellia, chiefly from seeds produced by 'Anemoniflora'. As this variety never has anthers of its own, I fertilised its blossoms with pollen of *C. reticulata* and Sp. *maliflora*." Although most of Macarthur's seedling varieties have been lost to cultivation, some are still popular today, including 'Aspasia Macarthur' (named after him).*[11]

A well-known camellia nursery in Sydney was "Camellia Grove", set up in 1852 by Silas Sheather who leased land adjoining the Parramatta River on what was originally part of Elizabeth Farm.*[13] *Fuller's Sydney Handbook* of 1877 describes his nursery as having 59 varieties of camellias.*[14] Camellia and other flowers from Sheather's nursery were sent by steamship downriver to florists at Sydney Markets, tied in bunches and suspended from long pieces of wood which were hung up about the decks.*[13]*[15] Silas Sheather developed a number of camellia cultivars, the most popular (and still commercially grown) were *C. japonica* 'Prince Frederick William' and *C. japonica* 'Harriet Beecher Sheather', named after his daughter.*[14]*[16] The area in the vicinity of Sheather's nursery was eventually made a suburb and named Camellia, in honor of Camellia Grove nursery.*[17]*[18]

By 1883, Shepherd and Company, the leading nurserymen in Australia at the time, listed 160 varieties of *Camellia japonica*.*[12]

Associate Professor Eben Gowrie Waterhouse was a scholar, linguist, garden designer and camellia expert who brought about a worldwide revival of interest in the genus in the first half of the twentieth century.*[19] The E.G. Waterhouse National Camellia Garden in Sydney, Australia is named after him.*[20]

Europe

According to a research conducted in 1959, by Dr. Frederick Meyer, of the United States Department of Agriculture, the camellias of Campo Bello (Portugal) are the oldest known specimens in Europe, which would have been planted around 1550, that is to say, these trees are nowadays approximately 460 years old.*[21] However it is said that the camellia was first brought to the West in 1692 by Engelbert Kaempfer, Chief Surgeon to the Dutch East India Company. He brought details of over 30 varieties back from Asia.*[22] Camellias were introduced into Europe during the 18th century and had already been cultivated in the Orient for thousands of years. Robert James of Essex, England, is thought to have brought back the first live camellia to England in 1739. On his return from Dejima, Carl Peter Thunberg made a short trip to London where he made the acquaintance of Sir Joseph Banks. Thunberg donated to Kew Botanic Gardens four specimens of *Camellia japonica*. One of these was supposedly given in 1780 to the botanical garden of Pillnitz Castle near Dresden in Germany where it currently measures 8.9 metres (29 feet) in height and 11 metres (36 feet) in diameter.*[23]

Camellia japonica *in the garden of Pillnitz Castle, Germany*

The oldest trees of *Camellia japonica* in Europe can be found in Campobello (Portugal), Caserta (Italy) and Pillnitz (Germany).*[24] These were probably planted at the end of the 16th century.

United States

In the U.S.A., camellias were first sold in 1807 as greenhouse plants, but were soon distributed to be grown outdoors in the south.*[6]

In Charleston, South Carolina, the estate garden of Magnolia-on-the-Ashley introduced hundreds of new *Camellia japonica* cultivars from the 19th century onwards, and its recently restored collection has been designated an International Camellia Garden of Excellence. "Debutante", a popular variety, was originally introduced by Magnolia as "Sarah C. Hastie". The name was changed to give it more marketing appeal.

Cross-breeding of camellias has produced many cultivars which are tolerant of hardiness zone 6 winters. These camellia varieties can grow in the milder parts of the lower Midwest (St. Louis, for example), Pacific Northwest, NYC area (NYC/NJ/CT), and even Ontario, Canada (near edge of the Great Lakes).

3.20.4 Cultivars

Camellia japonica is valued for its flowers, which can be single, semi-double or double flowered.*[6] There are more than 2,000 cultivars developed from *C. japonica*. The shade of the flowers can vary from red to pink to white; they sometimes have multi-coloured stripes or specks. Cultivars include 'Elegans' with large pink flowers which often have white streaks, 'Giulio Nuccio' with red to pinkish petals and yellow stamens, 'Mathotiana Alba' with pure white flowers, and the light crimson semi-double-flowered 'The Czar'.*[25]

C. japonica 'Alba Plena' is nicknamed the "Bourbon Camellia". Captain Connor of the East Indiaman Carnatic.*[26] brought the flower to England in 1792.*[27] The flowers are pure white and about 3 to 4 inches across. It blooms earlier than most cultivated camellias, in the early winter or spring, and can flower for 4 to 5 months.*[28]

The zig-zag camellia or *C. japonica* 'Unryu' has different zig-zag branching patterns. "Unryu" means "dragon in the clouds" in Japanese; the Japanese believe it looks like a dragon climbing up to the sky. Another type of rare camellia is called the fishtail camellia or *C. japonica* 'Kingyotsubaki'. The tips of the leaves of this plant resemble a fish's tail.*[29]

The following cultivars have gained the Royal Horticultural Society's Award of Garden Merit:

Flower form or style

Camellia flower forms are quite varied but the main types are single, semi-double, formal double, informal double and elegans (or anemone) form.

Single   Single flowers have five to a maximum of eight petals in one row, petals loose, regular or irregular. May include petaloids; prominent display of stamens & pistils.

- 'Ashiya'

- 'Kamo-honnnami'

- 'Sekidotaroan'

- 'Yuletide'

Semi-Double   Two or more rows of large regular, irregular or loose outer petals (nine or more) with an uninterrupted cluster of stamens. May include petaloids; petals may overlap or be set in rows for 'hose in hose' effect.

- 'C.M. Wilson'

3.20. CAMELLIA JAPONICA

- 'The Czar'
-  'Dr. Tinsley'
-  'Dr. Clifford Parks'
-  'Mercury Supreme'
-  'Royal Velvet'
-  'Triphosa'
- 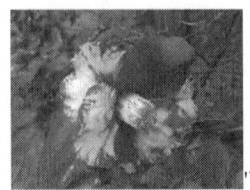 'Ville De Nantes'

Irregular Semi-Double A semi-double with one or more petaloids interrupting the cluster of stamens.

-  'Bob Hope'
-  'Drama Girl'
- 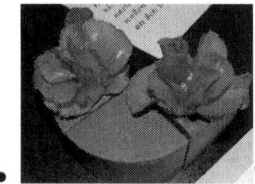 'Fred Sander'
-  Unidentified cultivar

Formal Double Many rows and number of petals (sometimes more than a hundred), regularly disposed, tiered or imbricated, but no visible stamens. Usually with a central cone of tightly furled petals.

-  'Hikarugenji'
-  'Black Lace'

94   CHAPTER 3. PLANTS USED IN BONSAI (IN ALPHABETICAL ORDER)

- 'Coquettii'

- 'Dahlohnega'

- 'Duchesse de Berry'

- 'White by the Gate'

Elegans Form One or more rows of large outer petals lying flat or undulating, with a mass of intermingled petaloids and stamens in the center. Previously called "Anemone Form".

- 'Althaeiflora'

- 'Bernhard Lauterbach'

- 'Chandler's Elegance'

- 'Nobilissima'

Informal Double A mass of raised petals with petaloids (parts of the flower that have assumed the appearance of small, narrow or twisted petals). Stamens may or may not be visible. Previously called "Peony Form".

- 'Ann Blair Brown Variegated'

- 'Colombo'

- 'Frankie Winn'

- 'Nuccio's Jewel'

3.20.5 Cultivation

Camellias should be planted in the shade in organic, somewhat acidic, semi-moist but well drained soil. If the soil is not well drained, it can cause the roots to rot.*[61]

As a *Camellia* species, *C. japonica* can be used to make tea. Its processed leaves show aromatic fragrance. It contains caffeine and catechins of the same kind as *C. sinensis*.*[62]

Diseases

Some fungal and algal diseases include: Spot Disease, which gives the upper side of leaves a silver color and round spots, and can cause loss of leaves; Black Mold; Leaf Spot; Leaf Gall; Flower Blight, which causes flowers to become brown and fall; Root Rot; and Canker caused by the fungus *Glomerella cingulata*, which penetrates plants through wounds. Some insects and pests of *C. japonica* are the Fuller Rose Beetle *Pantomorus cervinus*, the mealybugs *Planococcus citri* and *Pseudococcus longispinus*, the weevils *Otiorhyncus salcatus* and *Otiorhyncus ovatus*, and the tea scale *Fiorinia theae*.

Some physiological diseases include salt injury which results from high levels of salt in soil; chlorosis which is thought to be caused lack of certain elements in the soil or insufficient acidity preventing their absorption by the roots; bud drop which causes loss or decay of buds, and can be caused by over-watering, high temperatures, or pot-bound roots. Other diseases are oedema and sunburn. Not much is known about viral diseases in *C. japonica*.*[63]

3.20.6 In culture and art

Camellias are seen as lucky symbols for the Chinese New Year and spring and were even used as offerings to the gods during the Chinese New Year. It is also thought that Chinese women would never wear a Camellia in their hair because it opened much later after the bud formed. This was thought to signify that she would not have a son for a long time.*[7]

One of the most important plants related to *Camellia japonica* is the *Camellia sinensis*, which is the plant tea comes from. This plant is not usually grown in gardens because it has small white flowers, unlike the *Camellia japonica*, which has larger, more beautiful flowers. It is not seen in art as often as the *Camellia japonica*, but it is shown in a painting called the *Song Hundred Flowers* which hangs in the Palace Museum in Beijing. *Camellia sinensis* may have been used as medicine during the Shang Dynasty. It was first used for drinking during the Zhou Dynasty.*[7]

The following is a poem written by English evangelical

C. japonica on a Japanese postage stamp.

Protestant writer Charlotte Elizabeth Tonna in 1834:*[64]

THE WHITE CAMELLIA JAPONICA.
Thou beauteous child of purity and grace,
What element could yield so fair a birth?
Defilement bore me —my abiding place
Was mid the foul clods of polluted earth.
But light looked on me from a holier sphere,
To draw me heavenward —then I rose and shone;
And can I vainly to thine eye appear,
Thou dust-born gazer? make the type thine own.
From thy dark dwelling look thou forth, and see
The purer beams that brings a lovelier change for thee.

3.20.7 See also

- List of Award of Garden Merit camellias

3.20.8 References

[1] *English Names for Korean Native Plants* (PDF). Pocheon: Korea National Arboretum. 2015. p. 385. ISBN 978-89-97450-98-5. Retrieved 4 January 2017 – via Korea Forest Service.

[2] Rushing, Felder and Jennifer Greer. *Alabama & Mississippi Gardener's Guide.* Cool Springs Press, 2005. 158. ISBN 1-59186-118-7

[3] *Botanica. The Illustrated AZ of over 10000 garden plants and how to cultivate them*, p 176-177. Könemann, 2004. ISBN 3-8331-1253-0

[4] Min, Tianlu; Bartholomew, Bruce. "*Camellia japonica*". http://www.efloras.org/florataxon.aspx?flora_id=2&taxon_id=200014034. Retrieved 2011-11-18. Missing or empty |title= (help), in Wu, Zhengyi; Raven, Peter H. & Hong, Deyuan, eds. (1994 onwards), *Flora of China*, Beijing; St. Louis: Science Press; Missouri Botanical Garden, retrieved 2011-10-01 Check date values in: |date= (help)

[5] Roubik, Sakai, and Abang A. Hamid Karim. *Pollination ecology and the rain forest.* New York: Springer Science + Business Media. 2005. 135. ISBN 0-387-21309-0

[6] Cothran, James R. *Gardens and historic plants of the antebellum South.* South Carolina: University of South Carolina Press. 2003. pages 166-167. ISBN 1-57003-501-6

[7] Valder, Peter. The Garden Plants of China. Oregon: Timber Press, 1999. ISBN 0-88192-470-9

[8] "Camellia" (PDF). *Flora of China.* **12**: 367–412. 2007.

[9] "Camellia rusticana". The Plant List. Retrieved 17 August 2014.

[10] Waterhouse, Eben Gowrie (August 1963). "Camellia rusticana - The "Snow-camellia" of Japan" (PDF). *The Camellia Bulletin.* **16** (4): 8.

[11] Tate, Ken. "The History of Camellias In Australia". Camellias Australia. Retrieved 19 August 2014.

[12] Hazelwood, Walter G. (1955). "Camellias in Australia" (PDF). *American Camellia Yearbook*: 65.

[13] Barker, Geoff (14 May 2014). "The Parramatta River 1848 to 1861 – Personal Observations by W S Campbell". Parramatta Heritage Centre. Retrieved 17 August 2014.

[14] Spencer, Roger (ed.) (1995). *Horticultural Flora of South-Eastern Australia: Flowering Plants Vol. 2.* UNSW Press. p. 324. ISBN 9780868403038.

[15] "Horticultur, Farming, Etc.". *The Sydney Morning Herald.* May 29, 1878. p. 1. Retrieved 17 August 2014.

[16] "President's report". *The Granville Guardian.* **18** (3): 1. April 2011.

[17] *The Book of Sydney Suburbs*, Compiled by Frances Pollen, Angus & Robertson Publishers, 1990, Published in Australia ISBN 0-207-14495-8

[18] McClymont, John (2009). "Camellia". *Sydney Journal.* **2** (1): 84.

[19] O'Neil, W.M. "Eben Gowrie Waterhouse". *Australian Dictionary of Biography.* Australian National University. Retrieved 19 September 2016.

[20] E. G. Waterhouse National Camellia Garden (official website)

[21] Jorge Garrido: "Portuguese Camellias, History&Beauty" Agro-Manual Publicaçoes, Lda, February 2014. Page: 1

[22] oakleafgardening.com

[23] "Die Pillnitzer Kamelie (Camellia japonica L.)" (in German). Staatliche Schlösser, Burgen und Gärten Sachsen. 2011. Retrieved 26 December 2011.

[24] P. Vela, J. L. Couselo, C. Salinero, M. González, M. J. Sainz: "Morpho-botanic and molecular characterization of the oldest camellia trees in Europe". In: *International Camellia Journal*, No. 41, 2009, pp. 51-57

[25] Nico Vermeulen. *The Complete Encyclopedia of Container Plants*, pp. 65-66. Rebo International, Netherlands, 1998. ISBN 90-366-1584-4

[26] http://www.internationalcamellia.org/camellia-japonica-alba-plena

[27] Booth, William B. History and Description of the Species of Camellia and Thea. Published by s.n., 1829. Original from Harvard University. Digitized Jun 4, 2007.

[28] The Magazine of horticulture, botany, and all useful discoveries and improvements in rural affairs. Published by Hovey., 1836. v. 2. Original from Harvard University. Digitized May 11, 2007.

[29] Kirton, Meredith. *Dig: Modern Australian Gardening.* Murdoch Books, 2004. 399. ISBN 1-74045-365-4

[30] "RHS Plant Selector - *Camellia japonica* 'Adelina Patti'". Retrieved 13 June 2013.

[31] "RHS Plant Selector - *Camellia japonica* 'Adolphe Audusson'". Retrieved 13 June 2013.

[32] "RHS Plant Selector - *Camellia japonica* 'Akashigata'". Retrieved 13 June 2013.

[33] "RHS Plant Selector - *Camellia japonica* 'Alexander Hunter'". Retrieved 13 June 2013.

[34] "RHS Plant Selector - *Camellia japonica* 'Annie Wylam'". Retrieved 13 June 2013.

[35] "RHS Plant Selector - *Camellia japonica* 'Australis'". Retrieved 13 June 2013.

[36] "RHS Plant Selector - *Camellia japonica* 'Berenice Boddy'". Retrieved 13 June 2013.

[37] "RHS Plant Selector - *Camellia japonica* 'Bob Hope'". Retrieved 13 June 2013.

[38] "RHS Plant Selector - *Camellia japonica* 'Bob's Tinsie'". Retrieved 13 June 2013.

[39] "RHS Plant Selector - *Camellia japonica* 'Bokuhan'". Retrieved 13 June 2013.

[40] "RHS Plant Selector - *Camellia japonica* 'C. M. Hovey'". Retrieved 13 June 2013.

[41] "RHS Plant Selector - *Camellia japonica* 'Carter's Sunburst'". Retrieved 13 June 2013.

[42] "RHS Plant Selector - *Camellia japonica* 'Commander Mulroy'". Retrieved 13 June 2013.

[43] "RHS Plant Selector - *Camellia japonica* 'Drama Girl'". Retrieved 13 June 2013.

[44] "RHS Plant Selector - *Camellia japonica* 'Gloire de Nantes'". Retrieved 13 June 2013.

[45] "RHS Plant Selector - *Camellia japonica* 'Grand Prix'". Retrieved 13 June 2013.

[46] "RHS Plant Selector - *Camellia japonica* 'Grand Slam'". Retrieved 13 June 2013.

[47] "RHS Plant Selector - *Camellia japonica* 'Guilio Nucco'". Retrieved 13 June 2013.

[48] "RHS Plant Selector - *Camellia japonica* 'Hagoromo'". Retrieved 13 June 2013.

[49] "RHS Plant Selector - *Camellia japonica* 'Hakurakuten'". Retrieved 13 June 2013.

[50] "RHS Plant Selector - *Camellia japonica* 'Joseph Pfingstl'". Retrieved 13 June 2013.

[51] "RHS Plant Selector - *Camellia japonica* 'Jupiter'". Retrieved 13 June 2013.

[52] "RHS Plant Selector - *Camellia japonica* 'Lavinia Maggi'". Retrieved 13 June 2013.

[53] "RHS Plant Selector - *Camellia japonica* 'Margaret Davies'". Retrieved 13 June 2013.

[54] "RHS Plant Selector - *Camellia japonica* 'Mars'". Retrieved 13 June 2013.

[55] "RHS Plant Selector - *Camellia japonica* 'Masayoshi'". Retrieved 13 June 2013.

[56] "RHS Plant Selector - *Camellia japonica* 'Mercury'". Retrieved 13 June 2013.

[57] "RHS Plant Selector - *Camellia japonica* 'Nuccio's Jewel'". Retrieved 13 June 2013.

[58] "RHS Plant Selector - *Camellia japonica* 'Sylva'". Retrieved 13 June 2013.

[59] "RHS Plant Selector - *Camellia japonica* 'Tricolor'". Retrieved 13 June 2013.

[60] "RHS Plant Selector - *Camellia japonica* 'Wilamina'". Retrieved 13 June 2013.

[61] Francko, David. A. *Palms won't grow here and other myths*. Oregon: Timber Press, Inc. 2003. ISBN 0-88192-575-6

[62] Major Components of Teas Manufactured with Leaf and Flower of Korean Native Camellia japonica L. Cha Young-Ju, Lee Jang-Won, Kim Ju-Hee, Park Min-Hee and Lee Sook-Young, Korean Journal of Medicinal Crop Science, Volume 12, Issue 3, 2004, pages 183-190 (abstract in English)

[63] Pirone, Pascal P. Diseases and pests of ornamental plants. Edition 5. John Wiley and Sons. 1978. 172-175.

[64] Elizabeth, Charlotte (1846). *Posthumous and Other Poems*. Seeley, Burnside, and Seeley. p. 91.

3.20.9 External links

Media related to Camellia cultivars at Wikimedia Commons

- The International Camellia Society

3.21 Camellia sasanqua

Camellia sasanqua, with common name **sasanqua camellia**,[1] is a species of *Camellia* native to China and Japan. It is usually found growing up to an altitude of 900 metres.

It is an evergreen shrub growing to 5 m tall. The leaves are broad elliptic, 3–7 cm long and 1.2–3 cm broad, with a finely serrated margin. The flowers are 5–7 cm diameter, with 5–8 white to dark pink petals.

3.21.1 History and uses

At the beginning of the Edo period, cultivars of *Camellia sasanqua* began appearing; the first record of the cultivars of this plant was made by Ihei Ito (1695–1733).[2] In Japan, it is not considered to be a true Camellia as the Japanese call it Sazanka (サザンカ, 山茶花).[3]

C. sasanqua was not known in western societies until in 1820 Captain Richard Rawes of the East Indiaman *Warren Hastings* brought "Camellia sasanqua, var. β. stricata" to his relation, Thomas Carey Palmer, of Bromley in Kent.[4] Then in 1869, Dutch traders imported some specimens into Europe. It is now also introduced to Australia and the United States.[3]

It has a long history of cultivation in Japan for practical rather than decorative reasons. The leaves are used to make tea while the seeds or nuts are used to make tea seed oil,*[5] which is used for lighting, lubrication, cooking and cosmetic purposes. Tea oil has a higher calorific content than any other edible oil available naturally in Japan.*[3]

C. sasanqua is valued in gardens for its handsome glossy green foliage, and fragrant single white flowers produced extremely early in the season. Various cultivars have been selected, of which 'Crimson King',*[6] 'Hugh Evans'*[7] and 'Jean May'*[8] have gained the Royal Horticultural Society's Award of Garden Merit.

3.21.2 See also

- List of Award of Garden Merit camellias

3.21.3 Citations and references

Citations

[1] *USDA GRIN Taxonomy*, retrieved 21 April 2015

[2] Winter Flowers *Camellia sasanqua*

[3] Botanic Gardens Trust—Camellias

[4] Bretschneider (1898), pp. 282-3.

[5] *Camellia sasanqua* in BoDD – Botanical Dermatology Database

[6] "RHS Plant Selector - *Camellia sasanqua* 'Crimson King'". Retrieved 13 June 2013.

[7] "RHS Plant Selector - *Camellia sasanqua* 'Hugh Evans'". Retrieved 13 June 2013.

[8] "RHS Plant Selector - *Camellia sasanqua* 'Jean May'". Retrieved 13 June 2013.

References

- Bretschneider, E. (1898) *History of European Botanical Discoveries in China, Volumes 1-2*. (Sampson Low, Marston and Company).

3.22 Carissa

This article is about the botanical genus. For other uses, see Carissa (disambiguation).

Carissa is a genus of shrubs or small trees native to tropical and subtropical regions of Africa, Australia and Asia. Until recently about 100 species were listed, but most of them have been relegated to the status of synonyms or assigned to other genera, such as *Acokanthera*.*[2]*[3]

Carissa bispinosa, *thorns and flowers*

Conkerberry *(C. spinarum) flowers in Shamirpet, Rangareddy district, Andhra Pradesh, India.*

3.22.1 Description

Different species of *Carissa* grow as shrubs or trees, attaining respective heights of 2 to 10 m tall. They bear smooth, sharp thorns that often are formidable; they are true botanical thorns, being modified branches, morphologically speaking. The thorns may be simple, as in *Carissa spinarum*, dichotomously forked as in *Carissa bispinosa*, or dichotomously branched as in *Carissa macrocarpa*.

The leaves are a rich, glossy, waxy green, smooth, simple, entire and elliptic to ovate or nearly lanceolate. They are 2–8 cm long, partly depending on the species, and generally are thick and leathery. In suitable climates some species flower through most of the year. The flowers are nearly sessile, 1–5 cm diameter, with a five-lobed white or pink-tinged corolla. They may be solitary or borne in clusters in an umbel or corymb.*[4] The flowers of some species some have a fragrance reminiscent of Gardenia, which adds to their popularity as garden plants. The fruit is a plum-like berry in the shape of a prolate spheroid, like that of a rugby ball. In colour they vary according to species. In some species they are red when ripe, whereas others turn a glossy purple-black. Typically they are 1.5–6 cm in length, and usually contain 1-4 flat brown seeds, but up to 16 in some species.

3.22.2 Fruit

The fruit of the carissa is an oblong berry which contains numerous small seeds.*[5] The green fruit is poisonous, sometimes dangerously so. The ripe fruit are edible but may be fairly tart, and taste like a giant cranberry, though some species have fruity flavours with overtones of strawberry or apple. They are rich in Vitamin C, calcium, magnesium and phosphorus. The fruit of *C. macrocarpa* are especially relished and eaten raw or used to make jelly. Various birds eat *Carissa* fruit and distribute the seed. If eaten before fully ripe, a bitter, poisonous latex is released from the skin. Other than the ripe fruit, the plant is poisonous, much like the related and dangerously poisonous genus *Acokanthera*.

Carissa carandas is grown in several Asiatic countries for its fruit, which is variously used in cooking and in folk medicine (see article).

3.22.3 Horticulture

Carissa species generally respond well to gardening and are valued in topiary and in forming strong, dense, decorative, thorny, flowering hedges. Some sprawling varieties are useful as ground covers.*[6] *Carissa* species are grown from seed or cuttings and tolerate slight frost.

3.22.4 Species

The following species are recognised.*[2]

1. *Carissa bispinosa* (L.) Desf. ex Brenan - widespread in E + S Africa from Kenya to Cape Province
2. *Carissa boiviniana* (Baill.) Leeuwenb. - Madagascar
3. *Carissa carandas* L. - India, Bangladesh; naturalized in S China, Mauritius, Nepal, Pakistan, Indochina, Java, Philippines, West Indies
4. *Carissa haematocarpa* (Eckl.) A.DC. - Namibia, Cape Province of South Africa
5. *Carissa macrocarpa* (Eckl.) A.DC. - Kenya + Zaire south to Cape Province; naturalized in S China, Ascension Island, Hawaii, Florida, Texas, Mexico, Central America, West Indies
6. *Carissa pichoniana* Leeuwenb. - Madagascar
7. *Carissa spinarum* L. - Africa, Arabian Peninsula, Indian Subcontinent, Indochina, New Guinea, New Caledonia, Australia
8. *Carissa tetramera* (Sacleux) Stapf - E + S Africa from Kenya to KwaZulu-Natal

Formerly included

- *Acokanthera oblongifolia* (Hochst.) Codd (as *C. oblongifolia* Hochst.)
- *Acokanthera schimperi* (A.DC.) Benth. & Hook.f. ex Schweinf. (as *C. schimperi* A.DC.)

3.22.5 References

[1] "World Checklist of Selected Plant Families". Retrieved May 21, 2014.

[2] Kew World Checklist of Selected Plant Families

[3] "The Plant List: A Working List of All Plant Species, Version 1". 2010.

[4] Dyer, R. Allen, The Genera of Southern African Flowering Plants". ISBN 0 621 02854 1, 1975

[5] Boning, Charles R. (2006). *Florida's Best Fruiting Plants: Native and Exotic Trees, Shrubs, and Vines.* Sarasota, Florida: Pineapple Press, Inc. p. 61. ISBN 1561643726.

[6] Floridata page for *Carissa macrocarpa*

3.23 Carissa macrocarpa

Carissa macrocarpa (**Natal Plum**), is a shrub native to South Africa, where it is commonly called the **Large Num-Num**. In Zulu, as well as in the Bantu tribes of Uganda, it is called ***Amathungulu*** or ***umThungulu oBomvu***. In Afrikaans the fruit is called ***Noem-Noem***.

C. macrocarpa deals well with salt-laden winds, making it a good choice for coastal areas. It is commonly found in the coastal bush of the Eastern Cape and Natal.*[1] It produces shiny, deep green leaves and snowy white flowers whose perfumed scent intensifies at night. Like other *Carissa* species, *C. macrocarpa* is a spiny, evergreen shrub containing latex. They bloom for months at a time. The ornamental plump, round, crimson fruit appears in summer and fall (autumn) at the same time as the blooms. In moderate, coastal areas the fruits appear through the year. The fruit can be eaten out of hand or made into pies, jams, jellies, and sauces.*[1] Some claim that other than the fruit, the plant is poisonous.*[2] However this claim is a myth, possibly based on similarities to other plants with milky sap.*[3] The College of Agricultural and Environmental Sciences at University of California, Davis rates the plant as mildly toxic.*[4] It appears in the South African National tree list as number 640.3.

A traditional food plant in Africa, this little-known fruit has potential to improve nutrition, boost food security, foster rural development and support sustainable landcare.*[5]

3.23.1 Distribution

Carissa macrocarpa grows mainly in coastal areas in South Africa. It can be found on sand dunes and on the edges of coastal forests in Eastern Cape Province northwards from Natal to Mozambique. Today the plant is also growing commonly in southern Florida and is cultivated in southern California and used widely as an ornamental in Central America and the Caribbean.*[5]

3.23.2 Horticultural aspects

Natal plum shrub

Propagation

Carissa macrocarpa is quite easy to grow. Its seeds germinate 2 to 4 weeks after sowing. The development of the seedlings is very slow at first. Plants cultivated from seeds are bearing fruits within the first 2 years. A vegetative propagation is possible and preferred. The most efficient method consists of notching young branchlets by cutting them halfway through. Then they are bent downwards and allowed to hang limply. After the young branchlets have built a callus, in approximately 2 months, the cutting has to be removed from the parent and planted in sand under moderate shade. Roots form within one month. *Carissa macrocarpa* will produce fruits within the first 2 years applying this reproduction method.*[5]

Fertilizing

The maintenance of *Carissa macrocarpa* is simple. The plant is indigenous and does not need fertiliser.

Pollination

In the homeland of *Carissa macrocarpa* night-flying insects pollinates the white, bisexual flowers. Out of its origin area unfruitfulness has been attributed to inadequate pollination. However, hand pollination is possible and in future poor pollination could be avoided by cultivation of floral structures that are highly favourable for self-fertilization.*[5]

Orchard design

Narrow hedges are recommended as orchard design for *Carissa macrocarpa* due to its prickles. Like this the access to the fruits which are growing on the top of the bush is much simpler. Pruning the plant is beneficial because it induces the development of more fruiting tips. Beyond cutting, little pruning work has to be done to restrain the bush from massive growth. This results in an increasing amount of fruits per plant.*[5]

Harvesting

With a minimal yield of 3 tons per hectare under commercial production in South Africa, the productivity is considered as high. The main fruit production is in summer with slightly varying ripening times. So each fruit must be picked when it is ripe. Under good growing conditions the plant also produces many fruits during the off-season. During the harvest attention must be paid to the ripe fruits' skin as it can be easily bruised and is highly perishable.*[5]

Cross section of a ripe fruit

Cultivars for crop-production

Horticultural Scientists in South Africa and the USA (Florida and California) have selected and named several Carissa types which tend to produce fruits more reliably. The fruits are larger, have a good texture and contain fewer seeds. In California they selected Fancy (many large fruits with few seeds), Torrey Pines (good crop-production and abundant pollen), Frank (good pollen supplier but low yield), Chelsey and Serena. In Florida Gifford is one of the best fruit bearers. In Africa *C. haematocarpa* is defined suitable for drier areas and *C. bispinosa* for higher altitudes.*[5]

3.23.3 Environmental requirements

Carissa macrocarpa requires warm, moist subtropical climate. It tolerates different exposures as full sun and fairly heavy shade. As a coastal plant it can deal very well with salty ocean spray.

3.23.4 References

[1] Sparrow, Jacqueline and Gil Hanly. (2002), *Subtropical Plants: A Practical Gardening Guide*, Portland, OR: Timber Press, Inc.

[2] Floridata page for *Carissa macrocarpa*

[3] *Carissa macrocarpa* (Eckl.) A.DC., University of Pretoria Botanical Garden, accessed 4 February 2013 Archived September 8, 2014, at the Wayback Machine.

[4] *Toxic Plants (by scientific name)*, UC Davis, accessed 4 November 2016

[5] National Research Council (2008-01-25). "Carissa". *Lost Crops of Africa: Volume III: Fruits*. Lost Crops of Africa.

3. National Academies Press. ISBN 978-0-309-10596-5. Retrieved 2008-07-15.

3.23.5 External links

- Desert-Tropicals.com
- "*Carissa macrocarpa*". *Plantz Afrika*. Retrieved 2010-02-12.
- "*Carissa macrocarpa*". *Ecocrop FAO*. Retrieved 2010-02-12.
- Images on iSpot
-
- Dressler, S.; Schmidt, M. & Zizka, G. (2014). "*Carissa macrocarpa*". *African plants – a Photo Guide*. Frankfurt/Main: Forschungsinstitut Senckenberg.

3.24 Carmona (plant)

Carmona is a genus of flowering plants in the borage family, Boraginaceae. Members of the genus are commonly known as **Scorpionbush**.

Carmona retusa (Fukien tea tree) is used in bonsai because of its ability to develop a thick and interesting trunk, small white flowers that bloom almost year-round, and tiny round green, red, or black fruits. The lobed leaves are shiny dark green and maintain their small size.

3.24.1 References

[1] "Genus: *Carmona* Cav." . *Germplasm Resources Information Network*. United States Department of Agriculture. 2006-04-02. Retrieved 2010-08-21.

- Species 2000

3.24.2 External links

Media related to *Carmona* at Wikimedia Commons Data related to *Carmona* at Wikispecies

Carmona bonsai

3.25 Carmona retusa

Carmona retusa, also known as the **Fukien tea tree** or **Philippine tea tree**, is a species of flowering plant in the borage family, Boraginaceae. Its specific epithet comes from the Latin *retusus* (blunt), with reference to the leaf apex.*[2]

3.25.1 Description

Carmona retusa is a shrub growing to 4 m height, with long, straggling, slender branches. It is deciduous during the dry season. Its leaves are usually 10–50 mm long and 5–30 mm wide, and may vary in size, texture, colour and margin. It has small white flowers 8–10 mm in diameter with a 4–5 lobed corolla, and drupes 4–6 mm in diameter, ripening brownish orange.*[2]*[3]

3.25.2 Distribution and habitat

The plant occurs widely in eastern and south-eastern Asia from India, Indochina, southern China, Taiwan and Japan, through Malesia, including the Australian territory of Christmas Island, reaching New Guinea, mainland Australia at the Cape York Peninsula, and the Solomon Islands. It has become an invasive weed in Hawaii where it is a popular ornamental plant and where the seeds are thought to be spread by frugivorous birds.*[3]

On Cape York Peninsula, the plant is recorded from semi-evergreen vine thickets. On Christmas Island, it favours dry sites on the terraces, and sometimes occurs in rainforest.*[4]

3.25.3 Uses

The plant is popular in Penjing in China. The leaves are used medicinally in the Philippines to treat cough, colic, diarrhea and dysentery.*[3]

3.25.4 References

Notes

[1] Masamune (1940).

[2] Flora of Australia Online.

[3] Starr *et al.* (2003).

[4] Advice to the Minister for the Environment from the TSSC.

3.25.5 Sources

- Masamune, G. (1940). *Transactions of the Natural History Society of Taiwan.* **30**: 61. Missing or empty |title= (help)

- Starr, Forest; Starr, Kim; & Loope, Lloyd (January 2003). "*Carmona retusa*" (PDF). United States Geological Survey. Retrieved 2010-12-02.

- "Carmona (*Carmona retusa*)". *Advice to the Minister for the Environment and Heritage from the Threatened Species Scientific Committee (TSSC).* Dept of the Environment, Water, Heritage and the Arts, Australia. 2005-09-15. Retrieved 2010-12-02.

- "*Carmona retusa* (Vahl) Masam.". *Flora of Australia Online.* Australian Biological Resources Study. 1993. Retrieved 2010-12-02.

3.26 Carpinus orientalis

Carpinus orientalis, known as the **Oriental Hornbeam**, is a hornbeam native to Hungary, the Balkans, Italy, Crimea, Turkey, Iran, and the Caucasus.*[1]*[2] and occurs usually on hot dry sites at lower altitudes in comparison to the *Carpinus betulus* (European Hornbeam).

3.26.1 Description

The *Carpinus orientalis* is a small tree, rarely over 10 m tall and often shrubby. It has minute, with small leaves, 3–5 cm long.

The seeds have a simple bract, not trilobed like *Carpinus betulus*, that is about 2 cm long.*[3]*[4]

Cultivation

In recent years, this species has been extensively used as an ornamental tree for Bonsai.

3.26.2 References

[1] http://apps.kew.org/wcsp/namedetail.do?name_id=34405

[2] "*Carpinus orientalis* at the NPGS/GRIN database" . USDA. Retrieved 2008-10-24.

[3] Czerepanov, S. K. 1981. Sosudistye Rasteniia SSSR. 509 pages. Nauka, Leningradskoe Otd-nie, Leningrad

[4] Browicz, Kasimierz. Flora Iranica : Flora des Iranischen Hochlandes und der Umrahmenden Gebirge : Persien, Afghanistan, Teile von West-Pakistan, Nord-Iraq, (cont) 97: 2. 1972.

3.27 Casuarina equisetifolia

Casuarina equisetifolia tree at Chikhaldara, Maharashtra

Casuarina equisetifolia or **Australian pine tree** is a she-oak species of the genus *Casuarina*. The native range extends from Burma and Vietnam throughout Malaysia east to French Polynesia, New Caledonia, and Vanuatu, and south to Australia (north of Northern Territory, north and east Queensland, and north-eastern New South Wales).*[1]

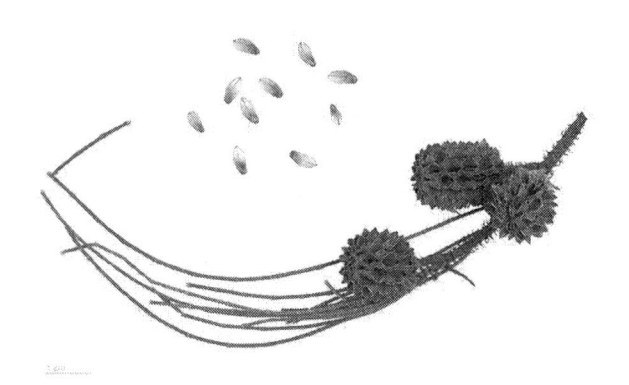

Casuarina equisetifolia - MHNT

Populations are also found in Madagascar, but it is doubtful if this is within the native range of the species.*[2]*[3] The species has been introduced to the Southern United States and West Africa.*[4] It is an invasive species in Florida*[5]*[6] and South Africa.*[7]

3.27.1 Taxonomy

Casuarina equisetifolia was officially described by Linnaeus in 1759 as *Casuarina equisefolia*. A type was designated by New South Wales botanist Lawrie Johnson in 1989.*[8] The specific name *equisetifolia* is derived from the Latin *equisetum*, meaning "horse hair" (referring to the resemblance of the drooping branchlets to horse tail).*[1] Common names include coast sheoak (coast she oak, coastal sheoak), beach casuarina, beach oak, beach sheoak (beach sheoak), whistling tree, horsetail she oak, horsetail beefwood, horsetail tree, Australian pine, ironwood, whistling pine, Filao tree, and agoho.*[1]*[8]*[9]

There are two subspecies:*[10]*[11]

- *Casuarina equisetifolia* subsp. *equisetifolia*. Large tree to 35 m (115 ft) tall; twigs 0.5–0.7 mm (0.020–0.028 in) diameter, hairless. Southeast Asia, northern Australia.*[12]

- *Casuarina equisetifolia* subsp. *incana* (Benth.) L.A.S.Johnson. Small tree to 12 m (39 ft) tall; twigs 0.7–1 mm (0.028–0.039 in) diameter, downy. Eastern Australia (eastern Queensland, New South Wales), New Caledonia, southern Vanuatu.*[13]

3.27.2 Description

Casuarina equisetifolia is an evergreen tree growing to 6–35 m (20–115 ft) tall. The foliage consists of slender, much-branched green to grey-green twigs 0.5–1 mm

Casuarina equisetifolia *leaf litter suppresses germination of understory plants using a biochemical means or allelopathy. This is one reason it can be such a damaging invasive species in places outside its native range.*

- *C. equisetifolia* subsp. *equisetifolia*
- *C. equisetifolia* stems and leaves
- *C. equisetifolia* fruits

(0.020–0.039 in) diameter, bearing minute scale-leaves in whorls of 6–8. The flowers are produced in small catkin-like inflorescences; the male flowers in simple spikes 0.7–4 cm (0.28–1.57 in) long, the female flowers on short peduncles. Unlike most other species of *Casuarina* (which are dioecious) it is monoecious, with male and female flowers produced on the same tree. The fruit is an oval woody structure 10–24 mm (0.39–0.94 in) long and 9–13 mm (0.35–0.51 in) in diameter, superficially resembling a conifer cone made up of numerous carpels each containing a single seed with a small wing 6–8 mm (0.24–0.31 in) long.*[2]*[14]

Like some other species of the Genus *Casuarina*, *Casuarina equisetifolia* is an actinorhizal plant able to fix atmospheric nitrogen. In contrast to species of the *Fabaceae* family of plants (e.g., beans, alfalfa, *Acacia*), Casuarina harbours a symbiosis with a *Frankia* actinomycete.

3.27.3 Distribution and habitat

Casuarina equisetifolia is found from Burma and Vietnam throughout Malesia east to French Polynesia, New Caledonia, and Vanuatu, and south into Australia (the northern parts of Northern Territory, north and east Queensland, and northeastern New South Wales, where it extends as far south as Laurieton.*[15]

3.27.4 Uses

Casuarina is widely used as a bonsai subject, particularly in South-east Asia and parts of the Caribbean. Indonesian specimens and those cultivated in Taiwan are regarded among the best in the bonsai world. The wood of this tree is used for shingles, fencing, and is said to make excellent hot-burning firewood. Among the islands of Hawaii, Casuarina are also grown for erosion prevention, and in general as wind breaking elements.

The legendary miraculous spear *Kaumaile* came with the hero Tefolaha on the South Pacific island Nanumea. He fought with it on the islands of Samoa and Tonga. As Tefolaha died, "Kaumaile" went to his heirs, then to their heirs, and on and on - 23 generations. It is about 1.80 meters long and about 880 years old and the tree was cut on Samoa.*[16]

3.27.5 References

[1] Boland, D. J.; Brooker, M. I. H.; Chippendale, G. M.; McDonald, M. W. (2006). *Forest trees of Australia* (5th ed.). Collingwood, Vic.: CSIRO Publishing. p. 82. ISBN 0-643-06969-0.

[2] "Casuarina equisetifolia L., Amoen. Acad. 143 (1759)". *Australian Biological Resources Study*. Australian National Botanic Gardens. Retrieved 23 April 2011.

[3] http://www.worldagroforestrycentre.org/sea/Products/AFDbases/AF/asp/SpeciesInfo.asp?SpID=477

[4] "Plant for the Planet: Billion Tree Campaign" (PDF). *United Nations Environment Programme*. Retrieved 23 April 2011.

[5] "Biological control of Australian native Casuarina species in the USA". *Commonwealth Scientific and Industrial Research Organisation*. 16 May 2007. Archived from the original on 5 June 2011. Retrieved 16 September 2010.

[6] Masterson, J. "Casuarina equisetifolia (Australian Pine)". Fort Pierce: Smithsonian Marine Station. Retrieved 5 May 2009.

[7] "SANBI:Declared Weeds & Invader Plants". South African National Biodiversity Institute. Retrieved 25 September 2014.

[8] "*Casuarina equisetifolia* L.". *Australian Plant Name Index (APNI), IBIS database*. Centre for Plant Biodiversity Research, Australian Government.

[9] "Casuarina equisetifolia". *World Agroforestry Centre*. Retrieved 23 April 2011.

[10] "Australian Plant Name Index (APNI)". *Australian National Botanic Gardens*. Retrieved 23 April 2011.

[11] "Taxon: Casuarina equisetifolia L.". *Germplasm Resources Information Network*. United States Department of Agriculture Agricultural Research Service. Retrieved 23 April 2011.

[12] "Casuarina equisetifolia L. subsp. equisetifolia". *Australian Biological Resources Study*. Australian National Botanic Gardens. Retrieved 23 April 2011.

[13] "Casuarina equisetifolia subsp. incana". *Australian Biological Resources Study*. Australian National Botanic Gardens. Retrieved 23 April 2011.

[14] Huxley, Anthony; Griffiths, Mark; Levy, Margot (1992). *The New Royal Horticultural Society dictionary of gardening. Volume 1*. London: Macmillan. ISBN 0-333-47494-5.

[15] K. L. Wilson & L. A. S. Johnson. "New South Wales Flora Online: *Casuarina equisetifolia*". Royal Botanic Gardens & Domain Trust, Sydney, Australia.

[16] "S dsee-Speer: Hamburger Forscher bestimmt Holzart - SPIEGEL ONLINE". *SPIEGEL ONLINE*. 30 May 2014. Retrieved 25 September 2014.

3.28 Cedrus

Cedrus (common name **cedar**) is a genus of coniferous trees in the plant family Pinaceae. They are native to the mountains of the western Himalayas and the Mediterranean region, occurring at altitudes of 1,500–3,200 m in the Himalayas and 1,000–2,200 m in the Mediterranean.[*][1]

3.28.1 Description

Foliage of Atlas cedar

Cedrus trees can grow up to 30–40 m (occasionally 60 m) tall with spicy-resinous scented wood, thick ridged or square-cracked bark, and broad, level branches. The shoots are dimorphic, with long shoots, which form the framework of the branches, and short shoots, which carry most of the leaves. The leaves are evergreen and needle-like, 8–60 mm long, arranged in an open spiral phyllotaxis on long shoots, and in dense spiral clusters of 15–45 together on short shoots; they vary from bright grass-green to dark green to strongly glaucous pale blue-green, depending on the thickness of the white wax layer which protects the leaves from desiccation. The seed cones are barrel-shaped, 6–12 cm long and 3–8 cm broad, green maturing grey-brown, and, as in *Abies*, disintegrate at maturity to release the winged seeds. The seeds are 10–15 mm long, with a 20–30 mm wing; as in *Abies*, the seeds have two or three resin blisters, containing an unpleasant-tasting resin, thought to be a defence against squirrel predation. Cone maturation takes one year, with pollination in autumn and the seeds maturing the same time a year later. The pollen cones are slender ovoid, 3–8 cm long, produced in late summer, and shedding pollen in autumn.[*][1][*][2]

3.28.2 Taxonomy

Cedars share a very similar cone structure with the firs (*Abies*) and were traditionally thought to be most closely related to them, but molecular evidence supports a basal position in the family.*[3]*[4]

Species and subspecies

The five taxa of *Cedrus* are assigned according to taxonomic opinion to between one and four different species:*[1]*[5]*[6]*[7]*[8]*[9]*[10]*[11]*[12]*[13]*[14]

- *Cedrus deodara* (syn. *C. l. deodara*) —deodar or deodar cedar, native to Western Himalaya, leaves are bright green to pale glaucous green, 25–60 mm; cones have slightly ridged scales

- *Cedrus libani* —Lebanon cedar or cedar of Lebanon, native to Mediterranean region mountains in Near East and Turkey, cones have smooth scales; two (or up to four) subspecies:

  - *C. l. libani* —Lebanon cedar, mountains of Lebanon, western Syria, and south-central Turkey, leaves dark green to glaucous blue-green, 10–25 mm

  - *C. l. stenocoma* —Turkish cedar, mountains of southwest Turkey, leaves glaucous blue-green, 8–25 mm

- *Cedrus brevifolia* —Cyprus cedar (syn. *C. l. brevifolia*, *C. libani* var. *brevifolia*), mountains of Cyprus, leaves glaucous blue-green, 8–20 mm

- *Cedrus atlantica* —Atlas cedar (syn. *C. l. atlantica*), Atlas mountains in Morocco and Algeria, leaves dark green to glaucous blue-green, 10–25 mm

A cedar in Lebanon

Glaucous Cedrus atlantica *trained as a bonsai*

3.28.3 Ecology

Cedars are adapted to mountainous climates; in the Mediterranean, they receive winter precipitation, mainly as snow, and summer drought, while in the western Himalaya, they receive primarily summer monsoon rainfall.*[1]

Cedars are used as food plants by the larvae of some Lepidoptera species including pine processionary and turnip moth (recorded on deodar cedar).

3.28.4 Uses

Cedars are very popular ornamental trees, widely used in horticulture in temperate climates where winter temperatures do not fall below about −25°C. The Turkish cedar is slightly hardier, to −30°C or just below. Extensive mortality of planted specimens can occur in severe winters where temperatures do drop lower.*[15] Areas with successful long-term cultivation include the entire Mediterranean region, western Europe north to the British Isles,

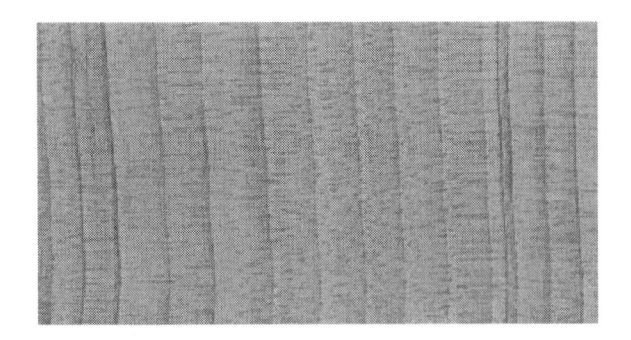

Cedar wood is not only scented, but also has an attractive colour and grain.

southern Australia and New Zealand, and southern and western North America.

Cedar wood and cedar oil are known to be a natural repellent to moths,*[16] hence cedar is a popular lining for modern-day cedar chests and closets in which woolens are stored. This specific use of cedar is mentioned in *The Iliad* (Book 24), referring to the cedar-roofed or lined storage chamber where Priam goes to fetch treasures to be used as ransom. However, the species typically used for cedar chests and closets in North America is *Juniperus virginiana*, which is different from the true cedars (note also common confusion with *Thuja* spp. below). Cedar is also commonly used to make shoe trees as it can absorb moisture and deodorise.

Many species of cedar trees are suitable for training as bonsai. They work well with many styles, including formal and informal upright, slanting, and cascading.*[17]

In North America, species of the genus *Thuja*, such as western red cedar, are commonly —though mistakenly — confused with genuine cedar, as is *J. virginiana*, typically known as red cedar or eastern red cedar. While some naturalized species of cedar (*Cedrus*, the true cedars) can be found in the Americas, no species is native.

3.28.5 Etymology

Both the Latin word *cedrus* and the generic name *cedrus* are derived from Greek κέδρος *kédros*. Ancient Greek and Latin used the same word, *kédros* and *cedrus*, respectively, for different species of plants now classified in the genera *Cedrus* and *Juniperus* (juniper). Species of both genera are native to the area where Greek language and culture originated, though as the word *kédros* does not seem to be derived from any of the languages of the Middle East, it has been suggested the word may originally have applied to Greek species of juniper and was later adopted for species now classified in the genus *Cedrus* because of the similarity of their aromatic woods.*[18] The name was similarly applied to citron and the word citrus is derived from the same root.*[19] However, as a loan word in English, cedar had become fixed to its biblical sense of *Cedrus* by the time of its first recorded usage in AD 1000.*[20]

The name "cedar" has more recently (since about 1700*[20]) been applied to many other trees (such as western red cedar; in some cases the botanical name alludes to this usage, such as the genus *Calocedrus* (meaning "beautiful cedar"), also known as incense cedar). Such usage is regarded by some authorities *[21] as a misapplication of the name to be discouraged.

3.28.6 See also

- Cedars of God
- Cedar wood

3.28.7 References

[1] Farjon, A. (1990). *Pinaceae. Drawings and Descriptions of the Genera*. Koeltz Scientific Books ISBN 3-87429-298-3.

[2] Frankis, M. & Lauria, F. (1994). The maturation and dispersal of cedar cones and seeds. *International Dendrology Society Yearbook* 1993: 43–46.

[3] Liston A., D.S. Gernandt, T.F. Vining, C.S. Campbell, D. Piñero. 2003. Molecular Phylogeny of Pinaceae and Pinus. In Mill, R.R. (ed.): *Proceedings of the 4th Conifer Congress. Acta Hort* **615**: Pp. 107-114.

[4] Wang, X.-Q., Tank, D. C. and Sang, T. (2000): Phylogeny and Divergence Times in Pinaceae: Evidence from Three Genomes. *Molecular Biology and Evolution* **17**:773-781. Available online

[5] Gymnosperm database *Cedrus*.

[6] NCBI Taxonomy Browser *Cedrus*.

[7] Flora of China vol. 4

[8] Qiao, C.-Y., Jin-Hua Ran, Yan Li and Xiao-Quan Wang (2007): Phylogeny and Biogeography of *Cedrus* (Pinaceae) Inferred from Sequences of Seven Paternal Chloroplast and Maternal Mitochondrial DNA Regions. *Annals of Botany* **100(3)**:573-580. Available online

[9] Farjon, A. (2008). *A Natural History of Conifers*. Timber Press ISBN 0-88192-869-0.

[10] Christou, K. A. (1991). The genetic and taxonomic status of Cyprus Cedar, *Cedrus brevifolia* (Hook.) Henry. Mediterranean Agronomic Institute of Chania, Greece.

[11] GRIN Taxonomy for Plants *Cedrus*.

[12] Güner, A., Özhatay, N., Ekim, T., & Başer, K. H. C. (ed.). 2000. *Flora of Turkey and the East Aegean Islands* 11 (Supplement 2): 5–6. Edinburgh University Press. ISBN 0-7486-1409-5

[13] Eckenwalder, J. E. (2009). *Conifers of the World: The Complete Reference*. Timber Press ISBN 0-88192-974-3.

[14] Sell, P. D. (1990). Some new combinations in the British Flora. *Watsonia* 18: 92.

[15] Ødum, S. (1985). Report on frost damage to trees in Denmark after the severe 1981/82 and 1984/85 winters. Hørsholm Arboretum, Denmark.

[16] Burfield, Tony (September 2002). "Cedarwood Oils". *www.users.globalnet.co.uk*. Retrieved 24 August 2016.

[17] Walston, Brent. "Cedars for Bonsai". *evergreengardenworks.com*. Retrieved 8 May 2015.

[18] Meiggs, R. 1982. Trees and Timber in the Ancient Mediterranean World.

[19] Andrews, A. C. 1961. Acclimatization of citrus fruits in the Mediterranean region. *Agricultural History* 35: 35–46.

[20] *Oxford English Dictionary*.

[21] Kelsey, H. P., & Dayton, W. A. (1942). *Standardized Plant Names*, second edition. American Joint Committee on Horticultural Nomenclature. Horace McFarland Company, Harrisburg, Pennsylvania.

3.28.8 External links

- **Media related to Cedrus at Wikimedia Commons**

- Karenplatt.co.uk: "Gold Fever" —*descriptions of golden or yellow-leaved Cedrus for gardens*.

3.29 Cedrus atlantica

Cedrus atlantica, the **Atlas cedar**, is a cedar native to the Atlas Mountains of Morocco (Middle Atlas, High Atlas), to the Rif, and to the Tell Atlas in Algeria.[2] A majority of the modern sources[3][4][5][6][7][8][9][10] treat it as a distinct species *Cedrus atlantica*, but some sources[11][12] consider it a subspecies of Lebanon cedar (*C. libani* subsp. *atlantica*).

3.29.1 Description

Fully grown, Atlas cedar is a large coniferous evergreen tree, 30–35 m (rarely 40 m) tall, with a trunk diameter of 1.5–2 m. It is very similar in all characters to the other varieties of Lebanon cedar; differences are hard to discern. The mean cone size tends to be somewhat smaller (although recorded to 12 cm,[2] only rarely over 9 cm long, compared to up to 10 cm in *C. brevifolia*, and 12 cm in *C. libani*, though with considerable overlap (all can be as short as 6 cm). The *Cedrus atlantica* leaf length (10–25 mm) is similar that of *C. libani* subsp. *stenocoma*, on average longer than *C. brevifolia* and shorter than *C. libani* subsp. *libani*, but again with considerable overlap.[2][8][13]

3.29.2 Ecology

Atlas cedar forms forests on mountainsides at 1,370 to 2,200 m, often in pure forests, or mixed with Algerian fir - *Abies numidica*, *Juniperus oxycedrus*, holm oak - *Quercus ilex*, and *Acer opalus*. These forests can provide habitat for the endangered Barbary macaque, *Macaca sylvanus*, a primate that had a prehistorically much wider distribution in northern Morocco and Algeria.[14]

Currently, Morocco has the highest total surface of Atlas cedar in the world, and it forms vast forests in the humid zones of the country, around the Middle-Atlas range, the oriental and Northern High-Atlas range, and in the Western and Central Rif mountain range. The current total area is around 163,000 hectares, of which around 115,000 hectares (80%) are situated in the Middle-Atlas mountains. The species is in danger of human use, wood mafia and fires. Data that go back to 1927 show higher number of Atlas cedars (more than 150,000 hectares) in the Middle-Atlas mountains only. The Rif mountains had one of the largest cedar forests in the past, but forests nowadays are much smaller, 15% of the total cedar forests in Morocco. Recently massive reforestation campaigns have taken place in the region of Ifrane Province.

In Algeria, the Atlas cedar has been in massive decline. According to data from 1966 the species inhabited 23,000 hectares, forming forests around the djurdjura Mountains in Kabylie and Aures Mountains. However, it is expected that it currently inhabits fewer than 15,000 hectares owing to extensive fires and human use.

3.29.3 Cultivation and uses

Landscape

C. atlantica is common in cultivation as an ornamental tree in temperate climates. In garden settings, often the glaucous forms are planted as ornamental trees, distinguished as the Glauca group, a cultivar group. Also, fastigiate, pendulous, and golden-leaf forms are in cultivation. The Atlas cedar is useful in cultivation because it is more tolerant of dry and hot conditions than most conifers.

Cedrus atlantica *foliage and mature female cone*

Male cones beginning to shed pollen

Many of the cultivated trees have glaucous (bluish) foliage, more downy shoots, and can have more leaves in each whorl; young trees in cultivation often have more ascending branches than many cultivated *C. atlantica* specimens.*[15]

An Atlas cedar is planted at the White House South Lawn in Washington, DC. President Carter ordered a tree house built within the cedar for his daughter Amy. The wooden structure was designed by the President himself, and is self-supporting so as not to cause damage to the tree.*[16]

Forestry

Cedar plantations, mainly with *C. atlantica*, have been established in southern France for timber production.

Cultural references

George Harrison references the species in his song "Beware of Darkness."

3.29.4 References

[1] Thomas, P. 2013. Cedrus atlantica. In: IUCN 2013. IUCN Red List of Threatened Species. Version 2013.1. <www.iucnredlist.org>. Downloaded on 13 July 2013.

[2] Gaussen, H. (1964). Genre *Cedrus*. Les Formes Actuelles. *Trav. Lab. For. Toulouse* T2 V1 11: 295-320

[3] Gymnosperm database *Cedrus*.

[4] GRIN Taxonomy for Plants *Cedrus*.

[5] NCBI Taxonomy Browser *Cedrus*.

[6] Flora of China vol. 4

[7] Qiao, C.-Y., Jin-Hua Ran, Yan Li and Xiao-Quan Wang (2007): Phylogeny and Biogeography of *Cedrus* (Pinaceae) Inferred from Sequences of Seven Paternal Chloroplast and Maternal Mitochondrial DNA Regions. *Annals of Botany* **100(3)**:573-580. Available online

[8] Farjon, A. (1990). *Pinaceae. Drawings and Descriptions of the Genera*. Koeltz Scientific Books ISBN 3-87429-298-3.

[9] Farjon, A. (2008). *A Natural History of Conifers*. Timber Press ISBN 0-88192-869-0.

[10] Christou, K. A. (1991). The genetic and taxonomic status of Cyprus cedar, *Cedrus brevifolia* (Hook.) Henry. Mediterranean Agronomic Institute of Chania, Greece.

[11] Güner, A., Özhatay, N., Ekim, T., & Başer, K. H. C. (ed.). 2000. *Flora of Turkey and the East Aegean Islands* 11 (Supplement 2): 5–6. Edinburgh University Press. ISBN 0-7486-1409-5

[12] Eckenwalder, J. E. (2009). *Conifers of the World: The Complete Reference*. Timber Press ISBN 0-88192-974-3.

[13] Schwarz, O. (1944). Anatolica. *Feddes Repertorium* 54: 26-34.

[14] C. Michael Hogan. 2008. *Barbary Macaque: Macaca sylvanus*, GlobalTwitcher.com, ed. N. Stromberg Archived August 31, 2009, at the Wayback Machine.

[15] Walters, W. M. (1986). *European Garden Flora* Vol 1. ISBN 0-521-24859-0.

[16] http://www.whitehousehistory.org/04/subs_pph/PresidentDetail.aspx?ID=39&imageID=4232

3.29.5 External links

- uconn.edu: *Cedrus atlantica* profile and gallery
- Gymnosperm Database - *Cedrus atlantica* (Atlas cedar) description
- PFAF Plant Database: *Cedrus atlantica* Atlas deodar cedar

3.30 Cedrus libani

Cedrus libani, commonly known as the **Cedar of Lebanon** is a species of cedar native to the mountains of the Eastern Mediterranean basin. It is an evergreen conifer that can reach 40 m in height. *Cedrus libani* is the national emblem of Lebanon and is widely used as an ornamental tree in parks and gardens.

3.30.1 Description

Cedrus libani *foliage*

Cedrus libani is an evergreen coniferous tree, it can reach 40 m (130 ft) in height with a massive monopodial columnar trunk up to 2.5 m (8 ft 2 in) in diameter.[2] The trunks of old trees ordinarily fork into several large, erect branches.[3] The rough and scaly bark is dark grey to blackish brown, it is run through by deep horizontal fissures that peel in small chips. The first-order branches are ascending in young trees; they grow to a massive size and take on a horizontal, wide-spreading disposition. Second-order branches are dense and grow in a horizontal plane. The crown is conical when young, becoming broadly tabular with age with fairly level branches; trees growing in dense forests maintain a more pyramidal shape. The shoots are dimorphic, with both long and short shoots. New shoots are pale brown, older shoots turn grey, grooved and scaly. *C. libani* has slightly resinous ovoid vegetative buds measuring 2 to 3 mm (0.079 to 0.118 in) long and 1.5 to 2 mm (0.059 to 0.079 in) wide enclosed by pale brown deciduous scales. The leaves are needle-like, arranged in spirals and concentrated at the proximal end of the long shoots, and in clusters of 15-35 on the short shoots; they are 5 to 35 mm (0.20 to 1.38 in) long and 1 to 1.5 mm (0.039 to 0.059 in) wide, rhombic in cross-section, and vary from light green to glaucous green with stomatal bands on all four sides.[2][4] *Cedrus libani* produces cones at around the age of 40; it flowers in autumn, the male cones appear in early September and the female ones in late September.[5][4] Male cones occur at the ends of the short shoots; they are solitary and erect approximately 4 to 5 cm (1.6 to 2.0 in) long and mature from a pale green to a pale brown color. The female seed cones also grow at the terminal ends of short shoots. The young seed cones are resinous, sessile and pale green; they require 17 to 18 months after pollination to mature. The mature woody cones are 8 to 12 cm (3.1 to 4.7 in) long and 3 to 6 cm (1.2 to 2.4 in) wide; they are scaly, resinous, ovoid or barrel shaped and gray-brown in color. Mature cones open from top to bottom, they disintegrate and lose their seed scales releasing the seeds until only the cone rachis remains attached to the branches.[3][4][5][6] The seed scales are thin, broad and coriaceous measuring 3.5 to 4 cm (1.4 to 1.6 in) long and 3 to 3.5 cm (1.2 to 1.4 in) wide. The seeds are ovoid, 10 to 14 mm (0.39 to 0.55 in) long and 4 to 6 mm (0.16 to 0.24 in) wide, attached to a light brown wedge-shaped wing that's 20 to 30 mm (0.79 to 1.18 in) long and 15 to 18 mm (0.59 to 0.71 in) wide.[6] *Cedrus libani* grows rapidly until the age of 45 to 50 years; growth becomes extremely slow after the age of 70 years.[5]

3.30.2 Taxonomy

Cedrus is the Latin name for true cedars.[7] The specific epithet refers the Lebanon mountain range where the species was first described by French botanist Achille

3.30. CEDRUS LIBANI

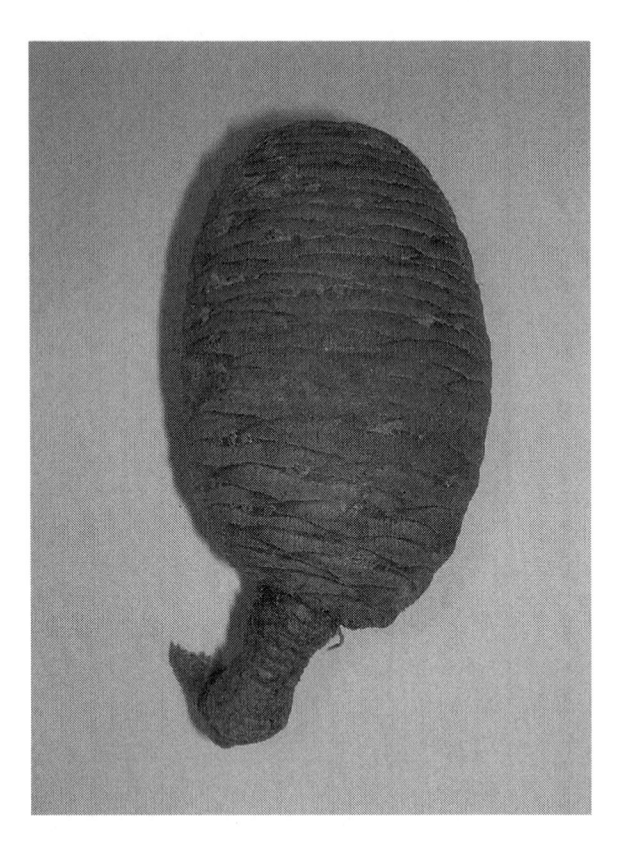

Cedar of Lebanon cone showing flecks of resin

3.30.3 Distribution and habitat

Cedrus libani var. *libani* is endemic to elevated mountains around the Eastern Mediterranean in Lebanon, Syria, and Turkey. The tree grows in well-drained calcareous lithosols on rocky, North and west-facing slopes and ridges and thrives in rich loam or a sandy clay in full sun.*[2]*[14] Its natural habitat is characterized by warm, dry summers and cool, moist winters with an annual precipitation of 1,000 to 1,500 mm (39 to 59 in); the trees get are blanketed by a heavy snow cover at the higher altitudes.*[2] In Lebanon and Turkey it occurs most abundantly at altitudes of 1,300 to 3,000 m (4,300 to 9,800 ft), where it forms pure forests or mixed forests with Cilician fir (*Abies cilicica*), European black pine (*Pinus nigra*), East Mediterranean pine (*Pinus brutia*) and several juniper species. In Turkey it can occur as low as 500 m (1,600 ft).*[15]*[2]

Cedrus libani var. *brevifolia* grows in similar conditions on medium to high mountains in Cyprus from altitudes ranging from 900 to 1,525 m (2,953 to 5,003 ft).*[15]*[2]

3.30.4 History and symbolism

Richard; the tree is commonly known as the Lebanon cedar or Cedar of Lebanon.*[2]*[8] There are two distinct types that are recognized as varieties: *C. libani* var. *libani* and *C. libani* var. *brevifolia*.*[2]

C. libani var. *libani*: Lebanon cedar, cedar of Lebanon – grows in Lebanon, western Syria, and south central Turkey. *C. libani* var. *stenocoma* (the Taurus cedar) considered a subspecies in earlier literature, is now recognized as an ecotype of *C. libani* var. *libani*. It usually has a spreading crown that doesn't flatten. This distinct morphology is a habit that's assumed to cope with the competitive environment since the tree occurs in dense stands mixed with the tall-growing *Abies cilicica,* or in pure stands of young cedar trees.*[6]

C. libani var. *brevifolia*: The Cyprus cedar occurs on the island's Troodos Mountains.*[6] This taxon was considered a separate species from *C.libani* because of morphological and ecophysiological tratit differences.*[9]*[10] It is characterized by slow growth, shorter needles and higher tolerance to drought and aphids.*[10]*[11] Genetic relationship studies however did not recognize *C. brevifolia* as a separate species, the markers being undistinguishable from those of *C. libani*.*[12]*[13]

Male cone of cedar of Lebanon

The Lebanon Cedar is mentioned several times in the Old Testament. Hebrew priests were ordered by Moses to use the bark of the Lebanon cedar in the treatment of leprosy.*[16] Solomon also procured cedar timber to build the Temple in Jerusalem.*[17] The Hebrew prophet Isaiah used the Lebanon cedar as a metaphor for the pride of the world,*[18] with the tree explicitly mentioned near the end of Psalm 92 as a symbol of the righteous.

National and regional significance

The Lebanon cedar is the national emblem of Lebanon, and is displayed on the flag of Lebanon and coat of arms of Lebanon. It is also the logo of Middle East Airlines (MEA), which is Lebanon's national carrier. Beyond that, it is also the main symbol of Lebanon's "Cedar Revolution" of 2005, along with many Lebanese political parties and movements, such as the Kataeb Party, the Lebanese Forces, the National Liberal Party, and the Future Movement. Finally, Lebanon is sometimes metonymically referred to as the Land of the Cedars.*[19]*[20]

3.30.5 Uses

The Lebanese flag, with the Lebanon cedar in the middle

Horticultural use

The Lebanon cedar is widely planted as an ornamental tree in parks and gardens.*[21]*[22]

It is unknown when the first cedar of Lebanon was planted in Britain, but it dates at least to 1664, when it is mentioned in *Sylva, or A Discourse of Forest-Trees and the Propagation of Timber*.*[23] In Britain, cedars of Lebanon are known for their use in London's Highgate Cemetery.*[21]

C. libani has gained the Royal Horticultural Society's Award of Garden Merit.*[24]

Other uses

Cedar wood is very prized for its fine grain, attractive yellow color and fragrance. It is exceptionally durable and immune to insect ravages. Wood from *C. libani* has a density of 560 kg/m^3; it is used for furniture, construction and handicrafts. In Turkey, shelterwood cutting and clearcutting techniques are used to harvest timber and promote uniform forest regeneration. Cedar resin (cedria) and cedar essential oil (cedrum) are prized extracts from the timber and cones of the cedar tree.*[25]*[26]

3.30.6 Ecology and conservation

Historically, there were various attempts at conserving the Lebanon cedars. The first was made by the Roman emperor Hadrian; he created an imperial forest and ordered it marked by inscribed boundary stones, two of which are in the museum of the American University of Beirut.*[27]

Over the centuries, extensive deforestation has occurred, with only small remnants of the original forests surviving. Deforestation has been particularly severe in Lebanon and on Cyprus; on Cyprus, only small trees up to 25 m (82 ft) tall survive, though Pliny the Elder recorded cedars 40 m (130 ft) tall there.*[28] Extensive reforestation of cedar is carried out in the Mediterranean region. In Turkey, over 50 million young cedars are planted annually; covering an area of approximately 300 square kilometres (74,000 acres).*[29]*[30] Lebanese cedar populations are also expanding through an active program combining replanting and protection of natural regeneration from browsing goats, hunting, forest fires, and woodworms.*[30] The Lebanese approach emphasizes natural regeneration by creating proper growing conditions. The Lebanese state has created several reserves including the Chouf Cedar Reserve, the Jaj Cedar Reserve, the Tannourine Reserve, the Ammouaa and Karm Shbat Reserves in the Akkar district, and the Forest of the Cedars of God near Bsharri.*[31]*[32]*[33]

3.30.7 Diseases and pests

C. libani is susceptible to a number of soil-borne, foliar and stem pathogens. The seedlings are prone to fungal attacks. *Botrytis cinerea*, a necrotrophic fungus that is known to cause considerable damage to food crops, attacks the cedar needles causing them to turn yellow and drop. *Armillaria mellea* (commonly known as honey fungus) is a basidiomycete that fruits in dense clusters at the base of trunks or stumps and attacks the roots of cedars growing in wet soils. The Lebanese cedar shoot moth (*Parasyndemis cedricola*) is a species of moth of the family Tortricidae found in the forests of Lebanon and Turkey; its larvae feed on young cedar leaves and buds.*[25]

3.30.8 See also

- Cedar Forest - Lebanon cedar forest that was home to the gods in Ancient Mesopotamian religion.
- Cedars of God - an old-growth *Cedrus libani* forest and World Heritage Site.
- Cedar (disambiguation)

3.30.9 References

[1] Gardner, M. (2013). "Cedrus libani". *IUCN Red List of Threatened Species*. IUCN. **2013**: e.T46191675A46192926. doi:10.2305/IUCN.UK.2013-1.RLTS.T46191675A46192926.en. Retrieved 27 August 2016.

[2] Farjon 2010, p.258

[3] Masri 1995

[4] Hemery & Simblet 2014, p.53

[5] CABI 2013, pp. 116

[6] Farjon 2010, p.259

[7] Farjon 2010, p.254

[8] Bory 1823, p.299

[9] Debazac 1964

[10] Ladjal 2001

[11] Fabre et al. 2001, pp. 88–89

[12] Fady et al. 2000

[13] Kharrat 2006, p.282

[14] "Cedrus libani Cedar Of Lebanon PFAF Plant Database". *pfaf.org*. Plants For A Future. Retrieved 2017-01-06.

[15] Conifer Specialist Group (1998). "*Cedrus libani*". *IUCN Red List of Threatened Species. Version 2006*. International Union for Conservation of Nature. Retrieved 12 May 2006.

[16] Leviticus 14:1-4

[17] "Welcome to Our Lady Of Lebanon Maronite Church's Homepage". Retrieved 19 July 2016.

[18] Isaiah 2:13

[19] Erman 1927, p.261

[20] Cromer 2004, p.58

[21] Hemery & Simblet 2014, p.55

[22] Howard 1955, p.168

[23] Hemery & Simblet 2014, p. 54.

[24] *Cedrus libani*: cedar of Lebanon, Royal Horticultural Society.

[25] CABI 2013, p. 117

[26] Coxe 1808, p.CED

[27] Shackley, p. 420–421

[28] Willan, R. G. N. (1990). The Cyprus Cedar. *Int. Dendrol. Soc. Yearbk*. 1990: 115-118.

[29] Anon. *History of Turkish Forestry*. Turkish Ministry of Forestry.

[30] Khuri, S., & Talhouk, S. N. (1999). Cedar of Lebanon. Pages 108-111 in Farjon, A., & Page, C. N. *Status Survey and Conservation Action Plan: Conifers*. IUCN/SSC Conifer Specialist Group. ISBN 2-8317-0465-0.

[31] Talhouk & Zurayk 2004, p.411–414

[32] Semaan, M. & Haber, R. 2003. In situ conservation on *Cedrus libani* in Lebanon. *Acta Hort*. 615: 415-417.

[33] Cedars of Lebanon Nature Reserve Archived 19 May 2012 at the Wayback Machine.

3.30.10 Bibliography

- CABI (2013-01-01). Praciak, Andrew, ed. *The CABI Encyclopedia of Forest Trees*. Centre for Agriculture and Bioscience International. ISBN 9781780642369.

- Coxe, John Redman (1808-01-01). *The Philadelphia Medical Dictionary: Containing a Concise Explanation of All the Terms Used in Medicine, Surgery, Pharmacy, Botany, Natural History, Chymistry, and Materia Medica*. Thomas Dobson; Thomas and George Palmer, printers.

- Cromer, Gerald (2004-01-01). *A War of Words: Political Violence and Public Debate in Israel*. Frank Cass. ISBN 9780714656311.

- Dagher-Kharrat, Magida Bou; Mariette, Stéphanie; Lefèvre, François; Fady, Bruno; March, Ghislaine Grenier-de; Plomion, Christophe; Savouré, Arnould (2006-11-21). "Geographical diversity and genetic relationships among Cedrus species estimated by AFLP". *Tree Genetics & Genomes*. **3** (3): 275–285. doi:10.1007/s11295-006-0065-x. ISSN 1614-2942.

- Debazac, E. F. (1964-01-01). *Manuel des conifères* (in French). École nationale des eaux et forêts.

- Eckenwalder, James E. (2009-11-14). *Conifers of the World: The Complete Reference*. Timber Press. ISBN 9780881929744.

- Erman, Adolf (1927-01-01). *The Literature of the Ancient Egyptians: Poems, Narratives, and Manuals of Instruction, from the Third and Second Millennia B. C.* Methuen & Company, Limited.

- Fabre, JP; Bariteau, M; Chalon, A; Thevenet, J (2001). "Possibilités de multiplication de pucerons Cedrobium laportei Remaudiére (Homoptera, Lachnidae) sur différentes provenances du genre Cedrus et sur deux hybrides d'espéces, perpectives d'utilisation en France". *International meeting on sylviculture of cork oak (Quercus suber L.) and Atlas cedar (Cedrus atlantica Manetti)*. Rabat, Morocco.

- Fady, B.; Lefèvre, F.; Reynaud, M.; Vendramin, G. G.; Bou Dagher-Kharrat, M.; Anzidei, M.; Pastorelli, R.; Savouré, A.; Bariteau, M. (2003-10-01). "Gene flow among different taxonomic units: evidence from nuclear and cytoplasmic markers in Cedrus plantation forests". *TAG. Theoretical and applied genetics. Theoretische und angewandte Genetik*. **107** (6): 1132–1138. doi:10.1007/s00122-003-1323-z. ISSN 0040-5752. PMID 14523524.

- Farjon, Aljos (2010-04-27). *A Handbook of the World's Conifers (2 Vols.)*. BRILL. ISBN 9004177183.

- Greuter, W.; Burdet, H.M.; Long, G., eds. (1984). "A critical inventory of vascular plants of the circum-mediterranean countries". *ww2.bgbm.org*. Botanic Garden and Botanical Museum, Berlin. Retrieved 2017-01-10.

- Güner, Adil, ed. (2001-04-09). *Flora of Turkey and the East Aegean Islands: Flora of Turkey, Volume 11* (1 ed.). Edinburgh University Press. ISBN 9780748614097.

- Hemery, Gabriel; Simblet, Sarah (2014-10-21). *The New Sylva: A Discourse of Forest and Orchard Trees for the Twenty-First Century*. A&C Black. ISBN 9781408835449.

- Howard, Frances (1955-01-01). *Ornamental Trees: An Illustrated Guide to Their Selection and Care*. University of California Press. ISBN 9780520007956.

- Mehdi, Ladjal, (2001-01-01). "Variabilité de l'adaptation à la sécheresse des cèdres méditerranéens (Cedrus atlantica, C. Brevifolia et C. Libani) : aspects écophysiologiques". *Doctorate thesis, Université Henri Poincaré Nancy 1. Faculté des sciences et techniques* – via www.theses.fr.

- Masri, Rania (1995), "The Cedars of Lebanon: significance, awareness and management of the Cedrus libani in Lebanon", *Cedars awareness and salvation effort lecture, Massachusetts Institute of Technology seminar on the environment in Lebanon*, Massachusetts Institute of Technology

- Shackley, Myra (2004-10-01). "Managing the Cedars of Lebanon: Botanical Gardens or Living Forests?". *Current Issues in Tourism*. **7** (4-5): 417–425. doi:10.1080/13683500408667995. ISSN 1368-3500.

- Saint-Vincent, Bory de (1823-01-01). *Dictionnaire classique d'histoire naturelle* (in French). **3**. Paris: Rey et Gravier. p. 299.

- Talhouk, Salma; Zurayk, Rami (2003). "Conifer conservation in Lebanon". *Acta Horticulturae*. International Society for Horticultural Science. **615**: 411–414. doi:10.17660/ActaHortic.2003.615.46.

3.30.11 External links

- *Cedrus libani* - information, genetic conservation units and related resources. European Forest Genetic Resources Programme (EUFORGEN)

3.31 Celtis

This article is about the genus of plants. For other uses, see Celtis (disambiguation).

Celtis, commonly known as **hackberries** or **nettle trees**, is a genus of about 60–70 species of deciduous trees widespread in warm temperate regions of the Northern Hemisphere, in southern Europe, southern and eastern Asia, and southern and central North America, south to central Africa, and northern and central South America. The genus is present in the fossil record at least since the Miocene of Europe, and Paleocene of North America and eastern Asia.[1][2][3]

Previously included either in the elm family (Ulmaceae) or a separate family, Celtidaceae, the APG III system places *Celtis* in an expanded hemp family (Cannabaceae).[4][5] The generic name originated in Latin and was applied by Pliny the Elder (23–79) to the unrelated *Ziziphus lotus*.[6]

3.31.1 Description

Celtis species are generally medium-sized trees, reaching 10–25 m (35–80 ft) tall, rarely up to 40 m (130 ft) tall.

3.31. CELTIS

The leaves are alternate, simple, 3–15 cm (1 ¼–6 in) long, ovate-acuminate, and evenly serrated margins. Diagnostically, *Celtis* can be very similar to trees in Rosaceae and other rose motif families.

Small monoecious flowers appear in early spring while the leaves are still developing. Male flowers are longer and fuzzy. Female flowers are greenish and more rounded.

The fruit is a small drupe 6–10 mm (¼–⅜ in) in diameter, edible in many species, with a dryish but sweet, sugary consistency, reminiscent of a date

3.31.2 Selected species

Clusters of staminate (male) flowers of C. africana, *with 4 tepals and 4 stamens each*

Leaf of C. occidentalis

- *Celtis africana* Burm.f. – white stinkwood (Afrotropical region)
- *Celtis australis* L. – European hackberry, European nettle tree or lote tree
- *Celtis balansae* Planch. (New Caledonia (Australia))
- *Celtis biondii* Pamp.
- *Celtis brasiliensis* Planch.
- *Celtis bungeana* L. – Bunge's hackberry
- *Celtis caucasica* L. – Caucasian hackberry
- *Celtis conferta* Planch. – cotton-wood
    - *Celtis conferta* subsp. *conferta* – New Caledonia
    - *Celtis conferta* subsp. *amblyphylla* – Lord Howe Island
- *Celtis durandii* Engl.
  [syn. *C. gomphophylla* Bak.]

- *Celtis ehrenbergiana* (Klotzsch) Liebm. – spiny hackberry, *granjeno* (Spanish) (southern US, Mexico, Greater Antilles, northern South America)
- *Celtis hypoleuca* Planch. (New Caledonia (Australia))
- *Celtis iguanaea* (Jacq.) Sarg. – iguana hackberry (Florida (US), Mexico, Caribbean, Central & South America)
- *Celtis integrifolia* L. – African hackberry
- *Celtis jessoensis* Koidz. – Japanese hackberry (Japan & Korea)
- *Celtis koraiensis* L. – Korean hackberry
- *Celtis labilis* L. – Hubei hackberry
- *Celtis laevigata* Willd. – southern or sugar hackberry (southern US / Texas), sugarberry (eastern USA, northeastern Mexico)

- *Celtis lindheimeri* Engelm. ex K.Koch – Lindheimer's hackberry (Texas (US), Coahuila (Mexico))

- *Celtis loxensis* C.C.Berg

- *Celtis luzonica* Warb. (Philippines)

- *Celtis mildbraedii* Engl.

- *Celtis occidentalis* L. – common or northern hackberry, false elm (eastern North America)

- *Celtis pallida* Torr. – desert or shiny hackberry (southwestern US / Texas, northern Mexico)

- *Celtis paniculata* (Endl.) Planch. – whitewood (eastern Malesia, eastern Australia, Micronesia, western Polynesia)

- *Celtis philippensis* Planch.

- *Celtis planchoniana* K.I.Chr. (eastern Europe & western Asia)

- *Celtis reticulata* Torr. – netleaf hackberry (western North America)

- *Celtis schippii* Standl.

- *Celtis sinensis* Pers. – Chinese or Japanese hackberry, Chinese nettle tree (China & Japan)
  [syn. *C. japonica* Planch.; *C. sinensis* var. *japonica* (Planch.) Nakai; *C. tetrandra* ssp. *sinensis* (Roxb.) Y.C.Tang]

- *Celtis tala* Gillet ex Planch. – tala (South America)

- *Celtis tenuifolia* Nutt. – dwarf hackberry (e North America)

- *Celtis tetranda* Roxb.

- *Celtis timorensis* Span. – kayu busok

- *Celtis tournefortii* L. – Oriental hackberry

- *Celtis triflora* (Klotzsch) Ruiz ex Miq.

- *Celtis trinervia* Lam. – almex

    additional list source[7][8]

Formerly placed here

- *Trema cannabina* Lour. (as *C. amboinensis* Willd.)

- *Trema lamarckiana* (Schult.) Blume (as *C. lamarckiana* Schult.)

- *Trema orientalis* (L.) Blume (as *C. guineensis* Schumach. or *C. orientalis* L.)

- *Trema tomentosa* (Roxb.) H.Hara (as *C. aspera* Brongn. or *C. tomentosa* Roxb.)[9]

3.31.3 Uses and ecology

Several species are grown as ornamental trees, valued for their drought tolerance. They are a regular feature of arboreta and botanical gardens, particularly in North America. Chinese hackberry (*C. sinensis*) is suited for bonsai culture, while a magnificent specimen in Daegu-myeon is one of the natural monuments of South Korea. Some, including common hackberry (*C. occidentalis*) and *C. brasiliensis*, are honey plants and pollen source for honeybees of lesser importance. Hackberry wood is sometimes used in cabinetry and woodworking.

The berries are often eaten locally. The Korean tea *gamro cha* (☒☒☒, 甘露茶) contains *C. sinensis* leaves.

Lepidoptera

Celtis species are used as food plants by the caterpillars of certain Lepidoptera. These include mainly brush-footed butterflies, most importantly the distinct genus *Libythea* (beak butterflies) and some Apaturinae (emperor butterflies):

*Common beak (*Libythea lepita*) caterpillars feed on* Celtis

- *Acytolepis puspa* (common hedge blue) – recorded on Chinese hackberry (*C. sinensis*)

- *Automeris io* (Io moth) – recorded on southern hackberry (*C. laevigata*)

- *Asterocampa celtis* (hackberry butterfly, hackberry emperor)

- A putative new taxon of the two-barred flasher (*Astraptes fulgerator*) cryptic species complex, provisionally called "CELT," has hitherto only been found on *C. iguanaea*.[10]

- *Libythea celtis* (European beak)

- *Libythea labdaca* (African beak)

- *Libythea lepita* (common beak)

- *Libythea myrrha* (club beak) – recorded on *C. tetranda*

- *Nymphalis xanthomelas* (scarce tortoiseshell) – recorded on European hackberry (*C. australis*)

- *Sasakia charonda* (great purple emperor) – recorded on Japanese hackberry (*C. jessoensis*) and pseudo-hackberry (*C. japonica*)

Pathogens

The plant pathogenic basidiomycete fungus *Perenniporia celtis* was first described from a *Celtis* host plant. Some species of *Celtis* are threatened by habitat destruction.

3.31.4 Gallery

- *Celtis aetnensis* with mature fruit

- Caucasian hackberry (*Celtis caucasica*) with immature fruit

- African hackberry (*Celtis integrifolia*)

- Chinese hackberry (*Celtis sinensis*)

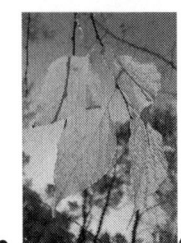

- *Celtis australis* autumn leaves

3.31.5 Footnotes

[1] Keeler (1900): pp.249–252.

[2] MacPhail et. al. (1994): pp. 231.

[3] Manchester, S. R., Akhmetiev, M. A., & Kodrul, T. M. (2002). Leaves and fruits of *Celtis aspera* (Newberry) comb. nov. (Celtidaceae) from the Paleocene of North America and eastern Asia. International Journal of Plant Sciences, 163(5), 725-736.

[4] Stevens, P.F., *Angiosperm Phylogeny Website: Cannabaceae*

[5] "Celtis" . *Germplasm Resources Information Network (GRIN)*. Agricultural Research Service (ARS), United States Department of Agriculture (USDA). Retrieved February 12, 2012.

[6] Quattrocchi, Umberto (2000). *CRC World Dictionary of Plant Names*. I A–C. CRC Press. p. 468. ISBN 978-0-8493-2675-2.

[7] "*Celtis ehrenbergiana* (Klotzsch) Liebm." . GRIN. USDA. 2002-01-10. Retrieved April 16, 2009.

[8] "*Celtis sinensis* Pers.". GRIN. USDA. Retrieved July 2, 2009.

[9] "GRIN Species Records of *Celtis*". *Germplasm Resources Information Network*. United States Department of Agriculture. Retrieved 2010-12-04.

[10] Hébert et al. (2004), Brower et al. (2006)

3.31.6 References

- Brower, Andrew V.Z. (2006). Problems with DNA barcodes for species delimitation: 'ten species' of *Astraptes fulgerator* reassessed (Lepidoptera: Hesperiidae). *Systematics and Biodiversity* **4**(2): 127–132. doi:10.1017/S147720000500191X PDF fulltext

- MacPhail, M. K., N. F. Alley, E. M. Truswell and I. R. K. Sluiter (1994). "Early Tertiary vegetation: evidence from spores and pollen." *History of the Australian Vegetation: Cretaceous to Recent.* Ed. Robert S. Hill. Cambridge University Press. pp. 189–261. ISBN 0521401976. Partially available on Google Books.

- Keeler, Harriet L. (1900). *Our Native Trees and How to Identify Them.* Originally published by Charles Scribner's Sons, New York. Facsimile edition from a scan of the first edition published 2005 by The Kent State University Press, Ohio. ISBN 0873388380. Available online through Google Books.

- Hébert, Paul D.N.; Penton, Erin H.; Burns, John M.; Janzen, Daniel H. & Hallwachs, Winnie (2004). Ten species in one: DNA barcoding reveals cryptic species in the semitropical skipper butterfly *Astraptes fulgerator*. *PNAS* **101**(41): 14812-14817. doi:10.1073/pnas.0406166101 PDF fulltext Supporting Appendices

3.32 Chaenomeles

Chaenomeles is a genus of three species of deciduous spiny shrubs, usually 1–3 m tall, in the family Rosaceae. They are native to Japan, Korea, China, Bhutan, and Burma. (Burmese: ▨▨▨▨▨▨▨▨) These plants are related to the quince (*Cydonia oblonga*) and the Chinese quince (*Pseudocydonia sinensis*), differing in the serrated leaves that lack fuzz, and in the flowers, borne in clusters, having deciduous sepals and styles that are connate at the base.

The leaves are alternately arranged, simple, and have a serrated margin. The flowers are 3–4.5 cm diameter, with five petals, and are usually bright orange-red, but can be white or pink; flowering is in late winter or early spring. The fruit is a pome with five carpels; it ripens in late autumn.

Chaenomeles is used as a food plant by the larvae of some Lepidoptera species including Brown-tail and the leafminer *Bucculatrix pomifoliella*.

3.32.1 Common names

Although all quince species have flowers, gardeners in the West often refer to these species as "flowering quince", since *Chaenomeles* are grown ornamentally for their flowers, not for their fruits. These plants have also been called "Japanese quince", and the name "japonica" (referring to *C. japonica*) was widely used for these plants in the 19th and 20th centuries, although this common name is not particularly distinctive, since *japonica* is a specific epithet shared by many other plants. The names "japonica" or "Japanese quince" were (and still are) often loosely applied to *Chaenomeles* in general, regardless of their species. The most commonly cultivated *Chaenomeles* referred to as "japonica" are actually the hybrid *C.* × *superba* and *C. speciosa*; *C. japonica* itself is not as commonly grown.

3.32.2 Species and hybrids

C. cathayensis is native to western China and has the largest fruit of the genus, pear-shaped, 10–15 cm long and 6–9 cm wide. The flowers are usually white or pink. The leaves are 7–14 cm long.

Chaenomeles japonica

C. japonica (Maule's Quince or Japanese Quince) is native to Japan, and has small fruit, apple-shaped, 3–4 cm diameter. The flowers are usually red, but can be white or pink. The leaves are 3–5 cm long.

C. speciosa (Chinese Flowering Quince; syn.: *Chaenomeles laganaria, Cydonia lagenaria, Cydonia speciosa, Pyrus japonica*) is native to China and Korea, and has hard green apple-shaped fruit 5–6 cm diameter. The flowers are shades of red, white, or flecked with red and white. The leaves are 4–7 cm long.

Four named hybrids have been bred in gardens. The most common is *C.* × *superba* (hybrid *C. speciosa* × *C. japonica*), while *C.* × *vilmoriniana* is a hybrid *C. speciosa* × *C. cathayensis*, and *C.* × *clarkiana* is a hybrid *C. japonica* × *C. cathayensis*. The hybrid *C.* × *californica* is a tri-species hybrid (*C.* × *superba* × *C. cathayensis*). Numerous named cultivars of all of these hybrids are available in the horticultural trade.

Chaenomeles *sp. bisected fruit, probably* C. speciosa *or cultivar*

Uses

The species have become popular ornamental shrubs in parts of Europe and North America, grown in gardens both for their bright flowers and as a spiny barrier. Some cultivars grow up to 2 m tall, but others are much smaller and creeping.

They are also suitable for cultivation as a bonsai.*[2]

The fruits are very hard and astringent and very unpleasant to eat raw, though they do soften and become less astringent after frost (when they are said to be "bletted"). They are, however, suitable for making liqueurs, as well as marmalade and preserves, as they contain more pectin than apples and true quinces. The fruits are sometimes used as a substitute for true quinces, though the fruit of flowering quinces is considered by some to be inferior in flavor compared to the fruit of true quinces. The fruit of flowering quinces also contains more vitamin C than lemons (up to 150 mg/100 g).

3.32.3 See also

- *Pseudocydonia sinensis* (sometimes called *Chaenomeles sinensis*)
- Quince (*Cydonia oblonga*)

3.32.4 References and external links

[1] Potter, D., et al. (2007). Phylogeny and classification of Rosaceae. *Plant Systematics and Evolution*. 266(1–2): 5–43. [Referring to the subfamily by the name "Spiraeoideae"]

[2] D'Cruz, Mark. "Ma-Ke Bonsai Care Guide for *Chaenomeles japonica*". Ma-Ke Bonsai. Retrieved 2011-07-08.

3.32.5 External links

- *Chaenomeles speciosa* entry in Plants for a Future database
- University of Arkansas Division of Agriculture: Flowering Quince, Japonica: *Chaenomeles speciosa*

3.33 Chamaecyparis obtusa

Chamaecyparis obtusa (**Japanese cypress**, **hinoki cypress***[2] or **hinoki**; Japanese: 檜 or 桧, *hinoki*) is a species of cypress native to central Japan.*[3]*[4]

It is a slow-growing tree which grows to 35 m tall with a trunk up to 1 m in diameter. The bark is dark red-brown. The leaves are scale-like, 2–4 mm long, blunt tipped (obtuse), green above, and green below with a white stomatal band at the base of each scale-leaf. The cones are globose, 8–12 mm diameter, with 8–12 scales arranged in opposite pairs. The related *Chamaecyparis pisifera* (sawara cypress) can be readily distinguished in its having pointed tips to the leaves and smaller cones.*[3]*[4]

3.33.1 Spreading and uses

Foliage; underside showing white stomatal lines

The plant is spread in Japan. A similar cypress found on Taiwan is treated by different botanists as either a variety of this species (as *Chamaecyparis obtusa* var. *formosana*) or as a separate species *Chamaecyparis taiwanensis*; it differs in having smaller cones (6–9 mm diameter) with smaller scales, and leaves with a more acute apex.[3][4]

It is grown for its very high quality timber in Japan, where it is used as a material for building palaces, temples, shrines, traditional *noh* theatres, baths, table tennis blades and masu. The wood is lemon-scented, light pinkish-brown, with a rich, straight grain, and is highly rot-resistant.

For example, Horyuji Temple and Osaka Castle are built from hinoki wood. The hinoki grown in Kiso, used for building Ise Shrine, are called 御神木 *go-shin-boku* "divine tree".

It is also a popular ornamental tree in parks and gardens, both in Japan and elsewhere in temperate climates, including western Europe and parts of North America. A large number of cultivars have been selected for garden planting, including dwarf forms, forms with yellow leaves, and forms with congested foliage. It is also often grown as bonsai.

Hinoki wood is used as a traditional Japanese stick incense for its light, earthy aroma.

Hinoki (and sugi) pollen is a major cause of hay fever in Japan.

Cultivars

Over 200 cultivars have been selected, varying in size from trees as large as the wild species, down to very slow-growing dwarf plants under 30 cm high. A few of the best known are:[5][6][7]

- *Crippsii* makes a broad conic golden-green crown with a vigorous leading shoot, growing to 15–20 m or more tall.

- *Flabelliformis* is a dwarf growing with pale green leaves.

- *Kosteri* is a dwarf with brilliant green foliage.

- *Lycopodioides* reaches up to 19 m tall, with somewhat fasciated foliage.

- *Minima* under 10 cm after 20 years with mid-green foliage.

- *Nana Aurea* has golden tips to the fans and a bronze tone in winter.

- *Nana Gracilis* has crowded fans of tiny branches producing richly textured effects; it is often cited as a dwarf but has reached 11 m tall in cultivation in Britain.

- *Nana Lutea* A compact, slow-growing, golden yellow selection which has become very popular. A yellow counterpart to 'Nana gracilis'.

- *Spiralis* is an erect, stiff dwarf tree.

- *Tempelhof* which grows to 2–4 metres has a green-yellow foliage that turns bronze in winter.

- *Tetragona Aurea* grows to around 18 m tall, with a narrow crown and irregular branching, the scale leaves in 4 equal ranks and branchlets tightly crowded, green and gold.

3.33.2 Chemistry

The lignans chamaecypanones A and B, obtulignolide and isootobanone can be found in the heartwood of *Chamaecyparis obtusa var. formosana*.[8] The biflavones sciadopitysin, ginkgetin, isoginkgetin, podocarpusflavone B, 7,7"-O-dimethylamentoflavone, bilobetin, podocarpusflavone A, 7-O-methylamentoflavone, amentoflavone and hinokiflavone have been confirmed in the leaves of the plant.[9]

3.33.3 Images

- *Chamaecyparis obtusa* 'Nana Gracilis'

- Cypress bark is used as a traditional roofing material (*hiwadabuki*) at Tō-ji in Kyoto

- Illustration

-  Bonsai
-  Japanese cypress, hinoki
-  Hinoki cypress, Tanzawa Mountains, Japan

3.33.4 References

[1] Conifer Specialist Group (2000). "*Chamaecyparis obtusa*". *IUCN Red List of Threatened Species. Version 2006*. International Union for Conservation of Nature. Retrieved 11 May 2006.

[2] "BSBI List 2007". Botanical Society of Britain and Ireland. Archived from the original (xls) on 2015-02-25. Retrieved 2014-10-17.

[3] Farjon, A. (2005). *Monograph of Cupressaceae and Sciadopitys*. Kew: Royal Botanic Gardens. ISBN 1-84246-068-4.

[4] Rushforth, K. (1987). *Conifers*. Helm. ISBN 0-7470-2801-X.

[5] Lewis, J. (1992). *The International Conifer Register Part 3: The Cypresses*. London: Royal Horticultural Society.

[6] Welch, H.; Haddow, G. (1993). *The World Checklist of Conifers*. Landsman's. ISBN 0-900513-09-8.

[7] Tree Register of the British Isles

[8] Kuo, Y.-H.; Chen, C.-H.; Chiang Y.-M. (September 2001). "Three novel and one new lignan, chamaecypanones A, B, obtulignolide and isootobanone from the heartwood of Chamaecyparis obtusa var. formosana". *Tetrahedron Lett.* **42** (38): 6731–6735. doi:10.1016/S0040-4039(01)01272-2.

[9] Krauze-Baranowska, M.; Pobłocka, L.; El-Hela, A. A. (September–October 2005). "Biflavones from Chamaecyparis obtusa". *Z. Naturforsch. C.* **60** (9–10): 679–685. PMID 16320608.

3.33.5 External links

Media related to Chamaecyparis obtusa at Wikimedia Commons

3.34 Chamaecyparis pisifera

Chamaecyparis pisifera (**sawara cypress** or **sawara** Japanese: サワラ *Sawara*) is a species of false cypress, native to central and southern Japan, on the islands of Honshū and Kyūshū.[1][2]

It is a slow-growing coniferous tree growing to 35–50 m tall with a trunk up to 2 m in diameter. The bark is red-brown, vertically fissured and with a stringy texture. The foliage is arranged in flat sprays; adult leaves are scale-like, 1.5–2 mm long, with pointed tips (unlike the blunt tips of the leaves of the related *Chamaecyparis obtusa* (hinoki cypress), green above, green below with a white stomatal band at the base of each scale-leaf; they are arranged in opposite decussate pairs on the shoots. The juvenile leaves, found on young seedlings, are needle-like, 4–8 mm long, soft and glaucous bluish-green. The cones are globose, 4–8 mm diameter, with 6–10 scales arranged in opposite pairs, maturing in autumn about 7–8 months after pollination.[1]

A related cypress found on Taiwan, *Chamaecyparis formosensis* (Formosan cypress), differs in longer ovoid cones 6–10 mm long with 10–16 scales.[1] The extinct Eocene species *Chamaecyparis eureka*, known from fossils found on Axel Heiberg Island in Canada, is noted to be very similar to *C. pisifera*.[3]

3.34.1 Uses

It is grown for its timber in Japan, where it is used as a material for building palaces, temples, shrines and baths, and making coffins, though less valued than the timber of *C. obtusa*. The wood is lemon-scented and light-colored with a rich, straight grain, and is rot resistant.[4]

It is also a popular ornamental tree in parks and gardens, both in Japan and elsewhere in temperate climates including western Europe and parts of North America. A large number of cultivars have been selected for garden planting, including dwarf forms, forms with yellow or blue-green leaves, and forms retaining the juvenile needle-like foliage; particularly popular juvenile foliage cultivars include 'Plumosa', 'Squarrosa' and 'Boulevard'.*[4]

3.34.2 References

[1] Farjon, A. (2005). *Monograph of Cupressaceae and Sciadopitys*. Royal Botanic Gardens, Kew. ISBN 1-84246-068-4

[2] Conifer Specialist Group (1998). "*Chamaecyparis pisifera*". *IUCN Red List of Threatened Species*. Version 2006. International Union for Conservation of Nature. Retrieved 12 May 2006.

[3] Kotyk, M.E.A.; Basinger, J.F.; McIlver, E.E. (2003). "Early Tertiary *Chamaecyparis* Spach from Axel Heiberg Island, Canadian High Arctic". *Canadian Journal of Botany*. **81**: 113–130. doi:10.1139/B03-007.

[4] Dallimore, W., & Jackson, A. B. (1966). *A Handbook of Coniferae and Ginkgoaceae* 4th ed. Arnold.

-  Grove of 80-year-old trees
- 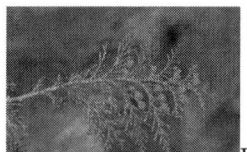 Foliage and cones
-  Central trunk of a tree
-  Bark
-  Bonsai example
-  Foliage of the juvenile cultivar 'Boulevard', with soft feathery needle-like leaves
-  Cultivar 'Golden Charm'
-  Cultivar 'Filifera aurea'
-  leaves of the Filifera aurea

3.34.3 External links

- Conifers Around the World: Chamaecyparis pisifera - sawara cypress.

3.35 Cherry blossom

"Cherry Blossom" and "Sakura" redirect here. For other uses, see Cherry Blossom (disambiguation) and Sakura (disambiguation).

3.35. CHERRY BLOSSOM

A **cherry blossom** is the flower of any of several trees

Cherry blossoms at the Tokyo Imperial Palace

The Miharu Takizakura in Fukushima

Cherry blossom tree in bloom at the Pittock Mansion in Oregon

of genus *Prunus*, particularly the **Japanese cherry**, *Prunus serrulata*, which is called **sakura** after the Japanese (桜 or 櫻; さくら).*[1]*[2]*[3]

Currently it is widely distributed, especially in the temperate zone of the Northern Hemisphere including Japan, China, Korea, Europe, West Siberia, India, Canada, and the United States.*[4]*[5] Along with the chrysanthemum, the cherry blossom is considered the national flower of Japan.*[6]

Many of the varieties that have been cultivated for ornamental use do not produce fruit. Edible cherries generally come from cultivars of the related species *Prunus avium* and *Prunus cerasus*. Cherry blossom are also closely related to other Prunus trees such as the almond, peach, plum and apricot and more distantly to apples, pears and roses.

Cherry blossoms in Fukushima

Yachounomori Garden, Tatebayashi, Gunma, Japan

Woodblock print of Mount Fuji and cherry blossom from Thirty-six Views of Mount Fuji *by Hiroshige*

3.35.1 Flower viewing

Main article: Hanami

"Hanami" is the centuries-old practice of picnicking under a blooming *sakura* or *ume* tree. The custom is said to have started during the Nara Period (710–794) when it was *ume* blossoms that people admired in the beginning. But by the Heian Period (794–1185), cherry blossoms came to attract more attention and *hanami* was synonymous with *sakura*.*[7] From then on, in both waka and haiku, "flowers" (花 *hana*) meant "cherry blossoms". The custom was originally limited to the elite of the Imperial Court, but soon spread to samurai society and, by the Edo period, to the common people as well. Tokugawa Yoshimune planted areas of cherry blossom trees to encourage this. Under the *sakura* trees, people had lunch and drank sake in cheerful feasts.

Every year the Japanese Meteorological Agency and the public track the *sakura zensen* (cherry blossom front) as it moves northward up the archipelago with the approach of warmer weather via nightly forecasts following the weather segment of news programs. The blossoming begins in Okinawa in January and typically reaches Kyoto and Tokyo at the end of March or the beginning of April. It proceeds into areas at the higher altitudes and northward, arriving in Hokkaidō a few weeks later. Japanese pay close attention to these forecasts and turn out in large numbers at parks, shrines, and temples with family and friends to hold flower-viewing parties. *Hanami* festivals celebrate the beauty of the cherry blossom and for many are a chance to relax and enjoy the beautiful view. The custom of *hanami* dates back many centuries in Japan. The eighth-century chronicle *Nihon Shoki* (日本書紀) records *hanami* festivals being held as early as the third century AD.

Most Japanese schools and public buildings have cherry blossom trees outside of them. Since the fiscal and school year both begin in April, in many parts of Honshū, the first day of work or school coincides with the cherry blossom season.

The Japan Cherry Blossom Association developed a list of Japan's Top 100 Cherry Blossom Spots*[8] with at least one location in every prefecture.

3.35.2 Symbolism

A 100 yen coin depicting cherry blossom

In Japan, cherry blossoms symbolize clouds due to their nature of blooming *en masse*, besides being an enduring metaphor for the ephemeral nature of life,*[9] an aspect of Japanese cultural tradition that is often associated with Buddhist influence,*[10] and which is embodied in the concept of *mono no aware*.*[11] The association of the cherry blossom with *mono no aware* dates back to 18th-century scholar Motoori Norinaga.*[11] The transience of the blossoms, the exquisite beauty and volatility, has often been associated with mortality*[9] and graceful and readily acceptance of destiny and karma; for this reason, cherry blossoms are richly symbolic, and have been utilized often in Japanese art, manga, anime, and film, as well as at musical performances for ambient effect. There is at least one popular folk song, originally meant for the shakuhachi (bamboo flute), titled "Sakura", and several pop songs. The flower is also represented on all manner of consumer goods in Japan, including kimono, stationery, and dishware.

Cherry blossoms at Himeji Castle, Japan

The *Sakurakai* or Cherry Blossom Society was the name chosen by young officers within the Imperial Japanese Army in September 1930 for their secret society established with the goal of reorganizing the state along totalitarian militaristic lines, via a military coup d'état if necessary.*[12]

During World War II, the cherry blossom was used to motivate the Japanese people, to stoke nationalism and militarism among the populace.*[13] Even prior to the war, they were used in propaganda to inspire "Japanese spirit," as in the "Song of Young Japan,"exulting in "warriors"who were "ready like the myriad cherry blossoms to scatter." *[14] In 1932, Akiko Yosano's poetry urged Japanese soldiers to endure sufferings in China and compared the dead soldiers to cherry blossoms.*[15] Arguments that the plans for the Battle of Leyte Gulf, involving all Japanese ships, would expose Japan to serious danger if they failed, were countered with the plea that the Navy be permitted to "bloom as flowers of death."*[16] The last message of the forces on Peleliu was "Sakura, Sakura"—cherry blossoms.*[17] Japanese pilots would paint them on the sides of their planes before embarking on a suicide mission, or even take branches of the trees with them on their missions.*[13] A cherry blossom painted on the side of the bomber symbolized the intensity and ephemerality of life;*[18] in this way, the aesthetic association was altered such that falling cherry petals came to represent the sacrifice of youth in suicide missions to honor the emperor.*[13]*[19] The first kamikaze unit had a subunit called *Yamazakura* or wild cherry blossom.*[19] The government even encouraged the people to believe that the souls of downed warriors were reincarnated in the blossoms.*[13]

In its colonial enterprises, imperial Japan often planted cherry trees as a means of "claiming occupied territory as Japanese space" .*[13]

Cherry blossoms are a prevalent symbol in Irezumi, the traditional art of Japanese tattoos. In tattoo art, cherry blossoms are often combined with other classic Japanese symbols like koi fish, dragons or tigers.*[20]

3.35.3 Varieties and blooming

The following species, hybrids, and varieties are used for *sakura*:*[21]*[22]*[23]*[24]*[25]

- *Prunus apetala* var. *pilosa*
- *Prunus campanulata*
- *Prunus* ×*furuseana*
- *Prunus incisa* var. *incisa*
- *Prunus incisa* var. *kinkiensis*
- *Prunus* ×*introrsa*
- *Prunus* ×*kanzakura*

- *Prunus ×miyoshii*
- *Prunus padus*
- *Prunus ×parvifolia*
- *Prunus pendula*
- *Prunus ×sacra*
- *Prunus sargentii*
- *Prunus serrulata*
- *Prunus ×sieboldii*
- *Prunus ×subhirtella*
- *Prunus ×syodoi*
- *Prunus ×tajimensis*
- *Prunus ×takenakae*
- *Prunus verecunda*
- *Prunus ×yedoensis*

White cherry blossoms (sakura)

Japan has a wide variety of cherry blossoms (*sakura*); well over 200 cultivars can be found there.*[26] The most popular variety of cherry blossom in Japan is the *Somei Yoshino*. Its flowers are nearly pure white, tinged with the palest pink, especially near the stem. They bloom and usually fall within a week, before the leaves come out. Therefore, the trees look nearly white from top to bottom. The variety takes its name from the village of Somei (now part of Toshima in Tokyo). It was developed in the mid- to late-19th century at the end of the Edo period and the beginning of the Meiji period. The *Somei Yoshino* is so widely associated with cherry blossoms that *jidaigeki* and other works of fiction often depict the variety in the Edo period or earlier; such depictions are anachronisms.

Winter *sakura* or *fuyuzakura* (*Prunus subhirtella autumnalis*) begins to bloom in the fall and continues blooming sporadically throughout the winter. It is said to be a cross between *edohiganzakura*, the Tokyo Higan cherry (*P. incisa*) and *mamezakura* (*P. pendula*).*[27]

Other categories include *yamazakura*, *yaezakura*, and *shidarezakura*. The **yaezakura** have large flowers, thick with rich pink petals. The *shidarezakura*, or weeping cherry, has branches that fall like those of a weeping willow, bearing cascades of pink flowers.

3.35.4 By country

Australia

Panoramic view from the Symbolic Mountain at the Japanese gardens. The view takes in the gardens and the plains of the Cowra district across to the nearby mountains.

During World War II, a prisoner of war (POW) camp near the town of Cowra in New South Wales, Australia was the site of one of the largest prison escapes of the war, on 5 August 1944. During the Cowra breakout and subsequent rounding up of POWs, four Australian soldiers and 231 Japanese soldiers died and 108 prisoners were wounded. The Japanese War Cemetery holding the dead from the Breakout was tended to after WWII by members of the Cowra RSL and ceded to Japan in 1963. In 1971 the Cowra Tourism Development decided to celebrate this link to Japan, and proposed a Japanese garden for the town. The Japanese government agreed to support this development as a sign of thanks for the respectful treatment of their war dead; the development also received funding from the Australian government and private entities.

The garden was designed by Ken Nakajima (1914–2000), a world-renowned designer of Japanese gardens at the time. The first stage was opened in 1979, with a second stage opened in 1986.

The gardens were designed in the style of the Edo period and are a *kaiyū-shiki* or strolling garden. They are designed to show all of the landscape types of Japan. At five hectares (12 acres), the Cowra Japanese Garden is the largest Japanese garden in the Southern Hemisphere. An annual cherry blossom festival is a major event in Cowra's tourism calendar and is held in the gardens during September.

Brazil

Cherry blossom in the Botanical Garden of Curitiba, Southern Brazil

With the Japanese diaspora to Brazil, many immigrants brought seedlings of cherry trees. In São Paulo State, home to the largest Japanese community outside Japan, it is common to find them in Japan-related facilities and in some homes, usually of the cultivars *Prunus serrulata* 'Yukiwari' and *Prunus serrulata* var. *lannesiana* 'Himalaya'. Some cities, as Garça*[28] and Campos do Jordão,*[29] have annual festivals to celebrate the blooming of the trees and the Japanese culture. In the Parana State (in southern Brazil), many cities received many of these immigrants, who planted the trees, as in Apucarana,*[30] Maringá, Cascavel*[31] and especially in the capital city of Curitiba.*[32]

In the capital city of Parana, the first seedlings were brought by Japanese immigrants in the first half of the 20th century, but large quantities of them were only planted from the 1990s, with the opening of the Botanical Garden of Curitiba.*[32] Nowadays the seedlings are produced locally and used in afforestation*[33] of streets and squares – as in the Japanese Square, where there are more than 30 cherry trees around the square which were sent by the Japanese Empire to Curitiba.*[34]

Canada

Vancouver, BC is famous for its thousands of cherry trees (estimated 50,000) lining many streets and in many parks, including Queen Elizabeth Park and Stanley Park. Van-

Cherry blossoms in Vancouver

couver holds the Vancouver Cherry Blossom Festival every year.*[35] With multiple varieties and a temperate climate, they begin to bloom in February yearly and peak in April.

High Park in Toronto, Ontario features many Somei-Yoshino cherry trees (the earliest species to bloom and much loved by the Japanese for their fluffy white flowers) that were given to Toronto by Japan in 1959. Through the Sakura Project, the Japanese Consulate donated a further 34 cherry trees to High Park in 2001, plus cherry trees to various other locations like Exhibition Place, McMaster University, York University (near Calumet College and on Ottawa Road near McLaughlin College) and the University of Toronto's main (next to Robarts Library) and Scarborough campuses. Niagara Falls also has many near the Falls itself. Royal Botanical Gardens in Burlington and Hamilton was also the recipient of a number of Somei-Yoshino cherry trees that were donated by the Consulate-General of Japan in Toronto as part of the Sakura Project. The trees are located in the Arboretum and the Rock Garden and were planted to celebrate the continual strengthening of friendship between Japan and Canada. Peak bloom time at Royal Botanical Gardens is normally around the last week of April or the first week of May.

China

Cherry trees naturally grow in the middle northern or southern part of China, the area nearby the sea. However, the most famous cherry blossom parks in China reflect Japan's brief occupation of parts of China during the first half of the 20th century or the donation from Japan thereafter:

- Longwangtang Cherry Blossom Park in Lushun, Dalian, Liaoning

- East Lake Cherry Blossom Park near Wuhan University, in Donghu District, Wuhan, Hubei

A Mughal imperial poet seated in a cherry blossom garden

- Wuhan University, in Donghu District, Wuhan, Hubei
- Nanshan Botanical Garden in Nan'an District, Chongqing
- Multiple locations across Taiwan.

France

Parc de Sceaux, located in a suburb of Paris, has two orchards of cherry trees, one for white cherry blossoms (Prunus avium) and one for pink cherry blossoms (Prunus serrulata), the later with about 150 trees that attract many visitors when they bloom in early April.

Germany

The cherry blossom is a major tourist attraction in Germany's Altes Land orchard region. The largest Hanami in Germany, in Hamburg, with Japanese-style fireworks, organized by the German-Japanese society, draws tens of thousands spectators every spring. Starting in 2015, Hamburg will be allowed to bestow the title of "Cherry Blossom Queen" by the Japan Cherry Blossom Association, one of only three cities worldwide to receive this privilege. The first Cherry Blossom Queen of Hamburg will be crowned by the Cherry Blossom Queen of Japan on May 23.*[36]

In 1990, along prior sections of the Berlin Wall, Japan donated cherry blossoms to express appreciation of German

Blooming cherry blossom trees in Parc de Sceaux, France

reunification. The gift was supported by donations from the Japanese people allowing for over 9000 trees to be planted. The first trees were planted in November of that year near Glienicker Bridge. *[37]

India

Oriental white-eye in a wild Himalayan cherry

In India, cherry blossom is an attraction as well, most

notably in Himalayan states like Himachal Pradesh, Uttarakhand, Jammu & Kashmir, Sikkim & northern districts of West Bengal of Jalpaiguri and Darjeeling. Temple towns like Kalpa, Sarahan, Chitkul, Sangla and Narkanda are notable for their wild cherry blossom during spring covering Himalayan foothills. They can also be seen in various British-era botanical gardens especially in Nilgiri Hills, Garo Hills, Khasi Hills as well as in some hill stations in the Western Ghats.*[38]

Prunus cerasoides is **wild Himalayan cherry** and **sour cherry**,*[39] known in Hindi as **padma** or **padmakashtha**,*[40] is a deciduous cherry tree found in parts of East, South and Southeast Asia. It is of the family *Rosaceae* and the genus *Prunus*. Recently Kolkata municipal department and the forest department planted cherry blossoms across main city places like Rajarhat.They were in full bloom in this year (1st week of march 2017)

Netherlands

In the year 2000, the Japan Women's Club (JWC) donated 400 cherry blossom trees to the city of Amstelveen. The trees have been planted in the cherry blossom park in the Amsterdamse Bos. A special detail is that every tree has a name —200 trees have female Japanese names, 200 trees have female Dutch names.

New Zealand

In New Zealand Japanese native Yoshino cherry is called *awanui cherry* after the place the cherry trees were planted.*[41]

Korea

Cherry blossoms at POSTECH, South Korea

The origins of cherry blossoms in South Korea is contentious. The Japanese planted Yoshino cherry trees at Seoul's Changgyeonggung Palace and the viewing of cherry blossoms was introduced to Korea during Japanese rule.*[42] The festivals continued even after the Japanese surrendered at the end of WWII but have been controversial, and many cherry trees were cut down to celebrate the fiftieth anniversary of the Japanese surrender because they were seen as symbols of the occupation.*[43]*[44] Yet Koreans continued to plant Yoshino cherry trees and festivals began attracting a wide range of tourists. Many Korean media assert that the Yoshino cherry is the same species as a Korean indigenous, endangered species called king cherry, whose mass production is still being studied.*[45]*[46]*[47]*[48] In 2007, a study conducted on the comparison of king cherry and Yoshino cherry concluded that these trees were categorized as distinct species.*[49] In 2016, a study on DNA analyses suggested the independent origin between king cherry and yoshino cherry each other.*[50] In 2016, a new scientific name *Cerasus × nudiflora* was given to King cherry to distinguish it from Yoshino cherry (*Prunus × Yedoensis*). *[51] In Korea most of the places for cherry blossom festivals, including Yeouido and Jinhae, are still planted with Yoshino cherry trees.*[52]

Turkey

Cherry blossoms in Turkey. (Ankara/Dikmen Vâdisi, Spring 2016)

In 2005, Japanese cherry trees were presented by Japan to the Nezahat Gökyiğit Botanical Garden in Istanbul, Turkey. Each tree represents one sailor of the frigate *Ertogrul* which was a famous frigate of the Ottoman Turkish navy. On the way back from a goodwill visit to Japan in 1890 she ran into a typhoon and sank with loss of 587 Ottoman Turkish sailors. That loss is being remembered at every anniversary. The Japanese cherry trees represent memory of those who died and provide remembrance.

United Kingdom

Batsford Arboretum in Gloucestershire (England), holds the national collection of Japanese village cherries, sato-sakura group.*[53] Keele University in Staffordshire (England), has one of the UK's largest collections of flowering cherries, with more than 150 varieties.*[54]

United States

Cherry blossoms in Washington, D.C.

Japan gave 3,020 cherry blossom trees as a gift to the United States in 1912 to celebrate the nations' then-growing friendship, replacing an earlier gift of 2,000 trees which had to be destroyed due to disease in 1910. These trees were planted in Sakura Park in Manhattan and line the shore of the Tidal Basin and the roadway in East Potomac Park in Washington, D.C. The first two original trees were planted by first lady Helen Taft and Viscountess Chinda on the bank of the Tidal Basin. The gift was renewed with another 3,800 trees in 1965.*[55]*[56] In Washington, D.C. the cherry blossom trees continue to be a popular tourist attraction (and the subject of the annual National Cherry Blossom Festival)

Cherry blossoms in Washington D.C.

when they reach full bloom in early spring.*[57] Just outside of Washington, D.C., the suburb of Kenwood in Bethesda, Maryland has roughly 1,200 trees that are popular with locals and tourists.*[58]

New Jersey's Branch Brook Park, which is maintained by the Essex County, is the oldest county park in the United States and is home to the nation's largest collection of cherry blossom trees, with about 4,300.*[59]*[60]*[61]

Also, Balboa Park of San Diego has 2,000 cherry blossom trees that blossom in mid to late March. In Los Angeles, over 2,000 trees are located at Lake Balboa in Van Nuys. These trees were donated by an anonymous Japanese benefactor and were planted in 1992. They originated from a single parent tree and were developed to grow in warm climates.*[62]

Philadelphia is also home to over 2,000 flowering Japanese cherry trees, half of which were a gift from the Japanese government in 1926 in honor of the 150th anniversary of American independence, with the other half planted by the Japan America Society of Greater Philadelphia between 1998 and 2007. Philadelphia's cherry blossoms are located within Fairmount Park, and the annual Subaru Cherry Blossom Festival of Greater Philadelphia celebrates the blooming trees. The University of Washington in Seattle also has cherry blossoms in its Quad.

Other US cities have an annual cherry blossom festival (or *sakura matsuri*), including the International Cherry Blossom Festival in Macon, Georgia, which features over 300,000 cherry trees. The Brooklyn Botanic Garden in New York City also has a large, well-attended festival.*[63] Portsmouth, New Hampshire, is the site of the peace conference that produced the Treaty of Portsmouth, for which the original Washington, DC cherry trees were given in thanks. Several cherry trees planted on the bank of the tidal pond next to Portsmouth City Hall were the gift of Portsmouth's Japanese sister city of Nichinan—the hometown of Marquis Komura Jutarō, Japan's representative at

Cherry blossoms in Newark, New Jersey

Cherry blossoms in Owensboro, Kentucky

the conference.*[64] Ohio University in Athens, Ohio, has 200 somei yoshino trees, a gift from its sister institution, Japan's Chubu University.*[65]

3.35.5 Culinary use

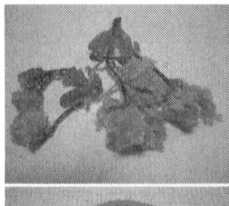

Pickled blossoms

A cup of sakurayu

Cherry blossoms and leaves are edible and both are used as food ingredients in Japan:

- The blossoms are pickled in salt and umezu (ume vinegar), and used for coaxing out flavor in wagashi, (a traditional Japanese confectionery,) or anpan, (a Japanese sweet bun, most-commonly filled with red bean paste.)

- Salt-pickled blossoms in hot water are called sakurayu, and drunk at festive events like weddings in place of green tea.

- The leaves, mostly from the Ōshima cherry because of the softness, are also pickled in salted water and used for sakuramochi.

Since the leaves contain coumarin, which is toxic in large doses, it is not recommended to eat them in great quantities.

3.35.6 See also

- Kabazaiku: sakura wood craftsmanship
- Kigo: discussion of the role of *sakura* in Japanese poetry
- List of Award of Garden Merit flowering cherries
- Ohka: Special Attack Aircraft of World War II
- Sakura Square
- Subaru Cherry Blossom Festival of Greater Philadelphia
- The Cherry Orchard

3.35.7 References

[1] The history and cultural symbolism of both the seven wild species and the hundreds of forms known for centuries as *sato-zakura*, or garden cherries and information about growing and propagating is found in Kuitert, Wybe (2015-03-06). "Japanese Flowering Cherries". Timber Press.

[2] "Sakura". *Webster's Third New International Dictionary, Unabridged*. Merriam-Webster. 2002. Retrieved 2008-04-02. Japanese flowering cherry

[3] "Japanese flowering cherry". *Webster's Third New International Dictionary, Unabridged*. Merriam-Webster. 2002. Retrieved 2008-04-02. any of certain ornamental hybrid cherries developed in Japan chiefly from two species (*Prunus serrulata* and *P. sieboldii*) that bear a profusion of white or pink usually double and often fragrant flowers followed by small inedible fruit...

[4] "財団法人日本花の会—The Flower Association of Japan". *hananokai.or.jp*.

[5] "さくらの基礎知識 - 公益財団法人日本さくらの会—JAPAN Cherry Blossom Association". *sakuranokai.or.jp*.

[6] Honoca. "The beauty and history of sakura, Japan's national flower". *Tsunagu Japa*. Retrieved 6 January 2016.

[7] Brooklyn Botanic Garden (2006). *Mizue Sawano: The Art of the Cherry Tree*. Brooklyn Botanic Garden. p. 12. ISBN 1-889538-25-6.

[8] "Japan's Top 100 Cherry Blossom Spots – GoJapanGo (English language version of list)". *Japan's Top 100 Cherry Blossom Spots – GoJapanGo*. Mi Marketing Pty Ltd. Retrieved 9 November 2011.

[9] Choy Lee, Khoon. *Japan—between Myth and Reality*. 1995, page 142.

[10] Young, John and Nakajima-Okano, Kimiko. *Learn Japanese: New College Text*. 1985, page 268.

[11] Slaymaker, Douglas. *The Body in Postwar Japanese Fiction*. 2004, page 122.

[12] James L. McClain, *Japan: A Modern History* p 414 ISBN 0-393-04156-5

[13] Ohnuki-Tierney, Emiko. *Kamikaze, Cherry Blossoms, and Nationalisms*. 2002, page 9-10.

[14] Piers Brendon, *The Dark Valley: A Panorama of the 1930s*, p441 ISBN 0-375-40881-9

[15] James L. McClain, *Japan: A Modern History* p 427 ISBN 0-393-04156-5

[16] John Toland, *The Rising Sun: The Decline and Fall of the Japanese Empire 1936–1945* p 539 Random House New York 1970

[17] Meirion and Susie Harries, *Soldiers of the Sun: The Rise and Fall of the Imperial Japanese Army* p 424 ISBN 0-394-56935-0

[18] Sakamoto, Kerri: *One Hundred Million Hearts*. Vintage Book, 2004. ISBN 0-676-97512-7.

[19] Ivan Morris, *The Nobility of Failure: Tragic Heroes in the History of Japan*, p290 Holt, Rinehart and Winston, 1975

[20] "Cherry Blossom Tattoo Designs". Freetattoodesigns.org. Retrieved 2013-06-14.

[21] Origins of Japanese flowering cherry (*Prunus* subgenus *Cerasus*) cultivars revealed using nuclear SSR markers

[22] "Clone identification in Japanese flowering cherry (*Prunus* subgenus *Cerasus*) cultivars using nuclear SSR markers".

[23] "サクラ栽培品種の分類体系の再編とデータベース化" (PDF).

[24] "桜の新しい系統保全—形質・遺伝子・病害研究に基づく取組—" (PDF).

[25] "The observation of flowering dates in the Cherry Preservation Forest at the Tama Forest Science Garden over a 30 year period." (PDF).

[26] Brandow Samuels, Gayle.

[27] "Winter-flowering cherry". Retrieved 1 January 2008.

[28] "Festa da Cerejeira em Garça recebe mais de 150 mil visitantes" (in Portuguese). TV TEM. Retrieved 7 July 2015.

[29] "Festa da Cerejeira em Flor 2014 celebra a Cultura do Japão em Campos do Jordão" (in Portuguese). Guia de Campos do Jordão. Retrieved 7 July 2015.

[30] "Cerejeiras enfeitam cidade no norte do Paraná" (in Portuguese). Jornal Nacional. Retrieved 2011-07-15.

[31] "Cerejeiras enfeitam Cascavel" (in Portuguese). Globo Vídeos. Retrieved 2011-07-15.

[32] "Temporada das Cerejeiras em Curitiba" (in Portuguese). Diário Urbano. Retrieved 2011-07-15.

[33] "Novo colorido em parques e praças" (in Portuguese). Prefeitura de Curitiba. Retrieved 2011-07-15.

[34] "Japan Square". Prefeitura de Curitiba. Retrieved 2011-07-15.

[35] "Vancouver Cherry Blossom Festival – VCBF.CA". *vcbf.ca*. Retrieved 26 April 2010.

[36] "Aktuelles aus der Gesellschaft". Deutsch-Japanische Gesellschaft zu Hamburg e.V. Retrieved 2015-04-25.

[37] "The Sakura Campain - The State of Berlin". *Berlin.de*. Retrieved 2 April 2017.

[38] "Cherry Blossoms in Shillong". *mapsofindia.com*.

[39] GRIN. "*Prunus cerasoides* information from NPGS/GRIN". *Taxonomy for Plants*. USDA, ARS, National Genetic Resources Program. Retrieved January 24, 2014.

[40] Navendu Pāgé. "*Cerasus cerasoids* – Wild Himalayan Cherry". Flowers of India . Retrieved July 9, 2014. External link in |publisher= (help)

[41] "Prunus 'Awanui' (Flowering Cherry)". Moores Valley Nurseries.

[42] 가슴과어깨에벚꽃을꽃고희생다짐하는 18 세조종사 (in Korean). Joongang. Retrieved 2009-01-03.

[43] Ohnuki-Tierney, Emiko. *Kamikaze, Cherry Blossoms, and Nationalisms*. 2002, page 122-3.

[44] Choi Sung-Un (2008). "Biting the cherry: Cherry blossoms and their attendant festivals herald the spring in Korea despite associations with a dark chapter with the country's history". *IK-Journal*. Investkorea.org. Retrieved 2009-11-30.

[45] "[광복 70년・한일 50년 특별기획/제 1부 제주와 일본이야기](3) 왕벚나무 세계화" [[70 years liberation, 50 years diplomatic relations: Jeju and Japan story / Part 1. Globalization of King cherry of Jeju] (3) Outpost of Mass production]. Halla Ilbo. March 23, 2015.

[46] *Korean Red List of Threatened Species Second Edition* (PDF). National Institute of Biological Resources. 2014. p. 156. Prunus × yedoensis Matsumura, Rosales: Rosaceae, Prunus × yedoensis is a deciduous tree endemic to Korea that only about 5 populations occur at Mt. Halla in Jeju-do. The estimated number of individuals is very small. This species is found in deciduous broadleaf forests at 450-900 m above sea level. The species is assessed as EN B2ab(iv). There are currently no regional conservation measures.

[47] Kim, Chan-Soo (2009). "Vascular Plant Diversity of Jeju Island, Korea" (PDF). *Korean Journal of Plant Resources*. **22** (6): 558〜570.

[48] 몰락한왕조궁궐에핀사쿠라일제는갔어도벚꽃놀이는 남아 (in Korean). 中央日報. Retrieved 2009-05-11.

[49] Roh, M.S., Cheong, E.J., Choi, I-Y and Young, Y.H. (2007). "Characterization of wild *Prunus yedoensis* analyzed by inter-simple sequence repeat and chloroplast DNA.". *Scientia Horticulturae*. **114** (2): 121–128. doi:10.1016/j.scienta.2007.06.005. Retrieved 2011-04-19.

[50] Cho, Myong-suk; et al. (2016). "The origin of flowering cherry on oceanic islands: The saga continues in Jeju Island.". *Botany 2016*. Botanical Society of America.

[51] Katsuki, Toshio; et al. (December 2016). "Nomenclature of Tokyo cherry (Cerasus × yedoensis 'Somei-yoshino', Rosaceae) and allied interspecific hybrids based on recent advances in population genetics". *Taxon*. International Association for Plant Taxonomy. **65** (6): 1415–1419. doi:10.12705/656.13.

[52] "'벚꽃'한・일 -원조논쟁' 왜끝나지않나" [Cherry "Korea-Japan origin controversy" Why does not end?] (in Korean). Hankyoreh. April 3, 2015. 여의도와진해등 우리나라벚꽃축제의주인공은모두일본이만든 왕벚나무(소메이요시노). [The protagonists of Cherry Blossom Festivals in Korea including Yeouido and Jinhae are all cultivated Yoshino cherry made in Japan.]

[53] "Batsford Arboretum". Batsarb.co.uk. Retrieved 2009-11-30.

[54] "Keele University Arboretum flowering cherry collection". keele.ac.uk. Retrieved 2011-03-28.

[55] "nps.gov – Cherry Blossom History". Retrieved 13 January 2009.

[56] Jefferson, Roland M. and Alan F. Fusonie. (1977). "The Japanese Flowering Cherry Trees of Washington, D.C.: A Living Symbol of Friendship. National Arboretum Contribution No. 4." Washington: USDA, Agricultural Research Service.

[57] "The Nation's Greatest Springtime Celebration". National Cherry Blossom Festival. Retrieved 2013-06-14.

[58] Block, Deborah. "Spectacular Cherry Blossoms in Maryland Lure International Visitors". *VOA*. Retrieved 2016-03-24.

[59] "Student scientists track nation's largest collection of cherry blossom trees at Essex County park". The Star-Ledger. August 13, 2010. Retrieved 2012-04-10.

[60] Hinds, Kate (March 25, 2012). "Cherry Blossom Trees Flourish in Newark". WNYC. Retrieved 2012-04-10.

[61] Drew Anne, Scarantino (March 14, 2011), "In Full Bloom", *New Jersey Monthly*, retrieved 2012-04-10

[62] rap pr (2006-04-10). "The Big Bloom of Cherry Blossoms at Lake Balboa in Van Nuys". Laparks.blogspot.com. Retrieved 2013-06-14.

[63] "BBG.org". BBG.org. 2008-04-26. Retrieved 2013-06-14.

[64] Stephanie Seacord. "Cherry trees have historical significance". SeacoastOnline.com. Retrieved 2013-06-14.

[65] "Ohio University Outlook". Ohio.edu. Retrieved 2013-06-14.

3.35.8 External links

- Japanese Cherry Blossom Events & Locations
- Copenhagen Sakura Festival
- Flowering cherry Database, Forestry and Forest Products Research Institute
- Flowering cherry introduction, Forestry and Forest Products Research Institute
- International Cherry Blossom Festival Online, Information about the 300,000 Yoshino cherry trees in Macon, Georgia and the 10-day celebration held in mid-March
- Vancouver Cherry Blossom Festival, Information about the 37,000 cherry trees in Greater Vancouver (Canada), What's in bloom now, Cherry Scout reports and maps, Cultivar identification.
- Subaru Cherry Blossom Festival of Greater Philadelphia, Information about cherry trees and the annual two-week Subaru Cherry Blossom Festival of Greater Philadelphia.

3.36 Citrus

For other uses, see Citrus (disambiguation).

Citrus is a genus of flowering trees and shrubs in the rue family, Rutaceae. Plants in the genus produce **citrus fruits**, including important crops like oranges, lemons, grapefruit, pomelo and limes.

The most recent research indicates an origin in Australia, New Caledonia and New Guinea.*[1] Some researchers believe that the origin is in the part of Southeast Asia bordered by Northeast India, Burma (Myanmar) and the Yunnan province of China,*[2]*[3]*[4] and it is in this region that some commercial species such as oranges, mandarins, and lemons originated. Citrus fruit has been cultivated in an ever-widening area since ancient times.

3.36.1 History

At various times, citrus plants were thought to be native to Asia (where they were first domesticated), Europe, and Florida. But the European oranges (such as the bitter orange) were originally brought from India at around the time of Alexander the Great, and the "native" oranges of Florida actually originated with the Spanish Conquistadors.*[5]*[6] The lemon reached Europe during the time of classical Rome.

Name

The generic name originated from Latin, where it referred to either the plant now known as Citron (*C. medica*) or a conifer tree (*Thuja*). It is somehow related to the ancient Greek word for cedar, κέδρος (*kédros*). This may be due to perceived similarities in the smell of citrus leaves and fruit with that of cedar.*[7] Collectively, *Citrus* fruits and plants are also known by the Romance loanword **agrumes** (literally "sour fruits").

Evolution

The large citrus fruit of today evolved originally from small, edible berries over millions of years. Citrus plants diverged from a common ancestor about 15 million years ago, which was about when it diverged from the closely related severinia, for example the Chinese box orange. About 7 million years ago, citrus plants diverged into two groups, the main citrus genus and the ancestors of the Trifoliate orange (poncirus), which is closely enough related that it can still be hybridized with all other citrus. These estimates are made using genetic mapping of plant chloroplasts,*[8] and the evolution at that time is thought to have occurred somewhere in either southeastern Asia or Australia.*[9]

The three original species in the citrus genus that have been hybridized into most modern commercial citrus fruit are the mandarin orange, pummelo, and citron.*[10] Within the last few thousand years, all common citrus fruits (sweet oranges, lemons, grapefruit, limes, and so on) were created by crossing those original species. Something similar has occurred with the wide array of chili peppers originating in the hybridization of a few initial species.

3.36.2 Taxonomy

Main article: Citrus taxonomy

The taxonomy and systematics of the genus are complex

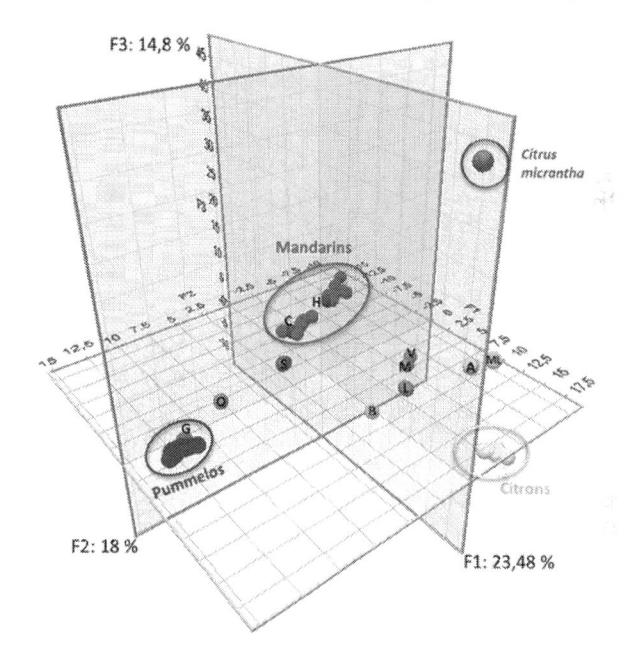

Citrus fruits clustered by genetic similarity (PCA of SNP diversity). Citrus micrantha (top right) is a papeda.

Hybrids are expected to plot between their parents. ML: 'Mexican' lime; A: 'Alemow'; V: 'Volkamer' lemon; M: 'Meyer' lemon; L: Regular and 'Sweet' lemons; B: Bergamot orange; H: Haploid clementine; C: Clementines; S: Sour oranges; O: Sweet oranges; G: Grapefruits.

and the precise number of natural species is unclear, as many of the named species are hybrids clonally propagated through seeds (by apomixis), and there is genetic evidence that even some wild, true-breeding species are of hybrid origin

Most cultivated *Citrus* seem to be natural or artificial hybrids of four core ancestral species*[11] —the citron, pummelo, mandarine, and papeda (see image).*[12] Natural and cultivated citrus hybrids include commercially important fruit such as oranges, grapefruit, lemons, limes, and some tangerines.

Apart from these four core citrus species, there are Australian limes and the recently discovered Mangshanyegan. Kumquats and *Clymenia sp.* are now generally considered to belong within the citrus genus.*[13] Trifoliate orange, which is often used as commercial rootstock, is an outgroup and may or may not be categorized as a citrus.

Phylogenetic analysis suggests the species of *Oxanthera* from New Caledonia should be transferred to the genus *Citrus*.*[14]

3.36.3 Description

Slices of various citrus fruits

Tree

These plants are large shrubs or small to moderate-sized trees, reaching 5–15 m (16–49 ft) tall, with spiny shoots and alternately arranged evergreen leaves with an entire margin. The flowers are solitary or in small corymbs, each flower 2–4 cm (0.79–1.57 in) diameter, with five (rarely four) white petals and numerous stamens; they are often very strongly scented.

Fruit

The fruit is a *hesperidium*, a specialised berry, globose to elongated, 4–30 cm (1.6–11.8 in) long and 4–20 cm (1.6–7.9 in) diameter, with a leathery rind or "peel" called a pericarp. The outermost layer of the pericarp is an "exocarp" called the flavedo, commonly referred to as the zest. The middle layer of the pericarp is the mesocarp, which in citrus fruits consists of the white, spongy "albedo", or "pith". The innermost layer of the pericarp is the endocarp. The segments are also called "liths", and the space inside each lith is a locule filled with juice vesicles, or "pulp". From the endocarp, string-like "hairs" extend into the locules, which provide nourishment to the fruit as it develops.*[15]*[16]

Citrus fruits are notable for their fragrance, partly due to flavonoids and limonoids (which in turn are terpenes) contained in the rind, and most are juice-laden. The juice contains a high quantity of citric acid giving them their characteristic sharp flavour. The genus is commercially important as many species are cultivated for their fruit, which is eaten fresh, pressed for juice, or preserved in marmalades and pickles.

They are also good sources of vitamin C and flavonoids. The flavonoids include various flavanones and flavones.*[17]

3.36.4 Cultivation

Further information: Citrus production

Citrus trees hybridise very readily – depending on the

Lemons are a citrus fruit native to Asia, but now common worldwide.

pollen source, plants grown from a Persian lime's seeds can produce fruit similar to grapefruit. Thus all commercial citrus cultivation uses trees produced by grafting the desired fruiting cultivars onto rootstocks selected for disease resistance and hardiness.

The colour of citrus fruits only develops in climates with a (diurnal) cool winter.*[18] In tropical regions with no winter at all, citrus fruits remain green until maturity, hence the tropical "green oranges". The Persian lime in particular is extremely sensitive to cool conditions, thus it is not usu-

Persian limes in a grocery store

Mediterranean Mandarin (Citrus ×deliciosa plantation, Son Carrió (Mallorca)

Leaf of Citrus tree

ally exposed to cool enough conditions to develop a mature colour. If they are left in a cool place over winter, the fruits will change colour to yellow.

The terms "ripe" and "mature" are usually used synonymously, but they mean different things. A mature fruit is one that has completed its growth phase. Ripening is the changes that occur within the fruit after it is mature to the beginning of decay. These changes usually involve starches converting to sugars, a decrease in acids and a softening and change in the fruit's colour.*[19]

Citrus fruits are non-climacteric and respiration slowly declines and the production and release of ethylene is gradual.*[20] The fruits do not go through a ripening process in the sense that they become "tree ripe." Some fruits, for example cherries, physically mature and then continue to ripen on the tree. Other fruits, like pears, are picked when mature but before they ripen, then continue to ripen off the tree. Citrus fruits pass from immaturity to maturity to over-maturity while still on the tree. Once they are separated from the tree, they will not increase in sweetness or continue to ripen. The only way change may happen after being picked is that they will eventually start to decay.

With oranges, colour cannot be used as an indicator of ripeness because sometimes the rinds turn orange long before the oranges are ready to eat. Tasting them is the only way to know whether or not they are ready to eat.

Citrus trees are not generally frost hardy. Mandarin oranges (*C. reticulata*) tend to be the hardiest of the common *Citrus* species and can withstand short periods down to as cold as −10 °C (14 °F), but realistically temperatures not falling below −2 °C (28 °F) are required for successful cultivation. Tangerines, tangors and yuzu can be grown outside even in regions with more marked sub-freezing temperatures in winter, although this may affect fruit quality. A few hardy hybrids can withstand temperatures well below freezing, but do not produce quality fruit. Lemons can be commercially grown in cooler-summer/moderate-winter, coastal Southern California, because sweetness is neither attained nor expected in retail lemon fruit. The related trifoliate orange (*Citrus trifoliata*) can survive below −20 °C (−4 °F); its fruit are astringent and inedible unless cooked but a few better-tasting cultivars and hybrids have been developed (see citranges).

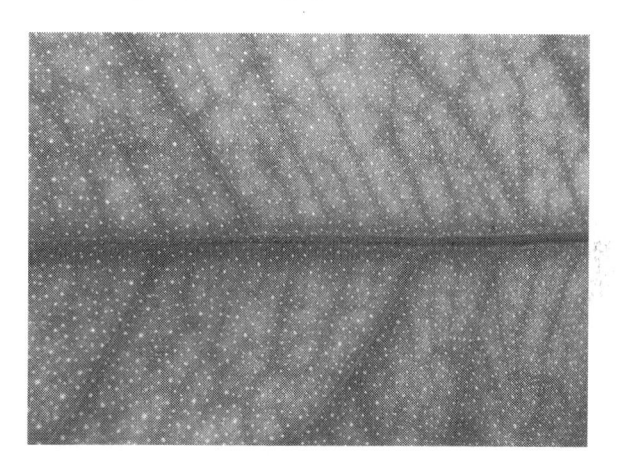

The trees thrive in a consistently sunny, humid environment with fertile soil and adequate rainfall or irrigation. Abandoned trees in valleys may suffer, yet survive, the dry summer of Central California's Inner Coast Ranges. At any age citrus grows well enough with infrequent irrigation in partial shade, but the fruit crop is smaller. Being of tropical and sub-tropical origin, oranges, like all citrus, are broadleaved and evergreen. They do not drop leaves except when stressed. The stems of many varieties have large sharp thorns. The trees flower in the spring, and fruit is set shortly afterward. Fruit begins to ripen in fall or early winter months, depending on cultivar, and develops increasing sweetness afterward. Some cultivars of tangerines ripen by winter. Some, such as the grapefruit, may take up to eighteen months to ripen.

Production

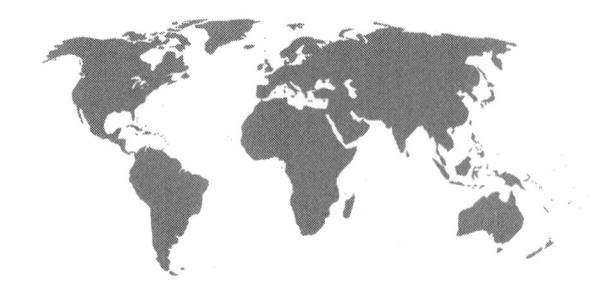

Major producer regions

See also: Citrus production

According to UN 2007 data, Brazil, China, the United States, Mexico, India, and Spain are the world's largest citrus-producing countries.

Major commercial citrus growing areas include southern China, the Mediterranean Basin (including southern Spain), South Africa, Australia, the southernmost United States, Mexico and parts of South America. In the United States, Florida, California, Arizona, and Texas are major producers, while smaller plantings are present in other Sun Belt states and in Hawaii.

As ornamental plants

Orangery of the Botanical Garden in Leuven (Belgium)

Citrus trees grown in tubs and wintered under cover were a feature of Renaissance gardens, once glass-making technology enabled sufficient expanses of clear glass to be produced. An orangery was a feature of royal and aristocratic residences through the 17th and 18th centuries. The *Orangerie* at the Palace of the Louvre, 1617, inspired imitations that were not eclipsed until the development of the modern greenhouse in the 1840s. In the United States the earliest surviving orangery is at the Tayloe House, Mount Airy, Virginia. George Washington had an orangery at Mount Vernon.

Some modern hobbyists still grow dwarf citrus in containers or greenhouses in areas where it is too cold to grow it outdoors. Consistent climate, sufficient sunlight, and proper watering are crucial if the trees are to thrive and produce fruit. Compared to many of the usual "green shrubs", citrus trees better tolerate poor container care. For cooler winter areas, limes and lemons should not be grown, since they are more sensitive to winter cold than other citrus fruits. Hybrids with kumquats (× *Citrofortunella*) have good cold resistance.

Pests and diseases

Main article: List of citrus diseases

Citrus plants are very liable to infestation by aphids,

Citrus canker is caused by the gammaproteobacterium Xanthomonas axonopodis

whitefly and scale insects (e.g. California red scale). Also rather important are the viral infections to which some of these ectoparasites serve as vectors such as the aphid-transmitted *Citrus tristeza virus* which when unchecked by proper methods of control is devastating to citrine plantations. The newest threat to citrus groves in the United States is the Asian citrus psyllid.

The Asian citrus psyllid is an aphid-like insect that feeds on the leaves and stems of citrus trees and other citrus-like plants – but the real danger lies in that it can carry a deadly, bacterial tree disease called Huanglongbing (HLB), also known as citrus greening disease."[21]

In August 2005 citrus greening disease was discovered in the south Florida region around Homestead and Florida

City. It has since spread to every commercial citrus grove in Florida. In 2004-2005 USDA Ag statistics reported the total Florida citrus production to be 169.1 million boxes of fruit. The estimate for all Florida citrus production in the 2015-2016 season is 86.4 million boxes—a 51% drop.

In June 2008, the psyllid was spotted dangerously close to California – right across the international border in Tijuana, Mexico. Only a few months later, it was detected in San Diego and Imperial counties, and has since spread to Riverside, San Bernardino, Orange, Los Angeles and Ventura counties sparking quarantines in those areas. The Asian citrus psyllid has also been intercepted coming into California in packages of fruit and plants, including citrus, ornamentals, herbs and bouquets of cut flowers, shipped from other states and countries.*[21]

The foliage is also used as a food plant by the larvae of Lepidoptera (butterfly and moth) species such as the Geometridae common emerald (*Hemithea aestivaria*) and double-striped pug (*Gymnoscelis rufifasciata*), the Arctiidae giant leopard moth (*Hypercompe scribonia*), *H. eridanus*, *H. icasia* and *H. indecisa*, many species in the family Papilionidae (swallowtail butterflies), and the black-lyre leafroller moth (*"Cnephasia" jactatana*), a tortrix moth.

Since 2000, the citrus leafminer (*Phyllocnistis citrella*) has been a pest in California,*[22] boring meandering patterns through leaves.

In eastern Australia, the bronze-orange bug (*Musgraveia sulciventris*) can be a major pest of citrus trees, particularly grapefruit. In heavy infestations it can cause flower and fruit drop and general tree stress.

European brown snails (*Cornu aspersum*) can be a problem in California, though laying female Khaki Campbell and other mallard-related ducks can be used for control.

Deficiency diseases Citrus plants can also develop a deficiency condition called chlorosis, characterized by yellowing leaves*[23] highlighted by contrasting leaf veins. The shriveling leaves eventually fall, and if the plant loses too many, it will slowly die. This condition is often caused by an excessively high pH (alkaline soil), which prevents the plant from absorbing iron, magnesium, zinc, or other nutrients it needs to produce chlorophyll. This condition can be cured by adding an appropriate acidic fertilizer formulated for citrus, which can sometimes revive a plant to produce new leaves and even flower buds within a few weeks under optimum conditions. A soil which is too acidic can also cause problems; citrus prefers neutral soil (pH between 6 and 8). Citrus plants are also sensitive to excessive salt in the soil. Soil testing may be necessary to properly diagnose nutrient deficiency diseases.*[24]

3.36.5 Uses

Culinary

Wedges of pink grapefruit, lime, and lemon, and a half orange (clockwise from top)

Citrus aurantifolia *in Kerala*

Many citrus fruits, such as oranges, tangerines, grapefruits, and clementines, are generally eaten fresh. They are typically peeled and can be easily split into segments. Grapefruit is more commonly halved and eaten out of the skin with a spoon.*[25] There are special spoons (grapefruit spoons) with serrated tips designed for this purpose. Orange and grapefruit juices are also very popular breakfast beverages. More acidic citrus, such as lemons and limes, are generally not eaten on their own. Meyer lemons can be eaten out of hand with the fragant skin; they are both sweet and sour. Lemonade or limeade are popular beverages prepared by diluting the juices of these fruits and adding sugar. Lemons and limes are also used as garnishes or in cooked dishes. Their juice is used as an ingredient in a variety of dishes; it can commonly be found in salad dressings and squeezed over cooked meat or vegetables.

A variety of flavours can be derived from different parts and treatments of citrus fruits. The rind and oil of the fruit is generally very bitter, especially when cooked, and so is often combined with sugar. The fruit pulp can vary from sweet and tart to extremely sour. Marmalade, a condiment derived from cooked orange and lemon, can be especially bitter, but is usually sweetened to cut the bitterness and produce a jam-like result. Lemon or lime is commonly used as a garnish for water, soft drinks, or cocktails. Citrus juices, rinds, or slices are used in a variety of mixed drinks. The colourful outer skin of some citrus fruits, known as zest, is used as a flavouring in cooking; the white inner portion of the peel, the pith, is usually avoided due to its bitterness. The zest of a citrus fruit, typically lemon or an orange, can also be soaked in water in a coffee filter, and drunk.

Medical

Citrus fruit intake has been associated with a 10% reduction in odds of developing breast cancer.[26]

Oranges were historically used for their high content of vitamin C, which prevents scurvy. Scurvy is caused by vitamin C deficiency, and can be prevented by having 10 milligrams of vitamin C a day. An early sign of scurvy is fatigue. If ignored, later symptoms are bleeding and bruising easily. British sailors were given a ration of citrus fruits on long voyages to prevent the onset of scurvy, hence the British nickname of Limey.

Pectin is a structural heteropolysaccharide contained in the primary cell walls of plants. Limes and lemons as well as oranges and grapefruits are among the highest in this level.[27]

After consumption, the peel is sometimes used as a facial cleanser.

Before the development of fermentation-based processes, lemons were the primary commercial source of citric acid.

Citrus fruit intake is associated with a reduced risk of stomach cancer.[28] Also, citrus fruit juices, such as orange, lime and lemon, may be useful for lowering the risk of specific types of kidney stones. Grapefruit is another fruit juice that can be used to lower blood pressure because it interferes with the metabolism of calcium channel blockers.[29] Lemons have the highest concentration of citrate of any citrus fruit, and daily consumption of lemonade has been shown to decrease the rate of kidney stone formation.[30]

3.36.6 Sweet and sour

The Moroccan professor Henri Chapot discovered that the acidity in the more common citrons or lemons is represented by red on the inner coat of seeds specifically on the chalazal spot, violet pigmentation on the outer side of the flower blossom, and also by the new buds that are reddish-purplish. The acidless varieties of citrus are completely lacking the red color in all the mentioned spots.[31] This designation was cited by Herbert John Webber and Leon Dexter Batchelor, the editors of the fundamental treatise on citrus, namely The Citrus Industry, which was published by the University of California, Riverside in 1967.[32]

3.36.7 Fossil record

A fossil leaf from the Pliocene of Valdarno (Italy) is described as †*Citrus meletensis*.[33] In China fossil leaf specimens of †*Citrus linczangensis* have been collected from coal-bearing strata of the Bangmai Formation in the Bangmai village, about 10 km northwest of Lincang City, Yunnan. The Bangmai Formation contains abundant fossil plants and is considered to be of late Miocene age, *Citrus linczangensis* and *C. meletensis* share some important characters, such as an intramarginal vein, an entire margin, and an articulated and distinctly winged petiole.[34]

3.36.8 List of citrus fruits

*This is a list by scientific names; there exists a list by **common names***

Main article: List of citrus fruits

The genus *Citrus* has been suggested to originate in Southeast Asia. Prior to human cultivation, it consisted of just a few species, namely:

- *Citrus crenatifolia* – species name is unresolved, from Sri Lanka

- *Citrus japonica* – Kumquats, from East Asia ranging into Southeast Asia (sometimes separated in 4–5 *Fortunella* species)

- *Citrus mangshanensis* – species name is unresolved, from Hunan Province, China.

- *Citrus maxima* – Pomelo (pummelo, shaddock), from the Malay Archipelago

Citrons (Citrus medica) for sale in Germany

Red Finger Lime (Citrus australasica), a rare delicacy from Australia

- *Citrus medica* – Citron, from India
- *Citrus platymamma* – Byeonggyul, from Jeju Island, Korea
- *Citrus reticulata* – Mandarin orange, from China
- *Citrus trifoliata* – Trifoliate orange, from Korea and adjacent China (often separated as *Poncirus*)
- Australian limes
  - *Citrus australasica* – Australian Finger Lime
  - *Citrus australis* – Australian Round lime
  - *Citrus glauca* – Australian Desert Lime
  - *Citrus garrawayae* – Mount White Lime
  - *Citrus gracilis* – Kakadu Lime or Humpty Doo Lime
  - *Citrus inodora* – Russel River Lime
  - *Citrus warburgiana* – New Guinea Wild Lime
  - *Citrus wintersii* – Brown River Finger Lime
- Papedas, including
  - *Citrus halimii* – limau kadangsa, limau kedut kera, from Thailand and Malaya
  - *Citrus indica* – Indian wild orange, from the Indian subcontinent*[35]
  - *Citrus macroptera* from Indochina and Melanesia*[35]
  - *Citrus micrantha* from the southern Philippines*[36]
  - *Citrus latipes* – Khasi Papeda, from Assam, Meghalaya, Burma*[35]

Hybrids and cultivars

See also: Citrus hybrid

Sorted by parentage. As each hybrid is the product of (at

Sweetie or Oroblanco is a pomelo-grapefruit hybrid.

least) two parent species, they are listed multiple times.

***Citrus maxima*-based**

- Amanatsu, natsumikan – *Citrus* ×*natsudaidai* (*C. maxima* × unknown)
- Cam sành – (*C. reticulata* × *C.* ×*sinensis*)
- Dangyuja – (*Citrus grandis Osbeck*)
- Grapefruit – *Citrus* ×*paradisi* (*C. maxima* × *C.* ×*sinensis*)
- Imperial lemon – (*C.* ×*limon* × *C.* ×*paradisi*)

3.36. CITRUS

The Etrog, or Citron, is central to the ritual of the Jewish Sukkot festival. Many varieties are used for this purpose (including the Yemenite variety pictured).

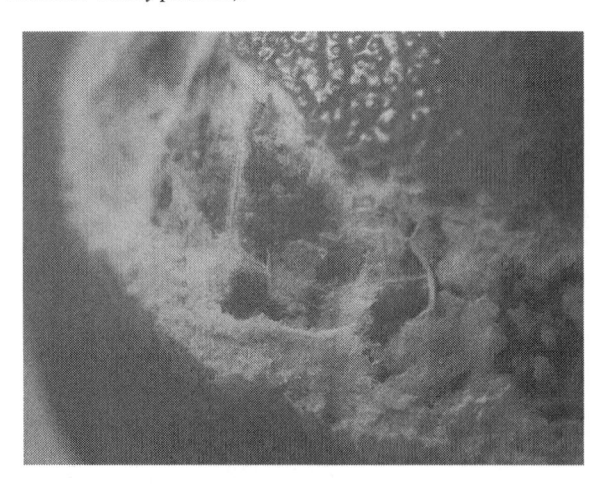

Clementines (Citrus ×clementina) have thinner skins than oranges.

- Kinnow – (*C.* ×*nobilis* × *C.* ×*deliciosa*)
- Kiyomi – (*C.* ×*sinensis* × *C.* ×*unshiu*)
- Lemon – *Citrus* ×*limon* (probably *C. maxima* × *C. medica*)
- Minneola tangelo – (*C. reticulata* × *C.* ×*paradisi*)
- Orangelo, Chironja – (*C.* ×*paradisi* × *C.* ×*sinensis*)
- Oroblanco, Sweetie – (*C. maxima* × *C.* ×*paradisi*)
- Sweet orange – *Citrus* ×*sinensis* (probably *C. maxima* × *C. reticulata*)
- Tangelo – *Citrus* ×*tangelo* (*C. reticulata* × *C. maxima* or *C.* ×*paradisi*)
- Tangor – *Citrus* ×*nobilis* (*C. reticulata* × *C.* ×*sinensis*)
- Ugli – (*C. reticulata* × *C. maxima* or *C.* ×*paradisi*)

Citrus medica-based

Mikan (Citrus ×unshiu), also known as satsumas

Sweet oranges (Citrus ×sinensis) are used in many foods. Their ancestors were probably pomelos and mandarin oranges.

- Buddha's hand – *Citrus medica* var. *sarcodactylus*, a fingered citron.

Cross section of Odichukuthi lime.

A pompia fruit

Odichukuthi fruit

- Citron varieties with sour pulp – Diamante citron, Florentine citron, Greek citron and Balady citron

- Citron varieties with sweet pulp – Corsican citron and Moroccan citron.

- Etrog, a group of citron cultivars that are traditionally used for a Jewish ritual. *Etrog* is Hebrew for citron in general.

- Fernandina – *Citrus ×limonimedica* (probably (*C. medica* × *C. maxima*) × *C. medica*)

- Ponderosa lemon – (probably (*C. medica* × *C. maxima*) × *C. medica*)

- Lemon – *Citrus ×limon* (probably *C. medica* × *C. maxima*)

- Key lime, Mexican lime, Omani lime – *Citrus ×aurantiifolia* (*C. medica* × *C. micrantha*)

- Lumia - a pear shaped lemon hybrid, (probably *C. medica* x *C. limon*)

- Rhobs el Arsa - bread of the garden, a Moroccan citron x lemon hybrid.

- Yemenite citron – a pulpless true citron.

Citrus reticulata-based

- Bergamot orange – *Citrus ×bergamia* (*C. limetta* × *C. ×aurantium*)

- Bitter orange, Seville Orange – *Citrus ×aurantium* (*C. maxima* × *C. reticulata*)

- Blood orange – *Citrus ×sinensis* cultivars

- Calamondin, Calamansi – (*Citrus reticulata* × *Citrus japonica*)

- Cam sành – (*C. reticulata* × *C. ×sinensis*)

- Chinotto – *Citrus ×aurantium* var. *myrtifolia* or *Citrus ×myrtifolia*

- ChungGyun – *Citrus reticulata* cultivar

- Clementine – *Citrus ×clementina*

- Cleopatra Mandarin – *Citrus ×reshni*

- Siranui – *Citrus reticulata* cv. 'Dekopon' (ChungGyun × Ponkan)

3.36. CITRUS

- Daidai – *Citrus ×aurantium* var. *daidai* or *Citrus ×daidai*
- Grapefruit – *Citrus ×paradisi* (*C. maxima* × *C. ×sinensis*)
- Hermandina – *Citrus reticulata* cv. 'Hermandina'
- Imperial lemon – ((*C. maxima* × *C. medica*) × *C. ×paradisi*)
- Kinnow, Wilking – (*C. ×nobilis* × *C. ×deliciosa*)
- Kiyomi – (*C. sinensis* × *C. ×unshiu*)
- Laraha – "*C. ×aurantium* ssp. *currassuviencis*
- Mediterranean mandarin, Willow Leaf – *Citrus ×deliciosa*
- Meyer lemon, Valley Lemon – *Citrus ×meyeri* ((*C. maxima* × *C. medica*) × *C. ×paradisi* or *C. ×sinensis*)
- Michal mandarin – *Citrus reticulata* cv. 'Michal'
- Mikan, Satsuma – *Citrus ×unshiu*
- Naartjie – (*C. reticulata* × *C. nobilis*)
- Nova mandarin, Clemenvilla
- Orangelo, Chironja – (*C. ×paradisi* × *C. ×sinensis*)
- Oroblanco, Sweetie – (*C. maxima* × *C. ×paradisi*)
- Ponkan – *Citrus reticulata* cv. 'Ponkan'
- Rangpur, Lemanderin, Mandarin Lime – *Citrus ×limonia* ((*C. reticulata* × *C. maxima*) × *C. medica*)
- Sweet orange – *Citrus ×sinensis* (probably *C. maxima* × *C. reticulata*)
- Tangelo – *Citrus ×tangelo* (*C. reticulata* × *C. maxima* or *C. ×paradisi*)
- Tangerine – *Citrus ×tangerina*
- Tangor – *Citrus ×nobilis* (*C. reticulata* × *C. ×sinensis*)
- Ugli – (*C. reticulata* × *C. maxima* or *C. ×paradisi*)
- Yuzu – *Citrus ×junos* (*C. reticulata* × *C. ×ichangensis*)

Other/Unresolved

- Alemow, Colo – *Citrus ×macrophylla*
- Djeruk limau – *Citrus ×amblycarpa*
- Gajanimma, Carabao Lime – *Citrus ×pennivesiculata*
- Hyuganatsu, Hyuganatsu pumelo – *Citrus tamurana*

- Ichang lemon, Ichang Papeda – *Citrus ×ichangensis*
- Imperial lemon – (*C. ×limon* × *C. ×paradisi*)
- Iyokan, *anadomikan* – *Citrus ×iyo*
- Kabosu – *Citrus ×sphaerocarpa*
- Kaffir lime, *makrut* – *Citrus ×hystrix*
- Limetta, Sweet Lemon, Sweet Lime, mosambi – *Citrus ×limetta*
- Palestine sweet lime – *Citrus ×limettioides* Tanaka
- Odichukuthi – *Citrus Odichukuthi* from Malayalam
- Ougonkan – *Citrus flaviculpus* hort ex.Tanaka
- Persian lime, Tahiti Lime – *Citrus ×latifolia*
- Pompia – *Citrus monstruosa*, a *nomen nudum*
- Rough lemon – *Citrus ×jambhiri* Lush.
- Sakurajima komikan orange
- Shekwasha, Hirami Lemon, Taiwan Tangerine – *Citrus ×depressa*
- Shonan gold – (Ougonkan) *Citrus flaviculpus* hort ex. Tanaka × (Imamura unshiu), *Citrus unshiu* Marc
- Sudachi – *Citrus ×sudachi*
- Sunki, Suenkat – *Citrus ×sunki*
- Tachibana orange – *Citrus ×tachibana* (Mak.) Tanaka
- Volkamer lemon – *Citrus ×volkameriana*

For hybrids with kumquats, see ×*Citrofortunella*. For hybrids with the Trifoliate Orange, see citrange.

3.36.9 See also

- *Citrus* – Wikipedia book
- Japanese citrus
- List of lemon dishes and beverages

3.36.10 Footnotes

[1] Liu, Y.; Heying, E.; Tanumihardjo, S. (2012). "History, Global Distribution, and Nutritional Importance of Citrus Fruits". *Comprehensive Reviews in Food Science and Food Safety*. **11**: 6. doi:10.1111/j.1541-4337.2012.00201.x.

[2] Gmitter, Frederick; Hu, Xulan (1990). "The possible role of Yunnan, China, in the origin of contemporary *Citrus* species (Rutaceae)". *Economic Botany*. **44** (2): 267–277. doi:10.1007/bf02860491.

[3] United Nations Conference on Trade and Development. Market Information in the Commodities Area: Citrus fruits

[4] Scora, Rainer W. (1975). "On the history and origin of citrus". *Bulletin of the Torrey Botanical Club*. **102** (6): 369–375. doi:10.2307/2484763. JSTOR 2484763.

[5] University of South Florida: Fruit
Contrary to general belief, the orange tree is not indigenous to Florida but was introduced into the state from Valencia by the Spanish colonists.

[6] History of the Citrus and Citrus Tree Growing in America
Many of these wild orange groves were seen by the early American explorer, William Bartram, according to his book, Travels, in 1773, while traveling down the Saint John's River in Florida. Bartram mistakenly thought these orange trees were native to Florida; however, they were established centuries earlier by the Spanish explorers.

[7] Spiegel-Roy, Pinchas; Eliezer E. Goldschmidt (1996). *Biology of Citrus*. Cambridge University Press. p. 4. ISBN 978-0-521-33321-4.

[8] A phylogenetic analysis of 34 chloroplast genomes elucidates the relationships between wild and domestic species within the genus Citrus

[9] Where Did Citrus Fruits Originate From?

[10] The origin and evolution of select citrus species.

[11] "International Citrus Genomics Consortium". *ucr.edu*.

[12] "Citron Cultivation, Production and Uses in the Mediterranean Region". *springer.com*.

[13] Andrés García Lor (2013). *Organización de la diversidad genética de los cítricos* (PDF) (Thesis). p. 79.

[14] Bayer, R. J., et al. (2009). A molecular phylogeny of the orange subfamily (Rutaceae: Aurantioideae) using nine cpDNA sequences. *American Journal of Botany* 96(3), 668-85.

[15] "Citrus fruit diagram". *ucla.edu*.

[16] "Lith". *TheFreeDictionary.com*.

[17] "Flavonoid Composition of Fruit Tissues of Citrus Species".

[18] "Citrus". Retrieved 2015-04-13.

[19] Helgi Öpik; Stephen A. Rolfe; Arthur John Willis; Herbert Edward Street (2005). *The physiology of flowering plants*. Cambridge University Press. pp. 309–. ISBN 978-0-521-66251-2. Retrieved 31 July 2010.

[20] Pinchas Spiegel-Roy; Eliezer E. Goldschmidt (1996). *Biology of citrus*. Cambridge University Press. pp. 101–. ISBN 978-0-521-33321-4. Retrieved 31 July 2010.

[21] "About the Asian Citrus Psyllid and Huanglongbing". *californiacitrusthreat.org*.

[22] "Citrus Leafminer – UC Pest Management".

[23] Online at SumoGardener "How to Avoid Yellow Leaves on Citrus Trees".

[24] Mauk, Peggy A.; Tom Shea. "Questions and Answers to Citrus Management (3rd ed.)" (PDF). University of California Cooperative Extension. Retrieved 2014-05-24.

[25] "American Indian Health – Health". Aihd.ku.edu. Retrieved 2011-12-17.

[26] Song, Jung-Kook; Bae, Jong-Myon (2013-03-01). "Citrus fruit intake and breast cancer risk: a quantitative systematic review". *Journal of Breast Cancer*. **16** (1): 72–76. doi:10.4048/jbc.2013.16.1.72. ISSN 1738-6756. PMC 3625773. PMID 23593085.

[27] Morgan, Laura (March 15, 2011). "What Fruits & Vegetables Contain Pectin?". Demand Media. Retrieved 2011-07-22.

[28] González CA, Sala N, Rokkas T (2013). "Gastric cancer: epidemiologic aspects". *Helicobacter*. **18** (Supplement 1): 34–38. doi:10.1111/hel.12082. PMID 24011243.

[29] "Grapefruit and Medication". *Total Health*. **27** (2): 39–39. 2005.

[30] Carr, Jackie (April 22, 2010). "Five Ways to Prevent Kidney Stones". UC San Diego. Retrieved 2010-12-03.

[31] *Un curieux cedrat Marocain* (1950) Rev. Intl. Bot. Appl. Agr. Trop. 30:506–514.

[32] Available online at The Citrus Industry, see title "Sugar or Acidless Oranges"

[33] Citrus meletensis (Rutaceae), a new species from the Pliocene of Valdarno (Italy) Fischer, T.C. & Butzmann, Plant Systematics and Evolution - March 1998, Volume 210, Issue 1, pp 51–55. doi:10.1007/BF00984727

[34] Citrus linczangensis sp. n., a Leaf Fossil of Rutaceae from the Late Miocene of Yunnan, China by Sanping Xie, Steven R Manchester, Kenan Liu and Bainian Sun - International Journal of Plant Sciences 174(8):1201-1207 October 2013.

[35] GRIN. "Species list in GRIN for genus *Citrus*". *Taxonomy for Plants*. National Germplasm Resources Laboratory, Beltsville, Maryland: USDA, ARS, National Genetic Resources Program. Retrieved Jan 6, 2011.

[36] P. J. Wester (1915), "Citrus Fruits In The Philippines", *Philippine Agricultural Review*, **8**

3.36.11 References

- Andrews, A.C. (1961). "Acclimatization of citrus fruits in the Mediterranean region". *Agricultural History*. **35** (1): 35–46.

- Araújo, De; Freitas, E.; de Queiroz, L. Paganucci; Machado, M.A. (2003). "What is *Citrus*? Taxonomic implications from a study of cp-DNA evolution in the tribe Citreae (Rutaceae subfamily Aurantioideae)". *Organisms Diversity & Evolution*. **3** (1): 55–62. doi:10.1078/1439-6092-00058.

- Nicolosi, E.; Deng, Z.N.; Gentile, A.; La Malfa, S.; Continella, G.; Tribulato, E. (2000). "*Citrus* phylogeny and genetic origin of important species as investigated by molecular markers". *Theoretical and Applied Genetics*. **100** (8): 1155–1166. doi:10.1007/s001220051419.

3.36.12 Further reading

- Calabrese, Francesco (2002): Origin and history. *In:* Dugo, Giovanni & Di Giacomo, Angelo (eds.) (2002): *Citrus*. Taylor & Francis. ISBN 0-415-28491-0

- Ellis, R.H.; Hong, T.D. & Roberts, E.H. (1985): Chapter 64. Rutaceae. *In: Handbook of Seed Technology for Genebanks* (Volume II: Compendium of Specific Germination Information and Test Recommendations). International Board for Plant Genetic Resources, Rome, Italy. HTML fulltext

- Frison, E.A. & Taher, M.M. (eds.) (1991): *FAO/IBPGR Technical Guidelines for the Safe Movement of Citrus Germplasm*. FAO, IOCV, IPGRI. PDF fulltext

- International Plant Genetic Resources Institute (IPGRI) (1999): Descriptors for Citrus (*Citrus spp.*). PDF fulltext

- Janick, Jules (2005): Purdue University Tropical Horticulture Lecture 32: Citrus

- Luro, F.; Laigret, F.; Bové, J.M. & Ollitrault, P. (1995): RFLP analysis of cytoplasmic and nuclear genomes used for citrus taxonomy. *In: Mandarines – développements scientifiques récents, résumés oraux et posters*: 12–13. CIRAD-FLHOR, San Nicolao, France. HTML abstract

- Molina, A.B.; Roa, V.N.; Bay-Petersen, J.; Carpio, A.T. & Joven, J.E.A. (eds.) (2000): *Citrus, Proceedings of a regional workshop on disease management of banana and citrus through the use of disease-free planting materials held in Davao City, Philippines, 14–16 October 1998*. INIBAP. PDF fulltext

- Sackman. Douglas Cazaux (2005): *Orange Empire: California and the Fruits of Eden*.

- University of California Division of Agricultural Sciences (UC-DAS) (1967–1989): *The Citrus Industry*. HTML fulltext of Vol. 1, 2, & Vol. 5, Chapter 5

3.36.13 External links

- Effects of pollination on Citrus plants Pollination of Citrus by Honey Bees

- Citrus Research and Education Center of IFAS (largest citrus research center in world)

- Citrus Variety Collection by the University of California

- Citrus (Mark Rieger, Professor of Horticulture, University of Georgia)

- Fundecitrus – Fund for Citrus Plant Protection is an organization of citrus Brazilian producers and processors.

- *Citrus* – taxonomy fruit anatomy at GeoChemBio

- Home Citrus Growers

- Citrus Variety Information Season of Maturity • Seeds / Fruit Information • Fruit Size • Fruit and Tree Insight

- "The Citrus Route. China-Middle East-Spain-The Americas" The history of citrus by Enrique García Ballesteros

- Porcher Michel H.; et al. (1995). "Multilingual Multiscript Plant Name Database (M.M.P.N.D) – A Work in Progress". School of Agriculture and Food Systems, Faculty of Land & Food Resources, The University of Melbourne. Australia.

3.37 Cornus

For other uses, see Cornus (disambiguation).
"Dogwood" redirects here. For other uses, see Dogwood (disambiguation).

Cornus is a genus of about 30–60 species*[Note

In species such as this Cornus unalaschkensis, *the tiny four-petaled flowers are clustered in a tightly packed, flattened cyme at the center of four showy white petal-like bracts.*

Cornus mas

1] of woody plants in the family Cornaceae, commonly known as **dogwoods**, which can generally be distinguished by their blossoms, berries, and distinctive bark.*[2] Most are deciduous trees or shrubs, but a few species are nearly herbaceous perennial subshrubs, and a few of the woody species are evergreen. Several species have small heads of inconspicuous flowers surrounded by an involucre of large, typically white petal-like bracts, while others have more open clusters of petal-bearing flowers. The various species of dogwood are native throughout much of temperate and boreal Eurasia and North America, with China and Japan and the southeastern United States particularly rich in native species.

Cornus florida *in spring*

Cornus drummondii *in flower*

Mature and immature flowers of Cornus canadensis, *Bonnechere Provincial Park, Ontario*

Species include the common dogwood *Cornus sanguinea* of Eurasia, the widely cultivated flowering dogwood *(Cornus*

3.37. CORNUS

Cornus canadensis *fruit*

Spring budding

florida) of eastern North America, the Pacific dogwood *Cornus nuttallii* of western North America, the Kousa dogwood *Cornus kousa* of eastern Asia, and two low-growing boreal species, the Canadian and Eurasian dwarf cornels (or bunchberries), *Cornus canadensis* and *Cornus suecica* respectively.

Depending on botanical interpretation, the dogwoods are variously divided into one to nine genera or subgenera; a broadly inclusive genus *Cornus* is accepted here.

3.37.1 Common name "dogwood"

The name "dog-tree" entered the English vocabulary before 1548, becoming "dogwood" by 1614. Once the name dogwood was affixed to this kind of tree, it soon acquired a secondary name as the Hound's Tree, while the fruits came to be known as **dogberries** or **houndberries** (the latter a name also for the berries of black nightshade, alluding to Hecate's hounds). Another theory advances the view that "dogwood" was derived from the Old English **dagwood,** from the use of the slender stems of its very hard wood for making "dags" (daggers, skewers, and arrows).*[3]*[4] Another, earlier name of the dogwood in English is the **whipple-tree.** Geoffrey Chaucer uses "whippletree" in *The Canterbury Tales* ("The Knight's Tale", verse 2065) to refer to the dogwood. A *whippletree* is an element of the traction of a horse-drawn cart, linking the drawpole of the cart to the harnesses of the horses in file; these items still bear the name of the tree from which they are commonly carved.

Cherokee Princess dogwood

3.37.2 Characteristics

Dogwoods have simple, untoothed leaves with the veins curving distinctively as they approach the leaf margins. Most dogwood species have opposite leaves, while a few, such as *Cornus alternifolia* and *C. controversa*, have their leaves alternate. Dogwood flowers have four parts. In many species, the flowers are borne separately in open (but often dense) clusters, while in various other species (such as the flowering dogwood), the flowers themselves are tightly clustered, lacking showy petals, but surrounded by four to six large, typically white petal-like bracts.

The fruits of all dogwood species are drupes with one or two seeds, often brightly colorful. The drupes of species in the subgenera *Cornus* are edible. Many are without much flavor. *Cornus kousa* and *Cornus mas* are sold commercially as edible fruit trees. The fruits of *Cornus kousa* have a sweet, tropical pudding like flavor in addition to hard pits. The fruits of *Cornus mas* are both tart and sweet when completely ripe. They have been eaten in Eastern Europe for centuries, both as food and medicine to fight colds and flus. They are very high in vitamin C. However, those of species in subgenus *Swida* are mildly toxic to people, though readily eaten by birds.

Dogwoods are used as food plants by the larvae of some species of butterflies and moths, including the Emperor moth, the Engrailed, the small angle shades, and the following case-bearers of the genus *Coleophora*: *C. ahenella*, *C. salicivorella* (recorded on *Cornus canadensis*), *C. albiantennaella*, *C. cornella* and *C. cornivorella,* with the latter three all feeding exclusively on *Cornus*.

3.37.3 Uses

Dogwoods are widely planted horticulturally, and the dense wood of the larger-stemmed species is valued for certain specialized purposes. Cutting boards and other fine turnings can be made from this fine grained and beautiful wood. Over 32 different varieties of game birds, including quail, feed on the red seeds.*[5]

Symbol: British Columbia's Provincial Flower

The Dogwood flower motif was adopted as British Columbia's provincial flower in 1956. Actually a flowering tree, the Pacific Dogwood is known for its white blooms, brilliant red berries and bright foliage in the fall. It stands about eight to ten metres high, and blossoms in April and May.

Horticulture

Various species of *Cornus,* particularly the flowering dogwood *(Cornus florida),* are ubiquitous in American gardens and landscaping; horticulturist Donald Wyman stated, "There is a dogwood for almost every part of the U.S. except the hottest and driest areas" .*[6] In contrast, in England the lack of sharp winters and hot summers makes *Cornus florida* very shy of flowering.*[7]

Other *Cornus* species are stoloniferous shrubs that grow naturally in wet habitats and along waterways. Several of these are used along highways and in naturalizing landscape plantings, especially those species with bright red or bright yellow stems, particularly conspicuous in winter, such as *Cornus stolonifera*.

Fruits

The species *Cornus mas* is commonly cultivated in southeastern Europe for its edible berries, which can be turned into jam, fermented into a wine, or eaten raw after slight bletting.

Wood

Dense and fine-grained, dogwood timber has a density of 0.79 and is highly prized for making loom shuttles, tool handles, roller skates and other small items that require a very hard and strong wood.*[8] Though it is tough for woodworking, some artisans favor dogwood for small projects such as walking canes, arrow making, mountain dulcimers and fine inlays. Dogwood wood is an excellent substitute for persimmon wood in the heads of certain golf clubs ("woods"). Dogwood lumber is rare in that it is not readily available with any manufacturer and must be cut down by the person(s) wanting to use it.

Larger items have also been occasionally made of dogwood, such as the screw-in basket-style wine or fruit presses. The first kinds of laminated tennis rackets were also made from this wood, cut into thin strips.

Dogwood twigs were used by pioneers to brush their teeth. They would peel off the bark, bite the twig and then scrub their teeth.*[9]

Medicinal

The bark of *Cornus* species is rich in tannin and has been used as a substitute for quinine.*[10] During the American civil war confederate soldiers would make a tea from the bark to treat pain and fevers, and dogwood leaves in a poultice to cover wounds.*[11]

The Japanese cornel, *C. officinalis*, is used extensively in traditional Chinese medicine as "shān zhū yú," (山茱萸) where it is used for weakness, dizziness, pain of the lower back and knees, and to astringe excessive sweating, uterine bleeding, and bladder incontinence.*[12]

3.37.4 Classification

The following classification recognizes a single, inclusive genus *Cornus,**[13]*[14] with four subgroups and ten subgenera supported by molecular phylogeny.*[15]*[16] Geographical ranges as native plants are given below. In addition, cultivated species occasionally persist or spread from plantings beyond their native ranges, but are rarely if ever locally invasive.*[Note 2]

Blue- or White-fruited Dogwoods

Paniculate or corymbose cymes; bracts minute, nonmodified; fruits globose or subglobose, white, blue, or black:

- **Subgenus *Yinquania*.** Leaves opposite to subopposite; fall blooming.
    - *Cornus oblonga.*
    - *Cornus peruviana.* Costa Rica and Venezuela to Bolivia.*[17]*[18]

3.37. CORNUS

- **Subgenus *Kraniopsis*.** Leaves opposite; summer blooming.

  - *Cornus alba**[Note 3] (Siberian dogwood). Siberia and northern China.
  - *Cornus amomum**[Note 4] (silky dogwood). Eastern U.S. east of the Great Plains except for the Deep South.
  - *Cornus asperifolia* (toughleaf dogwood). Southeastern U.S.
  - *Cornus austrosinensis* (South China dogwood). East Asia.
  - *Cornus bretschneideri* (Bretschneider's dogwood). Northern China.
  - *Cornus coreana* (Korean dogwood). Northeast Asia.
  - *Cornus drummondii* (roughleaf dogwood). U.S. between the Appalachia and the Great Plains, and southern Ontario, Canada.
  - *Cornus excelsa*.
  - *Cornus foemina* (stiff dogwood) Southeastern and southern United States.
  - *Cornus glabrata* (brown dogwood or smooth dogwood). Western North America.
  - *Cornus hemsleyi* (Hemsley's dogwood). Southwest China.
  - *Cornus koehneana* (Koehne's dogwood). Southwest China.
  - *Cornus macrophylla* (large-leafed dogwood; Chinese: 梾椋; pinyin: *jiáliáng or jiàliáng*). East Asia.
  - *Cornus obliqua**[Note 5] (pale dogwood). Northeastern and central U.S., and southeastern Canada.
  - *Cornus paucinervis*. China.
  - *Cornus racemosa* (northern swamp dogwood or gray dogwood). Northeastern and central U.S., and extreme southeastern Canada.
  - *Cornus rugosa* (round-leaf dogwood). Northeastern and north-central U.S., and southeastern Canada.
  - *Cornus sanguinea* (common dogwood). Europe.
  - *Cornus sericea**[Note 6] (red osier dogwood). Northern and western North America, except Arctic regions.
  - *Cornus walteri* (Walter's dogwood). Central China.
  - *Cornus wilsoniana* (Wilson's dogwood). Central China.

- **Subgenus *Mesomora*.** Leaves alternate; summer blooming.

  - *Cornus alternifolia* (pagoda dogwood or alternate-leaf dogwood). Eastern U.S. and southeastern Canada.
  - *Cornus controversa* (table dogwood). East Asia.

Cornelian Cherries

Umbellate cymes; bracts modified, non-petaloid; fruits oblong, red; stone walls filled with cavities:

- **Subgenus *Afrocrania*.** Dioecious, bracts 4.

  - *Cornus volkensii*.

- **Subgenus *Cornus*.** Plants hermaphroditic, bracts 4 or 6

  - *Cornus eydeana*.
  - *Cornus mas* (European cornel or Cornelian-cherry). Mediterranean.
  - *Cornus officinalis* (Japanese cornel). China, Japan, Korea.
  - †*Cornus piggae* (Late Paleocene, North Dakota)*[19]
  - *Cornus sessilis* (blackfruit cornel). California.

- **Subgenus *Sinocornus*.** Plants hermaphroditic, bracts 4 or 6

  - *Cornus chinensis* (Chinese cornel). China.

Big-bracted Dogwoods

Capitular cymes:

- **Subgenus *Discocrania*.** Bracts 4, modified, non-petaloid; fruits oblong, red.

  - *Cornus disciflora*.

- **Subgenus *Cynoxylon*.** Bracts 4 or 6, large and petaloid, fruits oblong, red.

  - *Cornus florida* (flowering dogwood). U.S. east of the Great Plains, north to southern Ontario.
  - *Cornus nuttallii* (Pacific dogwood). Western North America, from British Columbia to California.

- **Subgenus *Syncarpea*.** Bracts 4, large and petaloid, fruits red, fused into a compound multi-stoned berry.

- *Cornus capitata* (Himalayan flowering dogwood). Himalaya.
- *Cornus elliptica*
- *Cornus hongkongensis* (Hong Kong dogwood). Southern China, Laos, Vietnam.
- *Cornus kousa* (Kousa dogwood). Japan and (as subsp. *chinensis*) central and northern China.
- *Cornus multinervosa*.

Dwarf Dogwoods

Minute corymbose cymes; bracts 4, petaloid; fruit globose, red; rhizomatous herb:

- **Subgenus *Arctocrania*.**
    - *Cornus canadensis* (Canadian dwarf cornel or bunchberry) Northern North America, southward in the Appalachian and Rocky Mountains.
    - *Cornus suecica* (Eurasian dwarf cornel or bunchberry). Northern Eurasia, locally in extreme northeast and northwest North America.
    - *Cornus* × *unalaschkensis* (Hybrid: *C. canadensis* × *C. suecica*). Aleutian Islands (Alaska), Greenland, and Labrador and Newfoundland in Canada.

Incertae sedis (**unplaced**)

- †*Cornus clarnensis* (Middle Eocene, Central Oregon)*[20]

Horticultural hybrids

Cornus × *rutgersensis* (Hybrid: *C. florida* × *C. kousa*). Horticulturally developed.*[21]

3.37.5 Cultural references

The inflorescence ("flower") of the Pacific dogwood (*Cornus nuttallii*) is the official flower of the province of British Columbia. The flowering dogwood (*Cornus florida*) and its inflorescence are the state tree and the state flower respectively for the U.S. Commonwealth of Virginia. It is also the state tree of Missouri and the state flower of North Carolina, and the State Memorial Tree of New Jersey.

The poet Virgil makes reference to a haunted copse of cornel and myrtle in Book III of the Aeneid. The hero Aeneas attempts to break off boughs to decorate an altar, but instead the wood drips with black blood.*[22] Anne Morrow Lindbergh gives a vivid description of the dogwood tree in her poem "Dogwood".*[23]

A Christian legend of unknown origin proclaims that the cross used to crucify Jesus was constructed of dogwood.*[24] As the story goes, during the time of Jesus, the dogwood was larger and stronger than it is today and was the largest tree in the area of Jerusalem. After his crucifixion, Jesus changed the plant to its current form: he shortened it and twisted its branches to assure an end to its use for the construction of crosses.*[25] He also transformed its inflorescence into a representation of the crucifixion itself, with the four white bracts cross-shaped representing the four corners of the cross, each bearing a rusty indentation as of a nail, the red stamens of the flower representing Jesus' crown of thorns, and the clustered red fruit representing his blood.*[26]*[27]

In the Victorian era, flowers or sprigs of dogwood were presented to unmarried women by male suitors to signify affection. The returning of the flower conveyed indifference on the part of the woman; if she kept it, it became a sign of mutual interest.

The term "dogwood winter", in colloquial use in the American Southeast, is sometimes used to describe a cold snap in spring, presumably because farmers believed it was not safe to plant their crops until after the dogwoods blossomed.*[28]

3.37.6 Etymology

Cornus is the ancient Latin word for the Cornelian cherry, *Cornus mas*. 'Cornus' means 'horn'.*[29]

3.37.7 Notes

[1] 58 species according to Xiang *et al.* (2006)*[1]

[2] For further detail on distributions of native North American dogwoods, see *Cornus* in BONAP's North American Plant Atlas.

[3] *Cornus sericea*, treated separately here, is sometimes included in a more broadly taken concept of *Cornus alba*, which in that sense is also native in North America.

[4] *Cornus obliqua*, here recognized separately, has been included in a broader concept of *C. amomum* by some botanists. Canadian reports for *C. amomum* are apparently all based on plants here classified as *C. obliqua*.

[5] *Cornus obliqua* is sometimes included in a more broadly taken concept of *C. amomum*, also in the eastern U.S.

[6] *Cornus sericea* (including *C. stolonifera*) is sometimes itself included in a more broadly taken concept of the otherwise Eurasian *Cornus alba*.

3.37.8 References

[1] Qiu-Yun (Jenny) Xiang, David T. Thomas, Wenheng Zhang, Steven R. Manchester and Zack Murrell (2006). "Species level phylogeny of the genus *Cornus* (Cornaceae) based on molecular and morphological evidence – implications for taxonomy and Tertiary intercontinental migration". *Taxon*. **55** (1): 9–30. doi:10.2307/25065525. JSTOR 25065525.

[2] "Notable Characteristics of Dogwood Trees". answers.com. Retrieved August 24, 2014.

[3] Vedel, H., & Lange, J. (1960). *Trees and Bushes in Wood and Hedgerow*. Metheun & Co. Ltd., London.

[4] Fernald, Merritt Lyndon (1950). *Gray's Manual of Botany (8th ed.)*. New York: American Book Company.

[5] "Wildlife Dogwood Trees". Prepper Gardens. Retrieved January 8, 2013.

[6] Wyman's Garden Encyclopedia, *s.v.* "Cornus"

[7] Alice M. Coats, *Garden Shrubs and their Histories* (1964) 1992, *s.v.* "Cornus".

[8] "Dogwood."McGraw-Hill Concise Encyclopedia of Science and Technology. New York: McGraw-Hill, 2006. Credo Reference. Web. 17 September 2012.

[9] Gunn, John C. (1835). *Gunn's Domestic Medicine* (4th ed.). p. 523.

[10] "dogwood or cornel." The Columbia Encyclopedia. New York: Columbia University Press, 2008. Credo Reference. Web. 17 September 2012.

[11] "Medicinal Dogwood Trees". Prepper Gardens. Retrieved January 8, 2013.

[12] Schafer, Peg (2011). *The Chinese Medicinal Herb Farm: A Cultivator's Guide to Small-scale Organic Herb Production*. Chelsea Green Publishing. pp. 312 (page 150). ISBN 9781603583305.

[13] Richard H. Eyde (1987). "The case for keeping *Cornus* in the broad Linnaean sense". *Systematic Botany*. **12** (4): 505–518. doi:10.2307/2418886. JSTOR 2418886.

[14] Richard H. Eyde (1988). "Comprehending *Cornus*: puzzles and progress in the systematics of the dogwoods". *Botanical Review*. **54** (3): 233–351. doi:10.1007/bf02868985. JSTOR 4354115.

[15] Fan, Chuanzhu; Xiang, Qiu-Yun (2001). "Phylogenetic relationships within *Cornus* (Cornaceae) based on 26S rDNA sequences.". *American Journal of Botany*. **88** (6).

[16] Zhiang, Qiu-Yun; Thomas, David T.; Zhang, Wenheng; Manchester, Steven R.; Murrell, Zack (2006). "Species level phylogeny of the genus Cornus (Cornaceae) based on molecular and morphological evidence—implications for taxonomy and Tertiary intercontinental migration." (PDF). *Taxon*. **55** (1). Retrieved 29 January 2016.

[17] "Tropicos | Name - Cornus peruviana J.F. Macbr.". *www.tropicos.org*. Retrieved 2016-01-29.

[18] Macbride, J.F. (1959). "Cornaceae". *Flora of Peru*. 13 pt.5 no.1. Field Museum. pp. 44–45.

[19] Manchester, S.R.; Xiang, X-P.; Xiang, Q-Y (2010). "Fruits of Cornelian Cherries (Cornaceae: *Cornus* Subg. *Cornus*) in the Paleocene and Eocene of the Northern Hemisphere" (PDF). *International Journal of Plant Sciences*. **171** (8): 882–891. doi:10.1086/655771.

[20] Manchester, S.R. (1994). "Fruits and Seeds of the Middle Eocene Nut Beds Flora, Clarno Formation, Oregon". *Palaeontographica Americana*. **58**: 30–31.

[21] "*Cornus florida* × *Cornus kousa*". Landscape Plants: Images, identification, and information. Oregon State University. Retrieved 20 May 2011.

[22] Aeneid III 22-23: Forte fuit iuxta tumulus, quo cornea summo virgulta et densis hastilibus horrida myrtus.

[23] Morrow, Anne (1956). *Dogwood*. 333 6th Avenue, New York 14, N.Y.: Pantheon Books. pp. 38–39.

[24] The Old Legend of the Dogwood

[25] Jeffrey G. Meyer (2004). *The Tree Book: A Practical Guide to Selecting and Maintaining the Best Trees for Your Yard and Garden*. Simon and Schuster. pp. 258–. ISBN 978-0-7432-4974-4.

[26] Thomas E. Barden (1991). *Virginia Folk Legends*. University of Virginia Press. pp. 61–. ISBN 978-0-8139-1335-3.

[27] Ronald L. Baker (1 August 1984). *Hoosier Folk Legends*. Indiana University Press. pp. 7–. ISBN 0-253-20334-1.

[28] http://www.farmersalmanac.com/weather/2011/04/25/what-is-dogwood-winter/

[29] Gledhill, David (2008). "The Names of Plants". Cambridge University Press. ISBN 9780521866453 (hardback), ISBN 9780521685535 (paperback). pp 121

3.37.9 External links

- Dogwood history and uses
- Asian dogwoods
- The Medicinal Benefits for Growing Your Own Remedy: Dogwood Tree

3.38 Cycas revoluta

This article is about the cycad sago palm. For the "true sago palm", see Metroxylon sagu.

Cycas revoluta (**Sotetsu** [Japanese ソテツ], **sago palm, king sago, sago cycad, Japanese sago palm**), is a species of gymnosperm in the family Cycadaceae, native to southern Japan including the Ryukyu Islands. It is one of several species used for the production of sago, as well as an ornamental plant.

3.38.1 Names

Cycads are not closely related to the true palms (Arecaceae). The Latin specific epithet *revoluta* means "curled back",[2] in reference to the leaves. This is also called Kungi (comb) Palm in Urdu speaking areas.[3]

3.38.2 Description

This very symmetrical plant supports a crown of shiny, dark green leaves on a thick shaggy trunk that is typically about 20 cm (7.9 in) in diameter, sometimes wider. The trunk is very low to subterranean in young plants, but lengthens above ground with age. It can grow into very old specimens with 6–7 m (over 20 feet) of trunk; however, the plant is very slow-growing and requires about 50–100 years to achieve this height. Trunks can branch multiple times, thus producing multiple heads of leaves.[4]

Cycas revoluta

The leaves are a deep semiglossy green and about 50–150 cm (20–59 in) long when the plants are of a reproductive age. They grow out into a feather-like rosette to 1 m (3.3 ft) in diameter. The crowded, stiff, narrow leaflets are 8–18 cm (3.1–7.1 in) long and have strongly recurved or revolute edges. The basal leaflets become more like spines. The petiole or stems of the sago cycad are 6–10 cm (2.4–3.9 in) long and have small protective barbs.

Roots are called *coralloid* with an *Anabaena* symbiosis allowing nitrogen fixation.[5] Tannins-rich cells are found on either side of the algal layer to resist the algal invasion.

As with other cycads, it is dioecious, with the males bearing pollen cones (strobilus) and the females bearing groups of megasporophylls. Pollination can be done naturally by insects or artificially.

3.38.3 Cultivation and uses

Propagation of *Cycas revoluta* is either by seed or by removal of basal offsets. It is one of the most widely cultivated cycads, grown outdoors in warm temperate and subtropical regions, or under glass in colder areas. It grows best in sandy, well-drained soil, preferably with some organic matter. It needs good drainage or it will rot. It is fairly drought-tolerant and grows well in full sun or outdoor shade, but needs bright light when grown indoors. The leaves can bleach somewhat if moved from indoors to full sun outdoors.

Cycas revoluta also called **Kangi Palm** *covered with snow.*

Of all the cycads, *C. revoluta* is the most popular in cultivation. It is seen in almost all botanical gardens, in both temperate and tropical locations. In many areas of the world, it is heavily promoted commercially as a landscape plant. It is also quite popular as a bonsai plant. First described in the late 18th century, it is tolerant of mild to somewhat cold temperatures, provided the ground is dry. Frost damage can occur at temperatures below −10 °C (14 °F), and several healthy plants have been grown with little protection as far north as St. Louis Missouri and New York, New York, both in USDA zone 7b. *C. revoluta* usually defoliates in this temperate climate, but will usually flush (or grow) several new leaves by spring.

This plant has gained the Royal Horticultural Society's Award of Garden Merit.*[6]

The pith contains edible starch, and is used for making sago. Before use, the starch must be carefully washed to leach out toxins contained in the pith. Extracting edible starch from the sago cycad requires special care due to the poisonous nature of cycads. Cycad sago is used for many of the same purposes as palm sago. Sago is extracted from the sago cycad by cutting the pith from the stem, root and seeds of the cycads, grinding the pith to a coarse flour and then washing it carefully and repeatedly to leach out the natural toxins. The starchy residue is then dried and cooked, producing a starch similar to palm sago/sabudana. The cycad seed contains cycasin toxin and should not be eaten as it is possible for cycasin toxin to survive the most vigorous of repeated washings. Cycasin toxin can cause ALS, Parkinson's, prostate cancer and fibrolemellar hepatocellular carcinoma.

Aulacaspis yasumatsui is a scale insect feeding on *C. revoluta*, and unchecked is able to destroy the plant.*[7]

3.38.4 Chemistry

Example of a full-grown tree

The hydro-alcoholic extract of leaves of *C. revoluta* shows the presence of alkaloids, steroids and tannins while the chloroform extract shows the presence of saponins, tannins and sugars.*[8] Leaflets also contain biflavonoids.*[9] Estragole is the primary volatile compound emitted from the male and female cones of *C. revoluta*.*[10]

3.38.5 Toxicity

Cycad sago is extremely poisonous to animals (including humans) if ingested. Pets are at particular risk, since they seem to find the plant very palatable.*[11] Clinical symptoms of ingestion will develop within 12 hours, and may include vomiting, diarrhea, weakness, seizures, and liver failure or hepatotoxicity characterized by icterus, cirrhosis, and ascites. The pet may appear bruised, have nose bleeds (epistaxis), melena (blood in the stool), hematochezia (bloody straining), and hemarthrosis (blood in the joints).*[12] The ASPCA Animal Poison Control Center estimates a fatality rate of 50 to 75% when ingestion of the sago palm is involved. If any quantity of the plant is ingested, a poison control center or doctor should be contacted immediately. Effects of ingestion can include permanent internal damage and death.

All parts of the plant are toxic; however, the seeds contain the highest level of the toxin cycasin. Cycasin causes gastrointestinal irritation, and in high enough doses, leads to liver failure.*[13] Other toxins include Beta-methylamino L-alanine, a neurotoxic amino acid, and an unidentified toxin which has been observed to cause hindlimb paralysis in cattle.*[14]

3.38.6 References

[1] Hill (2003). *"Cycas revoluta"*. *IUCN Red List of Threatened Species. Version 2006*. International Union for Conservation of Nature. Retrieved 11 May 2006.

[2] D. Gledhill *The Names of Plants*, p. 329, at Google Books

[3] Harrison, Lorraine (2012). *RHS Latin for gardeners*. United Kingdom: Mitchell Beazley. p. 224. ISBN 9781845337315.

[4] Thunberg, Carl Peter. 1782. Verhandelingen uitgegeeven door de hollandse maatschappy der weetenschappen, te Haarlem 20(2): 424, 426–427.

[5] Ultrastructure and phenolic histochemistry of the Cycas revoluta-Anabaena symbiosis. M. Obukowicz, M. Schaller and G.S. Kennedy, New Phytologist, April 1981, Volume 87, Issue 4, pages 751–759, doi:10.1111/j.1469-8137.1981.tb01711.x

[6] *"Cycas revoluta"*. Royal Horticultural Society. Retrieved 22 July 2013.

[7] Aulacaspis yasumatsui (Hemiptera: Sternorrhyncha: Diaspididae), a Scale Insect Pest of Cycads Recently Introduced into Florida. Forrest W. Howard, Avas Hamon, Michael Mclaughlin, Thomas Weissling and Si-lin Yang, The Florida Entomologist, March 1999, Vol. 82, No. 1, pages 14-27 (article)

[8] Leaves Of Cycas revoluta: Potent Antimicrobial And Antioxidant Agent. Manoj K Mourya, Archana Prakash, Ajay Swami, Gautam K Singh and Abhishek Mathur, World Journal of Science and Technology, 2011, Vol 1, No 10, pages 11-20 (article)

[9] Phytochemical Investigation of Cycas circinalis and Cycas revoluta Leaflets: Moderately Active Antibacterial Biflavonoids. Abeer Moawad, Mona Hetta, Jordan K. Zjawiony, Melissa R. Jacob, Mohamed Hifnawy, Jannie P. J. Marais and Daneel Ferreira, Planta Med., 2010, 76(8), pages 796-802, doi:10.1055/s-0029-1240743

[10] Estragole (4-allylanisole) is the primary compound in volatiles emitted from the male and female cones of Cycas revoluta. Hiroshi Azuma and Masumi Kono, Journal of Plant Research, November 2006, Volume 119, Issue 6, pages 671-676, doi:10.1007/s10265-006-0019-2

[11] *Suspected cycad (Cycas revoluta) intoxication in dogs*, Botha CJ, Naude TW, Swan GE, et al.| J S Afr Vet Assoc | 1991

[12] Muller-Esneault, Susan (2009). "Cycas Revoluta: The Sago Palm, or Cycad Toxicity" . Critterology.com.

[13] *Selected poisonous plant concerns small animals*, Knight MW, Dorman DC | Vet Med | 1997 | 92(3):260-272

[14] *Toxicology Brief: Cycad toxicosis in dogs*, Hany Youssef| Veterinary Medicine | May 1, 2008 |

- The Cycad Pages: *Cycas revoluta*

- Sago Palm: University of Arizona Pima County Cooperative Extension

- The Sago Palm, *Cycas revoluta* by Phil Bergman

- Cycads: their evolution, toxins, herbivores and insect pollinators. Schneider D, Wink M, Sporer F, Lounibos P. Naturwissenschaften. 2002 Jul;89(7):281-94. Review.PMID 12216856

3.38.7 External links

- MicrosporophyllMacrosporophyllSeedsVideos - Flavon's Wild herb and Alpine plants

- line drawing of *Cycas revoluta*, Manual of Vascular Plants of the Lower Yangtze Valley China Illustration fig. 31

- line drawing of *Cycas revoluta*, Flora of China Illustrations vol. 4, fig. 2, 1-6

- Female reproductive structure

- New leaves

-

-

3.39 Ebenopsis ebano

Ebenopsis ebano is a species of flowering plant in the pea family, Fabaceae,*[1] that is native to the coastal plain of southern Texas in the United States and eastern Mexico.*[2] It is commonly known as **Texas Ebony** or **Ébano** (in Spanish).*[1]

3.39.1 Description

Texas Ebony is a small, evergreen tree that reaches a height of 7.6–9.1 m (25–30 ft) and a crown width of 1.8–4.6 m (5.9–15.1 ft).*[3]

Texas Ebony (Chloroleucon Ebano)

3.39.2 Habitat and range

The range of *E. ebano* stretches from Laredo and Corpus Christi, Texas*[4] south through the states of Tamaulipas, Nuevo León, San Luis Potosí, Veracruz, Campeche, and Yucatán in Mexico.*[5] It can be found in the Tamaulipan matorral,*[6] Tamaulipan mezquital,*[7] Veracruz dry forests, and Yucatán dry forests ecoregions.*[8] Its habitat extends from sea level to 1,000 m (3,300 ft), averages 20 to 27 °C (68 to 81 °F) in temperature, and receives a mean of 900 mm (35 in) of annual rainfall.*[5]

3.39.3 Uses

Texas Ebony is cultivated in xeriscaping for its dense foliage and fragrant flowers.*[9] It is also used in bonsai.*[10]

3.39.4 Ecology

E. ebano is a host plant for the caterpillars of the Coyote Cloudywing (*Achalarus toxeus*)*[11] and *Sphingicampa blanchardi*.*[12] The seedpods host the bean weevils *Stator beali* and *S. limbatus*. Despite the native range of Texas Ebony overlapping with that of the latter, *S. limbatus* only feeds upon it in locales where it is grown as an ornamental and is not native.*[13] *E. ebano* is also a preferred host of the epiphyte Bailey's Ball Moss (*Tillandsia baileyi*).*[14]

3.39.5 References

[1] "Genus: *Ebenopsis ebano* (Berland.) Barneby & J.W.Grimes". *Germplasm Resources Information Network*. United States Department of Agriculture. 2002-06-28. Retrieved 2009-11-25.

[2] "*Ebenopsis ebano* (Texas Ebony)". *Native Plant Database*. Lady Bird Johnson Wildflower Center. Retrieved 2009-07-06.

[3] Irish, Mary (2008). *Trees and Shrubs for the Southwest: Woody Plants for Arid Gardens*. Timber Press. pp. 178–179. ISBN 978-0-88192-905-8.

[4] "*Ebenopsis ebano* (Berl.) Barneby & Grimes Texas ebony". *The PLANTS Database*. United States Department of Agriculture. Retrieved 2010-11-25.

[5] "*Ebenopsis ebano* (Berl.) Britton et Rose" (PDF). *Reforestación: Fichas Técnicas* (in Spanish). CONAFOR. Retrieved 2009-07-09.

[6] García Pérez, Jaime F.; Óscar Aguirre Calderón; Eduardo Estrada Castillón; Joel Flores Rivas; Javier Jiménez Pérez; Enrique Jurado Ybarra (2007). "Germinación y establecimiento de plantas nativas del matorral tamaulipeco y una especie introducida en un gradiente de elevación" (PDF). *Madera y Bosques* (in Spanish). **13** (1): 99–117.

[7] Lentz, David Lewis (2000). *Imperfect Balance: Landscape Transformations in the Precolumbian Americas*. Columbia University Press. p. 79. ISBN 978-0-231-11157-7.

[8] Beletsky, Les (2006). *Southern Mexico: the Cancún Region, Yucatán Peninsula, Oaxaca, Chiapas, and Tabasco*. Interlink Books. p. 23. ISBN 978-1-56656-640-7.

[9] Miller, George Oxford (2007-03-15). *Landscaping with Native Plants of the Southwest*. MBI Publishing Company. p. 63. ISBN 978-0-7603-2968-9.

[10] Mahler, Robert; Julian Velasco (2008). Pat Lucke Morris; Sigrun Wolff Saphire, eds. *Growing Bonsai Indoors*. Brooklyn Botanic Garden. pp. 48–49. ISBN 978-1-889538-42-6.

[11] "Coyote Cloudywing *Achalarus toxeus* (Plötz, 1882)". Butterflies and Moths of North America. Retrieved 2010-03-30.

[12] "Sphingicampa blanchardi *Sphingicampa blanchardi*". Butterflies and Moths of North America. Retrieved 2010-03-30.

[13] Fox, Charles W. (2006). "Colonization of a new host by a seed-feeding beetle: Genetic variation, maternal experience, and the effect of an alternate host" (PDF). *Annales Zoologici Fennici*. **43**: 239–247.

[14] Sill, Sue (May 2009). "*Tillandsia baileyi* rose - Texas's Disappearing Native Air-Plant" (PDF). *The Sabal*. Native Plant Project. **26** (5): 1–5.

3.39.6 External links

- "Texas Ebony, Ebano, Ebony Blackbeard, Ebony Apes-earring *Pithecellobium flexicaule*". *Benny Simpson's Native Trees of Texas*. Texas A&M University.

- "Pithecellobium flexicaule" (PDF). *Digital Representations of Tree Species Range Maps from "Atlas of United States Trees" by Elbert L. Little, Jr. (and other publications)*. United States Geological Survey.

3.40 Ficus aurea

Ficus aurea, commonly known as the **Florida strangler fig** (or simply **strangler fig**), **golden fig**, or ***higuerón***,*[3] is a tree in the family Moraceae that is native to the U.S. state of Florida, the northern and western Caribbean, southern Mexico and Central America south to Panama.*[4] The specific epithet *aurea* was applied by English botanist Thomas Nuttall who described the species in 1846.

3.40. FICUS AUREA

Ficus aurea is a strangler fig. In figs of this group, seed germination usually takes place in the canopy of a host tree with the seedling living as an epiphyte until its roots establish contact with the ground. After that, it enlarges and strangles its host, eventually becoming a free-standing tree in its own right. Individuals may reach 30 m (100 ft) in height. Like all figs, it has an obligate mutualism with fig wasps: figs are only pollinated by fig wasps, and fig wasps can only reproduce in fig flowers. The tree provides habitat, food and shelter for a host of tropical lifeforms including epiphytes in cloud forests and birds, mammals, reptiles and invertebrates. *F. aurea* is used in traditional medicine, for live fencing, as an ornamental and as a bonsai.

3.40.1 Description

Ficus aurea *sapling showing elliptic leaf shape at Long Key, Florida*

Ficus aurea is a tree which may reach heights of 30 m (98 ft).*[5] It is monoecious: each tree bears functional male and female flowers.*[6] The size and shape of the leaves is variable. Some plants have leaves that are usually less than 10 cm (4 in) long while others have leaves that are larger. The shape of the leaves and of the leaf base also varies—some plants have leaves that are oblong or elliptic with a wedge-shaped to rounded base, while others have heart-shaped or ovate leaves with cordate to rounded bases. *F. aurea* has paired figs*[4] which are green when unripe, turning yellow as they ripen.*[7] They differ in size (0.6–0.8 cm [0.2–0.3 in], about 1 cm [0.4 in], or 1.0–1.2 cm [0.4–0.5 in] in diameter); figs are generally sessile, but in parts of northern Mesoamerica figs are borne on short stalks known as peduncles.*[4]

3.40.2 Taxonomy

With about 750 species, *Ficus* (Moraceae) is one of the largest angiosperm genera (David Frodin of Chelsea Physic Garden ranked it as the 31st largest genus).*[8] *Ficus aurea* is classified in the subgenus *Urostigma* (the strangler figs) and the section *Americana*.*[4] Recent molecular phylogenies have shown that subgenus *Urostigma* is polyphyletic, but have strongly supported the validity of section *Americana* as a discrete group (although its exact relationship to section *Galoglychia* is unclear).*[9]

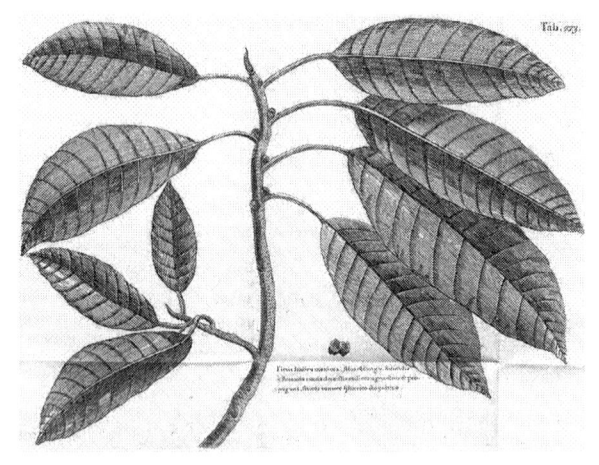

Engraving of Ficus maxima indica *after a drawing by Hans Sloane, the earliest published illustration of* Ficus aurea *and the basis of Thomas Miller's* Ficus maxima. *The unpaired figs in the illustration led to confusion as to the identity of the species described by Miller.*

Thomas Nuttall described the species in the second volume of the his 1846 work *The North American Sylva**[10] with specific epithet *aurea* ('golden' in Latin).*[11] In 1768, Scottish botanist Philip Miller described *Ficus maxima*, citing Carl Linnaeus' *Hortus Cliffortianus* (1738) and Hans Sloane's *Catalogus plantarum quæ in insula Jamaica* (1696). Sloane's illustration of the species, published in 1725, depicted it with figs borne singly, a characteristic of the *Ficus* subgenus *Pharmacosycea*.*[12] As a member of the subgenus *Urostigma*, *F. aurea* has paired figs. However, a closer examination of Sloane's description led Cornelis Berg to conclude that the illustration depicted a member of the subgenus *Urostigma* (since it had other diagnostic of that subgenus), almost certainly *F. aurea*, and that the illustration of singly borne figs was probably artistic license. Berg located the plant collection upon which Sloane's illustration was based and concluded that Miller's *F. maxima* was, in fact, *F. aurea*.*[10] In his description of *F. aurea*, which was based on plant material collected in Florida, Thomas Nuttall considered the possibility that his plants belonged to the species that Sloane had described, but came to the conclusion that it was a new species.*[10] Under the rules of botanical nomenclature, the name *F. maxima* has priority over *F. aurea* since Miller's description was published in 1768, while Nuttall's description was published in 1846.

In their 1914 *Flora of Jamaica*, William Fawcett and Alfred

Barton Rendle linked Sloane's illustration to the tree species that was then known as *Ficus suffocans*, a name that had been assigned to it in August Grisebach's *Flora of the British West Indian Islands*.[13] Gordon DeWolf agreed with their conclusion and used the name *F. maxima* for that species in the 1960 *Flora of Panama*.[14] Since this use has become widespread, Berg proposed that the name *Ficus maxima* be conserved in the way DeWolf had used it,[10] a proposal that was accepted by the nomenclatural committee.[2]

Reassigning the name *Ficus maxima* did not leave *F. aurea* as the oldest name for this species, as German naturalist Johann Heinrich Friedrich Link had described *Ficus ciliolosa* in 1822. Berg concluded that the species Link described was actually *F. aurea*, and since Link's description predated Nuttall's by 24 years, priority should have been given to the name *F. ciliolosa*. Since the former name was widely used and the name *F. ciliolosa* had not been, Berg proposed that the name *F. aurea* be conserved.[10] In response to this, the nomenclatural committee ruled that rather than conserving *F. aurea*, that it would be better to reject *F. ciliolosa*. Conserving *F. aurea* would mean that precedence would be given to that name over all others. By simply rejecting *F. ciliolosa*, the committee left open the possibility that the name *F. aurea* could be supplanted by another older name, if one were to be discovered.[2]

Synonyms

In 1920, American botanist Paul C. Standley described three new species based on collections from Panama and Costa Rica—*Ficus tuerckheimii*, *F. isophlebia* and *F. jimenezii*.[15] DeWolf concluded that they were all the same species,[14] and Berg synonymised them with *F. aurea*.[4] These names have been used widely for Mexican and Central American populations, and continue to be used by some authors. Berg suspected that *Ficus rzedowskiana* Carvajal and Cuevas-Figueroa may also belong to this species, but he had not examined the original material upon which this species was based.[4]

Berg considered *F. aurea* to be a species with at least four morphs. "None of the morphs", he wrote, "can be related to certain habitats or altitudes." [4] Thirty years earlier, William Burger had come to a very different conclusion with respect to *Ficus tuerckheimii*, *F. isophlebia* and *F. jimenezii*—he rejected DeWolf's synonymisation of these three species as based on incomplete evidence. Burger noted that the three taxa occupied different habitats which could be separated in terms of rainfall and elevation.[16]

3.40.3 Reproduction and growth

Figs have an obligate mutualism with fig wasps, (Agaonidae); figs are only pollinated by fig wasps, and fig wasps can only reproduce in fig flowers. Generally, each fig species depends on a single species of wasp for pollination. The wasps are similarly dependent on their fig species in order to reproduce. *Ficus aurea* is pollinated by *Pegoscapus mexicanus* (Ashmead).[17]

Figs have complicated inflorescences called syconia. Flowers are entirely contained within an enclosed structure. Their only connection with the outside is through a small pore called ostiole. Monoecious figs like *F. aurea* have both male and female flowers within the syconium.[18] Female flowers mature first. Once mature, they produce a volatile chemical attractant.[19] Female wasps squeeze their way through the ostiole into the interior of the syconium. Inside the syconium, they pollinate the flowers, lay their eggs in some of them, and die. The eggs hatch and the larvae parasitise the flowers in which they were laid. After four to seven weeks (in *F. aurea*), adult wasps emerge. Males emerge first, mate with the females, and cut exit holes through the walls of the fig. The male flowers mature around the same time as the female wasps emerge. The newly emerged female wasps actively pack their bodies with pollen from the male flowers before leaving through the exit holes the males have cut and fly off to find a syconium in which to lay their eggs. Over the next one to five days, figs ripen.[19] The ripe figs are eaten by various mammals and birds which disperse the seeds.

Phenology

Figs flower and fruit asynchronously.[6] Flowering and fruiting is staggered throughout the population. This fact is important for fig wasps—female wasps need to find a syconium in which to lay their eggs within a few days of emergence, something that would not be possible if all the trees in a population flowered and fruited at the same time. This also makes figs important food resources for frugivores (animals that feed nearly exclusively on fruit); figs are one of the few fruit available at times of the year when fruit are scarce.

Although figs flower asynchronously as a population, in most species flowering is synchronised within an individual. Newly emerged female wasps must move away from their natal tree in order to find figs in which to lay their eggs. This is to the advantage of the fig, since it prevents self-pollination.[18] In Florida, individual *F. aurea* trees flower and fruit asynchronously.[6] Within-tree asynchrony in flowering is likely to raise the probability of self-pollination, but it may be an adaptation that allows the species to maintain an adequate population of wasps at low population densities or in strongly seasonal climates.*[6]

Flowering phenology in *Ficus* has been characterised into five phases. In most figs, phase A is followed almost immediately by phase B. However, in *F. aurea* immature inflorescences can remain dormant for more than nine months.*[6]

A Florida strangler fig with abundant adventitious roots at Villa Vizcaya, Miami

Growth

Ficus aurea is a fast-growing tree.*[20] As a hemiepiphyte it germinates in the canopy of a host tree and begin life as an epiphyte before growing roots down to the ground. *F. aurea* is also a strangler fig (not all hemiepiphytic figs are stranglers)—the roots fuse and encircle the host tree. This usually results in the death of the host tree, since it effectively girdles the tree. Palms, which lack secondary growth, are not affected by this, but they can still be harmed by competition for light, water and nutrients.*[21] Following Hurricane Andrew in 1992, *F. aurea* trees regenerated from root suckers and standing trees.*[22]

3.40.4 Distribution

Ficus aurea ranges from Florida, across the northern Caribbean to Mexico, and south across Central America. It is present in central and southern Florida and the Florida Keys,*[23] The Bahamas, the Caicos Islands, Hispaniola, Cuba, Jamaica, the Cayman Islands, San Andrés (a Colombian possession in the western Caribbean),*[4] southern Mexico,*[24] Belize, Guatemala, Honduras, Nicaragua, El Salvador, Costa Rica and Panama.*[25] It grows from sea level up to 1,800 m (5,500 ft) above sea level,*[4] in habitats ranging from Bahamian dry forests,*[26] to cloud forest in Costa Rica.*[27]

Ficus aurea is found in central and southern Florida as far north as Volusia County;*[28] it is one of only two native fig species in Florida.*[29] The species is present in a range of south Florida ecosystems, including coastal hardwood hammocks, cabbage palm hammocks, tropical hardwood hammocks and shrublands, temperate hardwood hammocks and shrublands*[30] and along watercourses.*[19] In The Bahamas, *F. aurea* is found in tropical dry forests on North Andros,*[31] Great Exuma*[26] and Bimini.*[32] *F. aurea* occurs in 10 states in Mexico, primarily in the south, but extending as far north as Jalisco.*[24] It is found in tropical deciduous forest, tropical semi-evergreen forest, tropical evergreen forest, cloud forest and in aquatic or sub-aquatic habitats.*[24]

3.40.5 Ecology

Rubber, or Banyan Tree, on Banana River, Florida—an 1893 photograph of what is now known as a Florida strangler fig

Ficus aurea is a strangler fig—it tends to establish on a host tree which it gradually encircles and "strangles", eventually taking the place of that tree in the forest canopy. While this makes *F. aurea* an agent in the mortality of other trees, there is little to indicate that its choice of hosts is species specific. However, in dry forests on Great Exuma in The Bahamas, *F. aurea* establishes exclusively on palms, in spite of the presence of several other large trees that should provide suitable hosts. Eric Swagel and colleagues attributed this to the fact that humus accumulates on the leaf bases of these palms and provides a relatively moist microclimate in a dry environment, facilitating seedling survival.*[26]

Figs are sometimes considered to be potential keystone species in communities of fruit-eating animals because of their asynchronous fruiting patterns.*[33] Nathaniel Wheelwright reports that emerald toucanets fed on unripe *F. aurea* fruit at times of fruit scarcity in Monteverde, Costa Rica.*[34] Wheelwright listed the species as a year-round food source for the resplendent quetzal at the same site.*[35] In the Florida Keys, *F. aurea* is one of five fruit species that dominate the diet fed by white-crowned pigeons to their nestlings.*[36] *F. aurea* is also important in the diet of mammalian frugivores—both fruit and young leaves are consumed by black howler monkeys in Belize.*[37]

The interaction between figs and fig wasps is especially well-known (see section on reproduction, above). In addition to its pollinators (*Pegoscapus mexicanus*), *F. aurea* is exploited by a group of non-pollinating chalcidoid wasps whose larvae develop in its figs. These include gallers, inquilines and kleptoparasites as well as parasitoids of both the pollinating and non-pollinating wasps.*[38]

The invertebrates within *F. aurea* syconia in southern Florida include a pollinating wasp, *P. mexicanus*, up to eight or more species of non-pollinating wasps, a plant-parasitic nematode transported by the pollinator, mites, and a predatory rove beetle whose adults and larvae eat fig wasps.*[39] Nematodes: *Schistonchus aureus* (Aphelenchoididae) is a plant-parasitic nematode associated with the pollinator *Pegoscapus mexicanus* and syconia of *F. aurea*.*[40] Mites: belonging to the family Tarsonemidae (Acarina) have been recognized in the syconia of *F. aurea* and *F. citrifolia*, but they have not been identified even to genus, and their behavior is undescribed.*[39] Rove beetles: *Charoxus spinifer* is a rove beetle (Coleoptera: Staphylinidae) whose adults enter late-stage syconia of *F. aurea* and *F. citrifolia*.*[41] Adults eat fig wasps; larvae develop within the syconia and prey on fig wasps, then pupate in the ground.*[42]

As a large tree, *F. aurea* can be an important host for epiphytes. In Costa Rican cloud forests, where *F. aurea* is "the most conspicuous component" of intact forest,*[27] trees in forest patches supported richer communities of epiphytic bryophytes, while isolated trees supported greater lichen cover.*[27]

Florida International University ecologist Suzanne Koptur reported the presence of extrafloral nectaries on *F. aurea* figs in the Florida Everglades.*[43] Extrafloral nectaries are structures which produce nectar but are not associated with flowers. They are usually interpreted as defensive structure and are often produced in response to attack by insect herbivores.*[44] They attract insects, primarily ants, which defend the nectaries, thus protecting the plant against herbivores.*[45]

3.40.6 Uses

The fruit of *Ficus aurea* is edible and was used for food by the indigenous people and early settlers in Florida; it is still eaten occasionally as a backyard source of native fruit. The latex was used to make a chewing gum, and aerial roots may have been used to make lashings, arrows, bowstrings and fishing lines. The fruit was used to make a rose-coloured dye.*[46] *F. aurea* was also used in traditional medicine in The Bahamas*[47] and Florida.*[46] Allison Adonizio and colleagues screened *F. aurea* for anti-quorum sensing activity (as a possible means of anti-bacterial action), but found no such activity.*[48]

Individual *F. aurea* trees are common on dairy farms in La Cruz, Cañitas and Santa Elena in Costa Rica, since they are often spared when forest is converted to pasture. In interviews, farmers identified the species as useful for fence posts, live fencing and firewood, and as a food species for wild birds and mammals.*[3]

Ficus aurea is used as an ornamental tree, an indoor tree and as a bonsai.*[7] Like other figs, it tends to invade built structures and foundations, and need to be removed to prevent structural damage.*[39] Although young trees are described as "rather ornamental",*[29] older trees are considered to be difficult to maintain (because of the adventitious roots that develop off branches) and are not recommended for small areas.*[7] However, it was considered a useful tree for "enviroscaping" to conserve energy in south Florida, since it is "not as aggressive as many exotic fig species," although it must be given enough space.*[20]

3.40.7 References

[1] "The Plant List".

[2] Brummitt, R.K. (2005). "Report of the Committee for Spermatophyta: 56". *Taxon*. **54** (2): 527–536. doi:10.2307/25065389. JSTOR 25065389.

[3] Harvey, C. A.; Haber, W. A. (1998). "Remnant trees and the conservation of biodiversity in Costa Rican pastures". *Agroforestry Systems*. **44** (1): 37–68. doi:10.1023/A:1006122211692.

[4] Berg, C.C. (2007). "Proposals for treating four species complexes in *Ficus* subgenus *Urostigma* section *Americanae* (Moraceae)". *Blumea*. **52** (2): 295–312. doi:10.3767/000651907X609034.

[5] Flora de Nicaragua database. Tropicos. (Spanish) Retrieved on 2008-07-02

[6] Bronstein, Judith L.; Patel, Aviva (1992). "Causes and Consequences of Within-Tree Phenological Patterns in the Florida Strangling Fig, Ficus aurea (Moraceae)". *American Journal of Botany*. **79** (1): 41–48. doi:10.2307/2445195. JSTOR 2445195.

[7] Gilman, Edward F.; Watson, Dennis G. (December 2006). "*Ficus aurea*: Strangler Fig". Institute of Food and Agricultural Sciences (ENH409). Retrieved 2008-06-10.

[8] Frodin, David G. (2004). "History and concepts of big plant genera". *Taxon*. **53** (3): 753–776. doi:10.2307/4135449. JSTOR 4135449.

3.40. FICUS AUREA

[9] Rønsted, N.; Weiblen, G. D.; Clement, W. L.; Zerega, N. J. C.; Savolainen, V. (2008). "Reconstructing the phylogeny of figs (Ficus, Moraceae) to reveal the history of the fig pollination mutualism" (PDF). *Symbiosis*. **45** (1–3): 45–56.

[10] Berg, Cornelis C. (May 2003). "(1587–1590) Proposals to conserve the names *Ficus citrifolia* against *F. caribaea*, *F. maxima* with a conserved type, *F. aurea* against *F. ciliolosa*, and *F. americana* against *F. perforata* (Moraceae)". *Taxon*. **52** (2): 368–370. doi:10.2307/3647421. JSTOR 3647421.

[11] Simpson DP (1979). *Cassell's Latin Dictionary* (5 ed.). London: Cassell Ltd. p. 883. ISBN 0-304-52257-0.

[12] Sloane, Hans (1725). *A voyage to the islands Madera, Barbados, Nieves, S. Christophers and Jamaica*. B.M.

[13] Grisebach, August (1859). *Flora of the British West Indian Islands*. **1**. London: L. Reeve & Co. Retrieved 2008-07-02.

[14] DeWolf, Gordon P., Jr. "Ficus (Tourn.) L." in Nevling, Lorin I., Jr. (1960). "Flora of Panama. Part IV. Fascicle II". *Annals of the Missouri Botanical Garden*. **47** (2): 81–203. doi:10.2307/2394704. JSTOR 2394704.

[15] Standley, Paul C. (1920). "The Mexican and Central American Species of Ficus". *Contributions from the United States National Herbarium*. **20** (1): 1–35.

[16] Burger, William C. (1974). "Ecological Differentiation in Some Congeneric Species of Costa Rican Flowering Plants". *Annals of the Missouri Botanical Garden*. **61** (2): 297–306. doi:10.2307/2395057. JSTOR 2395057.

[17] Jousselin, Emmanuelle; Hossaert-Mckey, Martine; Vernet, Didier; Kjellberg, Finn (2001). "Egg deposition patterns of fig pollinating wasps: implications for studies on the stability of the mutualism". *Ecological Entomology*. **26** (6): 602–608. doi:10.1046/j.1365-2311.2001.00368.x.

[18] Janzen, Daniel H. (1979). "How to be a fig". *Annual Review of Ecology and Systematics*. **10**: 13–51. doi:10.1146/annurev.es.10.110179.000305.

[19] Bronstein, Judith L.; Hossaert-McKey, Martine (1995). "Hurricane Andrew and a Florida Fig Pollination Mutualism: Resilience of an Obligate Interaction". *Biotropica*. **27** (3): 373–381. doi:10.2307/2388922. JSTOR 2388922.

[20] Broschat, Timothy K.; Alan W. Meerow; Robert J. Black (February 2007). "Enviroscaping to Conserve Energy: Trees for South Florida". Institute of Food and Agricultural Sciences (Circular EES-42). Retrieved 2008-06-10.

[21] Putz, Francis E.; N. Michele Holbrook (1989). "Strangler Fig Rooting Habits and Nutrient Relations in the Llanos of Venezuela". *American Journal of Botany*. **76** (6): 781–788. doi:10.2307/2444534. JSTOR 2444534.

[22] Horvitz, Carol C.; Pascarella, John B.; McMann, Stephen; Freedman, Andrea; Hofstetter, Ronald H. (1988). "Functional Roles of Invasive Non-Indigenous Plants in Hurricane-Affected Subtropical Hardwood Forests". *Ecological Applications*. **8** (4): 947–974. doi:10.1890/1051-0761(1998)008[0947:FROINI]2.0.CO;2. ISSN 1051-0761.

[23] Little, Elbert L., Jr. (1978). *Atlas of United States Trees, Volume 5: Florida*. Washington, D.C.: U.S. Forest Service. OCLC 241660.

[24] Serrato, Alejandra; Ibarra-Manríquez, Guillermo; Oyama, Ken (March 2004). "Biogeography and conservation of the genus *Ficus* (Moraceae) in Mexico". *Journal of Biogeography*. **31** (3): 475–485. doi:10.1046/j.0305-0270.2003.01039.x.

[25] Ficus aurea Nutt. Flora Mesoamericana: Lista Anotada. (Spanish) Retrieved on 2008-07-02

[26] Swagel, Eric N.; Bernhard, A. Van H.; Ellmore, George S. (1997). "Substrate water potential constraints on germination of the strangler fig *Ficus aurea* (Moraceae)". *American Journal of Botany*. **84** (5): 716–722. doi:10.2307/2445908. JSTOR 2445908.

[27] Sillett, Stephen C.; Gradstein, S. Rob; Griffin, Dana, III (1995). "Bryophyte Diversity of Ficus Tree Crowns from Cloud Forest and Pasture in Costa Rica". *The Bryologist*. **98** (2): 251–260. doi:10.2307/3243312. JSTOR 3243312.

[28] "*Ficus aurea*: Distribution Map". *Atlas of Florida Vascular Plants*. Institute for Systematic Botany, University of South Florid. Retrieved 2008-06-10.

[29] Bessey, Ernst A. (1908). "The Florida Strangling Figs". *Missouri Botanical Garden Annual Report*. **1908**: 25–33. doi:10.2307/2400063. JSTOR 2400063.

[30] Ken Rutchey; et al. (2006). "Vegetation Classification for South Florida Natural Areas". United States Geological Survey. Retrieved 2008-06-10. Open-File Report 2006-1240.

[31] Smith, Inge K.; Vankat, John L. (1992). "Dry Evergreen Forest (Coppice) Communities of North Andros Island, Bahamas". *Bulletin of the Torrey Botanical Club*. **119** (2): 181–191. doi:10.2307/2997030. JSTOR 2997030.

[32] Howard, Richard A. (1950). "Vegetation of the Bimini Island Group: Bahamas, B. W. I". *Ecological Monographs*. **20** (4): 317–349. doi:10.2307/1943569. JSTOR 1943569.

[33] Terborgh, John (1986). "Keystone plant resources in the tropical forests". In Michael E. Soulé (ed.). *Conservation Biology: The Science of Scarcity and Diversity*. Sunderland, Massachusetts: Sinauer Associates. pp. 330–344. ISBN 978-0-87893-795-0.

[34] Wheelwright, Nathaniel T. (June 1985). "Competition for dispersers, and the timing of flowering and fruiting in a guild of tropical trees" (PDF). *Oikos*. **44** (3): 465–477. doi:10.2307/3565788. JSTOR 3565788.

[35] Wheelwright, Nathaniel T. (1983). "Fruits and the Ecology of Resplendent Quetzals" (PDF). *The Auk.* **100** (2): 286–301.

[36] Bancroft, G. Thomas; Reed Bowman (1994). "Temporal Patterns in Diet of Nestling White-Crowned Pigeons: Implications for Conservation of Frugivorous Columbids" (PDF). *The Auk.* **111** (4): 844–52. doi:10.2307/4088816.

[37] Silver, S. C.; L. E. T. Ostro; C. P. Yeager; R. Horwich (1999). "Feeding ecology of the black howler monkey (*Alouatta pigra*) in Northern Belize" (PDF). *American Journal of Primatology.* **45** (3): 263–279. doi:10.1002/(SICI)1098-2345(1998)45:3<263::AID-AJP3>3.0.CO;2-U. PMID 9651649.

[38] Bronstein, Judith L. (1999). "Natural History of *Anidarnes bicolor* (Hymenoptera: Agaonidae), a Galler of the Florida Strangling Fig (*Ficus aurea*)" (PDF). *Florida Entomologist.* **82** (3): 454–461. doi:10.2307/3496871. JSTOR 3496871.

[39] Nadel, Hannah; Frank, J. Howard; Knight, R. J., Jr. (March 1992). "Escapees and Accomplices: The Naturalization of Exotic *Ficus* and Their Associated Faunas in Florida". *Florida Entomologist.* **75** (1): 29–38. doi:10.2307/3495478. JSTOR 3495478.

[40] Decrappeo, N.; Giblin-Davis, R. M. (2001). "*Schistonchus aureus* n. sp. and *S. laevigatus* n. sp. (Aphelenchoididae): Associates of native Floridian *Ficus* spp. and their *Pegoscapus* pollinators (Agaonidae)". *Journal of Nematology.* **33** (2–3): 91–103. PMC 2638131⊚. PMID 19266003.

[41] Frank, J. H.; Thomas, M. C. (1997). "A new species of *Charoxus* (Coleoptera: Staphylinidae) from native figs (*Ficus* spp.) in Florida". *Journal of the New York Entomological Society.* **104**: 70–78.

[42] Frank, J. H.; Nadel, Hannah (2012). "Life cycle and behaviour of Charoxus spinifer and Charoxus major (Coleoptera: Staphylinidae: Aleocharinae), predators of fig wasps (Hymenoptera: Agaonidae)". *Journal of Natural History.* **46** (9–10): 621–635. doi:10.1080/00222933.2011.651641.

[43] Koptur, Suzanne (1992). "Plants with Extrafloral Nectaries and Ants in Everglades Habitats" (PDF). *Florida Entomologist.* **75** (1): 38–50. doi:10.2307/3495479. JSTOR 3495479.

[44] Heil, Martin (2007). "Indirect defence via tritrophic interactions". *New Phytologist.* **178** (1): 41–61. doi:10.1111/j.1469-8137.2007.02330.x. PMID 18086230.

[45] Bronstein, Judith L.; Alarcón, Ruben; Geber, Monica (2006). "The evolution of plant–insect mutualisms". *New Phytologist.* **172** (3): 412–428. doi:10.1111/j.1469-8137.2006.01864.x. PMID 17083673.

[46] Allen, Ginger M.; Bond, Michael D.; Main, Martin B. (December 2002). "50 Common Native Plants Important In Florida's Ethnobotanical History". Institute of Food and Agricultural Sciences (Circular 1439). Retrieved 2008-06-10.

[47] Eldridge, Joan (October 1975). "Bush medicine in the Exumas and Long Island, Bahamas. A field study". *Economic Botany.* **29** (4): 307–332. doi:10.1007/BF02862180.

[48] Adonizio, Allison L.; Downum, Kelsey; Bennett, Bradley C.; Mathee, Kalai (2006). "Anti-quorum sensing activity of medicinal plants in southern Florida". *Journal of Ethnopharmacology.* **105** (3): 427–435. doi:10.1016/j.jep.2005.11.025. PMID 16406418.

3.40.8 External links

- Interactive Distribution Map for Ficus aurea

3.41 Ficus benjamina

Ficus benjamina, commonly known as **weeping fig**, **benjamin fig**[2] or **Ficus tree**, and often sold in stores as just **ficus**, is a species of flowering plant in the family Moraceae, native to Asia and Australia.[3] It is the official tree of Bangkok. The species is also naturalized in the West Indies and in the States of Florida and Arizona in the United States.[4][5]

Ficus benjamina is a tree reaching 30 metres (98 ft) tall in natural conditions, with gracefully drooping branchlets and glossy leaves 6–13 cm (2–5 in), oval with an acuminate tip. In its native range, its small fruit are favored by some birds, such as the superb fruit dove, wompoo fruit dove, pink-spotted fruit dove, ornate fruit dove, orange-bellied fruit dove, Torresian imperial pigeon, purple-tailed imperial pigeon (Frith *et al.* 1976).

3.41.1 Cultivation

In tropical latitudes, the weeping fig makes a very large and stately tree for parks and other urban situations, such as wide roads. It is often cultivated for this purpose.

Ficus benjamina is a very popular houseplant in temperate areas, due to its elegant growth and tolerance of poor growing conditions; it does best in bright, sunny conditions but will also tolerate considerable shade. It requires a moderate amount of watering in summer, and only enough to keep it from drying out in the winter. It does not need to be misted. The plant is sensitive to cold and should be protected from strong drafts. When grown indoors, it can grow too large for its situation, and may need drastic pruning or replacing. *Ficus benjamina* has been shown to effectively remove gaseous formaldehyde from indoor air.[6]

The fruit is edible, but the plant is not usually grown for its fruit. The leaves are very sensitive to small changes in light. When it is turned around or re-located it reacts by dropping many of its leaves and replacing them with new leaves adapted to the new light intensity.

Used as decorative plant in gardens in Hyderabad, India

There are numerous cultivars available (e.g. 'Danielle', 'Naomi', 'Exotica', and 'Golden King'). Some cultivars include different patterns of colouration on the leaves, ranging from light green to dark green, and various forms of white variegation.

In cultivation in the UK, this plant*[7] and the variegated cultivar 'Starlight'*[8] have gained the Royal Horticultural Society's Award of Garden Merit.

The miniature cultivars, especially 'Too Little', are among the most popular plants for indoor bonsai.

3.41.2 Destructive roots

The United States Forest Service states "Roots grow rapidly, invading gardens, growing under and lifting sidewalks, patios, and driveways." They conclude that its use in tree form is much too large for residential planting, therefore in these settings this species should only be used as a hedge or clipped screen.*[9]

3.41.3 Allergic Reactions

The plant is a major source of indoor allergens, ranking as the third most common cause of indoor allergies after dust and pets.*[10] Common allergy symptoms include rhinoconjunctivitis and allergic asthma. Ficus plants can be of particular concern to latex allergy sufferers due to the latex in the ficus plant, and should not be kept in the environment of latex allergy sufferers.*[10] In extreme cases, ficus exposure can cause anaphylactic shock in latex allergy sufferers.

Allergy to ficus plants develops over time and from exposure. The allergy was first observed in occupational settings amongst workers who regularly handled the plants. A study of workers at four plant-leasing firms showed that 27% of the workers had developed antibodies in response to exposure to the plants.*[11]

3.41.4 Gallery

-  tree in Hyderabad, India.
-  fig in Hyderabad, India.
-  leaves in Hyderabad, India.
- 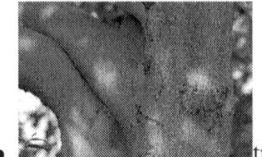 trunk in Hyderabad, India.

- Leaves

3.41.5 References

[1] *"Ficus benjamina* L.". *World Checklist of Selected Plant Families (WCSP)*. Royal Botanic Gardens, Kew. Retrieved 2015-07-19 – via The Plant List.

[2] "Ficus benjamina". *Germplasm Resources Information Network*. United States Department of Agriculture. 2009-01-16. Retrieved 2009-02-17.

[3] Flora of China, *Ficus benjamina* Linnaeus, 垂叶榕 chui ye

[4] Biota of North America Program 2014 county distribution map

[5] Flora of North America, *Ficus benjamina* Linnaeus, Mant. Pl. 129. 1767. Weeping fig

[6] Kwang Jin Kim, Mi Jung Kil, Jeong Seob Song, Eun Ha Yoo, Ki-Cheol Son, Stanley J. Kays (July 2008). "Efficiency of Volatile Formaldehyde Removal by Indoor Plants: Contribution of Aerial Plant Parts versus the Root Zone". *Journal of The American Society for Horticultural Science*. **133** (4): 521–526. ISSN 0003-1062.

[7] "*Ficus benjamina*". Royal Horticultural Society. Retrieved December 9, 2014.

[8] "*Ficus benjamina* 'Starlight' (v) Benjamin fig". Royal Horticultural Society. Retrieved December 9, 2014.

[9] Gilman, Edward F.; Watson, Dennis G. (November 1993). "*Ficus benjamina* Weeping Fig" (PDF). *Fact Sheet ST-251*. United States Forest Service. Retrieved December 6, 2014.

[10] Schenkelberger V, Freitag M, Altmeyer P. "*Ficus benjamina*--the hidden allergen in the house". *Hautarzt*. **49** (1): 2–5. doi:10.1007/s001050050692. PMID 9522185.

[11] http://www.phadia.com/en/Products/Allergy-testing-products/ImmunoCAP-Allergen-Information/Occupational-Allergens/Allergens/Ficus-spp-/. Missing or empty |title= (help)

3.41.6 Bibliography

- **Frith**, H.J.; Rome, F.H.J.C. & Wolfe, T.O. (1976): Food of fruit-pigeons in New Guinea. *Emu* **76**(2): 49-58. HTML abstract

3.42 Ficus coronata

For other uses of "sandpaper fig", see Sandpaper fig.

Ficus coronata, commonly known as the **sandpaper fig** or **creek sandpaper fig**, is a species of fig tree, native to Australia. It is found along the east coast from Mackay in Central Queensland, through New South Wales and just into Victoria near Mallacoota. It grows along river banks and gullies in rainforest and open forest. Its common name is derived from its rough sandpapery leaves, which it shares with the other sandpaper figs.

3.42.1 Taxonomy

Ficus coronata was first described by the Italian Marquese di Spigno in 1818. Its specific epithet the Latin *coronata* "crowned", referring to a ring of bristles around the apex of the fruit. *Ficus stephanocarpa* (also meaning 'crowned fruit') as described by the German botanist Otto Warburg is a synonym.[1]

3.42.2 Description

The sandpaper fig is a small tree which may reach the dimensions of 6–12 m (20–39 ft) tall by 3–5 m (9.8–16.4 ft) wide, although is generally smaller. The trunk is dark brown, and the ovate or elliptical leaves are 5–15 cm (2.0–5.9 in) long by 2–5 cm (0.79–1.97 in) wide and very scabrous (rough) like sandpaper on the upper side. The new growth is hairy. The succulent oval fruit is around 1.5 cm (0.59 in) long and covered in dense hairs.[1][2]

3.42.3 Distribution and habitat

The sandpaper fig is found along watercourses and gullies in rainforest, and less commonly in open forest. It may be associated with the rough-barked apple (*Angophora floribunda*).[3] It is found on limestone outcrops in Kanangra-Boyd National Park.[4] It is found from Mackay southwards through New South Wales and into eastern Victoria where it is listed as "threatened" under the Flora and Fauna Guarantee Act 1988.[5] There is one record from the Northern Territory.[1]

3.42.4 Ecology

Ficus coronata serves as a food plant for the caterpillars of the Queensland butterfly the common- or purple moonbeam (*Philiris innotatus*),*[6] The Australasian figbird (*Sphecotheres vieilloti*), green catbird (*Ailuroedus crassirostris*), olive-backed oriole (*Oriolus sagittatus*), topknot pigeon (*Lopholaimus antarcticus*), and grey-headed flying fox (*Pteropus poliocephalus*) are among those animals who consume the fruit.*[7]

3.42.5 Uses

The fruit is edible and palatable,*[8] and was consumed by local Aboriginal people.

A popular story holds that the fig's leaves were used as sandpaper for polishing wood or turtle shells by indigenous people, yet when tested by Bonsai and fig enthusiast Len Webber, they were too brittle and soft to function in this fashion.*[9]

The sandpaper fig's leaves are an attractive attribute which may be highlighted with bonsai, although the trunk may not thicken spontaneously.*[10] It is suited to a shady position in gardens, or medium to brightly lit indoor spaces.*[11] Like all figs in garden situations, they attract birds,*[12] such as species of silvereye and rainforest pigeon.*[13]

3.42.6 References

[1] Elliot, Rodger W; Jones, David L; Blake, Trevor (1986). *Encyclopaedia of Australian Plants Suitable for Cultivation: Volume 4 (Eu-Go)*. Port Melbourne: Lothian Press. pp. 213–X. ISBN 0-85091-589-9.

[2] Fairley, Alan; Moore, Philip (2000). *Native Plants of the Sydney District:An Identification Guide* (2nd ed.). Kenthurst, NSW: Kangaroo Press. pp. 61–62. ISBN 0-7318-1031-7.

[3] Benson, Doug; McDougall, Lyn (1998). "Ecology of Sydney plant species:Part 6 Dicotyledon family Myrtaceae" (PDF). *Cunninghamia*. 5 (4): 809–987. Archived from the original (PDF) on 2007-10-07. Retrieved 2008-02-19.

[4] Parks and Wildlife Division (2005). "Kowmung River, Kanangra-Boyd National Park: Wild River Assessment" (PDF). Department of Environment and Conservation (NSW). Retrieved 23 April 2012.

[5] "Threatened List March 2008" (PDF). *Flora and Fauna Guarantee Act 1988*. Department of Sustainability and Environment.

[6] Braby, Michael F. (2005). *The Complete Field Guide to Butterflies of Australia*. Collingwood, Victoria: CSIRO Publishing. p. 228. ISBN 0-643-09027-4.

[7] Floyd, Alex G. (2009). *Rainforest Trees of Mainland Southeastern Australia*. Lismore, NSW: Terania Rainforest Publishing. p. 230. ISBN 978-0-9589436-7-3.

[8] Lindsay, Lenore (March 1992). "Fancy a feast? Try a fig." . *Australian Plants*. **16** (130): 251–52.

[9] Webber, Len (1991). *Rainforest to Bonsai*. East Roseville, NSW: Simon and Schuster. p. 125. ISBN 0-7318-0237-3.

[10] Koreshoff, Dorothy and Vita (1984). *Bonsai with Australian native Plants*. Brisbane: Boolarong Publications. p. 52. ISBN 0-908175-66-3.

[11] Ratcliffe, David & Patricia (1987). *Australian Native Plants for Indoors*. Crows Nest, NSW: Little Hills Press. p. 89. ISBN 0-949773-49-2.

[12] Elliot, Rodger (1994). *Attracting Wildlife to Your Garden*. Melbourne: Lothian Books. p. 58. ISBN 0-85091-628-3.

[13] Dengate, John (1994). *Attracting Birds to Your Garden*. Kenthurst: New Holland Press. p. 23. ISBN 1-86436-411-4.

3.42.7 External links

- "Ficus coronata" . *Australian Plant Name Index (APNI), IBIS database*. Centre for Plant Biodiversity Research, Australian Government.

3.43 Ficus microcarpa

"Curtain fig" redirects here. For the Queensland, Australia strangler fig attraction, see Curtain Fig Tree.

Ficus microcarpa, also known as **Chinese banyan**, **Malayan banyan**, **Taiwan banyan**, **Indian laurel**, **curtain fig**, or **gajumaru** (ガジュマル), is a tree native in the range from China through Nepal, Bhutan, Sikkim, India, Sri Lanka, Taiwan, the Malay Archipelago, New Guinea, Australia,*[2] the Ryukyu Islands,*[3] and New Caledonia. It is widely planted as a shade tree*[2] and frequently misidentified as *F. retusa* or as *F. nitida* (*F. benjamina*).*[4]

3.43.1 Taxonomy

Ficus microcarpa has been described in 1782 by Carl Linnaeus the Younger. The species has a considerable number of synonyms. In 1965, E. J. H. Corner described seven varieties (and two forms of *Ficus microcarpa* var. *microcarpa*)*[5] which were regarded as synonyms under the name of *Ficus microcarpa* in the latest Flora Malesiana volume.

Hill's weeping fig was first formally described as a species, *Ficus hillii*, by Frederick Manson Bailey in the *Botany Bulletin* of the Queensland Department of Agriculture, based

Ficus microcarpa *with aerial roots.*

Ficus microcarpa *foliage and fruit.*

on the type specimen collected in the "scrubs of tropical Queensland'".*[6] In 1965, it was reassigned by E. J .H. Corner as a variety of *F. microcarpa*, namely ***F. microcarpa*** var. ***hillii***.*[5]

3.43.2 Distribution and habitat

Ficus microcarpa was widely distributed as an ornamental plant and is one of the most common street trees in warm climates. The symbiotic pollinating fig wasp, *Eupristina verticillata*, was introduced along with *F. microcarpa*. Such an introduction, however, can be delayed: in Brazil - where specimens of the tree had been used in gardening since the nineteenth century, when it was introduced by the architect Auguste François Marie Glaziou into various public parks of Rio de Janeiro - the appearance of saplings began only during the 1970s. Such saplings are considered to be very aggressive, as they can grow in the walls of buildings, bridges, highways, and other concrete structures.*[7]

The tree is considered a major invasive species in Hawaii, Florida, Bermuda, Central America, and South America. It's commonly used as a ornamental tree in most of Spain's mediterranean coast, as in the Balearic and the Canary islands. Ficus microcarpa can also be found on the Algarve, the southern coast of Sicily or in Cyprus. It is a common ornamental tree in the Tel Aviv, Israel area.

3.43.3 Ecology

The pollinating fig wasp associated with *Ficus microcarpa* is *Eupristina verticillata*. In addition, 19 non-pollinating fig wasp species parasitize *Ficus microcarpa* figs.*[8] These fig wasps are from different families. First, the Eurytomidae wasps are *Sycophila curta, Sycophila petiolata, Sycophila maculafacies* and *Bruchophagus sensoriae*. The wasps from the Pteromalidae family are the most speciose: *Acophila microcarpae, Eufroggattisca okinavensis, Meselatus bicolor, Micranisa degastris, Odontofroggatia corneri, Odontogroggatia gajimaru, Odontogroggatia galili, Odontofroggatia ishii, Philotrypesis emeryi, Philotrypesis okinavensis, Philotrypesis taiwanensis, Sycoryctes moneres, Sycoscapter gajimaru, Walkerella kurandensis*. Only one species from the Ormyridae family: *Ormyrus lini*.

In some parts of its introduced range, it is very attractive to avian wildlife: in São Paulo, Brazil, ten species of birds were listed as feeding on its fruits, especially *Turdus rufiventris, Pitangus sulphuratus, Turdus leucomelas, Thraupis sayaca* and *Celeus flavescens*.*[9] Its fruit and leaves are also sought after and eaten by the parrot *Aratinga leucophthalmus*.*[10] Although invasive, its hardiness makes it an important species for the attraction of avian wildlife in urban environments.*[11]

3.43.4 Cultivation

Ficus microcarpa is cultivated as an ornamental tree for planting in gardens, parks, and in containers as an indoor plant and bonsai specimen.

3.43.5 References

[1] *The Plant List: A Working List of All Plant Species*, retrieved 13 April 2016

[2] Zhengyi Wu; Zhe-Kun Zhou; Michael G. Gilbert, "*Ficus microcarpa* Linnaeus f., Suppl. Pl. 442. 1782", *Flora of China online*, **5**

[3] , Yokoyama, Jun, and Kunio Iwatsuki. "A faunal survey of fig-wasps (Chalcidoidea: Hymenoptera) distributed in Japan and their associations with figs (Ficus: Moraceae)." Entomological science 1.1 (1998): 37-46.

Ficus microcarpa *as an indoor landscape plant.*

[4] *"Ficus microcarpa* L. f." , *USDA GRIN Taxonomy*

[5] Corner, E. J. H. (1965). "Check-list of *Ficus* in Asia and Australasia with keys to identification" . *The Gardens' Bulletin Singapore.* (digitised, online, via biodiversitylibrary.org). **21** (1): 1–186. Retrieved 5 Feb 2014. pages 22–23

[6] *"Ficus microcarpa* var. *hillii* (F.M.Bailey) Corner" . *Australian Plant Name Index (APNI), IBIS database.* Centre for Plant Biodiversity Research, Australian Government.

[7] Carauta, Jorge Pedro Pereira & Diaz, B. Ernani, *Figueiras no Brasil, Rio de Janeiro, UFRJ, 2002, ISBN 85-7108-250-2, pg.155*

[8] Chen, Ying-Ru; Wen-Chung Chuang; Wen-Jer Wu (1999). "Chalcids wasps on *Ficus microcarpa* L. in Taiwan (Hymenoptera: Chalcidoidea)". *Journal of Taiwan Museum.* **52**: 39–79.

[9] Somenzari, Marina; Linda Lacerda da Silva & Rosanna G. Q. Benesi (2006). "Atração de aves por *Ficus elastica* Roxb. e *Ficus microcarpa* L. em ambiente urbano (abstract)" (PDF). *XIV Congresso Brasileiro de Ornitologia.* Archived from the original (PDF) on 2009-02-06.

[10] da Silva, Linda Lacerda; Sonia Maria de Amorim Gimenez & Sumiko Namba (2006). "Método quantitativo para a avaliacão da preferência alimentar de *Aratinga leucophthalmus* em cativeiro (abstract)" (PDF). *XIV Congresso Brasileiro de Ornitologia.* Archived from the original (PDF) on 2011-07-06.

[11] Frisch, Johan Dalgas & Frisch, Christian Dalgas, *Aves Brasileiras e Plantas que as Atraem*, São Paulo:2005, ISBN 85-85015-07-1 , pg.366

3.43.6 External links

- Plants of Hawaii: *Ficus microcarpa*, hear.org

- *Ficus microcarpa* L.f., Natural Resources Conservation Service of the U.S. Department of Agriculture

- Indian Laurel Invasive Plant Page, Bermuda Department of Conservation Services.

3.44 Ficus neriifolia

Ficus neriifolia is a species of fig (*Ficus*). It is native to Asia, including Bhutan, Burma, China, India, and Nepal.*[1]

3.44.1 Description

Ficus neriifolia grows as a tree up to 15 m (50 ft) tall with smooth, dark grey bark on its trunk. The hairless, leathery oval to lanceolate (spear-shaped) leaves are up to 8–18 cm (3 $\frac{1}{4}$–7 in) long by 3–6.5 cm (1 $\frac{1}{8}$–2 $\frac{1}{2}$ in) wide, and often asymmetrical in shape. The 8–10 cm (3 $\frac{1}{4}$–4 in) diameter figs are rounded, oval, or cylindrical and grow in pairs off older branches.*[1]

3.44.2 Taxonomy

James Edward Smith described *Ficus neriifolia* in 1810.

In 1965, E.H.Corner regarded the species as having three valid varieties : *F. neriifolia* var. *nemoralis, F. neriifolia* var. *fieldingii* and *F. neriifolia* var. *trilepis*. However, Wu and colleagues did not treat them as distinct in 2003. Chaudhary and colleagues observed that the receptacles are distinct and hence further investigation is needed.*[2]

3.44.3 Distribution and habitat

Ficus neriifolia is found in Mêdog County in southern Tibet and western Yunnan province in China, as well as Bhutan,

Myanmar,[1] central and western Nepal,[3] northeastern India including Sikkim,[1] Arunachal Pradesh, Assam, Meghalaya, Mizoram, Nagaland and Uttar Pradesh.[2]

It grows in forests of both coniferous and broadleaved trees at elevations of 1,700–2,900 m (5,600–9,500 ft) above sea level in China,[1] and 500–2,200 m (1,600–7,200 ft) above sea level in India.[2]

3.44.4 Ecology

The figs and leaves are eaten by the endangered black crested gibbon (*Nomascus concolor*) in Yunnan province, particularly between May and September where it is the most commonly eaten plant species.[4] It is also an important food item of the eastern hoolock gibbon (*Hoolock leuconedys*)[5]

3.44.5 Uses

Ficus neriifolia *as bonsai, San Diego*

The foliage of *Ficus neriifolia* is used as fodder and its wood used as fuel in Nepal. The juice of the stem bark is used as a folk remedy for conjunctivitis and boils[3] This fig tree is considered good for indoor bonsai in temperate climates, and it is easily shaped and pruned.[6]

3.44.6 References

[1] *Ficus neriifolia*. Flora of China.

[2] Chaudhary, Lal Babu, Jana Venkata Sudhakar, Anoop Kumar, Omesh Bajpai, Rinkey Tiwari, and G. V. S. Murthy (2012). "Synopsis of the genus *Ficus* L.(Moraceae) in India" (PDF). *Taiwania*. **57** (2): 193–216 [196].

[3] Kunwar, Ripu M.; Rainer W. Bussmann (2006). "*Ficus* (Fig) species in Nepal: a review of diversity and indigenous uses" (PDF). *Lyonia*. **11** (1): 85–97.

[4] Fan, Pengfei; Qingyong Ni; Guozheng Sun; Bei Huang & Xuelong Jiang (2009). "Gibbons under seasonal stress: the diet of the black crested gibbon (*Nomascus concolor*) on Mt. Wuliang, Central Yunnan, China" (PDF). *Primates*. **50** (1): 37–44. doi:10.1007/s10329-008-0114-1.

[5] Zhang, Dao; Han-Lan Fei; Sheng-Dong Yuan; Wen-Mo Sun; Qing-Yong Ni; Liang-Wei Cui & Peng-Fei Fan (2014). "Ranging behavior of eastern hoolock gibbon (*Hoolock leuconedys*) in a northern montane forest in Gaoligongshan, Yunnan, China" (PDF). *Primates*. **55** (2): 239–47. doi:10.1007/s10329-013-0394-y.

[6] Derderian, C. T. *Subtropical Bonsai for Indoor Gardening*. Arnold Arboretum, Harvard University. 1976.

3.45 Ficus obliqua

Ficus obliqua, commonly known as the **small-leaved fig**, is a tree in the family Moraceae, native to eastern Australia, New Guinea, eastern Indonesia to Sulawesi and islands in the southwestern Pacific Ocean. Previously known for many years as *Ficus eugenioides*, it is a banyan of the genus *Ficus*, which contains around 750 species worldwide in warm climates, including the edible fig (*Ficus carica*). Beginning life as a seedling, which grows on other plants (epiphyte) or on rocks (lithophyte), *F. obliqua* can grow to 60 m (200 ft) high and nearly as wide with a pale grey buttressed trunk, and glossy green leaves.

The small round yellow fruit ripen and turn red at any time of year, although they peak in autumn and winter (April to July). Known as a syconium, the fruit is an inverted inflorescence with the flowers lining an internal cavity. *Ficus obliqua* is pollinated by two species of fig wasp—*Pleistodontes greenwoodi* and *P. xanthocephalus*. Many species of bird, including pigeons, parrots and various passerines, eat the fruit. The range is along the east coast from Queensland, through New South Wales in rainforest, savanna woodland, sclerophyll forest and gallery forest. It is used as a shade tree in parks and public spaces, and is well-suited for use as an indoor plant or in bonsai. All parts of the tree have been used in traditional medicine in Fiji.

3.45.1 Taxonomy

Commonly known as the small-leaved fig, *Ficus obliqua* was described by German naturalist Georg Forster in 1786 based on type material collected in Vanuatu. Dutch botanist Friedrich Miquel described *Urostigma eugenioides* from

Albany Island in Queensland in 1861, which was reclassified by Victorian Government Botanist Ferdinand von Mueller as *Ficus eugenioides* in 1867, and it was known as this for many years. However, as Forster's name is older, it takes precedence. The specific epithet is the Latin adjective *obliquus*, meaning "oblique", although the attribute it refers to is unclear.*[2] Frederick Manson Bailey described *Ficus tryonii* in 1906, from a collection at altitude on Middle Percy Island in the Whitsunday Islands off central Queensland, which is now regarded as *F. obliqua*. Joseph Banks and Daniel Solander collected and named *Ficus virginea* from Booby Island in 1770, which was synonymised with *F. obliqua* by William Philip Hiern in 1901.*[3]

The species is currently regarded as monotypic. Three varieties of *Ficus obliqua* were recognised until 2001—*F. obliqua* var. *petiolaris*, *F. obliqua* var. *obliqua*, and *F. obliqua* var. *puberula* from Western Australia. A revision of the group led to the conclusion that *F. obliqua* var. *petiolaris* belonged in the species *F. rubiginosa*.*[4] *F. obliqua* var. *puberula* was found to be more distantly related to *obliqua* than *rubiginosa* and hence has been reclassified as a separate species, *Ficus brachypoda*.*[5]

With over 750 species, *Ficus* is one of the largest angiosperm genera.*[6] Based on morphology, English botanist E. J. H. Corner divided the genus into four subgenera,*[7] which was later expanded to six.*[8] In this classification, *Ficus obliqua* was placed in subseries *Malvanthereae*, series *Malvanthereae*, section *Malvanthera* of the subgenus *Urostigma*.*[9] In his reclassification of the Australian *Malvanthera*, Australian botanist Dale J. Dixon altered the delimitations of the series within the section, but left this species in the series *Malvanthereae*.*[7]

In a study published in 2008, Nina Rønsted and colleagues analysed the DNA sequences from the nuclear ribosomal internal and external transcribed spacers (ITS and ETS), and the glyceraldehyde-3-phosphate dehydrogenase (G3pdh) region, in the first molecular analysis of the section *Malvanthera*. They found *F. obliqua* to be most closely related to three species of the arid Northern Territory (*F. platypoda*, *F. subpuberula* and *F. lilliputiana*) and classified it in a new series *Obliquae* in the subsection *Platypodeae*. The species had remained a transitional rainforest species while its relatives radiated into dryer regions.*[9]

3.45.2 Description

Ficus obliqua is a tree, which may reach 15–60 m (49–197 ft) in height with a similar crown width.*[10] It has smooth thin grey bark with lighter-coloured lenticels, and a buttressed trunk, which may reach 3 m (9.8 ft) in diameter. The glossy green leaves are elliptic to oblong in shape and measure 5–8 cm (2.0–3.1 in) long by 2–3.5 cm (0.79–1.38

A large buttressed trunk of Ficus obliqua, *Allyn River, Barrington Tops, Australia.*

in) wide on 1–2 cm (0.39–0.79 in) petioles.*[10] They are alternately arranged on the stems.*[2] Growing in pairs, the round yellow fruit turn orange or orange-red dotted with darker red and reaches a diameter of 6 to 10 mm (0.24 to 0.39 in) upon ripening over April to July,*[10] although fruit can appear at other times of year.*[11] As is the case with all figs, the fruit is an inverted inflorescence known as a syconium, with tiny flowers arising from the inner surface.*[12] *Ficus obliqua* is monoecious—both male and female flowers are produced by the same plant, and in fact in the same fruit. Within any given fruit, female flowers mature several weeks before the male flowers.*[13]

Historically, there has been some confusion between *Ficus obliqua* and the related *F. rubiginosa*.*[5] *F. obliqua* can be distinguished by its smaller fruit on shorter stalks and its glabrous (hairless) leaves; in addition, the petioles have ascending hyaline hairs.*[12] Some forms of *F. rubiginosa* have both leaves and petioles glabrous while others have both covered in fine fur.*[5] The syconia of *F. obliqua* are smaller, measuring 4.3–11.9 mm long and 4.4–11.0 mm in diameter, compared with 7.4–17.3 mm long and 7.6–17.3 mm diameter for *F. rubiginosa*.*[5] *Ficus brachypoda* is a lithophytic plant from arid northern and western Australia, with a short petiole and leaf shape aligning it with *Ficus platypoda*.*[14]

3.45.3 Distribution and habitat

Ficus obliqua occurs from Mount Dromedary (36° S) in southern New South Wales northwards along the coast and Great Dividing Range to the tip of Cape York Peninsula in north Queensland. Outside Australia it occurs on New Guinea and offshore islands,*[12] through eastern Indonesia to Sulawesi in the west and east into the southwestern Pacific,*[15] where it is found in New Caledonia,*[16] Fiji,

Tonga, Samoa and Vanuatu.*[17] It had been thought to occur in Western Australia, but these collections have been now referred to *Ficus brachypoda*.*[5] Preferring soils with high nutrient and water content, it occurs on sandstone or latite soils in the Sydney region. The habitat is warm temperate to moist subtropical rainforest. Large specimens can rise above the canopy as emergent trees.*[11]

3.45.4 Ecology

Unripe fruit

The double-eyed fig parrot (*Cyclopsitta diophthalma*) eats the fruit of *Ficus obliqua*, steadily depositing fruity detritus on the ground.*[18] The rainbow lorikeet (*Trichoglossus moluccanus*) is another parrot that consumes the fruit and disperses the seeds;*[4] other Australian bird species include the southern cassowary (*Casuarius casuarius*),*[3] brown cuckoo-dove (*Macropygia phasianella*), rose-crowned fruit dove (*Ptilinopus regina*), wompoo fruit dove (*P. magnificus*), wonga pigeon (*Leucosarcia melanoleuca*), topknot pigeon (*Lopholaimus antarcticus*), silvereye (*Zosterops lateralis*), pied currawong (*Strepera graculina*), black-faced cuckoo-shrike (*Coracina novaehollandiae*), olive-backed oriole (*Oriolus sagittatus*), Australasian figbird (*Sphecotheres vieilloti*), green catbird (*Ailuroedus crassirostris*), regent bowerbird (*Sericulus chrysocephalus*), satin bowerbird (*Ptilonorhynchus violaceus*), and Lewin's honeyeater (*Meliphaga lewinii*).*[2] The tree is an important food source for the western Polynesian species the many-coloured fruit dove (*Ptilinopus perousii*)*[19] and crimson-crowned fruit dove (*P. porphyraceus*), and has been recommended for amenity planting in Tonga for these birds.*[20] The spectacled flying fox (*Pteropus conspicillatus*)*[21] and grey-headed flying fox (*Pteropus poliocephalus*) also eat the fruit.*[11]

Leaves of *Ficus obliqua* serve as a food source for the larvae of the butterfly species the common crow (*Euploea core*),*[22] the no-brand crow (*Euploea alcathoe*),*[23] and the Geometer moth species *Scopula epigypsa*.*[24] The thrips species *Gynaikothrips australis* feeds on the underside of new leaves of *F. obliqua*, as well as *F. rubiginosa* and *F. macrophylla*. As plant cells die, nearby cells are induced into forming meristem tissue. A gall results and the leaves become distorted and curl over. The thrips remain in the galls at night and wander about in the daytime before returning in the evening, possibly to different galls about the tree. The thrips begin feeding when the tree has flushes of new growth, and the life cycle is around six weeks. At other times, thrips reside on old leaves without feeding or pupate sheltered in the bark.*[25]

Reproduction and life span

A growing specimen that has begun as a lithophyte and has increasing numbers of roots reaching the ground, Watagan Mountains

Figs have an obligate mutualism with fig wasps (Agaonidae); figs are only pollinated by fig wasps, and fig wasps can only reproduce in fig flowers. Generally, each fig species depends on a single species of wasp for pollination. The wasps are similarly dependent on their fig species to reproduce.*[26] The assumption that fig species are usually pollinated by just one species of fig wasp has been challenged by the discovery of cryptic species complexes among what was previously thought to be single species of fig wasps.*[27] *Ficus obliqua* is pollinated by two species of fig wasp—*Pleistodontes greenwoodi* and *P. xanthocephalus*.*[26]

Female and male flowers in each syconium mature at different times. Female wasps enter the syconium and lay eggs in the female flowers as they mature. These eggs later hatch and the progeny mate. The females of the new generation collect pollen from the male flowers, which have matured by this point, and leave to visit other syconia and repeat the process. A field study in Brisbane found that *F. obliqua* trees often bore both male and female syconia at the same time—this could be beneficial for reproduction in isolated populations, such as those on islands. The same study found a slightly reduced number of male phase syconia in winter, thought due to increased mortality of the wasp pollinator in cooler months.*[13]

The animals that eat the figs disperse the seeds, which then germinate and grow on other plants (epiphytes) or on rocks (lithophytes). As the new plants develop, they send roots to the forest floor. Figs growing on other plants grow larger and larger until they strangle their hosts. *Ficus obliqua* is long-lived, and trees are thought to live in excess of 500 years.*[11]

3.45.5 Uses

Ficus obliqua *planted as a shade tree in a playground, Glebe, New South Wales*

Ficus obliqua is an elegant shade tree for parks or fields, and is adaptable to differing soils.*[10] A notable specimen in Mick Ryan Park, Milton on the New South Wales south coast stands 14 m (46 ft) tall and 38 m (125 ft) across,*[28] and is a local landmark.*[29] Like other fig species that grow into large trees, *Ficus obliqua* is not suitable for any but the largest gardens as its aggressive root system invades drains and garden beds. Fig trees also drop large quantities of fruit and leaves, leaving a mess underfoot.*[10] Although it is much less used in bonsai than *F. rubiginosa*,*[30] *F. obliqua* is well-suited for use in the medium; its small leaves and trunk's propensity to thicken give it attributes optimal for a tree 10–80 cm (3.9–31.5 in) in height. It is seen in bonsai nurseries mainly in the Brisbane area, where it is a locally common species, and is very highly regarded by at least one proponent, Bradley Barlow.*[31]*[32] Barlow entered a specimen from Brisbane to the Bonsai Clubs International competition in 2006, winning a prize.*[33] It is also suited for use as an indoor plant in low-, medium- or brightly lit indoor spaces.*[34] The timber is too soft for use in woodworking.*[10]

Known as *baka* or *baka ni viti* in Fiji, *Ficus obliqua* has many of its parts used in Fijian traditional medicine,*[17] and was previously held to be sacred there.*[35] Its white sap has been used for painful or swollen joints and limbs or boils, or diluted with water and drunk to improve breast milk. Liquid extracted from the root bark has been used for headaches or, when diluted, to improve health after childbirth, and the leaves are applied to venereal lesions. The species has been traditionally used for boils in Samoa and Tonga.*[17]

3.45.6 References

[1] "*Ficus obliqua* G.Forst.". *Australian Plant Name Index (APNI), IBIS database*. Centre for Plant Biodiversity Research, Australian Government. Retrieved 1 October 2013.

[2] Floyd, Alex G. (2009). *Rainforest Trees of Mainland Southeastern Australia*. Lismore, New South Wales: Terania Rainforest Publishing. p. 232. ISBN 978-0-9589436-7-3.

[3] Hyland, B. P. M.; Whiffin, T.; Zich, F. A.; et al. (Dec 2010). "Factsheet – *Ficus obliqua*". *Australian Tropical Rainforest Plants*. Edition 6.1, online version [RFK 6.1]. Cairns, Australia: Commonwealth Scientific and Industrial Research Organisation (CSIRO), through its Division of Plant Industry; the Centre for Australian National Biodiversity Research; the Australian Tropical Herbarium, James Cook University. Retrieved 16 March 2013.

[4] Cook, James M.; Rasplus, Jean-Yves (2003). "Mutualists with Attitude: Coevolving Fig Wasps and Figs" (PDF). *Trends in Ecology & Evolution*. **18** (5): 241–48. doi:10.1016/S0169-5347(03)00062-4.

[5] Dixon, Dale J.; Jackes, Betsy R.; Bielig, L. M. (2001). "Figuring Out the Figs: the *Ficus obliqua-Ficus rubiginosa* Complex (Moraceae: *Urostigma* sect. *Malvanthera*)". *Australian Systematic Botany*. **14** (1): 133–54. doi:10.1071/SB99029.

[6] Frodin, David G. (2004). "History and Concepts of Big Plant Genera". *Taxon*. **53** (3): 753–76. doi:10.2307/4135449. JSTOR 4135449.

[7] Dixon, Dale J. (2003). "A Taxonomic Revision of the Australian *Ficus* Species in the Section *Malvanthera* (*Ficus* subg. *Urostigma*: Moraceae)" (PDF). *Telopea*. **10** (1): 125–53.

[8] Rønsted, Nina; Weiblen, G. D.; Clement, W. L.; Zerega, N. J. C.; Savolainen, V. (2008). "Reconstructing the Phylogeny of Figs (*Ficus*, Moraceae) to Reveal the History of the Fig Pollination Mutualism" (PDF). *Symbiosis*. **45** (1–3): 45–56.

[9] Rønsted, Nina; Weiblen, George D.; Savolainen, V.; Cook, James M (2008). "Phylogeny, Biogeography, and Ecology of *Ficus* section *Malvanthera* (Moraceae)" (PDF). *Molecular Phylogenetics and Evolution*. **48** (1): 12–22. doi:10.1016/j.ympev.2008.04.005. PMID 18490180.

[10] Elliot, Rodger W.; Jones, David L.; Blake, Trevor (1986). *Encyclopaedia of Australian Plants Suitable for Cultivation: Volume 4 (Eu-Go)*. Port Melbourne, Victoria: Lothian Press. pp. 280, 287–88. ISBN 0-85091-589-9.

[11] Benson, Doug; McDougall, Lyn (1997). "Ecology of Sydney Plant Species Part 5: Dicotyledon Families Flacourtiaceae to Myrsinaceae" (PDF). *Cunninghamia*. **5** (2): 330–544.

[12] Fairley, Alan; Moore, Philip (2000). *Native Plants of the Sydney District: An Identification Guide* (2nd ed.). Kenthurst, New South Wales: Kangaroo Press. p. 62. ISBN 0-7318-1031-7.

[13] McPherson, John R. (2005). "Phenology of Six *Ficus* L., Moraceae, Species and its Effects on Pollinator Survival, in Brisbane, Queensland, Australia". *Geographical Research*. **43** (3): 297–305. doi:10.1111/j.1745-5871.2005.00329.x.

[14] Dixon, Dale J. (2001). "A chequered history: The taxonomy of *Ficus platypoda* and *F. Leucotricha* (Moraceae: *Urostigma* sect. *Malvanthera*) unravelled". *Australian Systematic Botany*. **14** (4): 535–63. doi:10.1071/SB00028.

[15] "*Ficus obliqua* G.Forst.". *Flora of Australia Online*. Department of the Environment and Heritage, Australian Government. Retrieved 1 October 2013.

[16] Morat, Philippe; Jaffre, Tanguy; Veillon, Jean-Marie (2001). "The flora of New Caledonia's calcareous substrates" (PDF). *Adansonia*. **23** (1): 109–27.

[17] Cambie, R.C.; Ash, Julian Edward (1994). *Fijian Medicinal Plants*. Collingwood, Victoria: CSIRO Publishing. p. 256. ISBN 0-643-05404-9.

[18] Forshaw, Joseph M.; Cooper, William T. (1978). *Parrots of the World* (2nd ed.). Melbourne, Victoria: Landsdowne Editions. p. 162. ISBN 0-7018-0690-7.

[19] Watling, Dick (2003). *A Guide to the Birds of Fiji and Western Polynesia*. Suva, Fiji: Environmental Consultants. p. 122. ISBN 982-9030-04-0.

[20] Steadman, David W. (1998). "Status of Land Birds on Selected Islands in the Ha'apai Group, Kingdom of Tonga" (PDF). *Pacific Science*. **52** (1): 14–34.

[21] Parsons, Jennifer G.; Cairns, Andi; Johnson, Christopher N.; et al. (2006). "Dietary Variation in Spectacled Flying Foxes (*Pteropus conspicillatus*) of the Australian Wet Tropics". *Australian Journal of Zoology*. **54** (6): 417–28. doi:10.1071/ZO06092. Retrieved 25 July 2010.

[22] Robinson, Gaden S.; Ackery, Phillip R.; Kitching, Ian J.; Beccaloni, George W.; Hernández, Luis M. "*Euploea core*". *HOSTS – a Database of the World's Lepidopteran Hostplants*. Natural History Museum. Retrieved 17 March 2012.

[23] Braby, Michael F. (2005). *The Complete Field Guide to Butterflies of Australia*. Collingwood, Victoria: CSIRO Publishing. p. 194. ISBN 0-643-09027-4.

[24] Robinson, Gaden S.; Ackery, Phillip R.; Kitching, Ian J.; Beccaloni, George W.; Hernández, Luis M. "*Scopula epigypsa*". *HOSTS – a Database of the World's Lepidopteran Hostplants*. Natural History Museum. Retrieved 12 July 2008.

[25] Tree, Desley J; Walter, G. H. (2009). "Diversity of Host Plant Relationships and Leaf Galling Behaviours within a Small Genus of Thrips –*Gynaikothrips* and *Ficus* in South East Queensland, Australia". *Australian Journal of Entomology*. **48** (4): 269–75. doi:10.1111/j.1440-6055.2009.00706.x.

[26] Lopez-Vaamonde, Carlos; Dixon, Dale J.; Cook, James M.; Rasplus, Jean-Yves (2002). "Revision of the Australian species of *Pleistodontes* (Hymenoptera: Agaonidae) Fig-pollinating Wasps and their Host-plant Associations". *Zoological Journal of the Linnean Society*. **136** (4): 637–83. doi:10.1046/j.1096-3642.2002.00040.x.

[27] Molbo, Drude; Machado, Carlos A.; Sevenster, Jan G.; Keller, Laurent; Herre, Edward Allen (2003). "Cryptic Species of Fig-pollinating Wasps: Implications for the Evolution of the Fig–wasp Mutualism, Sex Allocation, and Precision of Adaptation". *Proceedings of the National Academy of Sciences USA*. **100** (10): 5867–72. doi:10.1073/pnas.0930903100. PMC 156293. PMID 12714682.

[28] Ciampa, Bernadette (2009). "Fig – Small-leaved: Tree Details". *National Register of Big Trees: Australia's Champion Trees*. National Register of Big Trees. Retrieved 19 March 2012.

[29] "Artists gather under the fig- Celebration of special trees". *Milton Ulladulla Times*. Fairfax Media. 18 November 2004. Archived from the original on 21 April 2012. Retrieved 19 March 2012.

[30] Webber, Len (1991). *Rainforest to Bonsai*. East Roseville, New South Wales: Simon and Schuster. p. 109. ISBN 0-7318-0237-3.

[31] Koreshoff, Dorothy; Koreshoff, Vita (1984). *Bonsai with Australian Native Plants*. Brisbane, Queensland: Boolarong Publications. p. 52. ISBN 0-908175-66-3.

[32] Barlow, Bradley (2006). "Growing the Queensland Small leaf Fig as Bonsai in South-east Queensland". *ASGAP Australian Plants As Bonsai Study Group Newsletter* (10): 5–8. The Queensland Small-leaf Fig ... should be the first choice for more serious *Ficus* bonsai enthusiasts

[33] Hnatiuk, Roger (2006). "International Honours to Australians with Aussie Species as Bonsai". *ASGAP Australian Plants As Bonsai Study Group Newsletter* (11): 1.

[34] Ratcliffe, David; Ratcliffe, Patricia (1987). *Fancy a Feast? Try a Fig*. Australian Plants. **16**. Crows Nest, New South Wales: Little Hills Press. pp. 251–52.

[35] Blench, Roger (1999). *Archaeology and Language IV: Language Change and Cultural Transformation*. **35**. London, United Kingdom: Routledge. p. 203. ISBN 0-415-11786-0.

3.46 Ficus platypoda

Ficus platypoda, commonly known as the **desert fig** or **rock fig**, is a fig that is endemic to central and northern Australia. It is a lithophytic plant that grows on rocky outcrops, reaching 10 m in height.

3.46.1 Taxonomy

Dutch botanist Friedrich Anton Wilhelm Miquel described the desert fig in 1847 as *Urostigma platypodum*,*[1] from material collected on both the east and west coast of Australia. The material collected by Allan Cunningham from York Sound in Western Australia became the type material. E.J.H. Corner synonymised *F. platypoda* with *Ficus leucotricha*, which was described by Miquel in 1861, however as the former name is older, it has become the accepted name instead.*[2]

The various populations and subspecies of *Ficus platypoda* were examined genetically in 2001 and found to contain a number of distinct species. Hence *Ficus brachypoda*, *Ficus atricha* and *Ficus cerasicarpa* were described as separate species.*[2]

With over 750 species, *Ficus* is one of the largest angiosperm genera.*[3] Based on morphology, English botanist E. J. H. Corner divided the genus into four subgenera,*[4] which was later expanded to six.*[5] In this classification, *Ficus platypoda* was placed in subseries *Malvanthereae*, series *Malvanthereae*, section *Malvanthera* of the subgenus *Urostigma*.*[6] In his reclassification of the Australian *Malvanthera*, Australian botanist Dale J. Dixon altered the delimitations of the series within the section, but left this species in the series *Malvanthereae*.*[4]

In a study published in 2008, Nina Rønsted and colleagues analysed the DNA sequences from the nuclear ribosomal internal and external transcribed spacers (ITS and ETS), and the glyceraldehyde-3-phosphate dehydrogenase (G3pdh) region, in the first molecular analysis of the section *Malvanthera*. They found *F. platypoda* to be most closely related to the ancestor of two other arid Northern Territory species (*F. subpuberula* and *F. lilliputiana*) and classified it in a new series *Obliquae* in the subsection *Platypodeae*. The three species diverged from the ancestor of the transitional rainforest species *F. obliqua* and radiated into drier regions.*[6]

3.46.2 Description

F. platypoda *ripening fruit*

Ficus platypoda grows as a lithophytic shrub or tree to 10 m high. The branchlets are covered in fine hairs. The leaves are alternately arranged along the stems and are elliptical to oval in shape, measuring 5.3 to 16.7 cm long by 3.1 to 13.3 cm wide. The undersurface is furry. The oval to round figs pale can be various shades of yellow, orange, pink, red or purple and 0.9–2.8 cm long by 1–2.8 cm across.*[2]

3.46.3 Distribution and habitat

Within Australia, it is found across the Top End, from the Gulf Country around the Gulf of Carpentaria across the Northern Territory and into northern Western Australia.*[1] It generally found on sandstone outcrops, but has occasionally been found on limestone outcrops.*[2]

3.46.4 Ecology

The wasp species *Pleistodontes cuneatus* pollinates the rock fig.*[2]

3.46.5 Uses

The fruit can be eaten when soft and ripe.*[7] Horticulturally, it is suitable for use in bonsai; its tendency to form a wide trunk base and small leaves being attractive features.*[8] Specimens have been exhibited in at the 5th Annual Exhibition of Australian Native Plants as Bonsai in Canberra in November 2007.*[9]

3.46.6 References

[1] Hyland, B. P. M.; Whiffin, T.; Zich, F. A.; et al. (Dec 2010). "Factsheet – *Ficus platypoda*". *Australian Tropical Rainforest Plants*. Edition 6.1, online version [RFK 6.1]. Cairns, Australia: Commonwealth Scientific and Industrial Research Organisation (CSIRO), through its Division of Plant Industry; the Centre for Australian National Biodiversity Research; the Australian Tropical Herbarium, James Cook University. Retrieved 4 September 2015.

[2] Dixon, Dale J. (2001). "A Chequered History: the Taxonomy of *Ficus platypoda* and *F. leucotricha* (Moraceae: *Urostigma* sect. *Malvanthera*) Unravelled" (PDF). *Australian Systematic Botany*. **14**: 535–63. doi:10.1071/sb00028.

[3] Frodin, David G. (2004). "History and Concepts of Big Plant Genera". *Taxon*. **53** (3): 753–76. doi:10.2307/4135449. JSTOR 4135449.

[4] Dixon, Dale J. (2003). "A Taxonomic Revision of the Australian *Ficus* Species in the Section *Malvanthera* (*Ficus* subg. *Urostigma*: Moraceae)" (PDF). *Telopea*. **10** (1): 125–53.

[5] Rønsted, Nina; Weiblen, G. D.; Clement, W. L.; Zerega, N. J. C.; Savolainen, V. (2008). "Reconstructing the Phylogeny of Figs (*Ficus*, Moraceae) to Reveal the History of the Fig Pollination Mutualism" (PDF). *Symbiosis*. **45** (1–3): 45–56.

[6] Rønsted, Nina; Weiblen, George D.; Savolainen, V.; Cook, James M (2008). "Phylogeny, Biogeography, and Ecology of *Ficus* section *Malvanthera* (Moraceae)" (PDF). *Molecular Phylogenetics and Evolution*. **48** (1): 12–22. doi:10.1016/j.ympev.2008.04.005. PMID 18490180.

[7] Lindsay, Lenore (March 1992). "Fancy a feast? Try a fig.". *Australian Plants*. **16** (130): 251–52.

[8] Koreshoff, Dorothy and Vita (1984). *Bonsai with Australian native Plants*. Brisbane: Boolarong Publications. p. 52. ISBN 0-908175-66-3.

[9] Hnatiuk, Roger (2008). "APAB-N Gallery No. 5". *ASGAP Australian Plants As Bonsai Study Group Newsletter* (13): 13–14.

3.47 Ficus retusa

Ficus retusa is a species of evergreen woody plant in the fig genus, native to the Malay Archipelago and Malesia floristic region. The species name has been widely mis-applied to *Ficus microcarpa*.[2]

3.47.1 Description

Ficus retusa is a rapidly growing, rounded, broad-headed, evergreen shrub or tree that can reach 15 metres (49 ft) or more in height with an equal spread. The smooth, light grey trunk is quite striking, can grow to around 1 metre (3.3 ft) in diameter, and it firmly supports the massively spreading canopy.

The tree has small, dark green leaves which alternate up the stem and which are oval. It has a gray to reddish bark dotted with small, horizontal flecks, called lenticels, and are used by woody plant species for supplementary gas exchange through the bark. It is considered one of the easiest trees to keep as a bonsai.

3.47.2 Notes

[1] *The Plant List: A Working List of All Plant Species*, retrieved 13 April 2016

[2] "*Ficus microcarpa* L. f.", *USDA GRIN Taxonomy*

3.47.3 External links

3.48 Ficus rubiginosa

Ficus rubiginosa, commonly known as the **rusty fig** or **Port Jackson fig** (*damun* in the Dharug language), is a species of flowering plant native to eastern Australia in the genus *Ficus*. Beginning as a seedling that grows on other plants (hemiepiphyte) or rocks (lithophyte), *F. rubiginosa* matures into a tree 30 m (100 ft) high and nearly as wide with a yellow-brown buttressed trunk. The leaves are oval and glossy green and measure from 4 to 19.3 cm (1 ½–7 ½ in) long and 1.25 to 13.2 cm (½–5 ¼ in) wide.

The fruits are small, round and yellow, and can ripen and turn red at any time of year, peaking in spring and summer. Like all figs, the fruit is in the form of a syconium, an inverted inflorescence with the flowers lining an internal cavity. *F. rubiginosa* is exclusively pollinated by the fig wasp species *Pleistodontes imperialis*, which may comprise four cryptospecies. The syconia are also home to another fourteen species of wasp, some of which induce galls while others parasitise the pollinator wasps, and at least two species of nematode. Many species of bird, including pigeons, parrots and various passerines, eat the fruit. Ranging along the Australian east coast from Queensland to Bega in southern New South Wales (including the Port Jackson area, leading to its alternative name), *F. rubiginosa* grows in rainforest margins and rocky outcrops. It is used as a shade tree in parks and public spaces, and when potted is well-suited for use as an indoor plant or in bonsai.

3.48. FICUS RUBIGINOSA

Ficus rubiginosa *figs (syconia) and the rusty undersides of the leaves*

3.48.1 Taxonomy

Ficus rubiginosa was described by French botanist René Louiche Desfontaines in 1804,[2] from a type specimen whose locality is documented simply as "New Holland". In searching for the type specimen, Australian botanist Dale Dixon found one from the herbarium of Desfontaines at Florence Herbarium and one from the herbarium of Étienne Pierre Ventenat at Geneva. As Ventenat had used Desfontaines' name, Dixon selected the Florence specimen to be the type in 2001.[3] The specific epithet *rubiginosa* related to the rusty coloration of the undersides of the leaves.[4] Indeed, *rusty fig* is an alternate common name; others include *Illawarra fig* and *Port Jackson fig*.[4] It was known as *damun* (pron. "tam-mun") to the Eora and Darug inhabitants of the Sydney basin.[5]

In 1806, German botanist Carl Ludwig Willdenow gave it the botanical name *Ficus australis* in *Species Plantarum*,[6] but this is a *nomen illegitimum* as the species already had a validly published name.[1] Italian botanist Guglielmo Gasparrini broke up the genus *Ficus* in 1844, placing the species in the genus *Urostigma* as *U. rubiginosum*.[7] In 1862, Dutch botanist Friedrich Anton Wilhelm Miquel described *Urostigma leichhardtii* from material collected from Cape Cleveland, Queensland, noting it had affinities to *F. rubiginosa*.[8] In 1867, he placed *Urostigma* as a subgenus in the reunited *Ficus*, which resulted in the taxon becoming *Ficus leichhardtii*. Miquel also described *Ficus leichhardtii* variety *angustata* from Whitsunday Island,[9] later classified as *F. shirleyana* by Czech botanist Karel Domin.[10] Queensland state botanist Frederick Manson Bailey described *Ficus macrophylla* variety *pubescens* in 1911 from Queensland, Domin later renaming it *Ficus baileyana*.[11] All these taxa were found to be indistinguishable from (and hence reclassified as) *F. rubiginosa* by Dixon in 2001.[3]

In a study published in 2008, Nina Rønsted and colleagues analysed the DNA sequences from the nuclear ribosomal internal and external transcribed spacers, and the glyceraldehyde-3-phosphate dehydrogenase region, in the first molecular analysis of the section *Malvanthera*. They found *F. rubiginosa* to be most closely related to the rainforest species *F. watkinsiana* and two rock-growing (lithophytic) species of arid northern Australia (*F. atricha* and *F. brachypoda*). They classified these species in a new series *Rubiginosae* in the subsection *Platypodeae*. Relationships are unclear and it is uncertain into which direction the group radiated (into rainforest or into arid Australia).[12]

Joseph Maiden described variety *lucida* in 1902, and Bailey described variety *glabrescens* in 1913.[13] Both had diagnosed their varieties on the basis of their hairlessness. Maiden described a taxon totally devoid of hair, while Bailey described his as nearly glabrous (hairless). As Bailey's description more closely matched Dixon's findings (that these variants were only partly and not completely hairless), Dixon retained Bailey's name and reclassified it as *Ficus rubiginosa* forma *glabrescens* in 2001 as it differed only in the lack of hairs on new growth from the nominate form.[3]

3.48.2 Description

Variegated foliage of a cultivar

A spreading, densely-shading tree when mature, *F. rubiginosa* may reach 30 m (100 ft) or more in height,[14] although it rarely exceeds 10 m (30 ft) in the Sydney region.[15] The trunk is buttressed and can reach 1.5 m (4 ft 11 in) in diameter. The bark is yellow-brown.[4] It can also grow as on other plants as a hemiepiphyte,[3] or 1–5 m (3–16 ft) high lithophyte.[16] Alternately arranged on the stems, the ovate (egg-shaped), obovate (reverse egg-shaped) or oval-shaped leaves are anywhere from 4–19.3 cm (1 5/8–7 5/8 in) long and 1.25–13.2 cm (1/2–5 1/4 in) wide, on 7–8.2 cm (2 3/4–3 1/4 in)-long petioles (stalks that join the leaves to stems). They are smooth or bear tiny rusty hairs. There are 16 to 62 pairs of lateral veins that run off the midvein at an angle of 41.5–84.0°, while distinct basal veins run off the midvein at an angle of 18.5–78.9°.[3] As with all figs, the fruit (fig) is actually an inverted inflorescence (compound flower) known as a syconium, with tiny flowers arising from the fig's inner surface into a hollow cavity.[15] *F. rubiginosa* is monoecious—both male and female flowers are found on the same plant, and in fact in the same fruit, although they mature at different times.[17] Often growing in pairs, the figs are yellow initially and measure 4–10 mm (1/8–3/8 in) across.[18] Ripening to red in colour, they are tipped with a small nipple and on a 2–5 mm (1/8–1/4 in) stalk.[15] Fruits ripen throughout the year, although more so in spring and summer.[4] Some trees have ripe and unripe fruit at the same time.[18]

It closely resembles its relative, the Moreton Bay fig (*F. macrophylla*). Having similar ranges in the wild, they are often confused. The smaller leaves, shorter fruit stalks, and rusty colour of the undersides of the leaves of *F. rubiginosa* are the easiest distinguishing features.[15] It is also confused with the small-leaved fig (*F. obliqua*), the syconia of which are smaller, measuring 4–12 mm long and 4–11 mm in diameter, compared with 7–17 mm long and 8–17 mm diameter for *F. rubiginosa*.[3]

3.48.3 Distribution and habitat

Ficus rubiginosa's range spans the entire eastern coastline of Australia, from the top of the Cape York Peninsula in north Queensland to the vicinity of Bega on the south coast of New South Wales.[15] The range extends westwards to Porcupine Gorge National Park in Queensland and the far western plains in New South Wales.[3] *F. rubiginosa* f. *rubiginosa* and *F. rubiginosa* f. *glabrescens* are found over most of the range, though the latter does not occur south past the New South Wales-Queensland border region. Lithophytic, hemiepiphytic and tree forms can be found together in local populations of plants.[3]

F. rubiginosa is found in rainforest,[3] rainforest margins, gullies,[15] riverbank habitat, vine thickets,[3] and rocky hillsides.[15] It is found on limestone outcrops in

Lithophytic Ficus rubiginosa *growing on Narrabeen sandstone at Barrenjoey, New South Wales*

Kanangra-Boyd National Park.[19] Fig seedlings often grow from cracks in stone where seeds have been lodged, in locations such as cliffs and rock faces in natural environments,[4] or in brickwork on buildings and elsewhere in the urban environment. The soils it grows on are often well-drained and low in nutrients. They are derived from sandstone, quartzite and basalt. In the Sydney region, *F. rubiginosa* grows from sea level to 1000 m (3500 ft) altitude, in areas with an average yearly rainfall of 600–1,400 mm (24–55 in).[18] *F. rubiginosa* is largely sympatric with *F. obliqua*, though its range extends further west into dryer regions than the latter species.[3]

Outside its native range, *F. rubiginosa* has naturalised to some degree in urban Melbourne and Adelaide in Australia, as well as New Zealand, Hawaii and California, and Mediterranean Europe.[20] *F. rubiginosa* has been planted widely in Malta since the early 1990s but has not been observed to fruit.[21]

3.48.4 Ecology

The fruit is consumed by many bird species including the rose-crowned fruit-dove (*Ptilinopus regina*), wompoo fruit-dove (*P. magnificus*), wonga pigeon (*Leucosarcia melanoleuca*), topknot pigeon (*Lopholaimus antarcticus*), Pacific koel (*Eudynamys orientalis*),[4] Australasian swamphen (*Porphyrio melanotus*),[22] Australian king parrot (*Alisterus scapularis*),[23] Australasian figbird (*Sphecotheres vieilloti*), green catbird (*Ailuroedus crassirostris*), regent bowerbird (*Sericulus chrysocephalus*), satin bowerbird (*Ptilonorhynchus violaceus*) and pied currawong (*Strepera graculina*),[4] as well as the mammalian grey-headed flying fox (*Pteropus poliocephalus*),[18] and spectacled flying fox (*Pteropus conspicillatus*).[24] It is one of several plant species used as food by the endangered

Coxen's fig parrot.*[25] Many fruits drop onto the ground around the tree, though others are dispersed by animals that eat them.*[18]

The thrips species *Gynaikothrips australis* feeds on the underside of new leaves of *F. rubiginosa*, as well as *F. obliqua* and *F. macrophylla*. As plant cells die, nearby cells are induced into forming meristem tissue and a gall results, and the leaves become distorted and curl over. The thrips begin feeding when the tree has flushes of new growth, and live for around six weeks. At other times, thrips reside on old leaves without feeding. The species pupates sheltered in the bark. The thrips remain in the galls at night, wander about in the daytime and return in the evening, possibly to different galls about the tree.*[26] Psyllids have almost defoliated trees in the Royal Botanic Gardens in Sydney in spring.*[18]

Reproduction and life span

F. rubiginosa is exclusively pollinated in a symbiotic relationship with *Pleistodontes imperialis*, a species of fig wasp.*[27] Biologist Eleanor Haine and colleagues analysed the DNA of the wasp across the fig's range and determined four cryptic lineages forming what they term the *P. imperialis* species complex. They diverge to a greater degree than some distinct wasp species, yet form a monophyletic group; this indicates that the wasp lineages have split without a change of host.*[20]

Fertilised female wasps enter the receptive 'fig' (the syconium) through a tiny hole at the crown (the ostiole). They crawl around the inflorescenced interior of the fig, pollinating some of the female flowers,*[20] before laying eggs inside some of the flowers and dying. After several weeks' development in their galls, the male wasps emerge before the females. They chew holes in the galls containing females and fertilise them through the hole they have just chewed. Males return later to mated females, and enlarge the mating holes to enable the females to emerge. Some males then chew their way through the syconium wall, which allows the females to disperse after collecting pollen from the now fully developed male flowers.*[27] Females then have a short time (< 48 hours) to find a tree with receptive syconia to successfully reproduce and disperse pollen.*[17]

A field study in Brisbane found that *F. rubiginosa* trees often bore both male and female phase syconia at the same time,*[lower-alpha 1] which could be beneficial for reproduction in isolated populations. The same study found that male phase syconia development persisted through the winter, showing that its wasp pollinator tolerated cooler weather than those of more tropical fig species. *F. rubiginosa* itself can endure cooler climates than other members of the genus.*[17]

P. imperialis crossed the waters between Australia and New Zealand some time between 1960 and 1972, and seedlings of the previously infertile trees of *F. rubiginosa* began appearing in brick and stone walls, and on other trees, particularly in parks and gardens around Auckland. They have been recorded as far south as Napier.*[28] *P. imperialis* has been transported to Hawaii, California and Israel, where it has been observed to pollinate its host.*[27]

They can live to 100 years or more and have been known to resprout after bushfire, bearing fruit within three years.*[18]

Other life in the syconia

As with many other *Ficus* species, the community of wasps inside the figs of *F. rubiginosa* is made up mostly of pollinator wasps.*[16] These develop deep inside the syconium, presumably protected there from parasites.*[29] Also present are much smaller numbers of other wasp species, which do not pollinate the fig. At least fourteen species have been recorded,*[lower-alpha 2] of which four—two each belonging to the genera *Sycoscapter* and *Philotrypesis*—are common while others are rare.*[16] Investigation of *F. rubiginosa* syconia found that the fig seeds and parasitic wasps develop closer to the wall of the syconium. The wasps of the genera *Sycoscapter* and *Philotrypesis* are parasitic and are around the same size as the pollinator species.*[29] Their larvae are thought to feed on the larvae of the pollinator wasp.*[16] Male *Sycoscapter* and *Philotrypesis* wasps fight other males of the same species when they encounter each other in a *F. rubiginosa* fig.*[30] Several genera of uncommon larger wasp species enter the immature figs before other wasps and induce galls, which may impact on numbers of pollinator wasps in the fig later. An example of this is *Pseudidarnes minerva*,*[16] a metallic green wasp species.*[31]

Nematodes of the genus *Schistonchus* are found in the syconia (and the pollinator wasps) of many species of fig, with *F. rubiginosa* hosting two species. They appear to be less species-specific than wasps. *S. altermacrophylla* is generally associated with *F. rubiginosa* though it has been recorded on several other fig species.*[32]

3.48.5 Cultivation

Ficus rubiginosa was first cultivated in the United Kingdom in 1789, where it is grown in glasshouses.*[33] It is commonly used as a large ornamental tree in eastern Australia, in the North Island of New Zealand,*[28] and also in Hawaii and California, where it is also listed as an invasive species in some areas.*[34] It is useful as a shade tree in public parks and on golf courses.*[35] Not as prodigious as other

As bonsai, Auburn Botanic Gardens

figs, *F. rubiginosa* is suited to slightly more confined areas, such as lining car parks or suburban streets. However, surface roots can be large and intrusive and the thin bark readily damaged when struck. Tolerant of acid or alkaline soils, it is hardy to US Hardiness Zones 10B and 11, reaching 10 m (35 ft) high in 30 years. Planting trees 8–12 m (30–40 ft) apart will eventually result in a continuous canopy.*[36] The trees are of great value in providing fruit for birds and mammals, though drop large quantities of fruit and leaves, leaving a mess underfoot.*[33]

In a brief description, William Guilfoyle recorded a variegated fig from New South Wales "12–15 ft high" in 1911 as *F. rubiginosa* variety *variegata*.*[37] A variegated form is in cultivation on Australia's east coast,*[38] and in the United States.*[39] It is a chimera lacking in chlorophyll in the second layer of the leaf meristem.*[38] The leaves have an irregular central green patch along the midvein with irregular yellow and green elsewhere.*[33] Leaves that grow in winter generally have larger green patches than those that do in summer. The chimera is unstable, and branches of all-green growth appear sporadically.*[38]

Despite the relatively large size of the leaves, it is popular for bonsai work as it is highly forgiving to work with and hard to kill; the leaves reduce readily by leaf-pruning in early summer. Described as the best tree for a beginner to work with, it is one of the most frequently used native species in Australia.*[40] Its bark remains smooth, and does not attain a rugged, aged appearance. Known as "Little Ruby",*[41] a narrow-leaved form with its origins somewhere north of Sydney is also seen in cultivation.*[42]

F. rubiginosa is also suited for use as a houseplant in low, medium or brightly-lit spaces, although a variegated form requires brighter light.*[43] It has gained the Royal Horticultural Society's Award of Garden Merit.*[44] It is easily propagated by cuttings or aerial layering.*[4]

The light-coloured wood is soft and brittle. Lightweight, it has some value in the making of such items as toys and small boxes.*[14]

3.48.6 Notes

[1] The flowers within mature at different times, hence the syconium has male and female phase depending on the sex of the flowers at maturity.*[17]

[2] These are two species each of the genera *Sycoscapter*, *Philotrypesis* and *Watshamiella* of the subfamily Sycoryctinae, one species each of the genera *Eukoebelea* and *Pseudidarnes* in the subfamily Sycophaginae, one species each of the genera *Herodotia* and *Meselatus* in the subfamily Epichrysomallinae, all of the family Agaonidae, two species of the genus *Sycophila* of the family Eurytomidae, one species of *Megastigmus* of the family Torymidae and a species of the genus *Ormyrus* of the family Ormyridae.*[16]

3.48.7 References

[1] "Ficus rubiginosa". *Australian Plant Name Index (APNI), IBIS database*. Centre for Plant Biodiversity Research, Australian Government.

[2] Ventenat, E.P. (1804). *Jardin de la Malmaison* (in French). **2**. Paris, France: De l'imprimerie de Crapelet, et se trouve chez l'auteur. p. 114.

[3] Dixon, Dale J.; Jackes, Betsy R.; Bielig, L.M. (2001). "Figuring Out the Figs: the *Ficus obliqua-Ficus rubiginosa* Complex (Moraceae: Urostigma sect. Malvanthera)". *Australian Systematic Botany*. **14** (1): 133–54. doi:10.1071/SB99029.

[4] Floyd, Alex G. (2009). *Rainforest Trees of Mainland Southeastern Australia*. Lismore, New South Wales: Terania Rainforest Publishing. p. 233. ISBN 978-0-9589436-7-3.

[5] Troy, Jakelin (1993). *The Sydney Language*. Canberra: Self-published. p. 61. ISBN 0-646-11015-2.

[6] Willdenow, Carl Ludwig (1806). "2". *Species Plantarum*. **4** (4 ed.). Berlin, Germany: G.C. Nauk. pp. 1138–39.

[7] Gasparrini, Guglielmo (1844). *Nova Genera, quae super Nonnullis Fici Speciebus* (in Latin). Naples, Italy: Francisci. p. 7.

[8] Miquel, Friedrich Anton Wilhelm (1862). "Note sur le Figuiers de la *Nouvelle-Hollande*". *Journal de Botanique Neerlandaise* (in French). **1**: 230–43 [235].

[9] Miquel, Friedrich Anton Wilhelm (1867). "Annotationes de Ficus Speciebus". *Annales Musei Botanici Lugduno-Batavi* (in Latin). **3**: 260–84 [268].

[10] "*Ficus platypoda* variety *angustata* (Miq.) Corner". *Flora of Australia Online*. Department of the Environment and Heritage, Australian Government.

[11] "*Ficus baileyana* Domin". *Flora of Australia Online*. Department of the Environment and Heritage, Australian Government.

[12] Rønsted, Nina; Weiblen, George D.; Savolainen, V.; Cook, James M. (2008). "Phylogeny, Biogeography, and Ecology of *Ficus* section *Malvanthera* (Moraceae)". *Molecular Phylogenetics and Evolution*. **48** (1): 12–22. doi:10.1016/j.ympev.2008.04.005. PMID 18490180.

[13] Bailey, Frederick Manson (1913). *Comprehensive catalogue of Queensland plants, both indigenous and naturalised*. Brisbane, Queensland: A. J. Cumming, government printer. p. 486.

[14] Lake, Morris (2015). *Australian Rainforest Woods: Characteristics, Uses and Identification*. Collingwood, Victoria: CSIRO Publishing. p. 84. ISBN 1-4863-0180-0.

[15] Fairley, Alan; Moore, Philip (2000). *Native Plants of the Sydney District:An Identification Guide* (2nd ed.). Kenthurst, New South Wales: Kangaroo Press. p. 62. ISBN 0-7318-1031-7.

[16] Segar, Simon T.; Dunn, Derek W.; Darwell, Clive T.; Cook, James M. (2014). "How to be a fig wasp down under: The diversity and structure of an Australian fig wasp community". *Acta Oecologica*. **57**: 17–27. doi:10.1016/j.actao.2013.03.014.

[17] McPherson, John R. (2005). "Phenology of Six *Ficus* L., Moraceae, Species and its Effects on Pollinator Survival, in Brisbane, Queensland, Australia". *Geographical Research*. **43** (3): 297–305. doi:10.1111/j.1745-5871.2005.00329.x.

[18] Benson, Doug; McDougall, Lyn (1997). "Ecology of Sydney Plant Species Part 5: Dicotyledon Families Flacourtiaceae to Myrsinaceae" (PDF). *Cunninghamia*. **5** (2): 330–544 [525].

[19] Parks and Wildlife Division (2005). "Kowmung River, Kanangra-Boyd National Park: Wild River Assessment" (PDF). Department of Environment and Conservation (NSW). Retrieved 23 April 2012.

[20] Haine, Eleanor R.; Martin, Joanne; Cook, James M. (2006). "Deep mtDNA Divergences Indicate Cryptic Species in a Fig-pollinating Wasp". *BMC Evolutionary Biology*. **6** (1): 83. doi:10.1186/1471-2148-6-83. PMC 1626083. PMID 17040562.

[21] Mifsud, David; Falzon, Annushka; Malumphy, Chris; De Lillo, Enrico; Vovlas, Nicola; Porcelli, Francesco (2012). "On Some Arthropods Associated with *Ficus* Species (Moraceae) in the Maltese Islands" (PDF). *Bulletin of the Entomological Society of Malta*. **5**: 5–34.

[22] Barker, Robin Dale; Vestjens, Wilhelmus Jacobus Maria (1984). *The Food of Australian Birds: (I) Non-passerines*. Carlton, Victoria: Melbourne University Press. p. 207. ISBN 0-643-05007-8.

[23] Hornsby Shire Council. "Ficus rubiginosa – Port Jackson Fig" (PDF). *Bushland and Biodiversity*. Retrieved 1 May 2016.

[24] Parsons, Jennifer G.; Cairns, Andi; Johnson, Christopher N. (2006). "Dietary Variation in Spectacled Flying Foxes (*Pteropus conspicillatus*) of the Australian Wet Tropics". *Australian Journal of Zoology*. **54** (6): 417–28. doi:10.1071/ZO06092.

[25] Department of Environment and Heritage Protection (24 May 2011). "Double-eyed fig-parrot (Coxen's)". Queensland Government. Retrieved 1 May 2016.

[26] Tree, Desley J; Walter, G. H. (2009). "Diversity of Host Plant Relationships and Leaf Galling Behaviours within a Small Genus of Thrips –*Gynaikothrips* and *Ficus* in South East Queensland, Australia". *Australian Journal of Entomology*. **48** (4): 269–75. doi:10.1111/j.1440-6055.2009.00706.x.

[27] Lopez-Vaamonde, Carlos; Dixon, Dale J.; Cook, James M.; Rasplus, Jean-Yves (2002). "Revision of the Australian species of *Pleistodontes* (Hymenoptera: Agaonidae) Fig-pollinating Wasps and their Host-plant Associations". *Zoological Journal of the Linnean Society*. **136** (4): 637–83. doi:10.1046/j.1096-3642.2002.00040.x.

[28] Gardner, Rhys O.; Early, John W. (1996). "The Naturalisation of Banyan Figs (*Ficus* spp., Moraceae) and their Pollinating Wasps (Hymenoptera: Agaonidae) in New Zealand". *New Zealand Journal of Botany*. **34**: 103–10. doi:10.1080/0028825x.1996.10412697. Archived from the original on 19 July 2008. Retrieved 26 July 2010.

[29] Dunn, Derek W.; Segar, Simon T.; Ridley, Jo; Chan, Ruth; Crozier, Ross H.; Douglas, W. Yu; Cook, James M. (2008). "A Role for Parasites in Stabilising the Fig-pollinator Mutualism". *PLoS Biology*. **6** (3): e59. doi:10.1371/journal.pbio.0060059. PMC 2265770. PMID 18336072.

[30] Moore, Jamie C.; Obbard, Darren J.; Reuter, Caroline; West, Stuart A.; Cook, James M. (2008). "Fighting strategies in two species of fig wasp" (PDF). *Animal Behaviour*. **76** (2): 315–22. doi:10.1016/j.anbehav.2008.01.018.

[31] Farache, Fernando; Antoniolli, Henrique; Rasplus, Jean-Yves (2014). "Revision of the Australasian genus *Pseudidarnes* Girault, 1927 (Hymenoptera, Agaonidae, Sycophaginae)". *ZooKeys*. **404**: 31–70. doi:10.3897/zookeys.404.7204. PMC 4023259. PMID 24843270.

[32] Davies, Kerrie, Faerlie Bartholomaeus, Weimin Ye, Natsumi Kanzaki, and Robin Giblin-Davis

[33] Elliot, Rodger W.; Jones, David L.; Blake, Trevor (1986). *Encyclopaedia of Australian Plants Suitable for Cultivation: Volume 4 (Eu-Go)*. Port Melbourne, Victoria: Lothian Press. pp. 280, 290–91. ISBN 0-85091-589-9.

[34] Invasive Species Specialist Group (ISSG) (12 December 2005). "Ficus rubiginosa". *Global Invasive Species Database*. IUCN Species Survival Commission. Retrieved 3 April 2016.

[35] Halliday, Ivan (1989). *A Field Guide to Australian Trees*. Melbourne, Victoria: Hamlyn Australia. p. 200. ISBN 0-947334-08-4.

[36] Gilman, Edward F. (1997). *Trees for Urban and Suburban Landscapes*. Albany, New York: Delmar Publishers. p. 277. ISBN 0-8273-7053-9.

[37] Guilfoyle, William R. (1911). *Australian Plants suitable for gardens, parks, timber reserves, etc.* Christchurch, New Zealand: Whitcombe and Tombs Limited. p. 178.

[38] Beardsell, David; Norden, Ulla (2004). "*Ficus rubiginosa* 'Variegata', a Chlorophyll-deficient Chimera with Mosaic Patterns Created by Cell Divisions from the Outer Meristematic Layer". *Annals of Botany*. **94** (1): 51–58. doi:10.1093/aob/mch114. PMC 4242370. PMID 15145795.

[39] Gilman, Edward F.; Watson, Dennis G. (November 1993). "Ficus rubiginosa 'Variegata'" (PDF). Forest Service, US Department of Agriculture. Retrieved 11 February 2016.

[40] McCrone, Mark (2006). "Growing Port Jackson Fig as Bonsai in a Warm Temperate Climate". *ASGAP Australian Plants As Bonsai Study Group Newsletter* (11): 3–4.

[41] Kwong, Hoy Leong. *Ficus Bonsai in the Temperate Climate*. Caringbah, New South Wales: Bonsai South Nursery. p. 180. ISBN 978-0-646-47970-5.

[42] Webber, Len (1991). *Rainforest to Bonsai*. East Roseville, New South Wales: Simon and Schuster. p. 114. ISBN 0-7318-0237-3.

[43] Ratcliffe, David & Patricia (1987). *Australian Native Plants for Indoors*. Crows Nest, New South Wales: Little Hills Press. p. 90. ISBN 0-949773-49-2.

[44] Royal Horticultural Society (2015). "RHS Plant Selector - *Ficus rubiginosa*". Retrieved 15 October 2015.

3.48.8 External links

- Media related to *Ficus rubiginosa* at Wikimedia Commons
- Data related to *Ficus rubiginosa* at Wikispecies

3.49 Forsythia

(2010). "*Schistonchus* (Aphelenchoididae) from *Ficus* (Moraceae) in Australia, with description of *S. aculeata* sp. n." (PDF). *Nematology*. **12** (6): 935–58. doi:10.1163/138855410X498932.

For other uses, see Forsythia (disambiguation).

Forsythia (/fɔːrˈsɪθiə/[2] or /fɔːrˈsaɪθiə/) is a genus of flowering plants in the family Oleaceae (olive family). There are about 11 species, mostly native to eastern Asia, but one native to southeastern Europe.[1] The common name is also **forsythia**; the genus is named after William Forsyth.[3][4][5]

3.49.1 Description

Forsythia are deciduous shrubs typically growing to a height of 1–3 m (3 ft 3 in–9 ft 10 in) and, rarely, up to 6 m (20 ft) with rough grey-brown bark. The leaves are borne oppositely and are usually simple, though sometimes trifoliate with a basal pair of small leaflets; they range between 2 and 10 cm (0.79 and 3.94 in) in length and, rarely, up to 15 cm (5.9 in), with a margin that is serrated or entire (smooth).

The flowers are produced in the early spring before the leaves, bright yellow with a deeply four-lobed flower, the petals joined only at the base. These become pendent in rainy weather thus shielding the reproductive parts.

It is widely stated that forsythia flowers are able to produce lactose (the milk sugar). Lactose is very rarely established in other natural sources except milk. However, the presence of lactose could not be confirmed.[6] The actual fruit is a dry capsule, containing several winged seeds.[3][7]

The genus is named after William Forsyth (1737–1804), a Scottish botanist who was royal head gardener and a founding member of the Royal Horticultural Society.[8]

3.49.2 Species

1. *Forsythia europaea* Degen & Bald. Balkans in Albania and Serbia.
2. *Forsythia giraldiana* Lingelsh. Northwest China.
3. *Forsythia × intermedia*. Garden hybrid between *F. suspensa* and *F. viridissima*.
4. *Forsythia japonica* Makino. Japan.
5. *Forsythia koreana* (Nakai) T.B.Lee. Korea.
6. *Forsythia likiangensis* Ching & Feng ex P.Y.Bai. Southwest China.
7. *Forsythia × mandschurica* Uyeki. Northeast China.
8. *Forsythia mira* M.C.Chang. North central China.

3.49. FORSYTHIA

9. *Forsythia ovata* Nakai. Korea.
10. *Forsythia saxatilis* (Nakai) Nakai. Korea.
11. *Forsythia suspensa* (Thunb.) Vahl. Eastern and central China.
12. *Forsythia togashii* H.Hara. Japan (Shōdoshima).
13. *Forsythia velutina* Nakai. Korea.
14. *Forsythia viridissima* Lindley. Eastern China.

Sources:*[3]*[4]*[5]*[7]*[9]*[10]

A genetic study*[11] does not fully match the traditionally accepted species listed above, and groups the species in four clades: (1) *F. suspensa*; (2) *F. europaea*—*F. giraldiana*; (3) *F. ovata*—*F. japonica*—*F. viridissima*; and (4) *F. koreana* —*F. mandschurica*—*F. saxatilis*. Of the additional species, *F. koreana* is usually cited as a variety of *F. viridissima*, and *F. saxatilis* as a variety of *F. japonica*;*[12] the genetic evidence suggests they may be better treated as distinct species.

Forsythias are used as food plants by the larvae of some Lepidoptera species including Brown-tail and The Gothic.

3.49.3 Garden history

Forsythia in full bloom

Two species of forsythia are at the heart of the selected forms, for both species are variable, and garden hybrids: *Forsythia suspensa* and *F. viridissima*. "These two species are, as it were, the founder-members of the forsythia family" writes Alice Coats; they were the earliest species brought into Western gardens from the Far East and they have each played a role in the modern garden shrubs.*[13]

Forsythia suspensa, the first to be noticed by a Westerner, was seen in a Japanese garden by the botanist-surgeon Carl Peter Thunberg, who included it (as a lilac) in his *Flora Japonica* 1784. Thunberg's professional connections lay with the Dutch East India Company, and *F. suspensa* reached Holland first, by 1833. In England, when it was being offered by Veitch Nurseries in Exeter at mid-century, it was still considered a rarity. Not all the varieties of *suspensa* are splaying and drooping, best seen hanging over a retaining wall; an erect form found by Fortune near Peking in 1861 was for a time classed as a species—*F. fortunei*.*[13]

Forsythia viridissima, meanwhile, had overtaken it in European gardens. The Scottish plant-hunter Robert Fortune "discovered" it—in a mandarin's garden of the coastal city of Chusan (Zhoushan)—before he ever saw it growing wild in the mountains in Chusan's province, Zhejiang.*[13]

Forsythia × intermedia, as its name suggests, is a hybrid of *F. suspensa* and *F. viridissima*, introduced in continental Europe about 1880. Repeated crosses of the same two parents have made reiterations of *F. × intermedia* quite variable. A bud sport of a particularly showy (*spectabilis*) form is widely marketed as *F. × intermedia* 'Lynwood Variety'.*[13] This cultivar has gained the Royal Horticultural Society's Award of Garden Merit,*[14] as have *F. × intermedia* Week End 'Courtalyn'*[15] and *F.* MARÉE D'OR 'Courtasol'.*[16]

About the time of the First World War further species were discovered by plant hunters in China: *F. giraldian* (found in Gansu, 1910) and *F. ovata* (collected from seed in Korea by E.H. "Chinese" Wilson) have been particularly useful as seed parents in 20th-century American crosses.*[13]

3.49.4 Cultivation and uses

The hybrids *Forsythia × intermedia* (*F. suspensa* × *F. viridissima*) and *Forsythia × ×variabilis* (*F. ovata* × *F. suspensa*) have been produced in cultivation.*[7] *Forsythia intermedia* is a hybrid between *F. suspensa* and *F. viridissima*. Many cultivars have been selected from this cross including dwarf and compact forms.*[17]

Forsythias are popular early spring flowering shrubs in gardens and parks, especially during Eastertide; Forsythias are nicknamed the *Easter Tree* because its branches appear to be waving in praise of the resurrection of Jesus.*[18] Two are commonly cultivated for ornament, *Forsythia × intermedia* and *Forsythia suspensa*. They are both spring flowering shrubs, with yellow flowers. They are grown and prized for being tough, reliable garden plants. *Forsythia × intermedia* is the more commonly grown, is smaller, has an upright habit, and produces strongly coloured flowers. *Forsythia suspensa* is a large to very large shrub, can be grown as a weeping shrub on banks, and has paler flowers. Many named garden cultivars can also be found.*[7] Forsythia is frequently forced indoors in the early spring.

Commercial propagation is usually by cuttings, taken from

Autumn leaf color

green wood after flowering in late spring to early summer; alternatively, cuttings may be taken between November and February.*[7] Low hanging boughs often take root, and can be removed for transplanting. A common practice (known as layering) is to place a weight over a branch to keep it on the ground and, after it has rooted, to dig up the roots and cut the rooted part from the main branch; this can then be planted.

Forsythia suspensa is considered one of the 50 fundamental herbs in Chinese herbology. Forsythia sticks are used to bow a Korean string instrument called *ajaeng*.

3.49.5 Gallery

-  A young Forsythia shrub
-  *Forsythia × intermedia* flowers and young leaves
-  A Forsythia flower
-  The large size of a single, 50-year-old Forsythia
-  Forsythia flower

3.49.6 See also

- List of garden plants

3.49.7 References

[1] Kew World Checklist of Selected Plant Families

[2] *Sunset Western Garden Book,* 1995:606–607

[3] Flora of China: *Forsythia*

[4] Flora Europaea: *Forsythia*

[5] St Andrews Botanic Garden: Plant of the Month: *Forsythia*

[6] Toba, T., Nagashima, S. and Adachi, S. (1991), Is lactose really present in plants?. Journal of the Science of Food and Agriculture, 54: 305–308. doi:10.1002/jsfa.2740540217

[7] Huxley, A., ed. (1992). *New RHS Dictionary of Gardening*. Macmillan ISBN 0-333-47494-5.

[8] Forsythia by Green Deane at Eat the Weeds. Accessed April 2013

[9] University of Oxford, Oleaceae information site: *Forsythia*

[10] Government of Alberta, Agriculture and Rural Development

[11] Kim, K.-J. (1999). Molecular phylogeny of Forsythia (Oleaceae) based on chloroplast DNA variation. *P. Syst. Evol.* 218: 113-123. Abstract.

[12] Germplasm Resources Information Network: *Forsythia*

[13] Coats, Alice M. (1965). *Garden shrubs and their histories*. Dutton.

[14] "RHS Plant Selector – *Forsythia* × *intermedia* 'Lynwood Variety'". Retrieved 20 June 2013.

[15] "RHS Plant Selector – *Forsythia* × *intermedia* Week End 'Courtalyn'". Retrieved 20 June 2013.

[16] "RHS Plant Selector – *Forsythia* MARÉE D'OR 'Courtasol'". Retrieved 20 June 2013.

[17] "Arbor Day Foundation – *Forsythia* × *intermedia*". Retrieved 20 June 2013.

[18] Price, Mark (14 May 2014). "Birds, Bees, Flowers, and Faith". The United Methodist Church.

3.49.8 External links

- BBC – Forsythia page
- *Forsythia viridissima* Vanderbilt University – Forsythia page

3.50 Fraxinus hubeiensis

Fraxinus hubeiensis is a species of ash native to Hubei province in China.[1]

The species was first described in an obscure paper in 1979 with the name *Fraxinus hubeiensis*.[2] The description was republished the following year later in a more widely distributed journal, spelled *Fraxinus hupehensis*.[1][3] The latter is now considered a spelling variant, with *Fraxinus hubeiensis* the correct spelling.[4]

A molecular study shows it is most closely related to the Afghan ash (*Fraxinus xanthoxyloides*) which is found from North Africa to western China. The two are the only members of the section Sciadanthus.[5]

Fraxinus hubeiensis grows as a tree to 19 m (60 ft) high. It has compound leaves which are range from 7 to 15 cm (2.5–6 in) in length and are composed of 7 to 9 (or rarely 11) leaflets.[1]

It is used in penjing (a Chinese practice similar to the Japanese bonsai), but is at risk of overexploitation.[6]

3.50.1 References

[1] "Fraxinus hupehensis Ch'u & Shang & Su". *Flora of China*. eFlora. Retrieved 23 September 2012.

[2] S.Z.Qu, C.B.Shang & P.L.Su, 1979. Journal of the Nanjing Technological College of Forest Products 1979: 146 *Fraxinus hubeiensis*

[3] S.Z.Qu, C.B.Shang & P.L.Su. 1980. Acta Phytotaxonomica Sinica 28(3): 366, pl. 1 *Fraxinus hupehensis*

[4] "Fraxinus hubeiensis S.Z.Qu, C.B.Shang & P.L.Su". *The Plant List: A Working List of All Plant Species*. Royal Botanic Gardens, Kew and Missouri Botanical Garden. 2010. Retrieved 25 September 2012.

[5] Wallander, Eva (2008). "Systematics of *Fraxinus* (Oleaceae) and evolution of dioecy" (PDF). *Plant Syst Evol*. **273**: 25–49. doi:10.1007/s00606-008-0005-3.

[6] Ming Jun, Liao Hui Rong (1998). "On the present situation of *Fraxinus hupehensis* and its sustainable utilization". *Journal of Plant Resources and Environment*. **7**: 19–22.

3.51 Fuchsia

For other uses, see Fuchsia (color) and Fuchsia (disambiguation).

Fuchsia (pronunciation: /ˈfjuːʃə/) is a genus of flowering plants that consists mostly of shrubs or small trees. The first, *Fuchsia triphylla*, was discovered on the Caribbean island of Hispaniola (Haiti and the Dominican Republic) about 1696–1697 by the French Minim monk and botanist, Charles Plumier, during his third expedition to the Greater Antilles. He named the new genus after the renowned German botanist Leonhart Fuchs (1501–1566).[2][3]

3.51.1 Taxonomy

The fuchsias are most closely related to the northern hemisphere genus *Circaea*, the two lineages having diverged around 41 million years ago.[4]

3.51.2 Description

Almost 110 species of *Fuchsia* are recognized; the vast majority are native to South America, but a few occur north through Central America to Mexico, and also several from New Zealand to Tahiti. One species, *F. magellanica*, extends as far as the southern tip of South America, occurring on Tierra del Fuego in the cool temperate zone, but the majority are tropical or subtropical. Most fuchsias are

Fuchsia sp. in Japan

shrubs from 0.2 to 4 m (8 in to 13 ft 1 in) tall, but one New Zealand species, the kōtukutuku (*F. excorticata*), is unusual in the genus in being a tree, growing up to 12–15 m (39–49 ft) tall.

Fuchsia leaves are opposite or in whorls of three to five, simple lanceolate, and usually have serrated margins (entire in some species), 1–25 cm long, and can be either deciduous or evergreen, depending on the species. The flowers are very decorative; they have a pendulous "teardrop" shape and are displayed in profusion throughout the summer and autumn, and all year in tropical species. They have four long, slender sepals and four shorter, broader petals; in many species, the sepals are bright red and the petals purple (colours that attract the hummingbirds that pollinate them), but the colours can vary from white to dark red, purple-blue, and orange. A few have yellowish tones. The ovary is inferior and the fruit is a small (5–25 mm) dark reddish green, deep red, or deep purple berry, containing numerous very small seeds.

The fruit of all fuchsia species and cultivars is edible, with the berry of *F. splendens* reportedly among the best-tasting. Its flavor is reminiscent of citrus and black pepper, and it can be made into jam. The fruits of some other fuchsias are flavorless or leave a bad aftertaste.*[5]

3.51.3 Species

Fuchsia hybrida

The majority of *Fuchsia* species are native to Central and South America. A small additional number are found on Hispaniola (two species), in New Zealand (three species) and on Tahiti (one species). Philip A. Munz in his *A Revision of the Genus Fuchsia* classified the genus into seven sections of 100 species. More recent scientific publications, especially those by the botanists Dennis E. Breedlove of the University of California and, currently, Paul E. Berry of the University of Michigan, recognize 108 species and 122 taxa, organized into 12 sections. In New Zealand and Tahiti, section *Skinnera* now consists of only three species as *F.* × *colensoi* has been determined to be a naturally occurring hybrid between *F. excorticata* and *F. perscandens*. Also, *F. procumbens* has been placed into its own section, *Procumbentes*. Two other new sections are *Pachyrrhiza* and *Verrucosa*, each with one species. The Plant List, a cooperative endeavor by several leading botanical institutions to maintain a working list of all plant species, lists most currently accepted *Fuchsia* species and synonyms.*[6]

The vast majority of garden hybrids have descended from a few parent species.*[7]

Section 1: *Ellobium*

Mexico and Costa Rica. This section contains three species.

- *Fuchsia decidua*
- *Fuchsia fulgens*
- *Fuchsia splendens*
  - *F. splendens* var. *splendens*
  - *F. splendens* var. *cordifolia*

Section 2: *Encliandra*

Mexico to Panama. Flowers on the six species in this section have flat petals and short stamens and are reflexed into the tube. Fruits contain few seeds.

- *Fuchsia cyclindracea (synonym of F. parviflora)*
- *Fuchsia encliandra*
    - *Fuchsia encliandra* subsp. *encliandra*
    - *Fuchsia encliandra* subsp. *microphyloides*
    - *Fuchsia encliandra* subsp. *tetradactyla*
- *Fuchsia microphylla*
    - *Fuchsia microphylla* subsp. *aprica*
    - *Fuchsia microphylla* subsp. *chiapensis*
    - *Fuchsia microphylla* subsp. *hemsleyana*
    - *Fuchsia microphylla* subsp. *hidalgensis*
    - *Fuchsia microphylla* subsp. *microphylla*
    - *Fuchsia microphylla* subsp. *quercertorum*
- *Fuchsia obconica*
- *Fuchsia parviflora*
- *Fuchsia ravenii*
- *Fuchsia thymifolia*
    - *Fuchsia thymifolia* subsp. *minimiflora*
    - *Fuchsia thymifolia* subsp. *thymiflora*
- *Fuchsia × bacillaris*[8]

Section 3: *Fuchsia*

Northern Argentina to Colombia and Venezuela, and Hispaniola. With sixty-four currently recognized species, Sect. *Fuchsia* (syn. *Eufuchsia*) is the largest section within the genus.[9] The flowers are perfect, with convolute petals. The stamens are erect and may or may not be exserted from the corolla; the stamens opposite the petals are shorter. The fruit has many seeds.

- *Fuchsia abrupta*
- *Fuchsia ampliata*
- *Fuchsia andrei*
- *Fuchsia aquaviridis*
- *Fuchsia austromontana*

Fuchsia boliviana

- *Fuchsia ayavacensis*
- *Fuchsia boliviana*[10]
    - *F. boliviana* var. *boliviana (syn. of F. boliviana)*
    - *F. boliviana* var. *luxurians (syn. of F. boliviana*
- *Fuchsia campii*[11]
- *Fuchsia canescens*
- *Fuchsia caucana*
- *Fuchsia ceracea*
- *Fuchsia cinerea*
- *Fuchsia cochabambana*
- *Fuchsia confertifolia*
- *Fuchsia coriacifolia*[12]
- *Fuchsia corollata*
- *Fuchsia corymbiflora*
- *Fuchsia crassistipula*

- *Fuchsia cuatrecasaii*
- *Fuchsia decussata*
- *Fuchsia denticulata*
- *Fuchsia dependens*
- *Fuchsia ferreyrae*
- *Fuchsia fontinalis*
- *Fuchsia furfuracea*
- *Fuchsia gehrigeri*
- *Fuchsia glaberrima*
- *Fuchsia harlingii*
- *Fuchsia hartwegii*
- *Fuchsia hirtella*
- *Fuchsia hypoleuca*
- *Fuchsia lehmannii*
- *Fuchsia llewelynii*
- *Fuchsia loxensis*
- *Fuchsia macrophylla*
- *Fuchsia macropetala*
- *Fuchsia macrostigma*
- *Fuchsia magdalenae*
- *Fuchsia mathewsii*
- *Fuchsia nigricans*
- *Fuchsia orientalis*
- *Fuchsia ovalis*
- *Fuchsia pallescens*
- *Fuchsia petiolaris*
- *Fuchsia pilosa*
- *Fuchsia polyantha*
- *Fuchsia pringsheimii*
- *Fuchsia putamayensis*
- *Fuchsia rivularis*
  - *Fuchsia rivularis* subsp. *pubescens*
  - *Fuchsia rivularis* subsp. *rivularis*
- *Fuchsia sanctae-rosae*
- *Fuchsia sanmartina*
- *Fuchsia scabriuscula*
- *Fuchsia scherffiana*
- *Fuchsia sessifolia*
- *Fuchsia simplicicaulis*
- *Fuchsia steyermarkii*
- *Fuchsia summa*[11]
- *Fuchsia sylvatica*
- *Fuchsia tincta*
- *Fuchsia triphylla*
- *Fuchsia vargasiana*
- *Fuchsia venusta*
- *Fuchsia vulcanica*
- *Fuchsia wurdackii*

Section 4: *Hemsleyella*

Venezuela to Bolivia. The fifteen species in this section are characterised by a nectary that is fused with the base of the flower tube and petals that are partly or completely lacking.

- *Fuchsia apetala*
- *Fuchsia cestroides*
- *Fuchsia chloroloba*
- *Fuchsia garleppiana'*
- *Fuchsia huanucoensis*
- *Fuchsia inflata*
- *Fuchsia insignis*
- *Fuchsia juntasensis*
- *Fuchsia membranaceae*
- *Fuchsia mezae*
- *Fuchsia nana*
- *Fuchsia pilaloensis*
- *Fuchsia salicifolia*
- *Fuchsia tilletiana*
- *Fuchsia tunariensis*

3.51. FUCHSIA

Section 5: *Jimenezia*

Panama and Costa Rica.

- *Fuchsia jimenezii*

Section 6: *Kierschlegeria*

Coastal central Chile. This section is made up of a single species with pendulous axillary pedicels. The leaves are sparse. The sepals are reflexed and slightly shorter than the tube.

- *Fuchsia lycioides*

Section 7: *Pachyrrhiza*

Peru.

- *Fuchsia pachyrrhiza**[13]

Section 8: *Procumbentes*

New Zealand.

- *Fuchsia procumbens*

Section 9: *Quelusia*

Fuchsia regia

Southern Argentina and Chile, and Southeastern Brazil. The nine species in this section have the nectary fused to the base of the tube, or hypanthium. The hypanthium is cylindrical and is generally no longer than the sepals. The stamens are long and are exserted beyond the corolla.

- *Fuchsia alpestris*
- *Fuchsia bracelinae*
- *Fuchsia brevilobis*
- *Fuchsia campos-portoi*
- *Fuchsia coccinea*
- *Fuchsia glazioviana*
- *Fuchsia hatschbachii*
- *Fuchsia magellanica*
- *Fuchsia regia*
    - *Fuchsia regia* subsp. *regia*
    - *Fuchsia regia* subsp. *reitzii*
    - *Fuchsia regia* subsp. *serrae*

Section 10: *Schufia*

Mexico to Panama. These two species bear flowers in an erect, corymb-like panicle.

- *Fuchsia arborescens*
- *Fuchsia paniculata*
    - *Fuchsia paniculata* subsp. *mixensis*
    - *Fuchsia paniculata* subsp. *paniculata*

Section 11: *Skinnera*

New Zealand and Tahiti. The three living species have a floral tube with a swelling above the ovary. The sepals curve back on themselves and the petals are small or nearly absent. A new fossil species from the Early Miocene in New Zealand was described in October, 2013.

- †*Fuchsia antiqua**[14]
- *Fuchsia cyrtandroides*
- *Fuchsia excorticata*
- *Fuchsia perscandens*
- *Fuchsia* × *colensoi* - a natural hybrid

Section 12: *Verrucosa*

Venezuela and Colombia.

- *Fuchsia verrucosa*

3.51.4 Cultivation

Selection of cultivated fuchsias at BBC Gardeners' World in 2011

Fuchsias are popular garden shrubs, and once planted can live for years with a minimal amount of care. The British Fuchsia Society*[15] maintains a list of "hardy" fuchsias that have been proven to survive a number of winters throughout Britain and to be back in flower each year by July. Enthusiasts report that hundreds and even thousands of hybrids survive and prosper throughout Britain. In the United States, the Northwest Fuchsia Society maintains an extensive list of fuchsias that have proven hardy in members' gardens in the Pacific Northwest over at least three winters.*[16]

Fuchsias from sections *Quelusia* (*F. magellanica, F. regia*), *Encliandra, Skinnera* (*F. excorticata, F. perscandens*) and *Procumbentes* (*F. procumbens*) have especially proven to be hardy in widespread areas of Britain and Ireland, as well as in many other countries such as New Zealand (aside from its native species) or the Pacific Northwest region of the United States. A number of species will easily survive outdoors in agreeable mild temperate areas. Though some may not always flower in the average British summer, they will often perform well in other favorable climatic zones. Even in somewhat colder regions, a number of the hardier species will often survive as herbaceous perennials, dying back and reshooting from below ground in the spring.

Due to the favorably mild, temperate climate created by the North Atlantic Current, fuchsias grow abundantly in the West Cork region of Ireland and in the Scilly Isles, and have even colonised wild areas there. While *F. magellanica* is not widespread in Scotland it has been known to grow wild in sheltered areas, such as the banks of local streams in Fife.*[17] In the Pacific Northwest region of the United States, *F. magellanica* also easily survives regional winters.

Categories

Horticultural fuchsias may be categorised as upright and bushy, or trailing, and some can be trained as hedges, such as *F. magellanica*. Faster-growing varieties are easiest to train.*[18] Care should be taken to choose the hardier cultivars for permanent plantings in the garden as many popular upright Fuchsias such as 'Ernie', 'Jollies Nantes' and 'Maria Landy' are not reliably winter hardy,*[5] but rather extremely tender (hardiness zone 10).

3.51.5 Cultivars

Sixty cultivated varieties of fuchsia have gained the Royal Horticultural Society's Award of Garden Merit. Some cultivars popular in Great Britain include:

- 'Alice Hoffman'*[19] (pink sepals, white petals – hardy)
- 'Dollar Princess'*[20] (cerise sepals, purple petals – hardy)
- 'Garden News'*[21] (light pink sepals, double magenta petals – hardy)
- 'Genii'*[22]
- 'Hawkshead' (white self)*[23]
- 'Lady Thumb' (compact, pink sepals, white petals)*[24]
- 'Mrs Popple'*[25] (vigorous, red sepals, purple petals – hardy)
- 'Riccartonii'*[26] (crimson sepals, purple petals)
- 'Swingtime' (double, scarlet sepals, white petals)*[27]
- 'Thalia'*[28] (*tryphilla* group, orange)
- 'Tom Thumb' (compact, pink sepals, mauve petals)*[29]

3.51.6 Pests and diseases

Main article: List of fuchsia diseases

Fuchsias are eaten by the caterpillars of some Lepidoptera, such as the elephant hawk-moth (*Deilephila elpenor*) and the black-lyre leafroller moth (*"Cnephasia" jactatana*). Other major insect pests include aphids, mirid bugs such as *Lygocoris*, *Lygus* and *Plesiocoris* spp., vine weevils (*Otiorhynchus* spp.), and greenhouse whitefly (*Trialeurodes vaporariorum*). Problematic mites include the fuchsia gall mite (*Aculops fuchsiae*) and red spider mite (*Tetranychus urticae*).

Fuchsia with blossom opened

3.51.7 Pronunciation and spelling

While the original pronunciation from the word's German origin is *"fook-sya"* /ˈfʊksija/, the standard pronunciation for the common name in English is *"fyu-sha"* /ˈfjuːʃə/. As a consequence, *fuchsia* is often misspelled as *fuschia* in English.

When pronounced as scientific Latin name, the pronunciation would be *"fook-see-a"*, if one applies the rule that the root word in honorific Latin names should follow as much as possible the original pronunciation of the name of the person the plant is named for, plus the standard pronunciation of the Latin suffix. In practice, however, English-speaking botanists often pronounce it the same as the common name, *"fyu-sha"*.

3.51.8 History

Leonhart Fuchs, the eminent namesake of the genus, was born in 1501 in Wemding in the Duchy of Bavaria. A physician and professor, he occupied the chair of Medicine at the Tübingen University from his appointment at the age of 34 until his death in 1566. Besides his medical knowledge, according to his record of activities which was extensive for the time, he studied plants. This was usual for the period. Most remedies and medicines were herbal and the two subjects were often inseparable. In the course of his career Fuchs wrote the seminal *De Historia Stirpium Commentarii Insignes*, which was richly illustrated and published in *1542*. Along with Otto Brunfels (1489–1534) and Hieronymus Bock (1498–1554), also called Hieronymus Tragus, he is today considered one of the three fathers of botany.

It was in honour of Fuchs' and his work that the fuchsia received its name shortly before 1703 by Charles Plumier. Plumier compiled his *Nova Plantarum Americanum*, which was published in Paris in 1703, based on the results of his third plant-finding trip to the Caribbean in search of new

Leonhart Fuchs (1501–1566)

genera. In it he described *Fuchsia triphylla flore coccinea*.... Plumier's novel species was accepted by Linnaeus in 1753 but the long descriptive name was shortened in accordance with his binomial system.

The first fuchsia species were introduced into English gardens and glasshouses at the end of the 18th century. *Fuchsia coccinea* Aiton arrived at Kew Gardens in 1788 to be formally described in 1789. It was apparently shortly followed by *Fuchsia magellanica* Lam. There is much early confusion between these two similar-looking species in the Quelusia Section and they seem to have hybridized readily as well. *Fuchsia magellanica*, however, proved very hardy outdoors and its cultivars soon naturalized in favorable areas of the British Isles. Other species were quickly introduced to greenhouses. Of special interest is the introduction of *Fuchsia fulgens* Moç. & Sessé ex DC in the 1830s as it resulted in an outpouring of new cultivars when crossed with the existing species.

Philip Munz, in his *A Revision of the Genus Fuchsia*(1943), repeats the story that the fuchsia was first introduced into England by a sailor who grew it in a window where it was observed by a nurseryman from Hammersmith, a Mr. Lee, who succeeded in buying it and propagating it for the trade. This was supposedly either one of the short-tubed species such as *Fuchsia magellanica* or *Fuchsia coccinea*. The story given by Munz first appears in the 1850s and is embellished in various early publications. Captain Firth, a sailor, brought the plant back to England from one of his trips to his home in Hammersmith where he gave it to his wife. Later James Lee of St. Johns Wood, nurseryman and an astute businessman, heard of the plant and purchased it for £80. He then propagated as many as possible and sold them to the trade for prices ranging from £10 to £20 each. In the *Floricultural Cabinet*, 1855, there is a report which varies slightly from the above. There it is stated that *F. coccinea* was given to Kew Garden in 1788 by Captain Firth and that Lee acquired it from Kew. Other than a citation at Kew itself that *Fuchsia coccinea* was indeed given to it by a Captain Firth, there is no firm evidence to support any of these introduction stories.

Throughout the Nineteenth Century, plant-collecting fever spread throughout Europe and the United States. Many species of numerous genera were introduced, some as living plants, others as seed. The following fuchsias were recorded in England at Kew: *F. lycioides*, 1796; *F. arborescens*, 1824; *F. microphylla*, 1827; *F. fulgens*, 1830; *F. corymbiflora*, 1840; and *F. apetala*, *F. decussata*, *F. dependens* and *F. serratifolia* in 1843 and 1844, the last four species attributable to Messrs. Veitch of Exeter.

With the increasing numbers of differing species in England plant breeders began to immediately develop hybrids to develop more desirable garden plants. The first recorded experiments date to 1825 as *F. arborescens* X *F. macrostemma* and *F. arborescens* X *F. coccinea* where the quality of the resultant plants was unrecorded.

Between 1835 and 1850 there was a tremendous influx to England of both hybrids and varieties, the majority of which have been lost.

In 1848 Felix Porcher published the second edition of his book *Le Fuchsia son Histoire et sa Culture*. This described 520 species. In 1871 in later editions of M. Porchers book reference is made to James Lye who was to become famous as a breeder of fuchsias in England. In 1883 the first book of English fuchsias was published.

Between 1900 and 1914 many of the famous varieties were produced which were grown extensively for Covent Garden market by many growers just outside London. During the period between the world wars, fuchsia-growing slowed as efforts were made toward crop production until after 1949, when plant and hybrid production resumed on a large scale.*[7]

In the United States, Sidney Mitchell, a member of the newly formed American Fuchsia Society in San Francisco, shipped a large collection of fuchsias back to California from a nine-month trip to visit gardens in Europe in 1930. Almost immediately after the Society had been established in 1929, a thorough census and collection of fuchsias already growing in California gardens and nurseries had been undertaken under the scientific leadership and direction of Alice Eastwood. The census yielded ninety-one existing cultivars. Armed with that list, Mitchell acquired fifty-one new fuchsias; Forty-eight of his plants survived the long trip. These were doled out to members of the society and local businesses. Half were also cultivated at the University of California Botanical Garden in Berkeley and the other half at the Berkeley Horticultural Nursery. A wave of interest in fuchsia breeding was launched. Together with the hybrids already in California, many famous American hybrids of the Forties and Fifties are the descendants of this 1930 group.*[30]*[31]

3.51.9 References

[1] Clive A. Stace (2010). "*Fuchsia* L. – fuchsias". *New Flora of the British Isles* (3rd ed.). Cambridge University Press. p. 365. ISBN 978-0-521-70772-5.

[2] Charles Plumier. *Nova Plantarum Americanum Genera*, Paris, 1703.

[3] (1910) *The* Encyclopædia Britannica: *A Dictionary of Arts, Sciences, Literature and General Information, 11th Edition: Volume XI, Franciscans to Gibbons* The Encyclopædia Britannica Company: New York, page 272. Retrieved on 2007-09-25.

[4] Berry, Paul E., William J. Hahn, Kenneth J. Sytsma, Jocelyn C. Hall, and Austin Mast (2004). "Phylogenetic relationships and biogeography of *Fuchsia* (Onagraceae) based on noncoding nuclear and chloroplast DNA data". *American Journal of Botany*. **91** (4): 601–14. doi:10.3732/ajb.91.4.601. PMID 21653416.

[5] "*Fuchsia*". Royal Horticultural Society. Retrieved October 2, 2013.

[6] "The Plant List – Fuchsia". Retrieved 20 June 2013.

[7] A. G. Puttock (1959). *Lovely Fuchsias*. London: Gifford.

[8] *Fuchsia* × *bacillaris* is a natural hybrid between *F. microphylla* ssp. *microphylla* and *F. thymifolia* ssp. *thymifolia*.

[9] Berry P. E. (1982). "The systematics and evolution of *Fuchsia* Sect. *Fuchsia* (Onagraceae)". *Annals of the Missouri Botanical Garden*. **69** (1): 1–199. doi:10.2307/2398789.

[10] F. boliviana var. boliviana (Carrière 1877) and var. luxurians (Johnston 1925) are both synonyms of F. boliviana. Except for F. rivularis subsp. pubescens and subsp. rivularis (Berry & Hermsen 1999), there are currently no taxa of subspecific rank recognized within Section Fuchsia (Berry 1982).

[11] Berry, P. E. (1995). Two new species of *Fuchsia* section *Fuchsia* (Onagraceae) from southern Ecuador. *Novon: A Journal for Botanical Nomenclature* 5(4) 318–22, f. 2.

[12] Berry P. E. (1988). "Nomenclatural changes in the genus *Fuchsia*". *Annals of the Missouri Botanical Garden*. **75** (3): 1150. doi:10.2307/2399384.

[13] Berry P. E.; et al. (1988). "Fuchsia pachyrrhiza *(Onagraceae), a tuberous new species and section of* Fuchsia *from western Peru*". Systematic Botany. **13** *(4): 483–92*. *doi:10.2307/2419193*.

[14] Daphne E. Lee. "A fossil Fuchsia (Onagraceae) flower and an anther mass with in situ pollen from the early Miocene of New Zealand". amjbot.org.

[15] "British Fuchsia Society". Retrieved 20 June 2013.

[16] "Northwest Fuchsia Society". Retrieved 20 June 2013.

[17] "Gardening by the sea". Retrieved 20 June 2013.

[18] Bartlett, George (2005). *Fuchsias: a Colour Guide*. United Kingdom: Crowood Press. ISBN 1852239999.

[19] "RHS Plant Selector – *Fuchsia* 'Alice Hoffman'". Retrieved 20 June 2013.

[20] "RHS Plant Selector – *Fuchsia* 'Dollar Prinzessin'". Retrieved 20 June 2013.

[21] "RHS Plant Selector – *Fuchsia* 'Garden News'". Retrieved 20 June 2013.

[22] "RHS Plant Selector – *Fuchsia* 'Genii'". Retrieved 20 June 2013.

[23] "RHS Plant Selector – *Fuchsia* 'Hawkshead'". Retrieved 20 June 2013.

[24] "RHS Plant Selector - *Fuchsia* 'Lady Thumb'". Retrieved 20 June 2013.

[25] "RHS Plant Selector – *Fuchsia* 'Mrs Popple'". Retrieved 20 June 2013.

[26] "RHS Plant Selector – *Fuchsia* 'Riccartonii'". Retrieved 20 June 2013.

[27] "RHS Plant Selector – *Fuchsia* 'Swingtime'". Retrieved 20 June 2013.

[28] "RHS Plant Selector – *Fuchsia* 'Thalia'". Retrieved 20 June 2013.

[29] "RHS Plant Selector – *Fuchsia* 'Tom Thumb'". Retrieved 20 June 2013.

[30] Pam Peirce (2004). *Wildly Successful Plants: Northern California*. Seattle: Sasquatch Books.

[31] American Fuchsia Society (1945). *The Fuchsia Book*. Berkeley: American Fuchsia Society.

3.51.10 External links

Local and National Fuchsia Societies

- American Fuchsia Society
- The British Fuchsia Society
- Euro-Fuchsia - An Association of European Fuchsia Societies
- National Fuchsia Society of New Zealand
- Northwest Fuchsia Society (USA)
- Western Cape Fuchsia Society (South Africa)

Information Pages on Fuchsias

- Dave's Garden (USA) - Fuchsia information and reviews.
- Fuchsia Magic (UK) - Fuchsia photos.
- Fuchsias in the City (USA) - Extensive resource on all aspects of fuchsias.
- Lancaster, Morecambe & District Fuchsia Society (UK) - Fuchsia Flower: All you need to know.
- Nederlandse Kring van Fuchsiavrienden (NL) - Searchable database of fuchsia cultivars.
- Royal Horticultural Society (UK) - Fuchsia growing advice.
- Washington State University, Spokane County Extension (USA) - Fuchsia fact sheet.

3.52 Ginkgo biloba

This article is about the tree. For the Goethe poem, see Gingo biloba.

Ginkgo biloba, commonly known as **ginkgo** or **gingko**[*][3] (both pronounced /ˈɡɪŋkoʊ/), also known as the **ginkgo tree** or the **maidenhair tree**,[*][4] is the only living species in the division Ginkgophyta, all others being extinct. It is found in fossils dating back 270 million years. Native to China,[*][2] the tree is widely cultivated and was introduced early to human history. It has various uses in traditional medicine and as a source of food. The genus name *Ginkgo* is regarded as a misspelling of the Japanese *gin kyo*, "silver apricot".[*][5]

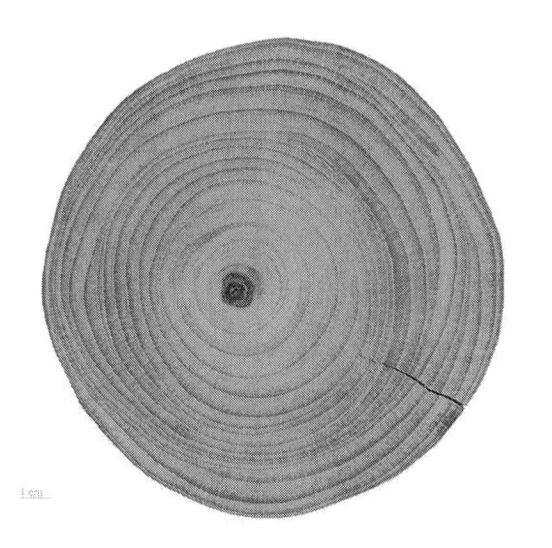

Ginkgo biloba *cross section of tree trunk (source: Muséum de Toulouse)*

3.52.1 Taxonomy and naming

The species was initially described by Carl Linnaeus in 1771, the specific epithet *biloba* derived from the Latin *bis*, "two" and *loba*, "lobed", referring to the shape of the leaves.*[6] Two names for the species recognise the botanist Richard Salisbury, a placement by Nelson as *Pterophyllus salisburiensis* and the earlier *Salisburia adiantifolia* proposed by James Edward Smith. The epithet of the latter may have been intended to denote a characteristic resembling *Adiantum*, the genus of maidenhair ferns.*[7]

The relationship of ginkgo to other plant groups remains uncertain. It has been placed loosely in the divisions Spermatophyta and Pinophyta, but no consensus has been reached. Since its seeds are not protected by an ovary wall, it can morphologically be considered a gymnosperm. The apricot-like structures produced by female ginkgo trees are technically not fruits, but are seeds that have a shell consisting of a soft and fleshy section (the sarcotesta), and a hard section (the sclerotesta).

The ginkgo is classified in its own division, the Ginkgophyta, comprising the single class Ginkgoopsida, order Ginkgoales, family Ginkgoaceae, genus *Ginkgo* and is the only extant species within this group. It is one of the best-known examples of a living fossil, because Ginkgoales other than *G. biloba* are not known from the fossil record after the Pliocene.*[8]*[9]

Chinese scientists published a draft genome of *Ginko biloba* in 2016.*[10] The tree has an exceptionally large genome of 10.6 billion DNA "letters" (the human genome has three billion) and about 41,840 predicted genes*[11] which enable a considerable number of antibacterial and chemical defense mechanisms.*[10]

Etymology and pronunciation

Despite its complicated spelling, which is due to an exceptionally complicated etymology including a transcription error, "ginkgo" is usually pronounced /ˈɡɪŋkoʊ/,*[3] which has given rise to the common other spelling "gingko". The spelling pronunciation /ˈɡɪŋkɡoʊ/ is however so widespread that it is recorded in some dictionaries, especially British ones, and no longer considered incorrect.

The older Chinese name for this plant is 銀果, meaning "silver fruit", pronounced *yínguǒ* in Mandarin or *Ngan-gwo* in Cantonese. The most usual names today are 白果 (*bái guǒ*), meaning "white fruit", and 銀杏 (*yínxìng*), meaning "silver apricot". The former name was borrowed directly in Vietnamese as *bạch quả*. The latter name was borrowed in Japanese ぎんなん (*ginnan*) and Korean ☒☒ (*eunhaeng*), when the tree itself was introduced from China.

The scientific name *Ginkgo* is the result of a spelling error that occurred three centuries ago. *Kanji* typically have multiple pronunciations in Japanese, and the characters 銀杏 used for *ginnan* can also be pronounced *ginkyō*. Engelbert Kaempfer, the first Westerner to investigate the species in 1690, wrote down this pronunciation in the notes that he later used for the *Amoenitates Exoticae* (1712) with the "awkward" spelling "ginkgo".*[12] This appears to be a simple error of Kaempfer; taking his spelling of other Japanese words containing the syllable "kyō" into account, a more precise romanization following his writing habits would have been "ginkio" or "ginkjo". Linné, who relied on Kaempfer when dealing with Japanese plants, adopted the spelling given in Kaempfer's "Flora Japonica" (*Amoenitates Exoticae*, p. 811).

3.52.2 Uses

Health

An extract of *Ginkgo biloba* leaf (GBE) is marketed in dietary supplement form with claims it can enhance cognitive function in people without known cognitive problems. Studies have failed to find such effects on memory or attention in healthy people.*[13]*[14]

A standardized medicinal extract of *Ginkgo biloba* leaf originally called EGb 761 has been studied as a possible treatment for dementia and Alzheimer's disease, with mixed results. Some reviews have concluded there is no good evidence supporting the use of Ginkgo in dementia,*[14]*[15]*[16]*[17] whereas others have concluded that the EGB761 extract may help people with dementia.*[18]*[19]*[20]

There is no good evidence supporting the use of Ginkgo for treating high blood pressure,*[21] menopause-related cognitive decline,*[22] tinnitus,*[23] post-stroke recovery,*[24] peripheral arterial disease,*[25] macular degeneration,*[26] or altitude sickness.*[27]*[28]

Cooking

Ginkgo seeds with sarcotesta removed

Ginkgo seeds served with boiled coconut flesh as a dessert in Thailand

The nut-like gametophytes inside the seeds are particularly esteemed in Asia, and are a traditional Chinese food. Ginkgo nuts are used in *congee*, and are often served at special occasions such as weddings and the Chinese New Year (as part of the vegetarian dish called Buddha's delight). In Chinese culture, they are believed to have health benefits; some also consider them to have aphrodisiac qualities. Japanese cooks add ginkgo seeds (called *ginnan*) to dishes such as *chawanmushi*, and cooked seeds are often eaten along with other dishes.

When eaten in large quantities or over a long period, the gametophyte (meat) of the seed can cause poisoning by 4'-O-methylpyridoxine (MPN). MPN is heat-stable and not destroyed by cooking.*[29] Studies have demonstrated the convulsions caused by MPN can be prevented or treated successfully with pyridoxine (vitamin B6).

Some people are sensitive to the chemicals in the sarcotesta, the outer fleshy coating. These people should handle the seeds with care when preparing the seeds for consumption, wearing disposable gloves. The symptoms are allergic contact dermatitis*[30]*[31] or blisters similar to that caused by contact with poison ivy. However, seeds with the fleshy coating removed are mostly safe to handle.

3.52.3 Side effects

Ginkgo may have undesirable effects, especially for individuals with blood circulation disorders and those taking anticoagulants such as aspirin or warfarin, although recent studies have found ginkgo has little or no effect on the anticoagulant properties or pharmacodynamics of warfarin in healthy subjects.*[32]*[33]

Additional side effects include increased risk of bleeding, gastrointestinal discomfort, nausea, vomiting, diarrhea, headaches, dizziness, heart palpitations, and restlessness.*[33]*[34]*[35] Ginkgo should be used with caution when combined with other herbs known to increase bleeding (e.g. garlic, ginseng, ginger).

According to a systemic review, the effects of ginkgo on pregnant women may include increased bleeding time, and it should be avoided during lactation because of inadequate safety evidence.*[36]

Allergic precautions and contraindications

Some authors claim that *Ginkgo biloba* extracts, which are co-administered with anticoagulant drugs such as warfarin or coumadin, increase the risk for bleeding because of their assumed antiplatelet activity. Concerns that standardized Ginkgo biloba preparations (GBE) significantly impact haemostasis or adversely affect the safety of anticoagulant drugs are however not supported by current medical literature.*[37]

The presence of amentoflavone in *G. biloba* leaves would indicate a potential for interactions with many medications through the strong inhibition of CYP3A4 and CYP2C9; however, no empirical evidence supports this. Further, at recommended doses, studies have shown, "[m]ultiple-dose administration of *Ginkgo biloba* did not affect cytochrome P-450 2D6 or 3A4 activity in normal volunteers."*[38] The concentration of amentoflavone found even in commercial ginkgo extracts possibly is too low to be pharmacologically active.

Ginkgo biloba leaves and sarcotesta also contain ginkgolic acids,*[39] which are highly allergenic, long-chain alkylphenols such as bilobol or adipostatin A*[40] (bilobol is a substance related to anacardic acid from cashew nut shells and urushiols present in poison ivy and other *Toxicodendron* spp.)*[31] Individuals with a history of strong allergic reactions to poison ivy, mangoes, cashews and other alkylphenol-producing plants are more likely to experience allergic reaction when consuming non-standardized ginkgo-containing preparations, combinations, or extracts thereof. The level of these allergens in standardized pharmaceutical preparations from *Ginkgo biloba* was restricted to 5 ppm by the Commission E of the former Federal German Health Authority.

3.52.4 Cultivation

Ginkgo biloba *in Morlanwelz-Mariemont Park, Belgium*

Ginkgo biloba *in Tournai, Belgium*

Symbol of Tokyo prefecture, representing a ginkgo leaf.

Ginkgo has long been cultivated in China; some planted trees at temples are believed to be over 1,500 years old. The first record of Europeans encountering it is in 1690 in Japanese temple gardens, where the tree was seen by the German botanist Engelbert Kaempfer. Because of its status in Buddhism and Confucianism, the ginkgo is also widely planted in Korea and parts of Japan; in both areas, some naturalization has occurred, with ginkgos seeding into natural forests.

In some areas, most intentionally planted ginkgos are male cultivars grafted onto plants propagated from seed, because the male trees will not produce the malodorous seeds. The popular cultivar "Autumn Gold" is a clone of a male plant.

The disadvantage of male *Ginkgo biloba* trees is that they are highly allergenic. Male *Ginkgo biloba* trees have an OPALS allergy scale rating of 7 (out of 10), whereas female trees, which can produce no pollen, have an OPALS allergy scale rating of 2.*[41]

Female cultivars include "Liberty Splendor", "Santa Cruz", and "Golden Girl", so named because of the striking yellow color of its leaves in the fall.

Ginkgos adapt well to the urban environment, tolerating pollution and confined soil spaces.*[42] They rarely suffer disease problems, even in urban conditions, and are attacked by few insects.*[43]*[44] For this reason, and for their general beauty, ginkgos are excellent urban and shade trees, and are widely planted along many streets.*[45]

Ginkgos are also popular subjects for growing as *penjing* and *bonsai*;*[46] they can be kept artificially small and tended over centuries. Furthermore, the trees are easy to propagate from seed.

The ginkgo leaf is the symbol of the Urasenke school of Japanese tea ceremony. The tree is the official tree of the Japanese capital of Tokyo, and the symbol of Tokyo is a ginkgo leaf.

3.52.5 Palaeontology

Ginkgo biloba *Eocene leaf from the McAbee, BC, Canada.*

The ginkgo is a living fossil, with fossils recognisably related to modern ginkgo from the Permian, dating back 270 million years. The most plausible ancestral group for the order Ginkgoales is the Pteridospermatophyta, also known as the "seed ferns", specifically the order Peltaspermales. The closest living relatives of the clade are the cycads,*[47]*:84 which share with the extant *G. biloba* the characteristic of motile sperm. Fossils attributable to the genus *Ginkgo* first appeared in the Early Jurassic, and the genus diversified and spread throughout Laurasia during the middle Jurassic and Early Cretaceous. It declined in diversity as the Cretaceous progressed, and by the Paleocene, *Ginkgo adiantoides* was

Fossil Ginkgo *leaves from the Jurassic of England*

the only *Ginkgo* species left in the Northern Hemisphere, while a markedly different (and poorly documented) form persisted in the Southern Hemisphere. At the end of the Pliocene, *Ginkgo* fossils disappeared from the fossil record everywhere except in a small area of central China, where the modern species survived. It is doubtful whether the Northern Hemisphere fossil species of *Ginkgo* can be reliably distinguished. Given the slow pace of evolution and morphological similarity between members of the genus, there may have been only one or two species existing in the Northern Hemisphere through the entirety of the Cenozoic: present-day *G. biloba* (including *G. adiantoides*) and *G. gardneri* from the Paleocene of Scotland.*[47]*:85

At least morphologically, *G. gardneri* and the Southern Hemisphere species are the only known post-Jurassic taxa that can be unequivocally recognised. The remainder may have been ecotypes or subspecies. The implications would be that *G. biloba* had occurred over an extremely wide range, had remarkable genetic flexibility and, though evolving genetically, never showed much speciation. While it may seem improbable that a species may exist as a contiguous entity for many millions of years, many of the ginkgo's life-history parameters fit. These are: extreme longevity; slow reproduction rate; (in Cenozoic and later times) a wide, apparently contiguous, but steadily contracting distribution coupled with, as far as can be demonstrated from the fossil record, extreme ecological conservatism (restriction to disturbed streamside environments).*[47]*:91

Modern-day *G. biloba* grows best in environments that are well-watered and drained,*[47]*:87 and the extremely similar fossil *ginkgo* favored similar environments: the sediment record at the majority of fossil *ginkgo* localities indicates it grew primarily in disturbed environments along streams and levees.*[47] ginkgo*, therefore, presents an "ecological paradox" because while it possesses some favorable traits for living in disturbed environments (clonal reproduction) many of its other life-history traits (slow growth, large seed size, late reproductive maturity) are the opposite of those exhibited by modern plants that thrive in disturbed settings.*[47]*:92

Given the slow rate of evolution of the genus, *ginkgo* possibly represents a preangiosperm strategy for survival in disturbed streamside environments. Ginkgo evolved in an era before flowering plants, when ferns, cycads, and cycadeoids dominated disturbed streamside environments, forming low, open, shrubby canopies. *Ginkgo*s large seeds and habit of "bolting" - growing to a height of 10 m before elongating its side branches - may be adaptions to such an environment. Because diversity in the genus *Ginkgo* drops through the Cretaceous (along with that of ferns, cycads, and cycadeoids) at the same time the flowering plants were on the rise, the notion that flowering plants with better adaptations to disturbance displaced *Ginkgo* and its associates over time is supported.*[47]*:93

Ginkgo has been used for classifying plants with leaves that have more than four veins per segment, while *Baiera* for those with fewer than four veins per segment. *Sphenobaiera* has been used to classify plants with a broadly wedge-shaped leaf that lacks a distinct leaf stem. *Trichopitys* is distinguished by having multiple-forked leaves with cylindrical (not flattened), thread-like ultimate divisions; it is one of the earliest fossils ascribed to the Ginkgophyta.

A digital recreation of Baiera *made from diverse images of fossils and academic descriptions*

3.52.6 Description

Ginkgos are large trees, normally reaching a height of 20–35 m (66–115 ft), with some specimens in China being over 50 m (160 ft). The tree has an angular crown and long, somewhat erratic branches, and is usually deep rooted and resistant to wind and snow damage. Young trees are often tall and slender, and sparsely branched; the crown becomes broader as the tree ages. During autumn, the leaves turn a bright yellow, then fall, sometimes within a short space of time (one to 15 days). A combination of resistance to disease, insect-resistant wood and the ability to form aerial roots and sprouts makes ginkgos long-lived, with some specimens claimed to be more than 2,500 years old.

Ginkgo is a relatively shade-intolerant species that (at least in cultivation) grows best in environments that are well-watered and well-drained. The species shows a preference for disturbed sites; in the "semiwild" stands at Tian Mu Shan, many specimens are found along stream banks, rocky slopes, and cliff edges. Accordingly, ginkgo retains a prodigious capacity for vegetative growth. It is capable of sprouting from embedded buds near the base of the trunk (lignotubers, or basal chi chi) in response to disturbances, such as soil erosion. Old individuals are also capable of producing aerial roots on the undersides of large branches in response to disturbances such as crown damage; these roots can lead to successful clonal reproduction upon contacting the soil. These strategies are evidently important in the persistence of ginkgo; in a survey of the "semi-wild" stands remaining in Tianmushan, 40% of the specimens surveyed were multistemmed, and few saplings were present.*[47]*:86–87

Phytochemicals

Extracts of ginkgo leaves contain phenolic acids, proanthocyanidins, flavonoid glycosides, such as myricetin, kaempferol, isorhamnetin and quercetin, and the terpene trilactones, ginkgolides and bilobalides.*[48]*[49] The leaves also contain unique ginkgo biflavones, as well as alkylphenols and polyprenols.*[49]

3.52.7 Branches

Ginkgo branches grow in length by growth of shoots with regularly spaced leaves, as seen on most trees. From the axils of these leaves, "spur shoots" (also known as short shoots) develop on second-year growth. Short shoots have very short internodes (so they may grow only one or two centimeters in several years) and their leaves are usually unlobed. They are short and knobby, and are arranged regularly on the branches except on first-year growth. Because of the short internodes, leaves appear to be clustered at the tips of short shoots, and reproductive structures are formed only on them (see pictures below - seeds and leaves are visible on short shoots). In ginkgos, as in other plants that possess them, short shoots allow the formation of new leaves in the older parts of the crown. After a number of years, a short shoot may change into a long (ordinary) shoot, or vice versa.

3.52.8 Leaves

Ginkgo leaves in autumn

Ginkgo leaves in summer

The leaves are unique among seed plants, being fan-shaped with veins radiating out into the leaf blade, sometimes bifurcating (splitting), but never anastomosing to form a network.[50] Two veins enter the leaf blade at the base and fork repeatedly in two; this is known as dichotomous venation. The leaves are usually 5–10 cm (2.0–3.9 in), but sometimes up to 15 cm (5.9 in) long. The old popular name "maidenhair tree" is because the leaves resemble some of the pinnae of the maidenhair fern, *Adiantum capillus-veneris*. Ginkgos are prized for their autumn foliage, which is a deep saffron yellow.

Leaves of long shoots are usually notched or lobed, but only from the outer surface, between the veins. They are borne both on the more rapidly growing branch tips, where they are alternate and spaced out, and also on the short, stubby spur shoots, where they are clustered at the tips. Leaves are green both on the top and bottom[51] and have stomata on both sides.[52]

3.52.9 Reproduction

Ginkgos are dioecious, with separate sexes, some trees being female and others being male. Male plants produce small pollen cones with sporophylls, each bearing two microsporangia spirally arranged around a central axis.

Female plants do not produce cones. Two ovules are formed at the end of a stalk, and after pollination, one or both develop into seeds. The seed is 1.5–2 cm long. Its fleshy outer layer (the sarcotesta) is light yellow-brown, soft, and fruit-like. It is attractive in appearance, but contains butyric acid[53] (also known as butanoic acid) and smells like rancid butter or vomit[54] when fallen. Beneath the sarcotesta is the hard sclerotesta (the "shell" of the seed) and a papery endotesta, with the nucellus surrounding the female gametophyte at the center.[55]

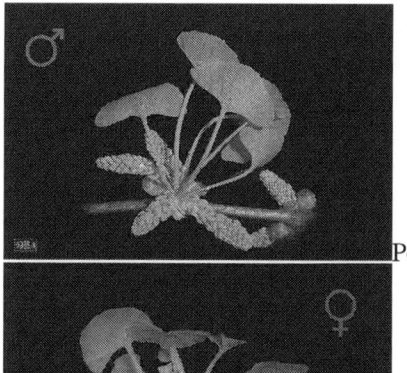

198   CHAPTER 3. PLANTS USED IN BONSAI (IN ALPHABETICAL ORDER)

Pollen cones

Ovules

The fertilization of ginkgo seeds occurs via motile sperm, as in cycads, ferns, mosses and algae. The sperm are large (about 70–90 micrometres)[*][56] and are similar to the sperm of cycads, which are slightly larger. Ginkgo sperm were first discovered by the Japanese botanist Sakugoro Hirase in 1896.[*][57] The sperm have a complex multi-layered structure, which is a continuous belt of basal bodies that form the base of several thousand flagella which actually have a cilia-like motion. The flagella/cilia apparatus pulls the body of the sperm forwards. The sperm have only a tiny distance to travel to the archegonia, of which there are usually two or three. Two sperm are produced, one of which successfully fertilizes the ovule. Although it is widely held that fertilization of ginkgo seeds occurs just before or after they fall in early autumn,[*][50][*][55] embryos ordinarily occur in seeds just before and after they drop from the tree.[*][58]

- Trunk bark

- Ginkgo pollen-bearing cones

- Bud in spring

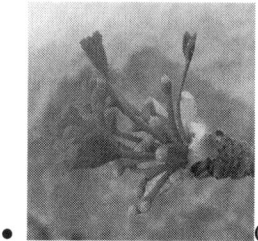

- Ovules ready for fertilization

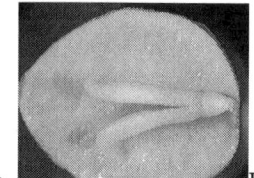

- Female gametophyte, dissected from a seed freshly shed from the tree, containing a well-developed embryo

- Immature ginkgo ovules and leaves

- Autumn leaves and fallen seeds

- A forest of saplings sprout among last year's seeds

-  Ginkgo tree in autumn

- 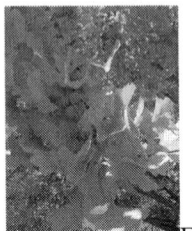 Fruit on tree

- 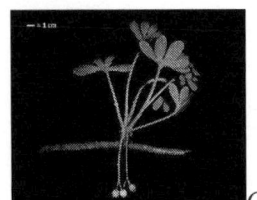 *Ginkgo yimaensis**[63]

- 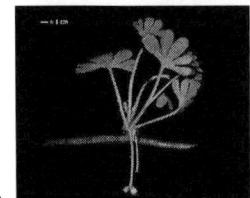 *Ginkgo apodes**[63]

- 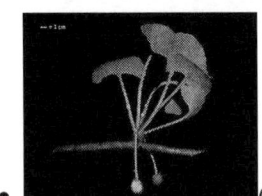 *Ginkgo adiantoides* or a new taxon from the USA, *G. cranei**[63]

- 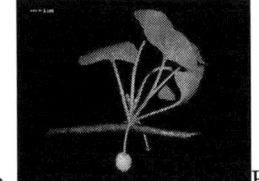 Extant *Ginkgo biloba**[63]

3.52.10 Distribution and habitat

Although *Ginkgo biloba* and other species of the genus were once widespread throughout the world, its range shrank until by two million years ago, it was restricted to a small area of China. For centuries, it was thought to be extinct in the wild, but is now known to grow in at least two small areas in Zhejiang province in eastern China, in the Tianmushan Reserve. However, recent studies indicate high genetic uniformity among ginkgo trees from these areas, arguing against a natural origin of these populations and suggesting the ginkgo trees in these areas may have been planted and preserved by Chinese monks over a period of about 1,000 years.*[59] This study demonstrates a greater genetic diversity in Southwestern China populations, supporting glacial refugia in mountains surrounding eastern Tibetan Plateau, where several old-growth candidates for wild populations have been reported.*[59]*[60] Whether native ginkgo populations still exist has not been demonstrated unequivocally, but evidence grows favouring these Southwestern populations as wild, from genetic data but also from history of those territories, with bigger *Ginkgo biloba* trees being older than surrounding human settlements.*[59]

Where it occurs in the wild, it is found infrequently in deciduous forests and valleys on acidic loess (i.e. fine, silty soil) with good drainage. The soil it inhabits is typically in the pH range of 5.0 to 5.5.*[61]

In many areas of China, it has been long cultivated, and it is common in the southern third of the country.*[61] It has also been commonly cultivated in North America for over 200 years and in Europe for close to 300, but during that time, it has never become significantly naturalized.*[62]

3.52.11 History

The first use as a medicine is recorded in the late 15th century in China; among western countries, its first registered medicinal use was in Germany in 1965. Despite use, controlled studies do not support the extract's efficacy for most of the indicated conditions.*[64]

Hiroshima

Further information: Atomic bombings of Hiroshima and Nagasaki

Extreme examples of the ginkgo's tenacity may be seen in Hiroshima, Japan, where six trees growing between 1– 2 km from the 1945 atom bomb explosion were among the few living things in the area to survive the blast. Although almost all other plants (and animals) in the area were killed, the ginkgos, though charred, survived and were soon healthy again, among other *hibakujumoku* (trees that survived the blast).

The six trees are still alive: they are marked with signs at Housenbou (報專坊) temple (planted in 1850), Shukkei-en (planted about 1740), Jōsei-ji (planted 1900), at the former site of Senda Elementary School near Miyukibashi, at the Myōjōin temple, and an Edo period-cutting at Anraku-ji temple.*[65]

3.52.12 1000-year-old ginkgo at Tsurugaoka Hachimangū

The stump of the ancient fallen ginkgo which has produced leaves in recent years

The ginkgo tree that had stood next to Tsurugaoka Hachiman-gū's stone stairway approximately from the Shinto shrine's foundation in 1063, and which appears in almost every old depiction of the shrine, was completely uprooted and irreparably damaged in March, 2010. According to an expert who analyzed the tree, the fall was likely due to rot.

Later, both the stump of the severed tree and a replanted section of the trunk sprouted leaves. The shrine is in the city of Kamakura, Kanagawa Prefecture, Japan.

The tree was nicknamed *kakure-ichō* (hiding ginkgo), deriving from an Edo period urban legend which told of a suspected assassin hiding behind it before striking his victim.

3.52.13 See also

- André Michaux, introduced the ginkgo to North America*[66]
- Ginkgo/Wanapum State Park in central Washington, USA
- Herbalism
- List of edible seeds

3.52.14 References

[1] Mustoe, G.E. (2002). "Eocene Ginkgo leaf fossils from the Pacific Northwest". *Canadian Journal of Botany.* **80** (10): 1078–1087. doi:10.1139/b02-097.

[2] Sun, W. 1998. *Ginkgo biloba*. The IUCN Red List of Threatened Species. Version 2015.2. Downloaded on 07 September 2015.

[3] American Heritage Dictionary

[4] "*Ginkgo biloba*". Natural Resources Conservation Service PLANTS Database. USDA. Retrieved 19 January 2016.

[5] Coombes, Allen J. (1994), *Dictionary of Plant Names*, London: Hamlyn Books, ISBN 978-0-600-58187-1

[6] Simpson DP (1979). *Cassell's Latin Dictionary* (5 ed.). London: Cassell Ltd. p. 883. ISBN 0-304-52257-0.

[7] Chandler, Brian (2000). "Ginkgo - origins". *Ginkgo pages*. Retrieved 22 November 2010.

[8] Zhou, Zhiyan; Zheng, Shaolin (2003). "Palaeobiology: The missing link in Ginkgo evolution". *Nature.* **423** (6942): 821–2. doi:10.1038/423821a. PMID 12815417.

[9] Julie Jalalpour; Matt Malkin; Peter Poon; Liz Rehrmann; Jerry Yu (1997). "Ginkgoales: Fossil Record". University of California, Berkeley. Retrieved 3 June 2008.

[10] Guan, Rui; Zhao, Yunpeng; Zhang, He; Fan, Guangyi; Liu, Xin; Zhou, Wenbin; Shi, Chengcheng; Wang, Jiahao; Liu, Weiqing (2016-01-01). "Draft genome of the living fossil Ginkgo biloba". *GigaScience.* **5**: 49. doi:10.1186/s13742-016-0154-1. ISSN 2047-217X.

[11] "Ginkgo 'living fossil' genome decoded". *BBC News*. 2016-11-21. Retrieved 2016-11-23.

[12] Engelbert Kaempfer (1721). *Amoenitates exoticae politico-physico-medicae* (in Latin). Lengoviae: Meyer.

[13] Laws KR, Sweetnam H, Kondel TK (November 2012). "Is Ginkgo biloba a cognitive enhancer in healthy individuals? A meta-analysis". *Hum Psychopharmacol* (Meta-analysis). **27** (6): 527–33. doi:10.1002/hup.2259. PMID 23001963.

[14] "Ginkgo". National Center for Complementary and Integrative Health, US National Institutes of Health. 2014. Retrieved 4 September 2014.

[15] Birks, J; Grimley Evans, J (January 21, 2009). "Ginkgo biloba for cognitive impairment and dementia.". *The Cochrane database of systematic reviews* (1): CD003120. doi:10.1002/14651858.CD003120.pub3. PMID 19160216.

[16] Cooper, C; Li, R; Lyketsos, C; Livingston, G (September 2013). "Treatment for mild cognitive impairment: systematic review.". *The British Journal of Psychiatry*. **203** (3): 255–64. doi:10.1192/bjp.bp.113.127811. PMID 24085737.

[17] Mancuso, C; Siciliano, R; Barone, E; Preziosi, P (May 2012). "Natural substances and Alzheimer's disease: from preclinical studies to evidence based medicine.". *Biochimica et Biophysica Acta*. **1822** (5): 616–24. doi:10.1016/j.bbadis.2011.09.004. PMID 21939756.

[18] Weinmann, S; Roll, S; Schwarzbach, C; Vauth, C; Willich, SN (2010). "Effects of Ginkgo biloba in dementia: systematic review and meta-analysis". *BMC geriatrics*. **10**: 14. doi:10.1186/1471-2318-10-14. PMC 2846949. PMID 20236541.

[19] Tan, MS; Yu, JT; Tan, CC; Wang, HF; Meng, XF; Wang, C; Jiang, T; Zhu, XC; Tan, L (August 11, 2014). "Efficacy and Adverse Effects of Ginkgo Biloba for Cognitive Impairment and Dementia: A Systematic Review and Meta-Analysis.". *Journal of Alzheimer's disease : JAD*. doi:10.3233/JAD-140837. PMID 25114079.

[20] Tan, et.al (2015). "Efficacy and adverse effects of ginkgo biloba for cognitive impairment and dementia: a systematic review and meta-analysis". *J Alzheimers Dis*. **43** (2): 589–603. doi:10.3233/JAD-140837. PMID 25114079.

[21] Xiong XJ, Liu W, Yang XC, et al. (September 2014). "Ginkgo biloba extract for essential hypertension: A systemic review". *Phytomedicine* (Systematic review). **21** (10): 1131–1136. doi:10.1016/j.phymed.2014.04.024. PMID 24877716.

[22] Clement, YN; Onakpoya, I; Hung, SK; Ernst, E (March 2011). "Effects of herbal and dietary supplements on cognition in menopause: a systematic review.". *Maturitas*. **68** (3): 256–63. doi:10.1016/j.maturitas.2010.12.005. PMID 21237589.

[23] Hilton, MP; Zimmermann, EF; Hunt, WT (March 28, 2013). "Ginkgo biloba for tinnitus.". *The Cochrane database of systematic reviews*. **3**: CD003852. doi:10.1002/14651858.CD003852.pub3. PMID 23543524.

[24] Zeng X, Liu M, Yang Y, Li Y, Asplund K (2005). "Ginkgo biloba for acute ischaemic stroke". *Cochrane Database Syst Rev* (Systematic review) (4): CD003691. doi:10.1002/14651858.CD003691.pub2. PMID 16235335.

[25] Nicolaï SP, Kruidenier LM, Bendermacher BL, et al. (2013). "Ginkgo biloba for intermittent claudication". *Cochrane Database Syst Rev* (Systematic review). **6**: CD006888. doi:10.1002/14651858.CD006888.pub3. PMID 23744597.

[26] Evans, JR (January 31, 2013). "Ginkgo biloba extract for age-related macular degeneration.". *The Cochrane database of systematic reviews*. **1**: CD001775. doi:10.1002/14651858.CD001775.pub2. PMID 23440785.

[27] Gertsch JH, Basnyat B, Johnson EW, Onopa J, Holck PS (April 3, 2004). "Randomised, double blind, placebo controlled comparison of ginkgo biloba and acetazolamide for prevention of acute mountain sickness among Himalayan trekkers: the prevention of high altitude illness trial (PHAIT).". *BMJ*. **328** (328(7443)): 797. doi:10.1136/bmj.38043.501690.7C. PMID 15070635.

[28] Seupaul, RA; Welch, JL; Malka, ST; Emmett, TW (April 2012). "Pharmacologic prophylaxis for acute mountain sickness: a systematic shortcut review.". *Annals of Emergency Medicine*. **59** (4): 307–317.e1. doi:10.1016/j.annemergmed.2011.10.015. PMID 22153998.

[29] Ginkgo Seed Poisoning. PEDIATRICS Vol. 109 No. 2 February 2002, pp. 325-327

[30] Lepoittevin, J. -P.; Benezra, C.; Asakawa, Y. (1989). "Allergic contact dermatitis to Ginkgo biloba L.: relationship with urushiol". *Archives of Dermatological Research*. **281** (4): 227–30. doi:10.1007/BF00431055. PMID 2774654.

[31] Schötz, Karl (2004). "Quantification of allergenic urushiols in extracts of Ginkgo biloba leaves, in simple one-step extracts and refined manufactured material(EGb 761)". *Phytochemical Analysis*. **15** (1): 1–8. doi:10.1002/pca.733. PMID 14979519.

[32] Jiang X, Williams KM, Liauw WS, Ammit AJ, Roufogalis BD, Duke CC, Day RO, McLachlan AJ (April 2005). "Effect of ginkgo and ginger on the pharmacokinetics and pharmacodynamics of warfarin in healthy subjects". *Br J Clin Pharmacol*. **59** (4): 425–32. doi:10.1111/j.1365-2125.2005.02322.x. PMC 1884814. PMID 15801937.

[33] "MedlinePlus Herbs and Supplements: Ginkgo (Ginkgo biloba L.)". National Institutes of Health. Retrieved 10 April 2008.

[34] "Ginkgo biloba". University of Maryland Medical Center. Retrieved 10 April 2008.

[35] Complete Ginkgo information from Drugs.com

[36] Dugoua, J. J.; Mills, E.; Perri, D.; Koren, G. (2006). "Safety and efficacy of ginkgo (Ginkgo biloba) during pregnancy and lactation". *Can J Clin Pharmacol*. **13** (3): e277–84. PMID 17085776. Retrieved 28 October 2014.

[37] Bone, KM (2008). "Potential interaction of Ginkgo biloba leaf with antiplatelet or anticoagulant drugs: what is the evidence?". *Mol Nutr Food Res*. **52** (7): 764–771. doi:10.1002/mnfr.200700098. PMID 18214851.

[38] Markowitz JS, Donovan JL, Lindsay DeVane C, Sipkes L, Chavin KD (Dec 2003). "Multiple-dose administration of Ginkgo biloba did not affect cytochrome P-450 2D6 or 3A4 activity in normal volunteers". *J Clin Psychopharmacol*. **23** (6): 576–81. doi:10.1097/01.jcp.0000095340.32154.c6. PMID 14624188.

[39] Xian-guo; et al. (2000). "High-Performance Liquid Chromatography-Electrospray Ionization-Mass Spectrometry Study of Ginkgolic Acid in the Leaves and Fruits of the Ginkgo Tree (Ginkgo biloba)". *Journal of Chromatographic Science*. **38** (4): 169–173. PMID 10766484.

[40] Tanaka, A; Arai, Y; Kim, SN; Ham, J; Usuki, T (2011). "Synthesis and biological evaluation of bilobol and adipostatin A". *Journal of Asian natural products research*. **13** (4): 290–6. doi:10.1080/10286020.2011.554828. PMID 21462031.

[41] Ogren, Thomas Leo (2000). *Allergy-Free Gardening*. Berkeley, California: Ten Speed Press. p. 112. ISBN 1-58008-166-5.

[42] Gilman, Edward F.; Dennis G. Watson (1993). "*Ginkgo biloba* 'Autumn Gold'" (PDF). US Forest Service. Archived from the original (PDF) on April 10, 2008. Retrieved 29 March 2008.

[43] Boland, Timothy, Laura E. Coit, Marty Hair (2002). *Michigan Gardener's Guide*. Cool Springs Press. ISBN 1-930604-20-3.

[44] "Examples of Plants with Insect and Disease Tolerance". *SULIS - Sustainable Urban Landscape Information Series*. University of Minnesota. Retrieved 29 March 2008.

[45] Ginkgo biloba trees in Barcelona (189 by 2015)

[46] D'Cruz, Mark. "Ma-Ke Bonsai Care Guide for Ginkgo biloba". Ma-Ke Bonsai. Retrieved 2013-09-12.

[47] Royer, Dana L.; Hickey, Leo J.; Wing, Scott L. (2003). "Ecological conservatism in the 'living fossil' *Ginkgo*". *Paleobiology*. **29** (1): 84–104. doi:10.1666/0094-8373(2003)029<0084:ECITLF>2.0.CO;2. ISSN 0094-8373.

[48] van Beek TA (2002). "Chemical analysis of Ginkgo biloba leaves and extracts". *J Chromatography A*. **967** (1): 21–55. doi:10.1016/S0021-9673(02)00172-3. PMID 12219929.

[49] van Beek TA, Montoro P (2009). "Chemical analysis and quality control of Ginkgo biloba leaves, extracts, and phytopharmaceuticals". *J Chromatography A*. **1216** (11): 2002–32. doi:10.1016/j.chroma.2009.01.013. PMID 19195661.

[50] Ginkgoales: More on Morphology

[51] "Ginkgo Tree". www.bio.brandeis.edu. Retrieved 2016-07-18.

[52] "Ginkgo Tree". prezi.com. Retrieved 2016-07-18.

[53] Raven, Peter H.; Ray F. Evert; Susan E. Eichhorn (2005). *Biology of Plants* (7th ed.). New York: W. H. Freeman and Company. pp. 429–430. ISBN 0-7167-1007-2.

[54] Plotnik, Arthur (2000). *The Urban Tree Book: An Uncommon Field Guide for City and Town* (1st ed.). New York: Three Rivers Press. p. 202. ISBN 0-8129-3103-3.

[55] Laboratory IX – *Ginkgo, Cordaites*, and the Conifers

[56] Vanbeek A. Vanbeek (2000). *Ginkgo Biloba (Medicinal and Aromatic Plants: Industrial Profiles)*. CRC Press. p. 37. ISBN 90-5702-488-8.

[57] History of Discovery of Spermatozoids In Ginkgo biloba and Cycas revoluta Archived March 31, 2015, at the Wayback Machine.

[58] Holt, B. F.; Rothwell, G. W. (1997). "Is Ginkgo biloba (Ginkgoaceae) Really an Oviparous Plant?". *American Journal of Botany*. **84** (6): 870–872. doi:10.2307/2445823. JSTOR 2445823.

[59] Shen, L; Chen, X-Y; Zhang, X; Li, Y-Y; Fu, C-X; Qiu, Y-X (2004). "Genetic variation of Ginkgo biloba L. (Ginkgoaceae) based on cpDNA PCR-RFLPs: inference of glacial refugia". *Heredity*. **94** (4): 396–401. doi:10.1038/sj.hdy.6800616. PMID 15536482.

[60] Tang, CQ; al, et (2012). "Evidence for the persistence of wild Ginkgo biloba (Ginkgoaceae) populations in the Dalou Mountains, southwestern China". *American Journal of Botany*. **99** (8): 1408–1414. doi:10.3732/ajb.1200168. PMID 22847538.

[61] Fu, Liguo; Li, Nan; Mill, Robert R. (1999). "Ginkgo biloba". In Wu, Z. Y.; Raven, P.H.; Hong, D.Y. *Flora of China*. **4**. Beijing: Science Press; St. Louis: Missouri Botanical Garden Press. p. 8.

[62] Whetstone, R. David (2006). "Ginkgo biloba". In Flora of North America Editorial Committee, eds. 1993+. *Flora of North America*. **2**. New York & Oxford: Oxford University Press.

[63] Approximate reconstructions by B. M. Begović Bego and Z. Zhou, 2010/2011. Source: B.M. Begović Bego, (2011). Nature's Miracle *Ginkgo biloba*, Book 1, Vols. 1–2, pp. 60–61.

[64] Committee on Herbal Medicinal Products. "Assessment report on Ginkgo biloba L., folium" (PDF). *European Medicines Agency*.

[65] "A-bombed Ginkgo trees in Hiroshima, Japan". *The Ginkgo Pages*.

[66] Huxley, Anthony. "He Gave Us the Gingko". *NY Times*. Retrieved 17 August 2015.

3.52.15 Bibliography

- Royer, Dana L.; Hickey, Leo J.; Wing, Scott L. (2003). "Ecological conservatism in the 'living fossil' *Ginkgo*". *Paleobiology*. **29** (1): 84–104. doi:10.1666/0094-8373(2003)029<0084:ECITLF>2.0.CO;2. ISSN 0094-8373.

3.52.16 External links

- Growing Ginkgoes from seed: by the Ottawa Horticultural Society
- Gymnosperm Database
- University of California Museum of Paleontology
- *Ginkgo biloba* information (Plants for a Future)
- *Ginkgo: MedlinePlus Supplements* - U.S. National Library of Medicine
- Ginkgo biloba Overview - University of Maryland Medical Center

3.53 Halleria lucida

Halleria lucida (also known as **tree fuchsia**, **umBinza** or **notsung**) is a small, attractive, evergreen tree that is indigenous to Southern Africa. It is increasingly grown as an ornamental tree in African gardens.

3.53.1 Appearance

This tree has lush, glossy, bright-green foliage on arching and drooping branches. It is often multi-stemmed and can eventually reach a height of over 15m. The way that the dense foliage droops from the hanging branches gives the tree a willowy appearance.
Notsung is unusual in producing its flowers and fruit, not from the tips of its branches like most flowering trees, but from its trunk, exhibiting what is known in botany as cauliflory. This characteristic is also found in other Southern African trees such as Stamvrug. The orange or purple flowers are rich in nectar and bi-sexual. The small, fleshy fruits are edible (but do not taste particularly good). It is a member of the Snapdragon family.

3.53.2 Distribution

The natural range of this tree extends throughout South Africa, as well as northwards through East Africa as far as Ethiopia.

Its natural habitats include deep afro-montane forest, forest fringes, open mountain slopes, gorges and river banks. Like many other trees, in a shady habitat (like deep forest) *Halleria lucida* grows tall and slender; while it forms a smaller shrub-like tree if grown in the open.

3.53.3 Growing *Halleria lucida*

On Table Mountain

Tough and easy to grow, *Halleria lucida* is becoming popular as an ornamental tree for gardens. It is undoubtedly one of the best trees in Africa for attracting birds, but it is usually grown more for its attractive foliage and flowers. It tolerates full sun as well as partial shade and, once established, it can also survive moderate drought. This makes it particularly suitable for growing in mildly arid areas. It is also a relatively fast-growing tree.

This is an excellent tree for bringing birds to the garden. Nectivorous birds such as sunbirds are attracted to the bright flowers, and the fruits attract a large range of other birds.

The leaves and fruits of *Halleria lucida* are an important component of traditional African medicine. In addition, it has a function in traditional Zulu religion, as the ceremonial burning of the leaves is believed to counter witchcraft and summon the protective spirits of dead ancestors. *[1]

3.53.4 Gallery

Flowers

Flowers

Foliage

Wood

Immature fruit

Bark

Cross-section

3.53.5 References

[1] "Halleria lucida". Plantzafrica.com. Retrieved 2013-07-16.

3.53.6 External links

•

- Dressler, S.; Schmidt, M. & Zizka, G. (2014). "*Halleria lucida*". *African plants – a Photo Guide*. Frankfurt/Main: Forschungsinstitut Senckenberg.

3.54 History of bonsai

Bonsai from the National Bonsai & Penjing Museum at the United States National Arboretum.

Bonsai (盆栽, "tray planting" ◀◎ pronunciation)*[1] is a Japanese art form using trees grown in containers. Similar practices exist in other cultures, including the Chinese tradition of *penjing* from which the art originated, and the miniature living landscapes of Vietnamese *hòn non bộ*. The term "bonsai" itself is a Japanese pronunciation of the earlier Chinese term *penzai*. The word *bonsai* is often used in English as an umbrella term for all miniature trees in containers or pots. This article focuses on the history of bonsai in Japan and, in modern times, worldwide.

3.54.1 History

Early versions

The earliest illustration of a penjing is found in the Qianling Mausoleum murals at the Tang-dynasty tomb of Crown Prince Zhanghuai, dating to 706.[2]*[3]*

The Japanese art of bonsai originated from the Chinese practice of penjing.*[4] From the 6th century onwards, Imperial embassy personnel and Buddhist students from Japan visited and returned from mainland China, bringing back souvenirs including container plantings.*[5] At least 17 diplomatic missions were sent from Japan to the Tang court between the years 603 and 839.*[5]

Japan's historical Shōsōin, which houses 7th, 8th, and 9th-century artifacts including material from Japan's Tenpyō period, contains an elaborate miniature tree display dating from this time.*[6] This artifact is composed of a shallow wooden tray serving as a base, carved wooden mountain models, and sand portraying a riverine sandbar. The artifact includes small tree sculptures in silver metal, which are meant to be placed in the sand to produce a table-top depiction of a treed landscape. Though this display is closer to the Japanese bonkei display than to a living bonsai, it does reflect the period's interest in miniature landscapes.

From about the year 970 comes the first lengthy work of fiction in Japanese, *Utsubo Monogatari* (*The Tale of the Hollow Tree*), which includes this passage: "A tree that is left growing in its natural state is a crude thing. It is only when it is kept close to human beings who fashion it with loving care that its shape and style acquire the ability to move one." The idea, therefore, was already established by this time that natural beauty becomes true beauty only when modified in accordance with a human ideal.*[7]

In the medieval period, recognizable bonsai began to appear in handscroll paintings like the *Ippen shonin eden* (1299).*[6] *Saigyo Monogatari Emaki* was the earliest known scroll to depict dwarfed potted trees in Japan. It dates from the year 1195, in the Kamakura period. Wooden tray and dish-like pots with dwarf landscapes on modern-looking wooden shelf/benches are shown in the 1309 *Kasuga-gongen-genki* scroll. These novelties show off the owner's wealth and were probably exotics imported from China.*[8]

Chinese Chan Buddhist monks also came over to teach at Japan's monasteries, and one of the monks' activities was to introduce political leaders of the day to the various arts of miniature landscapes as ideal accomplishments for men of taste and learning.*[9]*[10]

The c. 1300 rhymed prose essay, *Bonseki no Fu* (*Tribute to Bonseki*) written by celebrated priest and master of Chinese poetry, Kokan Shiren (1278–1346), outlined the aesthetic principles for what would be termed bonsai, bonseki and garden architecture itself. At first, the Japanese used miniaturized trees grown in containers to decorate their homes and gardens.*[10]*[11]*[12]

Criticism of the interest in curiously twisted specimens of potted plants shows up in one chapter of the 243-chapter compilation *Tsurezuregusa* (c. 1331). This work would become a sacred teaching handed down from master to student, through a limited chain of poets (some famous), until it was at last widely published in the early 17th century. Before then, the criticism had only a modest influence on dwarf potted tree cultures.

In 1351, dwarf trees displayed on short poles were portrayed in the *Boki Ekotoba* scroll.*[13] Several other scrolls and paintings also included depictions of these kinds of trees. Potted landscape arrangements made during the next hundred years or so included figurines after the Chinese fashion in order to add scale and theme. These miniatures would eventually be considered garnishes decidedly to be excluded by Japanese artists who were simplifying their creations in the spirit of Zen Buddhism.*[14]

Hachi-no-ki

Penjing specimen with decorated and relatively deep pot ("bowl")

Around the 14th century, the term for dwarf potted trees was "the bowl's tree" (鉢の木 *hachi no ki*).*[15] This denoted the use of a fairly deep pot, as opposed to the shallow pot denoted by the term *bonsai*.

Hachi no Ki (*The Potted Trees*) is also the title of a Noh play by Zeami Motokiyo (1363–1444), based on a story from c. 1383. It tells of an impoverished samurai who sacrifices his three last dwarf potted trees as firewood to provide warmth for a traveling monk on a winter night. The monk is an official in disguise who later rewards the samurai by giving him three lands whose names include the names of the three types of trees the samurai burnt: *ume* (plum), *matsu* (pine), and *sakura* (cherry). In later centuries, woodblock prints by several artists would depict this popular drama. There was even a fabric design of the same name.

Stories referring to bonsai began to appear more frequently

by the 17th century. *Shogun* Tokugawa Iemitsu (r. 1623–1651) was a *hachi no ki* enthusiast. A story tells of Okubo Hikozemon (1560–1639), councilor to the shogun, who threw one of Iemitsu's favorite trees away in the garden—in sight of the shogun—in order to dissuade him from spending so much time and attention on these trees. In spite of the servant's efforts, Iemitsu never gave up his beloved art form. Another story from this time tells of a samurai's gardener who killed himself when his master insulted a *hachi no ki* of which the artisan was especially proud.*[16]

Bonsai dating to the 17th century have survived to the present. One of the oldest-known living bonsai trees, considered one of the National Treasures of Japan, is in the Tokyo Imperial Palace collection.*[17] A five-needle pine (*Pinus pentaphylla* var. *negishi*) known as Sandai-Shogun-No Matsu is documented as having been cared for by Tokugawa Iemitsu. *[17]*[18] The tree is thought to be at least 500 years old and was first trained as a bonsai by, at latest, the year 1610.*[17] The earliest known report by a Westerner of a Japanese dwarf potted tree was made in 1692 by George Meister.*[19]

Chinese bonsai containers exported to Japan during the 17th and 18th centuries would become referred to as *kowatari* (古渡 "old crossing"). These were made between 1465 and about 1800. Many came from Yixing in Jiangsu province—unglazed and usually purplish-brown—and some others from around Canton, in particular, during the Ming dynasty.*[20]*[21] Miniature potted trees were called *hachi-ue* in a 1681 horticulture book. This book also stated that everyone at the time grew azaleas, even if the poorest people had to use an abalone shell as a container.*[22]*[23] Torii Kiyoharu's use of woodblock printing in Japan depicted the dwarf potted trees from horticultural expert Itō Ihei's nursery.*[24]

By the end of the 18th century, bonsai cultivation was quite widespread and had begun to interest the public. In the Tenmei era (1781–88), an exhibit of traditional dwarf potted pines began to be held every year in Kyoto. Connoisseurs from five provinces and neighboring areas would bring one or two plants each to the show in order to submit them to visitors for ranking.*[25]

Classical period

In Itami, Hyōgo (near Osaka), a group of scholars of Chinese arts gathered in the early 19th century to discuss recent styles in the art of miniature trees. Their version of these, which had been previously called "bunjin ueki" , "bunjin hachiue" , or other terms, were renamed "bonsai" (the Japanese pronunciation of the Chinese term penzai). This term had the connotation of a shallower container in which the Japanese could now more successfully style small trees.

White pine bonsai cultivated from 1855 (National Bonsai & Penjing Museum)

The term "bonsai" , however, would not become regularly used in describing their dwarf potted trees for nearly a century. Many others terms and compositions adopted by this group were derived from *Kai-shi-en Gaden*, the Japanese version of *Jieziyuan Huazhuan* (Manual of the Mustard Seed Garden).*[26]*[27]*[28]*[29]

In 1829, a significant book that first established classical bonsai art, *Sōmoku Kin'yō-shū* (草木錦葉集, *A Colorful Collection of Trees and Plants/Collection of tree leaves*), was published. It includes the basic criteria for the ideal form of the classical pine bonsai, in detail and with illustrations.*[30] That same year, small *tako-tsuki* (octopus-styled) trees with long, wavy-branches began to be offered by a grower in Asakusa Park, a north-eastern Edo suburb. Within 20 years that neighborhood became crowded with nurseries selling bonsai.*[31]*[32] The three-volume *Kinsei-Jufu,* possibly the first book of bonsai, tools, and pots, dates from 1833.*[33]

Numerous artists of the 19th century depicted dwarf potted trees in woodblock prints, including Yoshishige (who pictured each of the fifty-three classic stations of the Tōkaidō as miniature landscape) and Kunisada (who included mostly *hachi-no-ki* in some four dozen prints).*[34] The earliest known photograph from Japan depicting a dwarf potted tree dates from c. 1861 by Pierre Rossier.*[35]

On October 13, 1868, the Meiji Emperor moved to his new capital in Tokyo. Bonsai were displayed both inside and outside Meiji Palace, where they have since remained important in affairs of the Palace. Bonsai placed in the grand setting of the Imperial Palace had to be "Giant Bonsai,"

Meiji Palace in Tokyo

large enough to fill the grand space.*[36]*[37]*[38] The Meiji Emperor encouraged interest in bonsai. Government officials who did not appreciate bonsai fell out of favor. Soon all members of the ministry had bonsai whether they liked the tradition or not. Prince Itoh was an exception: Any bonsai that the emperor gave him were then passed to Kijoji Itoh. Kijoji Itoh was a statesman of great influence behind the scenes, and a noted bonsai collector who conducted research and experiments on these bonsai.*[39]*[40]

Bonsai shaping aesthetics and techniques were becoming more sophisticated. By the late 1860s, thick combed and wetted hemp fibers were used to roughly shape the trunk and branches of miniature trees by pulling and tying them. The process was tedious and bothersome, and the final product was unsightly. Tips of branches would only be opened flat. Long, wavy-branched *tako* (octopus)-style trees were mass-produced and designed in the [renamed capital] Tokyo for the increasing foreign trade, while the more subtle and delicate bunjin-style trees designed in Kyoto and Osaka were for use in Japan. Tokyo preferred big trunks out of proportion and did not approve of Kyoto's finely designed slender trunks. (This cultural rivalry would continue for a century.)*[41]*[42]*[43]

Pots exported from China between 1816 and 1911 (especially the late 19th century) were called *nakawatari* or *chūwatari* (both meaning "middle-crossing"), shallow rectangular or oval stoneware with carved feet and drainage holes. Unglazed pots of this type were used at ancestral shrines and treasured by the Chinese. After the mid-century, certain Japanese antiquities dealers imported them and instant popular approval for this type of container for bonsai created a huge demand. As a consequence, orders came from Japan to Yixing pottery centers specifically to make bonsai pots.*[44]*[45]

Through the later 19th century, Japanese participation in various international exhibitions introduced many in the U.S. and Europe to dwarf potted trees. Specimens from the displays went into Western hands following the closing of the fairs.*[46] Japanese immigrants to the U.S. West Coast and Hawaii Territory brought plants and cultivation experience with them. Export nurseries, the most notable one being the Yokohama Gardeners Association, provided increasingly good quality dwarf potted trees for Americans and Europeans—even if the buyers did not have enough information or experience to actually keep the trees alive long-term.*[47]*[48]

An Artistic Bonsai Concours was held in Tokyo in 1892 followed by the publication of a three-volume commemorative picture book. This demonstrated a new tendency to see bonsai as an independent art form.*[49] In 1903, the Tokyo association Jurakukai held showings of bonsai and ikebana at two Japanese-style restaurants. Three years later, *Bonsai Gaho* (1906 to c. 1913), became the first monthly magazine on the subject.*[50] It was followed by *Toyo Engei* and *Hana* in 1907, and *Bonsai* in 1921.*[51]

By 1907, "on the outskirts of Tokio [dwarf] tree artists have formed a little colony of from twenty to thirty houses, and from this centre their work finds its way to all parts of the world." "Its secrets are handed down from father to son in a few families, and are guarded with scrupulous care." *[52]

Count Ōkuma (1838–1922) maintained a famed collection of dwarf pines and dwarf plum trees.*[53]

In 1910, shaping with wire was described in the Sanyu-en Bonsai-Dan (History of Bonsai in the Sanyu nursery). Zinc-galvanized steel wire was initially used. Expensive copper wire was only used for trees that had real potential.*[54]*[55] Between 1911 and about 1940, mass-produced containers were exported from Yixing, China, and made to the specifications of Japanese dealers. These were called *Shinto* (*new crossing or arrival*) or *Shin-watare*. These were made for increasing numbers of enthusiasts. Some containers, including primitive style ones, were also being made in Formosa.*[56]*[57]

By 1914, "at the N.E. corner of Shiba Park is a permanent bazaar (the first of its kind established in Tokyo) where hosts of native-made gimcracks can be bought at fixed prices. The exhibits of potted plants and dwarf trees held here from time to time attract lovers of such things." In the same year, the first national annual bonsai show was held (an event repeated annually through 1933) in Tokyo's Hibiya Park.*[58]*[59] During this period, the tokonoma in formal rooms and tea rooms became the main place for bonsai display. The shaped trees now shared space with other items such as scrolls, incense burners, Buddhist statues and tea ceremony implements.*[60]

The first issue of *Bonsai* magazine was published in 1921 by Norio Kobayashi (1889–1972). This influential periodical would run for 518 consecutive issues. Copper wire was being extensively used by this time. Major changes to a tree's shape could now be accomplished with wiring. Trees could be precisely and aesthetically wired, and then sold immediately. A greater number of both collected and nursery trees could now be trained for bonsai. The number of hobbyists increased due to the increased ability to style with wire, but there was also an increase in damaged or scarred trees.*[36]*[61]

The 1923 Great Kantō earthquake and resulting fire devastated Tokyo, and gutted the downtown area where many bonsai specimens were grown. And so, two years later, a group of thirty families of downtown Tokyo professional growers established the Ōmiya Bonsai Village, northeast of the capital.*[62] The first great annual public exhibition of trees was held at the Asahi Newspaper Hall in Tokyo in 1927.*[63] The first of the very prestigious Kokufu-ten exhibitions were held in Tokyo's Ueno Park, beginning in 1934.*[64] By the following year, tokonoma display principles allowed for bonsai to be shown for the tree's individual beauty, not just for its spiritual or symbolic significance.*[65]

Toolsmith Masakuni I (1880–1950) helped design and produce the first steel tools specifically made for the developing requirements of bonsai styling.*[66]

By 1940, there were about 300 bonsai dealers in Tokyo, some 150 species of trees were being cultivated, and thousands of specimens annually were shipped to Europe and America. The first major book on the subject in English was published in the Japanese capital: *Dwarf Trees (Bonsai)* by Shinobu Nozaki (1895–1968).*[67] The first bonsai nurseries and clubs in the Americas were started by first and second-generation Japanese immigrants.

The caretaker of the Imperial bonsai collection, Kyūzō Murata (1902–1991), was one of very few persons allowed to take care of bonsai during the Pacific War. He gathered together and preserved many trees from the other Omiya growers and would water them under the protection of night. Throughout 1945, many old trees were the smallest casualties of the spring and summer napalm bombing of Tokyo (especially March 9/10) and sixty-six other cities. Gardeners protected the Imperial collection trees from fire by pouring water over them after the Palace caught fire when neighboring areas were bombed on May 25/26.*[68] Following the surrender of Japan, there began the post-war re-evaluation and reviving of damaged collections of trees —including the Imperial—which would continue for over a decade as Japan was rebuilt. Many of the Omiya growers did not continue their vocation.

During the Allied Occupation of Japan (through 1952) U.S. officers and their wives could take courses in bonsai, bonkei, ikebana, and other traditional arts and crafts as arranged by General MacArthur's headquarters. Many of the older and limited varieties of trees were no longer available, and the bonsai considered in fashion changed partly because of this shortage. Copper wire now largely replaced ordinary iron wire for shaping the better trees, but the latter still would be used for mass-produced commercial bonsai.*[37]*[69]*[70]*[71]

Modern bonsai

Following World War II, a number of trends made the Japanese tradition of bonsai increasingly accessible to Western and world audiences. One key trend was the increase in the number, scope, and prominence of bonsai exhibitions. For example, the Kokufu-ten bonsai displays reappeared in 1947 after a four-year cancellation and became annual affairs. These displays continue to this day, and are by invitation only for eight days in February.*[64] In October 1964, a great exhibition was held in Hibya Park by the private Kokufu Bonsai Association, reorganized into the Nippon Bonsai Association, to mark the Tokyo Olympics. A commemorative album titled *Gems of Bonsai and Suiseki* was published in Japanese and English. Other countries began presenting bonsai exhibitions as well, with recurring events now taking place in Taiwan and a number of other Asian countries, Australia, the United States, several European countries, and others.*[72] Currently, Japan continues to host regular exhibitions with the world's largest numbers of bonsai specimens and the highest recognized specimen quality.

Another key trend was the increase in books on bonsai and related arts, now being published for the first time in English and other languages for audiences outside Japan. In 1952, Yuji Yoshimura, son of a leader in the Japanese bonsai community, collaborated with German diplomat and author Alfred Koehn to give bonsai demonstrations. The first formal bonsai courses opened to the public and outsiders in Tokyo. Koehn had been an enthusiast before the war, and his 1937 book *Japanese Tray Landscapes* had been published in English in Peking. Yoshimura's 1957 book *The Art of Bonsai*, written in English with his student Giovanna M. Halford, addressed both cultivation and aesthetic aspects of bonsai growing and went on to be called the "classic Japanese bonsai bible for westerners" with over thirty printings.*[73]

The related art of saikei was introduced to English-speaking audiences in 1963 in Kawamoto and Kurihara's *Bonsai-Saikei*. This book described tray landscapes made with younger plant material than was traditionally used in bonsai, providing an alternative to the use of large, older plants, few of which had escaped war damage.

Other works in Japanese and English had been published by this time, and afterward a tremendous number of books saw print. Translations and original volumes in over two dozen languages were published over the following decades.*[74] Once Japanese was no longer the sole language of bonsai, the number of clubs outside of Asia increased and interaction increased between members of all levels of experience.

A third trend was the increasing availability of expert bonsai training, at first only in Japan and then more widely. In 1967 the first group of Westerners studied at an Ōmiya nursery. Returning to the U.S., these people established the American Bonsai Society. Other groups and individuals from outside Asia then visited and studied at the various Japanese nurseries, occasionally even apprenticing under the masters. These visitors brought back to their local clubs the latest techniques and styles, which were then further disseminated. Japanese teachers also traveled widely, bringing hands-on bonsai expertise to all six continents*[75]

By the beginning of the 1970s, these trends were beginning to merge. A large display of bonsai and suiseki was held as part of Expo '70, and formal discussion was made of an international association of enthusiasts. Three monthly magazines were started this year: *Bonsai Sekai, Satsuki Kenkyu,* and *Shizen to Bonsai.* In 1975, the first Gafu-ten (Elegant-Style Exhibit) of *shohin* bonsai (13–25 cm (5–10 in) tall) was held. So was the first Sakufu-ten (Creative Bonsai Exhibit), the only event in which professional bonsai growers exhibit traditional trees under their own names rather than under the name of the owner. It was organized by Hideo Kato (1918–2001) at Daimaru Department Store in Tokyo.*[76]

The First World Bonsai Convention was held in Osaka during the World Bonsai and Suiseki Exhibition in 1980.*[77] Nine years later, the first World Bonsai Convention was held in Omiya and the World Bonsai Friendship Federation (WBFF) was inaugurated. These conventions attracted several hundreds of participants from dozens of countries and have since been held every four years at different locations around the globe: 1993, Orlando, Florida; 1997, Seoul, Korea; 2001, Munich, Germany; 2005, Washington, D.C.; 2009, San Juan, Puerto Rico; 2013, Jitan, Jiangsu, China.*[77]*[78]

The final trend supporting world involvement in bonsai is the widening availability of specialized bonsai plant stock, soil components, tools, pots, and other accessory items. Bonsai nurseries in Japan advertise and ship specimen bonsai world-wide. Most countries have local nurseries providing plant stock as well, although finding specimen bonsai is more difficult outside Japan and bonsai enthusiasts will often start with local trees that have not been pre-shaped into candidate bonsai. Japanese bonsai soil components, such as Akadama clay, are available worldwide, and local suppliers also provide similar materials in many locations. Specialized bonsai tools are widely available from Japanese and Chinese sources. Potters around the globe provide material to hobbyists and specialists in many countries.*[79]

Bonsai has now reached a world-wide audience. There are over twelve hundred books on bonsai and the related arts in at least twenty-six languages available in over ninety countries and territories.*[68]*[80] A few dozen magazines in over thirteen languages are in print. Several score of club newsletters are available on-line, and there are at least that many discussion forums and blogs.*[81] Educational videos and just the appearance of dwarf potted trees in films and on television reach a wide audience.*[82] There are at least a hundred thousand enthusiasts in some fifteen hundred clubs and associations worldwide, as well as over five million unassociated hobbyists.*[83] Plant material from every location is being trained into bonsai and displayed at local, regional, national, and international conventions and exhibitions for enthusiasts and the general public.

3.54.2 See also

- Bonsai aesthetics – aesthetics of Japanese tradition in bonsai

- Bonsai cultivation and care – cultivation and care of small, container-grown trees

3.54.3 References

[1] Gustafson, Herbert L. (1995). *Miniature Bonsai.* Sterling Publishing Company, Inc. p. 9. ISBN 0-8069-0982-X.

[2] Taylor, Patrick (2008). *The Oxford companion to the garden* (2nd ed.). Oxford: Oxford University Press. p. 53. ISBN 978-0-19-955197-2.

[3] Hu, Yunhua (1987). *Chinese penjing: Miniature trees and landscapes.* Portland: Timber Press. p. 128. ISBN 978-0-88192-083-3.

[4] Keswick, Maggie; Oberlander, Judy; Wai, Joe (1990). *In a Chinese garden.* Vancouver: Dr. Sun Yat-Sen Garden Society of Vancouver. p. 59. ISBN 978-0-9694573-0-5.

[5] Yoshimura, Yuji (1991). "Modern Bonsai, Development Of The Art Of Bonsai From An Historical Perspective, Part 2". *International Bonsai* (4): 37.

[6] Kobayashi, Konio (2011). *Bonsai.* Tokyo: PIE International Inc. p. 15. ISBN 978-4-7562-4094-1.

[7] Nippon Bonsai Association (1989). *Classic Bonsai of Japan.* Kodansha International. p. 140.

[8] "Dwarf Potted Trees in Paintings, Scrolls and Woodblock Prints, to 1600". Magical Miniature Landscapes. Retrieved 2010-04-07.

[9] Covello, Vincent T. & Yuji Yoshimura (1984). *The Japanese Art of Stone Appreciation, Suiseki and Its Use with Bonsai*. Charles E. Tuttle. p. 20.

[10] Nippon Bonsai Association, pg. 144

[11] Yi, O-nyoung (1984) [1982]. *Smaller Is Better, Japan's Mastery of the Miniature (Chijimi shikoo no Nihonjin)* (First English ed.). Kodansha International, Ltd. p. 89.

[12] Del Tredici, Peter (1989). "Early American Bonsai: The Larz Anderson Collection of the Arnold Arboretum". *Arnoldia* (Summer).

[13] "Japanese Paintings: to 1600". Magical Miniature Landscapes. Retrieved 2010-04-07.

[14] Redding, Myron. "Art of the Mud Man". Art of Bonsai. Retrieved 2010-04-07.

[15] "Hachi-No-Ki". Magical Miniature Landscapes. Retrieved 2016-08-10.

[16] "Tokugawa Iemitsu's Pine". Magical Miniature Landscapes. Retrieved 2016-08-10.

[17] Naka, John Yoshio (1982). *Bonsai Techniques II*. Bonsai Institute of California. p. 258.

[18] "Oldest Bonsai trees". Bonsai Empire. Retrieved 2013-11-11.

[19] "George Meister's dwarf tree observations". Magical Miniature Landscapes. Retrieved 2016-08-10.

[20] Naka. *Bonsai Techniques II*. pp. 304–305, 322.

[21] Katayama, Tei'ichi (1974). *The Mini Bonsai Hobby*. Japan Publications, Inc. pp. 19–20.

[22] Naka, John and Richard K. Ota and Kenko Rokkaku (1979). *Bonsai Techniques for Satsuki*. Ota Bonsai Nursery. p. 32.

[23] Koreshoff, Deborah R. (1984). *Bonsai: Its Art, Science, History and Philosophy*. Timber Press, Inc. p. 8. ISBN 0-88192-389-3.

[24] "Dwarf Potted Trees in Paintings, Scrolls and Woodblock Prints, 1600 to 1800". Magical Miniature Landscapes. Retrieved 2016-08-10.

[25] Nippon Bonsai Association. *Classic Bonsai of Japan*. pp. 151–152.

[26] Covello, Vincent T. & Yuji Yoshimura (1984). *The Japanese Art of Stone Appreciation, Suiseki and Its Use with Bonsai*. Charles E. Tuttle. p. 25.

[27] Koreshoff. *Bonsai: Its Art, Science, History and Philosophy*. pp. 7–8.

[28] Naka, John (1989). "Bunjin-Gi or Bunjin Bonsai". *Bonsai in California*. **23**: 48.

[29] Dalby, Liza, ed. (1984). *All-Japan: The Catalogue of Everything Japanese*. Quarto Marketing, Inc. p. 44.

[30] "Bonsai Books 1800 to 1840". Phoenix Bonsai. Retrieved 2010-04-19.

[31] Nozaki, Shinobu (1940). *Dwarf Trees (Bonsai)*. Sanseido Company, Ltd. pp. 25–26.

[32] O'Connell, Jean (1970). "The Art of Bonsai". *Science Digest* (March): 38.

[33] "Bonsai Books 1800 to 1840". Magical Miniature Landscapes. Retrieved 2010-04-07.

[34] "Dwarf Potted Trees in Paintings, Scrolls and Woodblock Prints, 1800 to 1868". Magical Miniature Landscapes. Retrieved 2010-04-07.

[35] "Earliest Known Photograph from Japan that includes a Dwarf Potted Tree by Pierre Rossier, c.1861". Magical Miniature Landscapes. Retrieved 2016-09-01.

[36] Yamada, Tomio (2005). "Fundamentals of Wiring Bonsai". *International Bonsai* (4): 10–11.

[37] Hill, Warren (2000). "Reflections on Japan". *NBF Bulletin*. **XI**: 5.

[38] Yamanaka, Kazuki. "The Shimpaku Juniper: Its Secret History, Chapter II. First Shimpaku: Ishizuchi Shimpaku". World Bonsai Friendship Federation. Archived from the original on February 22, 2008. Retrieved 2011-09-29.

[39] Nozaki. *Dwarf Trees (Bonsai)*. p. 24.

[40] Itoh, Yoshimi (1969). "Bonsai Origins". *ABS Bonsai Journal*. **3** (1): 3.

[41] Koreshoff. *Bonsai: Its Art, Science, History and Philosophy*. p. 8.

[42] Nozaki. *Dwarf Trees (Bonsai)*. p. 43.

[43] Donovan, Earl H. (1978). "The Spirit of Bunjin". *ABS Bonsai Journal*. **12** (2): 30.

[44] Naka. *Bonsai Techniques II*. pp. 306, 322.

[45] Katayama. *The Mini Bonsai Hobby*. p. 20.

[46] "Expositions Known to Have Had Bonsai Present". Magical Miniature Landscapes. Retrieved 2016-09-01.

[47] "Bonsai Book of Days for February". Magical Miniature Landscapes. Retrieved 2016-09-01.

[48] "Dwarf Trees from Current Literature". Magical Miniature Landscapes. Retrieved 2016-09-13.

[49] Nippon Bonsai Association. *Classic Bonsai of Japan*. p. 153.

[50] "Bonsai and Other Magical Miniature Landscape Specialty Magazines, Part 1". Magical Miniature Landscapes. Retrieved 2016-09-13.

[51] Kobayashi, Konio (2011). *Bonsai*. Tokyo: PIE International Inc. p. 16. ISBN 978-4-7562-4094-1.

[52] Collins, Percy (1907). "The Dwarf-Tree Culture of Japan". *Windsor Magazine* (October): 540.

[53] ""Count Okuma's Dwarf Trees" from Francis E. Clark in The Independent". Magical Miniature Landscapes. Retrieved 2016-09-13.

[54] "The Books on Bonsai and Related Arts, 1900 - 1949". Magical Miniature Landscapes. Retrieved 2016-09-13.

[55] Yamada, Tomio (2005). "Fundamentals of Wiring Bonsai". *International Bonsai* (4): 10.

[56] Naka. *Bonsai Techniques II*. p. 322.

[57] Katayama, Tei'ichi (1974). *The Mini Bonsai Hobby*. Japan Publications, Inc. p. 20.

[58] Terry, Thomas Philip, F.R.G.S. *Terry's Japanese Empire*. Houghton Mifflin Company. p. 168. Retrieved 2010-04-07.

[59] Pessy, Christian & Rémy Samson (1992). *Bonsai Basics, A Step-by-Step Guide to Growing, Training & General Care*. Sterling Publishing Co., Inc. p. 17.

[60] Koreshoff. *Bonsai: Its Art, Science, History and Philosophy*. p. 242.

[61] Collins, Percy (1969). "The Dwarf-Tree Culture of Japan". *ABS Bonsai Journal* (1): 17.

[62] "Bonsai Book of Days for September". Magical Miniature Landscapes. Retrieved 2016-09-13.

[63] Koreshoff. *Bonsai: Its Art, Science, History and Philosophy*. p. 10.

[64] "Kokufu Bonsai Ten Shows, Part 1". Magical Miniature Landscapes. Retrieved 2016-09-16.

[65] Koreshoff. *Bonsai: Its Art, Science, History and Philosophy*. pp. 242–243.

[66] "Kyuzo Murata, the Father of Modern Bonsai in Japan, Part 1". Magical Miniature Landscapes. Retrieved 2016-09-16.

[67] Nozaki. *Dwarf Trees (Bonsai)*. pp. 6, 96.

[68] "The Imperial Bonsai Collection, Part 1". Magical Miniature Landscapes. Retrieved 2016-09-13.

[69] Nippon Bonsai Association. *Classic Bonsai of Japan*. p. 154.

[70] "Kyuzo Murata, the Father of Modern Bonsai in Japan, Part 1". Magical Miniature Landscapes. Retrieved 2016-09-13.

[71] "Some of the Serious Conditions in Japan After World War II". Magical Miniature Landscapes. Retrieved 2016-09-13.

[72] "The Conventions, Symposia, Demos, Workshops, & Exhibitions, Part VI". Magical Miniature Landscapes. Retrieved 2016-09-13.

[73] "Yuji Yoshimura, the Father of Popular Bonsai in the Non-Oriental World". Magical Miniature Landscapes. Retrieved 2016-09-13.

[74] "The Books on Bonsai and Related Arts". Magical Miniature Landscapes. Retrieved 2016-09-13.

[75] "Saburō Katō, International Bridge-builder, His Heritage and Legacy, Part 1". Magical Miniature Landscapes. Retrieved 2016-09-13.

[76] Elias, Thomas S. (2002). "The Best Bonsai and Suiseki Exhibits in Japan". *Bonsai Magazine*. **41** (May/June): 12.

[77] "Bonsai Book of Days for April". Magical Miniature Landscapes. Retrieved 2016-09-13.

[78] "The Conventions, Symposia, Demos, Workshops, and Exhibitions, Part 6". Magical Miniature Landscapes. Retrieved 2016-10-14.

[79] "About Bonsai Pots and Potters". Magical Miniature Landscapes. Retrieved 2016-09-13.

[80] "The Nations -- When Did Bonsai Come to the Various Countries and Territories?". Magical Miniature Landscapes. Retrieved 2016-09-13.

[81] "Club Newsletter On-Line". Magical Miniature Landscapes. Retrieved 2016-09-13.

[82] "To Boldly Grow: Some Celluloid Bonsai (An Overview)". Magical Miniature Landscapes. Retrieved 2016-09-13.

[83] "How Many Bonsai Enthusiasts Are There?". Magical Miniature Landscapes. Retrieved 2016-09-13.

3.55 Ilex mitis

Ilex mitis (commonly called **Cape holly**, **African holly**, **waterboom** or **umDuma**) is a tall, dense, evergreen tree that is indigenous to Southern Africa. It makes an excellent fast-growing hedge for gardens - growing tall, straight and dense. *[1]

3.55.1 Appearance

If not pruned, *Ilex mitis* can grow to a height of 20 meters or more. Its trunk is straight, grey or brown and usually spotted while it produces a dense, even canopy. Young growth and leaf-stalks tend to be purple or red. The simply shaped, pointed, shiny-green leaves have wavy margins that are sometimes slightly serrated. The tree can be identified by its purple or maroon leaf stalks and the leaves' strongly

If it is not occasionally pruned back, Ilex mitis *can eventually grow enormous.*

impressed midribs.

The small, white, scented flowers appear in spring. Ilex mitis is dioecious, with separate male and female trees.

The bright red fruits ripen in autumn, creating a colourful display and attracting a variety of birds.

3.55.2 Distribution

This is the only holly (*Ilex*) species from South Africa, where it grows naturally in all provinces, from Cape Town in the south, all the way up past Zimbabwe and Malawi in the north. It is usually found growing on the banks of rivers and in moist spots in Afro-montane forest.

3.55.3 Growing *Ilex mitis*

This is a fast-growing tree, growing nearly a meter a year in ideal conditions. It grows especially well in wet areas like beside lakes or rivers and it tolerates frost, making it suitable for colder climates. Fresh seed will usually germinate, but should first be dried out a bit. If kept moist after planting, the young plants usually sprout several weeks later. It transplants well, but needs to be protected from drying out and direct sun whilst young.

It has no known diseases or pests, though in the wild it is one of the favourite foods of elephants.

3.55.4 Pictures

-  A small *Ilex mitis*, growing un-pruned as a feature tree.

-  Foliage detail

- *Ilex mitis* blossoms.

3.55.5 References

[1] http://www.plantzafrica.com/planthij/ilexmitis.htm

3.55.6 External links

- *Ilex mitis* at PlantZAfrica.com

-

- Dressler, S.; Schmidt, M. & Zizka, G. (2014). "*Ilex mitis*". *African plants – a Photo Guide*. Frankfurt/Main: Forschungsinstitut Senckenberg.

3.56 Ilex vomitoria

Ilex vomitoria, commonly known as **yaupon** or **yaupon holly**, is a species of holly that is native to southeastern North America.[1] The word *yaupon* was derived from its Catawban name, *yopún*, which is a diminutive form of the word *yop*, meaning "tree". Another common name, **cassina**, was borrowed from the Timucua language[2] (despite this, it usually refers to *Ilex cassine*).

3.56.1 Description

Yaupon holly is an evergreen shrub or small tree reaching 5–9 meters tall, with smooth, light gray bark and slender, hairy shoots. The leaves are alternate, ovate to elliptical with a rounded apex and crenate or coarsely serrated margin, 1–4.5 cm long and 1–2 cm broad, glossy dark green above, slightly paler below. The flowers are 5–5.5 mm diameter, with a white four-lobed corolla. The fruit is a small round, shiny, and red (occasionally yellow) drupe 4–6 mm diameter containing four pits, which are dispersed by birds eating the fruit. The species may be distinguished from the similar *Ilex cassine* by its smaller leaves with a rounded, not acute apex.*[3]*[4]*[5]*[6]*[7]

3.56.2 Habitat and range

I. vomitoria occurs in the United States from Maryland south to Florida and west to Oklahoma *[6] and Texas. A disjunct population occurs in the Mexican state of Chiapas.*[1] It generally occurs in coastal areas in well-drained sandy soils, and can be found on the upper edges of brackish and salt marshes, sandy hammocks, coastal sand dunes, inner-dune depressions, sandhills, maritime forests, nontidal forested wetlands, well-drained forests and pine flatwoods.*[3]

3.56.3 Ecology

An eastern bluebird eating the bright red berries from an Ilex vomitoria.

The fruit are an important food for many birds, including Florida duck, American black duck, mourning dove, ruffed grouse, bobwhite quail, wild turkey, northern flicker, sapsuckers, cedar waxwing, eastern bluebird, American robin, gray catbird, northern mockingbird, and white-throated sparrow. Mammals that eat the fruit include nine-banded armadillo, American black bear, gray fox, raccoon and skunks. The foliage and twigs are browsed by white-tailed deer.*[3]

3.56.4 Cultivation and uses

Native Americans used the leaves and stems to brew a tea, commonly thought to be called *asi* or black drink for male-only purification and unity rituals. The ceremony included vomiting, and Europeans incorrectly believed that it was *Ilex vomitoria* that caused it (hence the Latin name). The active ingredients, like those of the related yerba mate and guayusa plants, are actually caffeine and theobromine,*[8]*[9] and the vomiting either was learned or resulted from the great quantities in which they drank the beverage coupled with fasting.*[3]*[10] Others believe the Europeans improperly assumed the black drink to be the tea made from *Ilex vomitoria* when it was likely an entirely different drink made from various roots and herbs and did have emetic properties.*[11]

Ornamental

Ilex vomitoria is a common landscape plant in the Southeastern United States. The most common cultivars are slow-growing shrubs popular for their dense, evergreen foliage and their adaptability to pruning into hedges of various shapes. These include:

- 'Folsom Weeping' – weeping cultivar

- 'Grey's Littleleaf'/'Grey's Weeping' – weeping cultivar

- 'Nana'/'Compacta' – dwarf female clone usually remaining below 1 m in height.

- 'Pride of Houston' – female clone similar to type but featuring improvements in form, fruiting, and foliage.

- 'Schilling's Dwarf'/'Stokes Dwarf' – dwarf male clone that grows no more than 0.6 m tall and 1.2 m wide.*[12]

- 'Will Flemming' – male clone featuring a columnar growth habit.

3.56.5 See also

- *Ilex paraguariensis* or *yerba mate* – a caffeinated holly native to subtropical South America.

- *Ilex guayusa* or guayusa – a caffeinated holly native to the Ecuadorian Amazon Rainforest.
- Kuding – a Chinese tisane made from *I. kudingcha*

3.56.6 References

[1] "Taxon: *Ilex vomitoria* Sol. ex Aiton". *Germplasm Resources Information Network*. United States Department of Agriculture. 2011-05-09. Retrieved 2011-09-19.

[2] Cutler, Charles L. (2000). *O Brave New Words!: Native American Loanwords in Current English*. University of Oklahoma Press. pp. 10, 163, 215. ISBN 978-0-8061-3246-4.

[3] "Yaupon *Ilex vomitoria*" (PDF). *USDA Plant Guide*.

[4] "Florida's Hollies". Florida Department of Environmental Protection.

[5] Martin, C.O.; Mott, S.P. (1997). "Section 7.5.10 Yaupon (*Ilex vomitoria*)". *U.S. Army Corps of Engineers Wildlife Resources Management Manual* (PDF). Vicksburg, MS: U.S. Army Engineer Waterways Experiment Station. Technical Report EL-97-16.

[6] "*Ilex vomitoria*". Oklahoma Biological Survey.

[7] Bioimages: *Ilex vomitoria*

[8] Wilford, JN (8 August 2012). "Ancient Energy Boost, Brewed From Toasted Leaves and Bark". *New York Times*.

[9] Crown PL, Emerson TE, Gu J, Hurst WJ, Pauketat TR, Ward T (August 2012). "Ritual Black Drink consumption at Cahokia". *Proc. Natl. Acad. Sci. U.S.A.* **109** (35): 13944–9. doi:10.1073/pnas.1208404109. PMC 3435207⊖. PMID 22869743.

[10] Hudson, C. M. (1976). *The Southeastern Indians*. University of Tennessee Press ISBN 0-87049-248-9.

[11] Gibbons, E. (1964). *Stalking the Blue-eyed Scallop*. David McKay. ISBN 0-911469-05-2.

[12] Flint, Harrison Leigh (1997). *Landscape Plants for Eastern North America* (2 ed.). John Wiley and Sons. pp. 282–283. ISBN 978-0-471-59919-7.

3.57 Jabuticaba

Plinia cauliflora, the **Brazilian grapetree**,[2] or **jabuticaba**,[2] is a tree in the family Myrtaceae, native to Minas Gerais and São Paulo states in Brazil.[2] Related species in the genus *Myrciaria*, often referred to by the same common names, are native to Brazil, Argentina, Paraguay, Peru and Bolivia. The tree is grown for its purplish-black, white-pulped fruits; they can be eaten raw or be used to make jellies, juice or wine.

3.57.1 Description

Tree

Jabuticaba tree

The tree is a slow-growing evergreen that can reach a height of 15 meters if not pruned. It has salmon-colored leaves when they are young, which turn green as they mature. The tree prefers moist, rich, lightly acidic soil. It is widely adaptable, however, and grows satisfactorily even on alkaline beach-sand type soils, so long as they are tended and irrigated. Its flowers are white and grow directly from its trunk in a cauliflorous habit. In an uncultivated state, the tree may flower and fruit only once or twice a year, but when continuously irrigated it flowers frequently, and fresh fruit can be available year round in tropical regions.

Fruit

The fruit is a thick-skinned berry and typically measures 3–4 cm in diameter. The fruit resembles that of a slip-skin grape. It has a thick, purple, astringent skin that encases a sweet, white or rosy pink gelatinous flesh. Embedded within the flesh are one to four large seeds, which vary in shape depending on the species.[3] Common in Brazilian markets, jabuticabas are largely eaten fresh; their popularity has been likened to that of grapes in the United States.

Jabuticaba tree

Leaves of Plinia cauliflora

Fresh fruit may begin to ferment 3 to 4 days after harvest, so they are often used to make jams, tarts, strong wines, and liqueurs. Due to the extremely short shelf-life, fresh jabuticaba fruit is very rare in markets outside of areas of cultivation. Traditionally, an astringent decoction of the sun-dried skins has been used as a treatment for hemoptysis, asthma, diarrhoea, and gargled for chronic inflammation of the tonsils.

Several potent antioxidant and anti-inflammatory anticancer compounds have been isolated from the fruit.[*][4] One that is unique to the fruit is jaboticabin.

In Brazil the fruit of several related species, namely *Myrciaria tenella* and *M. trunciflora*, share the same common name. While all jabuticaba species are subtropical and can tolerate mild, brief frosts, some species may be marginally more cold-tolerant. Commercial cultivation of the fruit in the Northern Hemisphere is more restricted by extremely slow growth and the short shelf-life of fruit than by temperature requirements. Grafted plants may bear fruit in 5 years; seed grown trees may take 10 to 20 years to bear fruit, though their slow growth and small size when immature make them popular as bonsai or container ornamental plants in temperate regions. Jabuticabas are fairly adaptable to various kinds of growing conditions, tolerating sand or rich topsoil. They are intolerant of salty soils or salt spray. They are tolerant of mild drought, though fruit production may be reduced, and irrigation will be required in extended or severe droughts.

3.57.2 Cultural aspects

The name jabuticaba, derived from the Tupi word *jabuti* (tortoise) + *caba* (place), meaning the place where you find tortoises. The Guarani name is *yvapurū*, where *yva* means fruit, and the onomatopoeic word *purū* for the crunching sound the fruit produces when bitten.

The jabuticaba tree, which appears as a charge on the coat of arms of Contagem, Minas Gerais, Brazil,[*][5] has become a widely used species in the art of bonsai, particularly in Taiwan and parts of the Caribbean.

3.57.3 References

[1] *The Plant List: A Working List of All Plant Species*, retrieved 23 April 2016

[2] "Taxon: *Plinia cauliflora* (Mart.) Kausel". *Germplasm Resources Information Network*. United States Department of Agriculture. Retrieved 2016-04-23.

[3] Boning, Charles (2006). *Florida's Best Fruiting Plants: Native and Exotic Trees, Shrubs and Vines*. Sarasota, Florida: Pineapple Press, Inc. p. 104.

[4] Reynertson KA, Wallace AM, Adachi S, Gil RR, Yang H, Basile MJ, D'Armiento J, Weinstein IB, Kennelly EJ. Bioactive depsides and anthocyanins from jaboticaba (Myrciaria cauliflora). J Nat Prod. 2006 Aug;69(8):1228-30 PMID 16933884 doi:10.1021/np0600999.

[5] Brazilian Flags

3.57.4 External links

- Jaboticaba California Rare Fruit Growers.
- Jaboticaba Features and growing conditions.

3.58 Juniperus californica

Juniperus californica, the **California juniper**, is a species of juniper native to southwestern North America.

3.58.1 Distribution

As the name implies, it is mainly found in numerous California habitats, although its range also extends through most of Baja California, a short distance into the Great Basin in southern Nevada, and into northwestern Arizona. In California it is found in: the Peninsular Ranges, Transverse Ranges, California Coast Ranges, Sacramento Valley foothills, Sierra Nevada, and at higher elevation sky islands in the Mojave Desert ranges.

It grows at moderate altitudes of 750–1,600 metres (2,460–5,250 ft). Habitats include: Pinyon-Juniper Woodland with Single-leaf pinyon (*Pinus monophylla*); Joshua Tree Woodland; and Foothill Woodlands, in the Montane chaparral and woodlands and Interior chaparral and woodlands subecoregions.

3.58.2 Description

Juniperus californica is a shrub or small tree reaching 3–8 metres (9.8–26.2 ft), but rarely up to 10 metres (33 ft) tall. The bark is ashy gray, typically thin, and appears to be "shredded".[1] The shoots are fairly thick compared to most junipers, between 1.5 and 2 millimeters (0.059 and 0.079 inches) in diameter.

Foliage is bluish-gray and scale-like. The leaves are arranged in opposite decussate pairs or whorls of three; the adult leaves are scale-like, 1 to 5 mm (0.039 to 0.197 in) long on lead shoots and 1 to 1.5 mm (0.039 to 0.059 in) broad. The juvenile leaves (on seedlings only) are needle-like, 5 to 10 mm (0.20 to 0.39 in) long.

The cones are berry-like, 7 to 13 mm (0.28 to 0.51 in) in diameter, blue-brown with a whitish waxy bloom, turning reddish-brown, and contain a single seed (rarely two or three).[1] The seeds are mature in about 8–9 months. The male cones are 2 to 4 mm (0.079 to 0.157 in) long, and shed their pollen in early spring. It is largely dioecious, producing cones of only one sex, but around 2% of plants are monoecious, with both sexes on the same plant.[2]

Branches and fruit

It is closely related to *Juniperus osteosperma* (Utah Juniper) from further east, which shares the stout shoots and relatively large cones, but differs in that Utah Juniper is largely monoecious, its cones take longer to mature (two growing seasons), and it's also markedly more cold-tolerant.

3.58.3 Uses

Juniperus californica provides food and shelter for a variety of native ground and avian wildlife. It is a larval host for the native moth Sequoia sphinx (*Sphinx sequoiae*).[1]

Native Americans

The plant was used as a traditional Native American medicinal plant, and as a food source, by the indigenous peoples of California, including the Cahuilla people, Kumeyaay people (*Diegueno*), and Ohlone people.[3] They gathered the berries to eat fresh and to grind into meal for baking.[1]

Cultivation

Juniperus californica is cultivated as an ornamental plant, as a dense shrub (and eventual tree) for use in habitat gardens, heat and drought-tolerant gardens, and in natural landscaping design.*[1] It is very tolerant of alkali soils, and can provide erosion control on dry slopes. California Juniper is also a popular species for bonsai.*[4]

Conservation

An IUCN Least concern listed species, and not considered globally threatened currently. However, one of the southernmost populations, formerly on Guadalupe Island off the Baja California Peninsula coast, was destroyed by feral goats in the late 19th century.*[5]

3.58.4 References

[1] University of Texas at Austin, Lady Bird Johnson Wildflower Center: *Juniperus californica*

[2] Charters (2007)

[3] University of Michigan, Dearborn; Ethnobotany of *Juniperus californica*

[4] Las Pilitas Horticultural Database: *Juniperus californica* (California Juniper)

[5] León de la Luz *et al.* (2003)

Further reading

- Adams, Robert P. (1993): 10. *Juniperus californica. In:* Flora of North America Editorial Committee (eds.): *Flora of North America North of Mexico* vol. 2.

- Adams, Robert P. (2004): *Junipers of the World: The genus* Juniperus. Trafford Publishing ISBN 1-4120-4250-X

- Charters, Michael L. (2007): Wildflowers and Other Plants of Southern California: *Juniperus californica*. Retrieved 2007-OCT-16.

- Conifer Specialist Group (1998). "*Juniperus californica*". *IUCN Red List of Threatened Species. Version 2006*. International Union for Conservation of Nature. Retrieved 12 May 2006.

- León de la Luz, José Luis; Rebman, Jon P. & Oberbauer, Thomas (2003): On the urgency of conservation on Guadalupe Island, Mexico: is it a lost paradise? *Biodiversity and Conservation* **12**(5): 1073–1082. doi:10.1023/A:1022854211166 (HTML abstract)

3.58.5 External links

- Calflora Database: *Juniperus californica* (California juniper)

- Jepson Manual eFlora (TJM2) treatment of *Juniperus californica*

- USDA Plants Profile for *Juniperus californica* (California juniper)

- Gymnosperm Database: *Juniperus californica*

- *Juniperus californica* —UC Photos gallery

3.59 Juniperus chinensis

Juniperus chinensis (**Chinese juniper**, ☒柏, 桧) is a juniper that grows as a shrub or tree with a very variable shape, reaching 1–20 m tall. This native of northeast Asia grows in China, Mongolia, Japan, Korea and the southeast of Russia.

3.59.1 Growth

It is a coniferous evergreen shrub. The leaves grow in two forms, juvenile needle-like leaves 5–10 mm long, and adult scale-leaves 1.5–3 mm long. Mature trees usually continue to bear some juvenile foliage as well as adult, particularly on shaded shoots low in the crown. This largely species often has dioecious either male and female plants, but some individual plants produce both sexes of flowers. The blue-black berry-like cones grow to 7–12 mm in diameter, have a whitish waxy bloom, and contain 2–4 seeds; they mature in about 18 months. The male cones, 2–4 mm long, shed their pollen in early spring.

3.59.2 Cultivation and uses

This popular ornamental tree or shrub in gardens and parks has more than 100 named cultivars selected for various characters, such as yellow foliage (e.g. cvs. 'Aurea', 'Tremonia'), permanently juvenile foliage (e.g. cv. 'Shoosmith'), columnar crown shape (cv. 'Columnaris'), abundant cones (e.g. cv. 'Kaizuka'), etc. Chinese juniper, as a non-native species in the U.S., should not be used there in natural plantings. The cultivar 'Shimpaku' is a very important bonsai subject. The Chinese juniper is widely used in bonsai, both as individual plants, such as the 250-year-old "Omiya tree" in the Birmingham Botanical Gardens in the UK, and in groups, such as the well-known *Goshin* on display at the National Bonsai and Penjing Museum at the US National Arboretum.

The following cultivars have gained the Royal Horticultural Society's Award of Garden Merit:-

The hybrid between *Juniperus chinensis* and *Juniperus sabina*, known as *Juniperus × pfitzeriana* (**Pfitzer Juniper**, synonym *J. × media*), is also very common as a cultivated plant. This hybrid grows only as a shrub, never a tree, making it suitable for smaller gardens:-

- *J. × pfitzeriana* 'Old Gold'*[7]
- *J. × pfitzeriana* 'Sulphur Spray'*[8]

- As a 250 year old bonsai in the Birmingham Botanical Gardens

- *J. × pfitzeriana* 'Old Gold'

- *J. chinensis* 'Expansa Variegata'

3.59.3 References

[1] "RHS Plant Selector Juniperus chinensis 'Aurea' AGM / RHS Gardening". Apps.rhs.org.uk. Retrieved 2012-07-12.

[2] "RHS Plant Selector Juniperus chinensis 'Blaauw' AGM / RHS Gardening". Apps.rhs.org.uk. Retrieved 2012-07-12.

[3] "RHS Plant Selector Juniperus 'Grey Owl' AGM / RHS Gardening". Apps.rhs.org.uk. Retrieved 2012-07-12.

[4] "RHS Plant Selector Juniperus chinensis 'Kaizuka' AGM / RHS Gardening". Apps.rhs.org.uk. Retrieved 2012-07-12.

[5] "RHS Plant Selector Juniperus chinensis 'Plumosa Aurea' AGM / RHS Gardening". Apps.rhs.org.uk. Retrieved 2012-07-12.

[6] "RHS Plant Selector Juniperus chinensis 'Pyramidalis' AGM / RHS Gardening". Apps.rhs.org.uk. Retrieved 2012-07-12.

[7] http://apps.rhs.org.uk/plantselector/plant?plantid=1083

[8] http://apps.rhs.org.uk/plantselector/plant?plantid=3303

3.59.4 Further reading

- Conifer Specialist Group (1998). "*Juniperus chinensis*". *IUCN Red List of Threatened Species. Version 2006*. International Union for Conservation of Nature. Retrieved 12 May 2006.

3.60 Juniperus procumbens

Juniperus procumbens is a low-growing shrubby juniper native to the southern Japan. Its status as a wild plant is disputed; some authorities treat it as endemic on high mountains on Kyūshū and a few other islands off southern Japan,*[2] while others consider it native to the coasts of southern Japan (north to Chiba Prefecture) and also the southern and western coasts of Korea.*[3] It is closely related to *Juniperus chinensis*, and is sometimes treated as a variety of it, as *J. chinensis* var. *procumbens*.*[2]*[3]

It is a prostrate plant, which usually grows between 20–30 cm tall, although sometimes as high as 50 cm; while it does not get very tall it can get quite wide, 2–4 m across or more, with long prostrate branches. The branches tend to intertwine and form a dense mat. The leaves are arranged in decussate whorls of three; all the leaves are juvenile form, needle-like, 6–8 mm long and 1-1.5 mm broad, with two white stomatal bands on the inner face. It is dioecious with separate male and female plants. The cones are berry-like, globose, 8–9 mm in diameter, dark blackish-brown with a pale blue-white waxy bloom, and contain two or three seeds (rarely one); they are mature in about 18 months. The male cones are 3–4 mm long, and shed their pollen in early spring. It is dioecious, producing cones of only one sex on each plant.*[2]*[3]*[4]

3.60.1 Cultivation and uses

A bonsai specimen of 'Nana'

Several cultivars have been selected, the most widely grown being 'Nana', a slow-growing procumbent plant.[3][5] Others include 'Bonin Isles', a strong-growing mat-forming plant collected on the Bonin Islands,[5] and 'Green Mound', which may just be a renaming of 'Nana'.[5] A variegated plant sold under the name *J. procumbens* 'Variegata' is actually a cultivar of *J. chinensis* misnamed.[5]

3.60.2 References

[1] Conifer Specialist Group (1998). "*Juniperus procumbens*". *IUCN Red List of Threatened Species*. Version 2006. International Union for Conservation of Nature. Retrieved 10 May 2006.

[2] Farjon, A. (2005). *Monograph of Cupressaceae and Sciadopitys*. Royal Botanic Gardens, Kew. ISBN 1-84246-068-4

[3] Adams, R. P. (2014), *Junipers of the World, 4th edition*, Trafford Publishing, p. 112, ISBN 1-4907-2325-0

[4] Gymnosperm Database: *Juniperus procumbens*

[5] Welch, H. & Haddow, G. (1993). *The World Checklist of Conifers*. ISBN 0-900513-09-8

3.60.3 External links

- Conifers Around the World: Juniperus procumbens - Japanese Mat Juniper.

3.61 Juniperus squamata

Juniperus squamata (**flaky juniper** or **Himalayan juniper**; Chinese: 高山柏 *gao shan bai*) is a species of juniper native to the Himalayas and China, from northeastern Afghanistan east to western Yunnan in southwestern China, and with disjunct populations north to western Gansu and east to Fujian. It grows at 1,600-4,900 m altitude.[1][2][3][4] It represents the provincial tree of Khyber Pakhtunkhwa (unofficial).

It is a coniferous evergreen shrub (rarely a small tree) reaching 2–10 m tall (rarely 15 m), with flaky brown bark, and a prostrate to irregularly conical crown. The leaves are broad needle-like, 3–9 mm long, arranged in six ranks in alternating whorls of three, and often strongly glaucous blue-green in colour. The cones are berry-like, globose to ovoid, 4–9 mm long and 4–6 mm diameter, glossy black, and contain one seed; they are mature in about 18 months. The male cones are 3–4 mm long, and shed their pollen in early spring. It is largely dioecious, with pollen and seed cones produced on separate plants, but occasionally monoecious.[1][2][3]

The Latin specific epithet *squamata* means small, scale-like leaves.[5]

Three to five varieties are accepted, with treatment differing between different authors:[1][2][3]

- *Juniperus squamata* var. *squamata* - leaves mostly 5–9 mm. Throughout the range.

- *Juniperus squamata* var. *fargesii* Rehder & E.H.Wilson - leaves mostly 3–5 mm. Confined to the eastern half of the range in China.

- *Juniperus squamata* var. *hongxiensis* Y.F.Yu & L.K.Fu; often included in var. *squamata*.[1]

- *Juniperus squamata* var. *parviflora* Y.F.Yu & L.K.Fu; often included in var. *squamata*.[1]

Juniperus morrisonicola Hayata from Taiwan is often treated as a synonym,[2] or a variety *Juniperus squamata* var. *morrisonicola* (Hayata) H.L.Li & H.Keng,[6] but is better treated as a distinct species as it has a distinct DNA profile.[1]

3.61.1 Cultivation and uses

Juniperus squamata is widely grown as an ornamental plant in Europe and North America, valued for its bluish foliage and compact habit. The following cultivars have gained the Royal Horticultural Society's Award of Garden Merit:-

- 'Blue carpet'*[7]
- 'Blue star'*[8]
- 'Holger'*[9]

3.61.2 References and external links

[1] Adams, R. P. (2004). *Junipers of the World*. Trafford. ISBN 1-4120-4250-X

[2] Farjon, A. (2005). *Monograph of Cupressaceae and Sciadopitys*. Royal Botanic Gardens, Kew. ISBN 1-84246-068-4

[3] Flora of China: *Juniperus squamata*

[4] Conifer Specialist Group (1998). "*Juniperus squamata*". *IUCN Red List of Threatened Species. Version 2006*. International Union for Conservation of Nature. Retrieved 12 May 2006.

[5] Harrison, Lorraine (2012). *RHS Latin for gardeners*. United Kingdom: Mitchell Beazley. p. 224. ISBN 9781845337315.

[6] Gymnosperm Database: *Juniperus squamata*

[7] "RHS Plant Selector - *Juniperus squamata* 'Blue Carpet'". Royal Horticultural Society. Retrieved 20 May 2013.

[8] "RHS Plant Selector - *Juniperus squamata* 'Blue Star'". Royal Horticultural Society. Retrieved 20 May 2013.

[9] "RHS Plant Selector - *Juniperus squamata* 'Holger'". Royal Horticultural Society. Retrieved 20 May 2013.

3.62 Juniperus virginiana

Juniperus virginiana —its common names include **red cedar**, **eastern redcedar**,*[2]*[3] **Virginian juniper**,*[4] **eastern juniper**, **red juniper**, **pencil cedar**, and **aromatic cedar** —is a species of juniper native to eastern North America from southeastern Canada to the Gulf of Mexico and east of the Great Plains.*[3] Further west it is replaced by the related *Juniperus scopulorum* (Rocky Mountain juniper) and to the southwest by *Juniperus ashei* (Ashe juniper).*[5]*[6]*[7]

3.62.1 Description

Juniperus virginiana is a dense slow-growing coniferous evergreen tree that may never become more than a bush on poor soil, but is ordinarily from 5–20 m or 16–66 ft tall, with a short trunk 30–100 cm or 12–39 inches in diameter (rarely to 27 m or 89 ft in diameter, and 170 cm or 67 inches tall). The oldest tree reported, from West Virginia, was 940 years old.*[8]*[9] The bark is reddish-brown, fibrous, and peels off in narrow strips. The leaves are of two types; sharp, spreading needle-like juvenile leaves 5–10 mm ($^3/_{16}$–$^3/_8$ in) long, and tightly adpressed scale-like adult leaves 2–4 mm ($^1/_{16}$–$^3/_{16}$ in) long; they are arranged in opposite decussate pairs or occasionally whorls of three. The juvenile leaves are found on young plants up to 3 years old, and as scattered shoots on adult trees, usually in shade. The seed cones are 3–7 mm ($^1/_8$–$^1/_4$ in) long, berry-like, dark purple-blue with a white wax cover giving an overall sky-blue color (though the wax often rubs off); they contain one to three (rarely up to four) seeds, and are mature in 6–8 months from pollination. The juniper berry is an important winter food for many birds, which disperse the wingless seeds. The pollen cones are 2–3 mm ($^1/_{16}$–$^1/_8$ in) long and 1.5 mm ($^1/_{16}$ in) broad, shedding pollen in late winter or early spring. The trees are usually dioecious, with pollen and seed cones on separate trees.*[5]*[6]*[7]

Juniperus virginiana foliage and mature cones

There are two varieties,*[2] which intergrade where they meet:*[5]*[6]*[7]

- *Juniperus virginiana* var. *virginiana* is called eastern juniper / redcedar. It is found in eastern North America, from Maine, west to southern Ontario and South Dakota, south to northernmost Florida and southwest into the post oak savannah of east-central Texas. Cones are larger, 4–7 mm ($^3/_{16}$–$^1/_4$ in); scale leaves are acute at apex and bark is red-brown.

- *Juniperus virginiana* var. *silicicola* (Small) E.Murray (syn. *Sabina silicicola* Small, *Juniperus silicicola* (Small) L.H.Bailey) is known as southern or sand juniper / redcedar. Habitat is along the Atlantic and Gulf coasts from the extreme Southeastern corner of Virginia,*[10] south to central Florida and west to southeast Texas. Cones are smaller, 3–4 mm ($^1/_8$–

$3/16$ in); scale leaves are blunt at apex and the bark is orange-brown. It is treated by some authors at the lower rank of variety, while others treat it as a distinct species.

3.62.2 Ecology

Characteristic shape in old field succession

Eastern juniper is a pioneer species, which means that it is one of the first trees to repopulate cleared, eroded, or otherwise damaged land. It is unusually long lived among pioneer species, with the potential to live over 900 years. It is commonly found in prairies or oak barrens, old pastures, or limestone hills, often along highways and near recent construction sites.*[5]*[6]*[11] It is an alternate host for cedar–apple rust, an economically significant fungal disease of apples, and some management strategies recommend the removal of *J. virginiana* near apple orchards*[12]

In many areas it is considered an invasive species, even if native. It is fire-intolerant, and was previously controlled by periodic wildfires. Low branches near the ground burn and provide a ladder that allows fire to engulf the whole tree. Grasses recover quickly from low severity fires that are characteristic of prairies that kept the trees at bay. With the urbanization of prairies, the fires have been stopped with roads, plowed fields, and other fire breaks, allowing *J. virginiana* and other trees to invade.*[13] Trees are destructive to grasslands if left unchecked, and are actively being eliminated by cutting and prescribed burning.*[14] The trees also burn very readily, and dense populations were blamed for the rapid spread of wildfires in drought stricken Oklahoma and Texas in 2005 and 2006.*[15]

Eastern juniper benefits from increased CO_2 levels, unlike the grasses with which it competes. Many grasses are C4 plants that concentrate CO_2 levels in their bundle sheaths to increase the efficiency of RuBisCO, the enzyme responsible for photosynthesis, while junipers are C3 plants that rely on (and may benefit from) the natural CO_2 concentrations of the environment, although they are less efficient at fixing CO_2 in general.*[16]

Damage done by *J. virginiana* includes outcompeting forage species in pastureland. The low branches and wide base occupy a significant portion of land area. The thick foliage blocks out most light, so few plants can live under the canopy. The needles that fall raise the pH of the soil, making it alkaline, which holds nutrients such as phosphorus, making it harder for plants to absorb them. *Juniperus virginiana* has been shown to remove nitrogen from the soil after invading prairies.*[17] It has also been found to reduce carbon stores in the soil. This reduction in soil nutrients also reduces the amount and diversity of microbial activity in the soil.*[18]

Cedar waxwings are fond of the "berries" of these junipers. It takes about 12 minutes for their seeds to pass through the birds' guts, and seeds that have been consumed by this bird have levels of germination roughly three times higher than those of seeds the birds did not eat. Many other birds (from bluebirds to turkeys) and many mammals also consume them.*[11]

3.62.3 Uses

The fine-grained, soft brittle pinkish- to brownish-red heartwood is fragrant, very light and very durable, even in contact with soil. Because of its rot resistance, the wood is used for fence posts. The aromatic wood is avoided by moths, so it is in demand as lining for clothes chests and closets, often referred to as cedar closets and cedar chests. If correctly prepared, it makes excellent English longbows, flatbows, and Native American sinew-backed bows. The wood is marketed as "eastern redcedar" or "aromatic cedar" . The best portions of the heartwood are one of the few woods good for making pencils, but the supply had diminished sufficiently by the 1940s that it was largely replaced by incense-cedar.*[11]

Juniper oil is distilled from the wood, twigs and leaves. The essential oil contains cedrol which has toxic and possibly

A log sawn in two and turned on a lathe, exposing the pale sapwood and the reddish heartwood

"Berries" of the 'Corcorcor' cultivar

carcinogenic properties.*[19] The cones are used to flavor gin.

Native American tribes have historically used juniper wood poles to mark out agreed tribal hunting territories. French traders named Baton Rouge, Louisiana, (meaning "red stick") from the reddish color of these poles. It is still used in ceremony by some Nations.

Among many Native American cultures, the smoke of the burning cedar is used to drive away evil spirits prior to conducting a ceremony, such as a healing ceremony.*[20]

During the Dust Bowl drought of the 1930s, the Prairie States Forest Project encouraged farmers to plant shelterbelts (wind breaks) made of eastern juniper throughout the Great Plains. They thrive under adverse conditions – both drought tolerant and cold tolerant, they grow well in rocky, sandy, and clay substrates. Competition between trees is minimal, so they can be planted in tightly spaced rows, and the trees still grow to full height, creating a solid windbreak in a short time.*[21]

A number of cultivars have been selected for garden planting, including 'Canaertii' (narrow conical; female) 'Corcorcor' (with a dense, erect crown; female), 'Goldspire' (narrow conical with yellow foliage), and 'Kobold' (dwarf). Some cultivars previously listed under this species, notably 'Skyrocket', are actually cultivars of *J. scopulorum*.*[22]

In the Missouri, Oklahoma and Arkansas Ozarks, eastern juniper is commonly used as a Christmas tree.

3.62.4 Allergen

The pollen is a known allergen, although not as potent as that of the related *Juniperus ashei* (Ashe juniper), which sheds pollen a month earlier. People allergic to one are usually allergic to both. *J. virginiana* sheds pollen as early as late winter and through early spring. Consequently, what begins as an allergy to Ashe juniper in the winter may extend into spring, since the pollination of the eastern juniper follows that of the Ashe juniper.

Contact with the leaves or wood can produce a mild skin rash in some individuals.

3.62.5 See also

- Cedar wood

3.62.6 References

[1] Farjon, A. (2011). "Juniperus virginiana". *IUCN Red List of Threatened Species*. IUCN. **2013**: e.T42257A2967510. doi:10.2305/IUCN.UK.2013-1.RLTS.T42257A2967510.en. Retrieved 11 November 2016.

[2] Flora of North America: *Juniperus virginiana*

[3] "*Juniperus virginiana*". Natural Resources Conservation Service PLANTS Database. USDA. Retrieved 22 January 2016.

[4] "BSBI List 2007". Botanical Society of Britain and Ireland. Archived from the original (xls) on 2015-02-25. Retrieved 2014-10-17.

[5] Farjon, A. (2005). *Monograph of Cupressaceae and Sciadopitys*. Royal Botanic Gardens, Kew. ISBN 1-84246-068-4

[6] Gymnosperm Database: *Juniperus virginiana*

[7] Adams, R. P. (2004). *Junipers of the World*. Trafford. ISBN 1-4120-4250-X

[8] "Juniperus virginiana" . *Eastern OLDLIST*. Retrieved 13 December 2015.

[9] Steelhammer, Rick (12 April 2012). "Oldest Table Mountain Pine in Pendleton". *Charleston Gazette-Mail*. Retrieved 13 December 2015.

[10] http://www.dof.virginia.gov/infopubs/_outside-pubs/USDA-FS-SRS-155_outpub.pdf

[11] Barlow, Virginia (Winter 2004). "Species in the Spotlight: Eastern Redcedar, *Juniperus virginiana*". *Northern Woodlands*. Center for Northern Woodlands Education. **11** (43): 37. Retrieved July 29, 2009.

[12] West Virginia University: Cedar-Apple Rust, *Gymnosporangium juniperi-virginianae*

[13] Forest Plan

[14] Noble Foundation: News Release

[15] "Wildfires Rip Through Oklahoma" . CNN. January 1, 2006. Retrieved April 11, 2007.

[16] McKinley, Duncan C., and John M. Blair. "Woody Plant Encroachment by *Juniperus virginiana* in a Mesic Native Grassland Promotes Rapid Carbon and Nitrogen Accrual." Ecosystems 11.3 (Apr. 2008): 454-468.

[17] Norris, Mark D., John M. Blair, and Loretta C. Johnson. "Altered Ecosystem Nitrogen Dynamics as a Consequence of Land Cover Change in Tallgrass Prairie." American Midland Naturalist 158.2 (Oct. 2007): 432-445.

[18] McKinley, Duncan C., and John M. Blair. "Woody Plant Encroachment by Juniperus virginiana in a Mesic Native Grassland Promotes Rapid Carbon and Nitrogen Accrual." Ecosystems 11.3 (Apr. 2008): 454-468.

[19] Sabine, J.R. (1975). "Exposure to an environment containing the aromatic red cedar, Juniperus virginiana: pro-carcinogenic, enzyme-inducing and insecticidal effects" . *Toxicology*. Elsevier. **5** (2): 221–235. doi:10.1016/0300-483X(75)90119-5. PMID 174251.

[20] Lyon, William S. (1998). *Encyclopedia of Native American Healing*. W.W. Norton & Company, Inc. p. 173. ISBN 0-393-31735-8.

[21] USDA Fact Sheet

[22] Welch, H., & Haddow, G. (1993). *The World Checklist of Conifers*. Landsman's. ISBN 0-900513-09-8.

3.62.7 External links

- PollenLibrary.com – Red Cedar distribution map and allergen information
- USDA Forest Service: Silvics of Trees of North America: *Juniperus virginiana*
- Interactive Distribution Map of *Juniperus virginiana*

3.63 Malus

"Crabapple" and "Wild apple" redirect here. For the cultivated fruit, see Apple. For the unrelated Australian tree, see Pouteria eerwah. For other uses, see Crabapple (disambiguation) and Malus (disambiguation)

Malus (/ˈmeɪləs/*[3] or /ˈmæləs/) is a genus of about 30–55 species*[4] of small deciduous apple trees or shrubs in the family Rosaceae, including the domesticated orchard apple (*M. pumila*). The other species are generally known as **crabapples**, crab apples, crabs, or wild apples.

The genus is native to the temperate zone of the Northern Hemisphere.

3.63.1 Description

Flowering crabapple blooms

Apple trees are typically 4–12 m (13–39 ft) tall at maturity, with a dense, twiggy crown. The leaves are 3–10 cm (1.2–3.9 in) long, alternate, simple, with a serrated margin. The flowers are borne in corymbs, and have five petals, which may be white, pink or red, and are perfect, with usually red stamens that produce copious pollen, and a half-inferior ovary; flowering occurs in the spring after 50–80 growing degree days (varying greatly according to subspecies and cultivar).

*Ripe Wild Crab Apples (*Malus sylvestris*)*

Baskets of crab apples for sale in Connecticut in 1939.

Trunk of malus

Apples require cross-pollination between individuals by insects (typically bees, which freely visit the flowers for both nectar and pollen); all are self-sterile, and (with the exception of a few specially developed cultivars) self-pollination is impossible, making pollinating insects essential. Several *Malus* species, including domestic apples, hybridize freely.[5] They are used as food plants by the larvae of a large number of Lepidoptera species; see list of Lepidoptera that feed on *Malus*.

The fruit is a globose pome, varying in size from 1–4 cm (0.39–1.57 in) diameter in most of the wild species, to 6 cm (2.4 in) in *M. sylvestris sieversii*, 8 cm (3.1 in) in *M. domestica*, and even larger in certain cultivated orchard apples. The centre of the fruit contains five carpels arranged star-like, each containing one or two seeds.

3.63.2 Cultivation

For the *Malus pumila* cultivars, the cultivated apples, see Apple.

Crabapples are popular as compact ornamental trees, providing blossom in Spring and colourful fruit in Autumn. The fruits often persist throughout Winter. Numerous hybrid cultivars have been selected, of which 'Evereste'*[6] and 'Red Sentinel'*[7] have gained The Royal Horticultural Society's Award of Garden Merit.

Other varieties are dealt with under their species names.

Some crabapples are used as rootstocks for domestic apples to add beneficial characteristics.*[8] For example, varieties of Baccata, also called Siberian crab, rootstock is used to give additional cold hardiness to the combined plant for orchards in cold northern areas.*[9]

They are also used as pollinizers in apple orchards. Varieties of crabapple are selected to bloom contemporaneously with the apple variety in an orchard planting, and the crabs are planted every sixth or seventh tree, or limbs of a crab tree are grafted onto some of the apple trees. In emergencies, a bucket or drum bouquet of crabapple flowering branches are placed near the beehives as orchard pollenizers. See also Fruit tree pollination.

Crabapples are small and sour tasting, and visually resemble a small apple, particularly some apples known as the "Lady Apple", which is also known as Pomme d'Api, Lady's Finger, Wax Apple and Christmas Apple.

3.63.3 Uses

Crabapple fruit is not an important crop in most areas, being extremely sour due to malic acid (which like the genus derives from the Latin name *mālum*), and in some species woody, and for this reason is rarely eaten raw. In some southeast Asian cultures they are valued as a sour condiment, sometimes eaten with salt and chili pepper, or shrimp paste.

Some crabapple varieties are an exception to the reputation of being sour, and can be very sweet, such as the 'Chestnut' cultivar.*[10]

Crabapples are an excellent source of pectin, and their juice can be made into a ruby-coloured preserve with a full, spicy flavour.*[11] A small percentage of crabapples in cider makes a more interesting flavour.*[12] As Old English *Wergulu*, the crab apple is one of the nine plants invoked in the pagan Anglo-Saxon *Nine Herbs Charm*, recorded in the 10th century.

Apple wood gives off a pleasant scent when burned, and smoke from an apple wood fire gives an excellent flavour to smoked foods.*[13] It is easier to cut when green; dry apple wood is exceedingly difficult to carve by hand.*[13] It is a good wood for cooking fires because it burns hot and slow, without producing much flame.*[13]

Because of the plentiful blossoms and small fruit, crabapples are popular for use in bonsai culture.*[14]*[15]*[16]

Crabapple bonsai tree taken in August

3.63.4 Species

- *Malus angustifolia* – Southern crabapple
- *Malus asiatica* – Chinese pearleaf crabapple
- *Malus baccata* – Siberian crabapple
- *Malus brevipes* – Shrub apple
- *Malus coronaria* – Sweet crabapple
- *Malus domestica* – synonym for *Malus pumila*, Orchard apple
- *Malus doumeri* – Taiwan crabapple
- *Malus florentina* – Florentine crabapple, hawthorn-leaf crabapple
- *Malus floribunda* – Japanese crabapple
- *Malus fusca* – Oregon or Pacific crabapple
- *Malus glabrata* – Biltmore's crabapple
- *Malus glaucescens* – Dunbar crabapple
- *Malus halliana* – Hall crabapple
- *Malus honanensis*
- *Malus hopa* – Flowering crabapple
- *Malus hupehensis* – Tea crabapple
- *Malus ioensis* – Prairie crabapple
- *Malus kansuensis* – Calva crabapple
- *Malus* × *micromalus* – Midget crabapple
- *Malus prattii* – Pratt's crabapple
- *Malus prunifolia* – plum-leaf crabapple, Chinese crabapple
- *Malus pumila* – Orchard apple
- *Malus rockii* – native to China and Bhutan
- *Malus sargentii* – Sargent crabapple
- *Malus sieboldii* – Toringo crabapple or Siebold's crabapple

- *Malus sieversii* – Asian wild or Almaty apple
- *Malus sikkimensis* – Sikkim crabapple
- *Malus spectabilis* – Asiatic apple, Chinese crabapple
- *Malus sublobata* – Yellow autumn crabapple
- *Malus sylvestris* – European wild apple
- *Malus toringoides* – Cut-leaf crabapple
- *Malus transitoria* – Cut-leaf crabapple
- *Malus trilobata* – Lebanese wild apple, erect crab apple, or three-lobed apple tree
- *Malus tschonoskii* – Chonosuki crabapple and pillar apple
- *Malus yunnanensis* – Yunnan crabapple

3.63.5 Cultivars

- *Malus* x *adstringens* 'Durleo' - Gladiator Crabapple*[17]
- *Malus* × *moerlandsii* Door. 'profusion' - Profusion crabapple

3.63.6 References

[1] Cirrus Digital Purple Prince Crabapple

[2] Potter, D., et al. (2007). Phylogeny and classification of Rosaceae. *Plant Systematics and Evolution*. 266(1–2): 5–43. [Referring to the subfamily by the name "Spiraeoideae"]

[3] *Sunset Western Garden Book,* 1995:606–607

[4] Phipps, J.B.; et al. (1990). "A checklist of the subfamily Maloideae (Rosaceae)". *Can. J. Bot.* **68** (10): 2209. doi:10.1139/b90-288.

[5] Ken Wilson and D.C. Elfving. "Crabapple Pollenizers for Apples". Ontario Ministry of Agriculture and Food. Retrieved 12 Sep 2013.

[6] "RHS Plant Selector - *Malus* 'Evereste'". Retrieved 20 July 2013.

[7] "RHS Plant Selector - *Malus* 'Red Sentinel'". Retrieved 20 July 2013.

[8] Apple Tree Rootstocks Ecogardening Factsheet #21, Summer 1999

[9] Alaska Department of Natural Resources

[10] "The Growing Guide". Stark Bro's Nurseries & Orchards Co.

[11] Rombauer, I.; Becker, M. R.; Becker, E. (2002) [2002]. *All About Canning & Preserving (The Joy of Cooking series)*. New York: Scribner. p. 72. ISBN 0-7432-1502-8.

[12] "The Science of Cidermaking". Andrew Lea. Retrieved November 14, 2013.

[13] Fraser, Anna (22 August 2005). "Properties of different trees as firewood". Retrieved 17 July 2008.

[14] Biel, John. "Collecting and Training Crab Apples | American Bonsai Society". *www.absbonsai.org*. American Bonsai Society. Retrieved 2 August 2016.

[15] "Crabapple (Malus) - Bonsai Empire". *www.bonsaiempire.com*. Retrieved 2 August 2016.

[16] Walston, Brent. "Crabapples for Bonsai". *evergreengardenworks.com*. Retrieved 2 August 2016.

[17] "Malus x adstringens 'Durleo' 'Gladiator Crabapple'". *Countryside Garden Centre*. Countryside Garden Centre. Retrieved 6 June 2016.

3.63.7 External links

- Germplasm Resources Information Network: *Malus*
- Flora of China: *Malus*
- Virginia Cooperative Extension - Disease resistant crabapples Archived 8 February 2007 at the Wayback Machine.
- The PRI disease resistant apple breeding program: a cooperative among Purdue University, Rutgers University, and the University of Illinois.

3.64 Olive

This article is about the tree and the fruit. For other uses, see Olive (disambiguation). For olive oil, see Olive oil. "Olive grove" and "Olive tree" redirect here. For other uses, see Olive grove (disambiguation) and Olive tree (disambiguation).

The **olive**, known by the botanical name ***Olea europaea***, meaning "European olive", is a species of small tree in the family Oleaceae, found in the Mediterranean Basin from Portugal to the Levant, the Arabian Peninsula, and southern Asia as far east as China, as well as the Canary Islands, Mauritius, and Réunion. The species is cultivated in many places and considered naturalized in all the countries of the Mediterranean coast, as well as in Argentina, Saudi Arabia, Java, Norfolk Island, California, and Bermuda.*[1]*[2]

Olea europeana sylvestris[3] is a subspecies that corresponds to a smaller tree bearing noticeably smaller fruits.

The olive's fruit, also called the olive, is of major agricultural importance in the Mediterranean region as the source of olive oil; it is one of the three core ingredients in Mediterranean cuisine. The tree and its fruit give their name to the plant family, which also includes species such as lilacs, jasmine, *Forsythia* and the true ash trees (*Fraxinus*). The word derives from Latin *ŏlīva* ("olive fruit" , "olive tree"; "olive oil" is *ŏlĕum*)[4] a borrowing from the Greek ἐλαία (*elaía*, "olive fruit", "olive tree") and ἔλαιον (*élaion*, "olive oil")[5] in the archaic form *ἐλαίϝα.[6] The oldest attested forms of the Greek words are the Mycenaean 𐀁𐀨𐀷, *e-ra-wa*, and 𐀁𐀨𐀺, *e-ra-wo* or 𐀁𐀨𐀂𐀺, *e-rai-wo*, written in the Linear B syllabic script.[7][8] The word "oil" in multiple languages ultimately derives from the name of this tree and its fruit.

3.64.1 Description

19th-century illustrations

The olive tree, *Olea europaea*, is an evergreen tree or shrub native to the Mediterranean, Asia and Africa. It is short and squat, and rarely exceeds 8–15 m (26–49 ft) in height. The *Pisciottana*, a unique variety comprising 40,000 trees found only in the area around Pisciotta in the Campania region of southern Italy often exceeds this, with correspondingly large trunk diameters. The silvery green leaves are oblong, measuring 4–10 cm (1.6–3.9 in) long and 1–3 cm (0.39–1.18 in) wide. The trunk is typically gnarled and twisted.

The small white, feathery flowers, with ten-cleft calyx and corolla, two stamens and bifid stigma, are borne generally on the previous year's wood, in racemes springing from the axils of the leaves.

The fruit is a small drupe 1–2.5 cm (0.39–0.98 in) long, thinner-fleshed and smaller in wild plants than in orchard cultivars. Olives are harvested in the green to purple stage. Canned black olives have often been artificially blackened (see below on processing) and may contain the chemical ferrous gluconate to improve the appearance. *Olea europaea* contains a seed commonly referred to in American English as a pit or a rock, and in British English as a stone.

3.64.2 Taxonomy

There are six natural subspecies of *Olea europaea* distributed over a wide range:[9][10]

- *Olea europaea* subsp. *europaea* (Mediterranean Basin)
- *Olea europaea* subsp. *cuspidata* (from South Africa throughout East Africa, Arabia to South West China)
- *Olea europaea* subsp. *guanchica* (Canaries)
- *Olea europaea* subsp. *cerasiformis* (Madeira)
- *Olea europaea* subsp. *maroccana* (Morocco)
- *Olea europaea* subsp. *laperrinei* (Algeria, Sudan, Niger)

The subspecies *maroccana* and *cerasiformis* are respectively hexaploid and tetraploid.[11]

Wild growing forms of the olive are sometimes treated as the species *Olea oleaster*.

Cultivars

Main article: List of olive cultivars

There are hundreds of cultivars of the olive tree (*Olea europaea*).[12][13] An olive's cultivar has a significant impact on its colour, size, shape, and growth characteristics, as well as the qualities of olive oil.[12] Olive cultivars may be used primarily for oil, eating, or both. Olives cultivated for consumption are generally referred to as **table olives**.[14]

Since many olive cultivars are self-sterile or nearly so, they are generally planted in pairs with a single primary cultivar and a secondary cultivar selected for its ability to fertilize the primary one. In recent times, efforts have been directed at producing hybrid cultivars with qualities such as resistance to disease, quick growth and larger or more consistent crops.

3.64.3 History

Prehistory

Fossil evidence indicates the olive tree had its origins some 20–40 million years ago in the Oligocene region corresponding to Italy and the eastern Mediterranean Basin.[15][16] The olive plant later was first cultivated some 7,000 years ago in Mediterranean regions.[15][17]

The edible olive seems to have coexisted with humans for about 5,000 to 6,000 years, going back to the early Bronze Age (3150 to 1200 BC). Its origin can be traced to the Levant based on written tablets, olive pits, and wood fragments found in ancient tombs.[18] At least one cookbook writer writes that the most ancient evidence of olive cultivation is found in Syria, Israel, and Crete.[19]

The immediate ancestry of the cultivated olive is unknown. It is assumed that *Olea europaea* may have arisen from *O. chrysophylla* in northern tropical Africa and that it was introduced into the countries of the Mediterranean Basin via Egypt and then Crete or the Levant, Tunisia and Asia Minor. Fossil Olea pollen has been found in Macedonia, and other places around the Mediterranean, indicating that this genus is an original element of the Mediterranean flora. Fossilized leaves of Olea were found in the palaeosols of the volcanic Greek island of Santorini (Thera) and were dated about 37,000 BP. Imprints of larvae of olive whitefly *Aleurolobus (Aleurodes) olivinus* were found on the leaves. The same insect is commonly found today on olive leaves, showing that the plant-animal co-evolutionary relations have not changed since that time.[20] Other leaves found on the same island are dated back to 60,000 BP, making them the oldest known olives from the Mediterranean.[21]

As far back as 3000 BC, olives were grown commercially in Crete; they may have been the source of the wealth of the Minoan civilization.[22]

Outside the Mediterranean

Olives are not native to the Americas. Spanish colonists brought the olive to the New World where its cultivation prospered in present-day Peru and Chile. The first seedlings from Spain were planted in Lima by Antonio de Rivera in 1560. Olive tree cultivation quickly spread along the valleys of South America's dry Pacific coast where the climate was similar to the Mediterranean.[23] Spanish missionaries established the tree in the 18th century in California. It was first cultivated at Mission San Diego de Alcalá in 1769 or later around 1795. Orchards were started at other missions but in 1838 an inspection found only two olive orchards in California. Cultivation for oil gradually became a highly successful commercial venture from the 1860s onward.[24] In Japan the first successful planting of olive trees happened in 1908 on Shodo Island which became the cradle of olive cultivation.[25] It is estimated that there are about 865 million olive trees in the world today (as of 2005), and the vast majority of these are found in Mediterranean countries, although traditionally marginal areas account for no more than 25% of olive planted area and 10% of oil production.[26]

3.64.4 Symbolic connotations

See also: Peace symbols

Olive oil has long been considered sacred. The olive branch was often a symbol of abundance, glory and peace. The leafy branches of the olive tree were ritually offered to deities and powerful figures as emblems of benediction and purification, and they were used to crown the victors of friendly games and bloody wars. Today, olive oil is still used in many religious ceremonies. Over the years, the olive has been the symbol of peace, wisdom, glory, fertility, power and purity.

Ancient Egypt

Leafy branches of the olive tree were found in Tutankhamun's tomb.

Ancient Israel and Hebrew Bible

The olive was one of the main elements in ancient Israelite cuisine. Olive oil was used for not only food and cooking, but also lighting, sacrificial offerings, ointment, and anointment for priestly or royal office.[27]

The olive tree is one of the first plants mentioned in the Hebrew Bible and in the Christian Old Testament, and one of the most significant. It was an olive leaf that a dove brought back to Noah to demonstrate that the flood was over (Book of Genesis, 8:11). The olive is listed in Deuteronomy 8:8 as one of the seven species that are noteworthy products of the Land of Israel.[28]

Ancient Greece

The ancient Greeks used to smear olive oil on their bodies and hair as a matter of grooming and good health.

Olive oil was used to anoint kings and athletes in ancient Greece. It was burnt in the sacred lamps of temples as well as being the "eternal flame" of the original Olympic Games. Victors in these games were crowned with its leaves.

In Homer's *Odyssey*, Odysseus crawls beneath two shoots of olive that grow from a single stock,*[29] and in the *Iliad*, (XVII.53ff) is a metaphoric description of a lone olive tree in the mountains, by a spring; the Greeks observed that the olive rarely thrives at a distance from the sea, which in Greece invariably means up mountain slopes. Greek myth attributed to the primordial culture-hero Aristaeus the understanding of olive husbandry, along with cheese-making and bee-keeping.*[30] Olive was one of the woods used to fashion the most primitive Greek cult figures, called *xoana*, referring to their wooden material; they were reverently preserved for centuries.*[31] It was purely a matter of local pride that the Athenians claimed that the olive grew first in Athens.*[32] In an archaic Athenian foundation myth, Athena won the patronship of Attica from Poseidon with the gift of the olive. According to the 4th-century BC father of botany, Theophrastus, olive trees ordinarily attained an age of about 200 years,*[33] he mentions that the very olive tree of Athena still grew on the Acropolis; it was still to be seen there in the 2nd century AD;*[34] and when Pausanias was shown it, c. 170 AD, he reported "Legend also says that when the Persians fired Athens the olive was burnt down, but on the very day it was burnt it grew again to the height of two cubits." *[35] Indeed, olive suckers sprout readily from the stump, and the great age of some existing olive trees shows that it was perfectly possible that the olive tree of the Acropolis dated to the Bronze Age. The olive was sacred to Athena and appeared on the Athenian coinage.

Theophrastus, in *On the Causes of Plants*, does not give as systematic and detailed an account of olive husbandry as he does of the vine, but he makes clear (in 1.16.10) that the cultivated olive must be vegetatively propagated; indeed, the pits give rise to thorny, wild-type olives, spread far and wide by birds. Theophrastus reports how the bearing olive can be grafted on the wild olive, for which the Greeks had a separate name, *kotinos*.*[36] In his *Enquiry into Plants* (2.1.2–4) he states that the olive can be propagated from a piece of the trunk, the root, a twig, or a stake.*[37]

Ancient Rome

According to Pliny the Elder, a vine, a fig tree and an olive tree grew in the middle of the Roman Forum; the latter was planted to provide shade (the garden plot was recreated in the 20th century).*[38] The Roman poet Horace mentions it in reference to his own diet, which he describes as very simple: "As for me, olives, endives, and smooth mallows provide sustenance." *[39] Lord Monboddo comments on the olive in 1779 as one of the foods preferred by the ancients and as one of the most perfect foods.*[40]

Vitruvius describes of the use of charred olive wood in tying together walls and foundations in his *De Architectura*:

Storing olives on Dere Street; Tacuinum Sanitatis, *14th century,*

The thickness of the wall should, in my opinion, be such that armed men meeting on top of it may pass one another without interference. In the thickness there should be set a very close succession of ties made of charred olive wood, binding the two faces of the wall together like pins, to give it lasting endurance. For that is a material which neither decay, nor the weather, nor time can harm, but even though buried in the earth or set in the water it keeps sound and useful forever. And so not only city walls but substructures in general and all walls that require a thickness like that of a city wall, will be long in falling to decay if tied in this manner.*[41]

New Testament

The Mount of Olives east of Jerusalem is mentioned several times in the New Testament. The Allegory of the Olive Tree in St. Paul's Epistle to the Romans refers to the scattering and gathering of Israel. It compares the Israelites to a tame olive tree and the Gentiles to a wild olive branch. The olive tree itself, as well as olive oil and olives, play an important role in the Bible.*[42]

Islam

The olive tree and olive oil are mentioned seven times in the Quran,*[43] and the olive is praised as a precious fruit. Olive tree and olive-oil health benefits have been propounded in Prophetic medicine. Muhammad is reported to have said: "Take oil of olive and massage with it – it is a blessed tree" (Sunan al-Darimi, 69:103).

Olives are substitutes for dates (if not available) during Ramadan fasting, and olive tree leaves are used as incense in some Muslim Mediterranean countries.*[44]

3.64.5 Oldest known olive trees

-  Kaštela, Croatia
-  Bar, Montenegro
-  Canneto Sabino, Italy
-  Karystos, Euboia, Greece
- 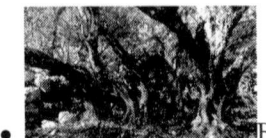 Bidnija, Malta
- Pelion, Greece

Olive trees in the groves around the Mediterranean sea can be centuries old and some have lived as long as 2000 years. The olive tree on the island of Brijuni (Brioni), Istria in Croatia, has a radiocarbon dating age of about 1,600 years. It still gives fruit (about 30 kg or 66 lb per year), which is made into top quality olive oil.*[45]

Pliny the Elder recorded a story about a sacred Greek olive tree that was 1,600 years old. An olive tree in west Athens, named "Plato's Olive Tree", is supposed to be a remnant of the grove within which Plato's Academy was situated, which would make it approximately 2,400 years old. The tree comprised a cavernous trunk from which a few branches were still sprouting in 1975, when a traffic accident caused a bus to uproot it. Since then, the trunk has been preserved and displayed in the nearby Agricultural University of Athens. A supposedly older tree, the "Peisistratos Tree", is located by the banks of the Cephisus River, in the municipality of Agioi Anargyroi, and is said to be a remnant of an olive grove that was planted by Athenian tyrant Peisistratos in the 6th century BC. Numerous ancient olive trees also exist near Pelion in Greece.*[46] The age of an olive tree in Crete, the Finix Olive is claimed to be over 2,000 years old; this estimate is based on archaeological evidence around the tree.*[47] The Olive tree of Vouves, also in Crete, has an age estimated between 2000 and 4000 years. An olive tree called *Farga d'Arió* in Ulldecona, Catalonia, Spain, has been dated (with laser-perimetry methods) as being 1,701 years old, namely it was planted when Constantine the Great was Roman Emperor.*[48]

Some Italian olive trees are believed to date back to Roman times, although identifying progenitor trees in ancient sources is difficult. A tree located in Santu Baltolu di Carana, in the municipality of Luras in Sardinia, Italy, is respectfully named in Sardinian as the *Ozzastru* by the islanders, and is claimed to be between 3,000 and 4,000 years old according to different studies. There are several other trees of about 1,000 years old within the same garden. The 15th-century trees of *Olivo della Linza*, at Alliste in the Province of Lecce in Apulia on the Italian mainland, were noted by Bishop Ludovico de Pennis during his pastoral visit to the Diocese of Nardò-Gallipoli in 1452.*[49]

The town of Bshaale, Lebanon claims to have the oldest olive trees in the world (4000 BC for the oldest), but no scientific study supports these claims. Other trees in the towns of Amioun appear to be at least 1,500 years old.[*][50][*][51]

There are dozens of ancient olive trees throughout Israel and Palestine whose age has earlier been estimated to be 1,600–2,000 years old; however, these estimates could not be supported by current scientific practices.[*][52] Ancient trees include two giant olive trees in Arraba and five trees in Deir Hanna, both in the Galilee region, which have been determined to be over 3,000 years old,[*][52] although there is no available data to support the credibility of the study that produced these age estimates and as such the 3000 years age estimate can not be considered valid.[*][53] All seven trees continue to produce olives.

Several trees in the Garden of Gethsemane (from the Hebrew words "gat shemanim" or olive press) in Jerusalem are claimed to date back to the purported time of Jesus.[*][54] A study conducted by the National Research Council of Italy in 2012 used carbon dating on older parts of the trunks of three trees from Gethsemane and came up with the dates of 1092, 1166 and 1198 AD, while DNA tests show that the trees were originally planted from the same parent plant.[*][55] According to molecular analysis, the tested trees showed the same allelic profile at all microsatellite loci analyzed which furthermore may indicate attempt to keep the lineage of an older species intact.[*][56] However Bernabei writes, "All the tree trunks are hollow inside so that the central, older wood is missing . . . In the end, only three from a total of eight olive trees could be successfully dated. The dated ancient olive trees do, however, not allow any hypothesis to be made with regard to the age of the remaining five giant olive trees." [*][57] Babcox concludes, "The roots of the eight oldest trees are possibly much older. Visiting guides to the garden often state that they are two thousand years old." [*][58]

The 2,000-year-old[*][59] Bidni olive trees, which have been confirmed through carbon dating,[*][60] have been protected since 1933,[*][61] and are also listed in UNESCO's Database of National Cultural Heritage Laws.[*][62] In 2011, after recognising their historical and landscape value, and in recognition of the fact that "only 20 trees remain from 40 at the beginning of the 20th century" ,[*][63] Maltese authorities declared the ancient Bidni olive grove at Bidnija, limits of Mosta, as a Tree Protected Area, in accordance with the provisions of the Trees and Woodlands Protection Regulations, 2011, as per Government Notice number 473/11.[*][64]

An olive tree in Bar, Montenegro, is claimed to be over 2,000 years old.[*][65]

An olive tree in Algarve, Portugal, is 2000 years old, according to radiocarbon dating.[*][66]

3.64.6 Uses

See also: Olive oil and Mediterranean cuisine

The olive tree, *Olea europaea*, has been cultivated for olive oil, fine wood, olive leaf, and the olive fruit. 90% of all harvested olives are turned into oil, while about 10% are used as table olives.[*][12] The olive is one of the "trinity" or "triad" of basic ingredients in Mediterranean cuisine, the other two being wheat for bread, pasta and couscous, and the grape for wine.[*][67][*][68]

green olives

black olives

Table olives

Table olives are classified by the IOC into 3 groups according to the degree of ripeness achieved before harvesting:[*][69]

1. **Green olives**. Picked when they have obtained full size, but before the ripening cycle has begun. Usually shades of green to yellow.

2. **Semi-ripe or turning-colour olives**. Picked at the beginning of the ripening cycle, when the colour has begun to change from green to multi-colour shades of red to brown. Only the skin is coloured as the flesh of the fruit lacks pigmentation at this stage, unlike that of ripe olives.

3. **Black olives** or **ripe olives**. Picked at full maturity when fully ripe. Found in assorted shades of purple to brown to black.*[69]

Traditional fermentation and curing

An olive vat room used for curing

Raw or fresh olives are naturally very bitter; to make them palatable, olives must be cured and fermented, thereby removing oleuropein, a bitter phenolic compound that can reach levels of 14% of dry matter in young olives.*[70] In addition to oleuropein, other phenolic compounds render freshly picked olives unpalatable and must also be removed or lowered in quantity through curing and fermentation. Generally speaking, phenolics reach their peak in young fruit and are converted as the fruit matures.*[71] Once ripening occurs, the levels of phenolics sharply decline through their conversion to other organic products which render some cultivars edible immediately.*[70] One example of an edible olive native to the island of Thasos is the *throubes* black olive, which when allowed to ripen in sun, shrivel, and fall from the tree, is edible.*[72]*[73]

The curing process may take from a few days, with lye, to a few months with brine or salt packing.*[74] With the exception of California style and salt cured olives, all methods of curing involve a major fermentation involving bacteria and yeast that is of equal importance to the final table olive product.*[75] Traditional cures, using the natural microflora on the fruit to induce fermentation, lead to two important outcomes: the leaching out and breakdown of oleuropein and other unpalatable phenolic compounds, and the generation of favourable metabolites from bacteria and yeast, such as organic acids, probiotics, glycerol and esters, which affect the sensorial properties of the final table olives.*[70] Mixed bacterial/yeast olive fermentations may have probiotic qualities.*[76]*[77] Lactic acid is the most important metabolite, as it lowers the pH, acting as a natural preservative against the growth of unwanted pathogenic species. The result is table olives which can be stored without refrigeration. Fermentations dominated by lactic acid bacteria are therefore the most suitable method of curing olives. Yeast-dominated fermentations produce a different suite of metabolites which provide poorer preservation, so they are corrected with an acid such as citric acid in the final processing stage to provide microbial stability.*[78]

There are many types of preparations for table olives depending on local tastes and traditions. The most important commercial examples are:

Spanish or Sevillian type (Olives with fermentation). Most commonly applied to green olive preparation. Around 60% of all the world's table olives are produced with this method.*[79] Olives are soaked in lye (dilute NaOH, 2–4%) for 8–10 hours to hydrolyse the oleuropein. They are usually considered "treated" when the lye has penetrated two-thirds of the way into the fruit. They are then washed once or several times in water to remove the caustic solution and transferred to fermenting vessels full of brine at typical concentrations of 8–12% NaCl.*[80] The brine is changed on a regular basis to help remove the phenolic compounds. Fermentation is carried out by the natural microbiota present on the olives that survive the lye treatment process. Many organisms are involved, usually reflecting the local conditions or "Terroir" of the olives. During a typical fermentation gram-negative enterobacteria flourish in small numbers at first, but are rapidly outgrown by lactic acid bacteria species such as *Leuconostoc mesenteroides, Lactobacillus plantarum, Lactobacillus brevis* and *Pediococcus damnosus*. These bacteria produce lactic acid to help lower the pH of the brine and therefore stabilize the product against unwanted pathogenic species. A diversity of yeasts then accumulate in sufficient numbers to help complete the fermentation alongside the lactic acid bacteria. Yeasts commonly mentioned include the teleomorphs *Pichia anomala, Pichia membranifaciens, Debaryomyces hansenii* and *Kluyveromyces marxianus*.*[78] Once fermented, the olives are placed in fresh brine and acid corrected, to be ready for market.

Sicilian or Greek type. (Olives with fermentation). Applied to green, semi-ripe and ripe olives. Almost identical to the Spanish type fermentation process, however the lye treatment process is skipped and the olives are placed directly in fermentation vessels full of brine (8–12% NaCl). The brine is changed on a regular basis to help remove the phenolic compounds. As the caustic treatment is avoided, lactic acid bacteria are only present in similar numbers to yeast and appear to be outcompeted by the abundant yeasts found on untreated olives. As there is very little acid produced by the yeast fermentation, lactic, acetic, or citric acid is often added to the fermentation stage to stabilize the process.*[75]

Picholine or directly-brined type. (Olives with fermentation). Can be applied to green, semi-ripe or ripe olives. Olives are soaked in lye typically for longer periods than Spanish style (e.g. 10–72 hours) until the solution has penetrated three-quarters of the way into the fruit. They are then washed and immediately brined and acid corrected with citric acid to achieve microbial stability. Fermentation still occurs carried out by acidogenic yeast and bacteria, but is more subdued than other methods. The brine is changed on a regular basis to help remove the phenolic compounds and a series of progressively stronger concentrations of NaCl are added until the product is fully stabilized and ready to be eaten.*[78]

Water-cured type. (Olives with fermentation). Can be applied to green, semi-ripe or ripe olives. Olives are soaked in water or weak brine and this solution is changed on a daily basis for 10–14 days. The oleuropein is naturally dissolved and leached into the water and removed during a continual soak-wash cycle. Fermentation takes place during the water treatment stage and involves a mixed yeast/bacteria ecosystem. Sometimes, the olives are lightly cracked with a hammer or a stone to trigger fermentation and speed up the fermentation process. Once debittered the olives are brined to concentrations of 8–12% NaCl and acid corrected, and are then ready to eat.*[75]

Salt-cured type. (Olives with minor fermentation). Applied only to ripe olives and usually produced in Morocco or Turkey and other eastern Mediterranean countries. Once picked, the olives are vigorously washed and packed in alternating layers with salt. The high concentrations of salt draw the moisture out of olives, dehydrating and shriveling them until they look somewhat analogous to a raisin. Once packed in salt, fermentation is minimal and only initiated by the most halophilic yeast species such as *Debaryomyces hansenii*. Once cured, they are sold in their natural state without any additives.*[78] So-called **Oil-cured olives** are cured in salt, and then soaked in oil.*[81]

California or "artificial ripening"type. (Olives without fermentation). Applied to green and semi-ripe olives. Olives are placed in lye and soaked. Upon their removal they are washed in water injected with compressed air. This process is repeated several times until both oxygen and lye have soaked through to the pit. The repeated, saturated exposure to air oxidises the skin and flesh of the fruit, turning it black in an artificial process that mimics natural ripening.

Once fully oxidised or "blackened", they are brined and acid corrected and are then ready for eating.*[75]

Olive wood

Olive wood is very hard and is prized for its durability, colour, high combustion temperature and interesting grain patterns. Because of the commercial importance of the fruit, and the slow growth and relatively small size of the tree, olive wood and its products are relatively expensive. Common uses of the wood include: kitchen utensils, carved wooden bowls, cutting boards, fine furniture, and decorative items.

The yellow or light greenish-brown wood is often finely veined with a darker tint; being very hard and close-grained, it is valued by woodworkers.*[82]

3.64.7 Cultivation

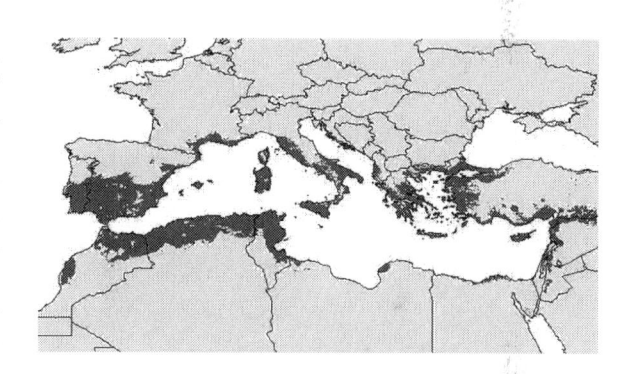

Potential distribution of olive tree over the Mediterranean Basin (Oteros, 2014)[83]*

The earliest evidence for the domestication of olives comes from the Chalcolithic Period archaeological site of Teleilat Ghassul in what is today modern Jordan. Farmers in ancient times believed that olive trees would not grow well if planted more than a certain distance from the sea; Theophrastus gives 300 stadia (55.6 km or 34.5 mi) as the limit. Modern experience does not always confirm this, and, though showing a preference for the coast, they have long been grown further inland in some areas with suitable climates, particularly in the southwestern Mediterranean (Iberia, northwest Africa) where winters are mild.

Olives are now cultivated in many regions of the world with Mediterranean climates, such as South Africa, Chile, Peru, Australia, and California and in areas with temperate climates such as New Zealand, under irrigation in the Cuyo region in Argentina which has a desert climate. They are also grown in the Córdoba Province, Argentina, which has a temperate climate with rainy summers and dry winters

3.64. OLIVE

Olive plantation in Andalucía, Spain

Olive trees on Thassos, Greece

(Cwa).*[84] The climate in Argentina changes the external characteristics of the plant but the fruit keeps its original features.*[85] The northernmost olive grove is placed in Anglesey, an island off the north west coast of Wales, in the United Kingdom:*[86] but it is too early to say if the growing will be successful, having been planted in 2006.

centuries and can remain productive for as long if they are pruned correctly and regularly.

There are only a handful of olive varieties that can be used to cross-pollinate. Pendolino olive trees are partially self-fertile, but pollenizers are needed for a large fruit crop. Other compatible olive tree pollenizers include Leccino and Maurino. Pendolino olive trees are used extensively as pollenizers in large olive tree groves.

Olives at a market in Toulon, France

Growth and propagation

Olive trees, *Olea europaea*, show a marked preference for calcareous soils, flourishing best on limestone slopes and crags, and coastal climate conditions. They grow in any light soil, even on clay if well drained, but in rich soils they are predisposed to disease and produce poorer oil than in poorer soil. (This was noted by Pliny the Elder.) Olives like hot weather and sunny positions without any shade while temperatures below −10 °C (14 °F) may injure even a mature tree. They tolerate drought well, thanks to their sturdy and extensive root system. Olive trees can live for several

Phenological development of Olive flowering, following BBCH standard scale. a-50, b-51, c-54, d-57, (<15% open flowers); f-65, (>15% open flowers); g-67, (<15% open flowers); h-68 (Oteros et al., 2013)[87]

Olives are propagated by various methods. The preferred ways are cuttings and layers; the tree roots easily in favourable soil and throws up suckers from the stump when cut down. However, yields from trees grown from suckers or seeds are poor; they must be budded or grafted onto other specimens to do well (Lewington and Parker, 114). Branches of various thickness cut into lengths of about 1 m (3.3 ft) planted deeply in manured ground soon vegetate. Shorter pieces are sometimes laid horizontally in shallow trenches and, when covered with a few centimetres of soil, rapidly throw up sucker-like shoots. In Greece, grafting the cultivated tree on the wild tree is a common practice. In Italy, embryonic buds, which form small swellings on the stems, are carefully excised and planted under the soil surface, where they soon form a vigorous shoot.

The olive is also sometimes grown from seed. To facilitate germination, the oily pericarp is first softened by slight rotting, or soaked in hot water or in an alkaline solution.

In situations where extreme cold has damaged or killed the olive tree the rootstock can survive and produce new shoots which in turn become new trees. In this way olive trees can regenerate themselves. In Tuscany in 1985 a very severe frost destroyed many productive, and aged, olive trees and ruined many farmers' livelihoods. However new shoots appeared in the spring and, once the dead wood was removed, became the basis for new fruit-producing trees. In this way an olive tree can live for centuries or even millennia.

Olives grow very slowly, and over many years the trunk can attain a considerable diameter. A. P. de Candolle recorded one exceeding 10 m (33 ft) in girth. The trees rarely exceed 15 m (49 ft) in height, and are generally confined to much more limited dimensions by frequent pruning.

The olive tree, *Olea europaea*, is very hardy: drought-, disease- and fire-resistant, it can live to a great age. Its root system is robust and capable of regenerating the tree even if the above-ground structure is destroyed. The older the olive tree, the broader and more gnarled the trunk becomes. Many olive trees in the groves around the Mediterranean are said to be hundreds of years old, while an age of 2,000 years is claimed for a number of individual trees; in some cases, this has been scientifically verified.*[66] See paragraph dealing with the topic.

The crop from old trees is sometimes enormous, but they seldom bear well two years in succession, and in many cases a large harvest occurs every sixth or seventh season.

Where the olive is carefully cultivated, as in Languedoc and Provence, the trees are regularly pruned. The pruning preserves the flower-bearing shoots of the preceding year, while keeping the tree low enough to allow the easy gathering of the fruit.

The spaces between the trees are regularly fertilized.

Pests, diseases, and weather

There are various pathologies that can affect olives. The most serious pest is the olive fruit fly (*Dacus oleae* or *Bactrocera oleae*) which lays its eggs in the olive most commonly just before it becomes ripe in the autumn. The region surrounding the puncture rots, becomes brown and takes a bitter taste making the olive unfit for eating or for oil. For controlling the pest the practice has been to spray with insecticides (organophosphates, e.g. dimethoate). Classic organic methods have now been applied such as trapping, applying the bacterium Bacillus thuringiensis and spraying with kaolin. Such methods are obligatory for organic olives.

A fungus, *Cycloconium oleaginum*, can infect the trees for several successive seasons, causing great damage to plantations. A species of bacterium, *Pseudomonas savastanoi* pv. *oleae*,*[88] induces tumour growth in the shoots. Certain lepidopterous caterpillars feed on the leaves and flowers.

A pest which spreads through olive trees is the black scale bug, a small black scale insect that resembles a small black spot. They attach themselves firmly to olive trees and reduce the quality of the fruit; their main predators are wasps. The curculio beetle eats the edges of leaves, leaving sawtooth damage.*[89]

Rabbits eat the bark of olive trees and can do considerable damage, especially to young trees. If the bark is removed around the entire circumference of a tree it is likely to die. Voles and mice also do damage by eating the roots of olives.

At the northern edge of their cultivation zone, for instance in Southern France and north-central Italy, olive trees suffer occasionally from frost. Gales and long-continued rains during the gathering season also cause damage.

As an invasive species

Olives as invasive weeds, Adelaide Hills, Australia

Since its first domestication, *Olea europaea* has been spreading back to the wild from planted groves. Its original wild populations in southern Europe have been largely swamped by feral plants.*[90]

In some other parts of the world where it has been introduced, most notably South Australia, the olive has become a major woody weed that displaces native vegetation. In South Australia, its seeds are spread by the introduced red fox and by many bird species, including the European starling and the native emu, into woodlands, where they germinate and eventually form a dense canopy that prevents regeneration of native trees.*[91] As the climate of South Australia is very dry and bushfire prone, the oil rich feral olive tree substantially increases the fire hazard of native sclerophyll woodlands.*[92]

Harvest and processing

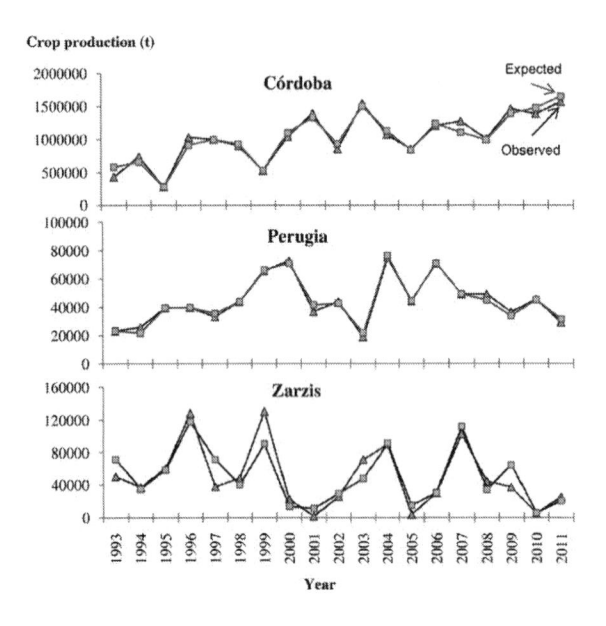

*Forecasting olive crop production based on aerobiological method (Oteros et al., 2014) *[93]*

Olives are harvested in the autumn and winter. More specifically in the Northern hemisphere, green olives are picked from the end of September to about the middle of November. Blond olives are picked from the middle of October to the end of November, and black olives are collected from the middle of November to the end of January or early February. In southern Europe, harvesting is done for several weeks in winter, but the time varies in each country, and with the season and the cultivar.

Most olives today are harvested by shaking the boughs or the whole tree. Using olives found lying on the ground can result in poor quality oil, due to damage. Another method involves standing on a ladder and "milking" the olives into a sack tied around the harvester's waist. This method produces high quality oil.*[94] A third method uses a device called an oli-net that wraps around the tree trunk and opens to form an umbrella-like catcher from which workers collect the fruit. Another method uses an electric tool, 'the oliviera', that has large tongs that spin around quickly, removing fruit from the tree. Olives harvested by this method are used for oil.

Table olive varieties are more difficult to harvest, as workers must take care not to damage the fruit; baskets that hang around the worker's neck are used. In some places in Italy, Croatia, and Greece, olives are harvested by hand because the terrain is too mountainous for machines. As a result, the fruit is not bruised, which leads to a superior finished product. The method also involves sawing off branches, which is healthy for future production.*[71]

The amount of oil contained in the fruit differs greatly by cultivar; the pericarp is usually 60–70% oil. Typical yields are 1.5–2.2 kg (3.3–4.9 lb) of oil per tree per year.*[47]

3.64.8 Global production

Olives are one of the most extensively cultivated fruit crops in the world.*[95] In 2011 there were about 9.6 million hectares planted with olive trees, which is more than twice the amount of land devoted to apples, bananas or mangoes. Only coconut trees and oil palms command more space.*[96] Cultivation area tripled from 2,600,000 to 7,950,000 hectares (6,400,000 to 19,600,000 acres) between 1960 and 1998 and reached a 10 million ha peak in 2008. The ten largest producing countries, according to the Food and Agriculture Organization, are all located in the Mediterranean region and produce 95% of the world's olives.

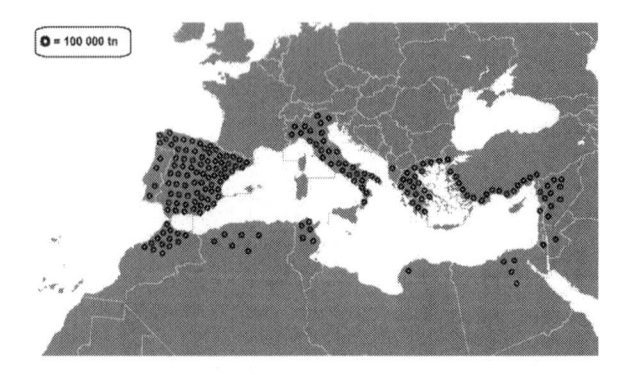

3.64.9 Nutrition

One hundred grams of cured green olives provide 146 calories, are a rich source of vitamin E (25% of the Daily Value, DV), and contain a large amount of sodium (104% DV); other nutrients are insignificant. Green olives are 75% water, 15% fat, 4% carbohydrates and 1% protein (table).

The polyphenol composition of olive fruits varies during fruit ripening and during processing by fermentation when olives are immersed whole in brine or crushed to produce oil.*[98] In raw fruit, total polyphenol contents, as measured by the Folin method, are 117 mg/100 g in black olives and 161 mg/100 g in green olives, compared to 55 and 21 mg/100 g for extra virgin and virgin olive oil, respectively.*[98] Olive fruit contains several types of polyphenols, mainly tyrosols, phenolic acids, flavonols and flavones, and for black olives, anthocyanins. The main bitter flavor of olives before curing results from oleuropein and its aglycone which total in content, respectively, 72 and 82 mg/100 g in black olives, and 56 and 59 mg/100 g in green olives.*[98]

During the crushing, kneading and extraction of olive fruit to obtain olive oil, oleuropein, demethyloleuropein and ligstroside are hydrolyzed by endogenous beta-glucosidases to form aldehydic aglycones. The aglycones become soluble in the oil phase, whereas the glycosides remain in the water phase.

Polyphenol content also varies with olive cultivar (Spanish Manzanillo highest) and the manner of presentation, with plain olives having higher contents than those that are pitted or stuffed.*[99]

3.64.10 Allergenic potential

Olive tree pollen is extremely allergenic, with an OPALS allergy scale rating of 10 out of 10.*[100] *Olea europaea* is primarily wind-pollinated,*[101] and their light, buoyant pollen is a strong trigger for asthma.*[100] One popular variety, "Swan Hill", is widely sold as an "allergy-free" olive tree; however, this variety does bloom and produce allergenic pollen.*[100]

3.64.11 Image gallery

-  Olive tree trunk
-  Olive flowers
-  Olivo della Linza. 15th century
-  A young olive plant, germinated from a seed
-  *Cailletier* cultivar, with an olive harvest net on the ground, Contes, France
-  Olive trees on Shōdo Island, Japan

3.64.12 See also

- Moria (tree)
- Oil-tree

3.64.13 References

[1] "Kew World Checklist of Selected Plant Families, Olea europaea". Kew Royal Botanic Gardens. Retrieved December 5, 2014.

[2] "*Olea europaea* (map)". Biota of North America Program. Retrieved December 5, 2014.

[3] Olea sylvestris Mill. —The Plant List

[4] oliva, oleum. Charlton T. Lewis and Charles Short. *A Latin Dictionary* on Perseus Project.

[5] ἐλαία, ἔλαιον. Liddell, Henry George; Scott, Robert; *A Greek–English Lexicon* at the Perseus Project

[6] OLD s.v. *oliva*, Ernout & Meillet s.v. *oleum*.

[7] "Mycenaean (Linear b) - English Glossary" (PDF). *www.explorecrete.com*.

[8] "The Linear B word e-ra-wa". "The Linear B word e-ra-wo". *Palaeolexicon. Word study tool of ancient languages*. "e-ra3-wo". Raymoure, K.A. "e-ra-wo". *Minoan Linear A & Mycenaean Linear B*. Deaditerranean.

[9] Green PS (2002). "A revision of Olea L. (Oleaceae)". *Kew Bulletin*. **57** (1): 91–140. doi:10.2307/4110824. JSTOR 4110824.

[10] Besnard G, Rubio de Casas R, Christin PA, Vargas P (2009). "Phylogenetics of Olea (Oleaceae) based on plastid and nuclear ribosomal DNA sequences: Tertiary climatic shifts and lineage differentiation times". *Annals of Botany*. **104** (1): 143–60. doi:10.1093/aob/mcp105. PMC 2706730. PMID 19465750.

[11] Besnard G, Garcia-Verdugo C, Rubio de Casas R, Treier UA, Galland N, Vargas P (2007). "Polyploidy in the Olive Complex (Olea europaea): Evidence from Flow Cytometry and Nuclear Microsatellite Analyses". *Annals of Botany*. **101** (1): 25–30. doi:10.1093/aob/mcm275. PMC 2701839. PMID 18024415.

[12] *World Olive Encyclopedia*, International Olive Council, 1996, ISBN 8401618819

[13] Fabrizia Lanza (15 March 2012), *Olive: A Global History*, Reaktion Books, pp. 106–110, ISBN 978-1-86189-972-9

[14] A. Garrido Fernandez; M.J. Fernandez-Diez; M.R. Adams (31 July 1997), *Table Olives: Production and Processing*, Springer, pp. 23–45, ISBN 978-0-412-71810-6

[15] Boskou, D., ed. (1996). *Olive Oil. Chemistry and Technology*. AOCS Press.

[16] Therios, Ioannis Nikolaos (2009-01-01). *Olives: Volume 18 of Crop Production Science in Horticulture (History of Olive Growing, page 1)*. CABI. ISBN 9781845936204.

[17] Di Giovacchino, Luciano (2013). "3". *Handbook of Olive Oil: Analysis & Properties* (2nd ed.). Springer Science & Business Media New York. p. 57.

[18] Vossen, Paul (2007). "Olive Oil: History, Production, and Characteristics of the World's Classic Oils". *HortScience*. **42** (5): 1093–1100.

[19] Lanza, Fabrizia (2011). *Olive: a global history*. London: Reaktion. p. 15.

[20] Friedrich W.L. (1978) Fossil plants from Weichselian interstadials, Santorini (Greece) II, published in the "Thera and the Aegean World II", London, pp. 109–128. Retrieved on 2011-12-07.

[21] "Mediterranean Museums of Olive". *www.oliveoilmuseums.gr*. Retrieved 2016-05-22.

[22] Gooch, Ellen (2005). "10+1 Things you may not know about olive oil". *Epikouria Magazine* (Fall/Spring). Retrieved December 5, 2014.

[23] Alfred W. Crosby (2003). *The Columbian Exchange: Biological and Cultural Consequencies of 1492*. Santa Barbara, CA: Praeger. p. 73. ISBN 978-0-27598-092-4.

[24] Nancy Carol Carter (2008). "San Diego Olives: Origins of a California Industry". *The Journal of San Diego History*. **54** (3): 138–140.

[25] "Shodoshima Town". *shodoshima.lg.jp*.

[26] "Olive Growing and Nursery Production". International Olive Council. Retrieved December 5, 2014.

[27] Macdonald, Nathan (2008). *What Did the Ancient Israelites Eat?*. pp. 23–24.

[28] Cooper, John (1993). *Eat and Be Satisfied: A Social History of Jewish Food*. New Jersey: Jason Aronson Inc. pp. 4–9. ISBN 0-87668-316-2.. See also both the Hebrew and English text in: Deut 8:8

[29] Homer, *Odyssey*, book 5".

[30] "He learned from the Nymphai how to curdle milk, to make bee-hives, and to cultivate olive-trees, and was the first to instruct men in these matters." (Diodorus Siculus, 4. 81. 1).

[31] Toward the end of the 2nd century AD, the traveler Pausanias saw many such archaic cult figures.

[32] "Indeed it is said that at that [ancient] time there were no olives anywhere save at Athens." (Herodotus, 5. 82. 1).

[33] Theophrastus, *On the Causes of Plants,*, 4.13.5., noted by Signe Isager and Jens Erik Skydsgaard, *Ancient Greek Agriculture, An introduction*, 1992, p. 38.

[34] "...which is still shown in the Pandroseion" (pseudo-Apollodorus, *Bibliotheke*, 3.14.1).

[35] Pausanias, *Description of Greece* 1. 27. 1.

[36] Isager and Skydsgaard 1992, p. 35.

[37] Hort, Sir Arthur (1916). *Theophrastus Enquiry into Plants*. William Heinemann. p. 107.

[38] "Ficus Ruminalis". *uchicago.edu*.

[39] "Me pascunt olivae, me cichorea levesque malvae." Horace, *Odes 1.31.15*, c. 30 BC

[40] *Letter from Lord Monboddo to John Hope*, 29 April 1779; reprinted by William Knight 1900 ISBN 1-85506-207-0

[41] Vitruvius Pollio, *The Ten Books on Architecture* Harvard University Press, (1914) Book1, Ch.V, Sec.3, p.22

[42] Balfour, John Hutton (1885) "Plants of the Bible".

[43] Viktoria Hassouna (2010). *Virgin Olive Oil.* p. 23.

[44] "Olive Leaf Burning".

[45] "Ancient Olive Tree". Brijuni National Park. Retrieved 27 May 2016.

[46] Koutoudis, Dennis. "The Pelion Estates". Retrieved 2012-11-10.

[47] Oliver Rackham; Jennifer Alice Moody (1996). *The making of the Cretan landscape*. Manchester University Press. ISBN 978-0-7190-3647-7. Retrieved 7 December 2011. cited in F. R. Riley (2002). "Olive Oil Production on Bronze Age Crete: Nutritional properties, Processing methods, and Storage life of Minoan olive oil". *Oxford Journal of Archaeology*. **21**: 63. doi:10.1111/1468-0092.00149.

[48] ARA, June 18, 2015. ARA-diari (2015-06-18). Retrieved on 2015-06-20.

[49] Diocese of Nardò–Gallipoli. GCatholic.org

[50] Al-BAB. "Ancient Olive Tree".

[51] Drinkwater, Carol (2006). *The Olive Route*. Weidenfeld & Nicholson. ISBN 0-297-84789-9.

[52] M. Kislew, Y. Tabak & O. Simhoni, *Identifying the Names of Fruits in Ancient Rabbinic Literature*, Leshonenu (Hebrew), vol. 69, p. 279

[53] Dr Shlomo Lee Abrahmov interviews with Prof. Mordechai Kislev (Kislew) 2010, Prof. Shimon Lavi 2012 and Dr. Jennifer Alice Moody, Crete 2012

[54] Lewington, A., & Parker, E. (1999) *Ancient Trees.*, pp 110–113, London: Collins & Brown Ltd. ISBN 1-85585-704-9

[55] Reuters (October 20, 2012). "Jerusalem olive trees among oldest in world". *Haaretz*.

[56] Petruccelli, Raffaella, et al. "Observation of eight ancient olive trees (Olea europaea L.) growing in the Garden of Gethsemane." Comptes rendus biologies 337.5 (2014): 311–317

[57] Bernabei, Mauro. "The age of the olive trees in the Garden of Gethsemane."Journal of Archaeological Science 53 (2015): 43–48

[58] Babcox, Wendy. "Every Olive Tree in the Garden of Gethsemane."Departures in Critical Qualitative Research 3.2 (2014): 111–115

[59] "2,000-year-old Trees still producing olives". The Malta Independent. Retrieved 14 May 2016.

[60] "Race to save endemic olive tree intensifies". The Times of Malta. Retrieved 10 August 2016.

[61] "List of Historical Trees Having an Antiquarian Importance". *Government of Malta*. Retrieved 14 May 2016.

[62] "List of Historical Trees Having an Antiquarian Importance". *UNESCO*. Retrieved 14 May 2016.

[63] "Rural Development Programme for Malta 2007–2013" (PDF). Ministry for Resources and Rural Affairs. 2009. Retrieved 10 May 2016.

[64] "Trees and Woodlands Protection Regulations, 2011" (PDF). The Government of Malta Gazette. 2011. Retrieved 10 May 2016.

[65] Municipality Bar, "Kod Starog Bara u Tombi (Mirovica) nalazi se maslina stara više od 2,000 godina" – Near the Old Bar in Tombi, there is an olive tree which is 2,000 years old. Bar.me. Retrieved on 2011-12-07.

[66] "Ecosfera", Público, May 13, 2010. Ecosfera.publico.clix.pt (2010-05-13). Retrieved on 2011-12-07 Archived May 31, 2010, at the Wayback Machine.

[67] Renfrew, Colin (1972). *The Emergence of Civilization; The Cyclades and the Aegean in the Third Millennium B.C.* Taylor & Francis. p. 280.

[68] Essid, Mohamed Yassine (2012). *Chapter 2. History of Mediterranean Food. MediTerra: The Mediterranean Diet for Sustainable Regional Development.* Presses de Sciences Po. p. 29. ISBN 9782724612486.

[69] "About Olives". International Olive Council. Retrieved December 5, 2014.

[70] Omar, Syed Haris. "Oleuropein in olive and its pharmacological effects." Scientia pharmaceutica 78.2 (2010).

[71] "Unusual Olives", *Epikouria Magazine*, Spring/Summer 2006

[72] "Throubes". Olives South Africa. Retrieved 2017-03-22.

[73] "Eat Like a Man". Esquire. Retrieved 22 September 2011.

[74] Yada, Sylvia; Harris, Linda. "Olives: Safe Methods for Home Pickling" (PDF). University of California, Division of Agricultural and Natural Resources. Retrieved December 6, 2014.

[75] Kailis, Stanley G., and David John Harris. Producing table olives. Landlinks Press, 2007.

[76] Bautista-Gallego, J., et al. "Screening of lactic acid bacteria isolated from fermented table olives with probiotic potential." Food Research International 50.1 (2013): 135–142.

[77] Silva, T., et al. "Characterization of yeasts from Portuguese brined olives, with a focus on their potentially probiotic behavior." LWT-Food Science and Technology 44.6 (2011): 1349–1354.

[78] Fernández, A. Garrido, M. J. Fernandez-Diez, and Martin R. Adams. Table olives: production and processing. Springer, 1997.

[79] Botta, Cristian, and Luca Cocolin. "Microbial dynamics and biodiversity in table olive fermentation: culture-dependent and-independent approaches." Frontiers in microbiology 3 (2012).

[80] University of Catania PhD in Food Science and Technology, Food Microbiology: "Isolation and characterization of yeasts isolated from naturally fermented olives with brine bioprotective function" Laboratory of Food Microbiology, DISPA, Agrarian Faculty.

[81] "Oil-Cured Olives: A Kalamata Substitute?". Cooks Illustrated. May 2016. Retrieved 27 November 2016.

[82] *EDIBLE TREES*. AnVi OpenSource Knowledge Trust. 1969. Retrieved 12 June 2016.

[83] Oteros Jose (2014) Modelización del ciclo fenológico reproductor del olivo (Tesis Doctoral). Universidad de Córdoba, Córdoba, España *Link*

[84] Enciclopedia Universal Europeo Americana. Volume 15. Madrid. 1981. Espasa-Calpe S.A. ISBN 84-239-4500-6 (Complete Encyclopedia) and ISBN 84-239-4515-4 (Volume 15)

[85] Discriminación de variedades de olivo a través del uso de caracteres morfológigos y de marcadores moleculares. 2001. Cavagnaro P., J. Juárez, M Bauza & R.W. Masuelli. AGRISCIENTA. Volume 18:27–35

[86] "First Welsh olive grove planted on Anglesey". Wales Online. Retrieved 2011-12-11.

[87] Oteros, J., García-Mozo, H., Vázquez, L., Mestre, A., Domínguez-Vilches, E., Galán, C. (2013). Modelling olive phenological response to weather and topography. Agriculture Ecosystems & Environment, 179: 62–68. *Link*

[88] Janse, J. D. (1982). "Pseudomonas syringae subsp. savastanoi (ex Smith) subsp. nov., nom. rev., the bacterium causing excrescences on Oleaceae and Nerium oleander L". *Int. J. Syst. Bacteriol.* **32** (2): 166–169. doi:10.1099/00207713-32-2-166.

[89] Burr, M. 1999. Australian Olives. A guide for growers and producers of virgin oils, 4th edition ISBN 0-9577583-0-8.

[90] Lumaret, Roselyne; Ouazzani, Noureddine (2001). "Ancient wild olives in Mediterranean forests". *Nature*. **413** (6857): 700. doi:10.1038/35099680. PMID 11607022.

[91] Spennemann, D. H. R.; Allen, L. R. (2000). "Feral olives (*Olea europaea*) as future woody weeds in Australia: a review". *Australian Journal of Experimental Agriculture*. **40** (6): 889–901. doi:10.1071/EA98141.

[92] Olives as Weeds Archived February 5, 2013, at the Wayback Machine. Animal and Plant Control Commission of South Australia

[93] Oteros, J., Orlandi, F., García-Mozo, H., Aguilera, F., Dhiab, A. B., Bonofiglio, T., ... & Galán, C. (2014). Better prediction of Mediterranean olive production using pollen-based models. Agronomy for sustainable development, 34(3), 685–694

[94] "Methods for harvesting olive fruit". olivemuseum.com. Retrieved 2 April 2014.

[95] "FAO, 2004". Apps3.fao.org. Retrieved 2009-05-18.

[96] Faostat.fao.org (2012-02-23). Retrieved on 2012-07-08

[97] FAOSTAT

[98] "Olives and olive oil". Phenol-Explorer. Retrieved December 5, 2014.

[99] Romero C, Brenes M, Yousfi K, García P, García A, Garrido A (2004). "Effect of cultivar and processing method on the contents of polyphenols in table olives". *J Agric Food Chem*. **52** (3): 479–84. doi:10.1021/jf030525l. PMID 14759136.

[100] Ogren, Thomas (2015). *The Allergy-Fighting Garden*. Berkeley, CA: Ten Speed Press. p. 159. ISBN 978-1-60774-491-7.

[101] Polito, V. "Pollination and Fruit Set" (PDF). Retrieved 12 May 2015.

3.64.14 External links

- Blue planet biomes: Olive trees —*Olea europaea* — *cultivation history + horticulture.*

- Agricultural Research Service (ARS); Germplasm Resources Information Network (GRIN): *Olea europaea* —*species treatment, native range, + links.*

- USDA Plants Profile for *Olea europaea* ssp. *europaea* (European olive)

- USDA Plants Profile for *Olea europaea* ssp. *cuspidata* (African olive)

- Olive trees (*Olea europaea*) —U.C. Photo gallery

- Olives at DMOZ

- "Olive". *Encyclopedia Americana*. 1920.

- *Olea europaea* ssp. *europaea* (Olive Scientific Information)

- Reproduction of the olive tree

3.65 Pemphis

Pemphis is a genus of maritime plants in family Lythraceae. It was recently thought have only one species (the type species, described in 1775, *Pemphis acidula*[*][2]) but is now believed to have at least two.[*][3]

Pemphis acidula, *bonsai*

Pemphis are highly adaptive. Depending on environmental factors, they are densely branched, or low and spreading bushes or short trees, with main stems that can be furcated and lie nearly prone, or develop into one erect trunk. Leaves can be small, fleshy and succulent, or larger, flat and not fleshy. All surfaces are covered generally in silky, colorless trichomes.[*][4] The fruits and bee-pollinated flowers are produced throughout the year. Seeds can float, and are sometimes propagated through water dispersal.[*][5]

3.65.1 Habitat

Most *Pemphis* live either at the verges of mangrove forests, well away from the forest-ocean interface; or they colonize beaches behind the intertidal zone, taking hold on rocks, gravel or sand, laterite or limestone, and frequently on promontories or crags.[*][5]

3.65.2 Range and distribution

They are not common, but far ranging from coastal, eastern Africa (including the Seychelles,[*][6] and the Zanzibar Archipelago[*][5]), states with Indian Ocean coastlines, to the Pacific (Philippines,[*][7] Cook Islands[*][8]), northwards up to Taiwan and the Ryukyu Islands[*][4] Other places reporting *Pemphis* include mainland coastal Tanzania, Thailand, Malaysia (Johore), Singapore, Indonesia (Papua, Sumatra, the Moluccas, Madura and Java), Papua New Guinea, Hong Kong and throughout tropical Australia. On Java in particular (where it is known as **stigi** or **santigi**), some areas are uncharacteristically abundant.[*][5]

3.65.3 Uses

Despite the difficulty presented for the prospective carver, wood from *Pemphis* species is highly prized for its extreme heaviness, toughness and resistance to warping. It is usually fashioned into walking canes, fence posts, tool handles, and even anchors, exhibiting a fine finish.[*][5]

Pemphis acidula is a valuable tropical species for bonsai, particularly in Asia.[*][9]

3.65.4 Species

This list is according to The Plant List.[*][3] Species that are as yet *unresolved* (*i.e.* neither *accepted* nor *synonyms*) are indicated by a red asterisk (*****); synonyms have been omitted.

- *Pemphis acidula* J.R.Forst. & G.Forst. (type)[*][2]

- *Pemphis hexandra* Mart. *ex* Koehne*****

- *Pemphis madagascariensis* (Baker) Koehne

- *Pemphis stachydifolia* Mart. *ex* Koehne*****

3.65.5 See also

- Mangroves

3.65.6 References

[1] "Plant name details for *Pemphis*". *IPNI*. Retrieved November 21, 2009.

[2] *Char. Gen. Pl.* 34. 1775 "Plant Name Details for *Pemphis acidula*". *IPNI*. Retrieved November 21, 2009.

[3] "TPL, treatment of *Pemphis*". *The Plant List; Version 1. (published on the internet)*. Royal Botanic Gardens, Kew and Missouri Botanical Garden. 2010. Retrieved 26 August 2013.

[4] Wu Zheng-yi & P. H. Raven et al., eds. (1994). "*Pemphis*". *Flora of China (English edition)*. Retrieved November 21, 2009.

[5] Wim Giesen; Stephan Wulffraat; Max Zieren; Liesbeth Scholten (2006). "Part 2: Description - Trees & shrubs". *Mangrove Guidebook for Southeast Asia*. Bangkok, Thailand: FAO, Regional Office for Asia and the Pacific; Wetlands International. ISBN 974-7946-85-8. Retrieved November 21, 2009.

[6] Piggott, C.J. (1961). "Notes on Some of the Seychelles Islands, Indian Ocean" (PDF). *Atoll Research Bulletin*. **83**: 1–10. doi:10.5479/si.00775630.83.1.

[7] "Kabantigi". *Herbarium Digital Library*. Philippines National Herbarium. May 1, 2005. Retrieved November 21, 2009.

[8] McCormack, Gerald (2007). "*Pemphis acidula*". *Cook Islands Biodiversity Database*. Vers. 2007.2. Bishop Museum, Rarotonga: Cook Islands National Heritage Trust. Retrieved November 21, 2009.

[9] Cheng Cheng-Kung (2007). "*Pemphis acidula* —A Tropical Classic" (PDF). *Bonsai Societies of Florida Magazine*. Cooper City, Florida: Bonsai Societies of Florida (BSF). XXXVIII; No. 4 (152 (Winter edition)).

3.66 Pemphis acidula

Pemphis acidula is a species of flowering plant in the family Lythraceae. The genus *Pemphis*, to which it belongs, was recently thought have only this single species, first described in 1775 and long considered the type species,[2] but is now believed to have at least one other.[3]

3.66.1 Distribution and habitat

Pemphis acidula is a halophyte bush found in coastal locations in the tropical areas of the Indo-Pacific. It is one of the types of shrubs growing in sandy and calcareous soils of the littoral zones of the Indian Ocean and the western and central Pacific Ocean. It is also found in mangroves.[4]

3.66.2 Uses

The wood of this species has been traditionally valued in many cultures for it is hard and heavy, as well as resistant to rot and warping. It also has naturally a fine finish and may be fashioned into walking canes, fence posts, tool handles, and even anchors.[5] In Réunion and Mauritius it is known as *bois matelot*[6] In the Maldives this hardy wood was used in traditional shipbuilding to hold the planks of the hull together, as well as to fashion "nails" in local sorcery.[7]

Pemphis acidula is also one of the plant species used in bonsai, particularly in Asia.[8]

3.66.3 Leaves, flowers and fruits

3.66.4 See also

- Mangroves

3.66.5 References

[1] IUCN Red List of Threatened Species

[2] *Char. Gen. Pl.* 34. 1775 "Plant Name Details for *Pemphis acidula*". *IPNI*. Retrieved November 21, 2009.

[3] "TPL, treatment of *Pemphis*". *The Plant List; Version 1. (published on the internet)*. Royal Botanic Gardens, Kew and Missouri Botanical Garden. 2010. Retrieved 26 August 2013.

[4] Piggott, C.J. (1961). "Notes on Some of the Seychelles Islands, Indian Ocean" (PDF). *Atoll Research Bulletin*. **83**: 1–10. doi:10.5479/si.00775630.83.1.

[5] Wim Giesen; Stephan Wulffraat; Max Zieren; Liesbeth Scholten (2006). "Part 2: Description - Trees & shrubs". *Mangrove Guidebook for Southeast Asia*. Bangkok, Thailand: FAO, Regional Office for Asia and the Pacific; Wetlands International. ISBN 974-7946-85-8. Retrieved November 21, 2009.

[6] xycol.net *Pemphis acidula* J.R. Forst., 1775 - Nom pilote : miki miki

[7] Xavier Romero-Frias, The Maldive Islanders, A Study of the Popular Culture of an Ancient Ocean Kingdom. NEI (1999), ISBN 84-7254-801-5

[8] Cheng Cheng-Kung (2007). "*Pemphis acidula* —A Tropical Classic" (PDF). *Bonsai Societies of Florida Magazine*. Cooper City, Florida: Bonsai Societies of Florida (BSF). XXXVIII; No. 4 (152 (Winter edition)).

3.67 Pinus clausa

Pinus clausa is a species of pine endemic to the Southeastern United States. Its common names include **sand pine**, **Florida spruce pine**,[1] **Alabama pine**, and **scrub pine**.[2]

3.67.1 Distribution

The tree is found in two separate locations, one across central peninsular Florida, and the other in the western Florida panhandle in the Alabama coast. There is a range gap of about 200 km (120 mi) between the populations (from Apalachicola to Cedar Key).

It is largely confined to very infertile, excessively well-drained, sandy habitats where competition from larger-growing species is minimized by the harsh growing conditions of hot sun, fast draining white sands, and frequent severe seasonal droughts. It is often the only canopy tree in the Florida scrub ecosystem.

3.67.2 Description

Pinus clausa is a small, often shrubby tree from 5–10 m (16–33 ft), exceptionally to 21 m (69 ft) tall.

The leaves are needle-like, in pairs, 5–10 cm (2.0–3.9 in) long, and its cones are 3–8 cm (1.2–3.1 in) long.[3]

Over much of its range, it is fire-adapted to stand-replacing wildfires, with the cones remaining closed for many years (*clausa* = closed), until a natural forest fire kills the mature trees and opens the cones. These then reseed the burnt ground. Some populations differ in having cones that open at maturity, with seed dispersal not relying on fires.[4]

3.67.3 Uses

Pinus clausa woodlands are an important part of the Florida scrub ecosystem, and provide habitat for the endangered Florida Sand Skink, among other species. It is one of the few canopy trees able to grow in arid, sandy, and hot locations with minimal care.

While the dense branching makes this tree unsuitable for wood production, it is often used for wood pulp.

3.67.4 References

[1] Farjon, A. 2013. *Pinus clausa*. The IUCN Red List of Threatened Species. Version 2015.2. Downloaded on 02 September 2015.

[2] *Pinus clausa*. USDA Germplasm Resources Information Network (GRIN).

[3] Flora of North America

[4] Moore, Gerry; Kershner, Bruce; Craig Tufts; Daniel Mathews; Gil Nelson; Spellenberg, Richard; Thieret, John W.; Terry Purinton; Block, Andrew (2008). *National Wildlife Federation Field Guide to Trees of North America*. New York: Sterling. p. 70. ISBN 1-4027-3875-7.

3.67.5 External links

- *Pinus clausa*. USDA PLANTS.
- *Pinus clausa*. Flora of North America.

3.68 Pinus mugo

For other uses, see Mountain pine (disambiguation).

Pinus mugo, known as **creeping pine**,[3] **dwarf mountainpine**,[4] **mugo pine**,[5] **mountain pine**, **scrub mountain pine** or **Swiss mountain pine**,[6] is a species of conifer, native to high elevation habitats from southwestern to Central Europe.

3.68.1 Distribution

Pinus mugo is native to the Pyrenees, Alps, Erzgebirge, Carpathians, northern Apennines, and higher Balkan Peninsula mountains. It is usually found from 1,000–2,200 m (3,281–7,218 ft), occasionally as low as 200 m (656 ft) in the north of the range in Germany and Poland, and as high as 2,700 m (8,858 ft) in the south of the range in Bulgaria and the Pyrenees.

Pinus mugo was planted in coastal Denmark for sand dune stabilization. It has naturalized and become invasive.

3.68.2 Subspecies

There are three subspecies:

- *Pinus mugo* subsp. *mugo* —in the east and south of the range (southern & eastern Alps, Balkan Peninsula), a low, shrubby, often multi-stemmed plant to 3–6 m (10–20 ft) tall with symmetrical cones.

3.66.6 External links

- Media related to Pemphis acidula at Wikimedia Commons

3.68. PINUS MUGO

- **Pinus mugo subsp.** *uncinata* —in the west and north of the range (from the Pyrenees northeast to Poland), a larger, usually single-stemmed tree to 20 m (66 ft) tall with asymmetrical cones (the scales are much thicker on one side of the cone than the other).

  Some botanists treat the western subspecies as a separate species, **Pinus uncinata**, others as only a variety, *Pinus mugo* var. *rostrata*. This subspecies in the Pyrenees marks the alpine tree line or timberline, the edge of the habitat at which trees are capable of growing.

- **Pinus mugo subsp.** *rotundata* —hybrid subspecies, of the two subspecies above that intergrade extensively in the western Alps and northern Carpathians.

Both subspecies have similar foliage, with dark green leaves ("needles") in pairs, 3–7 cm (1.2–2.8 in) long.

The cones are nut-brown, 2.5–5.5 cm (0.98–2.17 in) long: and in subsp. *mugo* are symmetrical, thin-scaled and matt textured; and in subsp. *uncinata* are asymmetrical with thick scales on the upper side of the cone, thin on the lower side, and glossy textured.

An old name for the species *Pinus montana* is still occasionally seen, and a typographical error "*mugho*" (first made in a prominent 18th century encyclopedia) is still repeated surprisingly often.

- *Pinus mugo* subsp. *mugo*. Romania.

- *Pinus mugo* subsp. *uncinata*.

- *Pinus mugo* subsp. *rotundata*. Swiss National Park.

- *Pinus mugo Turra*. Jakupica mountain, Republic of Macedonia.

3.68.3 Uses

Cultivation

Pinus mugo is widely cultivated as an ornamental plant, for use as a small tree or shrub, planted in gardens and in larger pots and planters. It is also used in Japanese garden style landscapes, and for larger bonsai specimens.

Cultivars Numerous cultivars have been selected. The cultivar *Pinus mugo* 'Mops' was given the Royal Horticultural Society Award of Garden Merit.[7]

Cultivars with seasonal changes in foliage color include *Pinus mugo* 'Wintergold' and *Pinus mugo* 'Ophir'.

Culinary use

A recent trend is the increase in use of the mugo pine in cooking. Buds and young cones are harvested from the wild in the spring and left to dry in the sun over the summer and into the fall. The cones and buds gradually drip syrup, which is then boiled down to a concentrate and combined with sugar to make pine syrup.[8][9] Menus also use the terms "pinecone syrup" [10] or "pine cone syrup" [11] to refer to this ingredient.

3.68.4 Invasive species

Pinus mugo is classed as a wilding conifer, an invasive species that spreads in the high country of New Zealand, in coastal Denmark and other Scandinavian areas.

3.68.5 Gallery

- *Pinus mugo* (subsp. *mugo*) habitat. Rila National Park in Bulgaria.

-  Female cones and young shoots
-  Male pollen producing strobili
-  Young cones

3.68.6 References

[1] "Pinus mugo (Mountain Pine)". *BioLib*. BioLib. 1999–2010. Retrieved 15 July 2010.

[2] "The Plant List: A Working List of All Plant Species".

[3] Andersson, F. (2005). *Coniferous Forests*. Elsevier. ISBN 9780444816276.

[4] "BSBI List 2007". Botanical Society of Britain and Ireland. Archived from the original (xls) on 2015-02-25. Retrieved 2014-10-17.

[5] "*Pinus mugo*". Natural Resources Conservation Service PLANTS Database. USDA. Retrieved 31 January 2016.

[6] "USDA GRIN Taxonomy".

[7] "RHS Plant Selector - *Pinus mugo* 'Mops'". Retrieved 27 May 2013.

[8] "Wild Mugolio Pine Syrup". *Zingerman's Mail Order*. Zingerman's Mail Order LLC. 2010. Retrieved 15 July 2010.

[9] "Wild Mugolio Pine Syrup". *Cube Marketplace*. Divine Pasta Company. 2008. Retrieved 15 July 2010.

[10] "Piccolo Restaurant - Minneapolis: Menu". Retrieved 15 July 2010.

[11] Colicchio, Tom (3 March 2009). "Tom Tuesday Dinner March 3, 2009" (PNG). *Tom Tuesday Dinner*. Retrieved 15 July 2010.

3.68.7 Sources

- Christensen, K. I. (1987). Taxonomic revision of the Pinus mugo complex and P. × rhaetica (P. mugo × sylvestris) (Pinaceae). *Nordic J. Bot.* 7: 383-408.

3.68.8 External links

- Gymnosperm Database - *Pinus mugo*
- Arboretum de Villadebelle - photos of cones (scroll down page)
- *Pinus mugo* and *Pinus uncinata* - information, genetic conservation units and related resources. European Forest Genetic Resources Programme (EUFORGEN)

3.69 Pinus parviflora

Pinus parviflora, also known as **five-needle pine**,[1] **Ulleungdo white pine**,[2] or **Japanese white pine**,[1] is a pine in the white pine group, *Pinus* subgenus *Strobus*, native to Korea and Japan.

It is a coniferous evergreen tree, growing to 15–25 m in height and is usually as broad as it is tall, forming a wide, dense, conical crown. The leaves are needle-like, in bundles of five, with a length of 5–6 cm. The cones are 4–7 cm long, with broad, rounded scales; the seeds are 8–11 mm long, with a vestigial 2–10 mm wing.

This is a popular tree for bonsai, and is also grown as an ornamental tree in parks and gardens. The [cultivar] 'Adcock's dwarf' has gained the Royal Horticultural Society's Award of Garden Merit.[3]

3.69.1 Gallery

-  *Pinus parviflora* cones
-  Japanese white pine bonsai tree

3.69.2 References

[1] "Pinus parviflora Siebold & Zucc.". *PLANTS*. United States Department of Agriculture. Retrieved 17 December 2016.

[2] *English Names for Korean Native Plants* (PDF). Pocheon: Korea National Arboretum. 2015. p. 575. ISBN 978-89-97450-98-5. Retrieved 17 December 2016 – via Korea Forest Service.

[3] "RHS Plant Selector – *Pinus parviflora* 'Adcock's Dwarf'". Retrieved 27 May 2013.

- Conifer Specialist Group (1998). "*Pinus parviflora*". *IUCN Red List of Threatened Species. Version 2006*. International Union for Conservation of Nature. Retrieved 9 May 2006.

3.70 Pinus ponderosa

This article is about the tree. For the plant community that is dominated by this tree, see Ponderosa pine forest.
"Ponderosa pines" redirects here. For the place, see Ponderosa Pines, Montana.

Pinus ponderosa, commonly known as the **ponderosa pine**,[1] **bull pine**, **blackjack pine**,[2] or **western yellow-pine**,[3] is a very large pine tree species of variable habitat native to the western United States and Canada. It is the most widely distributed pine species in North America.[4]:4

It grows in various erect forms from British Columbia southward and eastward through 16 western U.S. states and has been successfully introduced in temperate regions of Europe. It was first documented into modern science in 1826 in eastern Washington near present-day Spokane (of which it is the official city tree). On that occasion, David Douglas misidentified it as *Pinus resinosa* (red pine). In 1829, Douglas concluded that he had a new pine among his specimens and coined the name *Pinus ponderosa*[5] for its heavy wood. In 1836, it was formally named and described by Charles Lawson, a Scottish nurseryman.[6] It is the official state tree of Montana.[7]

3.70.1 Description

Pinus ponderosa is a large coniferous pine (evergreen) tree. The bark helps to distinguish it from other species. Mature to over-mature individuals have yellow to orange-red bark in broad to very broad plates with black crevices. Younger trees have blackish-brown bark, referred to as "blackjacks"

Pinus ponderosa *in Idaho*

by early loggers. Ponderosa pine's five subspecies, as classified by some botanists, can be identified by their characteristically bright, green needles (contrasting with blue-green needles that distinguish Jeffrey pine). The Pacific subspecies has the longest—19.8 cm or 7.8 in—and most flexible needles in plume-like fascicles of three. The Columbia ponderosa pine has long—12.0–20.5 cm or 4.7–8.1 in—and relatively flexible needles in fascicles of three. The Rocky Mountains subspecies has shorter—9.2–14.4 cm or 3.6–5.7 in—and stout needles growing in scopulate (bushy, tuft-like) fascicles of two or three. The southwestern subspecies has 11.2–19.8 cm or 4.4–7.8 in, stout needles in fascicles of three (averaging 69–89 mm (2.7–3.5 in)). The central High Plains subspecies is characterized by the fewest needles (1.4 per whorl, on average); stout, upright branches at narrow angles from the trunk; and long green needles —14.8–17.9 cm or 5.8–7.0 in—extending farthest along the branch, resembling a fox tail. Needles are widest, stoutest, and fewest (averaging 56–71 mm (2.2–2.8 in)) for the species.[8][9][10]

Sources differ on the scent of *P. ponderosa*, but it is more or less of turpentine, reflecting the dominance of terpenes (alpha- and beta-pinenes, and delta-3-carene).[11] Some state that it has no distinctive scent.[12]

Size

The National Register of Big Trees lists a ponderosa pine that is 235 ft (72 m) tall and 324 in (820 cm) in circumference.*[13] In January 2011, a Pacific ponderosa pine in the Rogue River–Siskiyou National Forest in Oregon was measured with a laser to be 268.35 ft (81.79 m) high. The measurement was performed by Michael Taylor and Mario Vaden, a professional arborist from Oregon. The tree was climbed on October 13, 2011, by Ascending The Giants (a tree-climbing company in Portland, Oregon) and directly measured with tape-line at 268.29 ft (81.77 m) high.*[14]*[15] This is the second tallest known pine after the sugar pine.

Cultivation

This species is grown as an ornamental plant in parks and large gardens.*[16]

Use in nuclear testing

During Operation Upshot–Knothole in 1953, a nuclear test was performed in which 145 ponderosa pines were cut down by the United States Forest Service and transported to Area 5 of the Nevada Test Site, where they were planted into the ground and exposed to a nuclear blast to see what the blast wave would do to a forest. The trees were partially burned and blown over.*[17]

3.70.2 Ecology and distribution

Pinus ponderosa is a dominant tree in the Kuchler plant association, the ponderosa shrub forest. Like most western pines, the ponderosa generally is associated with mountainous topography. However, it is found on banks of the Niobrara River in Nebraska. Scattered stands occur in the Willamette Valley of Oregon and in the Okanagan Valley and Puget Sound areas of Washington and British Columbia. Ponderosa covers 1,000,000 acres (400,000 ha), or 80%,*[18] of the Black Hills of South Dakota. It is found on foothills and mid-height peaks of the northern, central, and southern Rocky Mountains, in the Cascade Range, in the Sierra Nevada, and in the maritime-influenced Coast Range. In Arizona, it predominates on the Mogollon Rim and is scattered on the Mogollon Plateau and on mid-height peaks in Arizona and New Mexico. It does not extend into Mexico.*[19]

The fire cycle for ponderosa pine is 5 to 10 years, in which a natural ignition sparks a low-intensity fire.*[20]

Pinus ponderosa needles are the only known food of the

Subspecies P. p, scopulorum, Custer State Park, South Dakota

caterpillars of the gelechiid moth *Chionodes retiniella*.*[21] Blue stain fungus, *Grosmannia clavigera*, is introduced in sapwood of *P. ponderosa* from the galleries of all species in the genus *Dendroctonus* (Mountain Pine Beetle), which has caused much damage.

3.70.3 Taxonomy

Modern forestry research has identified five different taxa of *P. ponderosa*, with differing botanical characters and adaptations to different climatic conditions. Four of these have been termed "geographic races" in forestry literature. Some botanists historically treated some races as distinct species. In modern botanical usage, they best match the rank of subspecies and have been formally published.*[8]*[9]

Subspecies and varieties

1. *Pinus ponderosa* subsp. *brachyptera* Engelm. —southwestern ponderosa pine.*[22]

   - Range and climate: Four corners transition zone including

3.70. PINUS PONDEROSA

southern Colorado, southern Utah, northern and central New Mexico and Arizona, westernmost Texas, and a single disjunct population in the far northwestern Oklahoma panhandle.*[23] The Gila Wilderness contains one of the world's largest and healthiest forests.*[24] Hot with bimodal monsoonal rainfall; wet winters and summers contrast with dry springs and falls; mild winters.

1. *Pinus ponderosa* subsp. *critchfieldiana* Robert Z. Callaham subsp. novo —Pacific ponderosa pine.

    • Range and climate: western coastal parts of Washington State; Oregon west of the Cascade Range except for the southward-extending Umpqua–Tahoe Transition Zone; California except for both that transition zone and the Transverse-Tehahchapi Mountains Transition zone in southern California and Critchfield's far Southern California Race. Mediterranean hot, dry summers in California; mild wet winters with heavy snow in mountains.

1. *Pinus ponderosa* var. *pacifica* J.R. Haller & Vivrette —Pacific ponderosa pine.*[25]*[26]

    • Range and climate: 100–2,700 metres (330–8,860 ft) on coastal-draining slopes of major mountain ranges in California, and in southwestern Oregon, Washington.*[25]

1. *Pinus ponderosa* subsp. *ponderosa* Douglas ex C. Lawson —Columbia ponderosa pine, North plateau ponderosa pine.*[27]

    • Range and climate: southeast British Columbia, eastern Washington State and Oregon east of the Cascade Range, 1,200–1,900 metres (3,900–6,200 ft) in northeastern California, Arizona, northwestern Nevada, Idaho and west of the Helena, Montana, transition zone. Cool, relatively moist summers; very cold, snowy winters (except in the very hot and very dry summers of central Oregon, most notably near Bend, which also has very cold and generally dry winters).*[28]*[29]

1. *Pinus ponderosa* subsp. *readiana* Robert Z. Callaham subsp. novo —central High Plains ponderosa pine.

    • Range and climate: southern South Dakota and adjacent northern Nebraska and far eastern Colorado, but neither the northern and southern High Plains nor the Black Hills, which are in *P. p. scopulorun*. Hot, dry, very windy summers; continental cold, wet winters.

1. *Pinus ponderosa* var. *scopulorum* (Engelm. in S.Watson) E. Murray, Kalmia 12:23, 1982 —Rocky Mountains ponderosa pine.*[30]

- Range and climate: east of the Helena, Montana, transition zone, North & South Dakota, but not the central high plains, Wyoming, Nebraska, northern and central Colorado and Utah, and eastern Nevada. Warm, relatively dry summers; very cold, fairly dry winters.

1. *Pinus ponderosa* var. *washoensis* (H. Mason & Stockw.) J.R. Haller & Vivrette —Washoe pine.*[31]

    - Range and climate: predominantly in northeastern California, and into Nevada and Oregon, at 2,000–3,000 metres (6,600–9,800 ft), upper mixed-conifer to lower subalpine habitats.*[32]*[33]

Distributions of the subspecies in the United States are shown in shadow on the map. Distribution of ponderosa pine is from Critchfield and Little.*[34] The closely related five-needled Arizona pine (*Pinus arizonica*) extends southward into Mexico.

Before the distinctions between the North Plateau race and the Pacific race were fully documented, most botanists assumed that ponderosa pines in both areas were the same. When a botanist and a geneticist from California found in 1948 a distinct tree on Mt. Rose in western Nevada with some marked differences from the ponderosa pine they knew in California, they described it as a new species, Washoe pine *Pinus washoensis*. Subsequent research determined this to be one of the southern-most outliers of the typical North Plateau race of ponderosa pine.*[8]*:30–31*[35]*[36]*[37] Its current classification is *Pinus ponderosa* var. *washoensis*.*[31]*[32]*[33]

An additional variety, tentatively named *P. p.* var. *willamettensis*, found in the Willamette Valley in western Oregon, is rare.*[38] This is likely just one of the many islands of Pacific subspecies of ponderosa pine occurring in the Willamette Valley and extending north to the southeast end of Puget Sound in Washington.

Distinguishing subspecies

The subspecies of *P. ponderosa* can be distinguished by measurements along several dimensions:*[8]*:23–24*[9]*:17

Notes

Names of taxa and transition zones are on the map. Numbers in columns were derived from multiple measurements of samples taken from 10 (infrequently fewer) trees on a varying number of geographically dispersed plots. Numbers in each cell show calculated mean ± standard error and number of plots.

3.70.4 See also

- Southern yellow pine

3.70.5 References

[1] "*Pinus ponderosa*". Natural Resources Conservation Service PLANTS Database. USDA. Retrieved 31 January 2016.

[2] Moore, Gerry; Kershner, Bruce; Craig Tufts; Daniel Mathews; Gil Nelson; Spellenberg, Richard; Thieret, John W.; Terry Purinton; Block, Andrew (2008). *National Wildlife Federation Field Guide to Trees of North America*. New York, New York: Sterling. p. 89. ISBN 1-4027-3875-7.

[3] "BSBI List 2007". Botanical Society of Britain and Ireland. Archived from the original (xls) on 2015-02-25. Retrieved 2014-10-17.

[4] Safford, H.D. 2013. Natural Range of Variation (NRV) for yellow pine and mixed conifer forests in the bioregional assessment area, including the Sierra Nevada, southern Cascades, and Modoc and Inyo National Forests. Unpublished report. USDA Forest Service, Pacific Southwest Region, Vallejo, CA,

[5] Lauria, F. (1996). *The identity of* Pinus ponderosa *Douglas ex C. Lawson (Pinaceae)*. Linzer Biologische Beitraege.

[6] *The agriculturist's manual: being a familiar description of agricultural plants cultivated in Europe*. Edinburgh U.K.: William Blackwood and Sons. 1836.

[7] Dickson, Tom. "Ponderosa Pine". *Montana Outdoors*. Montana Fish, Wildlife & Parks. Retrieved February 18, 2015.

[8] Callaham, Robert Z. (September 2013). "Pinus ponderosa: A Taxonomic Review with Five Subspecies in the United States" (PDF). USDA Forest Service PSW RP-264.

[9] Callaham, Robert Z. (September 2013). "Pinus ponderosa: Geographic Races and Subspecies Based on Morphological Variation" (PDF). USDA Forest Service PSW RP-265.

[10] Eckenwalder, James (2009). *Conifers of the World*. Portland, Oregon: Timber Press. ISBN 978-0-88192-974-4.

[11] Smith, Richard H. (1977). *Monoterpenes of ponderosa pine in Western United States*. USDA Forest Service. Tech. Bull. 1532.

[12] Schoenherr, Allan A. (1995). *A Natural History of California*. University of California Press. p. 111.

[13] "Pacific ponderosa pine". *National Register of Big Trees*. American Forests.

[14] Gymnosperm Database – Pinus Ponderosa benthamiana

[15] Fattig, Paul (January 23, 2011). "Tallest of the tall". *Mail Tribune*. Medford, Oregon. Retrieved January 27, 2011.

[16] "Pinus ponderosa". *RHS Plant Selector*. Retrieved July 1, 2013.

[17] Finkbeiner, Ann (May 31, 2013). "How Do We Know Nuclear Bombs Blow Down Forests?". Slate.com. Retrieved May 31, 2013.

[18] Meierhenry, Mark (March 2008). "The Old Growth Pines". *South Dakota Magazine*.

[19] Perry, JP Jr. (1991). *Pines of Mexico and Central America*. Portland, Oregon: Timber Press.

[20] Stecker, Tiffany; ClimateWire (March 22, 2013). "U.S. Starts Massive Forest-Thinning Project". *Scientific American*. Retrieved April 19, 2014.

[21] Furniss, RL; Carolin, VM (1977). *Western Forest Insects*. US Department of Agriculture Forest Service. p. 177. Miscellaneous Publication 1339.

[22] USDA Plants Profile for *Pinus ponderosa* subsp. *brachyptera*, with distribution map.

[23] "Pinus ponderosa, ponderosa pine". *Catalog of the Woody Plants of Oklahoma*. Oklahoma Biological Survey.

[24] "Arizona Mountains forests". *Terrestrial Ecoregions*. World Wildlife Fund.

[25] Jepson eFlora (TJM2): *Pinus ponderosa* var. *pacifica*

[26] Calflora Database: *Pinus ponderosa* var. *pacifica* (Pacific ponderosa pine)

[27] Calflora Database: *Pinus ponderosa* subsp. *ponderosa* (North plateau ponderosa pine)

[28] Jepson eFlora (TJM2): *Pinus ponderosa* subsp. *ponderosa*

[29] USDA Plants Profile for *Pinus ponderosa* var. *ponderosa*, with distribution map.

[30] USDA Plants Profile for *Pinus ponderosa* var. *scopulorum*, with distribution map.

[31] Calflora Database: *Pinus ponderosa* var. *washoensis* (Washoe pine)

[32] Jepson eFlora (TJM2): *Pinus ponderosa* var. *washoensis*

[33] USDA Plants Profile for *Pinus ponderosa* var *washoensis* (Washoe pine), with distribution map.

[34] Critchfield, WB; Little, EL (1966). *Geographic distribution of the pines of the world*. USDA Forest Service. Miscellaneous Publication 991, p. 16 (Map 47).

[35] Haller, JR (1961). "Some recent observations on ponderosa, Jeffrey, and Washoe pines in northeastern California". *Madroño*. **16**: 126–132.

[36] Haller, JR (1965). "Pinus washoensis: taxonomic and evolutionary implications". *American Journal of Botany*. **52**: 646.

[37] Lauria, F (1997). "The taxonomic status of (Pinus washoensis) H. Mason & Stockw". *Annalen des Naturhistorischen Museums in Wien*. **99B**: 655–671.

[38] Ryan, Catherine (March 19, 2012). "Loggers give unique Oregon ponderosa pine a lifeline". *High Country News*. Paonia, Colorado. Retrieved March 28, 2012.

[39] Smith, R. H. (1981). "Variation in cone color of immature ponderosa pine (Pinaceae) in northern California and southern Oregon". *Madroño* 28: 272–275.

- Chase, J. Smeaton (1911). *Cone-bearing Trees of the California Mountains*. Chicago, Illinois: A. C. McClurg & Co. p. 99. LCCN 11004975. OCLC 3477527. LCC QK495.C75 C4, with illustrations by Carl Eytel – Kurut, Gary F. (2009), "Carl Eytel: Southern California Desert Artist", *California State Library Foundation*, Bulletin No. 95, pp. 17-20 (PDF), retrieved November 13, 2011

- Conifer Specialist Group (1998). "*Pinus ponderosa*". *IUCN Red List of Threatened Species. Version 2006*. International Union for Conservation of Nature. Retrieved May 12, 2006.

- Conkle, MT; Critchfield, WB (1988). "Genetic variation and hybridization of ponderosa pine". In Baumgartner, DM; Lotan, JE. *Ponderosa pine the species and its management*. Cooperative Extension, Washington State University. pp. 27–44.

- Critchfield, WB (1984). "Crossability and relationships of Washoe Pine". *Madroño*. **31**: 144–170.

- Critchfield, WB; Allenbaugh, GL (1965). "Washoe pine on the Bald Mountain Range, California". *Madroño*. **18**: 63–64.

- Farjon, A (2005). *Pines* (2nd ed.). Leiden & Boston: Brill. ISBN 90-04-13916-8.

- Haller, JR (1962). *Variation and hybridization in ponderosa and Jeffrey pines.* University of California Publications in Botany. **34**. pp. 123–166.

- Haller, JR (1965). "The role of 2-needle fascicles in the adaptation and evolution of ponderosa pine". *Brittonia.* **17** (4): 354–382. doi:10.2307/2805029. JSTOR 2805029.

- Haller, JR; Vivrette, NJ (2011). "Ponderosa pine revisited". *Aliso.* **29** (1): 53–57. doi:10.5642/aliso.20112901.07.

- Lauria, F (1991). "Taxonomy, systematics, and phylogeny of *Pinus* subsection *Ponderosae* Loudon (Pinaceae). Alternative concepts". *Linzer Biol. Beitr.* **23** (1): 129–202.

- Lauria, F (1996). "The identity of *Pinus ponderosa* Douglas ex C.Lawson (Pinaceae)". *Linzer Biol. Beitr.* **28** (2): 999–1052.

- Lauria, F (1996). "Typification of *Pinus benthamiana* Hartw. (Pinaceae), a taxon deserving renewed botanical examination". *Ann. Naturhist. Mus. Wien.* **98** (B Suppl.): 427–446.

- Mirov, NT (1929). "Chemical analysis of the oleoresins as a means of distinguishing Jeffrey pine and western yellow pine". *Journal of Forestry.* **27**: 176–187.

- Van Haverbeke, DF (1986). *Genetic variation in ponderosa pine: A 15-Year Test of provenances in the Great Plains.* USDA Forest Service. Research Paper RM-265.

- Wagener, WW (1960). "A comment on cold susceptibility of ponderosa and Jeffrey pines". *Madroño.* **15**: 217–219.

3.70.6 External links

- USDA Plants Profile for *Pinus* ponderosa (ponderosa pine)

- Gymnosperm Database: *Pinus ponderosa*

- Calflora Database: *Pinus ponderosa* (ponderosa pine, western yellow pine)

- Jepson Manual eFlora (TJM2) treatment of *Pinus ponderosa*

- UC CalPhotos Gallery – *Pinus ponderosa*

3.71 Pinus rigida

Pinus rigida, the **pitch pine**,[2][3] is a small-to-medium-sized (6–30 m [20–98 ft]) pine, native to eastern North America. This species occasionally hybridizes with other pine species such as loblolly pine (*Pinus taeda*), shortleaf pine (*Pinus echinata*), and pond pine (*Pinus serotina*); the last is treated as a subspecies of pitch pine by some botanists.

3.71.1 Distribution

Pitch pine is found mainly in the southern areas of the northeastern United States, from coastal Maine and Ohio to Kentucky and northern Georgia. A few stands occur in southern Quebec and Ontario. This pine occupies a variety of habitats from dry acidic sandy uplands to swampy lowlands, and can survive in very poor conditions; it is the primary tree of the New Jersey Pine Barrens.[4]

3.71.2 Description

The needles are in fascicles of three, about 6–13 cm (2.4–5.1 in) in length, and are stout (over 1 mm (0.039 in) broad) and often slightly twisted. The cones are 4–7 cm (1.6–2.8 in) long and oval with prickles on the scales. Pitch pine has an exceptionally high regenerative ability; if the main trunk is cut or damaged by fire it can re-sprout using epicormic shoots. This is one of its many adaptations to fire, which also includes a thick bark to protect the sensitive cambium layer from heat. Burnt trees often form stunted, twisted trees with multiple trunks as a result of the resprouting. This characteristic also makes it a popular species for bonsai.

Pitch pine is rapid-growing when young, gaining around one foot of height per year under optimal conditions until the tree is 50–60 years old, whereupon growth slows. By 90 years of age, the amount of annual height gain is minimal. Open-growth trees begin bearing cones in as little as three years, with shade-inhabiting pines taking a few years longer. Cones take two years to mature and seed dispersal occurs over the fall and winter and trees cannot self-pollinate. The total lifespan of pitch pine is about 200 years.

3.71.3 Uses

Pitch pine is not a major timber tree due to the frequency of multiple or crooked trunks; nor is it as fast-growing as other eastern American pines. However, it grows well on unfavorable sites. In the past, it was a major source of pitch and timber for ship building, mine timbers, and railroad ties because the wood's high resin content preserves it from decay. Pitch pine wood was also used for building radio towers in Germany, as at Muehlacker and Ismaning.

Pitch pine is currently used mainly for rough construction, pulp, crating, and fuel. However, due to its uneven growth, quantities of high quality can be very sought after, and large lengths of pitch pine can be very costly.

3.71.4 Gallery

- New growth and pollen cones

- Cone and needles

- View north from a fire tower on Apple Pie Hill in the New Jersey Pine Barrens. The vast pine forest is almost entirely made up of *Pinus rigida*.

3.71.5 References

[1] Farjon, A. (2013). "Pinus rigida". *IUCN Red List of Threatened Species. Version 2013.1*. International Union for Conservation of Nature. Retrieved 17 July 2013.

[2] *"Pinus rigida"*. Natural Resources Conservation Service PLANTS Database. USDA. Retrieved 31 January 2016.

[3] "BSBI List 2007". Botanical Society of Britain and Ireland. Archived from the original (xls) on 2015-02-25. Retrieved 2014-10-17.

[4] Moore, Gerry; Kershner, Bruce; et al. (2008). *National Wildlife Federation Field Guide to Trees of North America*. New York: Sterling. p. 756. ISBN 1-4027-3875-7.

3.71.6 External links

3.72 Pinus strobus

Pinus strobus, commonly denominated the **eastern white pine**, **northern white pine**, **white pine**, **Weymouth pine** (British), and **soft pine**[1] is a large pine native to eastern North America. It occurs from Newfoundland, Canada west through the Great Lakes region to southeastern Manitoba and Minnesota, United States, and south along the Appalachian Mountains and upper Piedmont to northernmost Georgia and perhaps very rarely in some of the higher elevations in northeastern Alabama.[2]

The Native American Haudenosaunee denominated it the "Tree of Peace". It is known as the "Weymouth pine" in the United Kingdom,[3] after Captain George Weymouth of the British Royal Navy, who brought its seeds to England from Maine in 1605.[4]

3.72.1 Distribution

Native eastern white pine, Sylvania Wilderness, Michigan

Pinus strobus is found in the nearctic temperate broadleaf and mixed forests biome of eastern North America. It prefers well-drained or sandy soils and humid climates, but can also grow in boggy areas and rocky highlands. In mixed forests, this dominant tree towers over many others, including some of the large broadleaf hardwoods. It provides food and shelter for numerous forest birds, such as the red crossbill, and small mammals such as squirrels.

Eastern White Pine forests originally covered much of north-central and north-eastern North America. Only one percent of the old-growth forests remain after the extensive logging operations of the 18th century to early 20th century.

Old growth forests, or virgin stands, are protected in Great Smoky Mountains National Park. Other protected ar-

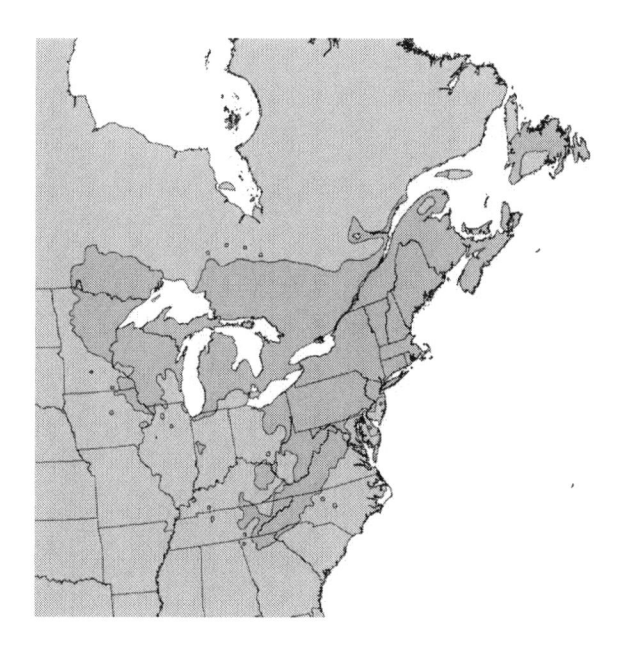

Partial distribution map of Pinus strobus *in North America*

eas with known virgin forests, as confirmed by the Eastern Native Tree Society, include Algonquin Provincial Park, Quetico Provincial Park, and Algoma Highlands in Ontario, Canada; Estivant Pines, Huron Mountains, Porcupine Mountains State Park, and Sylvania Wilderness Area in the Upper Peninsula of Michigan, United States; Hartwick Pines State Park in the Lower Peninsula of Michigan; Menominee Indian Reservation in Wisconsin; Lost 40 Scientific and Natural Area (SNA) and Boundary Waters Canoe Area Wilderness in Minnesota; White Pines State Park, Illinois; Cook Forest State Park, Hearts Content Scenic Area, and Anders Run Natural Area in Pennsylvania; and the Linville Gorge Wilderness in North Carolina.

Small groves or individual specimens of old growth Eastern White Pines are found across the range of the species in the USA, including in Ordway Pines, Maine; Ice Glen, Massachusetts; and Adirondack Park, New York. Many sites with conspicuously large specimens represent advanced old field ecological succession. The tall stands in Mohawk Trail State Forest and William Cullen Bryant Homestead in Massachusetts are examples.

As an introduced species, *Pinus strobus* is now naturalizing in the Outer Eastern Carpathians subdivision of the Carpathian Mountains in Czech Republic and southern Poland. It has spread from specimens planted as ornamental trees.

3.72.2 Description

Like all members of the white pine group, *Pinus* subgenus *Strobus*, the leaves ("needles") are in fascicles (bundles) of 5, or rarely 3 or 4, with a deciduous sheath. They are flexible, bluish-green, finely serrated, 5–13 cm (2–5 in) long, and persist for 18 months, i.e., from the spring of one season until autumn of the next, when they abscise.

The cones are slender, 8–16 cm (3 $\frac{1}{4}$–6 $\frac{1}{4}$ in) long (rarely longer than that) and 4–5 cm (1 $\frac{1}{2}$–2 in) broad when open, and have scales with a rounded apex and slightly reflexed tip. The seeds are 4–5 mm ($\frac{5}{32}$–$\frac{3}{16}$ in) long, with a slender 15–20 mm ($\frac{5}{8}$–$\frac{3}{4}$ in) wing, and are dispersed by wind. Cone production peaks every 3 to 5 years.

While Eastern White Pine is self-fertile, seeds produced this way tend to result in weak, stunted, and malformed seedlings.

Mature trees are often 200–250 years old, and some live to over 400 years. A tree growing near Syracuse, New York was dated to 458 years old in the late 1980s and trees in Michigan and Wisconsin were dated to approximately 500 years old.

Dimensions

Measuring the circumference of an Eastern White Pine

The Eastern White Pine has the distinction of being the

tallest tree in eastern North America. In natural precolonial stands it is reported to have grown as tall as 70 m (230 ft). There is no means of accurately documenting the height of trees from these times, but Eastern White Pine may have reached this height on rare occasions. Even greater heights have been reported in popular, but unverifiable, accounts such as Robert Pike's "Tall Trees, Tough Men".

Total trunk volumes of the largest specimens are approximately 28 m^3 (990 cu ft), with some past giants possibly reaching 37 or 40 m^3 (1,300 or 1,400 cu ft). Photographic analysis of giants suggests volumes closer to 34 m^3 (1,200 cu ft).

Height *Pinus strobus* grows approximately 1 m (3.3 ft) annually between the ages of 15 and 45 years, with slower height increments before and after that age range.*[5] The tallest presently living specimens are 50–57.55 m (164 ft 1 in–188 ft 10 in) tall, as determined by the Native Tree Society (NTS).*[6] Three locations in southeastern United States and one site in northeastern United States have trees that are 55 m (180 ft) tall.

The southern Appalachian Mountains have the most locations and the tallest trees in the present range of *Pinus strobus*. One survivor is a specimen known as the "Boogerman Pine" in the Cataloochee Valley of Great Smoky Mountains National Park. At 57.55 m (188 ft 10 in) tall, it is the tallest accurately measured tree in North America east of the Rocky Mountains. It has been climbed and measured by tape drop by the Native Tree Society. Before Hurricane Opal broke its top in October 1995, Boogerman Pine was 63 m (207 ft) tall, as determined by Will Blozan and Robert Leverett using ground based measurements.

The tallest specimens in Hartwick Pines State Park in Michigan are 45–48 m (148–157 ft) tall.

In northeastern USA, 8 sites in 4 states currently have trees over 48 m (157 ft) tall, as confirmed by the Native Tree Society. The Cook Forest State Park of Pennsylvania has the most numerous collection of 45 m (148 ft) Eastern White Pines in the Northeast, with 110 trees measuring that height or more. The Park's "Longfellow Pine" is the tallest presently living Eastern White Pine in the Northeast, at 55.96 m (183 ft 7 in) tall, as determined by being climbed and measured by tape drop.*[7] The Mohawk Trail State Forest of Massachusetts has 83 trees measuring 45 m (148 ft) or more tall, of which 6 exceed 48.8 m (160 ft). The "Jake Swamp Tree" located there is 51.54 m (169 ft 1 in) tall.*[8]*[9] The Native Tree Society maintains precise measurements of it. A private property in Claremont, New Hampshire has approximately 60 specimens that are 45 m (148 ft) tall. Besides the aforementioned sites, sites with 45 m (148 ft) tall specimens typically have one to 15 specimens.

Diameter Diameters of the larger pines range from 1.0–1.6 m (3 ft 3 in–5 ft 3 in), which translates to a circumference (girth) range of 3.1–5.0 m (10 ft 2 in–16 ft 5 in). However, single-trunked white pines in both the Northeast and Southeast with diameters over 1.45 m (4 ft 9 in) are exceedingly rare. Notable big pine sites of 40 ha (99 acres) or less will often have no more than 2 or 3 trees in the 1.2 to 1.4 m (3 ft 11 in to 4 ft 7 in) diameter class.

White pine boughs, showing annual yellowing and abscission of older foliage in the autumn. Upstate New York, USA.

Unconfirmed reports from the colonial era gave diameters of virgin white pines of up to 2.4 m (8 ft).*[10]

3.72.3 Mortality and disease

Because the eastern white pine tree is somewhat resistant to fire, mature survivors are able to re-seed burned areas. In pure stands mature trees usually have no branches on the lower half of the trunk. The white pine weevil (*Pissodes strobi*) and white pine blister rust (*Cronartium ribicola*), an introduced fungus, can damage or kill these trees.

Blister rust

Mortality from white pine blister rust in mature pine groves was often 50–80% during the early 20th century. The fungus must spend part of its life cycle on alternate hosts of the *Ribes* genus, the native gooseberry or wild currant. Foresters proposed that if all the alternate host plants were removed that white pine blister rust might be eliminated. A very determined campaign was mounted and all land owners in commercial pine growing regions were encouraged to uproot and kill all native gooseberry and wild currant

An illustration dated 1902, showing a variety of insect pests affecting eastern white pine

plants.*[10]*[11] The ramifications for wildlife and habitat ecology were of less concern at the time than timber industry protection.

Today native wild currants are relatively rare plants in New England, and planting wild currants or wild gooseberries is strongly discouraged, or even illegal in some jurisdictions. As an alternative, new strains of commercial currants have been developed which are highly resistant to white pine blister rust. Mortality in white pines from rust is only about 3% today.*[11]

3.72.4 Historical uses

Lumber

In the 19th century, the harvesting of Midwestern white pine forests played a major role in America's westward expansion through the Great Plains. A quarter million white pines were harvested and sent to lumber yards in Chicago in a single year.*[12]

The white pine had aesthetic appeal to contemporary naturalists such as Henry David Thoreau ("There is no finer tree.")*[13] Beyond that, it had commercial applications. It was considered "the most sought and most widely utilized of the various forest growths of the northwest." *[14] Descriptions of its uses are quoted below from a contemporary source:

Being of a soft texture and easily worked, taking paint better than almost any other variety of wood, it has been found adaptable to all the uses demanded in the building art, from the manufacture of packing cases to the bearing timber and finer finish of a dwelling. Of light weight, it has borne transportation to the farms of the west, where it is used for building purposes in dwellings, barns and corn cribs, while as a fencing material it has no superior. Aside from those conditions which demand a dense strong timber, such as shipbuilding or in wagon-making, white pine has been found adaptable to all the economic uses in which lumber is required, not excluding its use in coarser articles of furniture. No wood has found greater favor or entered more fully into supplying all those wants of man which could be found in the forest growths.*[14]

The species was imported in 1620 to England by Captain George Weymouth, who planted it for a timber crop, but had little success because of white pine blister rust disease.

Old growth pine in the Americas, of various *Pinus* species, was a highly desired wood since huge, knot-free boards were the rule rather than the exception. Pine was common and easy to cut, thus many colonial homes used pine for paneling, floors and furniture. Pine was also a favorite tree of loggers since pine logs can still be processed in a lumber mill a year or more after being cut down. In contrast, most hardwood trees such as cherry, maple, oak, and ash must be cut into 1" thick boards immediately after felling or large cracks will develop in the trunk which can render the wood worthless.*[10]

Although eastern white pine was frequently used for flooring in buildings constructed before the U.S. Civil War, the wood is soft and will tend to cup over time with wear. George Washington opted for the much harder southern yellow pine at Mount Vernon instead.*[10]

Masts

During the age of square riggers, tall white pines with high quality wood in the Thirteen Colonies were known as *mast pines*. Marked by agents of the Crown with the broad arrow, these "mast pines" were reserved for the British Royal Navy.

Special barge-like vessels were built to ship up to 50 pine trunks destined to become masts. The wood was often squared immediately after felling to fit in the holds of ships better.*[10] A 30 m (100 ft) mast was about 91 cm × 91 cm (3 ft × 3 ft) at the butt and 61 cm × 61 cm (2 ft × 2 ft) at the top, while a 37 m (120 ft) mast was 1.2 m × 1.2 m (4 ft × 4 ft) by 76 cm (30 in) on its ends.

Marking of large specimens by the Crown was very controversial in the colonies, leading to the Pine Tree Riot in 1772; its act of rebellion played a significant role in the events leading to the American Revolution. During that conflict colonists cut down and hauled off many mast pines.[*][15][*][16]

The original masts on the USS *Constitution* were single trees but were later replaced by laminated spars to better withstand cannonballs. An unusual large, lone, white pine was found in colonial times in coastal South Carolina along the Black River, far east of its southernmost normal range. The king's mark was carved into it, giving rise to the town of Kingstree.[*][17]

3.72.5 Contemporary uses

Lumber

Board of Pinus strobus

Eastern white pine is now widely grown in plantation forestry within its native area.

Freshly cut eastern white pine is creamy white or a pale straw color but pine wood which has aged many years tends to darken to a deep rich golden tan. Occasionally one can find light brown pine boards with unusual yellowish-golden or reddish-brown hues. This is the famous "pumpkin pine". It is generally thought that slow growing pines in old-growth forests accumulate colored products in the heartwood, but genetic factors and soil conditions may also play a role in rich color development.[*][15]

This wood is also favored by pattern makers for its easy working.

Foods and medicines

Eastern white pine needles contain five times the amount of Vitamin C (by weight) of lemons and make an excellent herbal tea. The cambium is edible. It is also a source of resveratrol. Linnaeus noted in the 18th century that cattle and pigs fed pine bark bread grew well, but he personally did not like the taste. Caterpillars of Lusk's Pinemoth (*Coloradia luski*) have been found to feed only on *Pinus strobus*.

Pine tar is produced by slowly burning pine roots, branches, or small trunks in a partially smothered flame. Pine tar mixed with beer can be used to remove tapeworms (flat worms) or nematodes (round worms). Pine tar mixed with sulfur is useful to treat dandruff, and marketed in present-day products. Pine tar can also be processed to make turpentine.[*][18]

Native American traditional uses

The name "Adirondack" is an Iroquois word which means tree-eater and referred to their neighbors (more commonly known as the Algonquians) who collected the inner bark of this tree, *Picea rubens*, and others during times of winter starvation. The white soft inner bark (cambial layer) was carefully separated from the hard, dark brown bark and dried. When pounded this product can be used as flour or added to stretch other starchy products.[*][19][*][20]

The young staminate cones were stewed by the Ojibwe Indians with meat and were said to be sweet and not pitchy. In addition, the seeds are sweet and nutritious, but not as tasty as those of some of the western nut pines.[*][19]

Pine resin (sap) has been used by various tribes to waterproof baskets, pails, and boats. The Chippewa also used pine resin to successfully treat infections and even gangrenous wounds.[*][19] This is because pine resin apparently has a number of quite efficient antimicrobials. Generally a wet pulp from the inner bark, or pine tar mixed with beeswax or butter was applied to wounds and used as a salve to prevent infection.

Cultivation

Pinus strobus is cultivated by plant nurseries as an ornamental tree, for planting in gardens and parks.[*][21] The species is low-maintenance and rapid growing as a specimen tree. With regular shearing it can also be trained as a hedge. Some cultivars are used in bonsai. [*][22]

Cultivars Cultivars have been selected for small to dwarf mature forms, and foliage color characteristics.[*][22] They include:

- *Pinus strobus* Nana Group —ave. 91 cm (3 ft) tall by 1.2 m (4 ft) wide. MBG: *Pinus strobus* (Nana Group)
  - *Pinus strobus* 'Macopin' —30 to 91 cm (1 to 3 ft) tall & wide. MBG:*Pinus strobus* 'Macopin'
  - *Pinus strobus* 'Paul Waxman' —61 to 152 cm (2 to 5 ft) tall & wide. MBG: *Pinus strobus* 'Paul Waxman'

Christmas trees Smaller specimens are popular as live Christmas trees. Eastern white pines are noted for holding their needles well, even long after being harvested. They also are well suited for people with allergies, as they give little to no aroma. A standard 1.8-meter (6 ft) tree takes approximately 6 to 8 years to grow in ideal conditions. Sheared varieties are usually desired because of their stereotypical Christmas tree conical shape, as naturally grown ones can become too thick for larger ornaments, or grow bushy in texture.*[23] The branches of the eastern white pine are also widely used in making holiday wreaths and garland because of their soft, feathery needles.

3.72.6 Symbolism

Eastern White Pine is the Provincial Tree of Ontario, Canada.*[24]

In the United States it is the State Tree of Maine (as of 1945)*[25] and Michigan (as of 1955).*[26] Its "pine cone and tassel" is also the State Flower of Maine.*[27] Sprigs of Eastern White Pine were worn as badges as a symbol of Vermont identity during the Vermont Republic and are depicted in a stained glass window in the Vermont State House, on the Flag of Vermont, and on the naval ensign of the Commonwealth of Massachusetts.

The Native American Haudenosaunee (Iroquois Confederation) denominated it the "Tree of Peace".

3.72.7 See also

- Giants in the Land

3.72.8 References

[1] Carey, Jennifer H. 1993. *Pinus strobus*. In: Fire Effects Information System, [Online]. U.S. Department of Agriculture, Forest Service, Rocky Mountain Research Station, Fire Sciences Laboratory (Producer). 2013, August 12 accessed 12 August 2013

[2] "*Pinus strobus*". Natural Resources Conservation Service PLANTS Database. USDA. Retrieved 13 January 2013.

[3] Moore, Gerry; Kershner, Bruce; Craig Tufts; Daniel Mathews; Gil Nelson; Spellenberg, Richard; Thieret, John W.; Terry Purinton; Block, Andrew (2008). *National Wildlife Federation Field Guide to Trees of North America*. New York: Sterling. p. 77. ISBN 1-4027-3875-7.

[4] Elbert L. Little. *National Audubon Society Field Guide to North American Trees: Eastern Region*. "Eastern White Pine", page 296. (New York, New York: Alfred A. Knopf, 1980)

[5] Beck, D.E. (1971). "Height-Growth Patterns and Site Index of White Pine in the Southern Appalachians". *Forest Science*. **17** (2): 252–260.

[6] NTS—Native Tree Society

[7] Luthringer, D.J. 2009. Big Trees of Cook Forest. Pennsylvania Forests 100(3):8-12.

[8] Jake Swamp Tree: 51.54m in August 2008.

[9] The Jake Swamp Tree was climbed and measured by tape drop in November 1998 and October 2001. It was scheduled to be climbed and measured a third time in November 2008.

[10] Ling, H. 2003. The Eastern White Pine. Native Plant Society of NJ Newsletter Winter 2003 pp 2–3.

[11] Lombard K. and J. Bofinger. 1999. White Pine Blister Rust. NH Div. of Forests and Lands.

[12] Cronon, William (1991). *Nature's Metropolis: Chicago and the Great West*. New York, NY: W. W. Norton and Company. p. 183.

[13] Thoreau, Henry David (1861). *The Writings of Henry David Thoreau: Journal*. p. 33.

[14] Hotchkiss, George Woodward (1861). *History of the Lumber and Forest Industry of the Northwest*. p. 752.

[15] Nizalowski, E. 1997. The mystery of the Pumpkin Pine. Newark Valley Historical Society, Newark, NY.

[16] Sloane, E. 1965. A Reverence for Wood. Balantine Books, NY.

[17] "History". Retrieved November 10, 2011.

[18] Erichsen-Brown, C. 1979. Medicinal and Other Uses of North American Plants. Dover Publications, NY.

[19] Native American Ethnobotany (University of Michigan – Dearborn), accessed 1.13.2013

[20] Fernald, M., A. Kinsey, and R. Rollins. 1943. Edible Wild Plants. Harper & Row, NY.

[21] from Lady Bird Johnson Wildflower Center Native Plant Information Network (NPIN); species account, horticultural information, + photographs . accessed 1.13.2013

[22] MBG —Missouri Botanical Garden Kemper Center for Home Gardening: *Pinus strobus* (eastern white pine) . accessed 1.13.2013

[23] Christmas tree.org

[24] Ontario Symbols. Accessed 13 January 2013.

[25] White Pine

[26] Eastern White Pine

[27] Netstate.com: Maine State Flower

- Conifer Specialist Group (1998). "*Pinus strobus*". IUCN Red List of Threatened Species. Version 2006. International Union for Conservation of Nature. Retrieved 12 May 2006.

- Pinetum.org: Cone photo from Arboretum de Villardebelle

- Eastern Native Tree Society – Boogerman Pine photo gallery

- The Monday Garden: The Eastern White Pine

3.72.9 External links

- *Pinus strobus* at the Encyclopedia of Life
- USDA Plants Profile for *Pinus strobus* (eastern white pine)
- EFLORAS—Flora of North America: *Pinus strobus* treatment
- EFLORAS: *P. strobus* Distribution map
- Gymnosperm Database: *Pinus strobus*
- Bioimages.vanderbilt.edu: *Pinus strobus* images
- *Pinus strobus* —U.C. Photo gallery
- *Pinus strobus* - information, genetic conservation units and related resources. European Forest Genetic Resources Programme (EUFORGEN)

3.73 Pinus thunbergii

Pinus thunbergii (Syn: *Pinus thunbergiana*), also called **black pine**,[1] **Japanese black pine**,[2] and **Japanese pine**, is a pine native to coastal areas of Japan(Kyūshū, Shikoku and Honshū) and South Korea.[3]

It is called *gomsol*(곰솔) in Korean, *hēisōng*(黑松) in Chinese, and *kuromatsu*(黒松) in Japanese.

3.73.1 Description

Black pines can reach the height of 40 m, but rarely achieves this size outside its natural range. The needles are in fascicles of two with a white sheath at the base, 7–12 cm long; female cones are 4–7 cm in length, scaled, with small points on the tips of the scales, taking two years to mature. Male cones are 1–2 cm long borne in clumps of 12-20 on the tips of the spring growth. Bark is gray on young trees and small branches, changing to black and plated on larger branches and the trunk; becoming quite thick on older trunks.

3.73.2 Ecology

In North America this tree is subject to widespread mortality by the native American pinewood nematode, *Bursaphelenchus xylophilus*, spread by means of beetle vectors. Subsequently, blue stain fungus invades the plant, leading to a rapid decline and death. This nematode has also been introduced to Japan accidentally, leading to the species becoming endangered in its native area.

3.73.3 Uses

Because of its resistance to pollution and salt, it is a popular horticultural tree. In Japan it is widely used as a garden tree both trained as Niwaki and untrained growing as an overstory tree. The trunks and branches are trained from a young age to be elegant and interesting to view. It is one of the classic bonsai subjects, requiring great patience over many years to train properly.

3.73.4 Images

- Pinus thunbergii var. corticata Bonsai

- Pinus thunbergiana var. corticata Bonsai

- Well trimmed, small in Ichikawa, Chiba

- Close up of trunk in Enoshima

- Pinus thunbergii var. Thunderhead

3.73.5 Notes

[1] *English Names for Korean Native Plants* (PDF). Pocheon: Korea National Arboretum. 2015. p. 575. ISBN 978-89-97450-98-5. Retrieved 17 December 2016 – via Korea Forest Service.

[2] "*Pinus thunbergii*". Natural Resources Conservation Service PLANTS Database. USDA. Retrieved 31 January 2016.

[3] eFloras, 2009

3.73.6 References

- Conifer Specialist Group (1998). "*Pinus thunbergii*". *IUCN Red List of Threatened Species. Version 2006*. International Union for Conservation of Nature. Retrieved 12 May 2006.

- eFloras, Missouri Botanical Garden & Harvard University Herbaria (FOC Vol. 4 Page 21), *Pinus thunbergii*, retrieved 2009 Check date values in: |access-date=, |date= (help)

3.73.7 External links

- Conifers Around the World: *Pinus thunbergii - Japanese Black Pine.*

3.74 Pinus virginiana

Pinus virginiana (**Virginia pine, scrub pine, Jersey pine**) is a medium-sized tree, often found on poorer soils from Long Island in southern New York south through the Appalachian Mountains to western Tennessee and Alabama. The usual size range for this pine is 9–18 m, but can grow taller under optimum conditions. The trunk can be as large as 0.5 m diameter. This tree prefers well-drained loam or clay, but will also grow on very poor, sandy soil, where it remains small and stunted. The typical life span is 65 to 90 years.

The short (4–8 cm), yellow-green needles are paired in fascicles and are often twisted. Pinecones are 4–7 cm long and may persist on the tree for many years, often (though not always) releasing their seeds in the second year. In growth habit, some trees may be inclined with twisted trunks.

This pine is useful for reforesting and provides nourishment for wildlife. Its other main use is on Christmas tree farms, despite having sharp-tipped needles and yellowish winter color. It also can provide wood pulp and lumber. Like some other southern yellow pines, Virginia Pine lumber case hardens. That is it becomes very hard over time during wood drying. Wood from Virginia pine is not normally considered to resist rot unless treated with preservatives.

3.74.1 Introduction

Pinus virginiana is a species of Pine.[*][2] Common names for the *Pinus virginiana* are the Virginia, Scrub and Jersey Pine.[*][2] *Pinus virginiana* has the following synonyms, *Pinus inops*[*][3] *Pinus ruthenica* and *Pinus turbinate*.[*][4] *Pinus virginiana* is a species in the order Pinales and the family Pinaceae. Pines are an evergreen tree. In general, pine trees were thought to have arisen anywhere from 153.1 million years ago to 271 million years ago.[*][5] *Pinus virginiana* is a perennial tree, which means that it lives for numerous years. They are also gymnosperms. Gymnosperms produce seeds, but they do not protect these seeds with an ovary or with fruit and they lack flowers.

3.74.2 Description

Pinus virginiana is a distinct pine in the United States and can be identified by a key characteristic the relatively short needles are twisted and come in bunches of two. The needles are typically are two to eight centimeters in length. There is hair on the bracts and on the bud scales of the *P. virginiana*. The leaf sheath of the *P. virginiana* is greater than 2.5 millimeters long. The cones of the *P. virginiana* only open after they are mature. The branches of the *Pinus virginiana* are flexible. They will bend when pressure is added to them.*[6] *Pinus virginiana* are between 9 and 18 meters tall. The bark of *P. virginiana* is red and brown in color, and also has the tendency to be rough with relatively small bark scales. The pollen cones are circular, almost elliptical and are 10–20 millimeters in size. They are the same color as the bark, typically. Seed cones are spread throughout the tree. The mature seed cones (4–7 cm) are much larger than the pollen cones.*[7] The *P. virginiana* prefers to grow in poor soils and dry loam or clay. They can grow on sandy soil, but this usually causes the tree to be smaller than the average *P. virginiana*.*[8]

3.74.3 Taxonomy

Pinus virginiana is in the family Pinaceae and the order Pinales.*[2] A molecular phylogeny indicates that the sister taxa to *Pinus virginiana* are *Pinus clausa*, *Pinus contorta*, and *Pinus banksiana*.*[9] *Pinus banksiana* has shorter needles than *P. viginiana* at 2–3.5 centimeters in length, whereas *P. virginiana* is 2–8 centimeters in length. *P. banksiana* needles are not twisted, but curved, and has cones that are serotinous and unarmed. The leaf sheaths in *P. banksiana* are less than 2.5 millimeters long. In *P. virginiana* the needles are twisted and straight. The cones open at maturity, are not serotinous and the scales on the cones have prominent prickles. The sheaths of the *P. virginiana* are greater than 2.5 millimeters long. *Pinus clausa* has larger needles than the *P. virginiana*. The *Pinus clausa* has needles that are between 5 and 13 centimeters long, *P. virginiana* has needles that range between 2 and 8 centimeters long. *Pinus clausa* is also serotinous.*[2] Lastly, *Pinus virginiana* and *Pinus contorta* are distributed differently: *Pinus virginiana* are found on the eastern side of the United States, whereas *Pinus contorta* are found on the western side.*[10] A similarity between *Pinus virginiana* and *Pinus contorta* is that the needles of both species are twisted.

3.74.4 Distribution and habitat

Pinus virginiana inhabit dry forested areas. The tree occurs in New York, New Jersey, Pennsylvania, Virginia, West Virginia, Ohio, Illinois, Kentucky, Tennessee, North Carolina, Georgia, Alabama, Mississippi,*[2] Indiana, South Carolina, Maryland and Delaware.*[7] In locations where the *P. virginiana* lives, rainfall is typically between 890 and 1400 millimeters. The average temperatures in the summer are between 21–24 degrees Celsius and in the winter it is around −4 to 4 degrees Celsius. *Pinus virginiana* is poorly adapted to fire, but if the tree is larger they are able to survive. Between the ages of 65–90 years they no longer reproduce, but they are able to live up to 150 years. The oldest recorded was 150 years old.*[9]

3.74.5 Ethnobotany

Cherokee Indians used *P. virginiana* medicinally. They used it for many symptoms like diarrhea, stiffness of the body, colds, fevers, hemorrhoids, tuberculosis, and constipation. Cherokee Indians used *P. virginiana* in different ways including bathing in water that had been soaked in the bark, steams and oils, root and needle infusions, and for tar. They also used it in certain cultural rituals. In burial rituals *P. virginiana* branches were burned and the ashes were used for a fire in their homes. Also, they would infuse needles in apple juice and they would drink it. The Cherokee basically did that as a toast to the wind. Lastly, they used the root infusions as a stimulant and the needles were used as a soap.*[9]

3.74.6 Etymology

The etymology of the *Pinus virginiana* is as follows: *Pinus* is Latin for Pine and *virginiana* means of Virginia.*[11]

3.74.7 Uses

Pinus virginiana was used historically as mine timbers, for railroad ties, and for fuel and tar. Currently, it is being planted as in reclamation sites for coal mining operations. *Pinus virginiana* can also be used for wood pulp, which is used to make paper, and for lumber.*[3]

3.74.8 Conservation

On the IUCN Red List of Threatened Species, the *Pinus virginiana* is considered a species that is of least concern. It is a species of least concern due to relative commonness as an early successional species. In areas of abandoned farmland in the eastern US, *P. virginiana* tends to be common.*[12]

3.74.9 Gallery

-  Cone closeup
-  Cone and needles
-  Bark
-  Bark closeup
-  New growth and pollen cones

3.74.10 References

[1] Farjon, A. (2013). "Pinus virginiana". *IUCN Red List of Threatened Species. Version 2013.1*. International Union for Conservation of Nature. Retrieved 16 July 2013.

[2] "Plants Profile for Pinus virginiana (Virginia pine)". United States Department of Agriculture Natural Resources Conservation Service. Retrieved 2016-11-02.

[3] "IPNI Plant Name Details". *ipni.org*. Retrieved 2016-12-06.

[4] GBIF. "Pinus virginiana Mill. - Checklist View". *www.gbif.org*. Retrieved 2016-12-06.

[5] "Angiosperm Phylogeny Website". *www.mobot.org*. Retrieved 2016-12-06.

[6] "Plants Profile for Pinus virginiana (Virginia pine)". *plants.usda.gov*. Retrieved 2016-12-06.

[7] "UNC Herbarium". *herbarium.unc.edu*. Retrieved 2016-12-06.

[8] "Home —The Plant List". *www.theplantlist.org*. Retrieved 2016-12-06.

[9] "Pinus virginiana (Virginia pine) description". *www.conifers.org*. Retrieved 2016-12-06.

[10] "BioWeb Home". *bioweb.uwlax.edu*. Retrieved 2016-12-06.

[11] Schoennagel, Tania; Veblen, Thomas T.; Romme, William H. (July 2004). "The Interaction of Fire, Fuels, and Climate across Rocky Mountain Forests" (PDF). *BioScience*. **54** (7): 661–676. ISSN 0006-3568.

[12] "Pinus virginiana (Scrub Pine, Virginia Pine)". *www.iucnredlist.org*. Retrieved 2016-12-06.

3.74.11 External links

- Flora of North America, Profile and map: *Pinus virginiana*
- *Pinus virginiana* images at bioimages.vanderbilt.edu

3.75 Podocarpus costalis

Podocarpus costalis, locally known as *Arius*,[1] is a species of conifer in the family Podocarpaceae. It is native to the Philippines and Taiwan.[2]

This plant is a shrublike tree which grows in island scrub, low forest, and bluff habitat. It is also widely cultivated as a garden plant.[2] It is used in bonsai.[2] The fruit is edible.[1]

One threat to the survival of wild populations is overcollecting for horticulture; this practice is illegal throughout its native range.[2]

3.75.1 References

[1] dela Cruz, R. Potential food products from "Batanes berries" explored. BAR Chronicle. Bureau of Agricultural Research, Philippines. June, 2012.

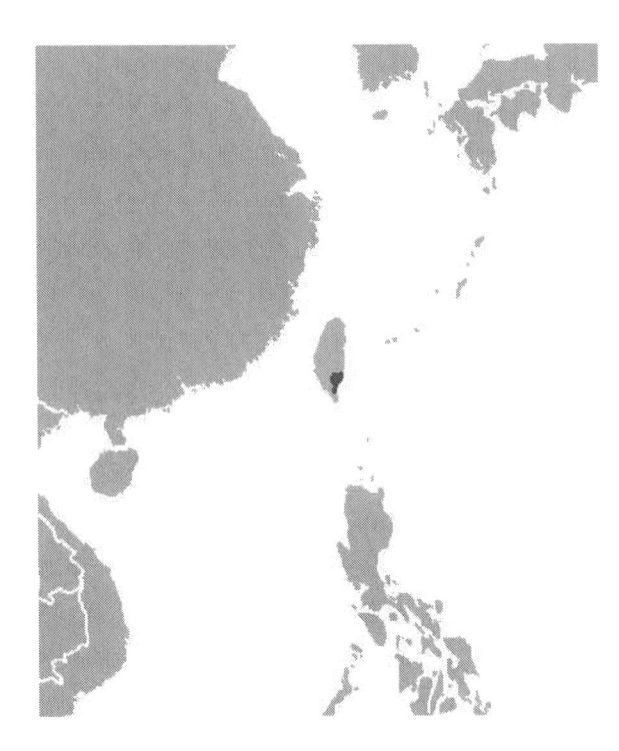

Podocarpus costalis *range*

[2] Carter, G. & Farjon, A. 2013. *Podocarpus costalis*. The IUCN Red List of Threatened Species. Version 2015.2. Downloaded on 03 September 2015.

3.76 Podocarpus latifolius

Podocarpus latifolius (**broad-leaved yellowwood** or **real yellowwood**, Afrikaans: *Opregte-geelhout*, Northern Sotho: *Mogôbagôba*, Xhosa: *Umcheya*, Zulu: *Umkhoba*)[*][1] is a large evergreen tree up to 35 m high and 3 m trunk diameter, in the conifer family Podocarpaceae; it is the type species of the genus *Podocarpus*.

The real yellowwood has been declared the national tree of South Africa and is protected here.[*][1]

3.76.1 Appearance

Detail of the characteristic foliage of the real yellowwood

The real yellowwood is a large evergreen tree that grows up to 30 meters in height. It grows relatively slowly but forms a wood of exceptional quality.

The leaves are strap-shaped, 25–40 mm long on mature trees, larger, to 100 mm long, on vigorous young trees, and 6–12 mm broad, with a bluntly pointed tip. The species name *"latifolius"* actually means *"wide-leaved"*. The bright-coloured foliage of new growth stands out against the dark leaves of mature foliage.

The cones of this dioecious tree are berry-like, with a single (rarely two) 7–11 mm seed apical on an 8–14 mm pink-purple aril; the aril is edible and sweet. The male (pollen) cones are 10–30 mm long.

3.76.2 Distribution

It is native to the moister southern and eastern areas of South Africa, from coastal areas of the Western Cape east to KwaZulu-Natal and north to eastern Limpopo. Pockets are naturally found further north in and around Zimbabwe.

It is commonly found in afro-temperate forests and often in mountainous areas. In harsh or exposed areas it tends to become stunted, small and dense.

3.76.3 Human usage

A young specimen growing on the slopes of Table Mountain

It is a slow-growing tree but exceptionally long-lived, and is increasingly grown as an ornamental feature in South African gardens. The unusual texture of the foliage is a reason for its growing popularity. The bright edible berries attract birds, which spread the seed.

The wood is hard, similar to yew wood, used for furniture, panelling, etc. Due to past over-exploitation, little is now cut.

3.76.4 References

[1] "Protected Trees" (PDF). Department of Water Affairs and Forestry, Republic of South Africa. 3 May 2013.

3.76.5 External links

- Conifer Specialist Group (1998). *"Podocarpus latifolius"*. *IUCN Red List of Threatened Species*. Version 2006. International Union for Conservation of Nature. Retrieved 12 May 2006.
- South African National Symbols
- *"Podocarpus latifolius"*. *Plantz Afrika*. Retrieved 2010-03-04.
- Images on iSpot
- Biodiversity Explorer

3.77 Pomegranate

For other uses, see Pomegranate (disambiguation).

The **pomegranate**, botanical name ***Punica granatum***, is

Young pomegranate trees

a fruit-bearing deciduous shrub or small tree in the family

Lythraceae that grows between 5 and 8 m (16 and 26 ft) tall.

The fruit is typically in season in the Northern Hemisphere from September to February,*[2] and in the Southern Hemisphere from March to May. As intact arils or juice, pomegranates are used in baking, cooking, juice blends, meal garnishes, smoothies, and alcoholic beverages, such as cocktails and wine.

The pomegranate originated in the region of modern-day Iran, and has been cultivated since ancient times throughout the Mediterranean region and northern India.*[3] It was introduced into Spanish America in the late 16th century and California, by Spanish settlers, in 1769.*[3]

Today, it is widely cultivated throughout the Middle East and Caucasus region, north and tropical Africa, the Indian subcontinent, Central Asia, the drier parts of southeast Asia, and parts of the Mediterranean Basin.*[3] It is also cultivated in parts of Arizona and California.*[4] In recent years, it has become more common in the commercial markets of Europe and the Western Hemisphere.*[3]*[4]

3.77.1 Etymology

An opened pomegranate

The name pomegranate derives from medieval Latin *pōmum* "apple" and *grānātum* "seeded".*[5] Possibly stemming from the old French word for the fruit, *pomme-grenade*, the pomegranate was known in early English as "apple of Grenada"—a term which today survives only in heraldic blazons. This is a folk etymology, confusing the Latin *granatus* with the name of the Spanish city of Granada, which derives from Arabic.*[6]

Garnet derives from Old French *grenat* by metathesis, from Medieval Latin *granatum* as used in a different meaning "of a dark red color". This derivation may have originated from *pomum granatum*, describing the color of pomegranate pulp, or from *granum*, referring to "red dye, cochineal".*[7]

The French term for pomegranate, *grenade*, has given its name to the military grenade.*[8]

3.77.2 Description

A shrub or small tree growing 6 to 10 m (20 to 33 ft) high, the pomegranate has multiple spiny branches and is extremely long-lived, with some specimens in France surviving for 200 years.*[3] *P. granatum* leaves are opposite or subopposite, glossy, narrow oblong, entire, 3–7 cm (1.2–2.8 in) long and 2 cm broad. The flowers are bright red and 3 cm in diameter, with three to seven petals.*[3] Some fruitless varieties are grown for the flowers alone.

The edible fruit is a berry, intermediate in size between a lemon and a grapefruit, 5–12 cm (2.0–4.7 in) in diameter with a rounded shape and thick, reddish skin.*[3] The number of seeds in a pomegranate can vary from 200 to about 1400.*[9] Each seed has a surrounding water-laden pulp —the edible sarcotesta that forms from the seed coat —ranging in color from white to deep red or purple. The seeds are "exarillate", i.e., unlike some other species in the order, Myrtales, no aril is present. The sarcotesta of pomegranate seeds consists of epidermis cells derived from the integument.*[10] The seeds are embedded in a white, spongy, astringent membrane.*[3]

3.77.3 Cultivation

P. granatum is grown for its fruit crop, and as ornamental trees and shrubs in parks and gardens. Mature specimens can develop sculptural twisted-bark multiple trunks and a distinctive overall form. Pomegranates are drought-tolerant, and can be grown in dry areas with either a Mediterranean winter rainfall climate or in summer rainfall climates. In wetter areas, they can be prone to root decay from fungal diseases. They can be tolerant of moderate frost, down to about −12 °C (10 °F).*[11]

Insect pests of the pomegranate can include the pomegranate butterfly *Virachola isocrates* and the leaf-footed bug *Leptoglossus zonatus*, and fruit flies and ants are attracted to unharvested ripe fruit.*[12] Pomegranate grows easily from seed, but is commonly propagated from 25 to 50 cm (9.8 to 19.7 in) hardwood cuttings to avoid the genetic variation of seedlings. Air layering is also an option for propagation, but grafting fails.*[3]

Illustration by Otto Wilhelm Thomé, 1885

and marketing, the most important of which are fruit size, exocarp color (ranging from yellow to purple, with pink and red most common), seed-coat color (ranging from white to red), hardness of seed, maturity, juice content and its acidity, sweetness, and astringency.*[15]

3.77.4 Cultural history

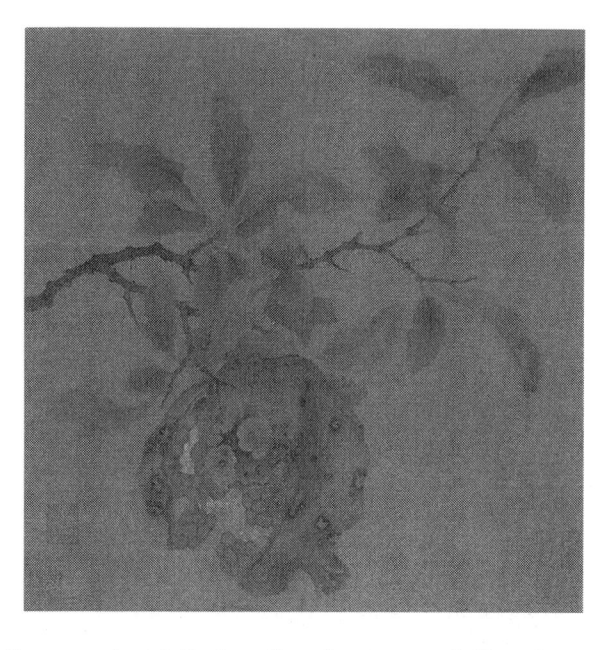

Pomegranate, *late Southern Song dynasty or early Yuan dynasty circa 1200–1340 (Los Angeles County Museum of Art)*

Pomegranate is native to a region from Iran to northern India.*[3] Pomegranates have been cultivated throughout the Middle East, South Asia, and Mediterranean region for several millennia, and also thrive in the drier climates of California and Arizona.*[3]*[16]*[17]

Carbonized exocarp of the fruit has been identified in early Bronze Age levels of Jericho in the West Bank, as well as late Bronze Age levels of Hala Sultan Tekke on Cyprus and Tiryns.*[18] A large, dry pomegranate was found in the tomb of Djehuty, the butler of Queen Hatshepsut in Egypt; Mesopotamian cuneiform records mention pomegranates from the mid-third millennium BC onwards.*[19]

It is also extensively grown in South China and in Southeast Asia, whether originally spread along the route of the Silk Road or brought by sea traders. Kandahar is famous in Afghanistan for its high-quality pomegranates.*[20]

Although not native to Korea or Japan, the pomegranate is widely grown there and many cultivars have been developed. It is widely used for bonsai because of its flowers and for the unusual twisted bark the older specimens can attain.*[21] The term "balaustine" (Latin: *balaustinus*) is

Varieties

P. granatum var. *nana* is a dwarf variety of *P. granatum* popularly planted as an ornamental plant in gardens and larger containers, and used as a bonsai specimen tree. It could well be a wild form with a distinct origin. It has gained the Royal Horticultural Society's Award of Garden Merit.*[13] The only other species in the genus *Punica* is the Socotran pomegranate (*P. protopunica*), which is endemic to the island of Socotra. It differs in having pink (not red) flowers and smaller, less sweet fruit.*[14]

Cultivars

P. granatum has more than 500 named cultivars, but evidently has considerable synonymy in which the same genotype is named differently across regions of the world.*[15]

Several characteristics between pomegranate genotypes vary for identification, consumer preference, preferred use,

3.77. POMEGRANATE

also used for a pomegranate-red color.*[22]

Coat of arms of Granada

The ancient city of Granada in Spain was renamed after the fruit during the Moorish period and today the province of Granada uses pomegranate as a charge in heraldry for its canting arms.

Spanish colonists later introduced the fruit to the Caribbean and America (Spanish America), but in the English colonies, it was less at home: "Don't use the pomegranate inhospitably, a stranger that has come so far to pay his respects to thee," the English Quaker Peter Collinson wrote to the botanizing John Bartram in Philadelphia, 1762. "Plant it against the side of thy house, nail it close to the wall. In this manner it thrives wonderfully with us, and flowers beautifully, and bears fruit this hot year. I have twenty-four on one tree... Doctor Fothergill says, of all trees this is most salutiferous to mankind." *[23]

The pomegranate had been introduced as an exotic to England the previous century, by John Tradescant the elder, but the disappointment that it did not set fruit there led to its repeated introduction to the American colonies, even New England. It succeeded in the South: Bartram received a barrel of pomegranates and oranges from a correspondent in Charleston, South Carolina, 1764. John Bartram partook of "delitious" pomegranates with Noble Jones at Wormsloe Plantation, near Savannah, Georgia, in September 1765. Thomas Jefferson planted pomegranates at Monticello in 1771: he had them from George Wythe of Williamsburg.*[24]

Culinary use

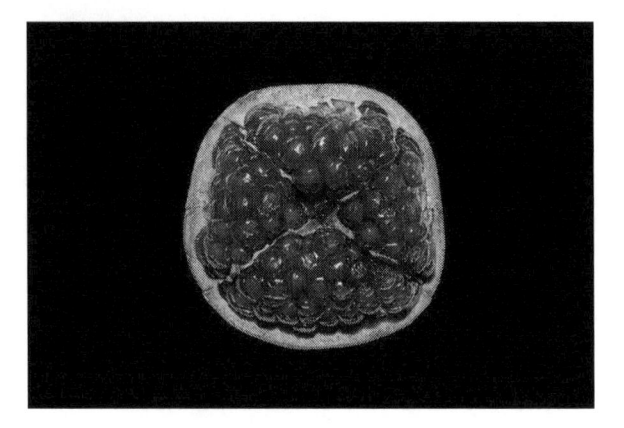

Half peeled pomegranate

Fresh pomegranate seeds revealed through peeling

After the pomegranate is opened by scoring it with a knife and breaking it open, the seeds are separated from the peel and internal white pulp membranes. Separating the seeds is easier in a bowl of water because the seeds sink and the inedible pulp floats. Freezing the entire fruit also makes it easier to separate. Another effective way of quickly harvesting the seeds is to cut the pomegranate in half, score each half of the exterior rind four to six times, hold the pomegranate half over a bowl, and smack the rind with a large spoon. The seeds should eject from the pomegranate directly into the bowl, leaving only a dozen or more deeply embedded seeds to remove.*[25] The entire seed is consumed raw, though the watery, tasty sarcotesta is the desired part. The taste differs depending on the variety or cultivar of pomegranate and its ripeness.

Pomegranate juice can be sweet or sour, but most fruits are moderate in taste, with sour notes from the acidic tannins contained in the juice. Pomegranate juice has long been a

A bowl of ash-e anar, *a Persian soup made with pomegranate juice*

popular drink in Europe, the Middle East and is now widely distributed in the United States and Canada.*[26]

Grenadine syrup long ago consisted of thickened and sweetened pomegranate juice, now is usually a sales name for a syrup based on various berries, citric acid, and food coloring, mainly used in cocktail mixing. In Europe, Bols still manufactures grenadine syrup with pomegranate.*[27] Before tomatoes, a New World fruit, arrived in the Middle East, pomegranate juice, molasses, and vinegar were widely used in many Iranian foods, and are still found in traditional recipes such as *fesenjān*, a thick sauce made from pomegranate juice and ground walnuts, usually spooned over duck or other poultry and rice, and in *ash-e anar* (pomegranate soup).*[28]*[29]

Pomegranate seeds are used as a spice known as *anardana* (from Persian: dana + anar, pomegranate + seed), most notably in Indian and Pakistani cuisine. Dried whole seeds can often be obtained in ethnic Indian subcontinent markets. These seeds are separated from the flesh, dried for 10–15 days, and used as an acidic agent for chutney and curry preparation. Ground *anardana* is also used, which results in a deeper flavoring in dishes and prevents the seeds from getting stuck in teeth. Seeds of the wild pomegranate variety known as *daru* from the Himalayas are regarded as quality sources for this spice.

Dried pomegranate seeds, found in some natural specialty food markets, still contain some residual water, maintaining a natural sweet and tart flavor. Dried seeds can be used in several culinary applications, such as trail mix, granola bars, or as a topping for salad, yogurt, or ice cream.

In the Caucasus, pomegranate is used mainly for juice.*[30] In Azerbaijan, a sauce from pomegranate juice *narsharab*, (from Persian: sharab + (a)nar, lit. "pomegranate wine") is usually served with fish*[31] or *tika kabab*. In Turkey, pomegranate sauce (Turkish: nar ekşisi) is used as a salad dressing, to marinate meat, or simply to drink straight. Pomegranate seeds are also used in salads and sometimes as garnish for desserts such as *güllaç*.*[32] Pomegranate syrup or molasses is used in *muhammara*, a roasted red pepper, walnut, and garlic spread popular in Syria and Turkey.*[33]

In Greece, pomegranate (Greek: ρόδι, *rodi*) is used in many recipes, including *kollivozoumi*, a creamy broth made from boiled wheat, pomegranates, and raisins, legume salad with wheat and pomegranate, traditional Middle Eastern lamb kebabs with pomegranate glaze, pomegranate eggplant relish, and avocado-pomegranate dip. Pomegranate is also made into a liqueur, and as a popular fruit confectionery used as ice cream topping, mixed with yogurt, or spread as jam on toast. In Cyprus and Greece, and among the Greek Orthodox Diaspora, ρόδι (Greek for pomegranate) is used to make *koliva*, a mixture of wheat, pomegranate seeds, sugar, almonds, and other seeds served at memorial services.

In Mexico, they are commonly used to adorn the traditional dish *chiles en nogada*, representing the red of the Mexican flag in the dish which evokes the green (poblano pepper), white (*nogada* sauce) and red (pomegranate seeds) tricolor.

In traditional medicine

In the Indian subcontinent's ancient Ayurveda system of traditional medicine, the pomegranate is frequently described as an ingredient in remedies.*[34]

3.77.5 Nutrition

A 100-g serving of pomegranate seeds provides 12% of the Daily Value (DV) for vitamin C, 16% DV for vitamin K and 10% DV for folate (table).

Pomegranate seeds are an excellent source of dietary fiber (20% DV) which is entirely contained in the edible seeds. People who choose to discard the seeds forfeit nutritional benefits conveyed by the seed fiber and micronutrients.*[35]

Pomegranate seed oil contains punicic acid (65.3%), palmitic acid (4.8%), stearic acid (2.3%), oleic acid (6.3%), and linoleic acid (6.6%).*[36]

3.77.6 Research

Juice

The most abundant phytochemicals in pomegranate juice are polyphenols, including the hydrolyzable tannins called ellagitannins formed when ellagic acid and/or gallic acid binds with a carbohydrate to form pomegranate ellagitannins, also known as punicalagins.*[37]

The red color of juice can be attributed to anthocyanins, such as delphinidin, cyanidin, and pelargonidin glycosides.*[38] Generally, an increase in juice pigmentation occurs during fruit ripening.*[38]

The phenolic content of pomegranate juice is adversely affected by processing and pasteurization techniques.*[39]

Peel

Compared to the pulp, the inedible pomegranate peel contains as much as three times the total amount of polyphenols,*[37] including condensed tannins,*[40] catechins, gallocatechins and prodelphinidins.*[41]

The higher phenolic content of the peel yields extracts for use in dietary supplements and food preservatives.*[42]*[43]*[44]

Health claims

Despite limited research data, manufacturers and marketers of pomegranate juice have liberally used results from preliminary research to promote products.*[45] In February 2010, the FDA issued a Warning Letter to one such manufacturer, POM Wonderful, for using published literature to make illegal claims of unproven anti-disease benefits.*[46]*[47]*[48]

3.77.7 Symbolism

Ancient Egypt

Ancient Egyptians regarded the pomegranate as a symbol of prosperity and ambition. According to the Ebers Papyrus, one of the oldest medical writings from around 1500 BC, Egyptians used the pomegranate for treatment of tapeworm and other infections.*[49]

Ancient and Modern Greece

The Greeks were familiar with the fruit far before it was introduced to Rome via Carthage, and it figures in multiple myths and artworks.*[50]

In Ancient Greek mythology, the pomegranate was known as the "fruit of the dead" and believed to have sprung from the blood of Adonis.*[49]*[51]

The myth of Persephone, the goddess of the underworld, prominently features the pomegranate. In one version of Greek mythology, Persephone was kidnapped by Hades and taken off to live in the underworld as his wife. Her mother, Demeter (goddess of the harvest), went into mourning for her lost daughter; thus all green things ceased to grow. Zeus, the highest-ranking of the Greek gods, could not allow the Earth to die, so he commanded Hades to return Persephone. It was the rule of the Fates that anyone who consumed food or drink in the underworld was doomed to spend eternity there. Persephone had no food, but Hades tricked her into eating six pomegranate seeds while she was still his prisoner, so she was condemned to spend six months in the underworld every year. During these six months, while Persephone sits on the throne of the underworld beside her husband Hades, her mother Demeter mourns and no longer gives fertility to the earth. This was an ancient Greek explanation for the seasons.*[52]

The number of seeds Persephone ate varies, depending on which version of the story is told. The number ranges from three to seven, which accounts for just one barren season if it is just three or four seeds, or two barren seasons (half the year) if she ate six or seven seeds. Dante Gabriel Rossetti's painting, *Persephona*, depicts Persephone holding the fatal fruit.

The pomegranate also evoked the presence of the Aegean Triple Goddess who evolved into the Olympian Hera, who is sometimes represented offering the pomegranate, as in the Polykleitos' cult image of the Argive Heraion (see below).

According to Carl A. P. Ruck and Danny Staples, the chambered pomegranate is also a surrogate for the poppy's narcotic capsule, with its comparable shape and chambered interior.*[53] On a Mycenaean seal illustrated in Joseph Campbell's *Occidental Mythology* (1964), figure 19, the seated Goddess of the double-headed axe (the labrys) offers three poppy pods in her right hand and supports her breast with her left. She embodies both aspects of the dual goddess, life-giving and death-dealing at once.

The Titan Orion was represented as "marrying" Side, a name that in Boeotia means "pomegranate", thus consecrating the primal hunter to the Goddess.

Other Greek dialects call the pomegranate *rhoa*; its possible connection with the name of the earth goddess Rhea, inexplicable in Greek, proved suggestive for the mythographer Karl Kerenyi, who suggested the consonance might ultimately derive from a deeper, pre-Indo-European language layer.

In the 5th century BC, Polycleitus took ivory and gold to sculpt the seated Argive Hera in her temple. She held a scepter in one hand and offered a pomegranate, like a "royal orb", in the other.*[54] "About the pomegranate I must say nothing," whispered the traveller Pausanias in the 2nd century, "for its story is somewhat of a holy mystery." *[54]

In the Orion story, Hera cast pomegranate-Side (an ancient city in Antalya) into dim Erebus — "for daring to rival Hera's beauty", which forms the probable point of connection with the older Osiris/Isis story. Since the ancient Egyptians identified the Orion constellation in the sky as Sah the "soul of Osiris", the identification of this section of the myth seems relatively complete. Hera wears, not a wreath nor a tiara nor a diadem, but clearly the calyx of the pomegranate that has become her serrated crown. The pomegranate has a calyx shaped like a crown. In Jewish tradition, it has been seen as the original "design" for the proper crown.*[55]

In some artistic depictions, the pomegranate is found in the hand of Mary, mother of Jesus.

A pomegranate is displayed on coins from the ancient city of Side, Pamphylia.*[56]

Within the Heraion at the mouth of the Sele, near Paestum, Magna Graecia, is a chapel devoted to the *Madonna del Granato*, "Our Lady of the Pomegranate", "who by virtue of her epithet and the attribute of a pomegranate must be the Christian successor of the ancient Greek goddess Hera", observes the excavator of the Heraion of Samos, Helmut Kyrieleis.*[57]

Girl with a pomegranate, *by William-Adolphe Bouguereau, 1875*

In modern times, the pomegranate still holds strong symbolic meanings for the Greeks. On important days in the Greek Orthodox calendar, such as the Presentation of the Virgin Mary and on Christmas Day, it is traditional to have at the dinner table *polysporia*, also known by their ancient name *panspermia*, in some regions of Greece. In ancient times, they were offered to Demeter and to the other gods for fertile land, for the spirits of the dead and in honor of compassionate Dionysus. When one buys a new home, it is conventional for a house guest to bring as a first gift a pomegranate, which is placed under/near the *ikonostasi* (home altar) of the house, as a symbol of abundance, fertility, and good luck. Pomegranates are also prominent at modern Greek weddings and funerals. When Greeks commemorate their dead, they make *kollyva* as offerings, which consist of boiled wheat, mixed with sugar and decorated with pomegranate. It is also traditional in Greece to break a pomegranate on the ground at weddings and on New Years. Pomegranate decorations for the home are very common in Greece and sold in most home goods stores.*[58]

Ancient Israel and Judaism

The pomegranate is mentioned or alluded to in the Bible many times. It is also included in coinage and various types of ancient and modern cultural works.

For example, pomegranates were known in Ancient Israel as the fruits which the scouts brought to Moses to demonstrate the fertility of the "promised land".*[59] The Book of Exodus*[60] describes the *me'il* ("robe of the ephod") worn by the Hebrew high priest as having pomegranates embroidered on the hem, alternating with golden bells which could be heard as the high priest entered and left the Holy of Holies. According to the Books of Kings,*[61] the capitals of the two pillars (Jachin and Boaz) that stood in front of Solomon's Temple in Jerusalem were engraved with pomegranates. Solomon is said to have designed his coronet based on the pomegranate's "crown" (calyx).*[55]

Some Jewish scholars believe the pomegranate was the forbidden fruit in the Garden of Eden.*[62] additionally, pomegranates are one of the Seven Species (Hebrew: שבעת המינים, *Shiv'at Ha-Minim*) of fruits and grains enumerated in the Hebrew Bible (Deuteronomy 8:8) as special products of the Land of Israel, and the Songs of Solomon contains this quote: "Thy lips are like a thread of scarlet, and thy speech is comely: thy temples are like a piece of a pomegranate within thy locks." (Song of Solomon 4:3).

It is traditional to consume pomegranates on Rosh Hashana because, with its numerous seeds, it symbolizes fruitfulness.*[62] Also, it is said to have 613 seeds, which corresponds with the 613 commandments of the Torah.*[63] This particular tradition is referred to in the opening pages of Ursula Dubosarsky's novel *Theodora's Gift*.*[64]

The pomegranate appeared on the ancient coins of Judea,

and when not in use, the handles of Torah scrolls are sometimes covered with decorative silver globes similar in shape to "pomegranates" (*rimmonim*).

Pomegranates symbolize the mystical experience in the Jewish mystical tradition, or kabbalah, with the typical reference being to entering the "garden of pomegranates" or pardes rimonim; this is also the title of a book by the 16th-century mystic Moses ben Jacob Cordovero.

In European Christian motifs

Detail from Madonna of the Pomegranate *by Sandro Botticelli, c. 1487 (Uffizi Gallery, Florence)*

In the earliest incontrovertible appearance of Christ in a mosaic, a 4th-century floor mosaic from Hinton St Mary, Dorset, now in the British Museum, the bust of Christ and the chi rho are flanked by pomegranates.[65] Pomegranates continue to be a motif often found in Christian religious decoration. They are often woven into the fabric of vestments and liturgical hangings or wrought in metalwork. Pomegranates figure in many religious paintings by the likes of Sandro Botticelli and Leonardo da Vinci, often in the hands of the Virgin Mary or the infant Jesus. The fruit, broken or bursting open, is a symbol of the fullness of Jesus' suffering and resurrection.[62]

In the Eastern Orthodox Church, pomegranate seeds may be used in *kolyva*, a dish prepared for memorial services, as a symbol of the sweetness of the heavenly kingdom.

Afghanistan

Main article: Pomegranate production in Afghanistan

Pomegranate, a favorite fall and winter fruit in Afghanistan, has mainly two varieties: one that is sweet and dark red with hard seeds growing in and around Kandhar province, and the other that has soft seeds with variable color growing in the central/northern region. The largest market for Afghan pomegranates is India followed by Pakistan, Russia, United Arab Emirates and Europe.

Armenia

The pomegranate is one of the main fruits in Armenian culture (alongside apricots and grapes). Its juice is famously used with Armenian food, heritage, or wine. The pomegranate is the symbol of Armenia and represents fertility, abundance, marriage. It is also a semi-religious icon.[66][67] For example, the fruit played an integral role in a wedding custom widely practiced in ancient Armenia: a bride was given a pomegranate fruit, which she threw against a wall, breaking it into pieces. Scattered pomegranate seeds ensured the bride future children.

The Color of Pomegranates, a movie directed by Sergei Parajanov, is a biography of the Armenian *ashug* Sayat-Nova (King of Song) which attempts to reveal the poet's life visually and poetically rather than literally.

Azerbaijan

Main article: Goychay Pomegranate Festival

Pomegranate is considered one of the symbols of Azerbaijan.[68] Annually in October, a cultural festival is held in Goychay, Azerbaijan known as the Goychay Pomegranate Festival. The festival features Azerbaijani fruit-cuisine mainly the pomegranates from Goychay, which is famous for its pomegranate growing industry. At the festival, a parade is held with traditional Azerbaijani dances and Azerbaijani music.[69] Pomegranate was depicted on the official logo of the 2015 European Games held in Azerbaijan.[70] Nar the Pomegranate was one of the two mascots of these games.[71] Pomegranates were also featured on the jackets worn by Azerbaijani male athletes at the games' opening ceremony.[72]

Iran and ancient Persia

Iran is the second largest producer and largest exporter of pomegranates in the world. The fruit's juice and paste have

Black pomegranate

a role in Iranian cuisine, e.g. chicken, ghormas, and refreshment bars. Pomegranate skins may be used to stain wool and silk in the carpet industry.

The Pomegranate Festival is an annual cultural and artistic festival held during October in Tehran, to exhibit and sell pomegranates, food products, and handicrafts.

Pakistan

The pomegranate (known as "anār" in Urdu) is a popular fruit in Pakistan. It is grown in Pakistan and is also imported from Afghanistan.

India

In some Hindu traditions, the pomegranate (Hindi: *anār*) symbolizes prosperity and fertility, and is associated with both *Bhoomidevi* (the earth goddess) and Lord Ganesha (*the one fond of the many-seeded fruit*).*[73]*[74] The Tamil name *maadulampazham* is a metaphor for a woman's mind. It is derived from, *maadhu*=woman, *ullam*=mind, which means as the seeds are hidden, it is not easy to decipher a woman's mind.

The pomegranate is regarded as a symbol of fertility in China

China

Introduced to China during the Tang Dynasty (618-907 AD), the pomegranate (Chinese: 石榴; pinyin: *shíliu*) in olden times was considered an emblem of fertility and numerous progeny. This symbolism is a pun on the Chinese character 子 (*zǐ*) which, as well as meaning seed, also means "offspring" thus a fruit containing so many seeds is a sign of fecundity. Pictures of the ripe fruit with the seeds bursting forth were often hung in homes to bestow fertility and bless the dwelling with numerous offspring, an important facet of traditional Chinese culture.*[75]

3.77.8 Gallery

- Pomegranate blossom before petal fall

- Pomegranate sepals and drying stamens after fertilization and petal fall

- Unripened pomegranate fruit on a small tree in India

- A mature pomegranate fruit

3.77.9 References

[1] "*Punica granatum* L., The Plant List, Version 1". Royal Botanic Gardens, Kew and Missouri Botanical Garden. 2010.

[2] "Pomegranate". Department of Plant Sciences, University of California at Davis, College of Agricultural & Environmental Sciences, Davis, CA. 2014. Retrieved 29 January 2017.

[3] Morton JF (1987). "Pomegranate, *Punica granatum* L.". *Fruits of Warm Climates*. Purdue New Crops Profile. pp. 352–5. Retrieved 2012-06-14.

[4] "Pomegranate. California Rare Fruit Growers". Crfg.org. Retrieved 2012-06-14.

[5] "Etymology of *pomegranate*". Online Etymology Dictionary, Douglas Harper. 2015.

[6] "All hail the Pomegranate, official symbol of Granada".

[7] Harper, Douglas. "garnet". *Online Etymology Dictionary*.

[8] Harper, Douglas (8 October 2011). "Grenade". *Online Etymology Dictionary*.

[9] "Does a larger pomegranate yield more seeds?". AquaPhoenix.

[10] Dahlgren, R. And R. F. Thorne; Thorne (1984). "The order Myrtales: circumscription, variation, and relationships". *Annals of the Missouri Botanical Garden*. **71** (3): 633–699. doi:10.2307/2399158. JSTOR 2399158.

[11] M.D. Sheets, former research assistant, M.L. DuBois, former research assistant, J.G. Williamson, professor, Horticultural Sciences Department, JCooperative Extension Service, Institute of Food and Agricultural Sciences, University of Florida Gainesville FL 32611 - "The Pomegranate" ([PDF]) - Retrieved December 24, 2012

[12] Ingels, Chuck, et. al. (2007). *The Home Orchard: Growing Your Own Deciduous Fruit and Nut Trees*. University of California Agriculture and Natural Resources. p. 26.

[13] "RHS Plant Selector - *Punica granatum* var. *nana*". Retrieved 27 June 2013.

[14] "Punica granatum - the Drops of Blood from Garden of Eden".

[15] Stover E, Mercure EW (August 2007). "The pomegranate: a new look at the fruit of paradise". *HortScience*. **42** (5): 1088–92.

[16] Doijode, S. D. (2001). *Seed storage of horticultural crops*. New York: Food Products Press. p. 77. ISBN 1-56022-883-0.

[17] George Ripley; Charles Anderson Dana (1875). *The American cyclopaedia: a popular dictionary of general knowledge, Volume 13*. Appleton. ... frequent reference is made to it in the Mosaic writings, and sculptured representations of the fruit are found on the ancient monuments of Egypt and in the Assyrian ruins. It is found in a truly wild state only in northern India ...

[18] Still, D. W. (2006). "Pomegranate: A botanical perspective". In Seeram, Navindra P.; Schulman, Risa N.; Heber, David. *Pomegranates: ancient roots to modern medicine*. CRC Press. pp. 199–2010. ISBN 978-0-8493-9812-4.

[19] Hopf, Maria; Zohary, Daniel (2000). *Domestication of plants in the old world: the origin and spread of cultivated plants in West Asia, Europe, and the Nile Valley* (3rd ed.). Oxford [Oxfordshire]: Oxford University Press. p. 171. ISBN 0-19-850356-3.

[20] "Pomegranate —Afghan Agriculture". *afghanag.ucdavis.edu*. University of California at Davis, International Programs. 2013. Retrieved 2017-02-17.

[21] "History of Science: Cyclopædia, or, An universal dictionary of arts and sciences". Digicoll.library.wisc.edu. Retrieved 2012-06-14.

[22] Osborne, Roy; Pavey, Don (2003). *On Colours 1528: A Translation from Latin*. Parkland, Fla: Universal Publishers. ISBN 1-58112-580-1.

[23] Leighton, Ann (1986). *American gardens in the eighteenth century: "for use or for delight"*. Amherst: University of Massachusetts Press. p. 242. ISBN 0-87023-531-1.

[24] Leighton, *American Gardens*, p. 272.

[25] "How to de-seed a pomegranate". Gourmet.com. 2008.

[26] Tundel, Nikki (2007-04-20). "The pomegranate hits the peak of popularity". Minnesota Public Radio News.

[27] "BOLS Grenadine Syrup". *www.bols.de* (in German). Retrieved 11 January 2014.

[28] Burke, Andrew (15 July 2008). *Iran*. Lonely Planet. p. 82. ISBN 978-1-74104-293-1. Retrieved 2010-11-29. The anar (pomegranate) is native to the region around Iran and is eaten fresh and incorporated in a range of Persian dishes most famously in *fesenjun*, but also in *ash-e-anar* (pomegranate soup) and in rich red *ab anar* (pomegranate juice).

[29] "Ash-e Anar". Internetserver.com. Retrieved 2012-06-14.

[30] Bulletin —Page 52 by United States Bureau of Plant Industry, Division of Plant Industry, Queensland

[31] *Culinary cultures of Europe*, Council of Europe, 2005, p. 72

[32] Akgün, Müge (2006-09-22). "Güllaç, a dainty and light dessert". *Turkish Daily News*. Istanbul: DYH. Archived from the original on 2008-05-23. Retrieved 2007-12-26.

[33] Malouf, Greg and Lucy (2006). *Saha*. Australia: Hardie Grant Books. p. 46. ISBN 0-7946-0490-0.

[34] K. K. Jindal; R. C. Sharma (2004). *Recent trends in horticulture in the Himalayas*. Indus Publishing. ISBN 81-7387-162-0. ... bark of tree and rind of fruit is commonly used in ayurveda ... also used for dyeing ...

[35] Nutrition data for raw pomegranate, Nutritiondata.com

[36] Antioxidant and eicosanoid enzyme inhibition properties of pomegranate seed oil and fermented juice flavonoids. Shay Yehoshua Schubert, Ephraim Philip Lansky and Ishak Neeman, Journal of Ethnopharmacology, Volume 66, Issue 1, July 1999, Pages 11–17, doi:10.1016/S0378-8741(98)00222-0

[37] Singh, R. P.; Chidambara Murthy, K. N.; Jayaprakasha, G. K. (2002). "Studies on the Antioxidant Activity of Pomegranate (Punica granatum) Peel and Seed Extracts Using in Vitro Models". *Journal of Agricultural and Food Chemistry*. **50** (1): 81–6. doi:10.1021/jf010865b. PMID 11754547.

[38] Hernández F, Melgarejo P, Tomás-Barberán FA, Artés F (1999). "Evolution of juice anthocyanins during ripening of new selected pomegranate (Punica granatum) clones". *European Food Research and Technology*. **210** (1): 39–42. doi:10.1007/s002170050529.

[39] Influence of processing and pasteurization on color values and total phenolic compounds of pomegranate juice. Neslihan Alper, K. Savas Bahçeci and Jale Acar, Journal of Food Processing and Preservation, October 2005, Volume 29, Issue 5-6, pages 357–368, doi:10.1111/j.1745-4549.2005.00033.x

[40] Quantitative determination of the polyphenolic content of pomegranate peel. C. Ben Nasr, N. Ayed, and M. Metche, Zeitschrift für Lebensmittel-Untersuchung und Forschung, 1996, Volume 203, Issue 4, pages 374-378, doi:10.1007/BF01231077

[41] Plumb GW, De Pascual-Teresa S, Santos-Buelga C, Rivas-Gonzalo JC, Williamson G (2002). "Antioxidant properties of gallocatechin and prodelphinidins from pomegranate peel". *Redox Rep*. **7** (41): 41–6. doi:10.1179/135100002125000172. PMID 11981454.

[42] Chidambara Murthy, K. N.; Jayaprakasha, G. K.; Singh, R. P. (2002). "Studies on Antioxidant Activity of Pomegranate (Punica granatum) Peel Extract Using in Vivo Models". *Journal of Agricultural and Food Chemistry*. **50** (17): 4791. doi:10.1021/jf0255735. PMID 12166961.

[43] Li, Y.; Guo, C.; Yang, J.; Wei, J.; Xu, J.; Cheng, S. (2006). "Evaluation of antioxidant properties of pomegranate peel extract in comparison with pomegranate pulp extract". *Food Chemistry*. **96** (2): 254. doi:10.1016/j.foodchem.2005.02.033.

[44] Negi, P. S.; Jayaprakasha, G. K.; Jena, B. S. (2003). "Antioxidant and antimutagenic activities of pomegranate peel extracts". *Food Chemistry*. **80** (3): 393. doi:10.1016/S0308-8146(02)00279-0.

[45] "Pomegranate: superfood or fad?". UK National Health Service (NHS).

[46] "Pom Wonderful Warning Letter". U.S. Food and Drug Administration. Retrieved 2011-03-24.

[47] "Understanding Front-of-Package Violations: Why Warning Letters Are Sent to Industry". Retrieved 2011-03-24.

[48] Starling S (March 3, 2010). "FDA says Pom Wonderful antioxidant claims not so wonderful". NutraIngredients.com. Retrieved March 6, 2010.

[49] Jayaprakasha, G. K.; Negi, P.S.; Jena, B.S. (2006). "Antimicrobial activities of pomegranate". In Seeram, Navindra P.; Schulman, Risa N.; Heber, David. *Pomegranates: ancient roots to modern medicine*. CRC Press. p. 168. ISBN 978-0-8493-9812-4.

[50] Hodgson, Robert Williard (1917). *The pomegranate. Issue 276 of Bulletin*. California Agricultural Experiment Station. p. 165.

[51] Graves, Robert (1992). *The Greek Myths*. Penguin Books. p. 95. ISBN 9780140171990.

[52] Ovid. *Metamorphoses*. **V**. pp. 385–571.

[53] Staples, Danny; Ruck, Carl A. P. (1994). *The world of classical myth: gods and goddesses, heroines and heroes*. Durham, N.C.: Carolina Academic Press. ISBN 0-89089-575-9.

[54] "Pausanias, Description of Greece". *2,17,4*. Loeb Classical Library. Retrieved 30 November 2011.

[55] *Parashat Tetzaveh*, Commentary by Peninnah Schram, Congregation B'nai Jeshurun, New York

[56] Sear, David R. (1978). *Greek coins and their values*. London: Seaby. ISBN 0-900652-46-2.

[57] Kyrieleis, "The Heraion at Samos" in *Greek Sanctuaries: New Approaches*, Nanno Marinatos and Robin Hägg, eds. 1993, p. 143.

[58] Christmas Traditions in Greece by folklorist Thornton B. Edwards

[59] *Why Hebrew Goes from Right to Left: 201 Things You Never Knew about Judaism*, Ronald H. Isaacs (Newark, 2008), page 129

[60] 28:33–34

[61] 7:13–22

[62] "A Pomegranate for All Religions" by Nancy Haught, *Religious News Service*

[63] "What's the Truth about ... Pomegranate Seeds?". *Ou.org*. June 5, 2008. Retrieved 2012-06-14.

[64] Dubosarsky, Ursula. *Theodora's Gift*. Retrieved July 6, 2012.

[65] Paul Stephenson, *Constantine, Roman Emperor, Christian Victor*, 2010:1 and fig. 1.

[66] Dewey, Susan (2008). *Hollow Bodies: Institutional Responses to Sex Trafficking in Armenia, Bosnia, and India*. Kumarian Press. p. 92. ISBN 9781565492653.

[67] Verotta, Luisella; Macchi, Maria Pia; Venkatasubramanian, Padma, eds. (2015). *Connecting Indian Wisdom and Western Science: Plant Usage for Nutrition and Health*. CRC Press. ISBN 1482299755.

[68] European Games goes Gaga, Azeris jeer Armenians. *Times of India*. 13 June 2015. Retrieved 1 September 2015.

[69] iguide.travel Goychay Activities: Pomegranate Festival

[70] Korram, Andy. "The "European Games, Baku 2015" disclosed their official logo". *en.mastaekwondo.com*. Retrieved 25 June 2014.

[71] "Baku 2015 European Games Unveils Official Mascots Jeyran And Nar". *www.baku2015.com*. Retrieved 26 November 2014.

[72] Lucie Janik. Azerbaijan National Team Wears Scervino. *WWD*. 11 June 2015. Retrieved 1 September 2015.

[73] Suresh Chandra (1998). *Encyclopaedia of Hindu Gods and Goddesses*. Sarup & Sons. ISBN 81-7625-039-2. ... *Bhumidevi (the earth goddess) ... Attributes: ... pomegranate ...*

[74] Vijaya Kumar (2006). *Thousand Names of Ganesha*. Sterling Publishers. ISBN 81-207-3007-0. ... *Beejapoori ... the pomegranate in His hand is symbolic of bounteous wealth, material as well as spiritual ...*

[75] Doré S.J., Henry; Kennelly, S.J. (Translator), M. (1914). *Researches into Chinese Superstitions*. Tusewei Press, Shanghai. Vol V p. 722

3.77.10 Further reading

- Seeram, N. P.; Schulman, R. N.; Heber, D., eds. (2006). *Pomegranates: Ancient Roots to Modern Medicine*. CRC Press. ISBN 978-0-8493-9812-4.

- Amos Fawole, Olaniyi; Linus Opara, Umezuruike (2013). "Developmental changes in maturity indices of pomegranate fruit: A descriptive review". *Sci. Hort.* **159**: 152–161. doi:10.1016/j.scienta.2013.05.016.

3.77.11 External links

- The dictionary definition of pomegranate at Wiktionary

- Media related to Punica granatum at Wikimedia Commons

- Pomegranate - Trusted Health Information (MedlinePlus)

3.78 Portulacaria afra

Portulacaria afra (known as **elephant bush**, **dwarf jade plant**, **porkbush** and *spekboom* in Afrikaans) is a small-leaved succulent plant found in South Africa.

3.78.1 Description

It is a soft-wooded, semi-evergreen upright shrub or small tree, usually 2.5–4.5 metres (8–15 ft) tall. Similar in appearance to the unrelated "jade plant" *Crassula ovata* (family Crassulaceae), *P. afra* has smaller and rounder pads and more compact growth (shorter internodal spaces, down to 1.5 mm). It is much hardier, faster growing, more loosely branched, and has more limber tapering branches than *Crassula* once established.*[1]

Within the genus *Portulacaria*, it has been shown to be an outlier, relatively unrelated to the other species in the genus, which are all restricted to small ranges in the arid far west of southern Africa.*[2]

3.78.2 Distribution and habitat

It is very widespread in the east of South Africa (including Swaziland). In this moist climate, it is relatively rare, and tends to favour dryer rocky outcrops and slopes.

It is also found in much denser numbers in the dryer southern Cape. Here it occurs from the "Little Karoo" of the Western Cape, eastwards up until the thicket vegetation of the Eastern Cape.*[3] Spekboom is found most prolifically in the Albany thickets, a woodland ecoregion, which locally is often called *noorsveld*, after the high number of succulent *Euphorbia* species, which are often called *noors* plants.

3.78.3 Cultivation and uses

"Prostrata" decumbent variety

In the wilds of South Africa, large plants do survive the winter frosts by growing dense enough to provide their own natural cover. Drought-tolerant and fire-resistant, it will endure desert sun and heat once established, which the jade plant will not. Cuttings root very easily in most potting media.

Ornamental

P. afra *cultivated as a bonsai*

It is popular as an indoor bonsai,*[4] and as a hardy xeriscaping plant. Several varieties exist - some bred in cultivation, others naturally occurring:*[5]

- "**Limpopo**": A variety with much larger leaves. It is the natural form from the far north of the species' range.

- "**Prostrata**": A low-lying, decumbent form that is frequently used as a ground-cover.

- "**Aurea**": A compact, upright form with rounded leaves that go bright yellow in the sun.

- "**Foliis variegatus**": A variegated form.

- "**Medio-picta**": Variegated with a lighter centre.

Food source

In southern Africa it is commonly eaten, usually as one component of a salad or a soup.

Carbon sequestration

It is capable of either C₃ or CAM carbon fixation, depending on factors such as the season and the age of the leaves.*[3]

3.78.4 References

[1] "*Portulacaria afra* Monograph". Pyramid Dancer. Retrieved 2011-01-20.

[2] P.Bruyns, M.Oliveira-Neto, G.F. Melo de Pinna, C.Klak: *Phylogenetic relationships in the Didiereaceae with special reference to subfamily Portulacarioideae.* Taxon 63 (5). October 2014. 1053-1064.

[3] Lonnie J. Guralnick, Patricia A. Rorabaugh & Zac Hanscom, III (1984). "Seasonal shifts of photosynthesis in *Portulacaria afra* (L.) Jacq.". *Plant Physiology.* **76** (3): 643–646. doi:10.1104/pp.76.3.643. PMC 1064348⊘. PMID 16663899.

[4] D'Cruz, Mark. "Ma-Ke Bonsai Care Guide for *Portulacaria afra*". Ma-Ke Bonsai. Retrieved 2010-12-07.

[5] "Portulacaria afra". Plantzafrica.com. Retrieved 2015-10-05.

3.79 Portulacaria pygmaea

Portulacaria pygmaea (previously *Ceraria pygmaea*), also known as the **Pygmy porkbush**, is a small-leaved dwarf succulent plant found on the border between Namibia and South Africa.

3.79.1 Description

It is a small, compact, soft-wooded, dwarf shrub with bisexual flowers. Its blue-green leaves are semi-evergreen. Its tiny compact branches spread, and often droop, staying close to the ground. It also develops a thick caudex or rootstock, which has led to it being a popular bonsai specimen.

Within the genus *Portulacaria* it is most closely related to its larger sister-species *Portulacaria fruticulosa.**[1]

3.79.2 References

[1] P.Bruyns, M.Oliveira-Neto, G.F. Melo de Pinna, C.Klak: *Phylogenetic relationships in the Didiereaceae with special reference to subfamily Portulacarioideae.* Taxon 63 (5). October 2014. 1053-1064.

3.80 Prunus serrulata

For cherry blossoms and their cultural significance to the Japanese, see sakura.

Prunus serrulata or **Japanese cherry**;*[1] also called **hill cherry**, **oriental cherry** or **East Asian cherry**, is a species of cherry native to Japan, Korea and China and is used for its spring cherry blossom displays and festivals.

3.80.1 Description

Prunus serrulata is a small deciduous tree with a short single trunk, with a dense crown reaching a height of 26–39 feet (7.9–11.9 m). The smooth bark is chestnut-brown, with prominent horizontal lenticels. The leaves are arranged alternately, simple, ovate-lanceolate, 5–13 cm long and 2.5–6.5 cm broad, with a short petiole and a serrate or doubly serrate margin. At the end of autumn, the green leaves turn yellow, red or crimson.

Flowers

Main article: Cherry blossom

The flowers are produced in racemose clusters of two to five together at nodes on short spurs in spring at the same time as the new leaves appear; they are white to pink, with five petals in the wild type tree. The fruit is a globose black drupe 8–10 mm diameter.

3.80.2 Cultivation

Prunus serrulata is widely grown as a flowering ornamental tree, both in its native countries and throughout the temperate regions of the world. Numerous cultivars have been selected, many of them with double flowers with the stamens replaced by additional petals.

In cultivation in Europe and North America, it is usually grafted on to *Prunus avium* roots; the cultivated forms rarely bear fruit. It is viewed as part of the Japanese custom of Hanami.

The National Cherry Blossom Festival is a spring celebration in Washington, D.C., commemorating the 1912 gift of *Prunus serrulata* Japanese cherry trees from Tokyo to the city of Washington. They are planted in the Tidal Basin park.

Varieties and cultivars

There are several varieties:

- *Prunus serrulata* var. *serrulata* (syn. var. *spontanea*). Japan, Korea, China.

- *Prunus serrulata* var. *hupehensis* (Ingram) Ingram. Central China. Not accepted as distinct by the *Flora of China*.

- *Prunus serrulata* var. *lannesiana* (Carrière) Makino (syn. *Cerasus lannesiana* Carrière; *Prunus lannesiana* (Carrière) E. H. Wilson). Japan.

- *Prunus serrulata* var. *pubescens* (Makino) Nakai. Korea, northeastern China.

- *Prunus serrulata* var. *spontanea* (Maxim.) E. H. Wilson (syn. *Prunus jamasakura* Siebold ex Koidz.)

Some important cultivars include:

- 'Amonogawa'. Fastigiate cherry, with columnar habit; flowers semi-double, pale pink.

- 'Kwanzan'. = 'Sekiyama', 'Kanzan', or 'Kansan'.[2] Kanzan Cherry. Flowers pink, double; young leaves bronze-coloured at first, becoming green.

- 'Kiku-shidare'. Cheal's Weeping Cherry. Stems weeping; flowers double, pink. Tends to be short-lived.

- 'Shirofugen'. Flowers double, deep pink at first, fading to pale pink.

- 'Shirotae'. Mt. Fuji Cherry. Very low, broad crown with nearly horizontal branching; flowers pure white, semi-double.

- 'Tai Haku'. Great White Cherry. Flowers single, white, very large (up to 8 cm diameter); young leaves bronze-coloured at first, becoming green.

- 'Ukon'.

3.80.3 References

[1] "BSBI List 2007". Botanical Society of Britain and Ireland. Archived from the original (xls) on 2015-02-25. Retrieved 2014-10-17.

[2] Arthur Lee Jacobson. "Plant of the Month: April 2005: Japanese Sato zakura in Seattle: Prunus cultivars". Retrieved 21 October 2011.

3.80.4 Further reading

- Rushforth, K. (1999). *Trees of Britain and Europe*. Collins ISBN 0-00-220013-9.

- Flora of China: *Cerasus serrulata*

- NC State University: *Prunus serrulata*

- Arborist's photo: size potential for *Prunus serrulata* 'Shirotae' ('Mt. Fuji')

3.80.5 Gallery

- *Prunus serrulata* – Cherry blossoms.

- 'Ukon' Prunus lannesiana Wilson cv. Grandiflora

- Typical autumn foliage

-  Buds on cultivar 'Kanzan'

-  Flower close up

- [image]

- [image]

- Leaf close up

-  Kurozome, the tree spirit of the Japanese Cherry Tree

-  Flowers on 'Kanzan'

-  Flowers on 'Kanzan'

3.80.6 External links

3.81 Pseudocydonia

Not to be confused with *Carica papaya*, papaya, which, like *Pseudocydonia sinensis*, is sometimes called *mugua*.

Not to be confused with *Chaenomeles speciosa*, Chinese flowering quince, which, like *P. sinensis*, is sometimes called *mugua*.

Pseudocydonia sinensis, the **Chinese quince**, is a

Chinese quince fruits

deciduous or semi-evergreen tree in the family Rosaceae, native to eastern Asia in China, and the sole species in the genus **Pseudocydonia**. It is closely related to the east Asian genus *Chaenomeles*, and is sometimes placed in *Chaenomeles* as *C. sinensis*,[3] but notable differences are the lack of thorns, and that the flowers are produced singly, not in clusters. The Chinese quince is also closely related to the European Quince genus *Cydonia*;[4] notable differences include the serrated leaves, and lack of fuzz.

In China, the species is called *"mugua"*, while in Korea, it is called *"mogwa"* (hangul: ⊠⊠; Chinese/hanja: 木瓜 - not to be confused with *"papaya"*, whose Chinese transliteration is also called 木瓜) which is used for medicine or for making beverages, such as mogwacha.*[5] In Japan, it is known as *"karin - 花梨"* (literally, "flowering pear" *[note 1]).

It grows to 10–18 m tall, with a dense, twiggy crown. The leaves are alternately arranged, simple, 6–12 cm long and 3–6 cm broad, and have a serrated margin. The flowers are 2.5–4 cm diameter, with five pale pink petals; flowering is in mid spring. The fruit is a large ovoid pome 12–17 cm long with five carpels; it gives off an intense, sweet smell and it ripens in late autumn.

3.81.1 Uses

The fruit is hard and astringent, though it does soften and becomes less astringent after a period of frost. It can be used in the same way as quince is used for making jam. It is also grown as an ornamental tree in southern Europe.

The wood of this plant is frequently used in Japan for making low-end shamisen.

The fruit is used extensively in Traditional Chinese Medicine to treat rheumatoid arthritis (termed as "damp bi syndrome").*[6] Recent pharmacological studies suggest extracts of phytochemicals in the fruit have antioxidant and antiviral properties.*[7]

3.81.2 See also

- the flowering quinces, genus *Chaenomeles*
- the "true" Quince (*Cydonia oblonga*)

3.81.3 References

[1] 花 - a flower, 梨 - the pear species, *Pyrus pyrifolia*, also called "Asian pear," or "nashi"

[1] Potter, D.; Eriksson, T.; Evans, R. C.; Oh, S.; Smedmark, J. E. E.; Morgan, D. R.; Kerr, M.; Robertson, K. R.; et al. (2007). "Phylogeny and classification of Rosaceae". *Plant Systematics and Evolution*. **266** (1–2): 5–43. doi:10.1007/s00606-007-0539-9. [Referring to the subfamily by the name "Spiraeoideae"]

[2] "USDA GRIN Taxonomy".

[3] Gu Cuizhi and Stephen A. Spongberg, 2003. *Flora of China* (entry under *Chaenomeles sinensis*)

[4] Campbell, C.S.; Evans, R.C.; Morgan, D.R.; Dickinson, T.A.; Arsenault, M.P. (2007). "Phylogeny of subtribe Pyrinae (formerly the Maloideae, Rosaceae): Limited resolution of a complex evolutionary history" (PDF). *Plant Systematics and Evolution*. **266** (1–2): 119–145. doi:10.1007/s00606-007-0545-y.

[5] http://herb.daegu.go.kr/kor/exhibit/herb.info.form.asp?h_code=75 (Korean)

[6] Lim, T. K. "Pseudocydonia sinensis." Edible Medicinal And Non-Medicinal Plants. Springer Netherlands, 2012. 515-522.

[7] Hamauzu, Yasunori, et al. "Reddish coloration of Chinese quince (Pseudocydonia sinensis) procyanidins during heat treatment and effect on antioxidant and antiinfluenza viral activities." Journal of agricultural and food chemistry 55.4 (2007): 1221-1226.

3.82 Quince

Not to be confused with quints. For other uses, see Quince (disambiguation).

The **quince** (/ˈkwɪns/; *Cydonia oblonga*) is the sole member of the genus ***Cydonia*** in the family Rosaceae (which also contains apples and pears, among other fruits). It is a small deciduous tree that bears a pome fruit, similar in appearance to a pear, and bright golden-yellow when mature. Throughout history the cooked fruit has been used as food, but the tree is also grown for its attractive pale pink blossoms and other ornamental qualities.

3.82.1 Description

The tree grows 5 to 8 metres (16 to 26 ft) high and 4 to 6 metres (13 to 20 ft) wide. The fruit is 7 to 12 centimetres (2.8 to 4.7 in) long and 6 to 9 centimetres (2.4 to 3.5 in) across.

The immature fruit is green with dense grey-white pubescence, most of which rubs off before maturity in late autumn when the fruit changes color to yellow with hard, strongly perfumed flesh. The leaves are alternately arranged, simple, 6–11 cm (2–4 in) long, with an entire margin and densely pubescent with fine white hairs. The flowers, produced in spring after the leaves, are white or pink, 5 cm (2 in) across, with five petals.

The seeds contain nitriles, which are common in seeds of the rose family. In the stomach, enzymes or stomach acid or both cause some of the nitriles to be hydrolyzed and produce hydrogen cyanide, which is a volatile gas. The seeds are only likely to be toxic if a large quantity is eaten.*[2]

Quince: botanical illustration

Quince foliage and ripening fruit

Quince flowers

3.82.2 Taxonomy

Four other species previously included in the genus *Cydonia* are now treated in separate genera. These are *Pseudocydonia sinensis* and the three flowering quinces of eastern Asia in the genus *Chaenomeles*. Another unrelated fruit, the bael, is sometimes called the "Bengal quince".

The modern name originated in the 14th century as a plural of *quoyn*, via Old French *cooin* from Latin *cotoneum malum / cydonium malum*, ultimately from Greek κυδώνιον μῆλον, *kydonion melon* "Kydonian apple".

3.82.3 Distribution and habitat

Quince is native to rocky slopes and woodland margins in South-West Asia, Armenia, Turkey, Georgia and Iran[3] although it thrives in a variety of climates and can be grown successfully at latitudes as far north as Scotland. It should not be confused with its relatives, the Chinese quince, *Pseudocydonia sinensis*, or the flowering quinces of genus *Chaenomeles*, either of which is sometimes used as culinary substitutes.

The fruit was known to the Akkadians, who called it *supurgillu*; Arabic سفرجل *al safarjal* "quinces" (collective plural).*[4]

3.82.4 Pests and diseases

Quince is used as a food plant by the larvae of some Lepidoptera species including brown-tail, *Bucculatrix bechsteinella*, *Bucculatrix pomifoliella*, *Coleophora cerasivorella*, *Coleophora malivorella*, green pug and winter moth.

While quince is a hardy shrub, it may develop fungal diseases in hot weather, resulting in premature leaf fall.*[5] Quince leaf blight, caused by fungus *Diplocarpon mespili*, presents a threat in wet summers, causing severe leaf spotting and early defoliation, also affecting fruit to a lesser extent. It may also affect other Rosaceae plants such as hawthorn and medlar, but is typically less damaging than on quince.*[6] Cedar-quince rust, caused by *Gymnosporangium clavipes*, requires two hosts to complete the fungal lifecycle, one being a cedar (most commonly a juniper, *Juniperus virginiana*) and the other a rosacea. Appearing as red excrescence on various parts of the plant, it may affect quinces grown in vicinity of junipers.*[7]

3.82.5 Cultivation

Quince is a hardy, drought-tolerant shrub which adapts to many soils of low to medium pH. It tolerates both shade and sun, but sunlight is required in order to produce larger flowers and ensure fruit ripening. It is a very tough plant that does not require much maintenance, and tolerates years without pruning or major insect and disease problems.*[5]

Quince is cultivated on all continents in warm-temperate and temperate climates. It requires a cooler period of the year, with temperatures under 7 °C (45 °F), to flower properly. Propagation is done by cuttings or layering; the former method produces better plants, but they take longer to mature than by the latter. Named cultivars are propagated by cuttings or layers grafted on quince rootstock. Propagation by seed is not used commercially. Quince forms thick bushes, which must be pruned and reduced into a single stem in order to grow fruit-bearing trees for commercial use. The tree is self-pollinated, but it produces better yields when cross-pollinated.*[5]

Fruits are typically left on the tree to ripen fully. In warmer climates, it may become soft to the point of being edible, but additional ripening may be required in cooler climates. They are harvested in late autumn, before first frosts.*[5]

Quince is also used as rootstock for certain pear cultivars.*[5]

In Europe, quinces are commonly grown in central and southern areas where the summers are sufficiently hot for the fruit to fully ripen. They are not grown in large amounts; typically one or two quince trees are grown in a mixed orchard with several apples and other fruit trees: so were they grown in the 18th-century New England colonies, where there was always a quince at the lower corner of the vegetable garden, Ann Leighton notes in records of Portsmouth, New Hampshire and Newburyport, Massachusetts.*[8] Charlemagne directed that quinces be planted in well-stocked orchards. Quinces in England are first recorded in about 1275, when Edward I had some planted at the Tower of London.*[9]

closeup of Russian quinces 'Aromatnaya'

3.82.6 Cultivars

The cultivar 'Vranja' Nenadovic has gained the Royal Horticultural Society's Award of Garden Merit.*[11]

3.82.7 Production

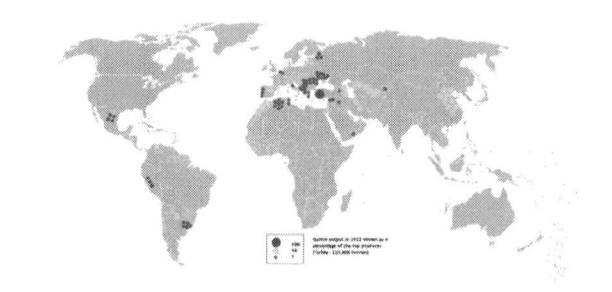

Quince output in 2012

3.82.8 Uses

Quinces are appreciated for their intense aroma and flavor. However, most varieties of quince are too hard and tart to be eaten raw; even ripe fruits should be subjected to bletting by frost or decay to be suitable for consumption. However, they may be cooked or roasted and used for jams, marmalade, jellies, or pudding.*[5]

As food

Some varieties of quince, such as 'Aromatnaya' and 'Kuganskaya' do not require cooking and can be eaten raw.*[13] However, most varieties of quince are too hard, astringent and sour to eat raw unless "bletted" (softened by frost and subsequent decay).*[14] High in pectin, they are used to make jam, jelly and quince pudding, or they may be peeled, then roasted, baked or stewed; pectin levels diminish as the fruit ripens.*[15] The flesh of the fruit turns red after a long cooking time. The very strong perfume means they can be added in small quantities to apple pies and jam to enhance the flavor. Adding a diced quince to apple sauce will enhance the taste of the apple sauce with the chunks of relatively firm, tart quince. The term "marmalade", originally meaning a quince jam, derives from *marmelo*, the Portuguese word for this fruit.*[16]*[17]

Quince cheese

Quince cheese is firm, sticky, sweet reddish hard paste made of the quince fruit, originating from the Iberian peninsula. It is known as *dulce de membrillo* across the Spanish-speaking world, where it is used in a variety of recipes, eaten in sandwiches and with cheese, traditionally manchego cheese, or accompanying fresh curds. It is also encountered in many regional variations across Europe. In Chile, boiled quince is popular in desserts such as the *murta con membrillo* that combines Chilean guava with quince.

In Kashmir, quinces are grown in abundance and are a seasonal fruit. They are called 'Bum-choonth' and are cooked with brinjals and enjoyed as a delicacy by Kashmiri Pundits.

As drink

In the Balkans and elsewhere, quince eau-de-vie (rakija) is made. For a quince *rakija*, ripe fruits of sweeter varieties are washed and cleared from rot and seeds, then crushed or minced, mixed with cold or boiling sweetened water and winemaking yeast, and left for several weeks to ferment. Fermented mash is distilled twice to obtain an approximately 60% alcohol-by-volume (ABV) liquor. It may be diluted with distilled water to obtain the final product, containing 42-43% ABV.*[18]

In the Alsace region of France and the Valais region of Switzerland, *liqueur de coing* made from quince is used as a *digestif*.

In Carolina in 1709, John Lawson allowed that he was "not a fair judge of the different sorts of Quinces, which they call Brunswick, Portugal and Barbary", but he noted "of this fruit they make a wine or liquor which they call Quince-Drink, and which I approve of beyond any that their country affords, though a great deal of cider and perry is there made, The Quince-Drink most commonly purges." *[19]

Ornamental

Quince is one of the most popular species for deciduous bonsai specimens,*[5] along with related Chinese quince and Japanese quince, native to Eastern Asia.

3.82.9 Cultural associations

- In Turkey, the expression *ayvayı yemek* (literally "to eat the quince") is used as a derogatory term indicating any unpleasant situation or a malevolent incident to avoid. This usage is likened to the rather bitter aftertaste of a quince fruit inside the mouth.

- When a baby is born in the Balkans, a quince tree is planted as a symbol of fertility, love and life.*[5]

- Ancient Greek poets (Ibycus, Aristophanes, *e.g.*) used quinces (*kydonia*) as a mildly ribald term for teenage breasts.

- Although the Book of Genesis does not name the specific type of the fruit that Adam and Eve ate from the Tree of Knowledge of Good and Evil in the Garden of Eden, some ancient texts suggest Eve's fruit of temptation might have been a quince.*[20]

- In Plutarch's *Lives*, Solon is said to have decreed that "bride and bridegroom shall be shut into a chamber, and eat a quince together." *[21]

- In the famous children's poem, "The Owl and the Pussycat" by Edward Lear (1871), "they dined on mince and slices of quince ..."

3.82.10 See also

- List of culinary fruits

3.82.11 References

[1] Potter, D., et al. (2007). Phylogeny and classification of Rosaceae. *Plant Systematics and Evolution*. 266(1–2): 5–43. [Referring to the subfamily by the name "Spiraeoideae"]

[2] "Cydonia oblonga Quince PFAF Plant Database". *pfaf.org*.

[3] *RHS A-Z encyclopedia of garden plants*. United Kingdom: Dorling Kindersley. 2008. p. 1136. ISBN 1405332964.

[4] Olivier Lauffenburger, 2006. The Hittite Grammar Homepage, Akkadian dictionary, entry for supurgillu

[5] Carlton, Deb (25 April 2013). Cumo, Christopher, ed. *Encyclopedia of Cultivated Plants: From Acacia to Zinnia [3 Volumes]: From Acacia to Zinnia*. ABC-CLIO. pp. 885–858. ISBN 978-1-59884-775-8.

[6] "Quince leaf blight". Royal Horticultural Society. 2016. Retrieved 22 November 2016.

[7] "Cedar-Quince Rust". RMissouri Botanical Garden. 2016. Retrieved 22 November 2016.

[8] Leighton 1986:243.

[9] Hugh Fearnley-Whittingstall. "Quince recipes - Hugh Fearnley-Whittingstall". *the Guardian*.

[10] "Agroforestry news quince cydonia oblonga". *agroforestry.co.uk*.

[11] "*Cydonia oblonga* 'Vranja' Nenadovic". Royal Horticultural Society. Retrieved 22 July 2013.

[12] "Statistics from: Food And Agricultural Organization of United Nations: Economic And Social Department: The Statistical Division". UN Food and Agriculture Organization Corporate Statistical Database. Archived from the original on September 6, 2015.

[13] USDA, ARS, National Genetic Resources Program. Germplasm Resources Information Network (GRIN). [Online Database] National Germplasm Resources Laboratory, Beltsville, Maryland. Available: http://www.ars-grin.gov/cgi-bin/npgs/acc/search.pl?accid=%20CCYD+131 (20 February 2011)

[14] "Quince". *herbs2000.com*.

[15] Alexander, S. The cook's companion. Penguin Australia. P.609

[16] Wilson, C. Anne. *The Book of Marmalade: Its Antecedents, Its History and Its Role in the World Today (Together with a Collection of Recipes for Marmalades and Marmalade Cookery)*, University of Pennsylvania Press, Philadelphia. Revised Edition 1999. ISBN 0-8122-1727-6

[17] "Marmalade" in Online Etymology Dictionary, © 2001 Douglas Harper apud Dictionary.com

[18] "Dunjevača izuzetne arome i ukusa" [Quince brandy of exceptional aroma and taste] (in Serbian). Poljoprivreda.info. 22 November 2003. Retrieved 22 November 2016.

[19] Lawson, *A New Voyage to Carolina*, 1709, quoted in Ann Leighton, *American Gardens in the 18th Century: 'for Use or For Delight'*, 1986:242f.

[20] Cyclopaedia of Biblical, theological, and ecclesiastical literature, Volume 1 By James Strong

[21] Wikisource: *Lives* by Plutarch, translated by John Dryden: *Solon*

3.82.12 External links

- Media related to Cydonia oblonga at Wikimedia Commons
- Cornell article
- Quince history

3.83 Rapanea melanophloeos

Rapanea melanophloeos, commonly known as **Cape Beech**, **Kaapse Boekenhout** or **IsiCalabi**, is a dense, graceful, evergreen tree that is native to the afromontane forests of Southern Africa.

3.83.1 Distribution

The natural range of this stately tree is from Cape Town in the south, to Zambia in the north. In the Eastern Cape it is sometimes found alongside its smaller coastal relative, *Rapanea gilliana*. Despite its common name it is not a close relative of the familiar Beech tree of the northern hemisphere, and it is actually more closely related to the Rhododendrons.

3.83.2 Description

Rapanea melanophloeos is a dense, graceful, evergreen tree. Its leaves, stalks and berries often have a purple or maroon color. This tree is usually dioecious (male and female flowers on different trees) and birds are attracted by its tiny, dark purple berries. The specific name 'melanophloeos' means 'black bark' and resulted from a mistaken identification of the source tree as Swartbas (*Diospyros whyteana*).

3.83.3 Cultivation

Rapanea melanophloeos is cultivated as an ornamental tree and screening shrub in gardens, and as a potted bonsai specimen. It is hardy and grows well in windy areas and near the coast. Once established, the plant is reasonably drought tolerant and has low maintenance needs.

3.83. RAPANEA MELANOPHLOEOS

Fully grown Rapanea melanophloeos *in native afro-temperate forest near Cape Town.*

Rapanea melanophloeos *tree in Harold Porter Botanical Gardens.*

The plant sends up suckers from its roots that eventually become new trees, and so is best not planted adjacent to paving. *[1] Rapanea grows easily from seed.

3.83.4 Gallery

Fruits

Fruits and seeds

3.83.5 References

[1] PlantzAfrica-rapanmelan

3.83.6 External links

- *Rapanea melanophloeos* at PlantZAfrica.com

3.84 Rhaphiolepis indica

Rhaphiolepis indica, the **Indian hawthorn**, **India hawthorn** or **Hong Kong hawthorn**, is an evergreen shrub in the family Rosaceae. The species is native to an area from southern China, Japan, Laos, Cambodia, Thailand and Vietnam.[1] It is grown for its decorative pink flowers, and is popular in bonsai culture. The fruit is edible when cooked, and can be used to make jam.

Indian hawthorn is a mainstay horticultural specimen in southern United States. It is often found in commercial as well as in private landscapes. Often it is trimmed into small compact hedges or balls for foundation plants. It has been successfully pruned into a standard form as well as small dwarf-like trees up to 15 feet in height. It is apt to develop leaf spot.

An Indian hawthorn bush at a distance

Rhaphiolepis indica *blooming in Hong Kong*

3.84.1 References

[1] Cuizhi Gu; Chaoluan Li; Lingdi Lu; Shunyuan Jiang; Crinan Alexander; Bruce Bartholomew; Anthony R. Brach; David E. Boufford; Hiroshi Ikeda; Hideaki Ohba; Kenneth R. Robertson & Steven A. Spongberg. "Flora of China". |chapter= ignored (help)

3.85 Robinia pseudoacacia

Robinia pseudoacacia, commonly known in its native territory as **black locust**,[1] is a medium-sized deciduous tree native to the southeastern United States, but it has been widely planted and naturalized elsewhere in temperate North America, Europe, Southern Africa[2] and Asia and is considered an invasive species in some areas.[3] Another common name is **false acacia**,[4] a literal translation of the specific name (*pseudo* meaning fake or false and *acacia* referring to the genus of plants with the same name.) It was introduced into Britain in 1636.[5]

3.85.1 History and naming

The name 'locust' is said to have been given to *Robinia* by Jesuit missionaries, who fancied that this was the tree that supported St. John in the wilderness, but it is native only to North America. The locust tree of Spain (*Ceratonia siliqua* or carob tree), which is also native to Syria and the entire Mediterranean basin, is supposed to be the true locust of the *New Testament*.

Robinia is now a North American genus, but traces of it are found in the Eocene and Miocene rocks of Europe.[6]

3.85.2 Distribution and invasive habit

The black locust is native to the eastern United States, but the exact native range is not accurately known[7] as the tree has been cultivated and is currently found across the continent, in all the lower 48 states, eastern Canada, and British Columbia.[1] The native range is thought to be two separate populations, one centered about the Appalachian Mountains, from Pennsylvania to northern Georgia, and a second westward focused around the Ozark Plateau and Ouachita Mountains of Arkansas, Oklahoma and Missouri.

Black locust's current range has been expanded by humans distributing the tree for landscaping and now includes: Australia, Canada, China, Europe, India, Northern and South Africa, temperate regions in Asia, New Zealand, Southern South America.[8]

Black locust is an interesting example of how one plant can be considered an invasive species even on the same continent it is native to. For example, within the western United States, New England region, and in the Midwest, black locust is considered an invasive species. In the prairie and savanna regions of the Midwest black locust can dominate and shade open habitats.[9] These ecosystems have been decreasing in size and black locust is contributing to this, when black locust invades an area it will convert the grassland ecosystem into a forested ecosystem where the grasses

Tree in flower

Robinia spines

are displaced.*[10] Black locust has been listed as invasive in Connecticut and prohibited in Massachusetts.*[1]

In Australia black locust has become naturalized within Victoria, New South Wales, South, and Western Australia. It is considered an environmental weed there.*[8] In South Africa, it is regarded as a weed because of its habit suckering.*[11]

3.85.3 Description

Black locust reaches a typical height of 40–100 feet (12–30 m) with a diameter of 2–4 feet (0.61–1.22 m).*[12] Exceptionally, it may grow up to 52 metres (171 ft) tall*[13] and 1.6 metres (5.2 ft) diameter in very old trees. It is a very upright tree with a straight trunk and narrow crown which grows scraggly with age.*[5] The dark blue-green compound leaves with a contrasting lighter underside give this tree a beautiful appearance in the wind and contribute to its grace.

Black locust is a shade intolerant species*[7] and therefore is typical of young woodlands disturbed areas where sunlight is plentiful and soil is dry, in this sense, black locust can often grow as a weed tree. It also often spreads by underground shoots or suckers which contribute to the weedy character of this species.*[5] Young trees are often spiny, however, mature trees often lack spines. In the early summer black locust flowers; the flowers are large and appear in large, intensely fragrant (reminiscent of orange blossoms), clusters. The leaflets fold together in wet weather and at night (nyctinasty) as some change of position at night is a habit of the entire leguminous family.

Although similar in general appearance to the honey locust, it lacks that tree's characteristic long branched thorns on the trunk, instead having the pairs of short prickles at the base of each leaf; the leaflets are also much broader then honey locust. It may also resemble Styphnolobium japonicum which has smaller flower spikes and lacks spines.

Detailed description

- The **bark** is dark gray brown and tinged with red or orange in the grooves. It is deeply furrowed into grooves and ridges which run up and down the trunk and often cross and form diamond shapes.*[5]

- The **roots** of black locust contain nodules which allow it to fix nitrogen as is common within the pea family.

- The **branches** are typically zig-zagy and may have ridges and grooves or may be round.*[5] When young, they are at first coated with white silvery down, this soon disappears and they become pale green and afterward reddish or greenish brown.

288   CHAPTER 3. PLANTS USED IN BONSAI (IN ALPHABETICAL ORDER)

One black locust leaf showing 13 leaflets

- **Prickles** may or may not be present on young trees, root suckers, and branches near the ground; typically, branches high above the ground rarely contain prickles. *R. pseudoacacia* is quite variable in the quantity and amount of prickles present as some trees are densely prickly and other trees have no prickles at all. The prickles typically remain on the tree until the young thin bark to which they are attached is replaced by the thicker mature bark. They develop from stipules*[14] (small leaf like structures which grow at the base of leaves) and since stipules are paired at the base of leaves, the prickles will be paired at the bases of leaves. They range from .25–.8 inches (0.64–2.03 cm) in length and are somewhat triangular with a flared base and sharp point. Their color is of a dark purple and they adhere only to the bark.*[14]

- **Wood**: Pale yellowish brown; heavy, hard, strong, close-grained and very durable in contact with the ground. The wood has a specific gravity of 0.7333, and a weight of approximately 45.7 pounds per cubic foot.

- The **leaves** are compound, meaning that each leaf contains many smaller leaf like structures called leaflets, the leaflets are roughly paired on either side of the stem which runs through the leaf (rachis) and there is typically one leaflet at the tip of the leaf (odd pinnate). The leaves are alternately arranged on the stem. Each leaf is 6–14 inches (15–36 cm) long and contains 9-19 leaflets, each being 1–2 inches (2.5–5.1 cm)long, and .25–.75 inches (0.64–1.91 cm) wide. The leaflets are rounded or slightly indented at the tip and typically rounded at the base. The leaves come out of the bud folded in half, yellow green, covered with silvery down which soon disappears. Each leaflet initially has a minute stipel, which quickly falls, and is connected to the (rachis) by a short stem or petiolule. The leaves are attached to the branch with slender hairy petioles which is grooved and swollen at the base. The stipules are linear, downy, membranous at first and occasionally develop into prickles. The leaves appear relatively late in spring.

- The **leaf color** of the fully grown leaves is a dull dark green above and paler beneath. In the fall the leaves turn a clear pale yellow.

- The **flowers** open in May or June for 7–10 days, after the leaves have developed. They are arranged in loose drooping clumps (racemes) which are typically 4–8 inches (10–20 cm) long.*[5] The flowers themselves are cream-white (rarely pink or purple) with a pale yellow blotch in the center and imperfectly papilionaceous in shape. They are about 1 inch (2.5 cm) wide, very fragrant, and produce large amounts of nectar. Each flower is perfect, having both stamens and a pistil (male and female parts). There are 10 stamens enclosed within the petals; these are fused together in a diadelphous configuration, where the filaments of 9 are all joined to form a tube and one stamen is separate and above the joined stamens. The single ovary is superior and contains several ovules. Below each flower is a calyx which looks like leafy tube between the flower and the stem. It is made from fused sepals and is dark green and may be blotched with red. The pedicels (stems which connect the flower to the branch) are slender, .5 inches (1.3 cm), dark red or reddish green.

- The **fruit** is a typical legume fruit, being a flat and smooth pea-like pod 2–4 inches (5.1–10.2 cm) long

Closeup of flowers

and .5 inches (1.3 cm) broad. The fruit usually contains 4-8 seeds.*[5] The seeds are dark orange brown with irregular markings. They ripen late in autumn and hang on the branches until early spring.*[6] There are typically 25500 seeds per pound.*[15]

- **Winter buds**: Minute, naked (having no scales covering them), three or four together, protected in a depression by a scale-like covering lined on the inner surface with a thick coat of tomentum and opening in early spring. When the buds are forming they are covered by the swollen base of the petiole.

- **Cotyledons** are oval in shape and fleshy.

3.85.4 Reproduction and dispersal

Black locust produces both sexually via flowers, and asexually via root suckers. The flowers are pollinated by insects, primarily by Hymenopteran insects. The physical construction of the flower separates the male and female parts so that self-pollination will not typically occur.*[16] The seedlings grow rapidly but they have a thick seed coat which means that not all seeds will germinate. The seed coat can be weakened via hot water, sulfuric acid, or be mechanically scarified and this will allow a greater quantity of the seeds to grow.*[5]*[15] The seeds are produced in good crops every year or every-other year.

Root suckers are an important method of local reproduction of this tree. The roots may grow suckers after damage (by being hit with a lawn mower or otherwise damaged) or after no damage at all. The suckers are stems which grow from the roots, directly into the air and may grow into full trees. The main trunk also has the capability to grow sprouts and will do so after being cut down.*[12] This makes removal of black locust difficult as the suckers need to be continually removed from both the trunk and roots or the tree will regrow. This is considered an asexual form or reproduction.

The suckers allow black locust to grow into colonies which are often exclude other species. These colonies may form dense thickets which shade out competition.*[17] Black locust has been found to have either 2n=20 or 2n=22 chromosomes.

Human mediated dispersal

Black locust has been spread and used as a plant for erosion control as it is fast growing and generally a tough tree.*[15] The wood, considered the most durable wood in America, has been very desirable and motivated people to move the tree to areas where it is not native so the wood can be farmed and used.

3.85.5 Ecology

Robinia pseudoacacia *seeds*

When growing in sandy areas this plant can enrich the soil by means of its nitrogen-fixing nodules, allowing other species to move in.*[12] On sandy soils black locust may also often replace other vegetation which cannot fix nitrogen.*[15]

Black locust is a typical early successional plant, a pioneer species, it grows best in bright sunlight and does not handle shade well.*[7] It specializes in colonizing disturbed and edges of woodlots before it is eventually replaced with more shade tolerant species. It prefers dry to moist limestone soils but will grow on most soils as long as they are not wet or poorly drained.*[7] This tree tolerates a soil pH range of 4.6 to 8.2.*[15] Within its native range it will often grow on soils of Inceptisols, Ultisols, and Alfisols groups. Black locust does not do well on compacted, clayey or eroded soils. Black locust is a part of the Appalachian mixed mesophytic forests.

Black locust is not a particularly valuable plant for wildlife, but does provide valuable cover when planted on previously open areas. Its seeds are also eaten by bobwhite quail and other game birds and squirrels. Woodpeckers may also nest in the trunk since older trees are often infected by heart rot.

3.85.6 Pests

Locust leaf miner *Odontota dorsalis* attacks the tree in spring and turns the leaves brown by mid summer, it slows the growth of the tree but not seriously.*[15] The locust borer *Megacyllene robiniae* larvae carve tunnels into the trunk of the tree and make it more prone to being knocked down by the wind. Heart rot is the only significant disease affecting black locust.*[15] Black locust is also attacked by *Chlorogenus robiniae*, a virus which causes witch's broom growths, clear leaflet veins are a symptom of the disease.*[18]

3.85.7 Uses

Cultivation

Black locust is a major honey plant in the eastern US, and has been planted in European countries. In many European countries, it is the source of the renowned acacia honey. Flowering starts after 140 growing degree days. However, its blooming period is short (about 10 days) and it does not consistently produce a honey crop year after year. Weather conditions can have quite an effect on the amount of nectar collected, as well; in Ohio for example, good locust honey flow happens in one of five years.*[19]

It can be easily propagated from roots, softwood, or hardwood*[5]*[15] and this allows for easy reproduction of the plant. Cultivars may also be grafted as this ensures the parent and daughter plant will be genetically identical.

R. pseudoacacia is considered an excellent plant for growing in highly disturbed areas as an erosion control plant.*[15] The roots are shallow aggressive which help to hold onto soil and the tree grows quickly and on poor soils due to its ability to fix nitrogen.

The golden 'Frisia' cultivar planted as an ornamental tree

Black locust has nitrogen-fixing bacteria on its root system, so it can grow on poor soils and is an early colonizer of disturbed areas. With fertilizer prices rising, the importance of black locust as a nitrogen-fixing species is also noteworthy. The mass application of fertilizers in agriculture and forestry is increasingly expensive; therefore nitrogen-fixing tree and shrub species are gaining importance in managed forestry.*[20]

It is also planted for firewood because it grows rapidly, is highly resilient in a variety of soils, and it grows back even faster from its stump after harvest by using the existing root system.*[21] (see coppicing)

In Europe, it is often planted along streets and in parks, especially in large cities, because it tolerates pollution well.

Cultivars Several cultivars exist but 'Frisia' seems to be one of the most planted ones.

- 'Decaisneana' has been considered a cultivar but is more accurately a hybrid (*R. psudeoacacia* x *R. viscosa*). It has light rose-pink colored flowers and small or no prickles.*[22]

- 'Frisia', a selection with bright yellow-green leaves and red prickles, is occasionally planted as an ornamental tree.*[5]

- 'Purple robe' has dark rose-pink flowers and bronze red new growth. The flowers tend to last longer than on the wild tree.*[5]

- 'Tortuosa', a small tree with curved and distorted branches.*[5]*[23]

- 'Unifoliola', a plant with fewer leaflets, no prickles, and a shorter height.

Wood

Wood

Bark

The wood is extremely hard, being one of the hardest woods in Northern America. It is very resistant to rot, and durable, making it prized for furniture, flooring, paneling, fence posts, and small watercraft. Wet, newly cut planks have an offensive odor which disappears with seasoning. Black locust is still in use in some rustic handrail systems. In the Netherlands and some other parts of Europe, black locust is one of the most rot-resistant local trees, and projects have started to limit the use of tropical wood by promoting this tree and creating plantations. Flavonoids in the heartwood allow the wood to last over 100 years in soil.*[24] As a young man, Abraham Lincoln spent much of his time splitting rails and fence posts from black locust logs.

Black locust is highly valued as firewood for wood-burning stoves; it burns slowly, with little visible flame or smoke, and has a higher heat content than any other species that grows widely in the Eastern United States, comparable to the heat content of anthracite.*[25] For best results, it should be seasoned like any other hardwood, but black locust is also popular because of its ability to burn even when wet.*[20] In fireplaces, it can be less satisfactory because knots and beetle damage make the wood prone to "spitting" coals for distances of up to several feet. If the black locust is cut, split, and cured while relatively young (within 10 years), thus minimizing beetle damage, "spitting" problems are minimal.

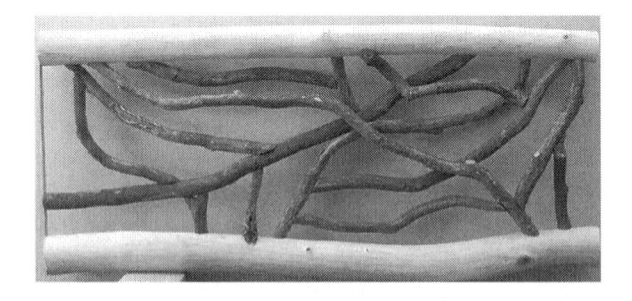

Locust railing

In 1900, the value of *Robinia pseudoacacia* was reported to be practically destroyed in nearly all parts of the United States beyond the mountain forests which are its home by locust borers which riddle the trunk and branches. Were it not for these insects, it would be one of the most valuable timber trees that could be planted in the northern and middle states. Young trees grow quickly and vigorously for a number of years, but soon become stunted and diseased, and rarely live long enough to attain any commercial value.*[6]

Food and Medicine

In traditional medicine of India, different parts of *R. pseudoacacia* are used as laxative, antispasmodic, and diuretic.[*][26]

In Romania the flowers are sometimes used to produce a sweet and perfumed jam. This means manual harvesting of flowers, eliminating the seeds and boiling the petals with sugar, in certain proportions, to obtain a light sweet and delicate perfume jam.

Although the bark and leaves are toxic, various reports suggest that the seeds and the young pods of the black locust are edible. Shelled seeds are safe to harvest from summer through fall, and are edible both raw and/or boiled.[*][27] Due to the small nature of the seeds, shelling them efficiently can prove tedious and difficult. In France and in Italy, *R. pseudoacacia* flowers are eaten as *beignets* after being coated in batter and fried in oil;[*][28] they are also eaten in Japan, largely as tempura.[*][29][*][30]

3.85.8 Toxicity

The bark, leaves, and wood are toxic to both humans and livestock.[*][31] Important constituents of the plant are the toxalbumin robin, which loses its toxicity when heated, and robinin, a nontoxic glucoside.[*][32]

Horses that consume the plant show signs of anorexia, depression, incontinence, colic, weakness, and cardiac arrhythmia. Symptoms usually occur about 1 hour following consumption, and immediate veterinary attention is required.

3.85.9 Flavonoids content

Black locust leaves contain flavone glycosides characterised by spectroscopic and chemical methods as the 7-O-β-d-glucuronopyranosyl-(1 → 2)[α-l-rhamnopyranosyl-(1 → 6)]-β-d-glucopyranosides of acacetin (5,7-dihydroxy-4′-methoxyflavone), apigenin (5,7,4′-trihydroxyflavone), diosmetin (5,7,3′-trihydroxy-4′-methoxyflavone) and luteolin (5,7,3′,4′-tetrahydroxyflavone).[*][33]

3.85.10 See also

- List of plants poisonous to equines
- *Megacyllene robiniae*

3.85.11 References

[1] "*Robinia pseudoacacia*". Natural Resources Conservation Service PLANTS Database. USDA. Retrieved 22 October 2015.

[2] http://www.biodiversityexplorer.org/plants/fabaceae/robinia_pseudoacacia.htm

[3] "*Robinia pseudoacacia*". *County-level distribution map from the North American Plant Atlas (NAPA)*. Biota of North America Program (BONAP). 2013.

[4] "BSBI List 2007" (xls). Botanical Society of Britain and Ireland. Retrieved 2014-10-17.

[5] Dirr, Michael A (1990). *Manual of woody landscape plants*. (4. ed., rev. ed.). Champaign, Illinois: Stipes Publishing Company. ISBN 0-87563-344-7.

[6] Keeler, Harriet L. (1900). *Our Native Trees and How to Identify Them*. New York: Charles Scriber's Sons. pp. 97–102.

[7] Huntley, J. C. (1990). "*Robinia pseudoacacia*". In Burns, Russell M.; Honkala, Barbara H. *Hardwoods. Silvics of North America*. Washington, D.C.: United States Forest Service (USFS), United States Department of Agriculture (USDA). **2**. Retrieved 14 July 2016 – via Northeastern Area State and Private Forestry (www.na.fs.fed.us).

[8] "Robinia pseudoacacia". *keyserver.lucidcentral.org*. Retrieved 2016-07-14.

[9] "black locust: Robinia pseudoacacia (Fabales: Fabaceae (Leguminosae)): Invasive Plant Atlas of the United States". *www.invasiveplantatlas.org*. Retrieved 2016-07-14.

[10] "PCA Alien Plant Working Group – Black Locust (Robinia pseudoacacia)". *www.nps.gov*. Retrieved 2016-07-14.

[11] http://www.arc.agric.za/home.asp?pid=1031

[12] "Robinia pseudoacacia". *www.eddmaps.org*. Retrieved 14 July 2016.

[13] "New tuliptree height record". Eastern Native Tree Society. Retrieved 2008-09-22.

[14] "*Robinia pseudoacacia*". *Flora of China*. Missouri Botanical Garden. Retrieved 14 July 2016 – via eFloras.org.

[15] "Robinia psudeoacacia factsheet" (PDF). *USDA*. Retrieved 14 July 2016.

[16] Houser, Cameron (August 2014). "GENETICALLY MEDIATED LEAF CHEMISTRY IN INVASIVE AND NATIVE BLACK LOCUST (ROBINIA PSEUDOACACIA L.) ECOSYSTEMS" (PDF). Retrieved 2016-07-15.

[17] "Black locust invasive species control" (PDF). Michigan DNR. Retrieved 14 July 2016.

[18] *Internationally dangerous forest tree diseases, Issues 911-940*. USDA. 1963.

[19] http://www.beeclass.com/DTS/blacklocust.htm

[20] "UN Food & Agriculture Organization's notes on Black Locust".

[21] "OSU: Managing Your Woodlot for Firewood" (PDF).

[22] "Ornamental Cultivar Details". *www.flemings.com.au*. Retrieved 14 July 2016.

[23] "Robinia pseudoacacia 'Tortuosa' – Plant Finder". *www.missouribotanicalgarden.org*. Retrieved 14 July 2016.

[24] "Black Locust: A Multi-purpose Tree Species for Temperate Climates". Retrieved 2007-06-27.

[25] "Heating the Home with Wood" (PDF).

[26] Wang L, Waltenberger B, Pferschy-Wenzig EM, Blunder M, Liu X, Malainer C, Blazevic T, Schwaiger S, Rollinger JM, Heiss EH, Schuster D, Kopp B, Bauer R, Stuppner H, Dirsch VM, Atanasov AG. Natural product agonists of peroxisome proliferator-activated receptor gamma (PPARγ): a review. *Biochem Pharmacol*. July 2014 . doi:10.1016/j.bcp.2014.07.018 PMID 25083916

[27] Thayer, Samuel (2006). *The Forager's Harvest*. W5066 State Hwy 86 Ogema, WI 54459: Forager's Harvest. p. 251. ISBN 0-9766266-0-8.

[28] http://www.cuisine-campagne.com/index.php?post/2007/05/07/250-beignets-de-fleurs-d-acacia

[29] ja: ニセアカシア

[30] http://cookpad.com/recipe/3179033

[31] "Toxicity of Black Locust". *www.woodweb.com*. Retrieved 5 July 2016.

[32] Medicinal and Poisonous Plants of Southern and Eastern Africa – Watt and Brandwijk

[33] Nigel C. Veitch, Peter C. Elliott, Geoffrey C. Kite & Gwilym P. Lewis (2010). "Flavonoid glycosides of the black locust tree, *Robinia pseudoacacia* (Leguminosae)". *Phytochemistry*. **71** (4): 479–486. doi:10.1016/j.phytochem.2009.10.024. PMID 19948349.

3.85.12 External links

- Purdue University
- *Robinia pseudoacacia* images at bioimages.vanderbilt.edu
- *Robinia pseudoacacia* images at Forestry Images
- *Robinia pseudoacacia* – US Forest Service Fire Effects Database
- *Robinia pseudoacacia* at USDA Plants Database
- Black locust – US Forest Service Silvics Manual
- Black Locust (as an invasive species)
- Interactive Distribution Map of *Robinia pseudoacacia*
- *Robinia pseudoacacia* flowers as food
- Black locust – Invasive species: Minnesota DNR
- *Robinia pseudoacacia* - information, genetic conservation units and related resources. European Forest Genetic Resources Programme (EUFORGEN)

3.86 Rosemary

For other uses, see Rosemary (disambiguation).

Rosmarinus officinalis, commonly known as **rosemary**, is a woody, perennial herb with fragrant, evergreen, needle-like leaves and white, pink, purple, or blue flowers, native to the Mediterranean region.

It is a member of the mint family Lamiaceae, which includes many other herbs. The name "rosemary" derives from the Latin for "dew"(*ros*) and "sea"(*marinus*), or "dew of the sea".*[2] The plant is also sometimes called **anthos**, from the ancient Greek word ἄνθος, meaning "flower".*[3] Rosemary has a fibrous root system.

3.86.1 Taxonomy

Rosmarinus officinalis is one of 2–4 species in the genus *Rosmarinus*.*[4] The other species most often recognized is the closely related, *Rosmarinus eriocalyx*, of the Maghreb of Africa and Iberia. The genus was named by the 18th-century naturalist and founding taxonomist Carl Linnaeus.

3.86.2 Description

Rosemary is an aromatic evergreen shrub with leaves similar to hemlock needles. It is native to the Mediterranean and Asia, but is reasonably hardy in cool climates. It can withstand droughts, surviving a severe lack of water for lengthy periods.*[5] Forms range from upright to trailing; the upright forms can reach 1.5 m (5 ft) tall, rarely 2 m (6 ft 7 in). The leaves are evergreen, 2–4 cm (0.8–1.6 in) long and 2–5 mm broad, green above, and white below, with dense, short, woolly hair. The plant flowers in spring and summer in temperate climates, but the plants can be in constant bloom in warm climates; flowers are white, pink, purple or deep blue.*[6] Rosemary also has a tendency to flower outside its normal flowering season; it has been known to flower as late as early December, and as early as mid-February (in the northern hemisphere).*[7]

Illustration from Köhler's Medicinal Plants

Rosmarinus officinalis prostratus

Flowering rosemary

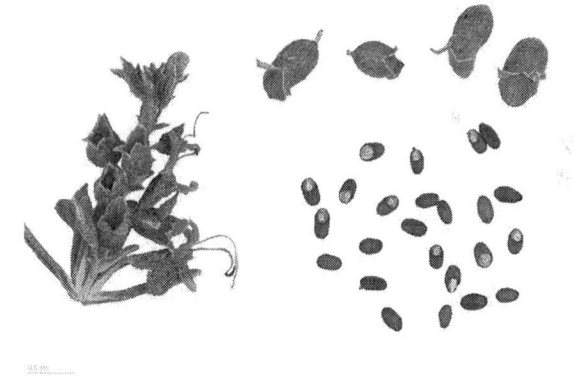

Rosmarinus officinalis – *MHNT*

3.86.3 Mythology

According to legend, it was draped around the Greek goddess Aphrodite when she rose from the sea, born of Uranus's semen. The Virgin Mary is said to have spread her blue cloak over a white-blossomed rosemary bush when she was resting, and the flowers turned blue. The shrub then became known as the "Rose of Mary".*[8]

3.86.4 Usage

Rosemary is used as a decorative plant in gardens where it may have pest control effects. The leaves are used to flavor various foods, such as stuffings and roast meats.

Cultivation

Since it is attractive and drought-tolerant, rosemary is used as an ornamental plant in gardens and for xeriscape land-

3.86. ROSEMARY

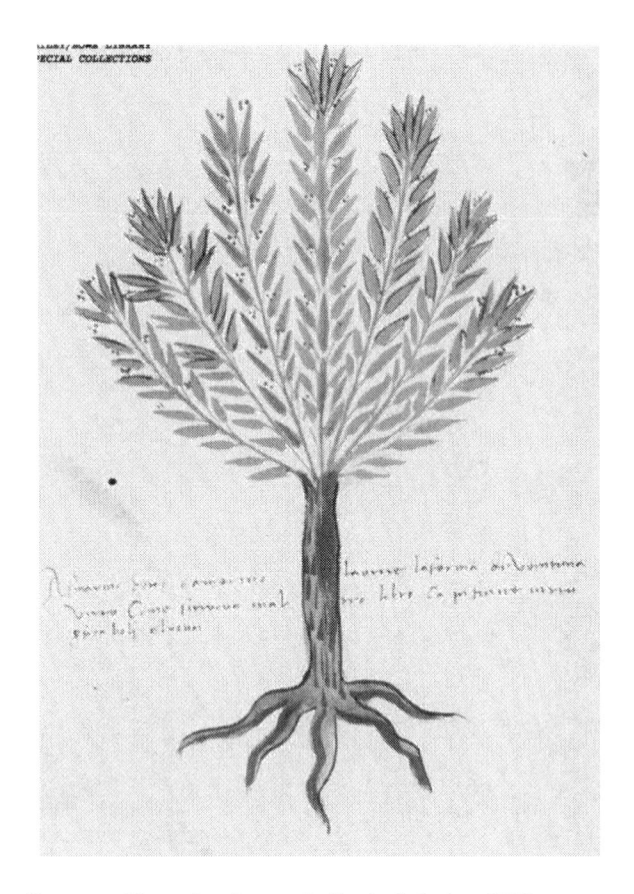

Rosemary illustration from an Italian herbal, circa 1500

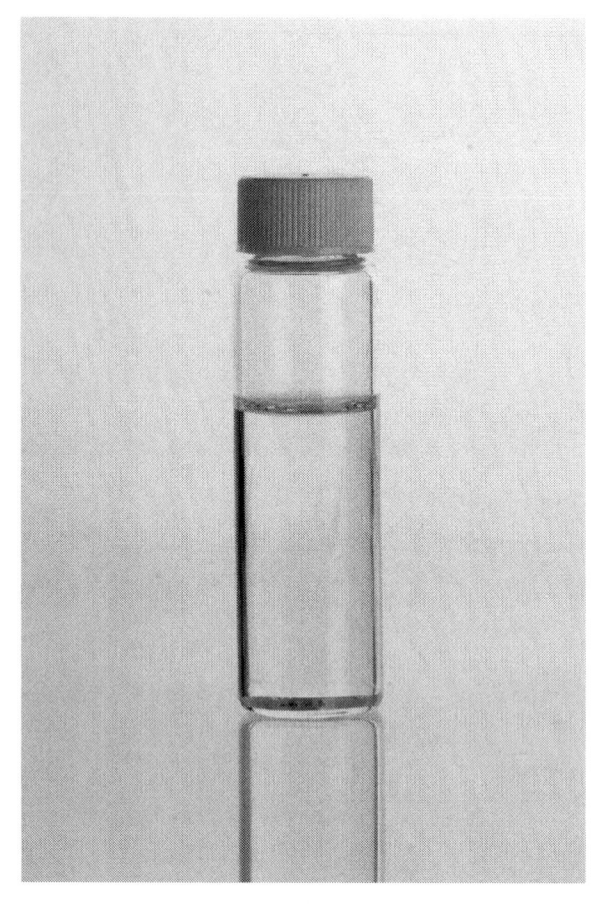

*Rosemary (*Rosmarinus officinalis*) essential oil*

scaping, especially in regions of Mediterranean climate. It is considered easy to grow and pest-resistant. Rosemary can grow quite large and retain attractiveness for many years, can be pruned into formal shapes and low hedges, and has been used for topiary. It is easily grown in pots. The groundcover cultivars spread widely, with a dense and durable texture.

Rosemary grows on friable loam soil with good drainage in an open, sunny position. It will not withstand waterlogging and some varieties are susceptible to frost. It grows best in neutral to alkaline conditions (pH 7–7.8) with average fertility. It can be propagated from an existing plant by clipping a shoot (from a soft new growth) 10–15 cm (4–6 in) long, stripping a few leaves from the bottom, and planting it directly into soil.

Cultivars Numerous cultivars have been selected for garden use. The following are frequently sold:

- 'Albus' – white flowers
- 'Arp' – leaves light green, lemon-scented
- 'Aureus' – leaves speckled yellow
- 'Benenden Blue' – leaves narrow, dark green
- 'Blue Boy' – dwarf, small leaves
- 'Blue Rain' – pink flowers
- 'Golden Rain' – leaves green, with yellow streaks
- 'Gold Dust' -dark green leaves, with golden streaks but stronger than 'Golden Rain'
- 'Haifa' – low and small, white flowers
- 'Irene' – low and lax, trailing, intense blue flowers
- 'Lockwood de Forest' – procumbent selection from 'Tuscan Blue'
- 'Ken Taylor' – shrubby
- 'Majorica Pink' – pink flowers
- 'Miss Jessop's Upright' – distinctive tall fastigiate form, with wider leaves.
- 'Pinkie' – pink flowers
- 'Prostratus' – lower groundcover

- 'Pyramidalis' (or 'Erectus') – fastigate form, pale blue flowers
- 'Remembrance' (or 'Gallipoli') – taken from the Gallipoli Peninsula[*][9]
- 'Roseus' – pink flowers
- 'Salem' – pale blue flowers, cold-hardy similar to 'Arp'
- 'Severn Sea' – spreading, low-growing, with arching branches, flowers deep violet
- 'Sudbury Blue' – blue flowers
- 'Tuscan Blue' – traditional robust upright form
- 'Wilma's Gold' – yellow leaves

The following cultivars have gained the Royal Horticultural Society's Award of Garden Merit:-

- 'Miss Jessop's upright'[*][10]
- 'Severn Sea'[*][11]
- 'Sissinghurst blue'[*][12]
- 'Benenden blue'[*][13]

Culinary use

Dried rosemary leaves

The leaves are used as a flavoring in foods such as stuffings and roast lamb, pork, chicken and turkey. Fresh or dried leaves are used in traditional Mediterranean cuisine. They have a bitter, astringent taste and a characteristic aroma which complements many cooked foods. Herbal tea can be made from the leaves. When roasted with meats or vegetables, the leaves impart a mustard-like aroma with an additional fragrance of charred wood compatible with barbecued foods.

In amounts typically used to flavor foods, such as one teaspoon (1 gram), rosemary provides no nutritional value.[*][14][*][15] Rosemary extract has been shown to improve the shelf life and heat stability of omega 3-rich oils which are prone to rancidity.[*][16]

Fragrance

Rosemary oil is used for purposes of fragrant bodily perfumes or to emit an aroma into a room. It is also burnt as incense, and used in shampoos and cleaning products.

Phytochemicals and traditional medicine

Rosemary contains a number of phytochemicals, including rosmarinic acid, camphor, caffeic acid, ursolic acid, betulinic acid, carnosic acid and carnosol.[*][17]

In traditional medicine, extracts and essential oil from flowers and leaves are used in the belief they may be useful to treat a variety of disorders.[*][17] Rosemary essential oil contains 10-20% camphor,[*][18] though the chemical composition can vary greatly between different samples, according to in vitro studies.[*][19]

Folklore and customs

In the Middle Ages, rosemary was associated with wedding ceremonies. The bride would wear a rosemary headpiece and the groom and wedding guests would all wear a sprig of rosemary. From this association with weddings, rosemary was thought to be a love charm.[*][20]

In myths, rosemary has a reputation for improving memory and has been used as a symbol for remembrance during war commemorations and funerals in Europe and Australia.[*][21] Mourners would throw it into graves as a symbol of remembrance for the dead. In Shakespeare's *Hamlet*, Ophelia says, "There's rosemary, that's for remembrance." (Hamlet, iv. 5.) In Australia, sprigs of rosemary are worn on ANZAC Day and sometimes Remembrance Day to signify remembrance; the herb grows wild on the Gallipoli Peninsula.[*][21]

Hungary water was first prepared for the Queen of Hungary Elisabeth of Poland to " ... renovate vitality of paralyzed limbs ... " and to treat gout. It was used externally and prepared by mixing fresh rosemary tops into spirits of wine.[*][22] Don Quixote (Part One, Chapter XVII) mixes it in his recipe of the miraculous balm of Fierabras.[*][23]

3.86.5 See also

- Four thieves vinegar
- Scented water

3.86.6 References

[1] "*Rosmarinus officinalis* information from NPGS/GRIN". www.ars-grin.gov. Retrieved 2008-03-03.

[2] Room, Adrian (1988). *A Dictionary of True Etymologies*. Taylor & Francis. p. 150. ISBN 978-0-415-03060-1.

[3] "The month." *The Pharmaceutical Journal and Transactions: A Weekly Record of Pharmacy and Allied Sciences*. Published by the Pharmaceutical Society of Great Britain. April 1887. 804–804

[4] Rosselló, J. A.; Cosín, R.; Boscaiu, M.; Vicente, O.; Martínez, I.; Soriano, P. (2006). "Intragenomic diversity and phylogenetic systematics of wild rosemaries (*Rosmarinus officinalis* L. S.l., Lamiaceae) assessed by nuclear ribosomal DNA sequences (ITS)". *Plant Systematics and Evolution*. **262**: 1. doi:10.1007/s00606-006-0454-5.

[5] "How to grow the herb rosemary". GardenAction. Retrieved 10 November 2011.

[6] Rosemary. BHG.com. Retrieved on 2014-06-03.

[7] McCoy, M. "Rosemary and its irritating growth habits". *The Gardenist*. Retrieved 10 April 2015.

[8] "Rosemary". ANZAC Day Commemoration Committee (Qld) Incorporated. 1988. Retrieved 10 November 2011.

[9] Rosemary. Gardenclinic.com.au. Retrieved on 2014-06-03.

[10] *Rosmarinus officinalis* 'Miss Jessop's Upright' AGM. Apps.rhs.org.uk. Retrieved on 2014-06-03.

[11] *Rosmarinus officinalis* 'Severn Sea' AGM. Apps.rhs.org.uk. Retrieved on 2014-06-03.

[12] *Rosmarinus officinalis* 'Sissinghurst Blue' AGM. Apps.rhs.org.uk. Retrieved on 2014-06-03.

[13] *Rosmarinus officinalis* var. *angustissimus* 'Benenden Blue' AGM. Apps.rhs.org.uk. Retrieved on 2014-06-03.

[14] "Nutrition Facts – Dried rosemary, one teaspoon (1 g)". *nutritiondata.com*. Conde Nast, USDA Nutrient Database, version SR-21. 2014.

[15] "USDA National Nutrient Database for Standard Reference". *NAL.usda.gov*. US Department of Agriculture. 2014. Retrieved 3 June 2014.

[16] "Oregano, rosemary extracts promise omega-3 preservation". 2007-11-20.

[17] Vallverdú-Queralt, A; Regueiro, J; Martínez-Huélamo, M; Rinaldi Alvarenga, J. F.; Leal, L. N.; Lamuela-Raventos, R. M. (2014). "A comprehensive study on the phenolic profile of widely used culinary herbs and spices: Rosemary, thyme, oregano, cinnamon, cumin and bay". *Food Chemistry*. **154**: 299–307. doi:10.1016/j.foodchem.2013.12.106. PMID 24518346.

[18] "Rosemary". Drugs.com. Retrieved 23 July 2016.

[19] Rašković, Aleksandar (7 July 2014). "Antioxidant activity of rosemary (Rosmarinus officinalis L.) essential oil and its hepatoprotective potential". *BMC Complementary and Alternative Medicine*. US Nat'l Institutes of Health. **14**: 225. doi:10.1186/1472-6882-14-225. PMC 4227022⊚. PMID 25002023. It should be emphasized that there have been considerable variations in the chemical composition of essential oils obtained from rosemary

[20] "History, Myths and Legends of Aromatherapy – Rosemary".

[21] "Rosemary". Australian War Memorial. Retrieved 10 November 2011.

[22] "Rosemary". *SuperbHerbs.net*.

[23] Capuano, Thomas (2005). "Las huellas de otro texto médico en Don Quijote: Las virtudes del romero". *Romance Notes*. **45** (3): 303–310.

3.86.7 External links

- Media related to Rosmarinus officinalis at Wikimedia Commons
- Chisholm, Hugh, ed. (1911). "rosemary". *Encyclopædia Britannica* (11th ed.). Cambridge University Press.
- Rosemary List of Chemicals (Dr. Duke's)
- History of Rosemary
- Description of characteristics, from Flora of China

3.87 Schefflera

Schefflera /ˈʃɛflərə/[1] is a genus of flowering plants in the family Araliaceae. The plants are trees, shrubs or lianas, growing 1–30 metres (3 ft 3 in–98 ft 5 in) tall, with woody stems and palmately compound leaves. The circumscription of the genus has varied greatly. Phylogenetic studies have shown that the widely used broad circumscription as a pantropical genus of over 700 species is polyphyletic, but it remains to be seen how this will affect the classification of the genus.[2][3]

Several species are grown in pots as houseplants, most commonly *Schefflera actinophylla* (Umbrella Tree) and *Schefflera arboricola* (Dwarf Umbrella Tree). Numerous cultivars have been selected for various characters, most popularly for variegated or purple foliage. *Schefflera* species are used as food plants by the larvae of some Lepidopteran species including *Batrachedra arenosella* (recorded on *S. stellata*). *Schefflera arboricola* and *Schefflera actinophylla* can be used to attract birds.*[4]

The genus is named in honor of Johann Peter Ernst von Scheffler (born in 1739), physician and botanist of Gdańsk, and later of Warsaw, who contributed plants to Gottfried Reyger for Reygers book, 'Tentamen Florae Gedanensis'.*[5]*[6]*[7]

3.87.1 Taxonomy

Schefflera venulosa, *details of inflorescence*

Schefflera gabriellae – *wood*

The genus has had a turbulent taxonomic history; the list of synonyms includes:

- *Actinomorphe* (Miq.) Miq.
- *Actinophyllum* Ruiz & Pav.
- *Agalma* Miq.
- *Astropanax* Seem.
- *Bakeria* Seem.
- *Brassaia* Endl.
- *Cephaloschefflera* (Harms) Merr.
- *Crepinella* Marchal
- *Didymopanax* Decne. & Planch.
- *Dizygotheca* N.E.Br.
- *Geopanax* Hemsl.
- *Heptapleurum* Gaertn.
- *Neocussonia* Hutch.
- *Nesopanax* Seem.
- *Octotheca* R.Vig.
- *Parapanax* Miq.
- *Paratropia* (Blume) DC.
- *Scheffleropsis* Ridl.
- *Sciadophyllum* P.Browne
- *Tupidanthus* Hook.f. & Thomson

3.87.2 References

[1] *Western Garden Book* (6th ed.). Sunset Pub Co. 1995. pp. 606–607. ISBN 978-0-376-03850-0.

[2] G. M. Plunkett, Porter P. Lowry II, D. G. Frodin & Jun Wen (2005). "Phylogeny and geography of *Schefflera*: pervasive polyphyly in the largest genus of Araliaceae". *Annals of the Missouri Botanical Garden*. **92** (2): 202–224. JSTOR 3298514.

[3] Pedro Fiaschi & Gregory M. Plunkett (2011). "Monophyly and phylogenetic relationships of Neotropical *Schefflera* (Araliaceae) based on plastid and nuclear markers". *Systematic Botany*. **36** (3): 806–817. doi:10.1600/036364411X583754.

[4] Johan Dalgas Frisch, Christian Dalgas Frisch (2005). *Aves Brasileiras e Plantas que as atraem*. São Paulo: Dalgas Ecotec. ISBN 85-85015-07-1.

[5] Forster. J.R. and Forster, G. Characteres Generum Plantarum. 1776

[6] Reyger, G. Tentamen Florae Gedanensis. vol. 2. 1766

[7] Schumann, E., ed. (1893). "Die einheimisclien Mitglieder der Gesellschaft, Lebensläufe". *Schriften der Naturforschenden Gesellschaft in Danzig*. **8** (2): 83.

3.87.3 Further reading

- Frodin, D. G. and R. Govaerts. 2004. World Checklist and Bibliography of Araliaceae. Kew Publishing. ISBN 978-1-84246-048-1

3.87.4 External links

3.88 Serissa

Serissa is a genus of flowering plants in the family Rubiaceae, containing only one species, ***Serissa japonica***. It is native to open sub-tropical woodlands and wet meadows in southeast Asia, from India, and China to Japan. It is commonly called the **snowrose**, **tree of a thousand stars**, or **Japanese boxthorn**; and was formerly called *Serissa foetida*. 'Foetida' referres to the unpleasant, vomit-like, odour that the trees give off if their leaves are pruned or bruised.

Snowrose and tree of a thousand stars are different cultivars. The only method of differentiating is measuring the difference in the shape and size of the flowers produced.

It is an evergreen or semi-evergreen shrub, 45–60 cm high, with oval, deep green, rather thick leaves that have an unpleasant smell if bruised (hence its name *foetida*). The upright stems branch in all directions and form a wide bushy dome. It is grown for its neat habit, good coverage of branches and long flowering time. It is also valued for its rough, grey trunk which tends to get lighter in colour with age.

Serissa flowers practically all year round, but particularly from early spring to near autumn. The 4- to 6-lobed flowers are funnel-shaped and 1 cm wide. They first appear as pink buds but turn to a profusion of white flowers. Fertilizing is especially important during the long flowering period.

Many cultivars with double flowers or variegated leaves are also available. 'Pink Snow Rose' has pale pink flowers and leaves edged off-white. Other cultivars include: 'Variegata', 'Variegated Pink', 'Pink Mystic', 'Snowflake', 'Snowleaves', 'Mt. Fuji', 'Kyoto' and 'Sapporo'.

Serissa is one of the most common bonsai, especially in Japan. It is not difficult to maintain as bonsai, but is very fussy. Many beginner bonsai enthusiasts will destroy a Serissa in their uninformed attempts to care for it. The trees respond adversely by dropping leaves if over-watered, under-watered, if it's too cold, too hot, or even if just moved to a new location. The plant usually grows back to health when put back to better conditions.[1][2]

Synonyms *Leptodermis nervosa, Leptodermis venosa, Buchozia coprosmoides, Serissa kawakamii, Serissa serissoides, Serissa democritea, Serissa foetida, Dysoda foetida, Dysoda fasciculata, Democritea serissoides, Serissa crassiramea, Serissa foetida forma plena, Serissa foetida forma pleniflora, Serissa foetida var. crassiramea*

3.88.1 Notes

[1] D'Cruz, Mark. "Ma-Ke Bonsai Care Guide for Serissa foetida". Ma-Ke Bonsai. Retrieved 2011-05-09.

[2] D'Cruz, Mark. "Ma-Ke Bonsai Care Guide for Serissa foetida Var. Mount Fuji". Ma-Ke Bonsai. Retrieved 2011-05-09.

3.88.2 External links

- http://www.bonsai-bci.com/species/serissa.html

- http://www.bonsai4me.com/SpeciesGuide/Serissa.html (Accessed 15 Sept 2006)

3.89 Syringa vulgaris

"Lilac" redirects here. For other uses, see Lilac (disambiguation).

Syringa vulgaris (**lilac** or **common lilac**) is a species of flowering plant in the olive family Oleaceae, native to the Balkan Peninsula, where it grows on rocky hills.[1][2][3] This species is widely cultivated as an ornamental and has been naturalized in other parts of Europe (including the United Kingdom, France, Germany, and Italy), as well as much of North America. It is not regarded as an aggressive species, found in the wild in widely scattered sites, usually in the vicinity of past or present human habitations.[4][5][6]

3.89.1 Description

S. vulgaris is a large deciduous shrub or multistemmed small tree, growing to 6–7 m (20–23 ft) high, producing secondary shoots ("suckers") from the base or roots, with stem diameters up to 20 cm (8 in), which in the course of decades may produce a small clonal thicket.[7] The bark is grey to grey-brown, smooth on young stems, longitudinally furrowed, and flaking on older stems. The leaves are simple, 4–12 cm (2–5 in) and 3–8 cm broad, light green to glaucous, oval to cordate, with pinnate leaf venation, a mucronate apex, and an entire margin. They are arranged in opposite pairs or occasionally in whorls of three. The flowers have a tubular base to the corolla 6–10 mm long with an open four-lobed apex 5–8 mm across, usually lilac to mauve, occasionally white. They are arranged in dense, terminal panicles 8–18 cm (3–7 in) long. The fruit is a dry, smooth, brown capsule, 1–2 cm long, splitting in two to release the two-winged seeds.*[1]*[8]

3.89.2 Taxonomy and naming

Syringa vulgaris was first formally described by Carl Linnaeus in 1753 and the description was published in *Species Plantarum*.*[9]*[10] The specific epithet (*vulgaris*) is a Latin word meaning "common" or "usual".*[11]

3.89.3 Garden history

Lilacs—both *S. vulgaris* and *S.* × *persica* the finer, smaller "Persian lilac", now considered a natural hybrid—were introduced into northern European gardens at the end of the 16th century, from Ottoman gardens, not through botanists exploring the Balkan habitats of *S. vulgaris*.*[12] The Holy Roman Emperor's ambassador, Ogier Ghiselin de Busbecq, is generally credited with supplying lilac slips to Carolus Clusius, about 1562. Well-connected botanists, such as the great herbalist John Gerard, soon had the rarity in their gardens: Gerard noted that he had lilacs growing "in very great plenty" in 1597, but lilacs were not mentioned by Shakespeare,*[13] and John Loudon was of the opinion that the Persian lilac had been introduced into English gardens by John Tradescant the elder.*[14] Tradescant's Continental source for information on the lilac, and perhaps ultimately for the plants, was Pietro Andrea Mattioli, as one can tell from a unique copy of Tradescant's plant list in his Lambeth garden, an adjunct of his *Musaeum Tradescantianum*; it was printed, though probably not published, in 1634: it lists *Lilac Matthioli*. That Tradescant's "lilac of Mattioli's" was a white one is shown by Elias Ashmole's manuscript list, *Trees found in Mrs Tredescants Ground when it came into my possession* (1662):*[15] "Syringa alba".

In the American colonies, lilacs were introduced in the 18th century. Peter Collinson, F.R.S., wrote to the Pennsylvania gardener and botanist John Bartram, proposing to send him some, and remarked that John Custis of Virginia had a fine "collection", which Ann Leighton interpreted as signifying common and Persian lilacs, in both purple and white, "the entire range of lilacs possible" at the time.*[16]

3.89.4 Cultivation

The lilac is a very popular ornamental plant in gardens and parks, because of its attractive, sweet-smelling flowers, which appear in early summer just before many of the roses and other summer flowers come into bloom."*[17]

In late summer, lilacs can be attacked by powdery mildew, specifically *Erysiphe syringae*, one of the Erysiphaceae.*[18] No fall color is seen and the seed clusters have no aesthetic appeal.

Common lilac tends to flower profusely in alternate years, a habit that can be improved by deadheading the flower clusters after the color has faded and before seeds, few of which are fertile, form. At the same time, twiggy growth on shoots that have flowered more than once or twice can be cut to a strong, outward-growing side shoot.

It is widely naturalised in western and northern Europe.*[8] In a sign of its complete naturalization in North America, it has been selected as the state flower of the state of New Hampshire, because it "is symbolic of that hardy character of the men and women of the Granite State".*[19] Additional hardiness, for Canadian gardens, was bred for in a series of *S. vulgaris* hybrids by Isabella Preston, who introduced many of the later-blooming varieties, whose later-developing flower buds are better protected from late spring frosts; the *Syringa* × *prestoniae* hybrids range primarily in the pink and lavender shades.*[20]

Cultivars

Most garden plants of *S. vulgaris* are cultivars, the majority of which do not exceed 4–5 m (13–16 ft) tall.*[21] Between 1876 and 1927, the nurseryman Victor Lemoine of Nancy introduced over 153 named cultivars, many of which are considered classics and still in commerce today. Lemoine's "French lilacs" extended the limited color range to include deeper, more saturated hues, and they also introduced double-flowered "sports", with the stamens replaced by extra petals.

These cultivars have gained the Royal Horticultural Society's Award of Garden Merit:

3.89.5 Gallery

• Flowers and heart-shaped leaves

S. vulgaris 'Alba'

S. vulgaris 'Charles Joly'

S. vulgaris 'Corondel'

S. vulgaris 'Etna'

S. vulgaris 'Mme. Francisque Morel'

S. vulgaris 'Maréchal Foch'

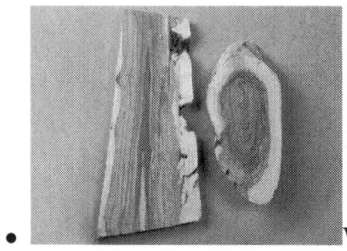

Wood of *Syringa*

Fasciation

Autumn foliage

3.89.6 References

[1] Rushforth, K. (1999). *Trees of Britain and Europe*. Collins ISBN 0-00-220013-9.

[2] Med-Checklist: *Syringa vulgaris*

[3] Flora Europaea: *Syringa vulgaris*

[4] Biota of North America Program, *Syringa vulgaris*

[5] Altervista Flora Italiana, *Syringa vulgaris*

[6] Illinois wildflowers, common lilac, *Syringa vulgaris*

[7] In second-growth woodlands of New England, a thicket of lilac may be the first indication of the cellar-hole of a vanished 19th-century timber-framed farmhouse.

[8] Blamey, M. & Grey-Wilson, C. (1989). *Flora of Britain and Northern Europe.* ISBN 0-340-40170-2.

[9] International Organization for Plant Information (IOPI). "Plant Name Search Results" (HTML). *International Plant Names Index.* Retrieved 27 December 2015.

[10] Linnaeus, Carl (1753). *Species Plantarum* (1 ed.). Stockholm: Laurentii Salvii. p. 9. Retrieved 27 December 2015.

[11] Brown, Roland Wilbur (1956). *The Composition of Scientific Words.* Washington, D.C.: Smithsonian Institution Press. p. 222.

[12] The botanic homeland of *S. vulgaris* was identified in 1828, when naturalist Anton Rocher found truly wild specimens in Balkans .

[13] Their first appearance by name in English print the *OED* dated to 1625.

[14] Loudon, *Arboretum* (1838:49), noted in R.T. Gunther, *Early British Botanists and their Gardens* (Oxford: Frederick Hall) 1922:339.

[15] Written in the endpapers of his copy of John Parkinson's *Paradisus*, in the Bodleian Library; printed in Gunther 1922:346

[16] Ann Leighton, *American Gardens in the Eighteenth Century* (University of Massachusetts Press) 1986:445

[17] *RHS A-Z encyclopedia of garden plants.* United Kingdom: Dorling Kindersley. 2008. p. 1136. ISBN 1405332964.

[18] B. Ing, "An Introduction to British Powdery Mildews" , in *The Mycologist* **5**.1 (1990:24–27).

[19] New Hampshire Revised Statute Annotated (RSA) 3:5

[20] Chicago Botanic Garden

[21] Huxley, A., ed. (1992). *New RHS Dictionary of Gardening.* Macmillan ISBN 0-333-47494-5.

[22] "RHS Plant Selector - *Syringa vulgaris* 'Andenken an Ludwig Späth'". Retrieved 17 July 2013.

[23] "RHS Plant Selector - *Syringa vulgaris* 'Firmament'". Retrieved 17 July 2013.

[24] "RHS Plant Selector - *Syringa vulgaris* 'Katherine Havemeyer'". Retrieved 17 July 2013.

[25] "RHS Plant Selector - *Syringa vulgaris* 'Madame Lemoine'". Retrieved 17 July 2013.

[26] "RHS Plant Selector - *Syringa vulgaris* 'Vestale'". Retrieved 17 July 2013.

3.89.7 External links

- "Lilac". *Encyclopædia Britannica* (11th ed.). 1911.

3.90 Taxodium ascendens

Taxodium ascendens, also known as **pond cypress**,[1] is a deciduous conifer of the genus *Taxodium*, native to North America. Many botanists treat it as a variety of bald cypress, *Taxodium distichum* (as *T. distichum* var. *imbricarium*) rather than as a distinct species, but it differs in ecology, occurring mainly in still blackwater rivers, ponds and swamps without silt-rich flood deposits. It predominates in cypress dome habitats.

3.90.1 Description

Taxodium ascendens reaches on average 15–18 metres (49–59 ft) in height. Compared to *T. distichum*, the leaves are shorter (3–10 mm long), slenderer and are on shoots that tend to be erect rather than spreading. The trunk is expanded at the base, even on young trees, assisting the tree in anchoring in the soft, muddy soil. The cones also tend to be smaller, not over 2.5 cm diameter. The bark is also a paler gray color. Like Bald Cypresses, Pond Cypresses growing in water have a characteristic growth trait called **cypress knees**; these are woody projections pneumatophores sent above the water from the roots, probably enabling this plant to breathe air in habitat with waterlogged soil. Maximum longevity of this plant is estimated at 1000 years. This figure may be an underestimate, as The Senator, until recently growing in Longwood, Florida's Big Tree Park, was estimated to be over 3,400 years old.

3.90.2 Distribution

This species is native to the southeastern United States, from southeastern Virginia to southeastern Louisiana and south into Florida except for the Florida Keys.

Stunted individuals of pond cypress are notable in the **dwarf cypress savanna** of the Everglades National Park.

3.90.3 Habitat

Taxodium ascendens occurs naturally in shallow ponds, lake margins, swamps and wetlands. It prefers wet, poorly drained and acidic soils, at an altitude of 0–30 metres (0–98 ft) above sea level.

3.90.4 References

[1] "*Taxodium ascendens*". Natural Resources Conservation Service PLANTS Database. USDA. Retrieved 8 December 2015.

3.91.1 Description

Taxodium distichum is a large slow-growing and long-lived tree typically reaching heights of 30–35 m (100–120 ft) and a trunk diameter of 1–2 m (3–6 ft). The bark is gray-brown to red-brown, thin and fibrous with a stringy texture, having a vertically interwoven pattern of shallow ridges and narrow furrows. The leaves are alternate and linear, with flat blades borne on the twig that are spirally arranged on the stem, but twisted at the base to lie in two horizontal ranks, 1–2 cm long and 1–2 mm broad. Unlike most other species in the family Cupressaceae, it is deciduous, losing its leaves in the winter months, hence the name 'bald'. It is monoecious (separate staminate and carpellate flowers are always found on the same plant), with male and female flowers forming on slender tassel-like structures near the edge of the branchlets. The male and female strobili are produced from buds formed in the late fall, with pollination in early winter, and mature in about 12 months. The seed cones are green maturing gray-brown, globular, and 2-3.5 cm in diameter. They have from 20 to 30 spirally arranged, four-sided scales, each bearing one or two (rarely three) triangular seeds. The number of seeds per cone ranges from 20 to 40. The cones disintegrate when mature to release the large seeds. The seeds are 5–10 mm long, the largest of any species in the cypress family, and are produced every year, but with heavy crops every three to five years. The seedlings have three to 9 (most often six) cotyledons.*[3]

The main trunks are surrounded by cypress knees.

The tallest known individual specimen, near Williamsburg, Virginia, is 44.11 m tall, and the stoutest known, in the Cat Island National Wildlife Refuge near Baton Rouge, Louisiana, has a diameter at breast height (DBH) of 521 cm.*[5] The oldest known specimen, located in Bladen County, North Carolina, is over 1,620 years old, making this one of the oldest living plants in eastern North America.*[7]

Taxodium ascendens in the Black Water, Okefenokee Swamp, Georgia, USA

- Flora of North America (as *T. distichum* var. *imbricarium*)
- Floridata
- File:The Senator Tree Longwood Florida.JPG

3.90.5 External links

- ITIS
- NCBI

3.91 Taxodium distichum

Taxodium distichum (**bald cypress**,*[2] **baldcypress**, **bald-cypress**, **cypress**, **southern-cypress**, **white-cypress**, **tidewater red-cypress**, **Gulf-cypress**, **red-cypress**, or **swamp cypress**) is a deciduous conifer in the family Cupressaceae that grows on saturated and seasonally inundated soils in the lowlands of the Southeastern and Gulf Coastal Plains of the United States.*[3]*[4]*[5]*[6]

3.91.2 Taxonomy

The closely related *Taxodium ascendens* (pond cypress) is treated by some botanists as a distinct species,*[8] while others classify it as merely a variety of bald-cypress,*[3]*[5] as *Taxodium distichum* var. *imbricatum* (Nutt.) Croom. It differs in shorter leaves borne on erect shoots, and in ecology, being largely confined to low-nutrient blackwater habitats. A few authors also treat *Taxodium mucronatum* as a variety of bald cypress, as *T. distichum* var. *mexicanum* Gordon, thereby considering the genus as comprising only one species.*[9]

3.91.3 Habitat

Bald cypress in Trap Pond State Park, Delaware

Bald cypress on the Texas side of Caddo Lake

Range

Bald cypress range

The native range extends from Delaware Bay south to Florida and west to East Texas and southeastern Oklahoma, and also inland up the Mississippi and Ohio Rivers north to southern Illinois and Indiana. Mature planted specimens are seen as far north as Pittsburgh,*[10] and Ottawa, Ontario.*[11] In Ottawa, in the Central Experimental Farm Arboretum, an average winter may kill back a quarter to half of new growth. Ancient bald cypress forests, with some trees more than 1,700 years old, once dominated swamps in the southeast US. The largest remaining old-growth stands are at Corkscrew Swamp Sanctuary, near Naples, Florida. and in the Three Sisters tract along eastern North Carolina's Black River. The Corkscrew trees are around 500 years of age and some exceed 40 m in height. The Black River trees were cored in 1986 by University of Arkansas dendrologists with dates ranging back to 364 AD.*[12] In the northern and more inland part of its range from Delaware and Maryland to Williamsburg, Virginia, it is found in groups growing in swamps and is accompanied by other hardwoods. In the southern parts of its range from extreme southeastern Virginia, Virginia Beach south to Florida and west to Texas, bald cypress can be found growing with loblolly pine and live oak, and it may be heavily covered in Spanish moss. This can be observed in the far northern part of its range at First Landing State Park, Virginia Beach, Virginia. From eastern North Carolina down throughout Florida and over to southeast and south Texas, bald cypress may be accompanied in forests by dwarf palmetto.

It is native to humid climates where annual precipitation ranges from about 760 mm (in Texas) to 1630 mm (along the Gulf Coast). Although it grows best in warm climates, the natural northern limit of the species is not due to a lack of cold tolerance, but to specific reproductive requirements; further north, regeneration is prevented by ice damage to seedlings. Larger trees are able to tolerate much lower temperatures and lower humidity.

In 2012 Scuba divers discovered an underwater forest several miles off the coast of Mobile, AL in 60 feet of water. The forest contains trees that could not be dated with radiocarbon methods since they are older than 50,000 years old, thus most likely lived in the early glacial interval of the last ice age. The forest contains trees so well-preserved that when they are cut, they still smell like fresh cypress. The team, which has not yet published their results in a peer-reviewed journal, is currently studying the site. It is estimated that they have less than two years before wood-burrowing marine animals destroy the submerged forest.*[13]

Soils and topography

Most bald cypress trees grow on flat ground on alluvial soils, usually at elevations of less than 50 m above sea level, although some stands may occur at elevations of 500 m in Texas.

Bald cypress occurs mainly along riparian (riverside) wetlands normally subject to periodic flooding by silt-rich 'brownwater' rivers, unlike the related *Taxodium ascendens*, which occurs in silt-poor blackwater rivers and ponds. *T. distichum* tolerates minor salinity, but does not grow in brackish or saline coastal waters.

3.91.4 Reproduction and early growth

Foliage in autumn just before shedding

Bald cypress is monoecious. Male and female strobili mature in one growing season from buds formed the previous year. The male catkins are about 2 mm (0.079 in) in diameter and are borne in slender, purplish, drooping clusters 7 to 13 cm (3 to 5 in) long that are conspicuous during the winter on this deciduous conifer. Pollen is shed in March and April. Female conelets are found singly or in clusters of two or three. The globose cones turn from green to brownish-purple as they mature from October to December. The cones are 13 to 36 mm (0.51 to 1.42 in) in diameter and consist of 9 to 15 four-sided scales that break away irregularly after maturity. Each scale can bear two irregular, triangular seeds with thick, horny, warty coats and projecting flanges.*[14]*[15]*[16]*[6]*[17] The number of seeds per cone averages 16 and ranges from two to 34. Cleaned seeds number from about 5600 to 18,430/kg (2,540 to 8,360/lb).*[6]*[15]*[16]*[17]

Seed production and dissemination

Some seeds are produced every year, and good seed crops occur at three- to five-year intervals.*[17] At maturity, the cone scales with their resin-coated seeds adhering to them, or sometimes entire cones, drop to the water or ground.*[18] This drop of mature seeds is often hastened by squirrels, which eat bald cypress seeds, but usually drop several scales with undamaged seeds still attached to each cone they pick.*[19] Floodwaters spread the scales or cones along streams and are the most important means of seed dissemination.*[16]

Seedling development

Germination is epigeal.*[17] Under swamp conditions, germination generally takes place on a sphagnum moss or a wet-muck seedbed. Seeds will not germinate under water, but some will remain viable for 30 months under water. On the other hand, seeds usually fail to germinate on better drained soils because of the lack of surface water. Thus, a soil saturated but not flooded for a period of one to three months after seedfall is required for germination.*[16]

Bald cypress swamp and Spanish moss at First Landing State Park in Virginia Beach, VA

After germination, seedlings must grow fast enough to keep at least part of their crowns above floodwaters for most of the growing season.*[20]*[21]*[22] Bald cypress seedlings can endure partial shading, but require overhead light for good growth.*[23] Seedlings in swamps often reach heights of 20 to 75 cm (8 to 29.5 in) their first year.*[24] Growth is checked when a seedling is completely submerged by flooding, and prolonged submergence kills the seedling.*[16]

In nurseries, *Taxodium* seeds show an apparent internal dormancy that can be overcome by various treatments, usually including cold stratification or submerging in water for 60 days. Nursery beds are sown in spring with pretreated seeds or in fall with untreated seeds. Seedlings usually reach 75 to 100 cm (29.5 to 39.5 in) in height during their first (and usually only) year in the nursery. Average size of 1-0 nursery-grown seedlings in a seed source test including 72 families was 81.4 cm (32.0 in) tall and 1.1 cm (0.43 in) in diameter.

Control of competing vegetation may be necessary for a year or more for bald cypress planted outside of swamps. Five years after planting on a harrowed and bedded, poorly drained site in Florida, survival was high, but heights had increased only 30 cm (12 in), probably because of heavy herbaceous competition. Seedlings grown in a crawfish pond in Louisiana, where weed control and soil moisture were excellent through June, averaged 2.9 m (9.5 ft) and 3.5 cm (1.4 in) diameter at breast height (DBH) after five years. However, a replicate of the same sources planted on an old soybean field, where weed control and soil moisture were poor, resulted in the same DBH, but a smaller average seedling height of 2.1 m (6.9 ft). When planted in a residential yard and weeded and watered, they averaged 3.7 m (12 ft) tall three years later.

Vegetative reproduction

Bald cypress is one of the few conifer species that sprouts. Thrifty sprouts are generally produced from stumps of young trees, but trees up to 60 years old also send up healthy sprouts if the trees are cut during the fall or winter. However, survival of these sprouts is often poor and those that live are usually poorly shaped and do not make quality sawtimber trees. Stumps of trees up to 200 years old may also sprout, but the sprouts are not as vigorous and are more subject to wind damage as the stump decays. In the only report on the rooting of bald cypress cuttings found in the literature, cuttings from trees five years old rooted better than those from older trees.

3.91.5 Ecology

The seeds remain viable for less than one year, and are dispersed in two ways. One is by water; the seeds float and move on water until flooding recedes or the cone is deposited on shore. The second is by wildlife; squirrels eat seeds, but often drop some scales from the cones they harvest. Seeds do not germinate under water and rarely germinate on well-drained soils; seedlings normally become established on continuously saturated, but not flooded, soils for one to three months. After germination, seedlings must grow quickly to escape floodwaters; they often reach a

A bald cypress in the Atchafalaya Basin of Louisiana

height of 20–75 cm (up to 100 cm in fertilized nursery conditions) in their first year. Seedlings die if inundated for more than about two to four weeks. Natural regeneration is therefore prevented on sites that are always flooded during the growing season. Although vigorous saplings and stump sprouts can produce viable seed, most specimens do not produce seed until they are about 30 years old. In good conditions, Bald-cypress grows fairly fast when young, then more slowly with age. Trees have been measured to reach 3 m in five years, 21 m in 41 years, and 36 m in height in 96 years; height growth has largely ceased by the time the trees are 200 years old. Some individuals can live over 1,000 years. Determination of the age of an old tree may be difficult because of frequent missing or false rings of stemwood caused by variable and stressful growing environments.

Bald cypress trees growing in swamps have a peculiarity of growth called cypress knees. These are woody projections from the root system project above the ground or water. Their function was once thought to be to provide oxygen to the roots, which grow in the low dissolved oxygen (DO) waters typical of a swamp (as in mangroves). However, evidence for this is scant; in fact, roots of swamp-dwelling specimens whose knees are removed do not decrease in

Bald cypress knees in duckweed

Bald cypress forest in winter, showing "knees" and (brown) high flood level, Lynches River, Johnsonville, South Carolina

oxygen content and the trees continue to thrive. Another more likely function is structural support and stabilization. Bald cypress trees growing on flood-prone sites tend to form buttressed bases, but trees grown on drier sites may lack this feature. Buttressed bases and a strong, intertwined root system allow them to resist very strong winds; even hurricanes rarely overturn them.*[25]

Many agents damage *T. distichum* trees. The main damaging (in some cases lethal) agent is the fungus *Stereum taxodii*, which causes a brown pocket rot known as "pecky cypress". It attacks the heartwood of living trees, usually from the crown down to the roots. A few other fungi attack the sapwood and the heartwood of the tree, but they do not usually cause serious damage. Insects such as the cypress flea beetle (*Systena marginalis*) and the bald cypress leafroller (*Archips goyerana*) (closely related to the fruit tree leafroller) can seriously damage trees by destroying leaves, cones or the bark. Nutrias also clip and unroot young bald cypress seedlings, sometimes killing a whole plantation in a short amount of time.*[25]

3.91.6 Conservation

In 2002, the Indiana Department of Natural Resources identified *T distichum* as a state protected plant with the status of Threatened.

3.91.7 Cultivation and uses

This species is a popular ornamental tree, grown for its light, feathery foliage and orange-brown to dull red fall color. In cultivation, it thrives on a wide range of soils, including well-drained sites where it would not grow naturally due to the inability of the young seedlings to compete with other vegetation. Cultivation is successful far to the north of its native range, north to southern Canada. It is also commonly planted in Europe, Asia and elsewhere with temperate to subtropical climates. It does, however, require hot summers for good growth; when planted in areas with cool summers oceanic climates, growth is healthy but very slow (some in northeastern England have only reached 4–5 m tall in about 50 years),*[26] and cones are not produced.

One of the oldest in Europe, was planted in the 1900s in the Arboretum de Pézanin, Burgundy, France.

Bald cypress has been noted for its high merchantable yields. In virgin stands, yields from 112 to 196 m^3/ha were common, and some stands might have exceeded 1000 m^3/ha. Bald cypress swamps are some of the world's most productive ecosystems.

The odorless wood of bald cypress, closely resembling that of *Cupressus* spp., has long been valued for its water resis-

Timber

tance, thus is called 'wood eternal'. Still-usable prehistoric wood is often found in swamps as far north as New Jersey, and occasionally as far as Connecticut, although it is more common in the southeast. The somewhat-mineralized wood is mined from some swamps in the southeast, and is highly prized for specialty uses such as wood carvings. Pecky cypress, caused by the fungus *Stereum taxodii* is used for decorative wall paneling.

The bald cypress was designated the official state tree of Louisiana in 1963.*[27] It is considered by some to be a symbol of the southern swamps.

Cypress trees can be used in the making of shingles. Joshua D. Brown, the first settler of Kerrville, Texas, made his living producing shingles from cypress trees growing along the Guadalupe River of the Texas Hill Country.*[28] Shingles produced from cypress were also one of the main industries for early pioneers in Kissimmee, Florida (near Walt Disney World). One of the main bodies of water in the area, Shingle Creek, is named in homage of their importance to the growth of the city.*[29]

3.91.8 References

[1] Conifer Specialist Group (1998). "*Taxodium distichum*". *IUCN Red List of Threatened Species. Version 2006.* International Union for Conservation of Nature. Retrieved 12 May 2006.

[2] "*Taxodium distichum*". Natural Resources Conservation Service PLANTS Database. USDA. Retrieved 8 December 2015.

[3] Farjon, A. (2005). *Monograph of Cupressaceae and Sciadopitys*. Royal Botanic Gardens, Kew. ISBN 1-84246-068-4

[4] "*Taxodium distichum*". *Flora of North America (FNA)*. Missouri Botanical Garden – via eFloras.org.

[5] Gymnosperm Database: *Taxodium distichum*

[6] Wilhite, L. P.; Toliver, J. R. (1990). "*Taxodium distichum*". In Burns, Russell M.; Honkala, Barbara H. *Conifers. Silvics of North America*. Washington, D.C.: United States Forest Service (USFS), United States Department of Agriculture (USDA). **1** – via Northeastern Area State and Private Forestry (www.na.fs.fed.us).

[7] http://www.ldeo.columbia.edu/~{}adk/oldlisteast/Spp/TADI.html

[8] USDA Plants Profiles: *Taxodium distichum*, *Taxodium ascendens*

[9] "*Taxodium*". *Flora of North America (FNA)*. Missouri Botanical Garden – via eFloras.org.

[10] http://www.pittsburghforest.org/userfiles/file/Lawrenceville%20Tree%20of%20the%20Month/LV_Tree_of_Month_03_Bald_Cypress.pdf

[11] Richard Hinchcliff (2007). *For the Love of Trees*. General Store Publishing. pp. 52–53. ISBN 978-1-897113-73-8.

[12] Paul Ferguson (2008). "Searching for Methuselah" (PDF). Pocosin Press. pp. 1–3. Retrieved 21 April 2011.

[13] "Primeval Underwater Forest Discovered in Gulf of Mexico". Live Science. Retrieved 11 July 2013.

[14] Faulkner, Stephen P. 1982. Genetic variation of cones, seed and nursery-grown seedlings of baldcypress [Taxodium distichum (L.) Rich.] provenances. M.S. Thesis, Louisiana State University, Baton Rouge. 71 p.

[15] Radford, Albert E., Harry E. Ahles, and C. Ritchie Bell. 1968. Manual of the vascular flora of the Carolinas. University of North Carolina Press, Chapel Hill. 1183 p.

[16] U.S. Department of Agriculture, Forest Service. 1965. Silvics of forest trees of the United States. H. A. Fowells, comp. U.S. Department of Agriculture, Agriculture Handbook 271. Washington, DC. 762 p.

[17] U.S. Department of Agriculture, Forest Service. 1974. Seeds of woody plants in the United States. C. S. Schopmeyer, tech. coord. U.S. Department of Agriculture, Agriculture Handbook 450. Washington, DC. 883 p.

[18] Stubbs, Jack. 1983. Personal communication. USDA Forest Service, Southeastern Forest Experiment Station, Clemson, SC.

[19] Brunswig, Norman L. 1983. Personal communication. National Audubon Society, Francis Beidler Forest, Harleyville, SC.

[20] Conner, William H, 1988, Natural and artificial regeneration of baldcypress [Taxodium distichum (L.) Rich.] in the Barataria and Lake Verret basins of Louisiana. Ph.D. Dissertation, Louisiana State University, Baton Rouge. 148 p.

[21] Conner, William H., and John R. Toliver. 1987. Vexar seedling protectors did not reduce nutria damage to planted baldcypress seedlings. USDA Forest Service, Tree Planter's Notes 38(3):26-29.

[22] Conner, William H., John R. Toliver, and Fred H. Sklar. 1986. Natural regeneration of baldcypress [Taxodium distichum (L.) Rich.] in a Louisiana swamp. Forest Ecology and Management 14:305-317.

[23] Williston, H. L., F. W. Shropshire, and W. E. Balmer. 1980. Cypress management: a forgotten opportunity. USDA Forest Service, Southeastern Area State and Private Forestry, Forestry Report SA-FR-8. Atlanta, GA. 8 p.

[24] Bull, H. 1949. Cypress planting in southern Louisiana. Southern Lumberman 179(2249):227-230.

[25] U.S. Forest Service Silvics Manual: *Taxodium distichum*

[26] Tree Register of the British Isles

[27] Calhoun, Milburn; Frois, Jeanne (31 May 2006). *Louisiana Almanac, 2006-2007* (17th ed.). Pelican Publishing. p. 431. ISBN 978-1-58980-307-7.

[28] Historical marker, Texas Historical Commission, Kerrville, Texas, 1971

[29] http://osceola.ifas.ufl.edu/pdfs/Natural%20Resources/Shingle%20Creek_Brochure_2013_final.pdf

3.91.9 External links

- Images of bald-cypress trees and swamps
- Interactive Distribution Map for Taxodium distichum
- Photos of remarkable bald-cypress trees worldwide
- *Taxodium distichum* - information, genetic conservation units and related resources. European Forest Genetic Resources Programme (EUFORGEN)

3.91.10 See also

- Battle Creek Cypress Swamp, Maryland
- Barley Barber Swamp, Florida

3.92 Taxus baccata

Taxus baccata is a conifer native to western, central and southern Europe, northwest Africa, northern Iran and southwest Asia.[*][2] It is the tree originally known as **yew**, though with other related trees becoming known, it may now be known as **English yew**,[*][3] or **European yew**.

3.92.1 Taxonomy and naming

The word *yew* is from Proto-Germanic **īwa-*, possibly originally a loanword from Gaulish **ivos*, compare Irish *ēo*, Welsh *ywen*, French *if* (see Eihwaz for a discussion). *Baccata* is Latin for *bearing red berries*. The word *yew* as it was originally used seems to refer to the color brown.[*][4] The yew (μίλος) was known to Theophrastus, who noted its preference for mountain coolness and shade, its evergreen character and its slow growth.[*][5]

Most Romance languages, with the notable exception of French, kept a version of the Latin word *taxus* (Italian *tasso*, Corsican *tassu*, Occitan *teis*, Catalan *teix*, Gasconic *tech*, Spanish *tejo*, Portuguese *teixo*, Galician *teixo* and Romanian *tisă*) from the same root as *toxic*. In Slavic languages, the same root is preserved: Russian *tis* (*тис*), Slovakian *tis*, Slovenian *tisa*, Serbian-Croatian-Bosnian *tisa/muca*. Albanian borrowed it as *tis*.

In German it is known as Eibe.

In Iran, the tree is known as *sorkhdār* (Persian: سرخدار, literally "the red tree").

The common yew was one of the many species first described by Linnaeus. It is one of around 30 conifer species in seven genera in the family Taxaceae, which is placed in the order Pinales.

3.92.2 Description

It is a small to medium-sized evergreen tree, growing 10–20 metres (33–66 ft) (exceptionally up to 28 metres (92 ft)) tall, with a trunk up to 2 metres (6 ft 7 in) (exceptionally 4 metres (13 ft)) diameter. The bark is thin, scaly brown, coming off in small flakes aligned with the stem. The leaves are flat, dark green, 1–4 centimetres (0.39–1.57 in) long and 2–3 millimetres (0.079–0.118 in) broad, arranged spirally on the stem, but with the leaf bases twisted to align

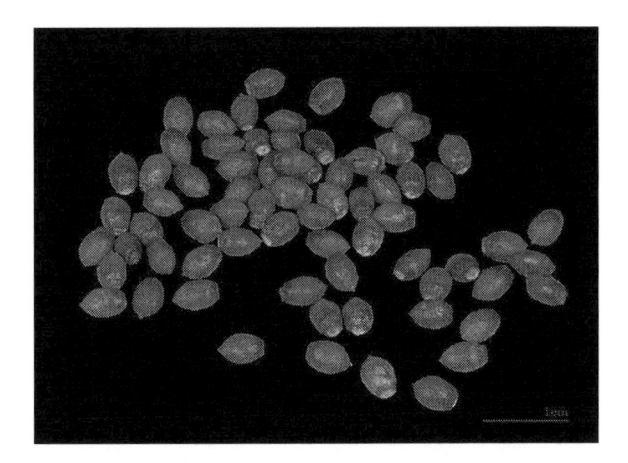

Seeds of Taxus baccata

the leaves in two flat rows either side of the stem, except on erect leading shoots where the spiral arrangement is more obvious. The leaves are poisonous.*[2]*[6]

The seed cones are modified, each cone containing a single seed, which is 4–7 millimetres (0.16–0.28 in) long, and partly surrounded by a fleshy scale which develops into a soft, bright red berry-like structure called an aril. The aril is 8–15 millimetres (0.31–0.59 in) long and wide and open at the end. The arils mature 6 to 9 months after pollination, and with the seed contained, are eaten by thrushes, waxwings and other birds, which disperse the hard seeds undamaged in their droppings. Maturation of the arils is spread over 2 to 3 months, increasing the chances of successful seed dispersal. The seeds themselves are poisonous and bitter, but are opened and eaten by some bird species including hawfinches,*[7] greenfinches and great tits.*[8] The aril is not poisonous, it is gelatinous and very sweet tasting. The male cones are globose, 3–6 millimetres (0.12–0.24 in) diameter, and shed their pollen in early spring. The yew is mostly dioecious, but occasional individuals can be variably monoecious, or change sex with time.*[2]*[6]*[9]

3.92.3 Longevity

Taxus baccata can reach 400 to 600 years of age. Some specimens live longer but the age of yews is often overestimated.*[10] Ten yews in Britain are believed to predate the 10th century.*[11] The potential age of yews is impossible to determine accurately and is subject to much dispute. There is rarely any wood as old as the entire tree, while the boughs themselves often become hollow with age, making ring counts impossible. Evidence based on growth rates and archaeological work of surrounding structures suggests the oldest yews, such as the Fortingall Yew in Perthshire, Scotland, may be in the range of 2,000 years,*[12]*[13]*[14] placing them among the oldest plants in Europe. One characteristic contributing to yew's longevity is that it is able to split under the weight of advanced growth without succumbing to disease in the fracture, as do most other trees. Another is its ability to give rise to new epicormic and basal shoots from cut surfaces and low on its trunk, even at an old age.

3.92.4 Significant trees

The Llangernyw Yew

The Fortingall Yew in Perthshire, Scotland, has the largest recorded trunk girth in Britain and experts estimate it to be 2,000 to 3,000 years old, although it may be a remnant of a post-Roman Christian site and around 1,500 years old.*[15] The Llangernyw Yew in Clwyd, Wales, can be found at an early saint site and is about 1,500 years old.*[16] Other well known yews include the Ankerwycke Yew, the Balderschwang Yew, the Caesarsboom, the Florencecourt Yew, and the Borrowdale Fraternal Four, of which poet William Wordsworth wrote. The Kingley Vale National Nature Reserve in West Sussex has one of Europe's largest yew woodlands.

The oldest specimen in Spain is located in Bermiego, Asturias. It is known as *Teixu l'Iglesia* in the Asturian language. It stands 15 m (49 ft) tall with a trunk diameter of 6.82 m (22.4 ft) and a crown diameter of 15 m. It was declared a Natural Monument on April 27, 1995 by the Asturian Government and is protected by the Plan of Natural Resources.*[17]

A unique forest formed by *Taxus baccata* and European box (*Buxus sempervirens*) lies within the city of Sochi, in the Western Caucasus.

Estry Yew, Normandy, around 1,600 years old

3.92.5 Allergenic potential

Yews in this genus are primarily separate-sexed, and males are extremely allergenic, with an OPALS allergy scale rating of 10 out of 10. Completely female yews have an OPALS rating of 1, and are considered "allergy-fighting".*[18] Male yews bloom and release abundant amounts of pollen in the spring; completely female yews only trap pollen while producing none.*[18]

3.92.6 Toxicity

All parts of a yew plant are toxic to humans with the exception of the yew berries (however, their seeds are toxic); additionally, male and monoecious yews in this genus release cytotoxic pollen, which can cause headaches, lethargy, aching joints, itching, and skin rashes; it is also a trigger for asthma.*[18]*[19] These pollen granules are extremely small, and can easily pass through window screens.*[18]

The foliage itself remains toxic even when wilted, and toxicity increases in potency when dried.*[20] Ingestion and subsequent excretion by birds whose beaks and digestive systems do not break down the seed's coating are the primary means of yew dispersal.*[21] The major toxin within the yew is the alkaloid taxine.*[22] Horses have a relatively low tolerance to taxine, with a lethal dose of 200–400 mg/kg body weight; cattle, pigs, and other livestock are only slightly less vulnerable.*[23] Several studies*[24] have found taxine LD_{50} values under 20 mg/kg in mice and rats.

Symptoms of yew poisoning include an accelerated heart rate, muscle tremors, convulsions, collapse, difficulty breathing, circulation impairment and eventually cardiac arrest. However, there may be no symptoms, and if poisoning remains undetected death may occur within hours.*[25] Fatal poisoning in humans is very rare, usually occurring after consuming yew foliage. The leaves are more toxic than the seed.*[22]

3.92.7 Uses and traditions

Foliage of Irish yew, Taxus baccata *'Fastigiata'; note the leaves spreading all round the erect shoots*

In the ancient Celtic world, the yew tree (*eburos) had extraordinary importance; a passage by Caesar narrates that Catuvolcus, chief of the Eburones poisoned himself with yew rather than submit to Rome (*Gallic Wars* 6: 31). Similarly, Florus notes that when the Cantabrians were under siege by the legate Gaius Furnius in 22 BC, most of them took their lives either by the sword, by fire, or by a poison extracted *ex arboribus taxeis*, that is, from the yew tree (2: 33, 50–51). In a similar way, Orosius notes that when the Astures were besieged at *Mons Medullius*, they preferred to die by their own swords or by the yew tree poison rather than surrender (6, 21, 1).

Religion

The yew is traditionally and regularly found in churchyards in England, Wales, Scotland, Ireland and Northern France (more specifically in Normandy). Some examples can be found in La Haye-de-Routot or La Lande-Patry. It is said that up to 40 people could stand inside one of the La-Haye-de-Routot yew trees and the Le Ménil-Ciboult yew is probably the largest one (13 m diameter*[26]). Indeed, some of these trees are exceptionally large (over 5 m diameter) and may be over 2,000 years old. Sometimes monks planted yews in the middle of their cloister, as at

Door of the Chapel in a Norman yew, poisoned in 2013 by glyphosate

Muckross Abbey (Ireland) or abbaye de Jumièges (France, Normandy). Some ancient yew trees are located at St Mary the Virgin Church, Overton-on-Dee in Wales.

In Asturian tradition and culture the yew tree has had a real link with the land, the people, the ancestors and the ancient religion. It was tradition on All Saints Day to bring a branch of a yew tree to the tombs of those who had died recently so they will find the guide in their return to the Land of Shadows. The yew tree has been found near chapels, churches and cemeteries since ancient times as a symbol of the transcendence of death, and is usually found in the main squares of the villages where people celebrated the open councils that served as a way of general assembly to rule the village affairs.*[27]

It has been suggested that the Sacred Tree at the Temple at Uppsala was an ancient yew tree.*[28]*[29] The Christian church commonly found it expedient to take over existing pre-Christian sacred sites for churches. It has also been suggested that yews were planted at religious sites as their long life was suggestive of eternity, or because being toxic they were seen as trees of death.*[30] Another suggested explanation is that yews were planted to discourage farmers and drovers from letting animals wander onto the burial grounds, the poisonous foliage being the disincentive. A further possible reason is that fronds and branches of yew were often used as a substitute for palms on Palm Sunday.*[31]*[32]*[33]

In traditional Germanic paganism, Yggdrasill was often seen as a giant ash tree. Many scholars now agree that in the past an error has been made in the interpretation of the ancient writings, and that the tree is most likely a European yew (*Taxus baccata*). This mistake would find its origin in an alternative word for the yew tree in the Old Norse, namely needle ash (*barraskr*). In addition, ancient sources, including the Eddas, speak about a *vetgrønster vida* which means "evergreen tree". An ash sheds its leaves in the winter, while yew trees retain their needles.

Conifers were in the past often seen as sacred, because they never lose their green. In addition, the tree of life was not only an object from the stories, but also believers often gathered around an existing tree. The yew releases gaseous toxins (taxine) on hot days. Taxine is in some instances capable of causing hallucinations. This has some similarities with the story that Odin had a revelation (the wisdom of the runes) after having been hanging from the tree for nine days.

Medical

Certain compounds found in the bark of yew trees were discovered by Wall and Wani in 1967 to have efficacy as anticancer agents. The precursors of the chemotherapy drug paclitaxel (taxol) was later shown to be synthesized easily from extracts of the leaves of European yew,*[34] which is a much more renewable source than the bark of the Pacific yew (*Taxus brevifolia*) from which they were initially isolated. This ended a point of conflict in the early 1990s; many environmentalists, including Al Gore, had opposed the destructive harvesting of Pacific yew for paclitaxel cancer treatments. Docetaxel can then be obtained by semi-synthetic conversion from the precursors.

Woodworking and longbows

Wood from the yew is classified as a closed-pore softwood, similar to cedar and pine. Easy to work, yew is among the hardest of the softwoods; yet it possesses a remarkable elasticity, making it ideal for products that require springiness, such as bows.*[35]

One of the world's oldest surviving wooden artifacts is a Clactonian yew*[36] spear head, found in 1911 at Clacton-on-Sea, in Essex, UK. Known as the Clacton Spear, it is estimated to be over 400,000 years old.*[37]*[38]

Yew is also associated with Wales and England because of the longbow, an early weapon of war developed in north-

Bole of an ancient yew in Pont-de-Buis-lès-Quimerch, Brittany

ern Europe, and as the English longbow the basis for a medieval tactical system. The oldest surviving yew longbow was found at Rotten Bottom in Dumfries and Galloway, Scotland. It has been given a calibrated radiocarbon date of 4040 BC to 3640 BC and is on display in the National Museum of Scotland. Yew is the wood of choice for longbow making; the heartwood is always on the inside of the bow with the sapwood on the outside. This makes most efficient use of their properties as heartwood is best in compression whilst sapwood is superior in tension. However, much yew is knotty and twisted, and therefore unsuitable for bowmaking; most trunks do not give good staves and even in a good trunk much wood has to be discarded.

There was a tradition of planting yew trees in churchyards throughout Britain and Ireland, among other reasons, as a resource for bows. "Ardchattan Priory whose yew trees, according to other accounts, were inspected by Robert the Bruce and cut to make at least some of the longbows used at the Battle of Bannockburn." *[39]

The trade of yew wood to England for longbows was so robust that it depleted the stocks of good-quality, mature yew over a vast area. The first documented import of yew bowstaves to England was in 1294. In 1350 there was a serious shortage, and Henry IV of England ordered his royal bowyer to enter private land and cut yew and other woods. In 1423 the Polish king commanded protection of yews in order to cut exports, facing nearly complete destruction of local yew stock.*[40] In 1470 compulsory archery practice was renewed, and hazel, ash, and laburnum were specifically allowed for practice bows. Supplies still proved insufficient, until by the Statute of Westminster in 1472, every ship coming to an English port had to bring four bowstaves for every tun.*[41] Richard III of England increased this to ten for every tun. This stimulated a vast network of extraction and supply, which formed part of royal monopolies in southern Germany and Austria. In 1483, the price of bowstaves rose from two to eight pounds per hundred, and in 1510 the Venetians would only sell a hundred for sixteen pounds. In 1507 the Holy Roman Emperor asked the Duke of Bavaria to stop cutting yew, but the trade was profitable, and in 1532 the royal monopoly was granted for the usual quantity "if there are that many." In 1562, the Bavarian government sent a long plea to the Holy Roman Emperor asking him to stop the cutting of yew, and outlining the damage done to the forests by its selective extraction, which broke the canopy and allowed wind to destroy neighbouring trees. In 1568, despite a request from Saxony, no royal monopoly was granted because there was no yew to cut, and the next year Bavaria and Austria similarly failed to produce enough yew to justify a royal monopoly. Forestry records in this area in the 17th century do not mention yew, and it seems that no mature trees were to be had. The English tried to obtain supplies from the Baltic, but at this period bows were being replaced by guns in any case.*[42]

Horticulture

*An Irish yew (*Taxus baccata *'Fastigiata') planted at Kenilworth Castle*

Today European yew is widely used in landscaping and ornamental horticulture. Due to its dense, dark green, mature foliage, and its tolerance of even very severe pruning, it is used especially for formal hedges and topiary. Its relatively slow growth rate means that in such situations it needs to be clipped only once per year (in late summer).

Well over 200 cultivars of *T. baccata* have been named. The most popular of these are the Irish yew (*T. baccata* 'Fastigiata'), a fastigiate cultivar of the European yew selected from two trees found growing in Ireland, and the several cultivars with yellow leaves, collectively known as "golden yew".*[6]*[9] In some locations, e.g. when hemmed in by buildings or other trees, an Irish yew can reach 20 feet in height without exceeding 2 feet in diameter at its thickest point, although with age many Irish yews assume a fat cigar shape rather than being truly columnar.

The following cultivars have gained the Royal Horticultural Society's Award of Garden Merit:-

- *T. baccata**[43]
- *T. baccata* 'Fastigiata'*[44]
- *T. baccata* 'Fastigiata Aureomarginata'*[45]
- *T. baccata* 'Icicle'*[46]
- *T. baccata* 'Repandens'*[47]
- *T. baccata* 'Repens Aurea'*[48]
- *T. baccata* 'Semperaurea'*[49]
- *T. baccata* 'Standishii'*[50]

European yew will tolerate growing in a wide range of soils and situations, including shallow chalk soils and shade,*[51] although in deep shade its foliage may be less dense. However it cannot tolerate waterlogging, and in poorly-draining situations is liable to succumb to the root-rotting pathogen *Phytophthora cinnamomi*.

In Europe, *Taxus baccata* grows naturally north to Molde in southern Norway, but it is used in gardens further north. It is also popular as a bonsai in many parts of Europe and makes a handsome small to large sized bonsai.*[52]

Privies

In England, yew has historically been sometimes associated with privies, possibly because the smell of the plant keeps insects away.*[53]

Musical instruments

The late Robert Lundberg, a noted luthier who performed extensive research on historical lute-making methodology, states in his 2002 book *Historical Lute Construction* that yew was historically a prized wood for lute construction. European legislation establishing use limits and requirements for yew limited supplies available to luthiers, but it was apparently as prized among medieval, renaissance, and baroque lute builders as Brazilian rosewood is among contemporary guitar-makers for its quality of sound and beauty.

3.92.8 Conservation

Clippings from ancient specimens in the UK, including the Fortingall Yew, were taken to the Royal Botanic Gardens in Edinburgh to form a mile-long hedge. The purpose of this "Yew Conservation Hedge Project" is to maintain the DNA of *Taxus baccata*. The species is threatened by felling, partly due to rising demand from pharmaceutical companies, and disease.*[54]

Another conservation programme was run in Catalonia in the early 2010s, by the Forest Sciences Centre of Catalonia (CTFC), in order to protect genetically endemic yew populations, and preserve them from overgrazing and forest fires.*[55] In the framework of this programme, the 4th International Yew Conference was organised in the Poblet Monastery in 2014, which proceedings are available.

There has also been a conservation programme in northern Portugal.

3.92.9 See also

- List of plants poisonous to equines

3.92.10 Notes

[1] Benham, S. E., Houston Durrant, T., Caudullo, G., de Rigo, D., 2016. ***Taxus baccata* in Europe: distribution, habitat, usage and threats**. In: San-Miguel-Ayanz, J., de Rigo, D., Caudullo, G., Houston Durrant, T., Mauri, A. (Eds.), *European Atlas of Forest Tree Species*. Publ. Off. EU, Luxembourg, pp. e015921+

[2] Rushforth, K. (1999). *Trees of Britain and Europe*. Collins ISBN 0-00-220013-9.

[3] "*Taxus baccata*". Natural Resources Conservation Service PLANTS Database. USDA. Retrieved 8 December 2015.

[4] Douglas Simms. "A Celto-Germanic Etymology for Flora and Fauna which will Boar Yew". Retrieved 10 July 2008.

[5] Theophrastus, *Enquiry into Plants*, iii.10.2; iv.1.3, etc.

[6] Mitchell, A. F. (1972). *Conifers in the British Isles*. Forestry Commission Booklet 33.

[7] "The Hawfinch". Wbrc.org.uk. Retrieved 2010-07-22.

[8] Snow, David; Snow, Barbara (2010). *Birds and Berries*. London: A & C Black. pp. 29–30. ISBN 9781408138229.

[9] Dallimore, W., & Jackson, A. B. (1966). *A Handbook of Coniferae and Ginkgoaceae* 4th ed. Arnold.

[10] Mayer, Hannes (1992). *Waldbau auf soziologisch-ökologischer Grundlage* [*Silviculture on socio-ecological basis*] (in German) (4th ed.). Fischer. p. 97. ISBN 3-437-30684-7.

[11] Bevan-Jones, Robert (2004). *The ancient yew: a history of Taxus baccata.* Bollington: Windgather Press. p. 28. ISBN 0-9545575-3-0.

[12] Harte, J. (1996). How old is that old yew? *At the Edge* 4: 1–9.online.

[13] Kinmonth, F. (2006). Ageing the yew – no core, no curve? *International Dendrology Society Yearbook* 2005: 41–46.

[14] Lewington, A., & Parker, E. (1999). *Ancient Trees: Trees that Live for a Thousand Years.* London: Collins & Brown Ltd. ISBN 1-85585-704-9

[15] Bevan-Jones, Robert (2004). *The ancient yew: a history of Taxus baccata.* Bollington: Windgather Press. p. 38. ISBN 0-9545575-3-0.

[16] Bevan-Jones, Robert (2004). *The ancient yew: a history of Taxus baccata.* Bollington: Windgather Press. p. 49. ISBN 0-9545575-3-0.

[17] "Monumentos Naturales" (in Spanish). Gobierno del Principado de Asturias. Retrieved 14 March 2013. Contains Word document "Monumento Natural Teixu de Bermiego".

[18] Ogren, Thomas (2015). *The Allergy-Fighting Garden.* Berkeley, CA: Ten Speed Press. p. 205. ISBN 9781607744917.

[19] "Yew poisoning". US National Library of Medicine. Retrieved 2015-04-05.

[20] "Yew". Provet. Retrieved 23 March 2013.

[21] Thomas, Peter A.; Packham, John R. (2007). *Ecology of Woodlands and Forests: Description, Dynamics and Diversity.* Cambridge [u.a.]: Cambridge Univ. Press. pp. 226–227. ISBN 0521542316.

[22] "How poisonous is the yew?". Ancient-yew.org. Retrieved 2010-07-22.

[23] Tiwary, A. K.; Puschner, B.; Kinde, H.; Tor, E. R. (2005). "Diagnosis of *Taxus* (Yew) poisoning in a horse" (pdf). *Journal of Veterinary Diagnostic Investigation.* **17** (3): 252–255. doi:10.1177/104063870501700307. PMID 15945382.

[24] TAXINE - National Library of Medicine HSDB Database, section "Animal Toxicity Studies"

[25] "Taxus baccata, yew - THE POISON GARDEN website". Thepoisongarden.co.uk. Retrieved 2010-07-22.

[26] List of world largest trees

[27] Abella Mina, I. Árboles De Junta Y Concejo. Las Raíces De La Comunidad. Libros del Jata, First Edition, 2016. ISBN 9788416443024

[28] Ohlmarks, Å. (1994). *Fornnordiskt lexikon.* p 372.

[29] Hellquist, O. (1922). *Svensk etymologisk ordbok.* p 266

[30] Andrews, W.(ed.)(1897) 'Antiquities and Curiosities of the Church, William Andrews & Co., London 1897; pp. 256-278: 'Amongst the ancients the yew, like the cypress, was regarded as the emblem of death... As, to the early Christian, death was the harbinger of life; he could not agree with his classic forefathers in employing the yew or the cyprus, "as an emblem of their dying for ever." It was the very antithesis of this, and as an emblem of immortality, and to show his belief in the life beyond the grave, that led to his cultivation of the yew in all the burying grounds of those who died in the new faith, and this must be regarded as the primary idea of its presence there... Evelyn's opinion is more decisive: — "that we find it so universally planted in our churchyards, was doubtless, from its being thought a symbol of immortality, the tree being so lasting and always green."'

[31] Andrews, W.(ed.)(1897) 'The majority of authorities agree that in England; branches of yew were generally employed; and some express the opinion, that the principal object of the tree being planted in churchyards, was to supply branches of it for this purpose.'

[32] "Palm Sunday: All About Palm Sunday of the Lord's Passion". Churchyear.net. Retrieved 2010-07-22.

[33] Dún Laoghaire Parks Some yew trees were actually there before the church was built...King Edward 1st ordered yew trees to be planted in churchyards to offer some protection to the buildings... Yews are poisonous so by planting them in the churchyards cattle that were not allowed to graze on hallowed ground were safe from eating yew. Yew was the traditional wood used for making long bows – planting in churchyards ensured availability in times of need. Yew branches on touching the ground take root and sprout again – this became the symbol of death, rebirth and therefore immortality.

[34] National Non-Food Crops Centre, "Yew". Retrieved on 2009-04-23.

[35] The Wood Database: European Yew

[36] "THE CLACTON SPEAR TIP".

[37] White, T.S.; Boreham, S.; Bridgland, D. R.; Gdaniec, K.; White, M. J. (2008). "The Lower and Middle Palaeolithic of Cambridgeshire" (PDF). English Heritage Project. Retrieved 23 March 2013.

[38] Laing, Lloyd; Laing, Jennifer (1980). *The Origins of Britain.* Book Club Associates. pp. 50–51. ISBN 0710004311.

[39] Transactions of the Gaelic Society of Inverness, Volume 62. 2004. Page 35.

[40] Romuald Sztyk. Obrót nieruchomościami w świetle prawa o ochronie środowiska. "Rejent - Miesięcznik Notariatu Polskiego". 10 (150), October 2003

[41] "...because that our sovereign lord the King, by a petition delivered to him in the said parliament, by the commons of the

same, hath perceived That the great scarcity of bowstaves is now in this realm, and the bowstaves that be in this realm be sold as an excessive price...", Statutes at Large

[42] *Yew: A History.* Hageneder F. Sutton Publishing, 2007. ISBN 978-0-7509-4597-4.

[43] "RHS Plant Selector - *Taxus baccata*". Retrieved 5 June 2013.

[44] "RHS Plant Selector - *Taxus baccata* 'Fastigiata'". Retrieved 5 June 2013.

[45] "RHS Plant Selector - *Taxus baccata* 'Fastigiata Aureomarginata'". Retrieved 5 June 2013.

[46] "RHS Plant Selector - *Taxus baccata* 'Icicle'". Retrieved 10 March 2016.

[47] "RHS Plant Selector - *Taxus baccata* 'Repandens'". Retrieved 5 June 2013.

[48] "RHS Plant Selector - *Taxus baccata* 'Repens Aurea'". Retrieved 5 June 2013.

[49] "RHS Plant Selector - *Taxus baccata* 'Semperaurea'". Retrieved 5 June 2013.

[50] "RHS Plant Selector - *Taxus baccata* 'Standishii'". Retrieved 5 June 2013.

[51] Hillier Nurseries, "The Hillier Manual Of Trees And Shrubs", David & Charles, 1998, p863

[52] D'Cruz, Mark. "Ma-Ke Bonsai Care Guide for Taxus baccata". Ma-Ke Bonsai. Retrieved 2011-11-19.

[53] "Cerne Privies". *Barnwells House and Garden.* Retrieved 2016-12-26.

[54] "Ancient yew DNA preserved in hedge project". United Press International. 7 November 2008. Retrieved 27 September 2013.

[55] Casals, Pere; Camprodon, Jordi; Caritat, Antonia; Rios, Ana; Guixe, David; Garcia-Marti, X; Martin-Alarcon, Santiago; Coll, Lluis (2015). "Forest structure of Mediterranean yew (Taxus baccata L.) populations and neighbor effects on juvenile yew performance in the NE Iberian Peninsula." (PDF). *Forest systems.* **24** (3). doi:10.5424/fs/2015243-07469.

3.92.11 References

- Chetan, A. and Brueton, D. (1994) *The Sacred Yew*, London: Arkana, ISBN 0-14-019476-2

- Conifer Specialist Group (1998) *Taxus baccata*, In: IUCN 2006/UCN Red List of Threatened Species, WWW page (Accessed 3 February 2007)

- Hartzell, H. (1991) *The yew tree: a thousand whispers: biography of a species*, Eugene: Hulogosi, ISBN 0-938493-14-0

- Simón, F. M. (2005) Religion and Religious Practices of the Ancient Celts of the Iberian Peninsula, *e-Keltoi*, v. 6, p. 287-345, ISSN 1540-4889 online

- Casals, Pere; Camprodon, Jordi; Caritat, Antonia; Rios, Ana; Guixe, David; Garcia-Marti, X; Martin-Alarcon, Santiago; Coll, Lluis (2015). "Forest structure of Mediterranean yew (Taxus baccata L.) populations and neighbor effects on juvenile yew performance in the NE Iberian Peninsula." (PDF). *Forest systems.* **24** (3). doi:10.5424/fs/2015243-07469.

3.92.12 External links

- Monumentaltrees.com: Images and location details of ancient yews

- *Taxus baccata* at the Encyclopedia of Life

- Life+ TAXUS.cat: Taxus conservation programme in Catalonia

- Forest Sciences Centre of Catalonia (CTFC)—Biology Conservation Department

- *Taxus baccata —distribution map, genetic conservation units, and related resources.* European Forest Genetic Resources Programme (EUFORGEN)

3.93 Taxus chinensis

Taxus chinensis is a species of yew. It is commonly called the **Chinese yew**, though this term also refers to *Taxus celebica* or *Taxus sumatrana*.

(Taxus celebica), a large, ornamental evergreen shrub or tree of the yew family (Taxaceae), widespread in China at elevations up to 900 meters (3,000 feet). The tree is up to 14 m (46 ft) tall and wide and bushy when cultivated. The leaves are up to 4 centimeters (1 ½ inches) long—broader than those of most other yews—and often end in a very small, sharp point. The underside of each leaf has two broad yellow stripes and is densely covered with minute projections.

Taxifolin can be found in *Taxus chinensis var. mairei.*[2]

This plant is used against cancer.[3][4] Paclitaxel or Taxol can be produced. The tree can also be used in many other ways and is under special protection of national and international laws.

3.93.1 References

[1] Template:IUCN2013

[2] Chemistry of Chinese yew, Taxus chinensis var. mairei. Cunfang Li, Changhong Huo , Manli Zhang, Qingwen Shi, Biochemical Systematics and Ecology, Volume 36, Issue 4, April 2008, Pages 266–282, doi:10.1016/j.bse.2007.08.002

[3] "紅豆杉 Hongdoushan_School of Chinese Medicine".

[4] "⊠豆杉 _Baidu".

3.94 Taxus cuspidata

Taxus cuspidata, the **Japanese yew**[1] or **spreading yew**, is a member of the genus *Taxus*, native to Japan, Korea, northeast China and the extreme southeast of Russia.

It is an evergreen tree or large shrub growing to 10–18 m tall, with a trunk up to 60 cm diameter. The leaves are lanceolate, flat, dark green, 1–3 cm long and 2–3 mm broad, arranged spirally on the stem, but with the leaf bases twisted to align the leaves in two flattish rows either side of the stem except on erect leading shoots where the spiral arrangement is more obvious.

The seed cones are highly modified, each cone containing a single seed 4–8 mm long partly surrounded by a modified scale which develops into a soft, bright red berry-like structure called an aril, 8–12 mm long and wide and open at the end. The arils are mature 6–9 months after pollination. Individual trees from Sikhote-Alin are known to have been 1,000 years old.[2]

3.94.1 Uses

It is widely grown in eastern Asia and eastern North America as an ornamental plant.

- Closeup of the leaves on a stem

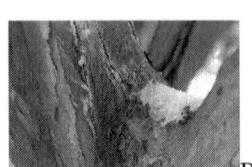

- Rough bark of the tree

3.94.2 Toxicity

The entire yew bush is toxic enough to kill a horse, except for the fleshy berry surrounding the seed.[3] For dogs, 2/5ths of an oz per 10 pounds of body weight is lethal. It is therefore advisable to keep domestic animals away from the plant. Undomesticated animals such as elk and moose have also reportedly been poisoned by yew.[4][5]

3.94.3 References

[1] "*Taxus cuspidata*". Natural Resources Conservation Service PLANTS Database. USDA. Retrieved 8 December 2015.

[2] http://wayback.archive.org/web/20070929092614/http://adm.khv.ru/invest2.nsf/pages/ru/rehabcentre.htm

[3] Yew

[4] "JAPANESE YEW PLANT POISONING - USA: (IDAHO) PRONGHORN ANTELOPE". ProMED-mail. 24 January 2016. Retrieved 25 January 2016.

[5] "PLANT POISONING, CERVID - USA: (ALASKA) ORNAMENTAL TREE, MOOSE". ProMED-mail. 22 February 2011. Retrieved 25 January 2016.

3.94.4 Further reading

- Conifer Specialist Group (1998). "*Taxus cuspidata*". *IUCN Red List of Threatened Species. Version 2006*. International Union for Conservation of Nature. Retrieved 5 May 2006.

3.95 Taxus × media

Taxus × media, more commonly known as the **Anglojap yew**[1] or simply *Taxus media*, is a conifer (more specifically, a yew) created by the hybridization of yew species *Taxus baccata* and *Taxus cuspidata*. This hybridization was thought to have been performed by the Massachusetts-based horticulturalist T.D. Hatfield in the early 1900s.[2]

3.95.1 Taxonomy and common naming

The *Taxus media* ("Anglojap") yew is a hybrid between *Taxus baccata* and *Taxus cuspidata*. The common name *Anglojap* is a portmanteau stemming from the national origin of *T. baccata* (a species native to England) and the national origin of *T. cuspidata* (a species native to Japan).[1]

3.95.2 Description

Like most yew species, *T. media* prefers well-drained and well-watered soils, but has some degree of drought tolerance and in fact may die in conditions of excessive precipitation if the soil beneath the plant is not sufficiently well-drained.*[1]

Taxus media is among the smallest extant species in the genus *Taxus* and (depending upon cultivar) may not even grow to the size of what one would consider a typical tree. Immature shrubs are very small and achieve (over the time span of ten to twenty years) heights of at most 20 feet and diameters of at most 8 feet, depending on the cultivar.*[2] Furthermore, *T. media* is known to grow rather slowly and is not injured by frequent pruning, making this hybrid a very desirable as a hedge in low-maintenance landscaping and also a good candidate for bonsai.*[1]

3.95.3 Toxicity

Taxus media also shares with its fellow yew trees a high level of taxine in its branches, needles, and seeds. Taxine is toxic to the mammalian heart.*[3]

3.95.4 Varieties (Cultivars)

- *Taxus media* var. *hicksii* (also known by the common name *Hicks's yew* or alternately, *Hicks yew*) is a common cultivar of this hybrid, and is the tallest and thinnest variety of *T. media*, limiting itself to a 4 foot (1.3 meter) diameter despite the fact it can achieve a height of close to 20 feet.*[2]*[4]

- Another commonly-planted cultivar of *T. Media* is the broader-spreading *densiformis* version, which can reach a diameter exceeding 10 feet; nonetheless, this cultivar does not grow much past 5 feet in height.*[2]

3.95.5 See also

- *Taxus baccata*
- *Taxus cuspidata*

3.95.6 References

[1] The Ohio State University Plant Facts: Anglojap Yew

[2] University of Connecticut Horticulture: Taxus Media

[3] Wilson, C. R.; Sauer, J.; Hooser, S. B. (2001). "Taxines: A review of the mechanism and toxicity of yew (*Taxus spp.*) alkaloids". *Toxicon*. **39** (2–3): 175–85. doi:10.1016/s0041-0101(00)00146-x. PMID 10978734.

[4] University of Illinois - Selecting Shrubs for Your Home

3.96 Tetraclinis

Tetraclinis forest at Al Hoceima National Park

Tetraclinis (also called arar,*[2] araar*[3] or Sictus tree) is a genus of evergreen coniferous trees in the cypress family Cupressaceae, containing only one species, ***Tetraclinis articulata***, also known as **Thuja articulata**,*[4] **sandarac**, **sandarac tree***[5] or **Barbary thuja**,*[6] endemic to the western Mediterranean region. It is native to northwestern Africa in the Atlas Mountains of Morocco, Algeria, and Tunisia, with two small outlying populations on Malta, and near Cartagena in southeast Spain. It grows at relatively low altitudes in a hot, dry subtropical Mediterranean climate.*[7]

Its closest relatives are *Platycladus, Microbiota*, and *Calocedrus*, with the closest resemblance to the latter. In older texts, it was sometimes treated in *Thuja* or *Callitris*, but it is less closely related to those genera.*[7]

It is a small, slow-growing tree, to 6–15 m (rarely 20 m) tall and 0.5 m (rarely 1 m) trunk diameter, often with two or more trunks from the base. The foliage forms in open sprays with scale-like leaves 1–8 mm long and 1–1.5 mm broad; the leaves are arranged in opposite decussate pairs, with the successive pairs closely then distantly spaced, so forming apparent whorls of four. The cones are 10–15 mm long, green ripening brown in about 8 months from pollination, and have four thick scales arranged in two opposite pairs. The seeds are 5–7 mm long and 2 mm broad, with a 3–4 mm broad papery wing on each side.*[7]*[8]

It is one of only a small number of conifers able to coppice (regrow by sprouting from stumps), an adaptation to survive

Tetraclinis cones at Al Hoceima National Park

wildfire and moderate levels of browsing by animals. Old trees that have sprouted repeatedly over a long period form large burls at the base, known as *lupias*.*[7]

3.96.1 Uses and symbolism

It is the national tree of Malta, where it is known as *għargħar* (derived from the Arabic name *araar*). It is now being used locally in afforestation projects.

The resin, known as sandarac, is used to make varnish and lacquer; it is particularly valued for preserving paintings.

The wood, known as thuya wood*[9] or citron wood,*[4] and historically also known as thyine wood, is used for decorative woodwork, particularly wood from burls at the base of the trunk. The market in Morocco is unsustainable, focusing as it does on the burl, and has resulted in mass deforestation of the species. The species is also threatened by overgrazing, which can kill the coppice regrowth before it gets tall enough to be out of the reach of livestock.*[7]

Cultivation

The species is cultivated to be grown as an ornamental tree, valued in hot, dry climates. It is also pruned in a hedge form, for privacy and security.*[8] The plant can be trained for use as bonsai specimens.

3.96.2 Fossil record

†*Tetraclinis salicornioides* leaf and cone fossils of Messinian age (ca. 5.7 Ma) have been uncovered in Monte Tondo and Borgo Tossignano, northern Apennines, Italy.*[10]

3.96.3 Gallery

- *Tetraclinis articulata* in the mountains of Cartagena, Spain

- A cup made of root burl wood from the Essaouira area of Morocco

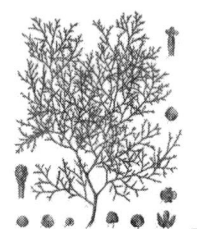

- Illustration from Koehler's *Medicinal-Plants* (1887)

- *Tetraclinis articulata* - Muséum de Toulouse

3.96.4 References

[1] http://www.iucnredlist.org/details/30318/0

[2] "Tetraclinis articulata" . *The Gymnosperm Database*. Retrieved 2011-02-13.

[3] but it is ambiguous arabic name also given to *Juniperus phoenicea*

[4] Memidex: sandarac (wood) Retrieved 2012-05-16

[5] Collins: sandarac and sandarac tree Retrieved 2012-05-16

[6] Jacques Blondel & James Aronson: *Biology and Wildlife of the Mediterranean Region*, Oxford University Press 1999 Retrieved 2012-05-16

[7] Farjon, A. (2005). *Monograph of Cupressaceae and Sciadopitys*. Royal Botanic Gardens, Kew. ISBN 1-84246-068-4

[8] Rushforth, K. (1999). *Trees of Britain and Europe*. Collins ISBN 0-00-220013-9.

[9] Arc-genesis: Thuya Wood Retrieved 2012-05-16

[10] Palaeoenvironmental analysis of the Messinian macrofossil floras of Tossignano and Monte Tondo (Vena del Gesso Basin, Romagna Apennines, northern Italy) - Vasilis Teodoridis, Zlatko Kvacek, Marco Sami and Edoardo Martinetto - December 2015 DOI: 10.14446/AMNP.2015.249.

3.97 Ulmus alata

Ulmus alata, the **winged elm** or **wahoo**, is a small- to medium-sized deciduous tree endemic to the woodlands of the southeastern and south-central United States. The species is tolerant of a wide range of soils, and of ponding, but is the least shade-tolerant of the North American elms. Its growth rate is often very slow, the trunk increasing in diameter by less than 5 mm (3/16 in) per year. The tree is occasionally considered a nuisance as it readily invades old fields, forest clearings, and rangelands, proving particularly difficult to eradicate with herbicides.*[1]

3.97.1 Description

As its common and scientific*[2] names imply, winged elm is most easily recognized by the very broad, thin pair of corky wings that form along the branchlets after a couple of years. The tree generally grows to a maximum height and breadth of about 13 m × 13 m (43 ft × 43 ft), although on fertile alluvial soils such as those of the Mississippi River Delta, some specimens have reached double this height (see 'Notable trees' below). The crown can be either rounded or pyramidal; the branches are pendulous.*[3]

The leaves are comparatively small for the genus, less than 6.5 cm (2 1/2 in) long and less than 2.0 cm (3/4 in) broad, oblong-lanceolate to narrowly elliptic, thin in texture, and smooth above. The wind-pollinated perfect apetalous flowers are borne on long pedicels in March and April before the leaves appear. The reddish samaras are also relatively small, less than 8 mm (5/16 in) long, narrowly elliptic with two long incurving stigmas at the tip,*[4] and usually disperse before the end of April.*[5]*[6]

The corky wings of Ulmus alata

3.97.2 Pests and diseases

Like the other North American species of elm, *U. alata* is very susceptible to Dutch elm disease and Elm Yellows (Elm phloem necrosis).*[7]

3.97.3 Cultivation

Ulmus alata is rarely cultivated beyond its natural range. It remains in commercial production in the USA, and is occasionally available in Europe; several specimens are also grown in New Zealand.*[8]

3.97.4 Notable trees

On the silty uplands of the Mississippi Delta, *Ulmus alata* can attain 27 m (89 ft) in height, although the trunk diameter rarely exceeds 60 cm (24 in) d.b.h. In the old growth Fernbank Forest in Atlanta, Georgia, the species attains heights up to 39 metres (128 ft). A tree measuring 40 metres (130 ft) high has been reported from the Congaree National Park in South Carolina.*[9] However, the USA National Champion, measuring 27 metres (89 ft) high in 2009, grows in Hopewell County, Virginia.*[10]

3.97.5 Cultivars

- Lace Parasol

3.97.6 Other uses

Ulmus alata is of minimal commercial significance, its hard timber considered no more remarkable than that of other American elms, and of limited use because of the commonly small size of the trees. However, owing to its resistance to splitting, it is used to make high-quality hockey sticks.

3.97.7 Accessions

North America

- Arnold Arboretum. Acc. no. 404-95, wild collected.
- Bartlett Tree Experts*[11] Acc. no. 1438, unrecorded provenance.
- Brooklyn Botanic Garden,*[12] New York City. Acc. nos. 730275, X00886
- Bernheim Arboretum and Research Forest, Clermont, Kentucky. No details available.
- Morton Arboretum. Acc. no. 116-96, wild collected Papoose Lake, Illinois.

Europe

- Brighton & Hove City Council, UK, NCCPG Elm Collection.*[13] One tree at East Brighton Park, UK champion 13 m (43 ft) high, 31 cm (12 $\frac{1}{4}$ in) d.b.h. in 2001.*[14]
- Grange Farm Arboretum, Sutton St James, Spalding, Lincolnshire, UK. Acc. no. 506
- Royal Botanic Garden Edinburgh. Acc. no. 20080092, from seed wild collected in USA.
- Thenford House, Northamptonshire, UK. No details available.

Australasia

- Manukau Cemetery & Crematorium, Auckland, New Zealand. No details available.

3.97.8 Nurseries

North America

Widely available.

Europe

- Arboretum Waasland, Nieuwkerken-Waas, Belgium.
- Grange Farm Plants, Spalding, Lincolnshire, UK.
- Plantentuin Esveld, Netherlands.

Seed suppliers

- Sheffield's Seeds Co. Inc., New York, USA.

3.97.9 References

[1] University of Florida, Environmental Horticulture Department (1994). *Fact Sheet ST-648*. Florida Cooperative Extension Service, Institute of Food and Agricultural Sciences.

[2] *Alata* is Latin for "winged".

[3]

[4] Photo of *U. alata* samarae, jimbotany.com/16-Catalog_Ra_through_Z-Ackn-LitCitd.htm,

[5] Elwes, H. J. & Henry, A. (1913). *The Trees of Great Britain & Ireland*. Vol. VII. 1848–1929. Republished 2014 Cambridge University Press, ISBN 978-1-108-06938-0

[6] Schnelle, M. (1999). Field Notes: Ulmus alata. *American Nurseryman*, page 1998, 1 March 1999. p. 98. Chicago

[7] "Elm Phloem Necrosis".

[8] Wilcox, Mike; Inglis, Chris (2003). "Auckland's elms" (PDF). *Auckland Botanical Society Journal*. Auckland Botanical Society. **58** (1): 38–45.

[9] http://www.nativetreesociety.org/events/congaree2009/NewCongMaxList.xls

[10] American Forests. (2012). The 2012 National Register of Big Trees.

[11]

[12]

[13] "List of plants in the {elm} collection". Brighton & Hove City Council. Retrieved 23 September 2016.

[14] Johnson, Owen (ed.) (2003). *Champion Trees of Britain & Ireland*. Whittet Press, ISBN 978-1-873580-61-5.

- Snow, G. A. (1990). *"Ulmus alata"*. In Burns, Russell M.; Honkala, Barbara H. *Hardwoods. Silvics of North America*. Washington, D.C.: United States Forest Service (USFS), United States Department of Agriculture (USDA). **2** – via Northeastern Area State and Private Forestry (www.na.fs.fed.us).

3.98 Ulmus crassifolia

Ulmus crassifolia Nutt., the **Texas cedar elm** or simply **cedar elm**, is a deciduous tree native to south central North America, mainly in southern and eastern Texas, southern Oklahoma, Arkansas and Louisiana, with small populations in western Mississippi, southwest Tennessee and north central Florida;*[1] it also occurs in northeastern Mexico.*[2]*[3] It is the most common elm tree in Texas. The tree typically grows well in flat valley bottom areas referred to as 'Cedar Elm Flats'. The common name 'cedar elm' is derived from the trees' association with juniper trees, locally known as cedars.*[4]

3.98.1 Description

The cedar elm is a medium to large deciduous tree growing to 24–27 m tall with a rounded crown. The leaves are small, 2.5–5 cm long by 1.3–2 cm broad, with an oblique base, and distinguish it from *Ulmus serotina* with which it readily hybridizes in the wild. Leaf fall is late, often in early winter. The wind-pollinated apetalous perfect flowers are produced in the late summer or early fall; they are small and inconspicuous, with a reddish-purple color. The fruit is a small winged samara 8–10 mm long, maturing quickly after the flowering in late fall.*[5]*[6]

- *U. crassifolia* bark

- Migrating monarch butterflies on a cedar elm in central Texas

3.98.2 Pests and diseases

Cedar elm is susceptible to Dutch elm disease (DED), though less so than American elm, and moderately damaged by the elm leaf beetle *Xanthogaleruca luteola*. The tree also suffers from a vascular wilt, the symptoms often confused with those of DED.

Cedar elms are very susceptible to mistletoe. Mistletoe is a parasite that roots itself in to the vascular system of the tree, thus stealing valuable nutrients and water. In some cases, if not removed the parasite can be devastating to large sections of trees and even fatal. They create club like branches that die out at the ends. These "club" branches create openings for future pests like the elm beetles and carpenter ants. There are no known treatments that are safe enough to kill mistletoe without killing the tree. Removing the mistletoe manually is not a guarantee, however it is the best known method for control.

3.98.3 Cultivation

Owing to Dutch elm disease, the cedar elm is now rarely cultivated in North America. It is extremely rare in cultivation in Europe,*[7] and Australasia.*[8] Henry (1913) and Bean (1988) note that it does not thrive in northern Europe, where the branchlets often die back.*[7]*[9] Specimens supplied by the Späth nursery to the Royal Botanic Garden Edinburgh in 1902 as *U. crassifolia* may survive in Edinburgh as it was the practice of the garden to distribute trees about the city (viz. the Wentworth Elm).*[10] A small elm with leaves matching the RBGE's 1902 herbarium specimens of Späth's clone (see **External links** below) stands in Calton Hill Park (2016), and may be regrowth from one of the three.

- Leaves matching Späth's 1902 *U. crassifolia*

3.98.4 Notable trees

The USA National Champion, measuring 37 m high in 2001, grows in the Meeman-Shelby Forest State Park Tennessee.*[11]

3.98.5 Cultivars

- Brazos Rim.

3.98.6 Hybrids

- *Ulmus* × *arkansana*

3.98.7 Accessions

North America

- Arnold Arboretum. Acc. nos. 511-2002, 758-86, both wild collected.
- Chicago Botanic Garden, Glencoe, Illinois. No details available.
- Bartlett Tree Experts. Acc. no. 90-1243, unrecorded provenance.
- Morton Arboretum. Acc. no. 385-68,*[12] 14-86
- New York Botanical Garden. Acc. no. 79617, unrecorded provenance.
- U S National Arboretum,*[13] Washington, D.C., United States. Acc. no. 37834

Europe

- Grange Farm Arboretum, Sutton St. James, Spalding, Lincolnshire, UK. Acc. no. 509
- Royal Botanic Garden Edinburgh. Acc. no. 20080090, from seed wild collected in USA.
- Sir Harold Hillier Gardens, UK. Acc. no. 1980-0443, (Brentry Field).
- University of Copenhagen Botanic Garden. No details available.

Australasia

- Manukau Cemetery & Crematorium, Auckland, New Zealand. No details available.

3.98.8 Nurseries

North America

Widely available

Europe

- Arboretum Waasland,*[14] Nieuwkerken-Waas, Belgium.

Australasia

None known.

3.98.9 References

[1] "Map: Ulmus crassifolia" . Efloras.org. Retrieved 2013-09-01.

[2] Todzia, C. A. & Panero, J. L. (2006). A new species of Ulmus (Ulmaceae) from southern Mexico and a synopsis of the species in Mexico. *Brittonia*, Vol 50, (3): 346

[3] "A New Species of Ulmus (Ulmaceae) from Southern Mexico and a Synopsis of the Species in Mexico" . JSTOR 2807778.

[4] http://npsot.org/wp/story/2011/1687/

[5] "Ulmus crassifolia in Flora of North America @". Efloras.org. Retrieved 2013-09-01.

[6] "Plants Profile for Ulmus crassifolia (cedar elm)". Plants.usda.gov. Retrieved 2013-09-01.

[7] Elwes, H. J. & Henry, A. (1913). *The Trees of Great Britain & Ireland*. Vol. VII. 1848–1929. Republished 2004 Cambridge University Press, ISBN 9781108069380

[8] Wilcox, Mike; Inglis, Chris (2003). "Auckland's elms" (PDF). *Auckland Botanical Society Journal*. Auckland Botanical Society. **58** (1): 38–45.

[9] Bean, W. J. (1988) *Trees and shrubs hardy in Great Britain*, 8th edition, Murray, London

[10] *Accessions book*. Royal Botanic Garden Edinburgh. 1902. pp. 45, 47.

[11] American Forests. (2012). The 2012 National Register of Big Trees.

[12] ""Ulmus crassifolia" at Morton Arboretum" . Cirrusimage.com. 2010-05-06. Retrieved 2013-09-14.

[13] Ramon Jordan. "US National Arboretum:". Usna.usda.gov. Retrieved 2013-09-01.

[14] "English" . Arboretum-waasland.be. Retrieved 2013-09-01.

3.98.10 External links

- "Herbarium specimen - E00824870". *Herbarium Catalogue*. Royal Botanic Garden Edinburgh. 1902, from Späth nursery

- "Herbarium specimen - E00824871". *Herbarium Catalogue*. Royal Botanic Garden Edinburgh. 1902, from Späth nursery

3.99 Ulmus parvifolia

Ulmus parvifolia, commonly known as the **Chinese elm**[1] or **lacebark elm**, is a species native to eastern Asia, including China, India, Taiwan, Japan, North Korea, and Vietnam.[2] It has been described as "one of the most splendid elms, having the poise of a graceful *Nothofagus*".[3]

The tree was introduced to the UK in 1794 by James Main, who collected in China for Gilbert Slater of Low Layton, Essex.[4][5]

3.99.1 Description

A small to medium deciduous, semi-deciduous (rarely semi-evergreen) tree growing to 10–18 m (33–59 ft) tall and 15–20 m (49–66 ft) wide with a slender trunk and crown. The leathery, lustrous green single-toothed leaves are small, 2–5 cm long by 1–3 cm broad, and often retained as late as December or even January in Europe and North America. The apetalous wind-pollinated perfect flowers are produced in early autumn, small and inconspicuous. The fruit is a samara, elliptic to ovate-elliptic, 10–13 mm long by 6–8 mm broad.[2] The samara is mostly glabrous, the seed at the centre or toward the apex, borne on a stalk 1–3 mm in length; it matures rapidly and disperses by late autumn. The trunk has a handsome, flaking bark of mottled greys with tans and reds, giving rise to its other common name, the lacebark elm, although scarring from major branch loss can lead to large canker-like wounds.[5][6][7][8][9]

- *U. parvifolia* juvenile

- Foliage and fruit

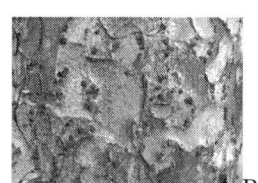

- Bark

Many nurserymen and foresters mistakenly refer to *Ulmus pumila*, the rapidly growing, disease-ridden, relatively short-lived, weak-wooded Siberian elm, as "Chinese elm." This has given the true Chinese elm an undeserved bad reputation. The two elms are very distinct and different species. Among other obvious differences, with age the Siberian elm's bark becomes deeply ridged and furrowed, and possesses a very rough, greyish-black appearance, while the Chinese elm's smooth bark becomes flaky and blotchy, exposing very distinctive, light-coloured mottling, hence the synonym *lacebark elm* for the real Chinese elm.[10]

3.99.2 Wood and timber

Elms, hickory and ash all have remarkably hard, tough wood that has made them popular for things like tool handles, bows and baseball bats. Chinese elm is considered the hardest of the elms. Owing to its superior hardness, toughness and resistance to splitting, Chinese elm is said to be the best of all woods for chisel handles and similar uses. Chinese elm lumber is used most for furniture, cabinets, veneer and hardwood flooring, as well as specialty uses such as long bow construction and tool handles. Most of the commercially milled lumber goes directly to manufacturers rather than to retail lumber outlets.

Chinese elm heartwood ranges in tone from reddish brown to light tan or flesh coloured, while the sapwood approaches off-white. The grain is often handsome and dramatic.[11] Unlike other elms, freshly cut Chinese elm has a peppery or spicy odour. While it turns easily and will take a nice polish off the lathe without any finish, and it holds detail well, the fibrous wood is usually considered too tough for carving or hand tools. Chinese elm contains silica which is hard on planer knives and chainsaws, but it sands fairly easily. Like other woods with interlocking grain, planes should be kept extra sharp to prevent tearing at the grain margins.

It steam-bends easily, holds screws well but pilot holes and countersinking are needed. It tends to be a "lively" wood, tending to warp and distort while drying. This water resistant wood easily takes most finishes and stains.

3.99.3 Taxonomy

Subspecies, varieties, and forms:

- *Ulmus parvifolia* var. *coreana* Nakai
- *Ulmus parvifolia* f. *lanceolata* Ueki

3.99.4 Pests and diseases

The Chinese elm is highly resistant, but not immune, to Dutch elm disease. It is also very resistant to the elm leaf beetle *Xanthogaleruca luteola*, but has a moderate susceptibility to elm yellows.*[12] In trials at the Sunshine Nursery, Oklahoma, the species was adjudged as having the best pest resistance of about 200 taxa *[13] However, foliage was regarded as only "somewhat resistant" to black spot by the Plant Diagnostic Clinic of the University of Missouri.*[14]

Cottony cushion scale or mealy bugs often protected and "herded" by ants exude a sticky, sweet "honeydew" which can mildew leaves and be a minor annoyance by dripping on cars and furniture. However, severe infestations on, or obvious damage to, otherwise healthy trees are not common.

3.99.5 Cultivation

The Chinese elm is a tough landscape tree, hardy enough for use in harsh planting situations such as parking lots, in small planters along streets and in plazas or patios. The tree is arguably the most ubiquitous of the elms, now found on all continents except Antarctica. It was introduced to Europe at the end of the 18th century as an ornamental, and is found in many botanical gardens and arboreta. In the United States, it appeared in the middle of the 19th century, and has proved very popular in recent years as a replacement for American elms killed by Dutch elm disease. The tree was sold in Australia at the beginning of the 20th century by Searl's Garden Emporium, Sydney. In New Zealand, it was found to be particularly suitable for windswept locations along the coast.

Ulmus parvifolia is one of the cold-hardiest of the Chinese species. In artificial freezing tests at the Morton Arboretum.*[15] the LT50 (temp. at which 50% of tissues die) was found to be −34 °C (−29 °F).

Bonsai

Owing to its versatility and ability to tolerate a wide range of temperatures, light, and humidity conditions, Chinese elm is a popular choice as a bonsai species, and is perhaps the single most widely available. It is considered a good choice for beginners because of its high tolerance of pruning.*[16]

- Chinese elm bonsai.
- Chinese elm bonsai
- Chinese elm bonsai

3.99.6 Cultivars

Numerous cultivars have been raised, mostly in North America:

- A. Ross Central Park = Central Park Splendor™, BSNUPF = Everclear™, Blizzard, Burgundy, Burnley Select, Catlin, Chessins, Churchyard, Cork Bark, D.B.Cole, Drake, Dwarf Weeper, Dynasty, Ed Wood, Elsmo, Emer I or Emerald Isle = Athena™, Emer II or Emerald Vase = Allee™, Emerald Prairie, Frosty, Garden City Clone, Geisha, Glory, Golden Rey, Hallelujah, Harzam = Harrison™, Hokkaido, Jade Empress, King's Choice, Littleleaf, Lois Hole, Matthew, Milliken, Nire-keyaki, Ohio, Orange Ribbon, Pathfinder, Pendens, Prairie Shade, Prince Richard, Red Fall, Sabamiki, Sagei, Seiju, Select 380, Sempervirens, Small Frye, State Fair, Stone's Dwarf, Taiwan, The Thinker, Todd, UPMTF = Bosque™, Ware's, Yarralumla, Yatsubusa, Zettler = Heritage™

Hybrid cultivars

An autumn flowering species, whereas most other elms flower in spring. Hybrids have accordingly been very few:

- Frontier
- Rebella

3.99.7 Accessions

North America

- Arnold Arboretum. Acc. nos. 1353-73, 17917, 195-90, 197-90.
- Bartlett Tree Experts. Acc. nos. 5546, 8109.
- Brenton Arboretum, Dallas Center, Iowa. No details available.
- Brooklyn Botanic Garden, New York. Acc. nos. 000880, 160001, 20020466, 850222, X00450, X00485, X02727, X02771.*[17]
- Chicago Botanic Garden, Glencoe, Illinois. 2 trees, no other details available.
- Dominion Arboretum, Ottawa, Canada. No acc. details.
- Fullerton Arboretum, California State University. Acc. no. 80-036.*[18]
- Holden Arboretum. Acc. nos. 57-1241, 80-665, 84-1214, 90-323.
- Longwood Gardens. Acc. nos. 1957-1058, 1959-1500, 1960-1138, 1991-0981.
- Missouri Botanical Garden, St. Louis. Acc. nos. 1986-0108, 1986-0276, 1986-0277, 1987-0019, 199-3195, 1996-3462.
- Morris Arboretum, University of Pennsylvania. Acc. no. 32-0052-A.*[19]
- Morton Arboretum. Acc. nos. 991-27, 772-54, 1231–57, 558-83, 52-96.
- New York Botanical Garden. Acc. nos. 195/56, 486/91, 68072.
- Phipps Conservatory. Acc. nos. 83-006, 83-058, 91-050, 2001-212UN.
- Scott Arboretum. Acc. nos. 62210, 71765, 71767, 71771, 75152, 64441.
- Smith College, acc. no. 42894.
- U S National Arboretum,*[20] Washington, D.C., United States. Acc. nos. 58000/1/2/3/4/5/6/7/8.

Europe

- Brighton & Hove City Council, UK, NCCPG Elm Collection.*[21]
- Cambridge Botanic Garden,*[22] University of Cambridge, UK. No accession details available.
- Dyffryn Gardens, Glamorgan. UK champion, 13 m high, 37 cm d.b.h., last surveyed 1997.*[23]
- Grange Farm Arboretum, Sutton St. James, Spalding, Lincolnshire, UK. Acc. no. 516.
- Hortus Botanicus Nationalis, Salaspils, Latvia. Acc. nos. 18150, 18151.
- Linnaean Gardens of Uppsala, Sweden. Acc. no. 2002-1542.
- Royal Botanic Gardens Kew. Acc. nos. 1979-1613, 1979-1614, 1982–8479, 1982-8505, 1982-6280, 1982-6284, 2002-137, 2003-1267, 2005-1076.
- Royal Botanic Gardens Kew Wakehurst Place. Acc. nos. 1969-33664, 1969-35133, 1973-21049, 1973-21525.
- Royal Horticultural Society Gardens, Wisley, UK. No details available.
- Strona Arboretum, University of Life Sciences, Warsaw, Poland. No accession details available.
- Tallinn Botanic Garden, Estonia.*[24] No accession details available.
- Thenford House arboretum, Banbury, UK. No details available.
- University of Copenhagen Botanic Garden. Acc. nos. S1956-1338, S1997-1304.
- Westonbirt Arboretum, Tetbury, Glos., UK. Planted 1981. No acc. no.*[25]

Australasia

- Eastwoodhill Arboretum, Gisborne, New Zealand. 9 trees, details not known.*[26]

3.99.8 Nurseries

Europe

- Pan-Global Plants, Frampton-on-Severn, Gloucestershire, UK.

3.99.9 References

[1] "PLANTS Profile for Ulmus parvifolia (Chinese elm)". *Natural Resources Conservation Service*. United States Department of Agriculture. Retrieved 20 September 2011.

[2] Fu, L., Xin, Y. & Whittemore, A. (2002). Ulmaceae, in Wu, Z. & Raven, P. (eds) *Flora of China*, Vol. 5 (Ulmaceae through Basellaceae). Science Press, Beijing, and Missouri Botanical Garden Press, St. Louis, USA; also available as Fu, L., Xin, Y. & Whittemore, A. "*Ulmus parvifolia*". *Flora of China*. Missouri Botanical Garden, St. Louis, MO & Harvard University Herbaria, Cambridge, MA. Retrieved 5 February 2015.

[3] *Hilliers' Manual of Trees & Shrubs*, 4th edition, 1977, David & Charles, Newton Abbot, England

[4] Elwes, H. J. & Henry, A. (1913). *The Trees of Great Britain & Ireland*. Vol. VII. 1848–1929. Republished 2004 Cambridge University Press, ISBN 9781108069380

[5] Bean, W. J. (1981). *Trees and shrubs hardy in Great Britain*, 7th edition. Murray, London.

[6] White, J & More, D. (2003). *Trees of Britain & Northern Europe*. Cassell's, London.

[7] http://www.cnr.vt.edu/dendro/dendrology/syllabus/uparvifolia.htm

[8] "Plants Profile for Ulmus pumila (Siberian elm)".

[9] *Ulmus parvifolia* photographs and fact-page, Michigan State University *Plant Encyclopedia*

[10] Leopold, D. J. (1980). "Chinese and Siberian elms". *Journal of Arboriculture*. **6** (7): 175–179.

[11] Images: wood OR lumber "chinese elm"

[12] Mittempergher, L; Santini, A (2004). "The history of elm breeding" (PDF). *Investigacion agraria: Sistemas y recursos forestales*. **13** (1): 161–177.

[13] http://www.greenbeam.com/rs/nm_pdfs/16338_013.pdf

[14] http://soilplantlab.missouri.edu/plant/diseases/resistant.htm

[15] Shirazi, A. M. & Ware, G. H. (2004). *Evaluation of New Elms from China for Cold Hardiness in Northern Latitudes*. International Symposium on Asian Plant Diversity & Systematics 2004, Sakura, Japan.

[16] D'Cruz, Mark. "Ma-Ke Bonsai Care Guide for Ulmus parvifolia". Ma-Ke Bonsai. Retrieved 2011-05-09.

[17] "Brooklyn Botanic Garden".

[18] "Fullerton Arboretum".

[19] The Morris Arboretum of the University of Pennsylvania

[20] http://www.usna.usda.gov/index.htm

[21] "List of plants in the {elm} collection". Brighton & Hove City Council. Retrieved 23 September 2016.

[22] "Cambridge University Botanic Garden".

[23] Johnson, Owen (ed.) (2003). *Champion Trees of Britain & Ireland*. Whittet Press, ISBN 978-1-873580-61-5.

[24] http://www.tba.ee/index.php?lang=eng

[25] Forestry Commission - The Forestry Commission - The National Arboreta

[26] Eastwoodhill | National Arboretum of New Zealand

3.99.10 External links

- "Ulmus parvifolia Jacq. (1854) K000852632". *Herbarium catalogue*. Board of Trustees of the Royal Botanic Gardens, Kew. Retrieved 17 October 2016.

- "Ulmus parvifolia Jacq. (1867) K000852633". *Herbarium catalogue*. Board of Trustees of the Royal Botanic Gardens, Kew. Retrieved 17 October 2016.

- "Ulmus sieboldii Daveau (1913) K000852631". *Herbarium catalogue*. Board of Trustees of the Royal Botanic Gardens, Kew. Retrieved 17 October 2016.

- "Herbarium specimen - E00824803". *Herbarium Catalogue*. Royal Botanic Garden Edinburgh. *Ulmus parvifolia* Jacq. (1909)

- "Herbarium specimen - E00824804". *Herbarium Catalogue*. Royal Botanic Garden Edinburgh. *Ulmus parvifolia* Jacq. (1902, Späth nursery)

- "Herbarium specimen - E00824805". *Herbarium Catalogue*. Royal Botanic Garden Edinburgh. *Ulmus parvifolia* Jacq. (1902, Späth)

- "Herbarium specimen - E00824802". *Herbarium Catalogue*. Royal Botanic Garden Edinburgh. *Ulmus parvifolia* Jacq. (1902, Späth)

3.100 Ulmus parvifolia 'Catlin'

The **Chinese Elm** cultivar ***Ulmus parvifolia* 'Catlin'** is a dwarf variety specifically raised as a bonsai plant by John Catlin, La Canada, California, circa 1950.

3.100.1 Description

The leaves are very small, < 12 mm long, and can remain evergreen on pot grown plants in California.[1]

3.100.2 Cultivation

The cultivar is not known to have been introduced to Europe or Australasia.

3.100.3 Accessions

North America

- Brooklyn Botanic Garden, New York. Acc. no. 900380.
- New York Botanical Garden. Acc. no. 1133/89
- U S National Arboretum, Washington, D.C., United States. Acc. no. 64443.

3.100.4 Nurseries

North America

- Japan Nursery

3.100.5 References

[1] Barrett, J. R., (1980), *Intern. Bonsai*, 2(3): 11, 1980.

3.100.6 External links

- http://rbg-web2.rbge.org.uk/multisite/multisite3.php Multi-site search engine

W. floribunda growing in Longwood Gardens

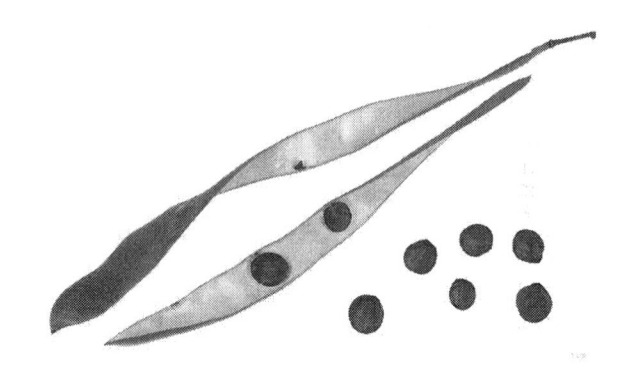

Wisteria floribunda - *MHNT*

3.101 Wisteria floribunda

Wisteria floribunda (common name **Japanese wisteria**) is a species of flowering plant in the pea family Fabaceae, native to Japan. Growing to 9 m (30 ft), it is a woody, deciduous twining climber. It was brought from Japan to the United States in 1830's.[1][2] Since then, it has become one of the most highly romanticized flowering garden plants. It is also a common subject for bonsai, along with *Wisteria sinensis* (Chinese wisteria).

The flowering habit of Japanese wisteria is perhaps the most spectacular of the Wisteria family. It sports the longest flower racemes of any wisteria; they can reach nearly half a meter in length. These racemes burst into great trails of clustered white, pink, violet, or blue flowers in early- to mid-spring. The flowers carry a distinctive fragrance similar to that of grapes. The early flowering time of Japanese wisteria can cause problems in temperate climates, where early frosts can destroy the coming years' flowers. It will also flower only after passing from juvenile to adult stage, a transition that may take many years just like its cousin Chinese wisteria.

Japanese wisteria can grow over 30m long over many supports via powerful clockwise-twining stems. The foliage consists of shiny, dark-green, pinnately compound leaves 10–30 cm in length. The leaves bear 9-13 oblong leaflets that are each 2–6 cm long. It also bears numerous poisonous, brown, velvety, bean-like seed pods 5–10 cm long that mature in summer and persist until winter. Japanese wisteria prefers moist soils and full sun in USDA plant hardiness zones 5-9.*[3] The plant often lives over fifty years.

3.101.1 *Wisteria floribunda* cultivars

Those marked agm have gained the Royal Horticultural Society's Award of Garden Merit.

1. 'Shiro Noda', 'Snow Showers' or 'Longissima Alba' agm*[4] - long white flower clusters
2. 'Kuchibeni' or 'Carnea' - pink flowers
3. 'Honbeni' or 'Rosea'agm*[5] - pale rose flowers tipped purple, 18 inches long
4. 'Issai Perfect' - light lavender flowers
5. 'Jako' or 'Ivory Tower'
6. 'Lawrence' - blue flowers, hardy cultivar
7. 'Macrobotrys' or 'Longissima' - reddish-violet flower clusters one meter or longer
8. 'Macrobotrys Cascade' - white and pinkish-purple flowers, vigorous grower
9. 'Multijuga'agm*[6] - violet flowers with darker markings
10. 'Nana Richins Purple' - purple flowers
11. 'Nishiki' - variegated foliage
12. 'Plena' or 'Violaceae Plena' - double blue flowers in dense clusters
13. 'Praecox' or 'Domino' - purple flowers
14. 'Purpurea' - unknown - May be Wisteria sinensis consequa which is sometimes labeled purpurea
15. 'Royal Purple' - purple flowers
16. 'Rubra'- unknown - may be Honbeni - sometimes labeled as Rubrum - deep pink to red flowers
17. 'Texas Purple' - may be a *sinensis* or a hybrid, short racemes, purple flowers, produced while the plant is still young
18. 'Violacea Plena' - double violet flowers, rosette-shaped
19. 'White with Blue Eye' - also known as Sekines Blue - very fragrant

3.101.2 External links

- Japanese Wisteria at MSU
- Japanese Wisteria as a pest
- University of Ohio fact sheet for *Wisteria* family

3.101.3 References

[1] "Wisteria floribunda, W. sinensis". United States Forest Service. Retrieved December 12, 2014.

[2] "Japanese Wisteria". National Park Service. Retrieved December 12, 2014.

[3] Growth Conditions

[4] "RHS Plant Selector - *Wisteria floribunda* 'Alba'". Retrieved 9 June 2013.

[5] "RHS Plant Selector - *Wisteria floribunda* 'Rosea'". Retrieved 9 June 2013.

[6] "RHS Plant Selector - *Wisteria floribunda* 'Multijuga'". Retrieved 9 June 2013.

3.102 Wisteria sinensis

Wisteria sinensis (**Chinese wisteria**) is a woody, deciduous, perennial climbing vine in the genus *Wisteria*, native to China in the provinces of Guangxi, Guizhou, Hebei, Henan, Hubei, Shaanxi, and Yunnan. While this plant is a climbing vine, it can be trained into a tree-like shape, usually with a wavy trunk and a flattened top.

It can grow 20–30 m long over supporting trees by counterclockwise-twining stems. The leaves are shiny, green, pinnately compound, 10–30 cm in length, with 9-13 oblong leaflets that are each 2–6 cm long. The flowers are white, violet, or blue, produced on 15–20 cm racemes before the leaves emerge in spring. The flowers on each raceme open simultaneously before the foliage has expanded, and have a distinctive fragrance similar to that of grapes. Though it has shorter racemes than *Wisteria floribunda* (Japanese wisteria), it often has a higher quantity of racemes. The fruit is a flattened, brown, velvety, bean-like pod 5–10 cm long with thick disk-like seeds around 1 cm in diameter spaced evenly inside; they mature in summer and crack and twist open to release the seeds; the empty pods often persist until winter. However seed production is often low, and most regenerative growth occurs through layering and suckering.

It is hardy in USDA plant hardiness zones 5-9, and prefers moist soils. It is considered shade tolerant, but will flower only when exposed to partial or full sun. It will also flower

Wisteria sinensis *and its variety* albiflora *(at the left) by Abraham Jacobus Wendel, 1868*

3.102.1 Gallery

- Season-impression animation of a free standing *Wisteria sinensis* at the Tsubo-en Zen garden

- *Wisteria sinensis* as a weed in South Carolina, U.S.A.

- The Sierra Madre Wistaria (the preferred spelling)

only after passing from juvenile to adult stage, a transition that may take up to 20 years. It can live for over a hundred years.

All parts of the plant contain a glycoside called wisterin which is toxic if ingested and may cause nausea, vomiting, stomach pains, and diarrhea. Wisterias have caused poisoning in children of many countries, producing mild to severe gastroenteritis.

Captain Richard Rawes of the East Indiaman *Warren Hastings* brought it from China to Britain in 1816, from where it spread to Europe and North America. It has secured for itself a place as one of the most popular vines for home gardens due to its flowering. It has however become an invasive species in some areas of the eastern United States[1] where the climate closely matches that of China.

A one-acre (4,000 m^2) specimen located in Sierra Madre, California is recognized by Guinness World Records as the world's largest blossoming plant.[2]

3.102.2 References

[1] "*Wisteria sinensis* (Sims) DC." . Natural Resources Conservation Service, United States Department of Agriculture. Retrieved December 13, 2014.

[2] Palma, Claudia (March 10, 2016). What to know if you're heading to Sierra Madre's Wistaria Festival. Retrieved August 21, 2016.

3.102.3 Further reading

Jiang, Yifan; Chen, Xinlu; Lin, Hong (2011). "Floral Scent in Wisteria: Chemical Composition, Emission Pattern, and Regulation" . *Journal of the American Society for Horticultural Science*. **136** (5): 307–314.

Zhang, Shu-yong; Xia, Jiang-bao; Zhou, Ze-fu; Zhang, Guang-can (September 2007). "Photosynthesis responses to various soil moisture in leaves of Wisteria sinensis" . *Journal of Forestry Research*. **18** (3): 217–220. doi:10.1007/s11676-007-0044-6.

3.102.4 External links

3.103 Zelkova serrata

"Keyaki" redirects here. For several Japanese ships, see Keyaki (ship).
For another plant called "Japanese elm", see Ulmus davidiana var. japonica.

Zelkova serrata (**Japanese zelkova**, **Japanese elm**[2] or **keyaki**; Japanese: 欅 (ケヤキ) *keyaki* /槻 (ツキ) *tsuki*; Chinese: 榉树/櫸樹 *jǔshù*; Korean: 느티나무 *neutinamu*) is a species of the genus *Zelkova* native to Japan, Korea, eastern China and Taiwan.[3][4] It is often grown as an ornamental tree, and used in bonsai. There are two varieties, *Zelkova serrata* var. *serrata* in Japan and mainland eastern Asia, and *Zelkova serrata* var. *tarokoensis* (Hayata) Li on Taiwan why differs from the type in its smaller leaves with less deeply cut serration on the margins.[4]

3.103.1 Description

Bark of mature Japanese zelkova

Foliage and flowers in spring

Zelkova serrata is a medium-sized deciduous tree usually growing to 30 m (98 ft) tall. It is characterized by a short trunk dividing into many upright and erect spreading stems forming a broad, round-topped head. The tree grows rapidly when young though the growth rate slows to medium upon middle age and maturity.[5]

It has alternately arranged leaves growing to 5 cm long and broad. The leaves themselves are simple and ovate to oblong-ovate with serrated or crenate margins, to which the tree owes its specific epithet *serrata*. The leaves are acuminate or apiculate, rounded or subcordate at the base, and contain 8-14 pairs of veins. The leaves are rough on top and glabrous or nearly glabrous on the underside. They are green to dark green in spring and throughout the summer, changing to yellows, oranges and reds in autumn. The petioles are 2–5 mm ($1/16$–$3/16$ in) long.[6]

Z. serrata develops monoecious flowers in spring with the leaves. Buds are ovoid, acutish, with many imbricate, dark brown scales.[5] They diverge at a 45 degree angle from the stem. The staminate flowers are shortly pedicellate and approximately 3mm in diameter, clustered in the axils of the lower leaves. The pistillate flowers are solitary or few in axils of the upper leaves, sessile and usually about 1.5 mm in diameter. The flowers are yellow-green, not showy, and occur in tight groups along new stems. They give rise to small, ovate, wingless drupes that ripen in late summer to autumn. The drupe is green maturing to brown, subsessile and 2.5 to 3.5 mm ($3/32$ to $1/8$ in) in diameter.

To identify *Zelkova serrata*, one would look for a short main trunk, low branching and a vase-shaped habit. The twigs are slender with small, dark conical buds in a zigzag pattern. The branches are usually glabrous. The bark is grayish white to grayish brown and either smooth with lenticels or exfoliating in patches to reveal orange inner bark. The branchlets are brownish-purple to brown.

3.103.2 Cultivation

This tree requires full to partial sun and prefers moist, well drained soils. A fertilizer rich in potassium and nitrogen encourages new vegetation and floral buds. It is adaptable and tolerant of heat, little water, nutrient poor soils and various pH. It should be periodically thinned to allow light into the inner canopy. *Zelkova serrata* is propagated by seeds, rooted stem cuttings and grafting. The seeds germinate without pretreatment, though the percentage is better when stratified at 5 °C (41 °F) for 60 days.*[5] Because germination requires stratification, the seed is best sown early in the year. To ensure survival it may be necessary to pot the tree and grow it in a greenhouse for its first winter. It may be reintroduced into its permanent habitat after the final frost.

3.103.3 Threats

The threats to this tree include colder temperature, which often result in twig dieback. It is highly resistant to Dutch elm disease, which makes it a good replacement tree for American elm. *Zelkova serrata* is similar in appearance to the elms, though may be distinguished by its unwinged fruit and leaves which are symmetrical rather than uneven at their base.*[7] *Zelkova serrata* also shows good resistance to elm leaf beetle and Japanese beetle.

3.103.4 Cultivation and uses

Zelkova serrata *bonsai from the United States National Arboretum*

Zelkova serrata is planted as a lawn or park tree for its attractive bark, leaf color and vase shape. It provides good shade and has an easy fall cleanup. It is easy to transport, and often available in burlap form. It is also commonly used for bonsai; its attractive shape and colors make it a popular choice for the art.*[3]*[4] It is often grown as an ornamental tree, both in its native area and in Europe and North America. The first cultivation outside of Asia was by Philipp Franz von Siebold, who introduced it to the Netherlands in 1830.*[4] Recently, it has been planted as a "street tree" in New York City.*[8] It has gained the Royal Horticultural Society's Award of Garden Merit.*[9]

Numerous cultivars have been selected, including

- 'Fuiri Keyaki' (variegated leaves)
- 'Goblin' (dwarf)
- 'Goshiki' (variegated leaves)
- 'Green Vase' (tall, narrow crown*[10])
- 'Green Veil' (pendulous branchlets)
- 'Iruma Sango' (fastigiate)
- 'Nire Keyaki' (semi-dwarf)
- 'Pulverulenta' (variegated leaves)
- 'Spring Grove' (upright crown)
- 'Variegata' (variegated leaves)
- 'Village Green' (grows more rapidly than ordinary seedlings and develops a straight smooth trunk. Hardier than trees of Japanese origin photos)
- 'Variegata' (weak growing, small leaved form with a narrow white rim around the margin of the leaf),
- 'Parkview' (selection with good vase-shape, size similar to species)
- 'Urban Ruby' (red autumn colour)
- 'Musashino' (Tightly columnar in form, fast growing)
- 'Ogon' (Bright green-yellow almost gold colored leaves all year, with a contrasting bronze colored bark)

It has also hybridised with *Zelkova carpinifolia* in Europe, the hybrid being named *Zelkova × verschaffeltii*.*[4]

Keyaki wood is valued in Japan and used often for furniture, such as tansu, as well as being considered the ideal wood for the creation of taiko drums.

The tree is a symbol of a number of Japanese cities and prefectures: Saitama Prefecture, Miyagi Prefecture, Fukushima Prefecture, Fukushima-shi, Abiko-shi, Tachikawa-shi, Yokohama-shi, Machida City in Tokyo Metropolis District, Takatsuki City and more.

3.103. ZELKOVA SERRATA

According to statistics data investigated by Korea Forest Service in 1989, the most numbers of old trees over 500 years were Zelkova serrata, while more than 10 old trees have been registered as Natural monuments of Korea.*[11]

3.103.5 Suppliers

Within the United Kingdom, the Royal Horticultural Society's Plantfinder currently lists 38 suppliers for the pure species and associated varieties.*[12]

3.103.6 Gallery

-  Autumn colour, November, Saitama Prefecture, Japan.
-  Trees lining an avenue in Sendai, Japan
-  Morton Arboretum acc. 10-54-1
-  A Japanese Sendai-dansu for kimono made from keyaki wood
-  Sasayama, Hyogo in the winter
-  An example of a mature tree

3.103.7 References

[1] Osaka Toyono County: Noma Keyaki (in Japanese; google translation)

[2] "BSBI List 2007". Botanical Society of Britain and Ireland. Archived from the original (xls) on 2015-02-25. Retrieved 2014-10-17.

[3] Flora of China: *Zelkova serrata*

[4] Andrews, S. (1994). Tree of the year: Zelkova. *Int. Dendrol. Soc. Yearbook* 1993: 11-30.

[5] Rehder, Alfred. Manual of Cultivated Trees and Shrubs. 2. New York: The Macmillan Company, 1949. Print.

[6] Dirr, Michael A. Manual of Woody Landscape Plants: Their Identification, Ornamental Characteristics, Culture, Propagation and Uses. 3. Champaign: Stipes Publishing Company, 1975. Print.

[7] "#820 Zelkova Serrata." Floridata. 01 25 2004. 4 May 2009 .

[8] New York City Parks Street Tree List

[9] "RHS Plant Selector - *Zelkova serrata*". Retrieved 10 June 2013.

[10] *Zelkova serrata* 'Green Vase' photos

[11] Lee, chang-bok(1989). ☒☒☒☒☒☒☒☒☒. 《☒☒ ☒☒》 16: 86. Accessed on October 9th, 2013

[12] Plantfinder

3.103.8 External links

- "Zelkova Serrata." The Ohio State University. 4 May 2009.
- "Family Ulmaceae." Zipcodezoo. 05 23 2009. 4 May 2009.

3.104 Zoysia 'Emerald'

Emerald Zoysia (*Zoysia* 'Emerald') is a cultivar of *Zoysia* grass with a thin bladed leaf that forms a very lush lawn. It shares the drought and shade resistance of the other varieties.

This grass has a fine, soft texture and can be left unmowed as it only grows to a height of 6–12 inches (15–30 cm). When left unmowed, it forms a humpy convoluted surface which is sometimes used in oriental landscapes (see picture on Zoysia page).

3.104.1 Adaptation and characteristics

Emerald Zoysia is adapted to zones 7-11*[1] and does well in warm, humid environments. It is an excellent grass for the southern and southeastern states. Once established it requires less water than St. Augustine but slightly more than Bermuda.*[2] It is drought tolerant due to its deep root structure.*[3] Browning may occur in triple digit heat, but adequate hydration can restore its vibrant green color in a matter of minutes. The grass is moderately shade tolerant, coming close to the shade tolerance of St. Augustine.*[4] However, it does not do well in full shade*[5] as compared to Rye and Fescue. An average of at least 3–4 hours of full sun per day is a good measure for healthy growth.*[6] Flooding is tolerated, but constant saturation will eventually weaken the grass. This zoysia has a moderate cold tolerance and can be damaged by hard freezes and is not hardy in transition zones. Emerald Zoysia is a very slow growing lawn grass. Zoysia grasses are generally slower growing than Bermuda and St. Augustine, with Emerald Zoysia being one of the slowest growing Zoysia grasses. The grass exhibits a dense creeping growth, rather than an aggressive upward, or sprawling growth. The blade density is much higher than other grasses, giving a very dense, carpet-like, or "hedgehog" appearance.

3.104.2 Care and maintenance

Due to the density of the grass, excess thatch can accumulate and should be removed every several weeks. Mowing can be performed every 7–10 days, with no more than 1/3 of the blade cut at one time. Recommended mowing height of this grass is between .75 and 2 inches (1.9 and 5.1 cm). Mowing the grass shorter than this height can produce a weaker less attractive product, whereas mowing the grass higher than this height will promote a less-dense, wispy appearance. The use of reel mowers are suggested since common rotary lawn mowers will tear the fine-blade grass and leave a grey/white tip instead of a clean cut.

Emerald Zoysia has an adverse reaction to excessive fertilization, requiring no more than two light distributions per year. 8-8-8 or 13-13-13 fertilizer is recommended. If over fertilized, it will turn yellow and could die. Since regrowth of this grass is slow, its best to err on the light side of fertilization than to over fertilize.

3.104.3 References

[1] "Archived copy". Archived from the original on January 5, 2009. Retrieved December 22, 2008.

[2] "Archived copy". Archived from the original on January 30, 2009. Retrieved December 22, 2008.

[3] http://plantanswers.tamu.edu/turf/publications/zoysia.html

[4] "Archived copy". Archived from the original on June 28, 2008. Retrieved December 22, 2008.

[5] "Archived copy". Archived from the original on October 17, 2008. Retrieved December 22, 2008.

[6] "Archived copy". Archived from the original on April 3, 2009. Retrieved December 22, 2008.

Chapter 4

Text and image sources, contributors, and licenses

4.1 Text

- **Bonsai** *Source:* https://en.wikipedia.org/wiki/Bonsai?oldid=773380703 *Contributors:* Kpjas, Mav, Tarquin, Rmhermen, Montrealais, Olivier, Spiff~enwiki, Infrogmation, Michael Hardy, Menchi, Ixfd64, TakuyaMurata, Delirium, Kistaro, Torge, Looxix~enwiki, Ahoerstemeier, John Webb, Ronz, Snoyes, Bueller 007, Aarchiba, Nikai, Lancevortex, Furrykef, Metasquares, Bloodshedder, Wetman, Robbot, Altenmann, Kokiri, Lowellian, Hippietrail, Kallgan, Exploding Boy, MPF, Fudoreaper, Lupin, Everyking, Niteowlneils, Leonard G., Revth, Henryhartley, Mboverload, Pascal666, Solipsist, Dainamo, Hereticam, Andycjp, Piotrus, Kusunose, Mzajac, Muijz, Mike Rosoft, Rich Farmbrough, Memobug, Vsmith, Francis Schonken, Xezbeth, Bender235, Mwanner, RoyBoy, Cacophony, Longhair, Func, John Vandenberg, Viriditas, Cmdrjameson, Ildefonse, Dungodung, Alphax, MPerel, Makersmark, Hooperbloob, Nsaa, HasharBot~enwiki, Danski14, Alansohn, Anthony Appleyard, Bonsaikc, Free Bear, Wiki-uk, Apoc2400, Mailer diablo, InShaneee, Cdc, Webslingr, Danhash, Gpvos, RainbowOfLight, Duff, BDD, RyanGerbil10, Woohookitty, Camw, Rocastelo, Acerperi, Clemmy, Aaroamal, Gimboid13, Gisling, Cshirky, Graham87, Sparkit, Deltabeignet, Magister Mathematicae, BD2412, Shandolad, Search4Lancer, Rjwilmsi, Pjetter, Gryffindor, Quiddity, VeritasEtAequitas, Trees4est, TheGWO, Yamamoto Ichiro, FlaBot, AdnanSa, DannyWilde, Fragglet, Hottentot, Andy85719, Ewlyahoocom, Karelj, Mitsukai, Maltmomma, Imnotminkus, DTOx, DVdm, Gdrbot, Schulte, Bgwhite, YurikBot, Wavelength, Icarus3, Hede2000, Kwb~enwiki, High5, Emmanuelm, Gaius Cornelius, Ksyrie, Bovineone, NawlinWiki, Fizan, Badagnani, Ragesoss, Retired username, Esthurin, Kingpomba, Dmaestoso, Zwobot, Mkill, Lockesdonkey, BOT-Superzerocool, Rayc, Cmcfarland, Djdaedalus, Nlu, Crisco 1492, Phgao, Meika, Chase me ladies, I'm the Cavalry, AnotherWaldo, MaverickLord, BorgQueen, GraemeL, LeonardoRob0t, Kungfuadam, Sam Weber, Ryūkotsusei, タチコマ robot, Sardanaphalus, SmackBot, InverseHypercube, Hydrogen Iodide, Deon Steyn, MeiStone, Lds, Eskimbot, Sam8, Paxse, Phanatical, Shai-kun, PeterSymonds, Gilliam, Portillo, Ohnoitsjamie, Hmains, ERcheck, Endroit, Thumperward, TheLeopard, DHN-bot~enwiki, Modest Genius, Can't sleep, clown will eat me, Egsan Bacon, Mulder416, Jmlk17, MrRadioGuy, Radagast83, Cybercobra, Khukri, Nibuod, Nakon, Tenmiles, Shadow1, Mini-Geek, Lcarscad, Drphilharmonic, RJBaran, Und3rlord, Zeamays, Mvp~enwiki, Curly Turkey, NeoVampTrunks, SashatoBot, Dcruz01, Vanished user 9i39j3, Kuru, Rodsan18, Bjankuloski06en~enwiki, Dally Horton, LuYiSi, Brockoali, Mr Stephen, Bell017, TastyPoutine, Ryulong, Cryo75, Twas Now, Gilabrand, Radiant chains, Tawkerbot2, Blackash, Makampec, VanHelsing.16, Godardesque, Michael J. Mullany, Omglazers, Gregbard, Cydebot, Grammaticus Repairo, Gogo Dodo, A Softer Answer, Denise23, Casliber, Thijs!bot, Epbr123, Wikid77, Pajz, Jedibob5, Danbonsai, Williamrayner, Marek69, Mr pand, BonsaiCenter, Noggon777, CharlotteWebb, Nick Number, Srose, WhaleyTim, Dawnseeker2000, Futurebird, Gossamers, AntiVandalBot, Mukake, AaronSmiley, Flondin, Prolog, HMAccount, Chill doubt, Spacecat2, Canadian-Bacon, JAnDbot, Candent shlimazel, MER-C, Charlene.fic, ZBryan2, SirNigpott~enwiki, Magioladitis, VoABot II, JanCK, AniBunny, Ling.Nut, TheOtherBob, SparrowsWing, Globalist1789, TyrocP, Fuzzyllama, Edward321, MidnightScott, Patstuart, IvoShandor, BobCatBobDog, RichMac, SquidSK, FisherQueen, MartinBot, Phantomsnake, Kiore, CommonsDelinker, Iwanafish, PrestonH, Boston, Matt57, J.delanoy, Kimse, Treetroll, DrKay, Meilanfang, Andreaelassar, Cocoaguy, AquamarineOnion, Jancellor, Acalamari, M C Y 1008, Ze-winnipeg, Dreko, Amake, Grosscha, Stormfin, Naniwako, Jon Ascton, Balthazarduju, Lucasio0, A302b, Luna tsukino, KylieTastic, Cometstyles, Littelinfo, Treisijs, MyDickHertz, Apocalyptic Destroyer, Signalhead, Asrobs, Sparky147, VolkovBot, Thedjatclubrock, ABF, Dogsgomoo, Jeff G., Indubitably, Kuebi, Harry harrington, TXiKiBoT, EvanCarroll, Mercy, Cinderella72, Anonymous Dissident, RealBigFlipsbrain, Mark waugh, Una Smith, Steven J. Anderson, Amagase~enwiki, Cybrix, Beechhouse, Muhammad Mahdi Karim, Geometry guy, Remilo, Funkydelux, Red minx, Andy Dingley, Seresin, Logan, PGWG, EmxBot, Yumao~enwiki, Top caty, SieBot, Iancuppleditch, Tresiden, Lindabonsai, BotMultichill, Jsc83, Yintan, Apollo Augustus Koo, Flyer22 Reborn, Fakeguy2, Oda Mari, Zurqoxn, Nuttycoconut, Hobartimus, Manway, Gomeying, StaticGull, Cyfal, Jacob.jose, Bisjoe, Wiki-Laurent, MUSASHIKOGANEI, Scuv, Phyte, ClueBot, The Thing That Should Not Be, Markkennerley, Der Golem, Sevilledade, Uncle Milty, Will Heath, Niceguyedc, Tiberio971, Auntof6, DragonBot, Vrevilla, Hal starkie, Excirial, Alexbot, Jusdafax, Lartoven, MacedonianBoy, Peter.C, World, TheRedPenOfDoom, SchreiberBike, Frongle, Zoezoo, Jlrmacias, NJGW, Apparition11, Black Knight takes White Queen, Crazy Boris with a red beard, XLinkBot, Scaramouche509, Chee Chahko, Krazyhurdler, Klundarr, Addbot, Ucla90024, Orlandobonsai, Cst17, WinterE229, Jasper Deng, Japanesewriter, Tide rolls, Lightbot, Megaman en m, Fryed-peach, Luckas-bot, Themfromspace, Ptbotgourou, Legobot II, Mmxx, THEN WHO WAS PHONE?, AnakngAraw, Tempodivalse, Rubypanther, AnomieBOT, Archon 2488, Jim1138, EdiPoo, LouPepe, BlazerKnight, Law, Flewis, Materialscientist, The National Bonsai and Penjing Museum, Citation bot, E2eamon, Xqbot, TinucherianBot II, Capricorn42, Drilnoth, DSisyphBot, Timmyshin, Sahara110, Vanished user xlkvmskgm4k, C+C, Malachia51, Apohran, Brutaldeluxe, White whirlwind, Shadowjams, Seric2, Samwb123, AdamFact, GT5162, FrescoBot, Cervelo21, TheJazzDalek, G1c2p3, Mfwitten, Gordys~enwiki, Bugfaced, Linksys567, Severv, Amplitude101, Pinethicket, Tom.Reding, Phoenix7777, Artdoiron, Kibi78304, RevJonny, کاشف عقیل, Yunshui, Animalparty, Jonkerz, Gtstewart, Tl1378, Vrenator, Rain drop 45, Reaper Eternal, DARTH SIDIOUS 2, RjwilmsiBot, TjBot, Polfeck, Peterrijks, Regancy42, Debanikray, EmausBot, Chan21cocjin, GoingBatty, Dcirovic, K6ka, Batikulon, Thecheesykid, Brandon Noah, Akerans, Wlnorm, Medeis, Arpit.arun.mishra, Gabriel.salinas, Tokonomascrolls, Rcsprinter123, Brandmeister, Coasterlover1994, Naturellement bonsaï, Anonimski, Graham Potter Bonsai, Whoop whoop pull up, Thevend, ClueBot NG, RodrigoVVSousa, This lousy T-shirt, Granthoganscot, A520, Frietjes, Delusion23, Thegoldenbonsai, CopperSquare, Widr, WikiPuppies, 祇園精舎, Ppikel, Helpful Pixie Bot, Bonsaiges, BlueMoonset, Titodutta, LittleOldManRetired, LEOThanhTiep, Mona Williams, Tuscanpistoia, Midwestbonsai~enwiki, Amp71, Zackp30, Cold Season, Larix21, Gledwood, BattyBot, Harry Franckaert, Justincheng12345-bot, StarryGrandma, Vanished user lt94ma34le12, Mrt3366, Cyberbot II, EuroCarGT, Umma rabeya, U2know, Dexbot, Mrmagikpants, Telamon456, SamRenBotch, Ansei, Me, Myself, and I are Here, Epicgenius, Pdecalculus, Ugog Nizdast, Dyveldi, Fpolson, TheEpTic, Monkbot, Thomaswilletts1989, JPNEX, Mixanobios, Julietdeltalima, Arifleshot, CallAng222, KasparBot, Chiriqui-david, Monkypluzz, Lourdes, Mrodriguez14, SaripBB, Ajrules30670 AJ, Bonsai trees, Duncan Bandojo and Anonymous: 751

- **Penjing** Source: https://en.wikipedia.org/wiki/Penjing?oldid=759563565 Contributors: Kowloonese, Ronz, Pratyeka, Wetman, Lowellian, Jxg, Kallgan, MPF, Leonard G., Henryhartley, Piotrus, Kusunose, Aranel, Surachit, Cacophony, Hintha, Caeruleancentaur, Etxrge, Fat pig73, Abstrakt, Pappa, RyanGerbil10, Gisling, Sparkit, Rjwilmsi, FlaBot, Wars, Benjwong, Bgwhite, RussBot, Emmanuelm, Ksyrie, SmackBot, Hmains, Chris the speller, Bluebot, Oatmeal batman, Midori, RJBaran, DavidCooke, Cydebot, Casliber, Marek69, Qarel, WinBot, Luna Santin, Airphloo, DuncanHill, Dekimasu, Nyttend, IvoShandor, Meilanfang, Yipely, Skier Dude, Apocalyptic Destroyer, Remilo, PericlesofAthens, Rstafursky, Gomeying, Lasalle202, Scuv, Der Golem, Sevilledade, TheRedPenOfDoom, Breakfasttea, Black Knight takes White Queen, Waterboyev, Addbot, Lightbot, Yobot, LlywelynII, Sahara110, Anna Frodesiak, Penjingfan, Omnipaedista, Kibi78304, ZhBot, Peacedance, RjwilmsiBot, Peterrijks, Look2See1, Rcsprinter123, ClueBot NG, CopperSquare, Helpful Pixie Bot, Mona Williams, Cold Season, Snow Rise, Mdy66, RudolfRed, FoCuSandLeArN, Me, Myself, and I are Here, Noyster, Monkbot, Opencooper, Doublestuff and Anonymous: 42

- **Bonsai aesthetics** Source: https://en.wikipedia.org/wiki/Bonsai_aesthetics?oldid=750196844 Contributors: Rmhermen, Montrealais, Ronz, MPF, Viriditas, Wiki-uk, Ragesoss, Chris the speller, ShelfSkewed, Gregbard, Prolog, Chill doubt, Storkk, Bus stop, Boston, Dogsgomoo, Harry harrington, Remilo, Pjoef, Jack Merridew, Gomeying, Panserbjorne51, Bob1960evens, Ost316, Yobot, Materialscientist, Citation bot, Sahara110, Dmazza, FrescoBot, Kwiki, Peterrijks, Look2See1, Griseum, Wlnorm, Tanoan, Helpful Pixie Bot, InternetArchiveBot, Myknowledgeshare, GreenC bot and Anonymous: 14

- **Bonsai cultivation and care** Source: https://en.wikipedia.org/wiki/Bonsai_cultivation_and_care?oldid=756010354 Contributors: Wiki-uk, BD2412, Kri, Chris the speller, GoodDay, Marek69, Bob1960evens, Sahara110, Look2See1, Auchansa, Helpful Pixie Bot, BG19bot, AK456, 3primetime3, MBlaze Lightning, GreenC bot, Kawsar Ahammad and Anonymous: 7

- **Bonsai styles** Source: https://en.wikipedia.org/wiki/Bonsai_styles?oldid=766173556 Contributors: Bearcat, Davidcannon, Malcolma, Chris the speller, Marek69, CommonsDelinker, Pjoef, Oda Mari, Ost316, Sahara110, Rilegator, RjwilmsiBot, John of Reading, Helpful Pixie Bot, Chris-Gualtieri, Puzzly, Myknowledgeshare, Thebestbonsai and Anonymous: 5

- **Acer buergerianum** Source: https://en.wikipedia.org/wiki/Acer_buergerianum?oldid=774212610 Contributors: William Avery, Ram-Man, MPF, JoJan, Closeapple, Circeus, Hesperian, ScottDavis, Rjwilmsi, Eubot, Abrahami, Dcruz01, -js-, Casliber, JAnDbot, Boston, Nadiatalent, Kyle the bot, ZSLF~enwiki, Alexbot, Addbot, LaaknorBot, ArthurBot, Xqbot, GrouchoBot, LucienBOT, PigFlu Oink, ZhBot, RjwilmsiBot, EmausBot, Look2See1, Jcaraballo, Justincheng12345-bot, Lukas[23], Jonnyroark, Joseph Laferriere, InternetArchiveBot, GreenC bot, Bender the Bot and Anonymous: 9

- **Acer campestre** Source: https://en.wikipedia.org/wiki/Acer_campestre?oldid=766175963 Contributors: William Avery, Silvonen, Topbanana, Robbot, Kristof vt, UtherSRG, Srtxg, MPF, JoJan, Closeapple, Circeus, Nicke Lilltroll~enwiki, Nk, Hesperian, HasharBot~enwiki, Jumbuck, Ricky81682, Lectonar, Stemonitis, Rjwilmsi, Ricardo Carneiro Pires, Eubot, Gdrbot, YurikBot, RussBot, Eupator, BOT-Superzerocool, Germore, Hirudo, Cazort, Chris the speller, Kitzke, Salvor, MalafayaBot, Hibernian, Colonies Chris, Dcruz01, Ptelea, Cydebot, Casliber, Thijs!bot, Headbomb, Escarbot, JAnDbot, Plantsurfer, Geniac, Magioladitis, Peter coxhead, Boston, Wlodzimierz, Bumper12, Nadiatalent, Jackaranga, STBotD, VolkovBot, Philip Trueman, TXiKiBoT, SieBot, Oculi, SoxBot III, Addbot, Numbo3-bot, Zorrobot, Luckas-bot, Yobot, Materialscientist, Eumolpo, Xqbot, Gigemag76, GrouchoBot, Galloramenu, I dream of horses, RedBot, SW3 5DL, Trappist the monk, Mishae, RjwilmsiBot, EmausBot, Look2See1, Dcirovic, Kmoksy, Matthewcgirling, عمرو بن كلثوم, Plantdrew, BG19bot, NotWith, Darorcilmir, Dexbot, Seacactus 13, Nicksola, Trixie05, Stamptrader, Joseph Laferriere, Monkbot, Impuls666666, Sunmist, Giovanni Caudullo, Tom elm, Otto Sheva2, Basotxerri, Mmurali1, Marrrrrra, InternetArchiveBot, Nina Lauridsen and Anonymous: 27

- **Acer circinatum** Source: https://en.wikipedia.org/wiki/Acer_circinatum?oldid=773763945 Contributors: William Avery, Nonenmac, Angilbas, MPF, JoJan, Famartin, Closeapple, Circeus, Longhair, Hesperian, Alaney2k, Eubot, Gdrbot, YurikBot, Chris Mealy, Wsiegmund, Mmcannis, Hirudo, EncycloPetey, Adamschneider, Dlc 73, Cydebot, Casliber, Thirdright, Athaenara, Nadiatalent, Liz de Quebec, TubularWorld, ClueBot, Fyyer, Excirial, Kbdankbot, Addbot, Yobot, ArthurBot, Ched, Pinethicket, MondalorBot, EmausBot, Look2See1, Sesamehoneytart, ZéroBot, Jsayre64, عمرو بن كلثوم, ClueBot NG, Plantdrew, Hillbillyholiday, Nightphoenix90, Joseph Laferriere, InternetArchiveBot, GreenC bot, Lavandulangustifolia and Anonymous: 17

- **Acer ginnala** Source: https://en.wikipedia.org/wiki/Acer_ginnala?oldid=742681554 Contributors: Edward, Robbot, MPF, JoJan, Closeapple, Circeus, Hesperian, Djlayton4, Eubot, Chobot, YurikBot, Hardyplants, Kevlar67, Ser Amantio di Nicolao, Sannab, WeggeBot, Casliber, Rosarinagazo, JAnDbot, Peter coxhead, Nadiatalent, Addbot, Culmensis, Erutuon, Lightbot, Yobot, Sprachpfleger, TaBOT-zerem, JMAN1156, Xqbot, Potejam, LucienBOT, Lotje, Glorioussandwich, EmausBot, AvicBot, ClueBot NG, Plantdrew, Darorcilmir, Mykola Swarnyk, Joseph Laferriere and Anonymous: 7

- **Acer monspessulanum** Source: https://en.wikipedia.org/wiki/Acer_monspessulanum?oldid=763543862 Contributors: William Avery, MPF, JoJan, OwenBlacker, Closeapple, Circeus, Hesperian, Deror avi, Stemonitis, Ricardo Carneiro Pires, Eubot, BOT-Superzerocool, Chris the speller, Rkitko, Kitzke, Casliber, Thijs!bot, Geniac, Magioladitis, Avicennasis, Peter coxhead, Boston, Nadiatalent, VolkovBot, CompactFish, Addbot, Luckas-bot, Yobot, AnomieBOT, RibotBOT, RedBot, EmausBot, WikitanvirBot, Look2See1, GoingBatty, AvicBot, ZéroBot, عمرو بن كلثوم, Ungoliant MMDCCLXIV, NotWith, Hossinhavashenasy, Joseph Laferriere, InternetArchiveBot, GreenC bot, Nina Lauridsen and Anonymous: 4

4.1. TEXT

- **Acer palmatum** *Source:* https://en.wikipedia.org/wiki/Acer_palmatum?oldid=774184725 *Contributors:* William Avery, Stan Shebs, Suisui, Bueller 007, Rl, Vargenau, Emperorbma, PuzzletChung, Chris 73, DocWatson42, MPF, Michael Devore, Jackol, Andycjp, JoJan, Gscshoyru, Oknazevad, Famartin, Closeapple, Circeus, Nk, Hesperian, Wtmitchell, Djlayton4, Timurberk~enwiki, LordAmeth, Stemonitis, Jeffrey O. Gustafson, Sdgjake, Schzmo, BD2412, Berserk798, Manualph, Eubot, Karelj, ChongDae, Chobot, Mhking, Gdrbot, Kummi, The Rambling Man, YurikBot, Huw Powell, RussBot, Gaius Cornelius, Ragesoss, Jpbowen, AdiJapan, SmackBot, Hu Gadarn, BeagleSoldier, EncycloPetey, Dansroka, Hardyplants, Gary2863, Gilliam, Chris the speller, Rkitko, SB Johnny, Bruce Marlin, Gsp8181, Khoikhoi, BesselDekker, Thor Dockweiler, Dcruz01, JorisvS, IronGargoyle, Ryulong, Joseph Solis in Australia, CapitalR, Lavateraguy, Jen1026, Dexnoodle, Casliber, Thijs!bot, Epbr123, Rosarinagazo, Marek69, Mnp~enwiki, David Shankbone, Interactbiz, Geniac, Magioladitis, Michael Goodyear, G.A.S, MartinBot, R'n'B, CommonsDelinker, Iwanafish, Boston, Benmdv, Skumarlabot, Paris1127, Gubbio, NewEnglandYankee, Nadiatalent, Lmbstl, Ja 62, Idioma-bot, Wikieditor06, VolkovBot, Coryjp, Barneca, Oshwah, Rei-bot, Una Smith, Jackfork, Jaguarlaser, Cnilep, Galamazoo12, Bfpage, Jack Merridew, Mywood, France3470, Jan Jansson, ClueBot, No such user, Jusdafax, InaMaka, Onozeki, Rui Gabriel Correia, Vanished User 1004, Ost316, Wyatt915, Addbot, John Stephen Dwyer, Veg grower, Bencohoon, Keds0, Nervous65, First Light, Bermicourt, Luckas-bot, Yobot, Fraggle81, Collieuk, Xqbot, Tomwsulcer, Anonymous from the 21st century, Pinethicket, Leegee23, Vladmirfish, Vrenator, AdrianoBruceLeonardo, Reaper Eternal, Diannaa, WikiKing1234, EmausBot, GoingBatty, RenamedUser01302013, Tommy2010, Marcusliou4, RaptureBot, JoeSperrazza, RCT3Rulez!, Donner60, Appalachiantrail73, KatPage, Sven Manguard, DASHBotAV, عمرو بن كلثوم, ClueBot NG, PaleCloudedWhite, Widr, Plantdrew, Christine217, Jumbopants123, Snow Blizzard, Darorcilmir, YFdyh-bot, EuroCarGT, Trixie05, Asp870, Todlichebujoku, Joseph Laferriere, Consciousobserver, Mattgible, Roryoza, InternetArchiveBot, GreenC bot, Ityoppyawit and Anonymous: 138

- **Acer rubrum** *Source:* https://en.wikipedia.org/wiki/Acer_rubrum?oldid=774189235 *Contributors:* Malcolm Farmer, Danny, Nonenmac, Camembert, Edward, Ixfd64, Ahoerstemeier, Pollinator, Kdebisschop, Angilbas, MPF, Chowbok, Yath, Gzuckier, JoJan, Famartin, Mike Rosoft, Discospinster, Rich Farmbrough, Fungus Guy, Closeapple, Swid, Jpgordon, Bobo192, Circeus, Hesperian, Alansohn, Djlayton4, Shoefly, Stemonitis, Firsfron, Mindmatrix, Schzmo, BD2412, Rjwilmsi, The wub, Gurch, Samwisebruce, CiaPan, Gdrbot, YurikBot, RobotE, Hede2000, C777, Gaius Cornelius, Curtis Clark, Dysmorodrepanis~enwiki, Closedmouth, Mmcannis, Hirudo, Mejor Los Indios, Sycthos, SmackBot, Amcbride, Eventer, Hardyplants, Canthusus, Cazort, Pcrooker, Andy M. Wang, Rkitko, SB Johnny, Bazonka, RedHillian, Noles1984, Rklawton, Dcruz01, Minna Sora no Shita, Darry2385, Iridescent, Baskaufs, Neelix, Cydebot, Teratornis, Kozuch, Casliber, Thijs!bot, Epbr123, Headbomb, Marek69, Vertium, Bobblehead, James086, E. Ripley, AntiVandalBot, Storkk, Altairisfar, Whilom, LeRoc, AuburnPilot, JamesBWatson, Ling.Nut, CTF83!, Edward321, Peter coxhead, Vicpeters, R'n'B, Vox Rationis, Masebrock, J.delanoy, Warren Lee, Uncle Dick, Floaterfluss, Nadiatalent, KylieTastic, CardinalDan, Funandtrvl, VolkovBot, TreasuryTag, Vlmastra, Vipinhari, Rei-bot, Karmos, Modal Jig, Corvus coronoides, Liz de Quebec, Ajrocke, Motorrad-67, Malcolmxl5, Legion fi, Taxodium, Keilana, Tiptoety, Lightmouse, IvanTortuga, ImageRemovalBot, Sfan00 IMG, ClueBot, Pan narrans, Middle Bill Hiccup, CounterVandalismBot, Iksnyzrog, Excirial, Ludwigs2, Rob rohrer, Thingg, Amaltheus, Berean Hunter, Epiphaross, Wikiuser100, Addbot, DOI bot, Download, Deinocheirus, Bencohoon, Erutuon, Lightbot, Fabiano Tatsch, Yobot, EdwardLane, 2D, Bunnyhop11, Cflm001, Bluerasberry, Citation bot, LilHelpa, Capricorn42, Jpon9, TonyHagale, Potejam, Slurrymaster, Citation bot 1, DigbyDalton, Pinethicket, Jonesey95, Trappist the monk, MApandr, Ewebs, DASHBot, Ftlombardo, Look2See1, Solarra, ZéroBot, Traxs7, H3llBot, عمرو بن كلثوم, ClueBot NG, Awwalter, Northamerica1000, Rubypeaches, Sheaden, Solistide, BattyBot, Darorcilmir, YFdyh-bot, Khazar2, Sminthopsis84, Promethean12232, Itc editor2, Nightphoenix90, Stamptrader, Joseph Laferriere, Monkbot, Spizaetus, Faune7, Sarr Cat, Deunanknute, Lena Key, Adam9007, GreenC bot, Bender the Bot, JStokes, EllenCat, Imminent77 and Anonymous: 129

- **Adenium** *Source:* https://en.wikipedia.org/wiki/Adenium?oldid=761995258 *Contributors:* SimonP, Stan Shebs, MPF, MathKnight, Gdr, Neutrality, Vsmith, Dara, Kwamikagami, Mairi, Hesperian, Jameselliot, Stemonitis, Rickjpelleg, Stdout, Rjwilmsi, Vuong Ngan Ha, FlaBot, Daderot, Eubot, DyluckTRocket, Gdrbot, Borgx, Shell Kinney, Handsome xxx, TDogg310, Lycaon, SmackBot, Ohnoitsjamie, MalafayaBot, Abrahami, Kingdon, SpiderJon, Titus III, JMK, Timothykinney, Ies~enwiki, Corpx, Casliber, Thijs!bot, CarbonX, LigerThai, JAnDbot, Ahmiguel, Aashish Ghosh, Tusbra, Anna Lincoln, Peter ja shaw, ClueBot, Musamies, Alexbot, DumZiBoT, XLinkBot, Little Mountain 5, Addbot, Siamadenium, Faforfun, Sugeesh, AdjustShift, Xqbot, TechBot, RibotBOT, Amada44, Recognizance, Reconsider the static, Trappist the monk, Jeffcraig, Glorioussandwich, Krisada 2002, Salvio giuliano, AvicBot, Gone2seed, Brandmeister, Spicemix, ClueBot NG, Widr, Helpful Pixie Bot, NotWith, WikiWhitney, Darorcilmir, Sminthopsis84, Makecat-bot, Dotti9, Snoopy6986, Joseph Laferriere, Sarr Cat, Sara Mary Ells Queen, Bender the Bot and Anonymous: 45

- **Adenium arabicum** *Source:* https://en.wikipedia.org/wiki/Adenium_arabicum?oldid=661769430 *Contributors:* Hectorthebat, Hesperian, Tabletop, Rjwilmsi, Multichill, Betacommand, Rkitko, OrphanBot, Kingdon, Túrelio, KP Botany, CommonsDelinker, ImageRemovalBot, Musamies, Stepheng3, Siamadenium, Glorioussandwich, Garygoh884, Sarr Cat and Anonymous: 7

- **Aesculus hippocastanum** *Source:* https://en.wikipedia.org/wiki/Aesculus_hippocastanum?oldid=774013405 *Contributors:* Amillar, William Avery, Schewek, Mrwojo, Wetman, PBS, Angilbas, DocWatson42, MPF, Gil Dawson, Ich, Grahame, Matthead, Manuel Anastácio, Sonjaaa, JoJan, Neale Monks, Deglr6328, Kostja, Bender235, Circeus, Hesperian, Ral315, Ricky81682, UTSRelativity, Dennis Bratland, Stemonitis, Isfisk, Mipmapped, Pixeltoo, DavidFarmbrough, SMC, Ricardo Carneiro Pires, FlaBot, Eubot, Hannu83, Chobot, Gdrbot, Korg, Theymos, YurikBot, Conscious, Eupator, ForteTwo, Terra Green, Gadget850, Asarelah, Orcaborealis, LeonardoRob0t, Argo Navis, West Virginian, Mangoe, Bomac, Eskimbot, Benjaminevans82, Bh3u4m, Rkitko, Melburnian, Deli nk, Bruce Marlin, Tlusťa, RossF18, Dcruz01, Mgiganteus1, JHunterJ, DGtal, Colonel Warden, George100, Baskaufs, Cydebot, Kupirijo, Alvesgaspar, DumbBOT, Casliber, Thijs!bot, Ebichu63, Epbr123, Floridasand, QuiteUnusual, Dyolf~enwiki, JAnDbot, Plantsurfer, Sarah777, JamesBWatson, Peter coxhead, MartinBot, Mschel, R'n'B, Nono64, Bumper12, Colchicum, Idioma-bot, VolkovBot, AlnoktaBOT, TXiKiBoT, FantasticAsh, Dclees, Modal Jig, Dirkbb, Gjames04, Jaguarlaser, The Random Editor, SieBot, IvanTortuga, Opuntia1, Cygnis insignis, Liekmudkipz, Richerman, Alexbot, DerBorg, Chhe, TFOWR, Thebestofall007, Addbot, Friginator, Oracle 45, Briancady413, Cuaxdon, Proxima Centauri, SamatBot, Numbo3-bot, Ssschhh, Lightbot, Vizu, Luckas-bot, Yobot, EdwardLane, Elizgoiri, AnomieBOT, Tom87020, ArthurBot, MauritsBot, Xqbot, Srich32977, かぬま, RibotBOT, FrescoBot, ქართული, Hallucegenia, Jauhienij, Sid the Obscure, Sp saunders, Dinamik-bot, Weakliesandcoldwalls, DARTH SIDIOUS 2, TjBot, Beyond My Ken, DASHBot, EmausBot, Look2See1, ZéroBot, Daonguyen95, Erianna, Rcsprinter123, Workshopalex, DASHBotAV, Michael Bailes, ClueBot NG, Gligan1, ElphiBot, MusikAnimal, Carystus, NotWith, Entomologger, Darorcilmir, WBeckon, Testem, Mogism, Fraser McFarlane, ArmbrustBot, BrittanyLou, Monkbot, BrayLockBoy, Impuls666666, SovalValtos, Giovanni Caudullo, Newrapid, Leifou, Sarah JPA, Marrrrrra, InternetArchiveBot, GreenC bot, P Caroline, Bender the Bot and Anonymous: 100

- **Aesculus indica** *Source:* https://en.wikipedia.org/wiki/Aesculus_indica?oldid=762880222 *Contributors:* Richard Avery, Rjwilmsi, Asarelah, Dcruz01, R'n'B, Frank R 1981, DerBorg, Addbot, Yobot, KamikazeBot, WikitanvirBot, ZéroBot, Helpful Pixie Bot, Plantdrew, Kgferg, InternetArchiveBot, GreenC bot and Anonymous: 3

- **Afrocarpus falcatus** *Source:* https://en.wikipedia.org/wiki/Afrocarpus_falcatus?oldid=755544619 *Contributors:* Jimfbleak, MPF, Tom Radulovich, Hesperian, Ricardo Carneiro Pires, Eubot, Bgwhite, NoahElhardt, JMK, Paul venter, Epistemos, VolkovBot, Jaguarlaser, Rotational, SchreiberBike, Pgallert, Addbot, Evangele19, Jkjambsj, Flakinho, ArthurBot, Oesjaar, FrescoBot, Andynct, DASHBot, AvicBot, Abu Shawka, Tortie tude, InternetArchiveBot and Anonymous: 4

- **Alnus cordata** *Source:* https://en.wikipedia.org/wiki/Alnus_cordata?oldid=764760739 *Contributors:* William Avery, MPF, JoJan, Circeus, Ricky81682, Stemonitis, Eubot, Gdrbot, SmackBot, Commander Keane bot, Rkitko, Gruzd, Abrahami, Dcruz01, Pcgardner, Peter coxhead, VolkovBot, Jaguarlaser, AlleborgoBot, SieBot, De728631, Muro Bot, Addbot, StraSSenBahn, Yobot, KamikazeBot, Unara, Xqbot, Erik9bot, LucienBOT, RedBot, RjwilmsiBot, EmausBot, Look2See1, AvicBot, M0rphzone, Darorcilmir, Joseph Laferriere, Monkbot, Giovanni Caudullo, Rubbish computer, InternetArchiveBot, GreenC bot, Nina Lauridsen and Anonymous: 2

- **Alnus glutinosa** *Source:* https://en.wikipedia.org/wiki/Alnus_glutinosa?oldid=769190521 *Contributors:* Wetman, Pigsonthewing, UtherSRG, Alan Liefting, MPF, Obli, Auximines, JoJan, DanielCD, Xezbeth, Hapsiainen, Circeus, Jumbuck, Etxrge, AnnaP, Ricky81682, SteinbDJ, Gene Nygaard, Stemonitis, Rocastelo, BD2412, JIP, Rjwilmsi, Coemgenus, Ricardo Carneiro Pires, FlaBot, Eubot, AdnanSa, Gdrbot, YurikBot, Russ-Bot, Dysmorodrepanis~enwiki, Bloodofox, Ormanbotanigi, Lt-wiki-bot, Wsiegmund, SmackBot, Hmains, Chris the speller, Rkitko, Gruzd, Bruce Marlin, Tlusťa, Flyguy649, Dcruz01, Titus III, Carnby, Mr Stephen, Rosser1954, Thijs!bot, JAnDbot, DuncanHill, Krasanen, WolfmanSF, Hekerui, Peter coxhead, R'n'B, Nono64, J Dezman, Chiswick Chap, Idioma-bot, VolkovBot, TXiKiBoT, Maksdo, Fraxinus Croat, Giancarlodessi, Jaguarlaser, SieBot, BotMultichill, ClueBot, Hafspajen, Alexbot, BodhisattvaBot, MystBot, ElMeBot, Addbot, Poco a poco, Ka Faraq Gatri, Peti610botH, First Light, Zorrobot, Ettrig, Luckas-bot, Yobot, TaBOT-zerem, AnomieBOT, ArthurBot, Xqbot, Brutaldeluxe, FrescoBot, Simuliid, Archaeodontosaurus, AstaBOTh15, Tom.Reding, RedBot, Trappist the monk, RjwilmsiBot, EmausBot, Look2See1, Dcirovic, ZéroBot, Peppigue, Sainsf, Rcsprinter123, ChuispastonBot, Cwmhiraeth, Movses-bot, Justincheng12345-bot, Darorcilmir, Dexbot, Lemnaminor, Impuls666666, Giovanni Caudullo, Gladamas, KasparBot, Srednuas Lenoroc, InternetArchiveBot, Nina Lauridsen and Anonymous: 26

- **Azalea** *Source:* https://en.wikipedia.org/wiki/Azalea?oldid=773117187 *Contributors:* Youssefsan, DWeir, Karen Johnson, William Avery, Sfdan, Tannin, Ixfd64, Lquilter, Arpingstone, Snoyes, Bogdangiusca, Dysprosia, Robbot, Dirgela, Xanzzibar, DocWatson42, MPF, Chinasaur, Alexf, Gdr, Quadell, Vina, Lynda Finn, Thincat, Famartin, Mike Rosoft, Shiftchange, DanielCD, Discospinster, CanisRufus, Bobo192, Yongxinge, Hesperian, Visviva, MIT Trekkie, New Age Retro Hippie, Stemonitis, Damicatz, BD2412, Bubba73, SchuminWeb, Eubot, RexNL, Zotel, Gdrbot, RussBot, Trudylan, Stephenb, Gaius Cornelius, NawlinWiki, Badagnani, Moe Epsilon, Quiettype, Phgao, SmackBot, KnowledgeOfSelf, Eventer, Jrkenti, Chris the speller, Rkitko, SB Johnny, Droll, PureRED, Raymie, Gruzd, Can't sleep, clown will eat me, Jennica, Warburger, Dreadstar, Esb, DMacks, Geofrog~enwiki, Virim, Nareek, Zahid Abdassabur, Dicklyon, Phuzion, Allenp109, CapitalR, Dan1679, Shrimp wong, Wiki name, Simply south, Figtab, Cdnrav4x4, Thijs!bot, Pstanton, Nerwen, Merbabu, JustAGal, Joel Bradshaw, Nipisiquit, Deflective, Hydro, Scanlan, Michael Goodyear, LarsMarius, Mjrmtg, KirinX, EagleFan, Joshuastar, Daemonic Kangaroo, Peter coxhead, Starrycupz, JosephCampisi, STBot, R'n'B, CommonsDelinker, Vox Rationis, Jrisbara, Thegreenj, Acalamari, Bottsjw, Nadiatalent, Treisijs, Hydango, JGHowes, Tesscass, Philip Trueman, Somanypeople, Rhodyman, Crispy park, SPNic, Tresiden, Viskonsas, Oxymoron83, Lightmouse, WingkeeLEE, Jan Jansson, ImageRemovalBot, ClueBot, Votecoffee, Sleepy cassell, Piledhigheranddeeper, Mathman10, Sdrtirs, Berean Hunter, DumZiBoT, XLinkBot, Wikiuser100, Libcub, Addbot, Cwalding, Crankelwitz, Favonian, Torfin, Msfitzsimons, 5 albert square, Joanieh, Tide rolls, Yobot, 松岡明芳, AnomieBOT, Acarmack, Xufanc, Materialscientist, Bob Burkhardt, Apothecia, Maddie!, Bigsmile20, Shi Gelei, Banks3369, Collegegirl87, Chipmunk2, Prari, Peachbird, Jameskbuck, FiestyBaby, OgreBot, Jcburcham, Priscilla0712, Daholley1s, Snowy133, Bgpaulus, Peace and Passion, PiRSquared17, VanArtGuy, Hoodedwarbler12, Kcs02s, Ithundir, Jawaun96, ExTexan66, Swambills, Solarra, QueryOne, Lancelotj~enwiki, Hobbykafe, MartinHR, PBS-AWB, Naviguessor, FidelIvanS, Cksweet, Sailsbystars, AndyTheGrump, Rmashhadi, ClueBot NG, Jack Greenmaven, Mathew105601, Widr, MerlIwBot, Pjefts, Plantdrew, InsooByun, Hi6334, Orangeknight78, Glacialfox, Allansdavid, Darorcilmir, KatofKnight, TheJJJunk, Aymankamelwiki, Aftabbanoori, Taylornelson, Who needs mates round here, Kjeongeun, MRD2014, TranquilHope, Leob123)87;)7));:.3:38, Yassssboo, Sarr Cat, InternetArchiveBot, Danricc, Librariandianne, Music for a Medium-Sized Ensemble and Anonymous: 153

- **Berberis** *Source:* https://en.wikipedia.org/wiki/Berberis?oldid=769282193 *Contributors:* Edward, TeunSpaans, Shyamal, Stan Shebs, Ehn, Imc, Nv8200pa, Wetman, Pigsonthewing, Naddy, Alan Liefting, Gwalla, MPF, Rpyle731, JoJan, DanielCD, EugeneZelenko, Mani1, Syp, CanisRufus, Kwamikagami, Circeus, Hesperian, HasharBot~enwiki, Larry Grossman, Anthony Appleyard, Civvi~enwiki, Mtiedemann, Stemonitis, Richard Barlow, Pixeltoo, Rtdrury, BD2412, Rjwilmsi, Ricardo Carneiro Pires, Eubot, Pvasshep, Gdrbot, Roboto de Ajvol, Kummi, YurikBot, Conscious, Dtrebbien, Badagnani, E rulez, BOT-Superzerocool, Asarelah, Emijrp, Waynesteele~enwiki, Shyam, Pmconoley, Luk, KnightRider~enwiki, SmackBot, Eskimbot, Kintetsubuffalo, Hank01, Yamaguchi 先生, Rkitko, Persian Poet Gal, Deli nk, Sct72, Duncancumming, Nima Baghaei, Bezapt, Gondooley, MTSbot~enwiki, Basicdesign, Chrumps, Thijs!bot, Cocoma, Nick Number, Smartse, Aelwyn, Spencer, Mutt Lunker, JAnDbot, Deflective, DuncanHill, Plantsurfer, Ericoides, TheEditrix2, Michael Goodyear, Urco, Peter coxhead, Gwern, Wiki wiki1, Serge925, The Behnam, Idioma-bot, VolkovBot, LeaveSleaves, Seb az86556, Earthdirt, AlleborgoBot, SieBot, Le Pied-bot~enwiki, Smf5000, Sphilbrick, Fangjian, Specac, E-cottage, Seanwal111111, RPSM, Alpha Ralpha Boulevard, LarryMorseDCOhio, Wikilumiwonder, MystBot, Addbot, No essential nature, Amorphagate, USchick, Zorrobot, Luckas-bot, Fraggle81, AnomieBOT, Bob Burkhardt, Helfiremart, Xqbot, GrouchoBot, Epp, Simuliid, Chenopodiaceous, Spirituscanis, EmausBot, WikitanvirBot, ZxxZxxZ, Djembayz, Checkingfax, SporkBot, ClueBot NG, Biopics, Rezabot, Go Phightins!, Widr, Onewhohelps, Darorcilmir, W.D., JYBot, Sminthopsis84, Mogism, Justicequaker, Хатхи, Joseph Laferriere, Monkbot, TeamFC, Sarr Cat, MKon, Ityoppyawit and Anonymous: 68

- **Birch** *Source:* https://en.wikipedia.org/wiki/Birch?oldid=772483238 *Contributors:* Magnus Manske, JeLuF, William Avery, Azhyd, Jaknouse, Hephaestos, Quercusrobur, Moravice, TeunSpaans, Liftarn, Ixfd64, (, Torge, Egil, Jadepearl, Andres, Palfrey, Hike395, Imc, Grendelkhan, SEWilco, Topbanana, Shafei, AlexPlank, Robbot, Globe199, UtherSRG, Alan Liefting, DocWatson42, MPF, Keith Edkins, Knutux, Gzuckier, Antandrus, Ex ottoyuhr, JoJan, Rdsmith4, DanielZM, Deirdre~enwiki, Rich Farmbrough, Guanabot, Cacycle, YUL89YYZ, Murtasa, Dbachmann, Bender235, Kwamikagami, Bobo192, Circeus, Robotje, Olve Utne, Hesperian, HasharBot~enwiki, Jumbuck, Alansohn, Velella, Fledgeling, Guthrie, Ghirlandajo, Kazvorpal, Luigizanasi, Brookie, SteveHFish, Stemonitis, Woohookitty, Richard Barlow, EnSamulili, Kelisi, Schzmo, BD2412, Bubba73, Czalex, The wub, Matt Deres, Mahlum~enwiki, FlaBot, Eubot, RobertG, Gurch, Hannu83, Chobot, DaGizza,

4.1. TEXT

DVdm, Gdrbot, Ahpook, YurikBot, Wavelength, RmM, Jon Peli Oleaga, RadioFan, Stephenb, Shaddack, Rsrikanth05, NawlinWiki, Dysmorodrepanis~enwiki, Wwilly, Janke, Bloodofox, Badagnani, Nick, Retired username, Mkill, DeadEyeArrow, Bota47, Asarelah, Mareklug, Wknight94, Tigershrike, Phgao, Theda, Xil, Thomas Blomberg, Fastifex, Zvika, Biddlesby, SmackBot, KnowledgeOfSelf, McGeddon, EncycloPetey, Eskimbot, Edgar181, Mikko-Petteri, Gilliam, Rkitko, Jprg1966, Berton, SchfiftyThree, Gruzd, ChristopherM, Langbein Rise, Can't sleep, clown will eat me, Jefffire, MeekSaffron, Khoikhoi, Clean Copy, NaySay, Doodle77, Bejnar, Ohconfucius, Jomegat, SashatoBot, Potosino, Microchip08, Žiga, J 1982, Jefe619, JoshuaZ, Nighthawknz, Bjankuloski06en~enwiki, IronGargoyle, Pennyforth, Physis, Langhorner, Boomshadow, Peter Horn, MTSbot~enwiki, Newone, Bajamircea, Tig528, Ü, George100, JForget, CWY2190, Phanu9000, NickW557, Richard Keatinge, Nilfanion, Cydebot, Gogo Dodo, Bridgecross, Dreadpiratetif, Devanatha, Mon4, Shirulashem, JodyB, Zalgo, Rosser1954, Thijs!bot, Epbr123, NJPharris, Chickenflicker, Sobreira, Neil916, X., RickinBaltimore, RoboServien, Escarbot, Hmrox, AntiVandalBot, Widefox, Opelio, Aelwyn, Storkk, Gökhan, Sluzzelin, JAnDbot, Deflective, Ekabhishek, Plantsurfer, Ericoides, ReignMan, VoABot II, Faizhaider, Think outside the box, Janadore, Ling.Nut, Michael Goodyear, Bcatabas, PatialaPeg, Mcfar54, Ksvaughan2, JaGa, Guitarspecs, Peter coxhead, FisherQueen, Notmyhandle, Gaidheal1, R'n'B, CommonsDelinker, Nono64, Lilac Soul, Dinkytown, J.delanoy, Pharaoh of the Wizards, Trusilver, Neiliyo, Victuallers, Psyclist112, Teol~enwiki, Larsenmax, MattDiClemente, STBotD, Bonadea, Squids and Chips, Idioma-bot, VolkovBot, Jehan60188, Philip Trueman, TXiKiBoT, Arnon Chaffin, Tatjak, Qxz, Corvus cornix, Werdtheogrecl, Seb az86556, Jigglypuffiscool, Maksdo, Vasantbarve, Malick78, Andy Dingley, Cantiorix, Brandonberti, SieBot, Birch21, Lost in a crowd, BotMultichill, Gerakibot, Kennkweder, CSPAClover, Bentogoa, Flyer22 Reborn, Nomadhacker, Hiddenfromview, JSpung, Dictionarydude1, Dmodderman, Juggler821, Dstlascaux, StaticGull, Choogler, Prof saxx, Lascorz, Atif.t2, Beeblebrox, ClueBot, Bob1960evens, The Thing That Should Not Be, Meekywiki, Drmies, Mild Bill Hiccup, DragonBot, No such user, Robert Skyhawk, Excirial, Alexbot, Verzannt, Slidinandridin06, Barbyr, Fastily, Rror, Wikiuser100, Robert of Ramsor, Addbot, Some jerk on the Internet, Ironholds, Leszek Jańczuk, Armankhan2008, Jim10701, CarsracBot, Alesiad123, AndersBot, Lucian Sunday, Rent A Troop, Numbo3-bot, Tide rolls, First Light, Bermicourt, Luckas-bot, Yobot, Luce nordica, Ptbotgourou, Fraggle81, TaBOT-zerem, Meotrangden, Worm That Turned, KamikazeBot, AnomieBOT, Jim1138, Piano non troppo, Ulric1313, Materialscientist, Hunnjazal, Billybobjhons, Citation bot, Tat1642, Fjames3, Zanderavia, Kakumaru, Oilybrash, Xqbot, Gigemag76, Anna Frodesiak, Make an account, Srich32977, Brout8, RadiX, GrouchoBot, Abce2, PCFleming05, RibotBOT, Marzedu, Hamamelis, SD5, FrescoBot, Riventree, Khalidmcs22, Simuliid, HJ Mitchell, Pinethicket, I dream of horses, Edderso, Jschnur, Jaguar, Serols, Jonkerz, Lotje, Mishae, Suffusion of Yellow, Tbhotch, Stroppolo, Alph Bot, Rwood128, DASHBot, EmausBot, Ghghnhhj, Super48paul, CaptRik, Solarra, Wikipelli, K6ka, Hooligandisco, Ganesh Paudel, Ebrambot, H3llBot, Rcsprinter123, Mahass1979, L Kensington, Donner60, Orange Suede Sofa, ChuispastonBot, DASHBotAV, E. Fokker, ClueBot NG, CocuBot, MelbourneStar, Movses-bot, ShellBP, Joseph Biddulph, U2beal999, Cattlemans123, GlassLadyBug, Vibhijain, Igotaboner, Titodutta, Gob Lofa, Plantdrew, BG19bot, Coolj2009, LittleMiss342, A2-33, Hghyux, Mediran, Torvalu4, Billyshiverstick, Dexbot, Valdemarr, TwoTwoHello, Andybard954, Jamesx12345, Flutide, Nalsenai, Telfordbuck, Epicgenius, Jiggly123, PhantomTech, HD259, Irisbox, George Parastatidis, Kingofaces43, Qubist, OmenBreeze, Baloney0007, Antrocent, Aleksander Kaasik, Joseph Laferriere, Lagoset, Monkbot, Vieque, Lor, Johnsoniensis, Sopmoo, Asdklf;, Adûnâi, Sarr Cat, Tammbeck, Abe0821, Helloroboto, Its bri9090, That blonde chick, Wasp32, Lighthammer18, Gavriil Khipés, Xx Bill Cosby xX, Gluons12, Alfie Gandon, Zeeslak, Rosco235, Hgvjygnkj and Anonymous: 385

- **Bougainvillea glabra** *Source:* https://en.wikipedia.org/wiki/Bougainvillea_glabra?oldid=750169279 *Contributors:* Eubot, Rkitko, Gurdjieff, AndrewHowse, Cydebot, Rosarinagazo, Mmcknight4, J.delanoy, Pachyderm13, Jaguarlaser, Tlustulimu, Chhe, Addbot, LaaknorBot, Flakinho, Alpalfour, Yobot, AnomieBOT, Materialscientist, Benny White, Plantmeister, I dream of horses, Look2See1, Jkadavoor, Xanchester, Fanwen619, Dudeskin8, InternetArchiveBot, GreenC bot and Anonymous: 11

- **Buxus** *Source:* https://en.wikipedia.org/wiki/Buxus?oldid=765589089 *Contributors:* William Avery, Ram-Man, Dominus, Ellywa, Stan Shebs, Docu, Magnus.de, Zoicon5, K1Bond007, Wetman, Robbot, Chris 73, Seglea, Pingveno, GerardM, MPF, Pethan, Picapica, DanielCD, Rich Farmbrough, Mani1, CanisRufus, Hesperian, HasharBot~enwiki, Alansohn, ESMtll, BD2412, Bubba73, Vuong Ngan Ha, Eubot, Gdrbot, YurikBot, Xoloz, RMcGuigan, Qwertzy2, David Pierce, Zwobot, Ms2ger, Vdegroot, Superp, Groyolo, Unyoyega, KVDP, Rkitko, Thumperward, Vietlong, Tamfang, Onorem, Gurdjieff, Ceoil, Bjankuloski06en~enwiki, Paul venter, CBM, Raz1el, Neelix, Smartse, Nipisiquit, JAnDbot, Ericoides, Krasanen, Pleather, Peter coxhead, Johnbod, Igno2, DadaNeem, Malerin, Richard New Forest, Funandtrvl, Deor, Andy Dingley, QualiaBot, Arjayay, DumZiBoT, Virginia-American, MystBot, MatthewVanitas, Addbot, MrOllie, Proxima Centauri, Karl gregory jones, Yobot, Jdeb901, AnomieBOT, Piano non troppo, Xufanc, Xqbot, Wcoole, GrouchoBot, FrescoBot, Simuliid, Plantmeister, Orenburg1, Jonkerz, EmausBot, WikitanvirBot, Dcirovic, ZéroBot, ClueBot NG, Helpful Pixie Bot, BG19bot, Darorcilmir, Prohairesius, Anne Delong, MacMorrow Mór, DivermanAU, Bender the Bot, GYeotu FCuucnkted and Anonymous: 43

- **Camellia japonica** *Source:* https://en.wikipedia.org/wiki/Camellia_japonica?oldid=763888585 *Contributors:* The Anome, Davidcannon, Chameleon, Gdr, JoJan, Rich Farmbrough, Hesperian, Stemonitis, Eubot, Bgwhite, Ytrottier, Dysmorodrepanis~enwiki, Doncram, Kaicarver, MalafayaBot, Melburnian, Epistemos, Bonás, Cydebot, Alvesgaspar, Oerjan, Rosarinagazo, JAnDbot, Magioladitis, Soulbot, Peter coxhead, VolkovBot, Jaguarlaser, SieBot, Whiteghost.ink, Rhanyeia, Tanvir Ahmmed, Neumeiko~enwiki, Addbot, Flakinho, Mps, Yobot, AnomieBOT, Xqbot, XZeroBot, Siwulek, Ibidwell, Maria8617, HRoestBot, Orenburg1, Lotje, EmausBot, John of Reading, Look2See1, Dewritech, ChuispastonBot, ClueBot NG, WIERDGREENMAN, Archie Barker, Very trivial, Undina-bird, Helpful Pixie Bot, Wikih101, Linear77, Darorcilmir, Edward1065, Sminthopsis84, Davidtrehane, Sanalyazici, Alayambo, Taylornelson, Monkbot, Bill Golladay, WordSeventeen, Sarr Cat, Caftaric, A,Ocram, Chlebosz, Bender the Bot, Ityoppyawit and Anonymous: 13

- **Camellia sasanqua** *Source:* https://en.wikipedia.org/wiki/Camellia_sasanqua?oldid=737425220 *Contributors:* MPF, Acad Ronin, Hesperian, ReyBrujo, Eubot, Meyer, Dysmorodrepanis~enwiki, Felicity4711, Hortlu, Sei Shonagon~enwiki, Shrimp wong, Bobo12345, Thijs!bot, David from Downunder, Jaguarlaser, Mild Bill Hiccup, Bagworm, Alexbot, Addbot, Flakinho, Luckas-bot, Yobot, JackieBot, Xqbot, GreenZmiy, PigFlu Oink, Lipsio, Look2See1, SchmidtRJ, ClueBot NG, Darorcilmir, Sminthopsis84, Davidtrehane, KasparBot and Anonymous: 13

- **Carissa** *Source:* https://en.wikipedia.org/wiki/Carissa?oldid=769935146 *Contributors:* Eugene van der Pijll, Mordomo, Carlossuarez46, Alan Liefting, MPF, Picapica, Mike Rosoft, DanielCD, Cmdrjameson, Hesperian, Pearle, Nsaa, Grutness, Alansohn, Craigy144, Stemonitis, Woohookitty, Rtdrury, BD2412, Eubot, DClement, Nihiltres, Jmorgan, Gdrbot, YurikBot, Qwertzy2, Dysmorodrepanis~enwiki, TDogg310, Closedmouth, EncycloPetey, Paxosmotic, Persian Poet Gal, Esb, Thejerm, Yodin, Tsands, Xcentaur, Lavateraguy, Basawala, Colorfulharp233, Thijs!bot, Epbr123, DRyan, Luna Santin, Bongwarrior, VoABot II, Peter coxhead, MartinBot, CommonsDelinker, J.delanoy, Pharaoh of the Wizards, TXiKiBoT, Sean D Martin, Cremepuff222, Wiae, Nagy, The Random Editor, SieBot, Ethel Aardvark, Exert, Wmpearl, ClueBot, Jmgarg1, Liempt, Auntof6, Excirial, Jusdafax, PixelBot, Arjayay, El bot de la dieta, Apparition11, TimTay, Pkreps, WikHead, Good Olfactory, Addbot, Fluffernutter, LaaknorBot, Flakinho, Yobot, AnomieBOT, JohnnyMorales, Obersachsebot, Xqbot, Samuelsidler, Plantmeister,

Dinamik-bot, Makki98, JonRichfield, Pokbot, ClueBot NG, Mark Marathon, Writ Keeper, NotWith, Maxx180, YFdyh-bot, Sminthopsis84, Cboning, Joseph Laferriere, Tanksinatra and Anonymous: 54

- **Carissa macrocarpa** *Source:* https://en.wikipedia.org/wiki/Carissa_macrocarpa?oldid=769480827 *Contributors:* Smallweed, Alan Liefting, Hesperian, Rjwilmsi, Eubot, Dysmorodrepanis~enwiki, SmackBot, Payxystaxna, Esb, JMK, Epistemos, Dancter, Marco Schmidt, Philipm, CommonsDelinker, PurpleHz, Deor, VolkovBot, Chango369w, Jaguarlaser, SieBot, Ethel Aardvark, Mdegraaf, Hippo99, EAKugler, Hercule, Chhe, Addbot, Flakinho, Yobot, Pganas, Plantmeister, Redrose64, Andynct, Makki98, Jesse V., Mcstayn, EmausBot, Look2See1, Abu Shawka, Thine Antique Pen, Galen777, Aristitleism, Suandre, Plantdrew, GuySh, AvocatoBot, Aftabbanoori, Gihan Jayaweera, InternetArchiveBot, NTRMK1, GreenC bot and Anonymous: 13

- **Carmona (plant)** *Source:* https://en.wikipedia.org/wiki/Carmona_(plant)?oldid=771564513 *Contributors:* Eugene van der Pijll, Alan Liefting, JoJan, Rich Farmbrough, Hesperian, Eubot, Ragesoss, TDogg310, Wknight94, SmackBot, Eskimbot, Rkitko, PrimeHunter, Fallen Reality, Shrimp wong, NJPharris, Maias, .anacondabot, LordAnubisBOT, Addbot, Dr CyCoe, I dream of horses, Pzrmd, Nodulation, Plantdrew, YFdyh-bot, Dexbot, InternetArchiveBot and Anonymous: 6

- **Carmona retusa** *Source:* https://en.wikipedia.org/wiki/Carmona_retusa?oldid=752866232 *Contributors:* Keith Edkins, Cydebot, Maias, Addbot, KamikazeBot, Ulric1313, Csigabi, DSisyphBot, Bellerophon, Hamamelis, Noder4, EmausBot, Dcirovic, ZéroBot, Plantdrew, BattyBot, Dexbot and Anonymous: 2

- **Carpinus orientalis** *Source:* https://en.wikipedia.org/wiki/Carpinus_orientalis?oldid=731459412 *Contributors:* Rkitko, Jeremy norbury, Krasanen, Addbot, SpBot, Flakinho, Luckas-bot, Yobot, Jackie, Robertito1965, FrescoBot, Ashkan P., EmausBot, WikitanvirBot, Look2See1, AvicBot, ChuispastonBot, *thing goes, Thatsha, Joseph Laferriere, Giovanni Caudullo and Anonymous: 1

- **Casuarina equisetifolia** *Source:* https://en.wikipedia.org/wiki/Casuarina_equisetifolia?oldid=769668730 *Contributors:* William Avery, MPF, Bkonrad, Shenme, Hesperian, Anthony Appleyard, Eubot, TDogg310, Bidgee, Rkitko, Melburnian, Riffic, Casliber, Smartse, DuncanHill, T L Miles, Bcsr4ever, Dawright12, TXiKiBoT, Synthebot, Dodger67, Jmgarg1, Addbot, LaaknorBot, Angrense, Luckas-bot, Yobot, Trinitrix, AnakngAraw, Rubinbot, Citation bot, ArthurBot, MauritsBot, Didactik, Trappist the monk, Look2See1, ZéroBot, Rcsprinter123, Chuck Entz, Spicemix, Rainbowwrasse, Helpful Pixie Bot, Mark Marathon, BG19bot, Ercé, ArmbrustBot, 115ash, Rawbliss, Yogdes, InternetArchiveBot, Bender the Bot and Anonymous: 11

- **Cedrus** *Source:* https://en.wikipedia.org/wiki/Cedrus?oldid=767541994 *Contributors:* Vicki Rosenzweig, Youssefsan, PierreAbbat, Ellmist, Quercusrobur, Lir, Menchi, Glenn, Marshman, Imc, Robbot, WormRunner, UtherSRG, Alan Liefting, DocWatson42, MPF, Isàm, Jonnyx, Varlaam, Niteowlneils, Yekrats, Gadfium, Yath, DanielZM, Ascánder, Kwamikagami, Bobo192, Robotje, Nk, Pearle, Alansohn, Sjschen, Mikeo, Tainter, Luigizanasi, Abanima, Richard Barlow, Schzmo, MarkusHagenlocher, BD2412, FlaBot, Eubot, Goudzovski, Gdrbot, Yurik-Bot, Sceptre, Hairy Dude, IanManka, Stephenb, Alynna Kasmira, Welsh, TDogg310, BOT-Superzerocool, DeadEyeArrow, Elkman, CLW, LeonardoRob0t, CharlieHuang, SmackBot, Brya, DCDuring, Iph, Betacommand, Eug, MalafayaBot, Melburnian, Harumphy, Klacquement, MJCdetroit, Rrburke, RedHillian, George, MrDarwin, Kuru, SilkTork, Xenocide wm, Noah Salzman, Peter Horn, Shoeofdeath, Fvasconcellos, Shandris, WeggeBot, Sa.vakilian, TheJC, Snehajp, Thijs!bot, Epbr123, Jaxsonjo, John254, Escarbot, Porqin, Just Chilling, Tangerines, Nelegene, JAnDbot, Ericoides, Andonic, Krasanen, Maias, LittleOldMe, VoABot II, Zanibas, Animum, Lenticel, Starry maiden Gazer, Paracel63, Jim.henderson, Kostisl, CommonsDelinker, Wlodzimierz, J.delanoy, Opps00, Adavidb, Numbo3, Acalamari, Nadiatalent, JavierMC, Idioma-bot, VolkovBot, Amikake3, Philip Trueman, TXiKiBoT, Taoshaman, Jpeeling, Falcon8765, BlingBling10, The Random Editor, SieBot, Calliopejen1, Elie plus, Ffaoe, Le Pied-bot~enwiki, OKBot, Altzinn, Amazonien, Tanvir Ahmmed, ClueBot, The Thing That Should Not Be, Ndenison, Pi zero, Auntof6, Alexbot, Sprotopapas, PunjabMuncher, Yoniw, SoxBot III, ProSvet, Spitfire, Rror, Addbot, Norahp, Favonian, Americanfreedom, Numbo3-bot, Flakinho, Tide rolls, Legobot, Luckas-bot, Yobot, TaBOT-zerem, Phiilyfreedom, AnomieBOT, Gpia7r, Ulric1313, Elostirion, Materialscientist, LilHelpa, Xqbot, Sionus, Loveless, GrouchoBot, Omnipaedista, Brambleshire, Brutaldeluxe, Doulos Christos, Rccapps, Epp, Orijentolog, LucienBOT, Hichamm, Amherst99, Chrispolicastro, Paragrapher, Jauhienij, TobeBot, كاشف عقيل, Pollytc, Okielina, Monty carlo, 1021on, Japmer, Look2See1, Jsayre64, Architect7, Helpful Pixie Bot, Myth59, Dzlinker, MusikAnimal, AvocatoBot, Darorcilmir, Lugia2453, Yamaha5, B14709, Eman235, Sarr Cat, Peter Paul John Obama, TLT2232, Snotgirl and Anonymous: 152

- **Cedrus atlantica** *Source:* https://en.wikipedia.org/wiki/Cedrus_atlantica?oldid=750351957 *Contributors:* Ram-Man, Skysmith, Imc, MPF, Rich Farmbrough, Hesperian, HenkvD, Drbreznjev, Tabletop, Graham87, Koavf, Ricardo Carneiro Pires, Eubot, Pburka, TDogg310, Mehdi1453, Rkitko, Paukrus, Ptelea, HennessyC, HitroMilanese, Ericoides, Krasanen, RebelRobot, R'n'B, Acalamari, 1000Faces, Ahuskay, Nadiatalent, Idioma-bot, Jaguarlaser, Le Pied-bot~enwiki, JSpung, TubularWorld, Estevoaei, Ouedbirdwatcher, SchreiberBike, Keeganza, Apparition11, Addbot, Luckas-bot, AnomieBOT, Elostirion, Xqbot, SassoBot, Brambleshire, Forstbirdo, Andromeas, FrescoBot, MastiBot, Stegop, 7mike5000, Look2See1, Reda Kerbouche, Dewritech, ZéroBot, Rcsprinter123, Helpful Pixie Bot, Darorcilmir, Khazar2, FC Casuario, Sizito, Srednuas Lenoroc, Sinneral, InternetArchiveBot, GreenC bot and Anonymous: 20

- **Cedrus libani** *Source:* https://en.wikipedia.org/wiki/Cedrus_libani?oldid=774672135 *Contributors:* Malcolm Farmer, Llywrch, Mulad, Imc, Raul654, M1shawhan, MykReeve, MPF, Bobblewik, Neutrality, Discospinster, Rich Farmbrough, Bender235, ESkog, Fenevad, MPS, Robotje, Hesperian, Ogress, Jérôme, Anthony Appleyard, Drbreznjev, Preost, Bobrayner, RM, Roylee, Woohookitty, Tbc2, Schzmo, Bluemoose, Erasmus, Cedrus-Libani, Mana Excalibur, Crzrussian, Rjwilmsi, Funnyhat, Yuber, Kbigdawg1, Eubot, CalJW, Folini, Karelj, Gdrbot, Yurik-Bot, RussBot, Hede2000, Gaius Cornelius, Thalter, Lexicon, Apokryltaros, TDogg310, Lockesdonkey, DRosenbach, CLW, Gergis, Footprintx, Mmcannis, SmackBot, Tom Lougheed, Slashme, Peter Isotalo, Portillo, Rkitko, SB Johnny, Melburnian, George, Thor Dockweiler, JMcFerran, Ser Amantio di Nicolao, MattHucke, A. Parrot, Dl2000, Hawkestone, Roxi2, Melicans, WeggeBot, Beastie Bot, Cydebot, Captainm, Casliber, Rosser1954, Oleksii0, Thijs!bot, AntiVandalBot, JAnDbot, Krasanen, Strafpeloton2, WolfmanSF, Fusionmix, Catgut, LorenzoB, Linaduliban, R'n'B, Nono64, Acalamari, Pyrospirit, Nadiatalent, DMCer, DASonnenfeld, Idioma-bot, Signalhead, Chengdi, Samisuccar, Jaguarlaser, Monty845, BlingBling10, Botev, SieBot, Elie plus, Barent, FunkMonk, Flyer22 Reborn, Finderskey, Lightmouse, Gabri118, Excirial, SchreiberBike, Chhe, DumZiBoT, Dthomsen8, Addbot, PhoeniciaReBorn, Americanfreedom, Tassedethe, Lightbot, Ameroffsky, Yobot, TaBOT-zerem, KamikazeBot, AnomieBOT, LlywelynII, ArthurBot, LilHelpa, Xqbot, SassoBot, Brambleshire, Brutaldeluxe, LucienBOT, StaticVision, Izzedine, HRoestBot, Tom.Reding, Jauhienij, Lpt101095, Lotje, Dinamik-bot, Norfolkbees, EmausBot, WikitanvirBot, Look2See1, ZéroBot, Erianna, Rcsprinter123, MALLUS, ChuispastonBot, عمرو بن كلشوم, ClueBot NG, Primergrey, Helpful Pixie Bot, Curb Chain, Plantdrew, BG19bot, Jacks1881, Dzlinker, TheGeneralUser, CitationCleanerBot, Gorobay, Greenknight dv, Friends147, Kooky2, BattyBot, Darorcilmir, Pratyya Ghosh, ADLB19882009, ChrisGualtieri, Busyclearsdfg, Groupbluesaxda, Makecat-bot, Yamaha5, AmaryllisGardener,

4.1. TEXT

YiFeiBot, Sam Sailor, Trinity Abbey, ChamithN, Unknownhbx369, Elmidae, Prinsgezinde, InternetArchiveBot, GreenC bot, Peter Paul John Obama, Bear-rings, Sfarjal, Familiars, Nina Lauridsen and Anonymous: 109

- **Celtis** *Source:* https://en.wikipedia.org/wiki/Celtis?oldid=773818192 *Contributors:* Hephaestos, Dominus, Bogdangiusca, Robbot, Peak, MPF, JoJan, DanielCD, Sten, Dannown, AnnaP, Geographer, Pixeltoo, Vuong Ngan Ha, Eubot, Chobot, Gdrbot, Mark Ironie, Eupator, Stephenb, Dysmodrepanis~enwiki, TDogg310, Jonathan Hornung, SmackBot, Notafly, EncycloPetey, Alsandro, Rkitko, SB Johnny, EncMstr, Solarapex, Kingdon, Sturm, Bejnar, Mgiganteus1, Iridescent, JMK, CzarB, Paul venter, Thricecube, Baskaufs, Ken Gallager, Myasuda, Rosarinagazo, Escarbot, Smartse, JAnDbot, Maias, Peter coxhead, Abestrobi, CommonsDelinker, Nadiatalent, Idioma-bot, Harold Eyster, Ninjatacoshell, Posterboy7, Fangjian, SchreiberBike, Addbot, Sapphosyne, Erutuon, Luckas-bot, Yobot, Lars1965, Nallimbot, Msbeier, Hamamelis, Dger, DrilBot, Wedson~enwiki, Makki98, Obsidian Soul, Thiridaz, EmausBot, Frietjes, Eocene guy, Helpful Pixie Bot, BG19bot, AvocatoBot, Facu unlp, Sminthopsis84, Ocotea, Gihan Jayaweera, Stamptrader, Sarr Cat, Belltoes, InternetArchiveBot, Manudouz, Eagle Pudding, Bender the Bot and Anonymous: 21

- **Chaenomeles** *Source:* https://en.wikipedia.org/wiki/Chaenomeles?oldid=750972581 *Contributors:* Vicki Rosenzweig, Paul A, Stan Shebs, Wetman, Pollinator, PuzzletChung, Nurg, Alan Liefting, MPF, DanielCD, CanisRufus, Yongxinge, Richard Barlow, Ricardo Carneiro Pires, Bhadani, Tommy Kronkvist, FlaBot, Eubot, SiGarb, Gdrbot, YurikBot, RussBot, Garglebutt, Apokryltaros, Meika, Verne Equinox, Rkitko, Melburnian, Cygnus78, Jeremy norbury, Dcruz01, Kevmin, Kanjy, MTSbot~enwiki, Skorpion87, Ü, Cydebot, Thijs!bot, Fayenatic london, JAnDbot, Nadiatalent, TXiKiBoT, SieBot, No such user, PixelBot, LarryMorseDCOhio, Addbot, Flakinho, Zorrobot, Luckas-bot, Yobot, TaBOT-zerem, Pomeapplepome, Xqbot, Epp, Izvora, TobeBot, Kiyoweap, EmausBot, Thos okapi, Richard asr, ClueBot NG, Darorcilmir, Sminthopsis84, Kamolea03 and Anonymous: 19

- **Chamaecyparis obtusa** *Source:* https://en.wikipedia.org/wiki/Chamaecyparis_obtusa?oldid=756634421 *Contributors:* Andre Engels, Pengo, MPF, Mintleaf~enwiki, Fg2, Dcfleck, BS Thurner Hof, Hesperian, Djlayton4, Ffbond, Jeffrey O. Gustafson, BD2412, Rjwilmsi, Gryffindor, Ricardo Carneiro Pires, Chobot, Gdrbot, Hede2000, Gaius Cornelius, DAJF, AdiJapan, TDogg310, Mkill, Emijrp, Can't sleep, clown will eat me, Carnby, Ryulong, Jjok, Beastie Bot, Cs california, Casliber, Thijs!bot, Fatidiot1234, Tillman, Michael Goodyear, Peter coxhead, VolkovBot, Jaguarlaser, HelloMojo, Rrogjenks, Arostron, Alexbot, EdChem, Wikiuser100, Addbot, Wakablogger2, Flakinho, Zorrobot, Luckas-bot, Jesielt, Citation bot, 陳炬燵, SassoBot, Nonoisense, Micromesistius, Tom.Reding, Lotje, RjwilmsiBot, Look2See1, ZéroBot, Hyronimus299, ClueBot NG, Auchansa, NotWith, Monkbot, KasparBot, MB298, InternetArchiveBot, GreenC bot and Anonymous: 11

- **Chamaecyparis pisifera** *Source:* https://en.wikipedia.org/wiki/Chamaecyparis_pisifera?oldid=755248560 *Contributors:* William Avery, Ram-Man, SEWilco, MPF, Manuel Anastácio, Hesperian, Djlayton4, Jeffrey O. Gustafson, GregorB, Rjwilmsi, Ricardo Carneiro Pires, Eubot, Gdrbot, YurikBot, Wavelength, TDogg310, Garchy, Carnby, Kevmin, Beastie Bot, Cs california, Casliber, Thijs!bot, Nipisiquit, Just H, Idioma-bot, VolkovBot, TubularWorld, DragonBot, Addbot, Flakinho, Zorrobot, Luckas-bot, Sanyi4, Micromesistius, Tom.Reding, MastiBot, Trappist the monk, Pc1878, RjwilmsiBot, Look2See1, GoingBatty, ZéroBot, メルビル, Pseudo75 and Anonymous: 4

- **Cherry blossom** *Source:* https://en.wikipedia.org/wiki/Cherry_blossom?oldid=773572684 *Contributors:* Ixfd64, TakuyaMurata, Ahoerstemeier, Jpatokal, Theresa knott, Marumari, Kingturtle, Darkwind, Julesd, Raven in Orbit, Agtx, Emperorbma, Fuzheado, WhisperToMe, Radiojon, Tpbradbury, Dinopup, PuzzletChung, Donarreiskoffer, Yas~enwiki, Moriori, Chris 73, Ianb, Postdlf, Rholton, SchmuckyTheCat, Aleron235, Mervyn, Jsonitsac, Kent Wang, Raeky, Davidcannon, Exploding Boy, MPF, Fudoreaper, Lupin, Bkonrad, Gilgamesh~enwiki, Gadfium, Manuel Anastácio, Andycjp, Sonjaaa, Piotrus, Kusunose, OwenBlacker, Eranb, Fg2, Neumannkun, Reflex Reaction, SYSS Mouse, Imroy, Maisnam, Rich Farmbrough, Kdammers, Rama, Tristan Schmelcher, Bender235, ESkog, Plugwash, *drew, Hayabusa future, Bendono, CeeGee, Bobo192, Imars, C S, PiccoloNamek, Apostrophe, Haham hanuka, Pearle, GK, Alansohn, Anthony Appleyard, Bathrobe, Lacrimulae, Water Bottle, Sligocki, Jaardon, Wtmitchell, LordAmeth, Alai, Outis~enwiki, Hijiri88, JALockhart, Weyes, Angr, Woohookitty, LOL, PoccilScript, Jersyko, BlankVerse, NeoChaosX, MONGO, Dlauri, Schzmo, Dtaw2001, Mandarax, KyuuA4, Feripe, BD2412, Plau, Rjwilmsi, Mayumashu, Sdornan, Bruce1ee, Nneonneo, ElKevbo, Asterism, Jwkpiano1, FlaBot, Eubot, DannyWilde, Nihiltres, Kerowyn, Mitsukai, Chong-Dae, Rrenner, Srleffler, NoseNuggets, Taichi, Gdrbot, Ahpook, Elfguy, Wavelength, Schmancy47, Sarranduin, Tyenkrovy, CambridgeBay-Weather, Schoen, Rsrikanth05, Pseudomonas, Wimt, Swollib, Curtis Clark, Julian Grybowski, Badagnani, Irishguy, DAJF, Tony1, Nate1481, Mkill, Rwalker, Wknight94, Uberlemur, Closedmouth, Mekugi, Brianlucas, Katieh5584, Tim1965, Tsm1128, Veinor, SmackBot, Inverse-Hypercube, Melchoir, Osarusan, David.Mestel, Lawrencekhoo, Piroteknix, Cla68, Kintetsubuffalo, BiT, Bryan Nguyen, Danikolt, Hmains, Rmdsc, Rmosler2100, Chris the speller, Endroit, AhmedHan, Rkitko, MalafayaBot, Hooriaj, Nbarth, Baa, Da Vynci, Aesshen, TKD, Dreadstar, IrisKawling, JakGd1, DMacks, Risker, Mikejmu, Autopilot, Shigeru~enwiki, MegA, Kuru, John, Keneckert, Linnell, Tasc, BeSherman, Kyoko, LightPhoenix, SolarAngel, Intranetusa, Ryulong, Vashtihorvat, Dl2000, DouglasCalvert, HelloAnnyong, Joseph Solis in Australia, Shoeofdeath, Dragonix, Lukewilbur, Neaco, Tawkerbot2, Weird0, JForget, CWY2190, Sbn1984, Old Guard, Iokseng, Ken Gallager, Bvbacon, Ph0kin, Slazenger, Cydebot, Fnlayson, Ganryuu, Marqueed, Cantras, Mr.weedle, Goldfritha, Dancter, DumbBOT, DBaba, Ebyabe, Vanished User jdksfajlasd, Picturetokyo, Epbr123, Jpark3909, HappyInGeneral, Luigifan, Nola chi, Escarbot, AntiVandalBot, Whats up skip, Luna Santin, Seaphoto, Poetic Decay, Parande, Merumerume, Objectiveye, OhanaUnited, Krisgrotius, Jarkeld, Acroterion, Bunny-chan, Propaniac, Bongwarrior, VoABot II, -Kerplunk-, Rivertorch, Tedickey, Dinosaur puppy, KConWiki, Catgut, Yunfeng, Alex Kov, DerHexer, Neyzenhasan, NatureA16, MartinBot, Mermaid from the Baltic Sea, AgarwalSumeet, Chikumaya, Shellwood, J.delanoy, Nightshadow28, Ashcraft, TriviaKing, Johnbod, McSly, Jwuthe2, Wincrest, Pygenot, DadaNeem, Nadiatalent, OneiroPhobia, Andy Marchbanks, Geeked, Idioma-bot, Djflem, Signalhead, Lights, Caspian blue, VolkovBot, CWii, Rikster2, Nburden, DarkArcher, Historiographer, Fran Rogers, TXiKiBoT, Giichi, Martin451, Nitramwin, Cercersan, Seberin, Wiae, Sieveking, MDfoo, Falcon8765, Piecemealcranky, Writingcritic, AgentCDE, Elevenit, Necmate, Galamazoo12, OlkhichaAppa, Gojapan, Triggersite, MrChupon, Z1x2c3, Calliopejen1, Yoyoyohi, Ellbeecee, Caltas, Quasirandom, Vanished User 8a9b4725f8376, Ode2joy, Zatch0214, Keilana, Flyer22 Reborn, Radon210, Masgatotkaca, Oda Mari, AlexWaelde, Moonraker12, Mimihitam, Bsherr, Oxymoron83, Frank94.kane, ZombieFeatures, Sakurafeig, Gomeying, Kjtobo, Dabomb87, Net99200, ClueBot, GorillaWarfare, The Thing That Should Not Be, Mattokunhayashi, Gaia Octavia Agrippa, Drmies, Yoshi Canopus, DanielDeibler, Bmayton, Bellatrix Kerrigan, Stayman Apple, Sseacord, Mr.Atoz, Drlosminasgangsta, Time for action, Excirial, Alexbot, Jusdafax, CrazyChemGuy, Pyroskyler, Razorflame, Tabunoki~enwiki, SchreiberBike, Craig James White, Thingg, Supergokuthree, Chyeager, Vanished user uih38riiw4hjlsd, GM Pink Elephant, XLinkBot, H.I.Remington, Jovianeye, Sakura Cartelet, Sergay, Frufru9700, WikiDao, ZooFari, Airplaneman, Sakuradawkins, Minorukjp, Addbot, HarueFukuiJapan~enwiki, Gsilverstone, Some jerk on the Internet, Jojhutton, Binary TSO, Download, Unkounkounko, Chamal N, Elan26, BobMiller1701, Royalcreed, Shekure, Luckas Blade, WikiDreamer Bot, HerculeBot, Mps, Qhilliq, Luckas-bot, Tohd8BohaithuGh1, Worm That Turned, AnakngAraw, AnomieBOT, Jim1138, Dwayne, Piano non troppo, Materialscientist, Bukubku, Tobirules39, ArthurBot, LilHelpa,

Xqbot, SLIMHANNYA, Capricorn42, TheWeakWilled, XZeroBot, Grim23, Itzjajon, GrouchoBot, RibotBOT, Momomomomistake, Erik9, FrescoBot, 青鬼よし, Batsford Arboretum, Sky Attacker, StaticVision, KuroiShiroi, Rmazurnal, Hanac12345, ポポマジン, Mincha91, Citation bot 1, Wrd234, Lucia Black, DrilBot, Pinethicket, Elockid, Phoenix7777, Tingchiyu, Crusoe8181, Easy2112, TankTrivia, Yunshui, Lotje, Vancouver Outlaw, WPPilot, AdrianoBruceLeonardo, Rain drop 45, Arided, Vanished user aoiowaiuyr894isdik43, Panchtatvam, Tbhotch, Obsidian Soul, Onel5969, Mean as custard, Dem907, CalicoCatLover, EmausBot, John of Reading, Fukoku Kyohei, WikitanvirBot, Look2See1, Racerx11, GoingBatty, RA0808, ZxxZxxZ, Dcirovic, K6ka, AvicBot, ZéroBot, H3llBot, Gray eyes, Lemony123, Faraleen, Donner60, Hannahkeele, Rorrima, Мурад 97, 28bot, Sonicyouth86, ClueBot NG, Veroribo, Satellizer, Chester Markel, Infinifold, Widr, Helpful Pixie Bot, Curb Chain, Plantdrew, Burstblue2, ChrisEngelsma, Maculosae tegmine lyncis, BG19bot, Gmcbjames, Ryush00, Mark Arsten, Nertrust, Polmandc, BattyBot, David.moreno72, Darorcilmir, Emilybelles, DoctorKubla, EuroCarGT, Uno b4, Dexbot, Thokara, Lugia2453, Epicgenius, I am One of Many, Retrolord, Tentinator, EvergreenFir, A.sky245, DavidLeighEllis, Moldy eyeballs, Thevideodrome, Kharkiv07, ㋛㋛㋛, 太田さく, Ingfbruno, HRae, Bladesmulti, Db9023, Qpc887, Keijhae, Hyeonjin Kim, Cdosborn, Diggy9302, Monkbot, FarahMG95, Wrestlingdude178, Party54321, Reginald.Witzersky, Seamtail, DoulosCore, Zppix, Ethel Mannin, Yogee-sikkim, Vivexdino, Infinite0694, Travelmite, Benjamin collier99, KasparBot, Jayeongwon, Dottie2, Fortunatestars, KentuckyKevin, CAPTAIN RAJU, EtherealGate, Tkaehfdl1234, CLCStudent, InternetArchiveBot, Banquet112, Axesrotor1, Reeses4500, Chrissymad, Kaboomnumber1, Gulumeemee, Seomun32, Portmoth14, Pkbwcgs, Twitbookspacetube, Tigger1199, Sukicakess, Jerte Valley Tourism, Valley Jerte tourism, Thomasjohnson977, Kwon Ye-rim and Anonymous: 586

- **Citrus** *Source:* https://en.wikipedia.org/wiki/Citrus?oldid=774584986 *Contributors:* Vicki Rosenzweig, Mav, Jeronimo, Rmhermen, Pierre-Abbat, Karen Johnson, William Avery, Roadrunner, Ben-Zin~enwiki, Ellmist, Stepnwolf, Heron, Henriette~enwiki, Edward, Dante Alighieri, Mahjongg, Gabbe, Menchi, Tomi, (, Ellywa, Ahoerstemeier, Jpatokal, Julesd, Ugen64, Marteau, Ffx, Ciphergoth, Tristanb, Jengod, Feedmecereal, Fuzheado, IceKarma, Tpbradbury, Marshman, Imc, Grendelkhan, Joy, Wetman, Pakaran, Secretlondon, Jerzy, UninvitedCompany, PuzzletChung, RedWolf, Nurg, Seglea, Dina, DocWatson42, MPF, BenFrantzDale, Jgritz, Yekrats, Dmmaus, AlistairMcMillan, Andycjp, Mendel, Yath, Phe, JoJan, PDH, Brooker, Picapica, ChrisRuvolo, Sparky the Seventh Chaos, DanielCD, Plexust, LindsayH, Bumhoolery, Bender235, Omnibus, Femto, Bobo192, Longhair, Fir0002, Cmdrjameson, K12u, Giraffedata, Hesperian, Haham hanuka, Nkedel, AnnaP, Hippophaë~enwiki, Mac Davis, Wtmitchell, TaintedMustard, Fledgeling, Kazvorpal, Geodejerry, Bastin, Woohookitty, Richard Barlow, Markfindlay, MONGO, Kralizec!, Chrkl, Graham87, BD2412, Sjö, Rjwilmsi, Koavf, Ricardo Carneiro Pires, DoubleBlue, Dracontes, Vuong Ngan Ha, Eubot, RobertG, Margosbot~enwiki, DannyWilde, Nihiltres, JdforresterBot, KFP, Atif.hussain, King of Hearts, Chobot, Bjwebb, Gdrbot, Wavelength, Sceptre, Phantomsteve, RussBot, Ashish Bakshi, CambridgeBayWeather, Eleassar, DERoss, Baru~enwiki, Curtis Clark, Dysmorodrepanis~enwiki, Aeusoes1, Dforest, Badagnani, Trovatore, Rjensen, Xeos, DAJF, TDogg310, Mahogany h00r, Bota47, MattReid, Open2universe, Palx, Vampyrium, Davidals, SmackBot, Melchoir, NorthernFire, Lawrencekhoo, Anastrophe, EncycloPetey, Hardyplants, Ávila, Francisco Valverde, Bryan Nguyen, Gilliam, Ohnoitsjamie, Keegan, Rkitko, Persian Poet Gal, Deli nk, Neo-Jay, DHN-bot~enwiki, Gruzd, Colonies Chris, Hengsheng120, Sunholm, Can't sleep, clown will eat me, Tamfang, Snowmanradio, TheKMan, Lesnail, VMS Mosaic, Tlusťa, Khoikhoi, Thegraham, SteveHopson, Adrigon, Zeamays, Wikiklaas, MrDarwin, Timofonic, Quasispace, Heimstern, Khono, Mat8989, Kevlarmry, Mgiganteus1, Dockingman, Newone, Phonix, Twas Now, Bruinfan12, Tawkerbot2, Hi2, JForget, CmdrObot, NickW557, WeggeBot, Spykumquat, Nauticashades, TJDay, Jon Stockton, Jayen466, Eulerianpath, Palaeologos, Roberta F., Manxmancelt, Casliber, 2z2z, Epbr123, Mojo Hand, Headbomb, Marek69, Icep, Escarbot, Luna Santin, Peter Moss, Gdo01, Mutt Lunker, John Moss, Sluzzelin, JAnDbot, Davewho2, Koibeatu, MER-C, Igodard, Coolhandscot, TheEditrix2, Acroterion, Bencherlite, Bongwarrior, Carlwev, Dekimasu, AtticusX, Faizhaider, Filousoph, Esanchez7587, Defenestrating Monday, Peter coxhead, MartinBot, Grandia01, STBot, Red Sunset, Speck-Made, Clarin, CommonsDelinker, J.delanoy, Pharaoh of the Wizards, Rod57, It Is Me Here, (jarbarf), Raining girl, Nwbeeson, SJP, AA, Nadiatalent, Juliancolton, Mr.Ripp, Halmstad, Funandtrvl, Postlebury, Lyonsbane, Philip Trueman, Somanypeople, TXiKiBoT, Vipinhari, Qxz, DamianLu, HLHJ, Martytheroo, LeaveSleaves, Cozbone43, Vgranucci, January2007, Cnilep, Brianga, Number1336, Docclabo, SieBot, Fabullus, Arpose, Packergreg, Poopypants1019, Strayan, RJaguar3, Flyer22 Reborn, DanBLOO, OKBot, Anchor Link Bot, 48states, Flcitrusmutual, Kanonkas, De728631, ClueBot, Johnbrewe, Moshe Yakob, Niceguyedc, LizardJr8, Excirial, Jusdafax, Cedro~enwiki, M.O.X, Thehelpfulone, Amaltheus, Berean Hunter, SoxBot III, Shoteh, XLinkBot, Wikiuser100, Duncan, Dthomsen8, Ost316, Libcub, SilvonenBot, Aitorbk, ZooFari, Kembangraps, Addbot, CubBC, Ronhjones, AndersBot, Favonian, Baffle gab1978, Koppas, Harrypotter445, Flakinho, HagiMalachi, Jarble, Se'hk, Luckas-bot, Yobot, Kristofferjay, Fraggle81, Synchronism, AnomieBOT, Floquenbeam, Kristen Eriksen, Jim1138, Chuckiesdad, Unara, Dinesh smita, BoxWear, GB fan, Xqbot, Manburger 486, WoodenPickle, Jeffrey Mall, Tomdo08, Anna Frodesiak, Srich32977, Garkeith, GrouchoBot, Nimmolo, Brambleshire, FrescoBot, Danielle001, Yara13, WikiDisambiguation, EricLaporteEn, Alxeedo, Talskubilos, Citation bot 1, Plantmeister, AstaBOTh15, Pinethicket, I dream of horses, RedBot, Tulipanos, Trappist the monk, Jonkerz, Vrenator, Rentzepopoulos, Weedgarden, Tbhotch, Gothgospel, DARTH SIDIOUS 2, Mean as custard, TjBot, BIGBALLSyummy, Idbdl2009, EmausBot, Techguy78, Gfoley4, Look2See1, Dancing pineapples, Jkadavoor, Dcirovic, Hiperpinguino, PBS-AWB, H3llBot, Wayne Slam, Matt the great IC, Erianna, Seanmcd27, Ayanoshihorina, Donner60, Mjbmr, ChuispastonBot, Jambolik, Neil P. Quinn, 28bot, Marmite1998, Will Beback Auto, ClueBot NG, Aflyhorse, Jasonrudd, Chandrawp, Reify-tech, Omar hoftun, Helpful Pixie Bot, Rutherfordgarfield, DBigXray, Mark Marathon, Greeneyes3, Plantdrew, BG19bot, Northamerica1000, Gir390907, 155blue, Midnight Green, CitationCleanerBot, Aranea Mortem, BattyBot, Ajaxfiore, Hyuganatsu, Hsp90, Ganjpar, 23mjbulls, Dexbot, Sminthopsis84, Lugia2453, えいえすあい, Sjonathanc, Brianaw, Pure genuine, M.Aurelius, Vice resident, Legoman 86, Gihan Jayaweera, Divine618, Huynp85, Trito1234567890, G S Palmer, Sean Br, Joseph Laferriere, Monkbot, Alan Merrit, BethNaught, Samsbanned, AwesoMan3000, Mrfluffy503, Kenneth miya1, Igmigwhm, Riversid, Julietdeltalima, Growscripts, Sarr Cat, Ehgarrick, Bgent16, Caftaric, Ktdempsey8, CLCStudent, Charlotte135, Karlfonza, Valliere71, Raccoon Zero, JJMC89 bot, Marissa streep, Tamatha rederboddon, Bmporter, Ollieleston, Sfarjal, Renamed user 0okmnji98u, Andycraft9999, Britt279, Lolpandas23 and Anonymous: 322

- **Cornus** *Source:* https://en.wikipedia.org/wiki/Cornus?oldid=772492627 *Contributors:* Malcolm Farmer, William Avery, Nonenmac, Adam-Retchless, Jaknouse, TeunSpaans, Menchi, Janko, Radiojon, SEWilco, Wetman, Pollinator, Mervyn, UtherSRG, MPF, Niteowlneils, PDH, Jossi, Rich Farmbrough, Xezbeth, Dbachmann, Bender235, Patton1138, Polypompholyx, CanisRufus, Dennis Brown, Bobo192, Circeus, Fir0002, Yongxinge, Nk, Hesperian, Pearle, Mrzaius, Istara, SonPraises, Fledgeling, Zntrip, Stemonitis, Woohookitty, Richard Barlow, Jpers36, Eras-mus, TheAlphaWolf, Tom Parks, Cuchullain, Rjwilmsi, Kugamazog, Bhadani, Eubot, Gurch, Choess, Joedeshon, Gdrbot, Wavelength, RussBot, Gaius Cornelius, Zingus, Thane, Welsh, Apokryltaros, Gadget850, IceCreamAntisocial, Wsiegmund, Garion96, Sassisch, SmackBot, CraigRorrer, EncycloPetey, Hardyplants, Swerdnaneb, Yamaguchi 先生, ERcheck, Bjmullan, Gruzd, Bruce Marlin, Scwlong, Addshore, Kcordina, Kevmin, Mgiganteus1, Special-T, Hu12, Runningonbrains, Baskaufs, Neelix, Darksyne, Satori Son, Epbr123, Osborne, AntiVandalBot, Majorly, Kauczuk, Skyjs, Arx Fortis, Melonseed, Plantsurfer, Max Hyre, Phennessy, VoABot II, Martin tamb, Michael Goodyear, Ali'i, Taamu, Yelir61, Peter coxhead, BunsenH, R'n'B, Mickaw2, Pharaoh of the Wizards, Frank R 1981, Ian.thomson, BrokenSphere, Kata-

4.1. TEXT

laveno, Bumper12, Idioma-bot, Rag47, VolkovBot, Drungarios, Sjones23, TXiKiBoT, Oshwah, Domdemase, JDAshton, Ask123, Poohmaeo, Akerbeltz, Lerdthenerd, Aqwfyj, Ashburnite, Sydneysart, Oda Mari, MaxFrear, Yerpo, AngelOfSadness, Gargaphy, Hamiltondaniel, KBYU, ClueBot, Fyyer, The Thing That Should Not Be, SuperHamster, Brewcrewer, LarryMorseDCOhio, Versus22, Wnt, DumZiBoT, Bilsonius, Wikiuser100, Rreagan007, SilvonenBot, Addbot, CubBC, Polinizador, Atethnekos, Dead Spec, Sabonarola, Funky Fantom, Yourbackup, Rufus1841, AndersBot, SpBot, Flakinho, Youngmike2k7, Erutuon, First Light, Luckas-bot, Yobot, Brougham96, AnomieBOT, Greenbreen, Piano non troppo, Sz-iwbot, ArthurBot, LilHelpa, Shimmin Beg, Teddks, AbigailAbernathy, Jezhotwells, Brutaldeluxe, Hamamelis, Thehelpfulbot, FrescoBot, Dger, Scarabocchio, Pinethicket, Jcf0987, Meaghan, Tim1357, Mlelao, FlameHorse, Puddinfudge, Reaper Eternal, EmausBot, Fatbrett2, Dudy001, NotAnonymous0, Tommy2010, Uleli, Princess Lirin, Wayne Slam, RaptureBot, ChuispastonBot, Architect7, ClueBot NG, Riverstyxx, Doh5678, Carsalesmanisme, Helpful Pixie Bot, Plantdrew, BG19bot, Sandere0, AvocatoBot, Mark Arsten, Cowisdog, Mascarponette, NotWith, Scotstout, Darorcilmir, Bigsky1965, AzseicsoK, Sminthopsis84, Corinne, Mattyboi7, Epicgenius, Khayyam.Bin.Saeed, HalfGig, Preppergardens, Lyonothamnus, Mitzi.humphrey, The bark is ruff, Sarr Cat, Mouthwash15, InternetArchiveBot, Bender the Bot, Hehe806, Lauriekingdon and Anonymous: 181

- **Cycas revoluta** *Source:* https://en.wikipedia.org/wiki/Cycas_revoluta?oldid=764630977 *Contributors:* Vt-aoe, MPF, Bradeos Graphon, Leonard G., DanielCD, Shuffdog, Kwamikagami, Hesperian, Djlayton4, Yousaf465, Miss Madeline, TheAlphaWolf, Rjwilmsi, Eubot, Karelj, CiaPan, Chobot, Jared Preston, Gdrbot, Whosasking, Hede2000, Gaius Cornelius, Prime Entelechy, Welsh, TDogg310, For7thGen, That Guy, From That Show!, SmackBot, Unyoyega, Hmains, Emufarmers, NaySay, MrDarwin, Rigadoun, Mgiganteus1, Rofl, Peyre, Mikael V, Paul venter, Igoldste, Beastie Bot, Cydebot, Nsaum75, Thijs!bot, Ufwuct, Escarbot, KP Botany, JAnDbot, Maias, Despedes, Japo, Drm310, Dracoverdi, Idioma-bot, Netmonger, VolkovBot, Al.locke, Una Smith, Jaguarlaser, Falcon8765, SieBot, ConfuciusOrnis, QualiaBot, Canglesea, Ralph24, Tyer, Hedwig Storch, Jotterbot, Columbiabotany, Sir Lestaty de Lioncourt, Addbot, Mentisock, Numbo3-bot, CountryBot, Leovizza, Luckas-bot, Yobot, Sanyi4, KDS4444, GB fan, Obersachsebot, Xqbot, Gigemag76, RibotBOT, Icaranious, Plantmeister, Tom.Reding, Tom Hulse, Pc1878, EmausBot, Danerikk, Lguipontes, Jsheffer2004, ClueBot NG, DavidAnstiss, Plantdrew, Umais Bin Sajjad, NotWith, BattyBot, Darorcilmir, Reallyoldplants, JPaestpreornJeolhlna, Piwaiwaka, Joseph Laferriere, Somepics, KasparBot, Robongio and Anonymous: 53

- **Ebenopsis ebano** *Source:* https://en.wikipedia.org/wiki/Ebenopsis_ebano?oldid=740794633 *Contributors:* Postdlf, BD2412, TDogg310, Rkitko, Myasuda, Cydebot, Robby, Mpinedag, Citation bot 1, Pinethicket, RjwilmsiBot, Look2See1, H3llBot, Helpful Pixie Bot, Tortie tude, Monkbot, Bender the Bot and Anonymous: 1

- **Ficus aurea** *Source:* https://en.wikipedia.org/wiki/Ficus_aurea?oldid=771284045 *Contributors:* Jimfbleak, Alan Liefting, Michael Devore, Andycjp, JoJan, Bender235, Art LaPella, Guettarda, Circeus, Alansohn, Gene Nygaard, Stemonitis, BD2412, Rjwilmsi, NawlinWiki, TDogg310, Hugh Manatee, SmackBot, Melchoir, Hmains, Rkitko, Melburnian, Snowmanradio, Risker, SandyGeorgia, Peter Horn, Makeemlighter, Neelix, Cydebot, Danrok, Amandajm, Casliber, Epbr123, Headbomb, Seaphoto, Moni3, WolfmanSF, Steven Walling, TinaSparkle, DrKay, Million Moments, GimmeBot, Mazarin07, Calliopejen1, Cb77305, ClueBot, NickCT, CarolSpears, Doseiai2, Piledhigheranddeeper, NuclearWarfare, Dana boomer, DumZiBoT, Addbot, DOI bot, Flakinho, Tide rolls, Lightbot, Luckas-bot, AnomieBOT, Ulric1313, Materialscientist, Citation bot, NocturneNoir, J04n, FrescoBot, LucienBOT, Parth24, Citation bot 1, December21st2012Freak, Tim1357, Vrenator, Tbhotch, RjwilmsiBot, Look2See1, Peterusso, Wackywace, SporkBot, AManWithNoPlan, Wayne Slam, Colinbnd, ClueBot NG, Caseman3333, The Truthteller 2000, Gassyfrog, Zackary O'Neil, VoteJagoffForMayor, Skytek4444, Sminthopsis84, Joseph Laferriere, Monkbot, 3 of Diamonds and Anonymous: 33

- **Ficus benjamina** *Source:* https://en.wikipedia.org/wiki/Ficus_benjamina?oldid=762886065 *Contributors:* Wapcaplet, Ahoerstemeier, Peregrine981, Imc, Jerzy, Securiger, Yosri, Xanzzibar, MPF, Duncharris, Bosniak, Yarnover, Arsene, DanielCD, CanisRufus, Hesperian, Methegreat, Alansohn, VsevolodSipakov, Rjwilmsi, Crazynas, MLRoach, Eubot, Kerowyn, Chobot, Gdrbot, Bgwhite, WriterHound, YurikBot, RussBot, Emmanuelm, Dysmorodrepanis~enwiki, TDogg310, SmackBot, Eskimbot, Rkitko, TheLeopard, Shrumster, Paul 012, Temp 64, Merchbow, Kirbytime, Bendzh, JMK, Kaarel, RekishiEJ, Oos, NTDOY Fanboy, WeggeBot, Cydebot, MoneySign, Casliber, J. W. Love, Escarbot, Nthep, J.delanoy, Frank R 1981, STBotD, VolkovBot, Rei-bot, BotKung, BotanyBot, CompassRose65, Jmgarg1, SchreiberBike, Thingg, ZooFari, Addbot, Betterusername, Hda3ku, Flakinho, Lightbot, Yobot, Xufanc, Pomeapplepome, Xqbot, Weepingraf, Noder4, Simuliid, Micromesistius, RjwilmsiBot, EmausBot, Look2See1, Werieth, Nikkolo, H3llBot, RaptureBot, Rcsprinter123, ClueBot NG, MerlIwBot, Declangi, Jimknows, Darorcilmir, Praveensdataworks, Illia Connell, Prabal123koirala, Passengerpigeon, Haminoon, Gihan Jayaweera, HalfGig, *thing goes, Joseph Laferriere, Koko Nigel, Monkbot and Anonymous: 42

- **Ficus coronata** *Source:* https://en.wikipedia.org/wiki/Ficus_coronata?oldid=757548240 *Contributors:* Nurg, Alan Liefting, Circeus, Hesperian, Alansohn, Choess, RussBot, Gaius Cornelius, Dysmorodrepanis~enwiki, BorgQueen, Chris the speller, Rkitko, Melburnian, Mr Stephen, JMK, Cydebot, Casliber, Jaguarlaser, Ethel Aardvark, SchreiberBike, Addbot, Flakinho, Lightbot, Ulric1313, Citation bot, Poyt448, LucienBOT, Dcirovic, H3llBot, Rcsprinter123, Mark Marathon, Monkbot, Felicitymcrowe, InternetArchiveBot and Anonymous: 1

- **Ficus microcarpa** *Source:* https://en.wikipedia.org/wiki/Ficus_microcarpa?oldid=762886553 *Contributors:* William Avery, Azhyd, Xavic69, Eugene van der Pijll, Guettarda, Hesperian, PMLF, BanyanTree, Tabletop, Eubot, Kerry Raymond, Dysmorodrepanis~enwiki, TDogg310, SmackBot, Rkitko, Melburnian, Esculapio, Ryulong, Lavateraguy, CBM, Cydebot, Macropneuma, Casliber, Thijs!bot, Nipisiquit, Parande, Maias, Frank R 1981, Sakletare, Efe, Addbot, Flakinho, Lightbot, First Light, Yobot, AnomieBOT, Xqbot, Noder4, Citation bot 1, Trappist the monk, EmausBot, Look2See1, Dcirovic, Bermudiana, Rcsprinter123, Daegil, Plantdrew, BG19bot, Declangi, Sminthopsis84, TechnicianGB, ArmbrustBot, Joseph Laferriere, InternetArchiveBot, Jd.varner44 and Anonymous: 15

- **Ficus neriifolia** *Source:* https://en.wikipedia.org/wiki/Ficus_neriifolia?oldid=739173202 *Contributors:* Quadell, Circeus, Alansohn, Rjwilmsi, Chobot, The Rambling Man, Emmanuelm, Dysmorodrepanis~enwiki, Rkitko, Cydebot, Casliber, Addbot, MGA73bot, Krish Dulal, EmausBot, Dcirovic, MelbourneStar, Daegil, Declangi, Tortie tude and Anonymous: 2

- **Ficus obliqua** *Source:* https://en.wikipedia.org/wiki/Ficus_obliqua?oldid=757548892 *Contributors:* Jimfbleak, Davidcannon, Bender235, Guettarda, Circeus, Hesperian, Alansohn, Woohookitty, Dmol, BD2412, Rjwilmsi, Choess, Gaius Cornelius, Dysmorodrepanis~enwiki, BorgQueen, SmackBot, Chris the speller, Rkitko, Melburnian, Colonies Chris, GoodDay, Snowmanradio, Thor Dockweiler, John, Mr Stephen, Sasata, J Milburn, Cydebot, Macropneuma, DumbBOT, Casliber, Headbomb, Bencherlite, Michael Goodyear, DrKay, Athaenara, GimmeBot, Jaguarlaser, Bfpage, Ethel Aardvark, Graham Beards, Niceguyedc, Piledhigheranddeeper, Alexbot, SchreiberBike, Another Believer, Addbot, Flakinho, Lightbot, AussieLegend2, Ulric1313, Westerness, Citation bot, Xqbot, Poyt448, Citation bot 1, Micromesistius, Tbhotch, RjwilmsiBot, Noommos, John of Reading, Dcirovic, Rcsprinter123, Chris857, ClueBot NG, Helpful Pixie Bot, Declangi, Jjcloudruns, Dexbot, Ginsuloft, Hareshrohan, Thewordsmith9, Monkbot, InternetArchiveBot and Anonymous: 7

- **Ficus platypoda** *Source:* https://en.wikipedia.org/wiki/Ficus_platypoda?oldid=757548912 *Contributors:* DennisDaniels, Guettarda, Circeus, Hesperian, Grutness, Alansohn, Rjwilmsi, The Rambling Man, JarrahTree, Rkitko, Melburnian, Cydebot, Casliber, WolfmanSF, TXiKiBoT, Jaguarlaser, Addbot, Queenmomcat, Citation bot, Look2See1, Dcirovic, Rcsprinter123, Helpful Pixie Bot, Mark Marathon, BG19bot, Monkbot, InternetArchiveBot and Anonymous: 2

- **Ficus retusa** *Source:* https://en.wikipedia.org/wiki/Ficus_retusa?oldid=717266562 *Contributors:* Xavic69, Ghormax, Gdr, Rich Farmbrough, Eubot, RobyWayne, Dysmorodrepanis~enwiki, Bookguy, SmackBot, EncycloPetey, Chris the speller, Bluebot, Rkitko, Thumperward, Greg5030, Casliber, Tiggrx, Jonnyboy5, Magioladitis, Kyle the bot, Whatsupmf, BotanyBot, SieBot, Addbot, Flakinho, Luckas-bot, Yobot, AnomieBOT, Erik9bot, Simuliid, Look2See1, Daegil, Plantdrew, Snow Rise, Pierre.becquart, Sayom, Earth100, Sminthopsis84, ArmbrustBot, NottNott, Treeenthusiast and Anonymous: 12

- **Ficus rubiginosa** *Source:* https://en.wikipedia.org/wiki/Ficus_rubiginosa?oldid=770901187 *Contributors:* Malcolm Farmer, Andrewa, Pollinator, Securiger, Davidcannon, MPF, MisfitToys, DanielCD, CanisRufus, Guettarda, Circeus, Giraffedata, Hesperian, Axl, BanyanTree, Schzmo, David Levy, Rjwilmsi, MWAK, Eubot, AndrewRaphael, Gdrbot, YurikBot, Welsh, NeilN, Ian Rose, Chris the speller, Rkitko, Snowmanradio, Kahuroa, Ceoil, Thor Dockweiler, JorisvS, JHunterJ, Mr Stephen, J Milburn, NTDOY Fanboy, Casliber, Thijs!bot, WolfmanSF, Oshwah, Hey jude, don't let me down, Jaguarlaser, BotanyBot, Phe-bot, FunkMonk, Invertzoo, Cygnis insignis, Mild Bill Hiccup, Piledhigheranddeeper, SchreiberBike, Dank, Addbot, Flakinho, Lightbot, Yobot, Materialscientist, Citation bot, Poyt448, Citation bot 1, Ypna, Serols, Gerda Arendt, Look2See1, Dcirovic, H3llBot, SporkBot, Rcsprinter123, Daegil, BG19bot, CitationCleanerBot, Darorcilmir, Cyberbot II, Dexbot, Sminthopsis84, TFA Protector Bot, Mevagiss, Monkbot, FACBot, GreenC bot, Paula William, Eoembem, Broman23 and Anonymous: 16

- **Forsythia** *Source:* https://en.wikipedia.org/wiki/Forsythia?oldid=771580984 *Contributors:* Kpjas, Amillar, Hephaestos, Ixfd64, Kingturtle, Imc, Joy, Wetman, David.Monniaux, Lumos3, PuzzletChung, Robbot, Naddy, DocWatson42, MPF, Mintleaf~enwiki, JoJan, Rdsmith4, Famartin, CanisRufus, Kwamikagami, Tigerente, Hesperian, Markj 87, Ceyockey, Stemonitis, Richard Barlow, Knuckles, TheAlphaWolf, Rjwilmsi, Eubot, No Swan So Fine, Chobot, Gdrbot, WriterHound, YurikBot, Wavelength, Huw Powell, Dnik, RussBot, Hede2000, Gaius Cornelius, Badagnani, E rulez, TDogg310, Gadget850, AjaxSmack, Heptazane, Sturmovik, Eskimbot, Hraefen, Manchild, Elatanatari, Melburnian, Avb, Salamurai, Goodnightmush, DavidOaks, Lavateraguy, CBM, Mhklein, Baskaufs, Cydebot, Thijs!bot, Barticus88, A Sniper, Osborne, Anupam, Rosarinagazo, Pemilligan, JAnDbot, Deflective, Magioladitis, Michael Goodyear, Nikevich, Wlodzimierz, Potatoswatter, BlackMetalWhiteGuy, JGHowes, Rlendog, ClueBot, Jbening, Comlag225, Arjayay, Tony Holkham, DumZiBoT, BodhisattvaBot, Addbot, Cuaxdon, MrOllie, FiriBot, Bencohoon, Tassedethe, Folypeelarks, Yobot, Noropdoropi, 松岡明芳, WizardOfOz, AnomieBOT, Nicholas24051979, Erud, JoeLoeb, Trafford09, Vinithehat, Barefoot gal, I.Sáček, senior, Tom.Reding, FoxBot, Tom Hulse, ZhBot, Stephen MUFC, EmausBot, WikitanvirBot, Stevenliuyi, ZéroBot, ClueBot NG, Raghith, PaleCloudedWhite, Plantdrew, Fortuitousrole, NotWith, Darorcilmir, Funk munkey, *thing goes, Joseph Laferriere, Gronk Oz, Sarr Cat, Cheesekates, Wilmadon, Bender the Bot and Anonymous: 51

- **Fraxinus hubeiensis** *Source:* https://en.wikipedia.org/wiki/Fraxinus_hubeiensis?oldid=711520227 *Contributors:* Rjwilmsi, Ptelea, Casliber, RjwilmsiBot, BG19bot, Joseph Laferriere and Sarr Cat

- **Fuchsia** *Source:* https://en.wikipedia.org/wiki/Fuchsia?oldid=773416073 *Contributors:* Kpjas, William Avery, Hephaestos, Tregoweth, Ahoerstemeier, Stan Shebs, Charles Matthews, Franz Xaver, Shizhao, Raul654, Robbot, Pigsonthewing, Naddy, David Gerard, DocWatson42, MPF, Elf, Yak, Wmahan, Gdr, Onco p53, JoJan, Kmweber, Pl212, Jim Horning, Mike Rosoft, O'Dea, WillDarlock, Florian Blaschke, MarkS, CanisRufus, Kwamikagami, Truthflux, Yongxinge, Shlomital, לערי ריינהארט, Pearle, Tom.k, Christian.ispir, Stemonitis, Georgia guy, LOL, TheAlphaWolf, Mandarax, Melesse, Rjwilmsi, TBHecht, MapsMan, FlaBot, Eubot, Nihiltres, Str1977, Gdrbot, Bgwhite, YurikBot, Peter G Werner, RussBot, Red Slash, John Quincy Adding Machine, Oni Lukos, Dysmorodrepanis~enwiki, Lijealso, IceCreamAntisocial, Katieh5584, Unyoyega, Eskimbot, Srnec, Ohnoitsjamie, Ckerr, Rkitko, Colonies Chris, KieferSkunk, OrphanBot, NoahElhardt, Richard001, Bejnar, MrDarwin, NutterguyIrl, BillFlis, Stupid Corn, Pjrm, CmdrObot, DathaiFrench, Cydebot, Casliber, Thijs!bot, NorwegianBlue, Sjoerd.klaveringa, CharlotteWebb, Nick Number, RoboServien, Escarbot, Rakey, Fru1tbat, Prolog, Chill doubt, Mutt Lunker, JAnDbot, Deflective, Michael Goodyear, Soulbot, F1alan, Daemonic Kangaroo, Peter coxhead, Starrycupz, Nehwyn, CommonsDelinker, Admc2006, Adavidb, Maproom, Tiptruck, Warut, 83d40m, Epibase, Tahnan, Million Moments, S (usurped also), Idioma-bot, VolkovBot, Somanypeople, Kumorifox, Penarc, MarieVelde, Agyle, Geanixx, HelloMojo, RicReilly, Flyer22 Reborn, Oxymoron83, Lightmouse, AutoYro, Denisarona, ClueBot, Jbening, Avenged Eightfold, GorillaWarfare, Monster boy1, No such user, Pamela Gardiner, Camboxer, Ost316, Libcub, Addbot, Hetus, Siderumhk, AndersBot, Flakinho, Erutuon, Tide rolls, Aviados, Drpickem, Yobot, 松岡明芳, Jim1138, Royote, ArthurBot, Xqbot, Hamamelis, Julcal, Primary key, AstaBOTh15, Lineslarge, Full-date unlinking bot, Kibi78704, Rasim1, Weedgarden, Reaper Eternal, RjwilmsiBot, John of Reading, WikitanvirBot, Look2See1, Gold Bernard, Dcirovic, Solomonfromfinland, Arsfuchsiae, ClueBot NG, 149AFK, BG19bot, Midnight Green, Darorcilmir, Redskin9999, Dexbot, Nomen ambiguum, Steve Bass Ellis, Hamsterhughey, Tortie tude, HalfGig, Savvyjack23, 1england12, Fanwen619, Sarr Cat, KasparBot, CAPTAIN RAJU, InternetArchiveBot, Bender the Bot and Anonymous: 84

- **Ginkgo biloba** *Source:* https://en.wikipedia.org/wiki/Ginkgo_biloba?oldid=774298046 *Contributors:* Kpjas, Dreamyshade, Vicki Rosenzweig, Bryan Derksen, Kowloonese, Christian List, PierreAbbat, Ben-Zin~enwiki, Robert Foley, Nonenmac, Jaknouse, Ram-Man, Lorenzarius, Infrogmation, Tim Starling, Llywrch, Menchi, Tannin, Ixfd64, Shoaler, Delirium, Ahoerstemeier, Stan Shebs, Anobo, Darkwind, Aarchiba, Wikidi, Glenn, Slusk, Jiang, Jouster, Hashar, Dcoetzee, Jukeboksi, Maximus Rex, Imc, Hyacinth, SEWilco, Claim~enwiki, Tjdw, Wiwaxia, Robbot, Fredrik, Chris 73, Kristof vt, WormRunner, Baldhur, ZimZalaBim, Ektar, Nurg, Kokiri, Hippietrail, UtherSRG, Fuelbottle, Davidcannon, Exploding Boy, Giftlite, Homsar2, DocWatson42, MPF, Jp~enwiki, Gilgamesh~enwiki, Dmmaus, Solipsist, Jmcnamera, Gyrofrog, Utcursch, Pgan002, Andycjp, Yath, Kusunose, Exigentsky, Rdsmith4, Bumm13, Pethan, Fanghong~enwiki, Famartin, Atrian, Shamino, DanielCD, Discospinster, Rich Farmbrough, Chowells, Murtasa, Xezbeth, Arthur Holland, Dlloyd, Bender235, Mykhal, Jarsyl, Neko-chan, Syp, Bendono, Jpgordon, R. S. Shaw, Gracee, Nk, Pschemp, Hesperian, Ogress, Espoo, Jumbuck, Alansohn, Etxrge, Corwin8, Fawcett5, Yummifruitbat, Djlayton4, Melaen, Velella, Cecil, Dinoguy2, Lerdsuwa, BDD, Iustinus, Adrian.benko, S.emmerson, Stemonitis, Dodiad, MONGO, Jean-Pol Grandmont, I64s, Kalmia, JIP, Pmj, Rjwilmsi, Astropithicus, DeadlyAssassin, Himasaram, Ligulem, Neuron132, Reinis, Yamamoto Ichiro, RCBot~enwiki, SchuminWeb, Musical Linguist, Nihiltres, Vandal B, Sunroofguy~enwiki, Choess, Ronebofh, Yuji, Chobot, Gdrbot, Bgwhite, WriterHound, CKorban, Vmenkov, EamonnPKeane, YurikBot, Wavelength, Freerick, Huw Powell, Conscious, Chris Capoccia, Moshe777, Gaius Cornelius, Shaddack, Tavilis, Alynna Kasmira, Curtis Clark, Dysmorodrepanis~enwiki, Cryptoid, Badagnani, Ospalh, JPMcGrath, EEMIV, Schnob Reider, Asarelah, Lt-wiki-bot, KekoDActyluS~enwiki, Ronasi, Josh3580, Tsunaminoai, Back ache, Wikipeditor, SmackBot, Asphaltbuffet, Indyguy, Herostratus, GoldenXuniversity, Slashme, Melchoir, Kimon, EncycloPetey, Chaosfeary, Nudimmud, Zekkelley, Kintetsubuffalo, Edgar181, ApersOn, Gilliam, Ohnoitsjamie, Skizzik, Viraz, Rkitko, NCurse, Thumperward, Melburnian,

MidgleyDJ, Hibernian, Deli nk, Nbarth, DHN-bot~enwiki, Bruce Marlin, Mike hayes, Can't sleep, clown will eat me, Tamfang, Abyssal, Sunny17152, Adamschneider, Addshore, Jeffblackadar, Greg5030, Kingdon, Alexandra lb, Paul H., BullRangifer, Zzorse, Ligulembot, Bezapt, Andrew Dalby, SashatoBot, Lambiam, Erimus, AThing, MrDarwin, U-571, Dcruz01, SilkTork, Ortho, Kevmin, JorisvS, Mgiganteus1, Bjankuloski06en~enwiki, Dysmachus, Smith609, BillFlis, Geeki, Godfrey Daniel, Boonukem, Novangelis, MTSbot~enwiki, Hu12, Iridescent, Igoldste, Tawkerbot2, Wspencer11, Falconus, Ceran, Igni, Picaroon, Baskaufs, Myasuda, Beastie Bot, Cydebot, Kupirijo, Lightblade, Gogo Dodo, DumbBOT, Narayanese, Damianrafferty, LHeyns, Cs california, Casliber, Thijs!bot, Wikid77, Parrt, Mactographer, TonyTheTiger, Bigwyrm, Mmmpie, Headbomb, Dimrof, Merkurix, Dfrg.msc, Urbanpoet, Nick Number, Escarbot, Mentifisto, Nbritton, AntiVandalBot, Smartse, Aelwyn, Canadian-Bacon, SincereGuy, Dreaded Walrus, JAnDbot, UCLABruin, Deflective, Leuko, MER-C, RebelRobot, SNP, Penubag, VoABot II, Meredyth, Dekimasu, MastCell, Sam Hyde, Robby, Caroldermoid, Wormcast, Animum, LookingGlass, Lelkesa, Jgnat, Cantwellma, Peter coxhead, Eduardo311, NatureA16, Yobol, Ligulem-s, Infopharm2, DandanxD, CotoNei, Nikpapag, Scenicguy24, Azalea pomp, R'n'B, Kolrobie, Nono64, ArcAngel, PrestonH, Thirdright, J.delanoy, Edgeweyes, Abidagus, Collegebookworm, JoeHigashi~enwiki, NewEnglandYankee, DadaNeem, Geekdiva, DorganBot, Khargas, Straw Cat, JMSchneid, Vlmastra, Philip Trueman, TXiKiBoT, Malljaja, JenniferFisher, Difranza, Rich Janis, Elphion, BwDraco, Fusionall, Greswik, Usmaankhan12, Jaguarlaser, Scipio7, Doc James, HelloMojo, SylviaStanley, Ultrapositive, Rmj03, SieBot, ZooKid6, Calliopejen1, YonaBot, Gerakibot, Yintan, LeadSongDog, Tv07, Djayjp, Omí Wale, Flyer22 Reborn, Alexbrn, Oda Mari, Darvijen, Brandonazz, Dravecky, Martinsmells1, IvanTortuga, Literaturegeek, Loren.wilton, ClueBot, Justin W Smith, CarolSpears, The Thing That Should Not Be, Cygnis insignis, Meekywiki, Sevilledade, Alpta, Lensicon~enwiki, Dr. B. R. Lang, Excirial, Jusdafax, Eggnog09, IVP, Estirabot, Sun Creator, Tianli, Prof Health, Rui Gabriel Correia, Thingg, Aitias, Dana boomer, Rocksteadyg, DumZiBoT, XLinkBot, Roxy the dog, Vanished 45kd09la13, Fro13, NellieBly, Anthony.page, Vianello, Porphyro, SplendidConfusion, Meow555, Omgholy, Addbot, Cantaloupe2, Some jerk on the Internet, DOI bot, Jame82, AndrewHZ, Globalsolidarity, Jncraton, Fluffernutter, Chamal N, Busterbarker2008, Sillyfolkboy, Dredog65, Blaylockjam10, Wakeham, Lights33, Craigsjones, BrianKnez, Lightbot, JEN9841, Bleujoy, Yegle, Legobot, Luckasbot, Yobol, 2D, UltraMagnus, Cyclechick, Bartdeb, AnomieBOT, DemocraticLuntz, Jim1138, Galoubet, Novel Zephyr, Materialscientist, Citation bot, Xqbot, ThePhoenixLives, Capricorn42, Gigemag76, Christian140, Teamjenn, Ched, Tyrol5, Cyphoidbomb, GrouchoBot, Omnipaedista, Zefr, SassoBot, Amaury, Brutaldeluxe, White whirlwind, Shadowjams, Hamamelis, Douglas W. Jones, CorporateM, Nagualdesign, Easyplantmapping, Simuliid, Gouerouz, HJ Mitchell, BenzolBot, Demonicspawn451, Citation bot 1, GroveWanderer, Ceydatiens, Pinethicket, Jonfischeruk, Micromesistius, Jonesey95, Chirochoi, Ginkgob, W Michel, Jauhienij, FoxBot, Trappist the monk, Agwoodliffe, Firstclasspimp23, Woodye06, Dieguico, Specs112, The Utahraptor, RjwilmsiBot, Steve03Mills, Max5600, EmausBot, Orphan Wiki, WikitanvirBot, Nick Moyes, Look2See1, ZeniffMartineau, Dr.n3no3, Medser, RA0808, Soulamon, Fpacifica, Empathictrust, Dcirovic, Falconjh, ZéroBot, Wackywace, Il-Iraute, AManWithNoPlan, Tolly4bolly, Ocdncntx, Brandmeister, Puffin, Fifty3, DemonicPartyHat, Papapaci, Thewarm, Michael Bailes, ClueBot NG, Raiden10, Muon, Asukite, Hwiseley, Masssly, Yarikata, WikiPuppies, Reify-tech, MerlIwBot, Helpful Pixie Bot, HMSSolent, Marranyoizer, Wbm1058, Plantdrew, Hyptis, BG19bot, Orthopteran, TCN7JM, MusikAnimal, Solistide, Hockeyguy128, NotWith, Xingchi Chen6650, SteveH37, BattyBot, Darorcilmir, Cyberbot II, EnzaiBot, Ultra Venia, Symphonic Spenguin, Mogism, Frosty, MartinMichlmayr, Absander, BurritoBazooka, Sbalfour, Ercé, Ruby Murray, Rod6807, Psatsankhya, Everymorning, ArmbrustBot, Babitaarora, Seppi333, Ginsuloft, Evergreenherbs, Krzysztof23, Japanseries, Monkbot, Impuls666666, Doppelich, Medgirl131, Ruff tuff cream puff, Veexkee, Firestar03, Elmidae, Ykbustanji, KasparBot, (jubi-net), Jeendanie, MZLTB, InternetArchiveBot, GreenC bot, Marvellous Spider-Man, Titanoptera, Bender the Bot, Mulus2lus, UpDownAndSideways, Johnnydev, Yellow Pearl, Zdmd2015, Dumas1945 and Anonymous: 558

- **Halleria lucida** *Source:* https://en.wikipedia.org/wiki/Halleria_lucida?oldid=761293551 *Contributors:* Tom Radulovich, Stemonitis, Joel7687, Asarelah, IceCreamAntisocial, Thor Dockweiler, Paul venter, Marco Schmidt, Addbot, OlEnglish, Yobot, Drakenwolf, TjBot, Androstachys, Abu Shawka, Rcsprinter123, Plantdrew, PhnomPencil, Joseph Laferriere and Nickwilso

- **History of bonsai** *Source:* https://en.wikipedia.org/wiki/History_of_bonsai?oldid=770584454 *Contributors:* GünniX, RJBaran, DuncanHill, CommonsDelinker, Katharineamy, Yobot, Sahara110, I dream of horses, StarryGrandma, Lourdes and Anonymous: 2

- **Ilex mitis** *Source:* https://en.wikipedia.org/wiki/Ilex_mitis?oldid=728830185 *Contributors:* Tom Radulovich, IceCreamAntisocial, JMK, Marco Schmidt, Jaguarlaser, Addbot, Yobot, Julia W, DSisyphBot, VernoWhitney, WikitanvirBot, Abu Shawka, Rcsprinter123 and Plantdrew

- **Ilex vomitoria** *Source:* https://en.wikipedia.org/wiki/Ilex_vomitoria?oldid=770048998 *Contributors:* Tedernst, Thehappysmith, MPF, DanielCD, Ziggurat, Hesperian, Josiahpugh, Stemonitis, Woohookitty, EWLwiki, Heah, Eubot, Gdrbot, WriterHound, RussBot, Trovatore, TDogg310, Asarelah, SmackBot, Kintetsubuffalo, RDBrown, Cybercobra, Zeamays, AThing, LadyofShalott, Lavateraguy, Baskaufs, Cydebot, Strongbad1982, Mereda, Ken Thomas, Altairisfar, WolfmanSF, Antepenultimate, TXiKiBoT, Deranged bulbasaur, Luteus, Cwkmail, JohnnyMrNinja, Kinkyturnip, Berean Hunter, Ost316, UhOhFeeling, Addbot, Cuaxdon, LaaknorBot, Laikayiu, Luckas-bot, Yobot, AnomieBOT, Pinethicket, RjwilmsiBot, Dcirovic, Erianna, Helpful Pixie Bot, KLBot2, Plantdrew, Me, Myself, and I are Here, Monkbot, Mropicki, Sarr Cat, Neurorebel, 8tx, Bender the Bot and Anonymous: 25

- **Jabuticaba** *Source:* https://en.wikipedia.org/wiki/Jabuticaba?oldid=769722907 *Contributors:* William Avery, Daniel C. Boyer, Alan Liefting, MPF, Jorge Stolfi, Gdr, Hesperian, Kazvorpal, Rjwilmsi, Ricardo Carneiro Pires, Eubot, Mr.Rocks, YurikBot, Aeusoes1, Tearlach, Apokryltaros, Rmky87, TDogg310, IceCreamAntisocial, Emijrp, Davidals, Gjs238, Happywaffle, Pieter1, Huon, Adamantiaf, Dantadd, Jidanni, Wkoide, DanielGSouza, Brandizzi, R2cyberpunk, Alaibot, Dyanega, Casliber, JamesAM, Thijs!bot, Jaboticaba~enwiki, Kzrt, Indon, LordAnubisBOT, Idioma-bot, Murderbike, Rumiton, Jaguarlaser, Lily02886, Cannonconsult, Lucasbfrbot, Alexbot, Addbot, Campola, Krenakarore, Luckas-bot, KamikazeBot, AnomieBOT, Cerme, ArthurBot, Quebec99, LilHelpa, Xqbot, Krydolf~enwiki, Abyssquick, Brutaldeluxe, FrescoBot, Markeilz, HRoest3bot, Makki98, EmausBot, John of Reading, GoingBatty, Akhilan, ZéroBot, Lguipontes, Mjbmrbot, Plantdrew, Dexbot, Sminthopsis84, Bruno.karklis, Cathry, Reiniger321, Zamanislam, Cboning, Lina Yab and Anonymous: 41

- **Juniperus californica** *Source:* https://en.wikipedia.org/wiki/Juniperus_californica?oldid=755118257 *Contributors:* Nonenmac, Ixfd64, Dino, MPF, DanielCD, Nyenyec, Hesperian, AnthonyWS, Eubot, Gdrbot, WriterHound, RussBot, Gaius Cornelius, Curtis Clark, Dysmorodrepanis~enwiki, Mmcannis, Beastie Bot, Cydebot, Cs california, Fractaloctal, Jcmenal, VolkovBot, BotanyBot, Mikemoral, Alexbot, Addbot, Mbinebri, Flakinho, First Light, Yobot, Rubinbot, Abce2, Pinethicket, Tom.Reding, EmausBot, Look2See1, ZéroBot, ClueBot NG, Plantdrew, Chaparral girl, Nightphoenix90, Trixie05, FloraWilde, AwesomesaucePlayz and Anonymous: 7

- **Juniperus chinensis** *Source:* https://en.wikipedia.org/wiki/Juniperus_chinensis?oldid=758641456 *Contributors:* William Avery, Robbot, MPF, Hesperian, Stephen Bain, Ghirlandajo, Isnow, Km1uk, Eubot, Chobot, Gdrbot, YurikBot, Ytrottier, Curtis Clark, Beastie Bot, Cydebot, Cs california, Casliber, Slaweks, Escarbot, Fractaloctal, Peter coxhead, Ef3, Sedgehead, BotanyBot, QualiaBot, Chhe, WikHead, MystBot, Addbot,

Cuaxdon, Flakinho, Luckas-bot, AnomieBOT, AThestral, Xqbot, GrouchoBot, Thehelpfulbot, Simuliid, Micromesistius, Tom.Reding, EmausBot, ZéroBot, Pescov, メルビル, Texasconverse, Plantdrew, NotWith, Darorcilmir, Sminthopsis84, Trixie05, KasparBot and Anonymous: 8

- **Juniperus procumbens** *Source:* https://en.wikipedia.org/wiki/Juniperus_procumbens?oldid=773430234 *Contributors:* SEWilco, Tomchiukc, MPF, Discospinster, Hesperian, Rydia, Gdrbot, SmackBot, Beastie Bot, Cs california, Casliber, KP Botany, Fractaloctal, Katharineamy, TXiKiBoT, BotanyBot, Addbot, Flakinho, Zorrobot, Yobot, D'ohBot, Tom.Reding, EmausBot, ZéroBot, ChrisGualtieri, Pseudo75, Sminthopsis84 and Anonymous: 4

- **Juniperus squamata** *Source:* https://en.wikipedia.org/wiki/Juniperus_squamata?oldid=758603336 *Contributors:* Centrx, MPF, D6, Hesperian, Eubot, Curtis Clark, Rathfelder, Victoriagirl, Beastie Bot, Cs california, Casliber, Thijs!bot, Fractaloctal, Vanished User 4517, BotanyBot, Addbot, LaaknorBot, Flakinho, First Light, Xqbot, GrouchoBot, PigFlu Oink, DrilBot, Tom.Reding, EmausBot, ZéroBot, Plantdrew, Darorcilmir, Sminthopsis84 and Anonymous: 7

- **Juniperus virginiana** *Source:* https://en.wikipedia.org/wiki/Juniperus_virginiana?oldid=764298925 *Contributors:* Nonenmac, Ram-Man, BoNoMoJo (old), Angela, Taxman, Pollinator, Hajor, Seglea, Mirv, Thehappysmith, MPF, Karl-Henner, Famartin, Liblamb, Fluzwup, Sten, Cmdrjameson, Hesperian, Stemonitis, Ricardo Carneiro Pires, Chobot, Gdrbot, WriterHound, Huw Powell, Jimp, Curtis Clark, Ragesoss, TDogg310, CorbieVreccan, Rallette, CLW, Ketsuekigata, West Virginian, Brya, Yamaguchi 先生, Ohnoitsjamie, Melburnian, Yaf, Greg5030, MrDarwin, John, Peter Horn, Baskaufs, Beastie Bot, Cydebot, Russian F, GRBerry, Cs california, Casliber, Thijs!bot, Horologium, AntiVandalBot, JAnDbot, Altairisfar, Natureguy1980, VoABot II, Zeandroid, Mjrmtg, -Bobby, Peter coxhead, R'n'B, Masebrock, Uncle Dick, Katalaveno, Kmanblue, Idioma-bot, ABF, Nburden, Philip Trueman, Disputantum, Vgranucci, Madhero88, Liz de Quebec, BotanyBot, SieBot, Neophyrigian, QualiaBot, IvanTortuga, Denisarona, ClueBot, The Thing That Should Not Be, Niceguyedc, DragonBot, Berean Hunter, Addbot, Some jerk on the Internet, GD 6041, Erutuon, Lightbot, Zorrobot, Kenraiz, Luckas-bot, Yobot, Jesielt, AnomieBOT, AdjustShift, Obersachsebot, Gigemag76, Wayne Roberson, Austin, Texas, GrouchoBot, Jthomp28, Elisaulal, MGA73bot, Citation bot 1, Pinethicket, Tom.Reding, BRUTE, RedBot, Kgrad, Mishae, 7mike5000, Romanbc, EmausBot, Look2See1, Peterusso, NicatronTg, ClueBot NG, Hackberry sampler, Plantdrew, Juniperandelton, BG19bot, BattyBot, Darorcilmir, Lago Mar, Boko80, ArmbrustBot, Nightphoenix90, ChamithN, Jcarter56633, Djadjko, Artheartsoul1 and Anonymous: 67

- **Malus** *Source:* https://en.wikipedia.org/wiki/Malus?oldid=766991971 *Contributors:* Llywrch, Menchi, Ixfd64, Marumari, Amcaja, Schneelocke, Radiojon, SEWilco, Pollinator, Nurg, Angilbas, Xanzzibar, DocWatson42, MPF, Leflyman, Golbez, JoJan, DanielCD, Florian Blaschke, Erolos, Kbh3rd, Kwamikagami, Man vyi, Retran, AnnaP, Radical Mallard, RainbowOfLight, Shoefly, BDD, Makanon, Alvis, Richard Barlow, Masterjamie, Kzollman, MrDarcy, Bytor, Cuvtixo, Jclemens, MarnetteD, Titoxd, Eubot, Chobot, Gdrbot, Tonync, RussBot, Dysmorodrepanis~enwiki, Bloodofox, Inhighspeed, E rulez, Raven4x4x, Rallette, Lt-wiki-bot, YolanCh, BorgQueen, SmackBot, Hardyplants, Gilliam, Anastasios~enwiki, Rkitko, Markp6, Bruce Marlin, OrphanBot, Kingdon, Krong, Jeremy norbury, Tova86, Gurdjieff, Marcus Brute, Andrew Dalby, Thor Dockweiler, ThurnerRupert, Kuru, Pepperjackcandy, Adamfenderson, Kevmin, IronGargoyle, RomanSpa, Maxxicum, Gogo Dodo, Roberta F., Editor at Large, PamD, Epbr123, Barticus88, Qwyrxian, MichaelMaggs, Escarbot, Yuanchosaan, Storkk, Dreaded Walrus, ShadowKinght, JAnDbot, Deflective, TensorProduct, Skyemoor, VoABot II, Caricologist, Animum, DerHexer, Gidip, Waystone, Wlodzimierz, Huzzlet the bot, J.delanoy, Severnjc, Kloisiie, Nadiatalent, Idioma-bot, Cmurphy10, VolkovBot, Butwhatdoiknow, Chango369w, XYer, TXiKiBoT, Muleattack, Red58bill, SieBot, Coffee, Vandalizor666, Alexbrn, Helikophis, Dust Filter, ClueBot, The Thing That Should Not Be, Excirial, Attenboroughii, PixelBot, Vanisheduser12345, Aurora2698, Jadeddissonance, XLinkBot, MystBot, Addbot, Proofreader77, Willking1979, DOI bot, Fyrael, CarsracBot, Lucian Sunday, Flakinho, Tide rolls, Ejir3j342490, Luckas-bot, Yobot, Ptbotgourou, TaBOT-zerem, Eng22, THEN WHO WAS PHONE?, AnomieBOT, Cottonapple4, RayvnEQ, Kingpin13, Materialscientist, Citation bot, Pomeapplepome, Jay L09, Xqbot, S h i v a (Visnu), Armbrust, Some standardized rigour, Prari, D'ohBot, Dger, Citation bot 1, Pinethicket, Jauhienij, Tim1357, FoxBot, Lotje, TBloemink, SeoMac, Fastilysock, Awesomeness19, Minimac, RjwilmsiBot, TjBot, Alph Bot, EmausBot, John of Reading, WikitanvirBot, RenamedUser01302013, TuHan-Bot, K6ka, Classedhaie, Bollyjeff, Koibryi, Kilo22, Unreal7, Surya Prakash.S.A., Erianna, AndyTheGrump, Evan-Amos, ClueBot NG, This lousy T-shirt, Plantdrew, Wehha, Argo752, 42GeoCPU, Pjh009, BattyBot, Darorcilmir, Qwerty12302, BlevintronBot, Sminthopsis84, Lugia2453, BJDJ1234, *thing goes, Monkbot, Riversid, Sarr Cat, KasparBot, Wnholmes, Aquajonah, GreenC bot, Marvellous Spider-Man, Prahlad balaji, Bender the Bot and Anonymous: 116

- **Olive** *Source:* https://en.wikipedia.org/wiki/Olive?oldid=774782435 *Contributors:* Magnus Manske, MichaelTinkler, Lee Daniel Crocker, Vicki Rosenzweig, Mav, Bryan Derksen, Andre Engels, PierreAbbat, William Avery, SimonP, Jaknouse, Youandme, Henriette~enwiki, Olivier, Edward, Michael Hardy, (, Stan Shebs, Mac, Ronz, Roger.wernersson, Docu, Andres, Adam Conover, Jengod, Adam Bishop, Tcassedy, Timc, Peregrine981, Tpbradbury, Marshman, Imc, Rnbc, Phoebe, Wetman, Robbot, Kristof vt, WormRunner, Stewartadcock, Rfc1394, Academic Challenger, Diderot, Hadal, UtherSRG, GerardM, Dd42, ManuelGR, Kevin Saff, DocWatson42, MPF, Marco Pellegrino, Bork, Meursault2004, Timpo, Binadot, Peruvianllama, Niteowlneils, Eequor, Macrakis, Foobar, Gyrofrog, Pgan002, Keith Edkins, Alexf, Zeimusu, Williamb, João Correia, JoJan, Kaldari, OwenBlacker, DragonflySixtyseven, Karl-Henner, Aramgutang, WpZurp, Neutrality, Slidewinder, Oknazevad, Jcw69, Marnevell, ELApro, Andylkl, Kate, Dr.frog, Imroy, DanielCD, Rich Farmbrough, LindsayH, Mani1, Bender235, Kaisershatner, Meamemg, Brian0918, CanisRufus, Kiand, Kwamikagami, Causa sui, Bobo192, Circeus, Smalljim, Olve Utne, StoatBringer, Cmdrjameson, Brim, Geocachernemesis~enwiki, Scott Ritchie, Nk, Darwinek, Hesperian, Caeruleancentaur, Justinc, Nickfraser, Alansohn, DLipovitch, Eric Kvaalen, Arthena, Hydriotaphia, Ricky81682, Wdfarmer, Snowolf, Velella, Hadlock, Matthias5, Ish ishwar, BDD, Gene Nygaard, Kazvorpal, Brookie, DanielVonEhren, Zntrip, Garrison Roo, Stemonitis, Gmaxwell, Nuno Tavares, Velho, Pekinensis, Woohookitty, Camw, Uncle G, Pol098, WadeSimMiser, Jeff3000, MONGO, Rickjpelleg, Tabletop, Jhortman, Pictureuploader, Graham87, Magister Mathematicae, BD2412, Jeanmi~enwiki, Mendaliv, Saperaud~enwiki, Cicada, Rjwilmsi, Zbxgscqf, Jake Wartenberg, MarSch, Salix alba, Himasaram, Boccobrock, Brighterorange, Eubot, Nihiltres, Gurch, Nick81, Nawwar, Mordicai, DVdm, Gdrbot, WriterHound, Elfguy, YurikBot, Wavelength, Butsuri, Al Silonov, Jimp, Sputnikcccp, DMahalko, Novastarj, Bhny, Frankh~enwiki, Casey56, Stephenb, Gaius Cornelius, Rsrikanth05, Bovineone, Wiki alf, The Ogre, Badagnani, Jaxl, Dogcow, Apokryltaros, Irishguy, E rulez, TDogg310, Zwobot, AntaineNZ, DeadEyeArrow, Bota47, Kewp, Tigershrike, Zello, TheOne, Open2universe, Chase me ladies, I'm the Cavalry, SMcCandlish, Wsiegmund, Skittle, Argo Navis, Tpayne, JDspeeder1, TravisTX, Veinor, Myrabella, SmackBot, FocalPoint, Aljosa, Narson, Honza Záruba, Reedy, Unyoyega, Ursatz, Delldot, Jab843, Frymaster, Alex earlier account, Surazeus, Gilliam, Ohnoitsjamie, Hmains, Ghosts&empties, Anwar saadat, Stevepeterson, Agateller, Rkitko, Robertissimo, Footodors, Oatmeal batman, A. B., Can't sleep, clown will eat me, Gmotamedi, Akhilleus, Snowmanradio, Constantine.Zakrasov, VMS Mosaic, Addshore, Jablair51, Monacat, Abrahami, Weirdy, Justin Stafford, Gabi S., Jiddisch~enwiki, AdeMiami, Ryan Roos, DMacks,

Primecoordinator, Kahuroa, Bejnar, Vidioman, Clicketyclack, Andrew Dalby, SashatoBot, Aldaniel, ArglebargleIV, Erimus, AThing, Anlace, Carnby, General Ization, DavidCooke, J 1982, JorisvS, Infidel taco, Accurizer, 16@r, A. Parrot, Slakr, Lampman, Dbo789, Optakeover, Tasty-Poutine, Jose77, DabMachine, Iridescent, Witblitz, MIckStephenson, Basicdesign, Digitalsurgeon, Igoldste, Ewulp, Gil Gamesh, Gilabrand, Rwst, Tawkerbot2, Astirmays, Beznas, JForget, Evilasiangenius, Ale jrb, BeenAroundAWhile, Neelix, Wingman358, Themightyquill, Cydebot, Peripitus, Peter-T, 663highland, Mziebell, Achangeisasgoodasa, Languagehat, Dnifan, Gogo Dodo, TicketMan, ST47, Amandajm, Dumb-BOT, Chrislk02, Damianrafferty, Viridae, Omicronpersei8, Reecel, Quaxmonster, Peeetar, Casliber, FrancoGG, Thijs!bot, Epbr123, LeeG, Marek69, Missvain, Edal, Ileanadu, VaneWimsey, Weasel5i2, Aquilosion, Tiamut, Escarbot, Mentifisto, AntiVandalBot, Seaphoto, Doc Tropics, Pintosal, Zizikos, Pro crast in a tor, Themadmanc, Gdo01, Natelewis, Sanctvs, Qwerty Binary, Kaini, JAnDbot, Deflective, Husond, Davewho2, DuncanHill, Omeganian, Fetchcomms, Andonic, Roleplayer, 100110100, F64too, PhilKnight, Photodude, LittleOldMe, Camerojo, KEKPΩΨ, Magioladitis, Murgh, Bongwarrior, VoABot II, JamesBWatson, Celebr8f8, Soulbot, Steven Walling, Ahecht, Sgr927, Nposs, Robotman1974, Logictheo, Cpl Syx, Lenticel, Gphoto, Peter coxhead, PeaceAnywhere, Palestine48, Dave, MartinBot, Bwtranch, CommonsDelinker, Thelastrights, Thirdright, Dr G~enwiki, Trusilver, Ali, Theo Mark, Whitebox, Gzkn, Acalamari, Rod57, Beaverboy not, Plasticup, Chiswick Chap, Colchicum, LeighvsOptimvsMaximvs, Ljgua124, Pfbasgen, Jackaranga, Shshshsh, Juliancolton, Corriebertus, WLRoss, Chatvisual, CardinalDan, Idioma-bot, Funandtrvl, Deor, VolkovBot, Gsapient, ABF, Macedonian, Shinju, Chango369w, Soliloquial, George Adam Horváth, Philip Trueman, Martinevans123, Michael.c.harris, DoorsAjar, TXiKiBoT, Oshwah, Zidonuke, Mercurywoodrose, Cosmic Latte, Codemu, Reibot, Nitin77, Henry Carrington, Frannyboy, Andreas Kaganov, Anna Lincoln, Martin451, Begewe1, Ch25kg, MsMichele, Aymerkez~enwiki, Rafaerts, Ilyasozgur, Ninjatacoshell, SexyPersonofthenorth, Olives101, Jaguarlaser, Enviroboy, Thanatos666, Andygharvey, Insanity Incarnate, EmxBot, Writer1966, CrossHouses, Al Ameer son, Sémhur, Pancholopez, Jokullmusic, Calliopejen1, Tiddly Tom, Elie plus, Arpose, Gerakibot, Rave92, Ricomalko, Dawn Bard, Yintan, Soler97, GlassCobra, Keilana, Not home, Oda Mari, Le Pied-bot~enwiki, Ferret, Oxymoron83, NBS, AlanUS, Vice regent, Sean.hoyland, Adammoftah, Jjlasne, Cngoulimis, Amazonien, ImageRemovalBot, Khirurg, Kinkyturnip, ClueBot, MBD123, Hippo99, Wikievil666, The Thing That Should Not Be, Nobodyishome, Liuzhou, Drmies, Der Golem, Blanchardb, Piledhigheranddeeper, Pras, Puchiko, Auntof6, No such user, Excirial, Kain Nihil, Ksjsoccer, Chefallen, Jotterbot, Wprlh, Lobbyworth, Jlamro, The Red, Audaciter, Hasanadnantaha, Rui Gabriel Correia, 1ForTheMoney, Adammacia, DerBorg, Mhockey, Yozer1, SoxBot III, Kcocsevol, XLinkBot, Wikiuser100, Dthomsen8, Avoided, SlimX, SilvonenBot, Thomas bonasera, MystBot, Urmajesty92, Ejosse1, HexaChord, Fedelosantos, Addbot, Xp54321, CWatchman, Mortense, Willking1979, Gahgeer, Yolgnu, Pipyblue, J4m35 80nd, TutterMouse, CanadianLinuxUser, Fluffernutter, Download, Favonian, Christopher140691, SamatBot, LinkFA-Bot, Acotanidis, Tide rolls, Mojail, Xenobot, Greyhood, Luckas-bot, Yobot, 2D, Una giornata uggiosa '94, TaBOT-zerem, Legobot II, THEN WHO WAS PHONE?, Eric-Wester, Agoldstand, AnomieBOT, Jim1138, Piano non troppo, RayvnEQ, Jpgcwiki, Materialscientist, Bazov, Yunus.sendag, ImperatorExercitus, Citation bot, Dromioofephesus, Bob Burkhardt, LilHelpa, ARAGONESE35, Parthian Scribe, Xqbot, Sketchmoose, Dhybhr, Gigemag76, Maddie!, Makeswell, GrouchoBot, Off2riorob, Kyragav, Omnipaedista, Vassobatt, Jackreichert, Zefr, The Interior, Davdde, Forstbirdo, Mash358, Brutaldeluxe, Sisi12345, Fobos92, Josh 2369, Adavis444, Shadowjams, Fkitselis, A.amitkumar, Ellcuisine, Dudedude112233, FrescoBot, Tobby72, Sky Attacker, Riverwhich!, Leonitice, Izzedine, MGA73bot, Resurr Section, Stephen Morley, Citation bot 1, Krish Dulal, Sopher99, AstaBOTh15, Pinethicket, I dream of horses, Titomuerte, Vidimian, Vladmirfish, Halfalah, Moonraker, Pteplitxy, RedBot, Imraneng007, Serols, Kgrad, Jonkerz, Lotje, Red Denim, Bluefist, Abc10, Oliverjew01, Wsaadnour, TKhaldi, Ripchip Bot, Beyond My Ken, CompAnatProf, CalicoCatLover, EmausBot, John of Reading, Dr Aaij, Gfoley4, Look2See1, Heracles31, Laszlovszky András, Shenl88, Uishaki, Doigel18, Winner 42, Dcirovic, Bobby8760, Lucas Thoms, Falconjh, ZéroBot, John Cline, PBS-AWB, Josve05a, Artman2002, Mar4d, Roskj001, Medeis, Wikfr, SporkBot, Tolly4bolly, Erianna, Rcsprinter123, Huskarl2000, L Kensington, Euzen, Wikiloop, Tigris08, JFB80, VictorianMutant, Aulinus12, TYelliot, Architect7, Motamot, ClueBot NG, Kiltedbiker, נרו, Uzma Gamal, CocuBot, ProudJewNo1, Edouard Albert, PaleCloudedWhite, Movses-bot, هاوية التـغذية, GoldenGlory84, Frietjes, Jfgahdsf, CopperSquare, Widr, Ryan Vesey, GeneC1, DavidAnstiss, Sameenahmedkhan, IeatYOUupx, Oddbodz, Helpful Pixie Bot, Calabe1992, Plantdrew, Gluonman, Ibarabi, BG19bot, Dennis koutou, TCN7JM, Hashem sfarim, Kaltenmeyer, Suitcivil133, Northamerica1000, Fromthehill, AvocatoBot, Kagundu, Alfonsoppp, Toastybites, Solistide, Arminden, Lolhugenoob, NotWith, Drakemiral, Alireza 80, Hybrid2712, Christos Oik, Averyhughson, Onthispage, Maurice Flesier, Glacialfox, Loriendrew, SHIVAM GANDHI, GeorgeJanney, Midatlanticdominance2, Triggerhippie4, Cyberbot II, Reuvengrish, ChrisGualtieri, EuroCarGT, MadGuy7023, Asisman, Shuayb twaissi, Shirokazan, Dexbot, SantoshBot, FoCuSandLeArN, Earth100, Sminthopsis84, Webclient101, Mogism, Fête, Morfusmax, Lugia2453, Vietspeits, Faloveka, Cathry, Generic1139, Perfecttwoegan, Cadillac000, TechnicianGB, Stenen Bijl, Rybec, Smartman1234567, Flat Out, Numerounobappu, Charlieminogue, Rebeccaxxniall, Ridha1981, NottNott, Metarese, Taohinton, DrRC, W. P. Uzer, HalfGig, AnnaPaw, Dough34, Zeusman6, Owselore, Rhondaneu, Frovac, Joseph Laferriere, Anon685, Aidepikiwereretetete, JMDGamotia, Rexstein, Paul H Andrews II, Lyonothamnus, Bordwall, Jamvirus, Eytzk, Mehsasharma13, Plainolejane, Jljpt1, Asum991, MRD2014, Harunabdr, Giovanni Caudullo, Ligaga91, Eteethan, Aimilios kampaxis, Therealwikimaster5, Cyrej, StevieJr11111, GeneralizationsAreBad, KasparBot, Sergeagle, 483747477478aaa, Equinox, Gail Platt of Coronation Street, CAPTAIN RAJU, A,Ocram, JoshMuirWikipedia, FozzaDAbeast, LIBERATEDARMENIA, Lakhish, Henrysucks, Geekgecko, Colonel Wilhelm Klink, KGirlTrucker81, GreenC bot, Music1201, Zelen-oko, PolluxWorld, Poddyellen, Bob is Fat, J947, Dante2326, Payton1819, Immcarle49, Tompop888, PersistantCorvid, SarahBKNYC and Anonymous: 853

- **Pemphis** *Source:* https://en.wikipedia.org/wiki/Pemphis?oldid=774247033 *Contributors:* Stemonitis, Rjwilmsi, Rkitko, Maias, R'n'B, Rochelimit, Mild Bill Hiccup, Addbot, Luckas-bot, Xufanc, Hamamelis, RjwilmsiBot, Ramon FVelasquez, ZéroBot, BG19bot, Declangi, BattyBot, Monkbot, Caftaric and Anonymous: 2

- **Pemphis acidula** *Source:* https://en.wikipedia.org/wiki/Pemphis_acidula?oldid=703344346 *Contributors:* Rkitko, Xufanc, Hamamelis and EmausBot

- **Pinus clausa** *Source:* https://en.wikipedia.org/wiki/Pinus_clausa?oldid=773182241 *Contributors:* Nonenmac, Hadal, Seth Ilys, MPF, Abigail-II, Hesperian, Schzmo, FlaBot, Eubot, Gdrbot, TDogg310, Sasata, Beastie Bot, Cydebot, Casliber, Altairisfar, Maias, Masebrock, Colchicum, PixelBot, Addbot, Flakinho, Xqbot, K Gator, Pinethicket, HRoestBot, RedBot, Carynvz, EmausBot, Look2See1, Dcirovic, Albert SN, BG19bot, Nightphoenix90, Ruff tuff cream puff and Anonymous: 13

- **Pinus mugo** *Source:* https://en.wikipedia.org/wiki/Pinus_mugo?oldid=761896750 *Contributors:* Bogdangiusca, SEWilco, Raul654, Naddy, Hadal, Alan Liefting, MPF, Abigail-II, Rich Farmbrough, Nk, Hesperian, Ricky81682, BDD, Stemonitis, Andrea.gf, Eubot, Choess, Gdrbot, YurikBot, Hydrargyrum, Bota47, CLW, Јованъ6, West Virginian, Rkitko, Salvor, MalafayaBot, Igrant, Winston.PL, NessieVL, Carnby, BananaFiend, Ken Gallager, Beastie Bot, Cydebot, Chasingsol, Casliber, AntiVandalBot, Ericoides, Appraiser, CommonsDelinker, Colchicum, Idioma-bot, SieBot, Bagatelle, Sanya3, Deminimis, Easyskanking, Niceguyedc, Estirabot, Addbot, SamatBot, Lightbot, Luckas-bot, Yobot, Ptbotgourou, AnomieBOT, Vihermarja, Xqbot, GrouchoBot, SassoBot, Brutaldeluxe, Noder4, GreenZmiy, LucienBOT, Doremo, Jordalena11,

Gerarcalis, Micromesistius, RedBot, Lotje, Dinamik-bot, EmausBot, John of Reading, Look2See1, Maxim Gavrilyuk, ZéroBot, ChuispastonBot, Plantdrew, NotWith, BattyBot, Darorcilmir, Dexbot, Sminthopsis84, Корінь, ArmbrustBot, RhinoMind, Filedelinkerbot, Giovanni Caudullo, Djadjko, Македонец, Nina Lauridsen and Anonymous: 17

- **Pinus parviflora** *Source:* https://en.wikipedia.org/wiki/Pinus_parviflora?oldid=755186270 *Contributors:* Hadal, MPF, Abigail-II, Hesperian, Anthony Appleyard, Djlayton4, BDD, MZMcBride, Eubot, Kri, Chobot, Gdrbot, Hede2000, Gaius Cornelius, Ragesoss, CLW, Eskimbot, DHN-bot~enwiki, Dicklyon, Beastie Bot, Cydebot, Casliber, Quentar~enwiki, Reedy Bot, Colchicum, STBotD, Jaguarlaser, SieBot, De728631, Addbot, Luckas-bot, Yobot, KamikazeBot, Isablidine, Xqbot, LucienBOT, Tom.Reding, MastiBot, Lotje, EmausBot, ZéroBot, عمرو بن كلثوم, CopperSquare, Plantdrew, Darorcilmir, Ityoppyawit and Anonymous: 7

- **Pinus ponderosa** *Source:* https://en.wikipedia.org/wiki/Pinus_ponderosa?oldid=754684174 *Contributors:* Mav, William Avery, Nonenmac, Erik Zachte, Menchi, Hike395, Jengod, Rei, MPF, Abigail-II, Antandrus, Scott Burley, DanielZM, Neutrality, Karl Dickman, Flyhighplato, Famartin, Zscout370, Shanes, NetBot, Clyde frogg, Runner1928, Hesperian, Alansohn, Buaidh, BlueCanoe, Woohookitty, T34, BD2412, Rjwilmsi, FlaBot, Eubot, Gdrbot, Bgwhite, YurikBot, RussBot, NawlinWiki, Curtis Clark, Dysmorodrepanis~enwiki, TDogg310, Kmmontandon, Wsiegmund, Mmcannis, Edward Waverley, SmackBot, Benjaminb, Eskimbot, Jamidwyer, Bazonka, Kukini, Thor Dockweiler, Valfontis, JohnCub, Dicklyon, Dabean, Sasata, RCopple, Beastie Bot, Cydebot, Cs california, PamD, Casliber, Thijs!bot, Headbomb, West Brom 4ever, Seaphoto, Txomin, Esprqii, MartinBot, J.delanoy, Globbet, McSly, Colchicum, Woahtoster, Idioma-bot, Burlywood, A4bot, Rei-bot, Ltvine, Broadbot, Breawycker, Flyer22 Reborn, Oxymoron83, ClueBot, Botanybob, Niceguyedc, Rockfang, Ktr101, Alexbot, John Nevard, Hans-Jürgen Hübner, ThreeWikiteers, DumZiBoT, Yarxia, Avoided, Helloperson212, Addbot, Non-dropframe, Crazyticktockclock, Erutuon, First Light, Luckas-bot, Yobot, Librsh, Amirobot, Vibrantspirit, AnomieBOT, DemocraticLuntz, Rubinbot, Bigdoog, 90 Auto, Citation bot, Eumolpo, Plumpurple, Jeffrey Mall, Anna Frodesiak, Srich32977, Arthropod, Benny White, LucienBOT, Dger, Pinethicket, I dream of horses, Tom.Reding, RedBot, Impala2009, Serols, Cnwilliams, Moerasbabe, Casey Duke, Ecologygirl, EmausBot, Look2See1, Tommy2010, Dcirovic, Richard asr, ZéroBot, Retto12, Refinnejann, Jsayre64, L Kensington, Rying~enwiki, ClueBot NG, Frietjes, Widr, Plantdrew, BG19bot, Vagobot, Declangi, Frze, Shazen27, Davidmoneyharris, BattyBot, ArdathK, Darorcilmir, Khazar2, ILIKEjuicyTHINGS, Sminthopsis84, Howpper, Me, Myself, and I are Here, Sosthenes12, Hottuna080, TheNyleve, Avi8tor, Trixie05, Rundmt, RZCallaham, Robert Callaham, FloraWilde, BD2412bot, Christ cssb and Anonymous: 95

- **Pinus rigida** *Source:* https://en.wikipedia.org/wiki/Pinus_rigida?oldid=769738717 *Contributors:* Nonenmac, Reinhard Kraasch, Sjorford, Seglea, Hadal, MPF, Abigail-II, Antandrus, Famartin, Mwanner, Dejitarob, Hesperian, Anthony Appleyard, Schzmo, ErikHaugen, Eubot, Gdrbot, Ragesoss, Ben Lunsford, Bota47, Mmcannis, West Virginian, Eskimbot, Gjs238, Sasata, Beastie Bot, Cydebot, Thijs!bot, Ri st, Ripogenus77, MartinBot, Emeraude, CommonsDelinker, Colchicum, Antepenultimate, Idioma-bot, Speciate, Indubitably, Rei-bot, Jaguarlaser, SieBot, JerrySteal, ClueBot, Gabodon, Drawn Some, Berean Hunter, Happymercury, MystBot, Addbot, Ronkonkaman, LaaknorBot, Xtimgx, Luckas-bot, TaBOT-zerem, ArthurBot, GnawnBot, Hamamelis, Elisaulal, LucienBOT, I dream of horses, Tom.Reding, Trappist the monk, Protarchaeopteryx-chan, EmausBot, Look2See1, Wikipelli, ZéroBot, Rcsprinter123, ChuispastonBot, ClueBot NG, Jamo58, Plantdrew, BG19bot, Makecat-bot, ArmbrustBot, Nightphoenix90, Endriksohn, CameronVlogZ and Anonymous: 32

- **Pinus strobus** *Source:* https://en.wikipedia.org/wiki/Pinus_strobus?oldid=773979743 *Contributors:* Nonenmac, Hephaestos, Ram-Man, Edward, Ahoerstemeier, Big iron, Pollinator, Bearcat, Naddy, Russellkanning, Ianml, Thehappysmith, Alan Liefting, MPF, Abigail-II, Everyking, Dratman, Kenneth Alan, Xinoph, Sonjaaa, Quadell, Gene s, Karl-Henner, Sam Hocevar, Famartin, QuartierLatin1968, Amerika, Meggar, Hesperian, Sam Korn, Alansohn, Wiki-uk, Gene Nygaard, Epimethius, BlueCanoe, Stemonitis, Woohookitty, Tabletop, Bennetto, Schzmo, Banpei~enwiki, T34, GeorgeTheCar, BD2412, FreplySpang, Mendaliv, Quiddity, Funnyhat, FlaBot, Eubot, RobertG, Crazycomputers, Chobot, Gdrbot, YurikBot, Huw Powell, RussBot, Hede2000, Gaius Cornelius, Dysmorodrepanis~enwiki, LiniShu, Welsh, Anetode, Brian Crawford, Asarelah, Phgao, Ninly, Dspradau, Mmcannis, West Virginian, SmackBot, Brya, KnowledgeOfSelf, Hardyplants, Gjs238, Hmains, TimBentley, Fluri, Melburnian, Flyguy649, Ggpauly, EMU CPA, Carnby, Mgiganteus1, IronGargoyle, Camazine, Sasata, Civil Engineer III, DangerousPanda, CmdrObot, Ale jrb, Baskaufs, OMGsplosion, Ken Gallager, Beastie Bot, Cydebot, Gogo Dodo, Synergy, Vashx14, Casliber, Thijs!bot, Epbr123, Ufwuct, Bob the Wikipedian, Natalie Erin, AntiVandalBot, Seaphoto, Emeraldcityserendipity, Jj137, Kariteh, JAnDbot, Fetchcomms, Andonic, TAnthony, 7severn7, Magioladitis, VoABot II, GearedBull, Pvmoutside, Ogdude, MartinBot, Petter Bøckman, J.delanoy, Trusilver, Piercetheorganist, Uncle Dick, Katalaveno, Colchicum, Sprucefrost, Cmichael, Tevonic, Vkt183, Idioma-bot, VolkovBot, Tristan705, BrineStans, Vipinhari, Karmos, Disputantum, LimStift, MDfoo, Liz de Quebec, Jaguarlaser, Ceranthor, Arjun024, Dawn Bard, Keilana, Happysailor, Neutralhomer, Redmarkviolinist, Ii386, ClueBot, Me5000, Cygnis insignis, R000t, I.i.mee, Gabodon, Excirial, Jusdafax, Yue Kudasaki, Erebus Morgaine, 7&6=thirteen, DonCBragg, SchreiberBike, Tgnil, Berean Hunter, Chhe, Boleyn, Wikiuser100, Dthomsen8, Skarebo, MystBot, Thatguyflint, Addbot, Pyfan, Ronhjones, Fieldday-sunday, CarTick, Erutuon, Tide rolls, GNews4BadTimes, Lightbot, Luckas-bot, Yobot, Ptbotgourou, Synchronism, AnomieBOT, AdjustShift, Kingpin13, Knowledgekid87, Nhfan367, Frankenpuppy, Gsmgm, Xqbot, JimVC3, RadiX, Crockermud, Samwb123, Elisaulal, FrescoBot, LucienBOT, Dger, DigbyDalton, Pinethicket, I dream of horses, Tom.Reding, A8UDI, Serols, FoxBot, Dinamik-bot, Reaper Eternal, Winteam, DARTH SIDIOUS 2, Whisky drinker, Noommos, Ecologygirl, EmausBot, Look2See1, Illogicalpie, Dcirovic, K6ka, ZéroBot, Fæ, Josve05a, Jshutton, Alpha Quadrant (alt), TyA, Macy184, Mappetop, ClueBot NG, Widr, Vibhijain, KLBot2, Plantdrew, BG19bot, MusikAnimal, ChrisGualtieri, AK456, Colo-Nesco, Sminthopsis84, Rich Monde, ChakaKong, ArmbrustBot, Nightphoenix90, Zenibus, Markbellis, Lenbehr, Prestinius, GoldCoastPrior, Chanteurdubois, JJMC89 bot, Jeanette2016, Nina Lauridsen, Tompop888 and Anonymous: 231

- **Pinus thunbergii** *Source:* https://en.wikipedia.org/wiki/Pinus_thunbergii?oldid=763828945 *Contributors:* MPF, Geographer, Woohookitty, EncycloPetey, Greg5030, Gurdjieff, SieBot, Kanguole, MystBot, Addbot, Flakinho, Luckas-bot, Yobot, AnomieBOT, Xqbot, FrescoBot, LucienBOT, Tom.Reding, Andrew69., EmausBot, ZéroBot, Plantdrew, BG19bot, AvocatoBot, Pseudo75, Enrico-lalla, Ityoppyawit and Anonymous: 3

- **Pinus virginiana** *Source:* https://en.wikipedia.org/wiki/Pinus_virginiana?oldid=768818513 *Contributors:* Nonenmac, Ram-Man, Radiojon, Smallweed, Hadal, UtherSRG, MPF, Abigail-II, Famartin, Hesperian, Anthony Appleyard, NovaEn, Sciurinæ, Gene Nygaard, Mazca, Schzmo, BD2412, Eubot, Nihiltres, Gdrbot, Ragesoss, Mmcannis, West Virginian, Dicklyon, Sasata, Baskaufs, Beastie Bot, Cydebot, Casliber, Altairisfar, Coppertwig, Colchicum, Tomer T, Mwilso24, ClueBot, Ideal gas equation, Berean Hunter, Addbot, Flakinho, Yobot, AnomieBOT, Eli17zn6, LilHelpa, Xqbot, LucienBOT, Amplitude101, Pinethicket, Tom.Reding, Spals11, EmausBot, Look2See1, Dcirovic, Jamo58, BG19bot, Nightphoenix90, AndreBerry, Isoetid, Rmccann15 and Anonymous: 18

4.1. TEXT

- **Podocarpus costalis** *Source:* https://en.wikipedia.org/wiki/Podocarpus_costalis?oldid=751291501 *Contributors:* Hesperian, Eubot, Alaibot, Rei-bot, BotanyBot, Polbot, TubularWorld, Addbot, Flakinho, Pc1878, EmausBot, Themodoccypress, George Ponderevo, Ruff tuff cream puff, TLT2232 and Anonymous: 2

- **Podocarpus latifolius** *Source:* https://en.wikipedia.org/wiki/Podocarpus_latifolius?oldid=748125093 *Contributors:* William Avery, Olivier, Ahoerstemeier, Angela, Rbraunwa, Alan Liefting, MPF, Tom Radulovich, Yath, Rich Farmbrough, Hesperian, Ricardo Carneiro Pires, FlaBot, Eubot, Gdrbot, Htonl, CLW, Bejnar, JMK, Kaarel, Epistemos, Neelix, Beastie Bot, Kyle the bot, MariusHR, Jaguarlaser, Yintan, Arnobarnard, Pgallert, Flakinho, Zorrobot, Legobot, Luckas-bot, FrescoBot, Andynct, Tom.Reding, Minimac, Abu Shawka, Rcsprinter123, ClueBot NG, MelbourneStar, Sunmist, CAPTAIN RAJU, QianCheng, Jimmy bro and Anonymous: 13

- **Pomegranate** *Source:* https://en.wikipedia.org/wiki/Pomegranate?oldid=774778944 *Contributors:* Jeronimo, Fcueto, Enchanter, Karen Johnson, William Avery, Zadcat, Montrealais, Bernfarr, Edward, Ubiquity, Llywrch, Skysmith, Ihcoyc, Ellywa, Mdebets, Ahoerstemeier, Ronz, Jadepearl, Jdforrester, Marteau, Error, Andres, Charles Matthews, Greenrd, Tpbradbury, Morwen, Karukera, Renke, Wetman, Gakrivas, Secretlondon, Eugene van der Pijll, Carlossuarez46, Robbot, Moriori, PBS, Chris 73, WormRunner, Nurg, Naddy, SchmuckyTheCat, Janos~enwiki, Hadal, Huckfinne, Fuelbottle, Jleedev, Jooler, Davidcannon, Giftlite, Dbenbenn, MPF, Martijn faassen, Jacob1207, Jfdwolff, Jorge Stolfi, Solipsist, Dash, Golbez, SoWhy, Andycjp, J. 'mach' wust, Yath, Antandrus, Mustafaa, JoJan, MisfitToys, Kaldari, Vina, Alex Cohn, CaribDigita, Rdsmith4, LHOON, Neutrality, Marcus2, Burschik, Okapi~enwiki, Joyous!, Neale Monks, Adashiel, Heegoop, Slady, DanielCD, EugeneZelenko, Discospinster, Rich Farmbrough, Emahyar, Hydrox, Parishan, Wk muriithi, Ahkond, Mani1, Tsujigiri~enwiki, Bender235, Martinman11, Furius, Brian0918, TOR, CanisRufus, Pjf, El C, Kwamikagami, Cacophony, Etz Haim, Bobo192, Fir0002, Sentience, Smalljim, Arcadian, Palmiro, Toh, NickSchweitzer, RaffiKojian, Pschemp, Hesperian, Pearle, Nsaa, Orangemarlin, Alansohn, Imfa1lingup, Ibn zareena, Joolz, Rd232, Intelligence3, Typhlosion, Spangineer, Malo, Shinjiman, Wtmitchell, Here, Pauli133, WayneMokane, Crosbiesmith, Abanima, Feezo, Stemonitis, Velho, Alvis, Woohookitty, 2004-12-29T22:45Z, RHaworth, Camw, Michaelkvance, WadeSimMiser, Jeff3000, MrDarcy, DonIncognito, Mb1000, TheAlphaWolf, とある白い猫, Marudubshinki, Emerson7, Graham87, BD2412, Amir85, Jorunn, Rjwilmsi, Londonbroil, ABot, Landon9720, SummitWulf, Sasanjan, Alhutch, Choess, Maltmomma, Lemmikkipuu, Le Anh-Huy, JM.Beaubourg, King of Hearts, Chobot, Drvgaikwad, PKM, Gdrbot, Bgwhite, Phantom Thief, WriterHound, Cornellrockey, Roboto de Ajvol, Andel, YurikBot, Paffka, Butsuri, Brandmeister (old), RussBot, Icarus3, Conscious, AVM, Eupator, CanadianCaesar, Hellbus, Stephenb, Gaius Cornelius, Cryptic, Anomalocaris, Dforest, Badagnani, TDogg310, Larsobrien, Kortoso, Bota47, IceCreamAntisocial, Creases, 2over0, Closedmouth, Mastercampbell, Rlove, Fram, Mursel, RunOrDie, Katieh5584, NeilN, Paul Erik, Patiwat, 8472, Nenamldu, Picardk, Phinnaeus, SmackBot, WilliamThweatt, AdamBlack, Kunalarya, Alyahyai, Melchoir, McGeddon, C.Fred, Loukinho, Ifnord, Eskimbot, Mgreenbe, Kintetsubuffalo, Edgar181, Gilliam, Ohnoitsjamie, Hmains, JAn Dudík, Durova, Chris the speller, Keegan, Rkitko, RDBrown, SweetP112, Jon513, Salvor, Deli nk, Anna05, Ralhazzaa~enwiki, Fk5k, Funper, Ted87, Spydermonkie, Talmage, KaiserbBot, Xiner, VMS Mosaic, Pnkrockr, Whpq, Abrahami, Magemirlen, Aldaron, Emre D., Cybercobra, Decltype, FiveRings, Nakon, MichaelBillington, Blake-, Andrew c, Zzorse, Leatherbear, Where, Vina-iwbot~enwiki, Mitsuki152, SashatoBot, Quendus, Ju98 5, MrDarwin, Kuru, Akendall, John, Rikardo gs~enwiki, BurningAfterTheDawn, Sir Nicholas de Mimsy-Porpington, Mgiganteus1, MkhitarSparapet, Alatius, Mallaccaos, Maksim L., Mets501, Neddyseagoon, Kiamlaluno, Pinkfloyd95209, Sasata, Koweja, Kevin W., Ginkgo100, Woodroar, Iridescent, Kencf0618, SriniG, Blehfu, Phoenixrod, Trialsanderrors, Gilabrand, Danlev, Tau'olunga, Kaze0010, TuckJ, Declic~enwiki, Dycedarg, Lavateraguy, BeenAroundAWhile, Nunquam Dormio, Sbn1984, Dgw, Myocastor, Slazenger, Cydebot, Hugeaux, DDugan, Phildm, Alvesgaspar, Chasingsol, Allpomegranate, HitroMilanese, Boplicity, Nsaum75, After Midnight, Omicronpersei8, Casliber, Thijs!bot, Epbr123, Barticus88, Biruitorul, Pstanton, Tkay, Blah3, Hugo.arg, Marek69, Tapir Terrific, Kborer, Dfrg.msc, Escarbot, Lawrenceraday, AntiVandalBot, The Obento Musubi, Fedayee, POM123, SummerPhD, Paul144, Myanw, Dfitzgerald, JAnDbot, Deflective, Husond, Demonkey36, ElComandanteChe, Plantsurfer, Avaya1, H3llbringer, Rajaramjana, PhilKnight, Y2kcrazyjoker4, .anacondabot, Magioladitis, YAM, Bongwarrior, VoABot II, Rhadamante, Englishmajor07, Froid, SwiftBot, Animum, Soulwar, Boffob, Styrofoam1994, MoralDecay, Bodox, Vssun, DerHexer, Philg88, WLU, Tapioca Dextrin, Vishvax, Peter coxhead, Seba5618, AliaGemma, Gjd001, Dcpirahna, B9 hummingbird hovering, EtienneDolet, Flowanda, Jerem43, Makalp, MartinBot, Vicpeters, AciSpades, R'n'B, CommonsDelinker, Nono64, Artaxiad, Huzzlet the bot, Etaicq, J.delanoy, Kosaran, DrKay, Trusilver, PRTkand, Bogey97, Oguz1, Nigholith, Athaenara, Cheeriokole, Sahdaquist, Morsels, Eskimospy, Acalamari, Rumpuscat, Miltonkeynes, Quialiss, Toosmoothgeo, Vanished User 4517, Richard D. LeCour, JSellers0, Sonabona, Elchin.az, Nadiatalent, Naturalscience, Pilisopa, Joshua Issac, STBotD, RB972, Tiggerjay, Sachinbhinge, Misha-Pan, TheNewPhobia, SoCalSuperEagle, Steel1943, Idioma-bot, Funandtrvl, Burlywood, Alradiox, X!, Ktkrysnskull, Caspian blue, 28bytes, XxNerdyDudexX, Kentmoraga, VolkovBot, Off-shell, Thedjatclubrock, Murderbike, AlnoktaBOT, Chango369w, Philip Trueman, TXiKiBoT, Oshwah, Rocketmagnet, Zidonuke, Hameryko, ClaireLaMarr, Kaktus999, Spleefmistress, Atabəy, Ann Stouter, Avdav, Captain Wikify, VartanM, Anna Lincoln, Melsaran, Martin451, Iheartlawyers, LeaveSleaves, Guest9999, Incremental Improvements, Solopiano, MearsMan, Butterscotch, Eubulides, Metzby, Synthebot, Jc iindyysgvxc, Falcon8765, Thanatos666, Why Not A Duck, Oyosef, AlleborgoBot, Road pancake, Kehrbykid, ZBrannigan, Scottywong, Demize, Edison9114, SieBot, Sonicology, Calliopejen1, EmilValdez, YourEyesOnly, Fullerenedream, SE7, Ashkani, Tataryn, Til Eulenspiegel, Flyer22 Reborn, Alexbrn, Jojalozzo, Big ossan, Prestonmag, Steven Crossin, Brice one, Mcbill88, Iknowyourider, Philly jawn, Vaedonz, X BSC x, Aiden p1, Denisarona, Vonones, Floodamanny, Amazonien, Ocdcntx, Martuni, Soph983, Nikuda, ClueBot, Badger Drink, Kafka Liz, TinyMark, Rivkystern, Wysprgr2005, Drmies, Mild Bill Hiccup, Malikbek, Boing! said Zebedee, Lamalo, Jimmy Hammerfist, DragonBot, Cabin Member, CrazyChemGuy, Katyenka99, Sundru, Lartoven, AZatBot~enwiki, NuclearWarfare, Bu mbarak, Muro Bot, Prof tpms, Rui Gabriel Correia, Thingg, MadDog1842, Rainbowsunshine86, SoxBot III, SherAbdul8, Editor2020, Evansad, DumZiBoT, Samichael95, XLinkBot, Kurdo777, AlexGWU, Namsos, Marschner, Little Mountain 5, Avoided, Zombie j, MystBot, Menthaxpiperita, Yes.aravind, Xommana, Addbot, ArticunoZapdosMoltres, Gabor.csorba, Umitiris, DOI bot, Szazaian, Ronhjones, Tutter-Mouse, Smarter1, Leszek Jańczuk, Ocedits, 007bistromath, Trevor Marron, John Chamberlain, Zasuwa, Download, Scarplark, PranksterTurtle, Glane23, Chzz, Debresser, Ks 7508, Nizil Shah, Tassedethe, Erutuon, Tide rolls, Lightbot, Nguyễn Thanh Quang, Mirza Barlas, Galloping Ghost U of I, Jcon1917, Ninetoyadome, CountryBot, Kozlov36, Cjabingham1973, Alfie66, Pomegranatebanana, Legobot, Aquamelli, GaiusGCaligula, Luckas-bot, Yobot, Ptbotgourou, Fraggle81, TaBOT-zerem, Hisgirlthursday, II MusLiM HyBRiD II, Guy1890, Ajh16, KeelNar, KamikazeBot, Plantscientist, AnomieBOT, Iamatom, Piano non troppo, Xufanc, Golb12, BobKilcoyne, Tatsundo h, NickK, CreativeSoul7981, Materialscientist, Hunnjazal, Citation bot, Pomeapplepome, Nrherron, OllieFury, I-rok-181, Bob Burkhardt, Odd Sound, Parthian Scribe, Xqbot, Historicist, Capricorn42, Gigemag76, Mspecial, Xashaiar, Toprewolf Tepmirk, Zefr, Bellerophon, White whirlwind, Marzedu, Verbum Veritas, Noder4, Griffinofwales, Mescalmarlowe, Nenya17, Prari, FrescoBot, Gky, Pouletic, Love2bird, Tekmeme, Thomasbbd194, Redbmk, Armenian King, M2545, Saulj42, Jnthn0898, Citation bot 1, Krish Dulal, Plantmeister, Pinethicket, LittleWink, Pzrmd, Jonesey95, Rastaman3000, A8UDI, Serols, HarshAJ, Reconsider the static, Kgrad, Trappist the monk, Zag1024, Fama Clamosa, Lotje, Gegik, Mandigirl313, Alborztv, Zvn, Extra999, Juybari, Cimorghe, Shimlalion, Diannaa, Tbhotch, Leeb106, The Utahraptor, RjwilmsiBot, Beyond My Ken, WildBot, Orphan Wiki, Immunize, Gfoley4, Look2See1, IncognitoErgoSum, RA0808, RenamedUser01302013, ZxxZxxZ, Anne the webkinz, Slightsmile, Dcirovic, K6ka, Catinhat95, Juky27, Comesturnruler, PBS-AWB, 4blossoms, Smelly1111, Tadpolesdeservetodie, Wayne Slam, Erianna, Jadraad, Jacobisq, L Kensington, Gator26, Donner60, Simeonhb, Diako1971, رو عم بن كل شوم, Michael Bailes, Sankarshansen, Motamot, LM2000, ClueBot NG, יהז, Molestash, Blarghyblargh, Globulenoire, RodrigoVVSousa, Satellizer, Movses-bot, Dikran.Kayfian, Cntras, Castncoot, Kasir, Costesseyboy, Widr, GlassLadyBug, Gunther26, Helpful Pixie Bot, Wbm1058, Aljlasefhkadshf, Pomegranatehealthbenefits, BG19bot, Kempf EK, Tiksn, M0rphzone, SSDPenguin, Brokz122, Umais Bin Sajjad, Shehroze khan, G.Raghav, Davidiad, Kagundu, Jahnavisatyan, DrPhen, Silvrous, AlexOlsen, Hesamghorbani, Zakamutt, Kukac, Fawwyb, 7noahsark, Writ Keeper, Panthayi, Snow Blizzard, NotWith, Granateple, Alireza 80, Imaadwhd, Harpieladyfan, Reemlb, Gotovikas, Evenflowmb, Candipopswasmyideafirst, AntanO, Connormanable, Jazmonik, جواد, BattyBot, Nocturnal781, Darorcilmir, Jeanloujustine, Birchhale, BenjaminBarrett12, JYBot, Stoneglasgow, E4024, Dexbot, Sminthopsis84, Webclient101, JohnVScott, TwoTwoHello, KWiki, Frosty, Bernadi, Wieldthespade, Noda1212, Farhadfarhangfar, RotlinkBot, Rheetuz, Aftabbanoori, Epicgenius, Thechickenontheroof, Katie7248, Michael!, Wikidamo, GinaJay, Melonkelon, Backgammon11, Horst59, Jakec, Wuerzele, Azaz.sayyad, Quranreading1, Firstchoice2similar, PLEASEGODHELPME, Varadaan, LouisAragon, Dingo101, Caitlinthough, NottNott, Gihan Jayaweera, Machho, Archlinux, Liquid poopie, Anush137, Stamptrader, Snowsuit Wearer, Bellus Delphina, Bnsmurthy, Nersesh, AmarantaEntertainment, Onuphriate, Arzashkun, Monkbot, Nestwiki, Wilmerdon, Steverci, Coo coo pigeon, MuseumGeek, MortalPayday, Sanskari, Falseinformationadder, Anupama.sheel, DangerousJXD, Krzyhorse22, Sholland123, FourViolas, Merp the unicorn, Haknguyen, Ligaga91, Blacknclick, Govindaharihari, JChecton, Sarr Cat, Mediavalia, ScrapIronIV, Jel49spa, Ted Gruen, Agulani, Jas.runningknight, Sro23, Tropicalkitty, ProgrammingGeek, WikiMaster 01, Imawikipediauser, Yallbetterwoke, 43jiyiy5, GreenC bot, Pacheco Torgal, Nagendra405, The Cynic Diogenes, UserDe, Jessesm28, Bukti.khan, Jujukrause, Iamaplayer33, Ksoheil, Sah7861, Glorkvorn and Anonymous: 1153

- **Portulacaria afra** *Source:* https://en.wikipedia.org/wiki/Portulacaria_afra?oldid=741982439 *Contributors:* Stemonitis, Rjwilmsi, Rsrikanth05, Apokryltaros, RJBaran, Dcruz01, Paul venter, Oosh, Keith D, Dodger67, Addbot, Ka Faraq Gatri, Xqbot, Drakenwolf, WikitanvirBot, Look2See1, ZéroBot, Abu Shawka, Wayne Slam, ClueBot NG, Philmarin, BG19bot, AvocatoBot, KH-1, Sarr Cat and Anonymous: 8

- **Portulacaria pygmaea** *Source:* https://en.wikipedia.org/wiki/Portulacaria_pygmaea?oldid=713452322 *Contributors:* Look2See1, Abu Shawka, Sarr Cat and Anonymous: 1

- **Prunus serrulata** *Source:* https://en.wikipedia.org/wiki/Prunus_serrulata?oldid=764848619 *Contributors:* William Avery, Bogdangiusca, Imc, SEWilco, PuzzletChung, Pigsonthewing, Chris 73, MPF, Sonjaaa, JoJan, Famartin, DanielCD, Plugwash, Sten, PiccoloNamek, Djlayton4, FlaBot, Eubot, ChongDae, Petrvs~enwiki, Chobot, Gdrbot, YurikBot, Gaius Cornelius, Myrabella, Melchoir, Eskimbot, Elk Salmon, Yamaguchi 先生, Cs-wolves, Melburnian, Abrahami, Thor Dockweiler, Kevmin, Kaarel, Casliber, NorwegianBlue, Escarbot, Merumerume, Peter coxhead, Shack, Nadiatalent, Prot D, Mdvaden, Jaguarlaser, Galamazoo12, BotMultichill, Oda Mari, Seedbot, Carlsbat, Chhe, Addbot, Captaintucker, First Light, Mps, KamikazeBot, Xufanc, Xqbot, Hamamelis, Abductive, RedBot, Lotje, EmausBot, Look2See1, ClueBot NG, MerlIwBot, Jean-Pol GRANDMONT, Curb Chain, Plantdrew, Ahora, Samuelbirkett, JWNoctis, Trixie05 and Anonymous: 20

- **Pseudocydonia** *Source:* https://en.wikipedia.org/wiki/Pseudocydonia?oldid=750972549 *Contributors:* Alan Liefting, MPF, Rjwilmsi, Ricardo Carneiro Pires, Eubot, Gdrbot, YurikBot, Badagnani, Apokryltaros, Rkitko, Abrahami, Gurdjieff, Kevmin, Stefan2, Cydebot, Mmcknight4, Paris1127, Nadiatalent, Caspian blue, VolkovBot, Tusbra, Jaguarlaser, Mycomp, Allmightyduck, No such user, Alexbot, Sasurai-bito, LarryMorseDCOhio, Addbot, Flakinho, Citation bot, Pomeapplepome, FrescoBot, Canyq, WikitanvirBot, Dcirovic, Plantdrew, NotWith, Slowlikemolasses, V Ryabish and Anonymous: 13

- **Quince** *Source:* https://en.wikipedia.org/wiki/Quince?oldid=774629796 *Contributors:* Tarquin, Rmhermen, William Avery, Heron, Hephaestos, Zeno Gantner, Stan Shebs, Jengod, Bemoeial, Dysprosia, Tpbradbury, Imc, Karukera, AnonMoos, Wetman, David.Monniaux, Pollinator, Owen, PuzzletChung, Gromlakh, Astronautics~enwiki, RedWolf, WormRunner, Altenmann, Mjgw, PedroPVZ, Ddstretch, Kent Wang, Srtxg, MPF, Emrys2, Kpalion, Gugganij, Quite, Ebear422, Antandrus, JoJan, Khaosworks, OwenBlacker, Marcus2, Oknazevad, Il hamster, Mike Rosoft, Boy in the bands, DanielCD, Rich Farmbrough, Mani1, Mwng, Syp, CanisRufus, Kwamikagami, Bobo192, Circeus, Fir0002, Nk, Hajenso, Idleguy, Bigtrick, Alansohn, Anthony Appleyard, Eleuthero, Keenan Pepper, Inky, Andrew Gray, Pwqn, Iustinus, Kazvorpal, Dismas, Ron Ritzman, Will-h, Richard Barlow, Jeff3000, TotoBaggins, JediKnyghte, Gillj, Rjwilmsi, Coemgenus, Lzz, Margosbot~enwiki, Nihiltres, Wgfcrafty, Lemmikkipuu, Gdrbot, WriterHound, Roboto de Ajvol, YurikBot, Wavelength, SkyCaptain~enwiki, Waitak, Garglebutt, Eupator, Hydrargyrum, Cryptic, Stassats, Tavilis, RattleMan, Badagnani, Apokryltaros, Rmky87, E rulez, Elizabeyth, Sotakeit, Bondegezou, DGaw, Fpenteado, ABehrens, SmackBot, Pwt898, Lapis, Melchoir, Yamaplos, Adammathias, Kintetsubuffalo, Yamaguchi 先生, Peter Isotalo, Anwar saadat, Cgoodwin, Brett.feldon, Rkitko, Deli nk, Nbarth, Can't sleep, clown will eat me, Msophelia, Esculapio, JonHarder, PiMaster3, Bigturtle, Kfasimpaur, Bdiscoe, Lambiam, BigDom, JzG, Žiga, Kevmin, Shlomke, Lisapollison, Beetstra, Jgrahn, MTSbot~enwiki, Nonpareil, Taran Wanderer, Saltlakejohn, Falconus, RCopple, SaintCahier, Neelix, Cydebot, Mjmarcus, Gogo Dodo, Devanatha, Daniel J. Leivick, Casliber, BetacommandBot, Barticus88, GentlemanGhost, Sobreira, Escarbot, AntiVandalBot, M.W.A., Gioto, Fayenatic london, Golf Bravo, Skyjs, Storkk, JAnDbot, Deflective, MER-C, Plantsurfer, Andonic, Ishikawaluvr, Ibrahim, Rothorpe, Dentren, Brashear, Matthias Blume, Ali 27, NatureA16, LiverpoolCommander, Ugajin, Burnedthru, CommonsDelinker, Gold-Horn, Wlodzimierz, Uncle Dick, Acalamari, Mikael Häggström, Nadiatalent, Cometstyles, Jlc999, Jacques23, VolkovBot, Macedonian, Jeff G., Chango369w, TXiKiBoT, March1291, Tusbra, LeaveSleaves, Mezzaluna, Maxim, Mazarin07, Hakanai, SkyViewOrphanage, SieBot, Tresiden, SuzanneIAM, Nummer29, Oblare90, Oda Mari, Oxymoron83, Yassertariq, DazMonroe, XagaEnergon, Akasolidus, Capitalismojo, Fangjian, Locaracle, Sfan00 IMG, ClueBot, Arakunem, Drmies, Mild Bill Hiccup, Niceguyedc, DifferCake, Rotational, Gordon Ecker, No such user, Gnome de plume, Advaughan, Khthelegend, AlexGWU, UGAdawg52, Rreagan007, Tkech, NebraskaDontAsk, Reporein, Laduqesa, Addbot, Willking1979, No essential nature, Tanhabot, Delfman, MrOllie, Colcas42, CarsracBot, Nickin, Xinos644, Ddrmaniac300, Tide rolls, Lightbot, Gkania, Willondon, Ben Ben, Pointer1, Luckasbot, Yobot, KamikazeBot, AnomieBOT, DemocraticLuntz, OpenFuture, Escarnafuncho, Materialscientist, Pomeapplepome, Bob Burkhardt, أحمد.غامدي24, ARAGONESE35, Xqbot, Mlevitt1, Skribunto, GrouchoBot, Omnipaedista, Croq, Basharh, LSG1-Bot, FrescoBot, Milimetr88, OgreBot, DrilBot, Pinethicket, Jusses2, Akunju, TobeBot, SeoMac, Miracle Pen, Mean as custard, EmausBot, Orphan Wiki, Sophie, Zollerriia, BaseballPie, PBS-AWB, Erianna, Rcsprinter123, L Kensington, Donner60, Michael Bailes, ClueBot NG, Wingtipvortex, Masssly, Helpful Pixie Bot, Vertevero, Mwells790, Mangee71, Plantdrew, AvocatoBot, Steak740, 86.** IP, Nbahaji, -quincey.v-, Aisteco, Darorcilmir, ZappaOMati, Mogism, AldezB, Amirs318, FruitGrower, Beezle24, 555Filk, Wuerzele, Soham, Avicenna Fellows, Khemzacek, Avi8tor, ReconditeRodent, Summergirl97, JeffingGood, BrayLockBoy, Lottiey, Godsentmb, Milanovicnenad, Swidran, Mndata, Julietdeltalima, Wanjabezdomnij, KasparBot, Nyxnax, InternetArchiveBot, GreenC bot, Bender the Bot and Anonymous: 312

4.1. TEXT

- **Rapanea melanophloeos** *Source:* https://en.wikipedia.org/wiki/Rapanea_melanophloeos?oldid=684982163 *Contributors:* Tom Radulovich, Choess, IceCreamAntisocial, Fram, Paul venter, Peter coxhead, Addbot, TjBot, Look2See1, Abu Shawka, RaqiwasSushi, Raymond Ellis and Anonymous: 5

- **Rhaphiolepis indica** *Source:* https://en.wikipedia.org/wiki/Rhaphiolepis_indica?oldid=751049470 *Contributors:* Smallweed, Quadell, Geographer, HenryLi, Eubot, SmackBot, Kevmin, Casliber, Erechtheus, Nadiatalent, Addbot, Flakinho, First Light, Farsight001, Pomeapplepome, Simuliid, EmausBot, Dcirovic, ZéroBot, ClueBot NG, Gareth Griffith-Jones, Plantdrew, Sminthopsis84 and Anonymous: 5

- **Robinia pseudoacacia** *Source:* https://en.wikipedia.org/wiki/Robinia_pseudoacacia?oldid=761899512 *Contributors:* Nonenmac, Jaknouse, Michael Hardy, Mkweise, Wik, Franz Xaver, Maximus Rex, Imc, SEWilco, Rei, J D, Finlay McWalter, Pollinator, Hadal, UtherSRG, Lady Tenar, DocWatson42, MPF, JoJan, PDH, Famartin, DanielCD, Bri, Guanabot, Tsho~enwiki, Vsmith, Duk, Drat, Shoefly, Adrian.benko, Stemonitis, Gmaxwell, Jean-Pol Grandmont, GregorB, Ketiltrout, Rjwilmsi, Eoghanacht, Ricardo Carneiro Pires, Vuong Ngan Ha, FlaBot, Eubot, Chobot, Gdrbot, Bgwhite, YurikBot, RussBot, Stephenb, Emmanuelm, Emijrp, Јованв6, Colin, Anclation~enwiki, ArielGold, NiTenIchiRyu, West Virginian, SmackBot, Cubs Fan, Eventer, Rkitko, Ron E, DHN-bot~enwiki, Coffee and TV, Jóna Þórunn, MrDarwin, Ktinga, Iridescent, Paul venter, CmdrObot, Tarchon, Baskaufs, Cydebot, Casliber, PoolDoc, Thijs!bot, Zupez zeta, JAnDbot, Altairisfar, Krasanen, Zorro CX, Catgut, Peter coxhead, Grandia01, Gidip, Vox Rationis, Nono64, J.delanoy, Adavidb, Tokyogirl79, Chiswick Chap, CardinalDan, Idioma-bot, Jmrowland, Rdnckj258, TXiKiBoT, Vyssotsky, Jaguarlaser, Struway, HelloMojo, Caltas, MaxFrear, Theologyguy, IvanTortuga, Fangjian, ClueBot, Rustic, Myokobill, Soaringbear, Otolemur crassicaudatus, Stevieray7b7, Psinu, Berean Hunter, The wranger rubicon, BodhisattvaBot, SilvonenBot, Addbot, Mortense, Fyrael, Ronkonkaman, AndersBot, Erutuon, Lightbot, Bff, Yobot, Ptbotgourou, Adam Hauner, Ulric1313, Materialscientist, Citation bot, ArthurBot, Obersachsebot, MauritsBot, GrouchoBot, Dzsi, RibotBOT, Brambleshire, Forstbirdo, Marmeladă, FrescoBot, Dger, Rosabell is me, Pinethicket, Hortiphile, Supernovagluon, Rob.HUN, Orenburg1, FoxBot, TjBot, DRAGON BOOSTER, Androstachys, EmausBot, John of Reading, Look2See1, Peterusso, ZéroBot, Jimmypader, Donner60, Dlwiii3, ClueBot NG, MerlIwBot, Rougenord, Plantdrew, BG19bot, Tekwani, Joydeep, Mehrajmir13, Scotstout, BattyBot, EuroCarGT, Dexbot, Robinia 1978, ArmbrustBot, Nightphoenix90, Mandruss, Popsie b, FungusBrew, Impuls666666, RenéeV, HoHey22, Xylowal, KasparBot, Martin Peter Clarke, Wasp32, Bender the Bot, Nina Lauridsen and Anonymous: 102

- **Rosemary** *Source:* https://en.wikipedia.org/wiki/Rosemary?oldid=774964528 *Contributors:* Tobias Hoevekamp, Marj Tiefert, Brion VIBBER, Josh Grosse, Perique des Palottes, Ewen, Liftarn, Menchi, Pagingmrherman, Keichwa, Ahoerstemeier, Stan Shebs, Ronz, Tpbradbury, Imc, Raul654, Pollinator, Jni, WormRunner, Seglea, Babbage, Rfc1394, Ojigiri~enwiki, DocWatson42, MPF, Orpheus, Patrick-br, Jfdwolff, Ryanaxp, Espetkov, Quadell, Williamb, JoJan, Eregli bob, Sam Hocevar, Iantresman, Joyous!, AliveFreeHappy, Shipmaster, Rich Farmbrough, Cacycle, Mani1, Martpol, Paul August, Bender235, Plugwash, CanisRufus, Bobo192, Circeus, Fir0002, Shenme, SpeedyGonsales, Man vyi, Hesperian, Conny, Jumbuck, Schissel, Alansohn, Hugowolf, Retran, DrGaellon, RyanGerbil10, Youngster68, Stemonitis, Richard Arthur Norton (1958-), Alvis, Woohookitty, Camw, LOL, SP-KP, Taragui, Graham87, Rjwilmsi, Strake, Loniceas, Darguz Parsilvan, Heah, Panterka, FlaBot, Celestianpower, RexNL, Gurch, Andham2000, CJLL Wright, Chobot, Gdrbot, WriterHound, NoAccount, Sceptre, NTBot~enwiki, RussBot, Hydrargyrum, Dotancohen, Wimt, Anomalocaris, Alynna Kasmira, ColonelKasatka, NawlinWiki, Seegoon, Rwalker, FF2010, 2over0, Extraordinary, Colin, LeonardoRob0t, RenamedUser jaskldjslak904, GrinBot~enwiki, SmackBot, Basmati~enwiki, Amcbride, Mangoe, Malkinann, McGeddon, Blue520, KocjoBot~enwiki, Edgar181, Francisco Valverde, Zephyris, Gilliam, Hmains, Skizzik, Rorybowman, Deli nk, Gruzd, Rrburke, VMS Mosaic, Abrahami, Noles1984, Richard001, AThing, U-571, Beetstra, Levineps, Mikael V, Tmangray, Cherry32, Sue in az, Gveret Tered, Markjoseph125, Cydebot, Kairotic, Jac4b, Octopod, Heroeswithmetaphors, Dikteren, Ericjs, Kanadano, Seaphoto, Amarto, Quintote, Tillman, Aelwyn, Ki4gmb, Gökhan, JAnDbot, MER-C, ElComandanteChe, JDrage, Kongurous, Magioladitis, Strangepalefighter, VoABot II, SladeMcGowan, JNW, Mcamorran, Ryan the rocket ship, Robby, Doug Coldwell, Prestonmcconkie, Catgut, Infiniteseries, ZackTheJack, Bill.matthews, Halogenated, Not telling, Peter coxhead, Jerem43, Grandia01, Yenisey, Roastytoast, Dlents, J.delanoy, Catmoongirl, Rhinestone K, Acalamari, McSly, Colchicum, NewEnglandYankee, MKoltnow, Nadiatalent, KylieTastic, Idioma-bot, VolkovBot, ABF, Jmrowland, Philip Trueman, Utgard Loki, Joe2832, Nitin77, Jestert9016, Monkey Bounce, Retiono Virginian, Sintaku, Peterbullockismyname, Delbert Grady, Saturn star, Tranquilidy, Spicedoctor, Cfp0608, Lokioak, Doc James, Vinayaraj, SieBot, MZ Lauren 120, Dawn Bard, Bestsugarweasel, Oolongy, Alexbrn, Brice one, StaticGull, BackToThePast, Lascorz, Tatterfly, ClueBot, Me5000, Incrediblehunk, Gor n bein, Sushilover boy, Joustin, Blanchardb, Mslice987, Kitsunegami, Excirial, Jusdafax, NathanWalther, Lartoven, Sun Creator, Razorflame, Bridgetsgirl, Dalyla, Berean Hunter, Humanisticmystic, Theking2, DumZiBoT, Alastar, Rilmadar, Ldbio130, XLinkBot, Rozenlime, Addbot, Frizzle101ac7, Ronhjones, Cuaxdon, Download, Supersqr, CarsracBot, Karl gregory jones, Baffle gab1978, Tassedethe, Numbo3-bot, Craigsjones, Tide rolls, Lightbot, Jchapin1, مإني, Czar Brodie, Teles, First Light, Bartledan, EJF (huggle), Luckas-bot, Yobot, TaBOT-zerem, DownUnderPete, Eric-Wester, AnomieBOT, Piano non troppo, Xufanc, Materialscientist, Biswarajib, Citation bot, Bob Burkhardt, Darmorrow, Quebec99, Xqbot, Janet Davis, JimVC3, Gigemag76, Anna Frodesiak, Gumruch, GrouchoBot, Itineranttrader, Zefr, Andromeas, Erik9, FrescoBot, Dogposter, Simuliid, Evan123465, Citation bot 1, Xxglennxx, SwineFlew?, Pinethicket, I dream of horses, Serols, Dhebold, Greco22, Lotje, Raidon Kane, Reaper Eternal, Petar43, Vlaaa, Sam'sTheJazzMan, Obsidian Soul, Mean as custard, RjwilmsiBot, EmausBot, Look2See1, CandyCorn1313, Joeywallace9, Slightsmile, Wikipelli, AvicBot, PBS-AWB, Mavrik33, EdEColbert, Sevenoclock, Soon waffles, IssyIsAwesome, CSJames9000, Surya Prakash.S.A., Wingman4l7, Erianna, Lizbeth2, L Kensington, Thomas Capuano, Donner60, ChuispastonBot, DASHBotAV, Celtics are the shizz, Michael Bailes, Biomarker, ClueBot NG, This lousy T-shirt, Mastringe, Kostdro, PaleCloudedWhite, Cntras, MerlIwBot, Helpful Pixie Bot, Calidum, Plantdrew, BG19bot, Hewhoamareismyself, CaraSchulz, IdealistCynic, BattyBot, Darorcilmir, TylerDurden8823, Dexbot, FoCuSandLeArN, Lugia2453, EntroDipintaGabbia, Ercé, Sweetearthbakery, Thecoolerjesse, DavidLeighEllis, Prokaryotes, AfadsBad, NutrientGirl, Monkbot, Rosemaryrose, Swwikip, Blockyblock567, Brewilson21, Julietdeltalima, Zppix, Sarr Cat, ChloeMcAllinway, Chronoclimate, Margalob, Ayebae123, Atudu, Wikieditshy, Bender the Bot, DakotaMalik, ImmernochEkelAlfred, Ksoheil, Roz1373 and Anonymous: 323

- **Schefflera** *Source:* https://en.wikipedia.org/wiki/Schefflera?oldid=723872946 *Contributors:* PierreAbbat, Shyamal, Imc, Eugene van der Pijll, MPF, D6, Kwamikagami, Hesperian, Stemonitis, Richard Barlow, FlaBot, Eubot, Gdrbot, Bgwhite, Qwertzy2, Sarefo, EncycloPetey, Melburnian, Colonies Chris, Kahuroa, MrDarwin, Rigadoun, Yodin, Paul venter, Neelix, Alaibot, Thijs!bot, Milton Stanley, Nipisiquit, AndreasWittenstein, Deflective, Jhansonxi, Oscargsol, VolkovBot, Haim Berman, Addbot, KellySaunders5, SpBot, Uroboros, Bff, Luckas-bot, Cerme, Xqbot, Inferno, Lord of Penguins, Innotata, Look2See1, Dcirovic, Allforrous, AManWithNoPlan, EdoBot, JonRichfield, BG19bot, Khazar2, Sminthopsis84, Nomen ambiguum, Ercé, Sarr Cat, Miscellanearium and Anonymous: 14

- **Serissa** *Source:* https://en.wikipedia.org/wiki/Serissa?oldid=768192312 *Contributors:* Tedernst, MPF, Jrdioko, JoJan, Kate, DanielCD, Hesperian, Djlayton4, Gautamgk, Pixeltoo, Rjwilmsi, Gdrbot, YurikBot, DanMS, Ragesoss, ColinFine, LeonardoRob0t, Eskimbot, MalafayaBot,

Gurdjieff, Dcruz01, Number36, .anacondabot, Magioladitis, STBotD, Phe-bot, Dodger67, ClueBot, Snigbrook, PixelBot, Winston365, Addbot, Lightbot, AnomieBOT, TechBot, RjwilmsiBot, ZéroBot, Plantdrew, NotWith, Sarr Cat, Jodie Y and Anonymous: 8

- **Syringa vulgaris** *Source:* https://en.wikipedia.org/wiki/Syringa_vulgaris?oldid=768504673 *Contributors:* Danny, Wetman, Robbot, DocWatson42, MPF, JoJan, Urhixidur, Famartin, Discospinster, Pokrajac, Hesperian, Kaf, Jjron, Ceyockey, Stemonitis, Isfisk, AnaZ, Ricardo Carneiro Pires, Panterka, Eubot, Chobot, Gdrbot, Limulus, Tavilis, TDogg310, Vanwaffle, Fuhghettaboutit, Kingdon, TenPoundHammer, Dylanmiller, Ptelea, IanOfNorwich, Cydebot, Rosarinagazo, Escarbot, JAnDbot, Huzzlet the bot, Antepenultimate, Epibase, Idioma-bot, Gothbag, VolkovBot, Jaguarlaser, Whiteghost.ink, Mx. Granger, BodhisattvaBot, Addbot, Cuaxdon, Turdman the Graffiti Artist, Luckas-bot, Andrey Korzun, AnomieBOT, FrescoBot, AstaBOTh15, Pinethicket, Booksrule9, John of Reading, PBS-AWB, Gderrin, ChuispastonBot, PaleCloudedWhite, Dominikmatus, Primergrey, Rm1271, Darorcilmir, Dexbot, Tortie tude, Library Guy, Joseph Laferriere, Piledhighandeep, Sarr Cat, 3 of Diamonds, Stikkyy and Anonymous: 27

- **Taxodium ascendens** *Source:* https://en.wikipedia.org/wiki/Taxodium_ascendens?oldid=755115227 *Contributors:* Rmhermen, Hike395, Big Bob the Finder, MPF, Gdr, DanielCD, TheParanoidOne, Stemonitis, Eubot, Gdrbot, YurikBot, TDogg310, Mmcannis, OrphanBot, Cydebot, Cs california, Casliber, Thijs!bot, Rosarinagazo, Altairisfar, R'n'B, Trilobitealive, Nadiatalent, Brickman1000, SieBot, Polly, Chhe, Addbot, Flakinho, Materialscientist, FrescoBot, Hectonichus, Candleabracadabra, Plantdrew, BG19bot, Nightphoenix90, Peacefulmatthew and Anonymous: 8

- **Taxodium distichum** *Source:* https://en.wikipedia.org/wiki/Taxodium_distichum?oldid=767951159 *Contributors:* Rmhermen, Ram-Man, Ubiquity, Raul654, Pollinator, Visuelya, Thehappysmith, MPF, Dick Bos, Joshuamcgee, Famartin, Mike Rosoft, Dcfleck, Hesperian, Jean-Pol Grandmont, Tbc2, Ryoung122, Rjwilmsi, The wub, Eubot, Gurch, Chobot, Gdrbot, DanMS, Gaius Cornelius, TDogg310, Mmcannis, SmackBot, Niro5, DLinth, Michael miceli, A. Parrot, Iridescent, Soapthgr8, Cartoonmaster, Baskaufs, Beastie Bot, Cydebot, Metanoid, Cs california, OhioAtty, Casliber, Mattisse, Epbr123, Omnijack, Ken Thomas, QuiteUnusual, Husond, Altairisfar, Ericoides, LeRoc, WolfmanSF, Esprqii, Mjrmtg, ChuckBiggs2, Sprocketq, Masebrock, Benmdv, Peter Chastain, Eric in SF, Nadiatalent, Black Kite, TXiKiBoT, Gottinou, Steven Weston, SieBot, IvanTortuga, Furado, ClueBot, The Thing That Should Not Be, Sloindo, Mocalo, Arapaima, Chhe, Addbot, Evergladesawareness, CarTick, Flakinho, Erutuon, Tide rolls, Lightbot, Nuberger13, مانى, Luckas-bot, Yobot, Ptbotgourou, AnomieBOT, DemocraticLuntz, Materialscientist, LilHelpa, Obersachsebot, Xqbot, Gigemag76, Almabot, RibotBOT, FrescoBot, Pinethicket, Tom.Reding, Jedi94, Greg.Hartley, Keteleeria, RjwilmsiBot, 7mike5000, Ecologygirl, Androstachys, Smd75jr, Look2See1, Peterusso, Wikipelli, ZéroBot, Akerans, Cksweet, Fitzgeoff, ChuispastonBot, Sandycheeks645, ClueBot NG, Helpful Pixie Bot, Plantdrew, BG19bot, MusikAnimal, AvocatoBot, Darorcilmir, Lago Mar, Rovere~enwiki, NJRobbie, Nightphoenix90, Mdomp, Congdinh2610, Rick oehler, Spizaetus, Nina Lauridsen and Anonymous: 83

- **Taxus baccata** *Source:* https://en.wikipedia.org/wiki/Taxus_baccata?oldid=774985510 *Contributors:* William Avery, Ewen, Llywrch, Mike Linksvayer, Rl, Imc, Ccady, Wetman, Donarreiskoffer, Robbot, Alan Liefting, MPF, Michael Devore, Varlaam, Jfdwolff, Geni, JoJan, Discospinster, Rich Farmbrough, Kostja, Dbachmann, Mani1, Bender235, Andrejj, Jnestorius, Syp, Pjf, Smalljim, Reinyday, Goblim, Vortexrealm, Hesperian, Alansohn, Hippophaë~enwiki, Velella, BlueCanoe, Stemonitis, Andrea.gf, Blacktav, Ricardo Carneiro Pires, Johnrpenner, Eubot, GünniX, Quuxplusone, Daycd, Gdrbot, Bgwhite, YurikBot, Wavelength, RussBot, Curtis Clark, TDogg310, Ormanbotanigi, Kortoso, Bota47, Grayson, KGasso, Altjira, Orcaborealis, LeonardoRob0t, Nsevs, Gaudio, Friman~enwiki, SmackBot, Brya, McGeddon, Jagged 85, Eventer, Stephanie pegg, Commander Keane bot, Gilliam, Hmains, Rkitko, Snori, Greatgavini, SundarBot, Grover cleveland, James M Barlow, Only, Tesseran, Crouchbk, Erimus, Anlace, Attys, Dcruz01, J. Finkelstein, Fuzzbox, Ian Dalziel, Ravenloft, Peter Horn, WahreJakob, Iridescent, Zh1yong, CmdrObot, Ballista, Richard Keatinge, Beastie Bot, Cydebot, Gogo Dodo, Ambo100, Casliber, Oxonhutch, Thijs!bot, Epbr123, Osborne, Steve Dufour, Colin Rowat, Nick Number, AntiVandalBot, KP Botany, Smartse, JAnDbot, Plantsurfer, Tadrámgo, Appraiser, Nyttend, Hekerui, Berig, Ultramarinblau1969, Peter coxhead, Myrkkyhammas, B9 hummingbird hovering, Paracel63, Ben MacDui, R'n'B, Vox Rationis, Nono64, Masebrock, Thirdright, Wlodzimierz, C.R.Selvakumar, DogNewTricks, Pardonmadame, Notreallydavid, John Tierney, Belovedfreak, Nwbeeson, Grey Maiden, Idioma-bot, X!, VolkovBot, Bacchus87, Philip Trueman, Kostaki mou, TXiKiBoT, Oshwah, Jalwikip, Kww, Vipinhari, Anonymous Dissident, Crocadillion, Jaguarlaser, SieBot, Janeleah, VVVBot, Phe-bot, Revent, Blago Tebi, Gerald Hogan, Ken123BOT, Graminophile, ClueBot, Czarkoff, Drmies, DrFO.Jr.Tn~enwiki, Blanchardb, Grandpallama, Excirial, Estirabot, SchreiberBike, Carriearchdale, SMTBSI, Versus22, Slayerteez, Pixixi, Ldbio130, BarretB, Jed 20012, Bvcde, HarlandQPitt, Alansplodge, Airplaneman, Snortymean, Tonsky, Addbot, Aceofhearts1968, Proxima Centauri, PRL42, Lightbot, Legobot, Luckas-bot, Yobot, Ptbotgourou, Jack5150, Jdeb901, Gerixau, Richigi, AnomieBOT, Normannus, Hadden, Jikkal, Maniadis, Xqbot, Zad68, Pontificalibus, Aragon121212125, Airascada, J04n, GrouchoBot, Diplogkop, Arthropod, Kak Dela?, Benny White, Ritenice, FrescoBot, Yardang, Codwangler, Simuliid, Archaeodontosaurus, Solaricon, Krish Dulal, Pinethicket, Arctic Night, Akkida, Lineslarge, Xune07, TobeBot, Lotje, Jaba1977, Mramz88, Yoyo9990, Editor XXV, Alistair45, EmausBot, Jdy17, Look2See1, Super48paul, ZxxZxxZ, Tommy2010, Dcirovic, K6ka, Jjcisneros, Matthewcgirling, Yew Logz Ftw, Earedelf123, Rasada Incogneta, Rcsprinter123, Τασουλα, Djapa84, Michaelandsandy, ChuispastonBot, ClueBot NG, PaleCloudedWhite, Ficatus, ArboreallyProcessed, Costesseyboy, Widr, Helpful Pixie Bot, Wbm1058, Plantdrew, Dayvey, Ugncreative Usergname, Solistide, Darorcilmir, Curritocurrito, Khazar2, Roboticman, Roboticracman, RotlinkBot, Reatlas, Scott Pringle Trotter, Mark viking, Hazelares, Mondiad, Pablo.alonso, Jayaguru-Shishya, Johnegbert1995, *thing goes, Monkbot, Mstoofan, Impuls666666, EarthWindAndPeaceYall, Snagglepuss88, Rygarris, Crystallizedcarbon, Giovanni Caudullo, Ewright17, Sarr Cat, Elmidae, Rosswhelan96, Djadjko, JJMC89 bot, Scday94, Ewa hermanowicz, Nina Lauridsen and Anonymous: 191

- **Taxus chinensis** *Source:* https://en.wikipedia.org/wiki/Taxus_chinensis?oldid=661170849 *Contributors:* Chowbok, Rich Farmbrough, Hesperian, Stemonitis, BD2412, Ricardo Carneiro Pires, Eubot, Jared Preston, Gdrbot, Qwertzy2, TDogg310, Alaibot, SGGH, VolkovBot, Addbot, Zorrobot, Laikayiu, Yobot, Xqbot, J04n, Erik9bot, Dodger641, Pc1878, Hannes Ulbricht, NotWith, Makecat-bot, Trixie05, Sarr Cat and Anonymous: 3

- **Taxus cuspidata** *Source:* https://en.wikipedia.org/wiki/Taxus_cuspidata?oldid=761949116 *Contributors:* William Avery, Ram-Man, Chris 73, MPF, Andycjp, Hesperian, Lectonar, Ghirlandajo, Eubot, Gdrbot, NSR, TDogg310, Brya, Eskimbot, Polyhedron, Beastie Bot, Thijs!bot, Peter coxhead, 10rudmar, Huzzlet the bot, KylieTastic, VolkovBot, Nicklin5, Galamazoo12, Cantor, DumZiBoT, Addbot, Mateussf, Flakinho, Gail, Zorrobot, Laikayiu, Fahadsadah, Materialscientist, Xqbot, Micromesistius, Tom.Reding, EmausBot, WikitanvirBot, Josve05a, BCLH, Kiwi128, ClueBot NG, Plantdrew, Makecat-bot, Trixie05, Sarr Cat, KasparBot and Anonymous: 9

- **Taxus × media** *Source:* https://en.wikipedia.org/wiki/Taxus_%C3%97_media?oldid=703025050 *Contributors:* Herrfous, Plantsurfer, Yobot, Faolin42, Plantdrew and Djadjko

4.2. IMAGES

- **Tetraclinis** *Source:* https://en.wikipedia.org/wiki/Tetraclinis?oldid=770814219 *Contributors:* MPF, Brian0918, RJHall, Hesperian, Graham87, FlaBot, Eubot, Gdrbot, YurikBot, RussBot, Thomas Blomberg, NeilN, Brya, Cs california, Rosarinagazo, Huttarl, Nanosanchez, Magioladitis, Lucyin, CommonsDelinker, Numbo3, Colchicum, Idioma-bot, TXiKiBoT, Mars11, AlleborgoBot, DumZiBoT, Addbot, Flakinho, Zorrobot, Luckas-bot, Yobot, KamikazeBot, Elostirion, LilHelpa, RibotBOT, Kokopelado, EmausBot, WikitanvirBot, Look2See1, Mathsum.mut, ZéroBot, SporkBot, Rcsprinter123, Omar hoftun, Plantdrew, NotWith, Ercé, Bender the Bot and Anonymous: 14

- **Ulmus alata** *Source:* https://en.wikipedia.org/wiki/Ulmus_alata?oldid=766825306 *Contributors:* Nonenmac, Asparagus, MPF, Valeriethe-Blonde, BD2412, MZMcBride, Eubot, Dtrebbien, Welsh, Rkitko, Colonies Chris, Dl2000, Ptelea, Mattbuck, Cydebot, Casliber, JamesAM, Altairisfar, Magioladitis, Masebrock, Gypsyware, Skumarlabot, Eric in SF, Kmanblue, Jaguarlaser, Miguel.v, Mild Bill Hiccup, LarryMorseDCOhio, Thingg, Addbot, Erutuon, Uksignpix, AnomieBOT, LucienBOT, Pinethicket, Jonesey95, Gaberlunzi, Helpful Pixie Bot, Plantdrew, BG19bot, Tom elm and Anonymous: 7

- **Ulmus crassifolia** *Source:* https://en.wikipedia.org/wiki/Ulmus_crassifolia?oldid=766825275 *Contributors:* Nonenmac, Topbanana, Eugene van der Pijll, Donarreiskoffer, MPF, Bookandcoffee, Damicatz, MauriceJFox3, Eubot, Gdrbot, Bgwhite, RussBot, Mmcannis, Rkitko, Derek R Bullamore, Ptelea, JoeBot, Cydebot, Torc2, Casliber, Ufwuct, Altairisfar, TAnthony, Masebrock, Jaguarlaser, ClueBot, SchreiberBike, Kingbuttzero, Dthomsen8, Addbot, Uksignpix, Luckas-bot, Yobot, AnomieBOT, Deribus, Pinethicket, Skyerise, Ftelia, Snotbot, Plantdrew, BG19bot, CitationCleanerBot, Cyberbot II, Tom elm and Anonymous: 13

- **Ulmus parvifolia** *Source:* https://en.wikipedia.org/wiki/Ulmus_parvifolia?oldid=766540496 *Contributors:* Magnus Manske, Goethean, MPF, Chowbok, Antandrus, Jossi, GeoGreg, Ukexpat, LJade728, Circeus, Pschemp, GregorB, BD2412, Rjwilmsi, Eubot, Chobot, Gdrbot, Bgwhite, Gaius Cornelius, Open2universe, West Virginian, Maxima m, EncycloPetey, Hardyplants, Rkitko, Melburnian, Gurdjieff, Dcruz01, Ptelea, ShelfSkewed, Grahamec, Casliber, Ken Thomas, TAnthony, Shadowcatcher~enwiki, JPG-GR, Tikiwont, 1000Faces, Philip Trueman, HelloMojo, SieBot, Oxymoron83, Phyte, Snigbrook, LarryMorseDCOhio, DumZiBoT, Addbot, Lightbot, Uksignpix, Yobot, AnomieBOT, Materialscientist, Xqbot, SciGuy013, FrescoBot, GreenZmiy, Wauw, Micromesistius, LittleWink, RjwilmsiBot, GoingBatty, Sesamehoneytart, ZéroBot, Helpful Pixie Bot, Plantdrew, Utar Sigmal, Tjbird9675, Cold Season, Darorcilmir, Dexbot, Captain rimmer, Hillbillyholiday, ArmbrustBot, Tom elm, Datbubblegumdoe and Anonymous: 27

- **Ulmus parvifolia 'Catlin'** *Source:* https://en.wikipedia.org/wiki/Ulmus_parvifolia_'Catlin'?oldid=740027403 *Contributors:* BD2412, Ptelea, Cydebot, TAnthony, BotanyBot, Lightbot, Yobot, Look2See1, Snotbot and Tom elm

- **Wisteria floribunda** *Source:* https://en.wikipedia.org/wiki/Wisteria_floribunda?oldid=725661726 *Contributors:* William Avery, Bogdangiusca, Raul654, Andycjp, B.d.mills, DanielCD, Kbh3rd, Guettarda, Djlayton4, Stemonitis, Crackerbelly, Bratsche, Ketiltrout, Eubot, Gdrbot, Draeco, Emijrp, Dav2008, Rkitko, Simon12, Raz1el, Cydebot, Casliber, Rosarinagazo, Altairisfar, Hydro, Michael Goodyear, TXiKiBoT, Mobiuschic42, SieBot, Winston365, Chhe, Addbot, Flakinho, Lightbot, Yobot, Pitke, LilHelpa, Suplilumas, Ripchip Bot, Look2See1, Thegm1, Plantdrew, BattyBot, Darorcilmir, Mogism, Ercé, HalfGig, Nickwilso and Anonymous: 8

- **Wisteria sinensis** *Source:* https://en.wikipedia.org/wiki/Wisteria_sinensis?oldid=774149125 *Contributors:* Ahoerstemeier, Grin, Franz Xaver, Nv8200pa, Davidcannon, MPF, Beland, Acad Ronin, Loren36, Guettarda, Inge-Lyubov, Stemonitis, Crackerbelly, Bratsche, Tbc2, Ketiltrout, Eubot, Gdrbot, Hede2000, Draeco, LeonardoRob0t, West Virginian, SmackBot, Rkitko, Writtenright, Simon12, JoeBot, Cydebot, Casliber, Thijs!bot, Rosarinagazo, Slaweks, Milton Stanley, RedCoat10, JAnDbot, Altairisfar, R'n'B, Nadiatalent, Umebo, PixelBot, Quelcrime, Newmans2001, Addbot, Tassedethe, Flakinho, Lightbot, Luckas-bot, AnomieBOT, Merube 89, Karesansui, Tom.Reding, MegaSloth, TjBot, Look2See1, GoingBatty, ZéroBot, Thine Antique Pen, ArmbrustBot, Hansmuller, JustBerry, HalfGig, Nickwilso, Jmc76, Ftuqan, Lezlierueda, JeffinNYC and Anonymous: 13

- **Zelkova serrata** *Source:* https://en.wikipedia.org/wiki/Zelkova_serrata?oldid=775011025 *Contributors:* Seglea, DocWatson42, MPF, Art LaPella, Geographer, Tabletop, Shikai shaw, Rjwilmsi, Eubot, DannyWilde, Gdrbot, Surge79uwf, Wavelength, Ytrottier, KevinCuddeback, NawlinWiki, Ragesoss, IceCreamAntisocial, Rkitko, Akanemoto, Bruce Marlin, OtherGuy1, Abrahami, Carnby, Skinsmoke, Ptelea, Casliber, Parande, T L Miles, Peter coxhead, LordAnubisBOT, KylieTastic, Idioma-bot, Broadbot, Kunchan, Jjw, Caveman55, Tdslk, DumZiBoT, Addbot, LaaknorBot, Zuidpoort, RockDeMarco, Flakinho, Luckas-bot, KamikazeBot, AnomieBOT, LilHelpa, Linguoboy, FrescoBot, Mar del Este, BoundaryRider, Sherlock1987, Micromesistius, Haaninjo, ZhBot, EmausBot, John of Reading, Absurdist1968, Fæ, Ted Barnes, Unbal3, 確認君, Darorcilmir, Mogism, KasparBot, Japonica, Bender the Bot, (Carlos Emanuel) and Anonymous: 26

- **Zoysia 'Emerald'** *Source:* https://en.wikipedia.org/wiki/Zoysia_'Emerald'?oldid=737838913 *Contributors:* Mrand, Eugene van der Pijll, MPF, Hesperian, Gblaz, Stemonitis, TDogg310, SmackBot, EncycloPetey, Zahid Abdassabur, TAnthony, Student7, Snideology, Anon lynx, Addbot, Lightbot, Russbach, DrilBot, Look2See1, ZéroBot, Plantdrew, InternetArchiveBot, GreenC bot and Anonymous: 7

4.2 Images

- **File:02_Camelia.jpg** *Source:* https://upload.wikimedia.org/wikipedia/commons/9/9d/02_Camelia.jpg *License:* CC-BY-SA-3.0 *Contributors:* Own work *Original artist:* Luis Miguel Bugallo Sánchez (Lmbuga Commons)(Lmbuga Galipedia)

- **File:07._Japanese_Garden_Pano,_Cowra,_NSW,_22.09.2006.jpg** *Source:* https://upload.wikimedia.org/wikipedia/commons/2/2f/07._Japanese_Garden_Pano%2C_Cowra%2C_NSW%2C_22.09.2006.jpg *License:* CC-BY-SA-3.0 *Contributors:* Own work *Original artist:* John O'Neill

- **File:100JPY.JPG** *Source:* https://upload.wikimedia.org/wikipedia/commons/0/0a/100JPY.JPG *License:* Public domain *Contributors:* Own work *Original artist:* Misogi

- **File:20071103Tradkrafta1.JPG** *Source:* https://upload.wikimedia.org/wikipedia/commons/8/89/20071103Tradkrafta1.JPG *License:* Public domain *Contributors:* Own work *Original artist:* Fyrverkarn

- **File:2007_Sakura_of_Fukushima-e_007_rotated.jpg** *Source:* https://upload.wikimedia.org/wikipedia/commons/3/3a/2007_Sakura_of_Fukushima-e_007_rotated.jpg *License:* CC-BY-SA-3.0 *Contributors:*

- 2007_Sakura_of_Fukushima-e_007.jpg *Original artist:* 2007_Sakura_of_Fukushima-e_007.jpg: Kropsoq
- **File:2009-11-04_20-View_north_from_the_top_of_the_Apple_Pie_Hill_fire_tower.jpg** *Source:* https://upload.wikimedia.org/wikipedia/commons/b/b2/2009-11-04_20-View_north_from_the_top_of_the_Apple_Pie_Hill_fire_tower.jpg *License:* CC BY 3.0 *Contributors:* Own work (Original text: *I (Famartin (talk)) created this work entirely by myself.*) *Original artist:* Famartin (talk)
- **File:2010.05.09_Horse_chestnut_blossom,_Kyiv,_Ukraine_001c.jpg** *Source:* https://upload.wikimedia.org/wikipedia/commons/b/b6/2010.05.09_Horse_chestnut_blossom%2C_Kyiv%2C_Ukraine_001c.jpg *License:* CC BY-SA 3.0 *Contributors:* Own work *Original artist:* William N. Beckon
- **File:2012quince.png** *Source:* https://upload.wikimedia.org/wikipedia/commons/6/63/2012quince.png *License:* CC BY-SA 4.0 *Contributors:* Own work *Original artist:* Swidran
- **File:2013-05-10_09_02_57_Pitch_Pine_new_growth_and_pollen_cones_along_the_Batona_Trail_in_Brendan_T._Byrne_State_Forest,_New_Jersey.jpg** *Source:* https://upload.wikimedia.org/wikipedia/commons/f/f5/2013-05-10_09_02_57_Pitch_Pine_new_growth_and_pollen_cones_along_the_Batona_Trail_in_Brendan_T._Byrne_State_Forest%2C_New_Jersey.jpg *License:* CC BY-SA 3.0 *Contributors:* Own work *Original artist:* Famartin
- **File:2013-05-10_10_32_15_Virginia_Pine_new_growth_and_pollen_cones_along_the_Mount_Misery_Trail_in_Brendan_T._Byrne_State_Forest,_New_Jersey.jpg** *Source:* https://upload.wikimedia.org/wikipedia/commons/b/b2/2013-05-10_10_32_15_Virginia_Pine_new_growth_and_pollen_cones_along_the_Mount_Misery_Trail_in_Brendan_T._Byrne_State_Forest%2C_New_Jersey.jpg *License:* CC BY-SA 3.0 *Contributors:* Own work *Original artist:* Famartin
- **File:2013-05-10_11_01_36_Virginia_Pine_along_the_Mount_Misery_Trail_in_Brendan_T._Byrne_State_Forest,_New_Jersey.jpg** *Source:* https://upload.wikimedia.org/wikipedia/commons/3/30/2013-05-10_11_01_36_Virginia_Pine_along_the_Mount_Misery_Trail_in_Brendan_T._Byrne_State_Forest%2C_New_Jersey.jpg *License:* CC BY-SA 3.0 *Contributors:* Own work *Original artist:* Famartin
- **File:2013-05-10_13_40_17_Immature_foliage_of_Red_Maple_in_Brendan_T_Byrne_State_Forest,_New_Jersey.jpg** *Source:* https://upload.wikimedia.org/wikipedia/commons/7/7a/2013-05-10_13_40_17_Immature_foliage_of_Red_Maple_in_Brendan_T_Byrne_State_Forest%2C_New_Jersey.jpg *License:* CC BY-SA 3.0 *Contributors:* Own work *Original artist:* Famartin
- **File:20130528Robinie_Hockenheim4.jpg** *Source:* https://upload.wikimedia.org/wikipedia/commons/c/ce/20130528Robinie_Hockenheim4.jpg *License:* CC0 *Contributors:* Own work *Original artist:* AnRo0002
- **File:2014-05-10_10_47_00_Flowering_Cherry_along_Terrace_Boulevard_in_Ewing,_New_Jersey.JPG** *Source:* https://upload.wikimedia.org/wikipedia/commons/4/40/2014-05-10_10_47_00_Flowering_Cherry_along_Terrace_Boulevard_in_Ewing%2C_New_Jersey.JPG *License:* CC BY-SA 3.0 *Contributors:* Own work *Original artist:* Famartin
- **File:2014-05-10_12_34_11_Flowering_Cherry_along_New_Jersey_Route_29_in_Hopewell_Township,_New_Jersey.JPG** *Source:* https://upload.wikimedia.org/wikipedia/commons/7/77/2014-05-10_12_34_11_Flowering_Cherry_along_New_Jersey_Route_29_in_Hopewell_Township%2C_New_Jersey.JPG *License:* CC BY-SA 3.0 *Contributors:* Own work *Original artist:* Famartin
- **File:2014-05-17_10_24_50_Pink-purple-flowered_and_red-flowered_Azaleas_in_front_of_an_old_house_on_Spruce_Street_(Mercer_County_Route_613)_in_Ewing,_New_Jersey.JPG** *Source:* https://upload.wikimedia.org/wikipedia/commons/8/80/2014-05-17_10_24_50_Pink-purple-flowered_and_red-flowered_Azaleas_in_front_of_an_old_house_on_Spruce_Street_%28Mercer_County_Route_613%29_in_Ewing%2C_New_Jersey.JPG *License:* CC BY-SA 3.0 *Contributors:* Own work *Original artist:* Famartin
- **File:2014-10-24_12_24_03_Lilac_foliage_in_autumn_in_Elko,_Nevada.JPG** *Source:* https://upload.wikimedia.org/wikipedia/commons/7/76/2014-10-24_12_24_03_Lilac_foliage_in_autumn_in_Elko%2C_Nevada.JPG *License:* CC BY-SA 4.0 *Contributors:* Own work *Original artist:* Famartin
- **File:2014-10-29_13_06_11_Forsythia_foliage_during_autumn_in_Ewing,_New_Jersey.JPG** *Source:* https://upload.wikimedia.org/wikipedia/commons/9/96/2014-10-29_13_06_11_Forsythia_foliage_during_autumn_in_Ewing%2C_New_Jersey.JPG *License:* CC BY-SA 4.0 *Contributors:* Own work *Original artist:* Famartin
- **File:2014-10-30_09_53_30_Kanzan_Cherry_foliage_during_autumn_along_Terrace_Boulevard_in_Ewing,_New_Jersey.JPG** *Source:* https://upload.wikimedia.org/wikipedia/commons/8/89/2014-10-30_09_53_30_Kanzan_Cherry_foliage_during_autumn_along_Terrace_Boulevard_in_Ewing%2C_New_Jersey.JPG *License:* CC BY-SA 4.0 *Contributors:* Own work *Original artist:* Famartin
- **File:2014-10-30_13_47_46_Red_Maple_during_autumn_along_Terrace_Boulevard_in_Ewing,_New_Jersey.JPG** *Source:* https://upload.wikimedia.org/wikipedia/commons/1/18/2014-10-30_13_47_46_Red_Maple_during_autumn_along_Terrace_Boulevard_in_Ewing%2C_New_Jersey.JPG *License:* CC BY-SA 4.0 *Contributors:* Own work *Original artist:* Famartin
- **File:2014-11-02_12_06_44_Ginkgo_during_autumn_at_the_Ewing_Presbyterian_Church_Cemetery_in_Ewing,_New_Jersey.jpg** *Source:* https://upload.wikimedia.org/wikipedia/commons/6/60/2014-11-02_12_06_44_Ginkgo_during_autumn_at_the_Ewing_Presbyterian_Church_Cemetery_in_Ewing%2C_New_Jersey.jpg *License:* CC BY-SA 4.0 *Contributors:* Own work *Original artist:* Famartin
- **File:2014-11-02_12_13_29_Ginkgo_foliage_and_fruit_during_autumn_at_the_Ewing_Presbyterian_Church_Cemetery_in_Ewing,_New_Jersey.JPG** *Source:* https://upload.wikimedia.org/wikipedia/commons/f/f1/2014-11-02_12_13_29_Ginkgo_foliage_and_fruit_during_autumn_at_the_Ewing_Presbyterian_Church_Cemetery_in_Ewing%2C_New_Jersey.JPG *License:* CC BY-SA 4.0 *Contributors:* Own work *Original artist:* Famartin
- **File:2014-11-02_14_12_30_Bald_Cypress_foliage_during_autumn_along_Hunters_Ridge_Drive_in_Hopewell_Township,_New_Jersey.jpg** *Source:* https://upload.wikimedia.org/wikipedia/commons/d/d4/2014-11-02_14_12_30_Bald_Cypress_foliage_during_autumn_along_Hunters_Ridge_Drive_in_Hopewell_Township%2C_New_Jersey.jpg *License:* CC BY-SA 4.0 *Contributors:* Own work *Original artist:* Famartin
- **File:2015-04-12_16_31_55_Male_Red_Maple_flowers_on_Bayberry_Road_in_Ewing,_New_Jersey.jpg** *Source:* https://upload.wikimedia.org/wikipedia/commons/a/af/2015-04-12_16_31_55_Male_Red_Maple_flowers_on_Bayberry_Road_in_Ewing%2C_New_Jersey.jpg *License:* CC BY-SA 4.0 *Contributors:* Own work *Original artist:* Famartin

4.2. IMAGES

- **File:2015-04-13_10_38_10_Female_Red_Maple_flowers_on_Madison_Avenue_in_Ewing,_New_Jersey.jpg** *Source:* https://upload.wikimedia.org/wikipedia/commons/e/eb/2015-04-13_10_38_10_Female_Red_Maple_flowers_on_Madison_Avenue_in_Ewing%2C_New_Jersey.jpg *License:* CC BY-SA 4.0 *Contributors:* Own work *Original artist:* Famartin
- **File:2015-10-30_16_27_33_Vine_Maple_foliage_during_autumn_along_Old_Brockway_Road_in_Truckee,_California.jpg** *Source:* https://upload.wikimedia.org/wikipedia/commons/e/ed/2015-10-30_16_27_33_Vine_Maple_foliage_during_autumn_along_Old_Brockway_Road_in_Truckee%2C_California.jpg *License:* CC BY-SA 4.0 *Contributors:* Own work *Original artist:* Famartin
- **File:2016-05-08_1452_Cherokee_Princess_dogwood.png** *Source:* https://upload.wikimedia.org/wikipedia/commons/8/8d/2016-05-08_1452_Cherokee_Princess_dogwood.png *License:* CC BY-SA 4.0 *Contributors:* Own work *Original artist:* Mitzi.humphrey
- **File:21-alimenti,_olio,Taccuino_Sanitatis,_Casanatense_4182..jpg** *Source:* https://upload.wikimedia.org/wikipedia/commons/e/e3/21-alimenti%2C_olio%2CTaccuino_Sanitatis%2C_Casanatense_4182..jpg *License:* Public domain *Contributors:* book scan *Original artist:* unknown master
- **File:237_Acer_campestre.jpg** *Source:* https://upload.wikimedia.org/wikipedia/commons/f/f5/237_Acer_campestre.jpg *License:* Public domain *Contributors:* «Bilder ur Nordens Flora» Stockholm *Original artist:* Carl Axel Magnus Lindman
- **File:Aardbei-bloemcloseup.jpg** *Source:* https://upload.wikimedia.org/wikipedia/commons/9/9d/Aardbei-bloemcloseup.jpg *License:* CC-BY-SA-3.0 *Contributors:* zelfgemaakte foto *Original artist:* Rasbak
- **File:Acer-campestre-flowers.JPG** *Source:* https://upload.wikimedia.org/wikipedia/commons/b/b8/Acer-campestre-flowers.JPG *License:* CC-BY-SA-3.0 *Contributors:* Own photo, taken in Jutland. *Original artist:* Sten Porse
- **File:Acer-campestre.JPG** *Source:* https://upload.wikimedia.org/wikipedia/commons/8/8a/Acer-campestre.JPG *License:* CC-BY-SA-3.0 *Contributors:* Own work *Original artist:* Sten Porse
- **File:Acer-palmatum-ssp.jpg** *Source:* https://upload.wikimedia.org/wikipedia/commons/0/05/Acer-palmatum-ssp.jpg *License:* CC BY-SA 2.5 *Contributors:* Own work *Original artist:* Abrahami
- **File:AcerPalmatum2.jpg** *Source:* https://upload.wikimedia.org/wikipedia/commons/7/79/AcerPalmatum2.jpg *License:* CC-BY-SA-3.0 *Contributors:* ? *Original artist:* ?
- **File:Acer_Palmatum_bonsai_2.JPG** *Source:* https://upload.wikimedia.org/wikipedia/commons/3/35/Acer_Palmatum_bonsai_2.JPG *License:* CC BY-SA 3.0 *Contributors:* Own work *Original artist:* Jeffrey O. Gustafson
- **File:Acer_buergerianum_leaf.jpg** *Source:* https://upload.wikimedia.org/wikipedia/commons/b/b0/Acer_buergerianum_leaf.jpg *License:* CC BY-SA 3.0 *Contributors:* Own work *Original artist:* Abrahami
- **File:Acer_buergerianum_seeds.jpg** *Source:* https://upload.wikimedia.org/wikipedia/commons/6/6c/Acer_buergerianum_seeds.jpg *License:* CC BY-SA 2.5 *Contributors:* No machine-readable source provided. Own work assumed (based on copyright claims). *Original artist:* No machine-readable author provided. Abrahami assumed (based on copyright claims).
- **File:Acer_campestre_(4).JPG** *Source:* https://upload.wikimedia.org/wikipedia/commons/6/62/Acer_campestre_%284%29.JPG *License:* CC BY-SA 4.0 *Contributors:* Own work *Original artist:* Marija Gajić
- **File:Acer_campestre_001.jpg** *Source:* https://upload.wikimedia.org/wikipedia/commons/e/ec/Acer_campestre_001.jpg *License:* CC BY-SA 2.5 *Contributors:* Own work *Original artist:* Willow
- **File:Acer_campestre_002.jpg** *Source:* https://upload.wikimedia.org/wikipedia/commons/2/26/Acer_campestre_002.jpg *License:* CC BY-SA 2.5 *Contributors:* Own work *Original artist:* Willow
- **File:Acer_campestre_003.jpg** *Source:* https://upload.wikimedia.org/wikipedia/commons/9/9f/Acer_campestre_003.jpg *License:* CC BY-SA 2.5 *Contributors:* Own work *Original artist:* Willow
- **File:Acer_campestre_004.jpg** *Source:* https://upload.wikimedia.org/wikipedia/commons/6/6c/Acer_campestre_004.jpg *License:* CC BY-SA 2.5 *Contributors:* Own work *Original artist:* Willow
- **File:Acer_campestre_005.jpg** *Source:* https://upload.wikimedia.org/wikipedia/commons/6/66/Acer_campestre_005.jpg *License:* CC BY-SA 2.5 *Contributors:* Own work *Original artist:* Willow
- **File:Acer_campestre_006.jpg** *Source:* https://upload.wikimedia.org/wikipedia/commons/d/df/Acer_campestre_006.jpg *License:* CC BY-SA 2.5 *Contributors:* Own work *Original artist:* Willow
- **File:Acer_campestre_007.jpg** *Source:* https://upload.wikimedia.org/wikipedia/commons/5/50/Acer_campestre_007.jpg *License:* CC BY-SA 2.5 *Contributors:* Own work *Original artist:* Willow
- **File:Acer_campestre_008.jpg** *Source:* https://upload.wikimedia.org/wikipedia/commons/3/36/Acer_campestre_008.jpg *License:* CC BY-SA 2.5 *Contributors:* Own work *Original artist:* Willow
- **File:Acer_campestre_009.jpg** *Source:* https://upload.wikimedia.org/wikipedia/commons/c/c5/Acer_campestre_009.jpg *License:* CC BY-SA 2.5 *Contributors:* Own work *Original artist:* Willow
- **File:Acer_campestre_010.jpg** *Source:* https://upload.wikimedia.org/wikipedia/commons/2/2d/Acer_campestre_010.jpg *License:* CC-BY-SA-3.0 *Contributors:* File:Unb6b.jpg *Original artist:* Ies
- **File:Acer_campestre_Weinsberg_20070419_1.jpg** *Source:* https://upload.wikimedia.org/wikipedia/commons/1/1a/Acer_campestre_Weinsberg_20070419_1.jpg *License:* CC BY 3.0 *Contributors:* Own work (own picture) *Original artist:* Rosenzweig
- **File:Acer_campestrie_L_ag1.jpg** *Source:* https://upload.wikimedia.org/wikipedia/commons/4/4e/Acer_campestrie_L_ag1.jpg *License:* Public domain *Contributors:* ? *Original artist:* ?
- **File:Acer_campestris1.jpg** *Source:* https://upload.wikimedia.org/wikipedia/commons/0/0d/Acer_campestris1.jpg *License:* CC-BY-SA-3.0 *Contributors:* ? *Original artist:* ?

356   *CHAPTER 4. TEXT AND IMAGE SOURCES, CONTRIBUTORS, AND LICENSES*

- **File:Acer_circinatum_03684.JPG** *Source:* https://upload.wikimedia.org/wikipedia/commons/2/25/Acer_circinatum_03684.JPG *License:* CC BY 2.5 *Contributors:* Own work *Original artist:* Walter Siegmund

- **File:Acer_circinatum_9468.JPG** *Source:* https://upload.wikimedia.org/wikipedia/commons/6/6f/Acer_circinatum_9468.JPG *License:* CC BY-SA 3.0 *Contributors:* Own work *Original artist:* Walter Siegmund (talk)

- **File:Acer_monspessulanum_subsp_turcomanicum_flower.jpg** *Source:* https://upload.wikimedia.org/wikipedia/commons/1/1b/Acer_monspessulanum_subsp_turcomanicum_flower.jpg *License:* CC BY-SA 2.5 *Contributors:* Own work *Original artist:* PiPi

- **File:Acer_palmatum_BotGartenMuenster_Faecherahorn_6691.jpg** *Source:* https://upload.wikimedia.org/wikipedia/commons/3/36/Acer_palmatum_BotGartenMuenster_Faecherahorn_6691.jpg *License:* CC BY-SA 2.5 *Contributors:* photo taken by Rüdiger Wölk, Münster, Germany *Original artist:* Rüdiger Wölk

- **File:Acer_palmatum_img.jpg** *Source:* https://upload.wikimedia.org/wikipedia/commons/9/9b/Acer_palmatum_img.jpg *License:* Public domain *Contributors:* Own work (Original text: *self-made*) *Original artist:* Iwanafish at English Wikipedia

- **File:Acer_rubrum.jpg** *Source:* https://upload.wikimedia.org/wikipedia/commons/f/f6/Acer_rubrum.jpg *License:* Public domain *Contributors:* No machine-readable source provided. Own work assumed (based on copyright claims). *Original artist:* No machine-readable author provided. Noles1984~commonswiki assumed (based on copyright claims).

- **File:Acer_rubrum_drummondii_drawing.png** *Source:* https://upload.wikimedia.org/wikipedia/commons/1/16/Acer_rubrum_drummondii_drawing.png *License:* Public domain *Contributors:* USDA *Original artist:* Britton, N.L., and A. Brown. 1913. *Illustrated flora of the northern states and Canada.* Vol. 2: 496.

- **File:Acerbark8344.jpg** *Source:* https://upload.wikimedia.org/wikipedia/commons/e/ee/Acerbark8344.jpg *License:* CC-BY-SA-3.0 *Contributors:* Transfered from en.wikipedia *Original artist:* Original uploader was Pollinator at en.wikipedia

- **File:AesculusHippocastanumTrunk.jpg** *Source:* https://upload.wikimedia.org/wikipedia/commons/6/6d/AesculusHippocastanumTrunk.jpg *License:* Public domain *Contributors:* Own work (Original text: *I created this work entirely by myself.*) *Original artist:* Chhe (talk)

- **File:Aesculus_hippocastanum-1.jpg** *Source:* https://upload.wikimedia.org/wikipedia/commons/0/05/Aesculus_hippocastanum-1.jpg *License:* CC BY 2.5 *Contributors:* Self-photographed *Original artist:* Alvesgaspar

- **File:Aesculus_hippocastanum_002.JPG** *Source:* https://upload.wikimedia.org/wikipedia/commons/d/de/Aesculus_hippocastanum_002.JPG *License:* CC BY-SA 3.0 *Contributors:* Own work *Original artist:* H. Zell

- **File:Aesculus_hippocastanum_PICT3472.jpg** *Source:* https://upload.wikimedia.org/wikipedia/commons/8/8d/Aesculus_hippocastanum_PICT3472.jpg *License:* CC-BY-SA-3.0 *Contributors:* Own work *Original artist:* Opuntia

- **File:Aesculus_hippocastanum_fruit.jpg** *Source:* https://upload.wikimedia.org/wikipedia/commons/1/14/Aesculus_hippocastanum_fruit.jpg *License:* CC BY-SA 2.0 *Contributors:* Own work *Original artist:* Solipsist

- **File:Afbeelding-011-Wisteria_sinensis.tiff** *Source:* https://upload.wikimedia.org/wikipedia/commons/7/7c/Afbeelding-011-Wisteria_sinensis.tiff *License:* Public domain *Contributors:* book H. Witte and A J Wendel: *Flora: afbeeldingen en beschrijvingen van boomen, heesters, éénjarige planten, enz. voorkomende in de Nederlandsche tuinen*, Groningen: Wolters, [1868]. *Original artist:* Abraham Jacobus Wendel

- **File:Afrocarpus_falcatus,_bas,_Nieuw_Muckleneuk,_a.jpg** *Source:* https://upload.wikimedia.org/wikipedia/commons/4/4d/Afrocarpus_falcatus%2C_bas%2C_Nieuw_Muckleneuk%2C_a.jpg *License:* CC BY-SA 3.0 *Contributors:* Own work *Original artist:* JMK

- **File:Afrocarpus_falcatus,_loof_en_bas,_LC_de_Villiers-sportsentrum.jpg** *Source:* https://upload.wikimedia.org/wikipedia/commons/c/ca/Afrocarpus_falcatus%2C_loof_en_bas%2C_LC_de_Villiers-sportsentrum.jpg *License:* CC BY-SA 3.0 *Contributors:* Own work *Original artist:* JMK

- **File:Akadama_dry_and_wet.JPG** *Source:* https://upload.wikimedia.org/wikipedia/commons/9/9a/Akadama_dry_and_wet.JPG *License:* CC BY-SA 3.0 *Contributors:* Own work *Original artist:* Abrahami

- **File:Alder_nodules2.JPG** *Source:* https://upload.wikimedia.org/wikipedia/commons/e/e2/Alder_nodules2.JPG *License:* CC BY-SA 3.0 *Contributors:* Own work *Original artist:* Cwmhiraeth

- **File:Alhucemas_(11).JPG** *Source:* https://upload.wikimedia.org/wikipedia/commons/8/80/Alhucemas_%2811%29.JPG *License:* GFDL *Contributors:* Own work *Original artist:* Kokopelado

- **File:Alhucemas_(9).JPG** *Source:* https://upload.wikimedia.org/wikipedia/commons/5/5f/Alhucemas_%289%29.JPG *License:* GFDL *Contributors:* Own work *Original artist:* Kokopelado

- **File:Alkottar.jpg** *Source:* https://upload.wikimedia.org/wikipedia/commons/0/04/Alkottar.jpg *License:* CC BY-SA 3.0 *Contributors:* Own work *Original artist:* EnDumEn

- **File:Alliste._Olivo_della_Linza.jpg** *Source:* https://upload.wikimedia.org/wikipedia/commons/8/8f/Alliste._Olivo_della_Linza.jpg *License:* CC-BY-SA-3.0 *Contributors:* Own work *Original artist:* Antonio47

- **File:Alnus_cordata_alder_tree.jpg** *Source:* https://upload.wikimedia.org/wikipedia/commons/9/9c/Alnus_cordata_alder_tree.jpg *License:* CC BY-SA 2.0 *Contributors:* [1] *Original artist:* AnemoneProjectors (<a href='//commons.wikimedia.org/wiki/User_talk:AnemoneProjectors' title='User talk:AnemoneProjectors'>talk</a>) (Flickr)

- **File:Alnus_glutinosa,_Munkholmen.jpg** *Source:* https://upload.wikimedia.org/wikipedia/commons/e/e1/Alnus_glutinosa%2C_Munkholmen.jpg *License:* CC BY-SA 3.0 *Contributors:* Own work *Original artist:* Esquilo

- **File:Alnus_glutinosa.jpg** *Source:* https://upload.wikimedia.org/wikipedia/commons/7/7b/Alnus_glutinosa.jpg *License:* CC BY 2.5 *Contributors:* No machine-readable source provided. Own work assumed (based on copyright claims). *Original artist:* No machine-readable author provided. MPF assumed (based on copyright claims).

- **File:Alnus_glutinosa_MHNT.BOT.2004.0.10a.jpg** *Source:* https://upload.wikimedia.org/wikipedia/commons/2/28/Alnus_glutinosa_MHNT.BOT.2004.0.10a.jpg *License:* CC BY-SA 4.0 *Contributors:* Own work *Original artist:* Didier Descouens

4.2. IMAGES

- **File:Alnus_glutinosa_R0015198.JPG** *Source:* https://upload.wikimedia.org/wikipedia/commons/b/b5/Alnus_glutinosa_R0015198.JPG *License:* CC-BY-SA-3.0 *Contributors:* No machine-readable source provided. Own work assumed (based on copyright claims). *Original artist:* No machine-readable author provided. TeunSpaans assumed (based on copyright claims).
- **File:Alnus_glutinosa_R0015202.JPG** *Source:* https://upload.wikimedia.org/wikipedia/commons/3/31/Alnus_glutinosa_R0015202.JPG *License:* CC-BY-SA-3.0 *Contributors:* No machine-readable source provided. Own work assumed (based on copyright claims). *Original artist:* No machine-readable author provided. TeunSpaans assumed (based on copyright claims).
- **File:Ambersweet_oranges.jpg** *Source:* https://upload.wikimedia.org/wikipedia/commons/4/43/Ambersweet_oranges.jpg *License:* Public domain *Contributors:* This image was released by the Agricultural Research Service, the research agency of the United States Department of Agriculture, with the ID k3644-12 <a class='external text' href='//commons.wikimedia.org/w/index.php?title=Category:Media_created_by_the_United_States_Agricultural_Research_Service_with_known_IDs,<span>,&,</span>,filefrom=k3644-12#mw-category-media'>(next)</a>. *Original artist:* ?
- **File:An_Indian_poet_seated_in_a_cherry_blossom_garden.jpg** *Source:* https://upload.wikimedia.org/wikipedia/commons/5/54/An_Indian_poet_seated_in_a_cherry_blossom_garden.jpg *License:* Public domain *Contributors:* http://www.granger.com/results.asp?inline=true&image=0119586&wwwflag=4&itemx=17 *Original artist:* Unknown<a href='https://www.wikidata.org/wiki/Q4233718' title='wikidata:Q4233718'><img alt='wikidata:Q4233718' src='https://upload.wikimedia.org/wikipedia/commons/thumb/f/ff/Wikidata-logo.svg/20px-Wikidata-logo.svg.png' width='20' height='11' srcset='https://upload.wikimedia.org/wikipedia/commons/thumb/f/ff/Wikidata-logo.svg/30px-Wikidata-logo.svg.png 1.5x, https://upload.wikimedia.org/wikipedia/commons/thumb/f/ff/Wikidata-logo.svg/40px-Wikidata-logo.svg.png 2x' data-file-width='1050' data-file-height='590' /></a>
- **File:Ancient_Olive_Tree_in_Pelion,_Greece.jpg** *Source:* https://upload.wikimedia.org/wikipedia/commons/f/f2/Ancient_Olive_Tree_in_Pelion%2C_Greece.jpg *License:* CC BY-SA 3.0 *Contributors:* Own work *Original artist:* Dennis koutou
- **File:Aoba-dori_Ave_2.JPG** *Source:* https://upload.wikimedia.org/wikipedia/commons/c/cc/Aoba-dori_Ave_2.JPG *License:* Public domain *Contributors:* Own work *Original artist:* Caveman2
- **File:Araar-root-burl-cup.jpg** *Source:* https://upload.wikimedia.org/wikipedia/commons/c/cf/Araar-root-burl-cup.jpg *License:* CC BY 2.5 *Contributors:* Own work *Original artist:* User:Huttarl
- **File:Arashiyama_Hanatōro,_Nison-in_☐☐☐☐☐☐☐☐_☐☐☐☐_DSCF5361.JPG** *Source:* https://upload.wikimedia.org/wikipedia/commons/1/19/Arashiyama_Hanat%C5%8Dro%2C_Nison-in_%E5%B5%90%E5%B1%B1%E8%8A%B1%E7%81%AF%E8%B7%AF%E3%83%BB%E4%BA%8C%E5%B0%8A%E9%99%A2_%E7%B4%85%E8%91%89%E3%81%A8%E6%9C%88_DSCF5361.JPG *License:* CC BY-SA 3.0 *Contributors:* Own work *Original artist:* 松岡明芳
- **File:Arms_of_Granada-_Coat_of_Arms_of_Spain_Template.svg** *Source:* https://upload.wikimedia.org/wikipedia/commons/a/a6/Arms_of_Granada-_Coat_of_Arms_of_Spain_Template.svg *License:* CC BY-SA 3.0 *Contributors:* Own work *Original artist:* Heralder
- **File:Asheanar.jpg** *Source:* https://upload.wikimedia.org/wikipedia/commons/5/5c/Asheanar.jpg *License:* CC-BY-SA-3.0 *Contributors:* ? *Original artist:* ?
- **File:Assorted_bonsai_pots.jpg** *Source:* https://upload.wikimedia.org/wikipedia/commons/7/7b/Assorted_bonsai_pots.jpg *License:* CC BY-SA 3.0 *Contributors:* Own work *Original artist:* Ragesoss
- **File:Atlas_Cedar,_GSBF-CN_120,_September_12,_2008.jpg** *Source:* https://upload.wikimedia.org/wikipedia/commons/6/68/Atlas_Cedar%2C_GSBF-CN_120%2C_September_12%2C_2008.jpg *License:* CC-BY-SA-3.0 *Contributors:* Own work *Original artist:* Sage Ross
- **File:Autumn_Blaze_Maple_in_Toronto.jpg** *Source:* https://upload.wikimedia.org/wikipedia/commons/3/39/Autumn_Blaze_Maple_in_Toronto.jpg *License:* CC BY-SA 4.0 *Contributors:* Own work *Original artist:* Deinocheirus
- **File:Azalea(2014).JPG** *Source:* https://upload.wikimedia.org/wikipedia/commons/c/ca/Azalea%282014%29.JPG *License:* CC BY-SA 3.0 *Contributors:* Own work *Original artist:* Kjeongeun
- **File:Azalea,_a_member_of_the_genus_Rhododendron.jpg** *Source:* https://upload.wikimedia.org/wikipedia/commons/1/17/Azalea%2C_a_member_of_the_genus_Rhododendron.jpg *License:* CC BY-SA 4.0 *Contributors:* Own work *Original artist:* i_am_jim
- **File:Azalea.750pix.jpg** *Source:* https://upload.wikimedia.org/wikipedia/commons/6/69/Azalea.750pix.jpg *License:* Public domain *Contributors:* Picture taken by Adrian Pingstone and released to the public domain. *Original artist:* Arpingstone at English Wikipedia
- **File:AzaleaFestivalNezuJinja.jpg** *Source:* https://upload.wikimedia.org/wikipedia/commons/2/23/AzaleaFestivalNezuJinja.jpg *License:* CC BY-SA 3.0 *Contributors:* Own work *Original artist:* Peachbird
- **File:Azaleas_JH.jpg** *Source:* https://upload.wikimedia.org/wikipedia/commons/6/65/Azaleas_JH.jpg *License:* Attribution *Contributors:* JGHowes *Original artist:* JGHowes, photographer
- **File:Baiera.jpg** *Source:* https://upload.wikimedia.org/wikipedia/commons/f/fb/Baiera.jpg *License:* CC BY-SA 3.0 *Contributors:* Own work *Original artist:* Rod6807
- **File:Bald_Cypress,_1987-2007.jpg** *Source:* https://upload.wikimedia.org/wikipedia/commons/b/b9/Bald_Cypress%2C_1987-2007.jpg *License:* CC BY-SA 3.0 *Contributors:* Own work *Original artist:* Ragesoss
- **File:Bald_Cypress.JPG** *Source:* https://upload.wikimedia.org/wikipedia/commons/3/37/Bald_Cypress.JPG *License:* CC BY-SA 3.0 *Contributors:* Own work *Original artist:* Kej605
- **File:Bald_Cypress_Leaves_2264px.jpg** *Source:* https://upload.wikimedia.org/wikipedia/commons/e/e3/Bald_Cypress_Leaves_2264px.jpg *License:* GFDL 1.2 *Contributors:* Own work *Original artist:* Photo by and (c)2006 Derek Ramsey (Ram-Man)
- **File:Bald_Cypress_Taxodium_distichum_Bark_Vertical.JPG** *Source:* https://upload.wikimedia.org/wikipedia/commons/c/ce/Bald_Cypress_Taxodium_distichum_Bark_Vertical.JPG *License:* CC BY-SA 4.0 *Contributors:* Self-photographed *Original artist:* Photo by and (c)2016 Derek Ramsey (Ram-Man)

- **File:Bald_Cypress_Taxodium_distichum_Fingers.JPG** *Source:* https://upload.wikimedia.org/wikipedia/commons/1/1b/Bald_Cypress_Taxodium_distichum_Fingers.JPG *License:* CC BY-SA 4.0 *Contributors:* Self-photographed *Original artist:* Photo by and (c)2016 Derek Ramsey (Ram-Man)
- **File:Bald_Cypress_swamp_and_Spanish_Moss.jpg** *Source:* https://upload.wikimedia.org/wikipedia/commons/f/f5/Bald_Cypress_swamp_and_Spanish_Moss.jpg *License:* CC BY-SA 3.0 *Contributors:* Own work *Original artist:* Lago Mar
- **File:Bald_cypress_Atchafalaya_Basin.jpg** *Source:* https://upload.wikimedia.org/wikipedia/commons/a/a8/Bald_cypress_Atchafalaya_Basin.jpg *License:* Public domain *Contributors:* U.S. Army Corps of Engineers Digital Visual Library
Image page
Image description page
Digital Visual Library home page *Original artist:* U.S. Army Corps of Engineers, photographer not specified or unknown
- **File:Bald_cypress_knees_in_duckweed.JPG** *Source:* https://upload.wikimedia.org/wikipedia/commons/b/bf/Bald_cypress_knees_in_duckweed.JPG *License:* Public domain *Contributors:* This image originates from the National Digital Library of the United States Fish and Wildlife Service
Original artist: Hillebrand, Steve - U.S. Fish and Wildlife Service
- **File:Baldcypress_cone.jpg** *Source:* https://upload.wikimedia.org/wikipedia/commons/6/65/Baldcypress_cone.jpg *License:* CC BY-SA 3.0 *Contributors:* Own work (Original text: *I created this work entirely by myself.*) *Original artist:* <a href='https://en.wikipedia.org/wiki/User:Docku' class='extiw' title='en:User:Docku'>Dock</a>*<a href='https://en.wikipedia.org/wiki/User_talk:Docku' class='extiw' title='en:User talk:Docku'>Hi</a>
- **File:Baldcypress_range.jpg** *Source:* https://upload.wikimedia.org/wikipedia/commons/2/28/Baldcypress_range.jpg *License:* Public domain *Contributors:* USGS *Original artist:* USGS
- **File:Bamboo_bonsai_Chengdu.jpg** *Source:* https://upload.wikimedia.org/wikipedia/commons/7/76/Bamboo_bonsai_Chengdu.jpg *License:* CC-BY-SA-3.0 *Contributors:* Own work *Original artist:* Felix Andrews (Floybix)
- **File:Bark_of_Pinus_thunbergii.jpg** *Source:* https://upload.wikimedia.org/wikipedia/commons/9/9f/Bark_of_Pinus_thunbergii.jpg *License:* CC BY-SA 3.0 *Contributors:* Self-photographed *Original artist:* Geographer
- **File:Bark_of_Zelkova_serrata.jpg** *Source:* https://upload.wikimedia.org/wikipedia/commons/c/ce/Bark_of_Zelkova_serrata.jpg *License:* CC BY-SA 3.0 *Contributors:* Self-photographed *Original artist:* Geographer
- **File:Berberis-aggregata.JPG** *Source:* https://upload.wikimedia.org/wikipedia/commons/a/a2/Berberis-aggregata.JPG *License:* CC-BY-SA-3.0 *Contributors:* Own work *Original artist:* Sten Porse
- **File:Berberis-thunbergii.JPG** *Source:* https://upload.wikimedia.org/wikipedia/commons/0/06/Berberis-thunbergii.JPG *License:* CC-BY-SA-3.0 *Contributors:* Own work *Original artist:* Sten Porse
- **File:Berberis-vulgaris-flowers.jpg** *Source:* https://upload.wikimedia.org/wikipedia/commons/f/f5/Berberis-vulgaris-flowers.jpg *License:* CC BY-SA 3.0 *Contributors:* Own photo, taken at Forstbotanisk Have, Århus. *Original artist:* Sten Porse
- **File:BerberisAculeata.jpg** *Source:* https://upload.wikimedia.org/wikipedia/commons/b/b4/BerberisAculeata.jpg *License:* CC BY-SA 3.0 *Contributors:* Own work *Original artist:* L. Shyamal
- **File:Berberis_gagnepainii_flowers.jpg** *Source:* https://upload.wikimedia.org/wikipedia/commons/c/c9/Berberis_gagnepainii_flowers.jpg *License:* CC-BY-SA-3.0 *Contributors:* http://en.wikipedia.org/wiki/Image:Berberis_gagn_fls.jpg *Original artist:* MPF
- **File:Berberis_gagnepainii_fruit.jpg** *Source:* https://upload.wikimedia.org/wikipedia/commons/4/42/Berberis_gagnepainii_fruit.jpg *License:* CC-BY-SA-3.0 *Contributors:* http://en.wikipedia.org/wiki/Image:Berberis_gagn_frt.jpg *Original artist:* MPF
- **File:Berberis_gagnepainii_thorn.jpg** *Source:* https://upload.wikimedia.org/wikipedia/commons/4/40/Berberis_gagnepainii_thorn.jpg *License:* CC-BY-SA-3.0 *Contributors:* http://en.wikipedia.org/wiki/Image:Berberis_gagn_thorn.jpg *Original artist:* =MPF
- **File:Berberis_valdiviana_120502-2.jpg** *Source:* https://upload.wikimedia.org/wikipedia/commons/8/8f/Berberis_valdiviana_120502-2.jpg *License:* CC0 *Contributors:* Own work *Original artist:* Peter coxhead
- **File:Berberis_verruculosa_leaves.jpg** *Source:* https://upload.wikimedia.org/wikipedia/commons/7/7c/Berberis_verruculosa_leaves.jpg *License:* CC-BY-SA-3.0 *Contributors:* http://en.wikipedia.org/wiki/Image:Berberis_verruculosa.jpg *Original artist:* MPF
- **File:Bidni_Tree_Trunks.png** *Source:* https://upload.wikimedia.org/wikipedia/commons/8/85/Bidni_Tree_Trunks.png *License:* CC BY-SA 4.0 *Contributors:* Own work *Original artist:* PolluxWorld
- **File:Birch_bark_document_210.jpg** *Source:* https://upload.wikimedia.org/wikipedia/commons/2/2a/Birch_bark_document_210.jpg *License:* Public domain *Contributors:* ? *Original artist:* ?
- **File:Birch_bark_front_rear.jpg** *Source:* https://upload.wikimedia.org/wikipedia/commons/7/7d/Birch_bark_front_rear.jpg *License:* CC BY-SA 3.0 *Contributors:* Own work *Original artist:* Choogler
- **File:Birke_Multiplex.JPG** *Source:* https://upload.wikimedia.org/wikipedia/commons/8/81/Birke_Multiplex.JPG *License:* CC BY-SA 3.0 *Contributors:* Own work *Original artist:* Lutzeputz
- **File:Black_Hills_Spruce_bonsai_forest_planting,_July_13,_2008.jpg** *Source:* https://upload.wikimedia.org/wikipedia/commons/5/56/Black_Hills_Spruce_bonsai_forest_planting%2C_July_13%2C_2008.jpg *License:* CC BY-SA 3.0 *Contributors:* Own work *Original artist:* Ragesoss
- **File:Black_Locust_Leaf_Close_Up.jpg** *Source:* https://upload.wikimedia.org/wikipedia/commons/8/86/Black_Locust_Leaf_Close_Up.jpg *License:* CC BY-SA 4.0 *Contributors:* Own work *Original artist:* HoHey22
- **File:Black_Pomegranate.JPG** *Source:* https://upload.wikimedia.org/wikipedia/commons/f/fa/Black_Pomegranate.JPG *License:* Public domain *Contributors:* Own work *Original artist:* Cimorghe

4.2. IMAGES

- **File:Black_alder_in_spring.JPG** *Source:* https://upload.wikimedia.org/wikipedia/commons/7/75/Black_alder_in_spring.JPG *License:* Public domain *Contributors:* Own work *Original artist:* peppigue
- **File:Blue_Atlas_Cedar,_1950-2007.jpg** *Source:* https://upload.wikimedia.org/wikipedia/commons/8/8c/Blue_Atlas_Cedar%2C_1950-2007.jpg *License:* CC-BY-SA-3.0 *Contributors:* Own work *Original artist:* Ragesoss
- **File:Bonsai33jf.JPG** *Source:* https://upload.wikimedia.org/wikipedia/commons/b/ba/Bonsai33jf.JPG *License:* CC BY-SA 3.0 *Contributors:* Own work *Original artist:* Ramon FVelasquez
- **File:BonsaiTridentMaple.jpg** *Source:* https://upload.wikimedia.org/wikipedia/commons/e/e1/BonsaiTridentMaple.jpg *License:* Public domain *Contributors:* This image was released by the Agricultural Research Service, the research agency of the United States Department of Agriculture, with the ID K10474-1 <a class='external text' href='//commons.wikimedia.org/w/index.php?title=Category:Media_created_by_the_United_States_Agricultural_Research_Service_with_known_IDs,<span>,&,</span>,filefrom=K10474-1#mw-category-media'>(next)</a>. *Original artist:* Peggy Greb, USDA
- **File:Bonsai_Besen-Form.svg** *Source:* https://upload.wikimedia.org/wikipedia/commons/6/68/Bonsai_Besen-Form.svg *License:* CC-BY-SA-3.0 *Contributors:* Own «transformation» png>svg plus colors *Original artist:* Original by de:Benutzer:Neitram, edited into svg by Simon Eugster --Simon 20:19, 20 July 2006 (UTC)
- **File:Bonsai_Doppelstamm-Form.svg** *Source:* https://upload.wikimedia.org/wikipedia/commons/d/d4/Bonsai_Doppelstamm-Form.svg *License:* CC-BY-SA-3.0 *Contributors:* Own «transformation» png>svg plus colors *Original artist:* Original by de:Benutzer:Neitram, edited into svg by Simon Eugster --Simon 20:19, 20 July 2006 (UTC)
- **File:Bonsai_Halbkaskaden-Form.svg** *Source:* https://upload.wikimedia.org/wikipedia/commons/1/1b/Bonsai_Halbkaskaden-Form.svg *License:* CC-BY-SA-3.0 *Contributors:* Own «transformation» png>svg plus colors *Original artist:* Original by de:Benutzer:Neitram, edited into svg by Simon Eugster --Simon 20:19, 20 July 2006 (UTC)
- **File:Bonsai_IMG_6394.jpg** *Source:* https://upload.wikimedia.org/wikipedia/commons/9/92/Bonsai_IMG_6394.jpg *License:* CC BY-SA 2.5 *Contributors:* ? *Original artist:* ?
- **File:Bonsai_IMG_6402.jpg** *Source:* https://upload.wikimedia.org/wikipedia/commons/3/34/Bonsai_IMG_6402.jpg *License:* CC BY-SA 2.5 *Contributors:* ? *Original artist:* ?
- **File:Bonsai_Juniperus_procumbens.jpg** *Source:* https://upload.wikimedia.org/wikipedia/commons/a/a2/Bonsai_Juniperus_procumbens.jpg *License:* CC BY-SA 2.5 *Contributors:* No machine-readable source provided. Own work assumed (based on copyright claims). *Original artist:* No machine-readable author provided. MPF assumed (based on copyright claims).
- **File:Bonsai_Kaskaden-Form.svg** *Source:* https://upload.wikimedia.org/wikipedia/commons/0/07/Bonsai_Kaskaden-Form.svg *License:* CC-BY-SA-3.0 *Contributors:* Own «transformation» png>svg plus colors *Original artist:* Original by de:Benutzer:Neitram, edited into svg by Simon Eugster --Simon 20:19, 20 July 2006 (UTC)
- **File:Bonsai_Literaten-Form.svg** *Source:* https://upload.wikimedia.org/wikipedia/commons/e/ef/Bonsai_Literaten-Form.svg *License:* CC-BY-SA-3.0 *Contributors:* Own «transformation» png>svg plus colors *Original artist:* Original by de:Benutzer:Neitram, edited into svg by Simon Eugster --Simon 20:19, 20 July 2006 (UTC)
- **File:Bonsai_United_States_National_Arboretum_7.JPG** *Source:* https://upload.wikimedia.org/wikipedia/commons/9/95/Bonsai_United_States_National_Arboretum_7.JPG *License:* GFDL *Contributors:* Own work *Original artist:* Abraham
- **File:Bonsai_display_with_Seiju_elm,_miniature_hosta_and_hanging_scroll,_12_July_2009.jpg** *Source:* https://upload.wikimedia.org/wikipedia/commons/7/70/Bonsai_display_with_Seiju_elm%2C_miniature_hosta_and_hanging_scroll%2C_12_July_2009.jpg *License:* CC BY-SA 3.0 *Contributors:* Own work *Original artist:* Sage Ross
- **File:Bonsai_locker_aufrechte_Form.svg** *Source:* https://upload.wikimedia.org/wikipedia/commons/b/bd/Bonsai_locker_aufrechte_Form.svg *License:* CC-BY-SA-3.0 *Contributors:* Own «transformation» png>svg plus colors *Original artist:* Original by de:Benutzer:Neitram, edited into svg by Simon Eugster --Simon 20:19, 20 July 2006 (UTC)
- **File:Bonsai_streng_aufrechte_Form.svg** *Source:* https://upload.wikimedia.org/wikipedia/commons/7/73/Bonsai_streng_aufrechte_Form.svg *License:* CC-BY-SA-3.0 *Contributors:* Own «transformation» png>svg plus colors *Original artist:* Original by de:Benutzer:Neitram, edited into svg by Simon Eugster --Simon 20:20, 20 July 2006 (UTC)
- **File:Bonsai_tools.jpg** *Source:* https://upload.wikimedia.org/wikipedia/commons/5/56/Bonsai_tools.jpg *License:* CC-BY-SA-3.0 *Contributors:* Own work *Original artist:* Ragesoss
- **File:Bonsai_tree2.jpg** *Source:* https://upload.wikimedia.org/wikipedia/commons/6/66/Bonsai_tree2.jpg *License:* CC BY-SA 3.0 *Contributors:* Own work *Original artist:* Japanexperterna.se
- **File:Bonsai_windgepeitschte_Form.svg** *Source:* https://upload.wikimedia.org/wikipedia/commons/7/78/Bonsai_windgepeitschte_Form.svg *License:* CC-BY-SA-3.0 *Contributors:* Own «transformation» png>svg plus colors *Original artist:* Simon Eugster --Simon 16:01, 20 July 2006 (UTC)
- **File:Botticelligranat_bild.jpg** *Source:* https://upload.wikimedia.org/wikipedia/commons/d/d2/Botticelligranat_bild.jpg *License:* Public domain *Contributors:* Web Gallery of Art: <a href='http://www.wga.hu/art/b/botticel/22/41pomegr.jpg' data-x-rel='nofollow'><img alt='Inkscape.svg' src='https://upload.wikimedia.org/wikipedia/commons/thumb/6/6f/Inkscape.svg/20px-Inkscape.svg.png' width='20' height='20' srcset='https://upload.wikimedia.org/wikipedia/commons/thumb/6/6f/Inkscape.svg/30px-Inkscape.svg.png 1.5x, https://upload.wikimedia.org/wikipedia/commons/thumb/6/6f/Inkscape.svg/40px-Inkscape.svg.png 2x' data-file-width='60' data-file-height='60' /></a> Image <a href='http://www.wga.hu/html/b/botticel/22/41pomegr.html' data-x-rel='nofollow'><img alt='Information icon.svg' src='https://upload.wikimedia.org/wikipedia/commons/thumb/3/35/Information_icon.svg/20px-Information_icon.svg.png' width='20' height='20' srcset='https://upload.wikimedia.org/wikipedia/commons/thumb/3/35/Information_icon.svg/30px-Information_icon.svg.png 1.5x, https://upload.wikimedia.org/wikipedia/commons/thumb/3/35/Information_icon.svg/40px-Information_icon.svg.png 2x' data-file-width='620' data-file-height='620' /></a> Info about artwork *Original artist:* Sandro Botticelli

- **File:BougainvilleaGlabraFlowers.jpg** *Source:* https://upload.wikimedia.org/wikipedia/commons/b/b5/BougainvilleaGlabraFlowers.jpg *License:* Public domain *Contributors:* Own work (Original text: *I (Chhe (talk)) created this work entirely by myself.*) *Original artist:* Chhe (talk)
- **File:BougainvilleaGlabraVine.jpg** *Source:* https://upload.wikimedia.org/wikipedia/commons/3/3f/BougainvilleaGlabraVine.jpg *License:* Public domain *Contributors:* Own work (Original text: *I (Chhe (talk)) created this work entirely by myself.*) *Original artist:* Chhe (talk)
- **File:Bougainvillea_glabra_(5).jpg** *Source:* https://upload.wikimedia.org/wikipedia/commons/7/7b/Bougainvillea_glabra_%285%29.jpg *License:* CC BY-SA 4.0 *Contributors:* Own work,http://www.flowersview.com/Bougainvillea%20glabra/Bougainvillea+glabra+%288%29.jpg.html *Original artist:* Fanwen619
- **File:Bougainvillea_glabra_at_Kadavoor.jpg** *Source:* https://upload.wikimedia.org/wikipedia/commons/e/e4/Bougainvillea_glabra_at_Kadavoor.jpg *License:* CC BY-SA 4.0 *Contributors:* Own work *Original artist:* **Jeevan Jose, Kerala, India**
- **File:Boulevard_cypress.jpg** *Source:* https://upload.wikimedia.org/wikipedia/commons/b/ba/Boulevard_cypress.jpg *License:* CC BY-SA 3.0 *Contributors:* Own work *Original artist:* MPF
- **File:Boxwood_Buxus_sempervirens_var._arborescens_Bark_2597px.jpg** *Source:* https://upload.wikimedia.org/wikipedia/commons/a/a1/Boxwood_Buxus_sempervirens_var._arborescens_Bark_2597px.jpg *License:* GFDL 1.2 *Contributors:* Self-photographed *Original artist:* Photo (c)2007 Derek Ramsey (Ram-Man)
- **File:Boxwood_Buxus_sempervirens_var._arborescens_Bark_Closeup_1825px.jpg** *Source:* https://upload.wikimedia.org/wikipedia/commons/9/92/Boxwood_Buxus_sempervirens_var._arborescens_Bark_Closeup_1825px.jpg *License:* GFDL 1.2 *Contributors:* Self-photographed *Original artist:* Photo (c)2007 Derek Ramsey (Ram-Man)
- **File:Briesetal_bei_Briese.JPG** *Source:* https://upload.wikimedia.org/wikipedia/commons/0/06/Briesetal_bei_Briese.JPG *License:* CC-BY-SA-3.0 *Contributors:* Own work *Original artist:* Bernd Schade
- **File:Bunchberry_plants.jpg** *Source:* https://upload.wikimedia.org/wikipedia/commons/b/b6/Bunchberry_plants.jpg *License:* CC BY-SA 3.0 *Contributors:* Own work *Original artist:* D. Gordon E. Robertson
- **File:Buxus-microphylla-sinica.JPG** *Source:* https://upload.wikimedia.org/wikipedia/commons/5/51/Buxus-microphylla-sinica.JPG *License:* CC-BY-SA-3.0 *Contributors:* Own work *Original artist:* Sten Porse
- **File:Buxus_henryi.jpg** *Source:* https://upload.wikimedia.org/wikipedia/commons/b/b3/Buxus_henryi.jpg *License:* Public domain *Contributors:* Own work *Original artist:* PiPi
- **File:Buxus_sempervirens.jpg** *Source:* https://upload.wikimedia.org/wikipedia/commons/f/fd/Buxus_sempervirens.jpg *License:* CC BY 2.5 *Contributors:* No machine-readable source provided. Own work assumed (based on copyright claims). *Original artist:* No machine-readable author provided. MPF assumed (based on copyright claims).
- **File:Buxus_sempervirens0.jpg** *Source:* https://upload.wikimedia.org/wikipedia/commons/a/a0/Buxus_sempervirens0.jpg *License:* CC-BY-SA-3.0 *Contributors:* ? *Original artist:* ?
- **File:Buxus_wallichiana.jpg** *Source:* https://upload.wikimedia.org/wikipedia/commons/9/92/Buxus_wallichiana.jpg *License:* CC-BY-SA-3.0 *Contributors:* Own work *Original artist:* MPF
- **File:CAMELLIA_japonica_'White_by_the_Gate'.jpg** *Source:* https://upload.wikimedia.org/wikipedia/commons/0/03/CAMELLIA_japonica_%27White_by_the_Gate%27.jpg *License:* CC BY-SA 4.0 *Contributors:* Own work *Original artist:* Bill Golladay
- **File:CYUS_PALM.JPG** *Source:* https://upload.wikimedia.org/wikipedia/commons/5/55/CYUS_PALM.JPG *License:* CC BY-SA 2.5 *Contributors:* No machine-readable source provided. Own work assumed (based on copyright claims). *Original artist:* No machine-readable author provided. Yousaf465 assumed (based on copyright claims).
- **File:Caddo_Lake-_Cypress.jpg** *Source:* https://upload.wikimedia.org/wikipedia/commons/6/6c/Caddo_Lake-_Cypress.jpg *License:* CC BY-SA 2.5 *Contributors:* Author *Original artist:* Jay Carriker (User:JCarriker)
- **File:Camelia_japonica_'Drama_Girl'_2006-05-03_032.jpg** *Source:* https://upload.wikimedia.org/wikipedia/commons/1/13/Camelia_japonica_%27Drama_Girl%27_2006-05-03_032.jpg *License:* CC-BY-SA-3.0 *Contributors:* Own work *Original artist:* BS Thurner Hof
- **File:Camelia_japonica_'Royal_Velvet'_2006-05-03_046.jpg** *Source:* https://upload.wikimedia.org/wikipedia/commons/6/67/Camelia_japonica_%27Royal_Velvet%27_2006-05-03_046.jpg *License:* CC-BY-SA-3.0 *Contributors:* Own work *Original artist:* BS Thurner Hof
- **File:Camelia_japonica_Dr._Tinsley_2006-04-8_200.jpg** *Source:* https://upload.wikimedia.org/wikipedia/commons/8/88/Camelia_japonica_Dr._Tinsley_2006-04-8_200.jpg *License:* CC-BY-SA-3.0 *Contributors:* Own work *Original artist:* BS Thurner Hof
- **File:Camelia_japonica_triphosa_2006-04-8_194.jpg** *Source:* https://upload.wikimedia.org/wikipedia/commons/6/6f/Camelia_japonica_triphosa_2006-04-8_194.jpg *License:* CC-BY-SA-3.0 *Contributors:* Own work *Original artist:* BS Thurner Hof
- **File:Camellia.japonica.cv.Ashiya.7166.jpg** *Source:* https://upload.wikimedia.org/wikipedia/commons/f/f6/Camellia.japonica.cv.Ashiya.7166.jpg *License:* CC-BY-SA-3.0 *Contributors:* picture taken by Olaf Leillinger at 2006-03-04 *Original artist:* Olaf Leillinger
- **File:Camellia.japonica.cv.Chandlers.Elegance.7167.jpg** *Source:* https://upload.wikimedia.org/wikipedia/commons/9/91/Camellia.japonica.cv.Chandlers.Elegance.7167.jpg *License:* CC-BY-SA-3.0 *Contributors:* ? *Original artist:* ?
- **File:Camellia.japonica.cv.Colombo.7168.jpg** *Source:* https://upload.wikimedia.org/wikipedia/commons/2/21/Camellia.japonica.cv.Colombo.7168.jpg *License:* CC-BY-SA-3.0 *Contributors:* ? *Original artist:* ?
- **File:Camellia_'Dahlohnega'.jpg** *Source:* https://upload.wikimedia.org/wikipedia/commons/5/54/Camellia_%27Dahlohnega%27.jpg *License:* CC0 *Contributors:* This file was derived from Kamelie in Pirna 10.JPG: <a href='//commons.wikimedia.org/wiki/File:Kamelie_in_Pirna_10.JPG' class='image'><img alt='Kamelie in Pirna 10.JPG' src='https://upload.wikimedia.org/wikipedia/commons/thumb/6/60/Kamelie_in_Pirna_10.JPG/50px-Kamelie_in_Pirna_10.JPG' width='50' height='38' srcset='https://upload.wikimedia.org/wikipedia/commons/thumb/6/60/Kamelie_in_Pirna_10.JPG/75px-Kamelie_in_Pirna_10.JPG 1.5x, https://upload.wikimedia.org/wikipedia/commons/thumb/6/60/Kamelie_in_Pirna_10.JPG/100px-Kamelie_in_Pirna_10.JPG 2x' data-file-width='2560' data-file-height='1920' /></a> *Original artist:* Kamelie_in_Pirna_10.JPG: Brücke-Osteuropa

4.2. IMAGES

- **File:Camellia_'Dr_Clifford_Parks'{}.jpg** *Source:* https://upload.wikimedia.org/wikipedia/commons/6/63/Camellia_%27Dr_Clifford_Parks%27.jpg *License:* CC BY-SA 3.0 *Contributors:* Own work *Original artist:* A. Barra
- **File:Camellia_'Duchesse_de_Berry'.jpg** *Source:* https://upload.wikimedia.org/wikipedia/commons/2/29/Camellia_%27Duchesse_de_Berry%27.jpg *License:* GFDL *Contributors:* Own work *Original artist:* A. Barra
- **File:Camellia_'Nuccio'{}s_Jewel'.JPG** *Source:* https://upload.wikimedia.org/wikipedia/commons/5/5f/Camellia_%27Nuccio%27s_Jewel%27.JPG *License:* CC0 *Contributors:* This file was derived from Kamelie in Pirna 10.JPG: <a href='//commons.wikimedia.org/wiki/File:Kamelie_in_Pirna_10.JPG' class='image'><img alt='Kamelie in Pirna 10.JPG' src='https://upload.wikimedia.org/wikipedia/commons/thumb/6/60/Kamelie_in_Pirna_10.JPG/50px-Kamelie_in_Pirna_10.JPG' width='50' height='38' srcset='https://upload.wikimedia.org/wikipedia/commons/thumb/6/60/Kamelie_in_Pirna_10.JPG/75px-Kamelie_in_Pirna_10.JPG 1.5x, https://upload.wikimedia.org/wikipedia/commons/thumb/6/60/Kamelie_in_Pirna_10.JPG/100px-Kamelie_in_Pirna_10.JPG 2x' data-file-width='2560' data-file-height='1920' /></a>
Original artist: Kamelie_in_Pirna_10.JPG: Brücke-Osteuropa
- **File:Camellia_'Sekidotaroan'1.jpg** *Source:* https://upload.wikimedia.org/wikipedia/commons/1/1a/Camellia_%27Sekidotaroan%271.jpg *License:* CC-BY-SA-3.0 *Contributors:* KENPEI's photo *Original artist:* KENPEI
- **File:Camellia_Japonica_'Ville_De_Nantes'{}.JPG** *Source:* https://upload.wikimedia.org/wikipedia/commons/3/3d/Camellia_Japonica_%27Ville_De_Nantes%27.JPG *License:* CC BY-SA 4.0 *Contributors:* Own work *Original artist:* Bill Golladay
- **File:Camellia_Japonica_-_Black_Lace.jpg** *Source:* https://upload.wikimedia.org/wikipedia/commons/1/14/Camellia_Japonica_-_Black_Lace.jpg *License:* CC BY-SA 2.5 *Contributors:* I took the picture at a public manifestation (41a Mostra Nazionale della Camelia, Verbania, Italy) *Original artist:* Rocco Pier Luigi
- **File:Camellia_japonica_'Ann_Blair_Brown_Variegated'.JPG** *Source:* https://upload.wikimedia.org/wikipedia/commons/3/38/Camellia_japonica_%27Ann_Blair_Brown_Variegated%27.JPG *License:* CC BY-SA 4.0 *Contributors:* Own work *Original artist:* Bill Golladay
- **File:Camellia_japonica_'Bob_Hope'.jpg** *Source:* https://upload.wikimedia.org/wikipedia/commons/9/9b/Camellia_japonica_%27Bob_Hope%27.jpg *License:* CC0 *Contributors:* Own work *Original artist:* Brücke-Osteuropa
- **File:Camellia_japonica_'C.M._Wilson'.JPG** *Source:* https://upload.wikimedia.org/wikipedia/commons/2/20/Camellia_japonica_%27C.M._Wilson%27.JPG *License:* CC BY-SA 4.0 *Contributors:* Own work *Original artist:* Bill Golladay
- **File:Camellia_japonica_'Coquettii'_01.jpg** *Source:* https://upload.wikimedia.org/wikipedia/commons/2/20/Camellia_japonica_%27Coquettii%27_01.jpg *License:* CC BY-SA 3.0 *Contributors:* Own work *Original artist:* Alicia Fagerving
- **File:Camellia_japonica_'Fred_Sander'.jpg** *Source:* https://upload.wikimedia.org/wikipedia/commons/a/a2/Camellia_japonica_%27Fred_Sander%27.jpg *License:* CC0 *Contributors:* Own work *Original artist:* Brücke-Osteuropa
- **File:Camellia_japonica_'Mercury_Supreme'.JPG** *Source:* https://upload.wikimedia.org/wikipedia/commons/d/dc/Camellia_japonica_%27Mercury_Supreme%27.JPG *License:* CC BY-SA 4.0 *Contributors:* Own work *Original artist:* Bill Golladay
- **File:Camellia_japonica_'Nobilissima'.jpg** *Source:* https://upload.wikimedia.org/wikipedia/commons/3/36/Camellia_japonica_%27Nobilissima%27.jpg *License:* CC-BY-SA-3.0 *Contributors:* Own work *Original artist:* Rasbak
- **File:Camellia_japonica_'The_Czar'.jpg** *Source:* https://upload.wikimedia.org/wikipedia/commons/3/39/Camellia_japonica_%27The_Czar%27.jpg *License:* CC BY 3.0 *Contributors:* Own work (digital photograph by author) *Original artist:* Melburnian
- **File:Camellia_japonica_'kamo-honnnami'.jpg** *Source:* https://upload.wikimedia.org/wikipedia/commons/3/3e/Camellia_japonica_%27kamo-honnnami%27.jpg *License:* CC-BY-SA-3.0 *Contributors:* KENPEI's photo *Original artist:* KENPEI
- **File:Camellia_japonica_Bernhard_Lauterbach_0503282_Kalenderkopie.jpg** *Source:* https://upload.wikimedia.org/wikipedia/commons/b/b8/Camellia_japonica_Bernhard_Lauterbach_0503282_Kalenderkopie.jpg *License:* CC-BY-SA-3.0 *Contributors:* Own work *Original artist:* BS Thurner Hof
- **File:Camellia_japonica_var._decumbens_3.JPG** *Source:* https://upload.wikimedia.org/wikipedia/commons/6/6d/Camellia_japonica_var._decumbens_3.JPG *License:* CC BY-SA 3.0 *Contributors:* Qwert1234's file *Original artist:* Qwert1234
- **File:Camellia_sasanqua_Yuletide_2.jpg** *Source:* https://upload.wikimedia.org/wikipedia/commons/6/6c/Camellia_sasanqua_Yuletide_2.jpg *License:* CC BY-SA 3.0 *Contributors:* Own work *Original artist:* by User:Stan Shebs
- **File:CarissaMacrocarpa.jpg** *Source:* https://upload.wikimedia.org/wikipedia/commons/1/17/CarissaMacrocarpa.jpg *License:* Public domain *Contributors:* Own work (Original text: *I created this work entirely by myself.*) *Original artist:* Chhe (talk)
- **File:Carissa_bispinosa_Uniondale_1168.jpg** *Source:* https://upload.wikimedia.org/wikipedia/commons/e/e0/Carissa_bispinosa_Uniondale_1168.jpg *License:* CC BY-SA 3.0 *Contributors:* Own work *Original artist:* JonRichfield
- **File:Carissa_macrocarpa,_vrug_deursnit,_TUT-kampus,_b.jpg** *Source:* https://upload.wikimedia.org/wikipedia/commons/7/75/Carissa_macrocarpa%2C_vrug_deursnit%2C_TUT-kampus%2C_b.jpg *License:* CC BY-SA 3.0 *Contributors:* Own work *Original artist:* JMK
- **File:Carissa_spinarum_near_Hyderabad_W_IMG_7612.jpg** *Source:* https://upload.wikimedia.org/wikipedia/commons/2/2b/Carissa_spinarum_near_Hyderabad_W_IMG_7612.jpg *License:* CC BY 3.0 *Contributors:* Own work *Original artist:* J.M.Garg
- **File:Castle_Himeji_sakura01_adjusted.jpg** *Source:* https://upload.wikimedia.org/wikipedia/commons/6/6b/Castle_Himeji_sakura01_adjusted.jpg *License:* CC-BY-SA-3.0 *Contributors:* Image:Castle_Himeji_sakura01.jpg *Original artist:* Taken by Miya.m, color correction by Gorgo, level-adjusted by Quasipalm
- **File:Casuarina_equisetifolia_-_Darwin_NT.jpg** *Source:* https://upload.wikimedia.org/wikipedia/commons/6/6f/Casuarina_equisetifolia_-_Darwin_NT.jpg *License:* CC BY 3.0 *Contributors:* Own work *Original artist:* Bidgee
- **File:Casuarina_equisetifolia_MHNT.BOT.2016.24.39.jpg** *Source:* https://upload.wikimedia.org/wikipedia/commons/c/c1/Casuarina_equisetifolia_MHNT.BOT.2016.24.39.jpg *License:* CC BY-SA 3.0 *Contributors:* Own work *Original artist:* Roger Culos

- File:Casuarina_equisetifolia_at_Chikhaldara,_Maharashtra02.jpg *Source:* https://upload.wikimedia.org/wikipedia/commons/2/24/Casuarina_equisetifolia_at_Chikhaldara%2C_Maharashtra02.jpg *License:* CC BY-SA 4.0 *Contributors:* Own work *Original artist:* Yogdes
- File:Casuarina_equisetifolia_fruits.jpg *Source:* https://upload.wikimedia.org/wikipedia/commons/5/56/Casuarina_equisetifolia_fruits.jpg *License:* CC-BY-SA-3.0 *Contributors:* ? *Original artist:* ?
- File:Casuarina_equisetifolia_leaves.jpg *Source:* https://upload.wikimedia.org/wikipedia/commons/1/1e/Casuarina_equisetifolia_leaves.jpg *License:* CC-BY-SA-3.0 *Contributors:* Own work *Original artist:* Eric Guinther
- File:Casuarina_litter.jpg *Source:* https://upload.wikimedia.org/wikipedia/commons/d/d8/Casuarina_litter.jpg *License:* CC-BY-SA-3.0 *Contributors:* Own work *Original artist:* Eric Guinther
- File:Cedar_of_Lebanon_cone.JPG *Source:* https://upload.wikimedia.org/wikipedia/commons/c/c4/Cedar_of_Lebanon_cone.JPG *License:* Public domain *Contributors:* self-made - Roger Griffith *Original artist:* Rosser1954
- File:Cedararz.jpg *Source:* https://upload.wikimedia.org/wikipedia/en/2/26/Cedararz.jpg *License:* PD *Contributors:*

    Own work

    Original artist:

    Yoniw (talk) (Uploads)
- File:Cedri_BMK.jpg *Source:* https://upload.wikimedia.org/wikipedia/commons/6/65/Cedri_BMK.jpg *License:* CC BY-SA 2.0 de *Contributors:* Own work (own picture) *Original artist:* User:BMK
- File:Cedrus_atlantica-Glauca-Bonsai.jpg *Source:* https://upload.wikimedia.org/wikipedia/commons/5/5d/Cedrus_atlantica-Glauca-Bonsai.jpg *License:* CC BY 2.0 *Contributors:* ? *Original artist:* ?
- File:Cedrus_atlantica2.jpg *Source:* https://upload.wikimedia.org/wikipedia/commons/0/06/Cedrus_atlantica2.jpg *License:* CC-BY-SA-3.0 *Contributors:* ? *Original artist:* ?
- File:Cedrus_atlantica_male_cones.jpg *Source:* https://upload.wikimedia.org/wikipedia/commons/2/27/Cedrus_atlantica_male_cones.jpg *License:* CC BY-SA 3.0 *Contributors:* Own work *Original artist:* Meneerke bloem
- File:Cedrus_libani_shoot.jpg *Source:* https://upload.wikimedia.org/wikipedia/commons/8/8d/Cedrus_libani_shoot.jpg *License:* CC-BY-SA-3.0 *Contributors:* ? *Original artist:* ?
- File:Cedrus_libani_ssp._atlantica_'Glauca'_cone_02_by_Line1.jpg *Source:* https://upload.wikimedia.org/wikipedia/commons/7/79/Cedrus_libani_ssp._atlantica_%27Glauca%27_cone_02_by_Line1.jpg *License:* CC BY 2.5 *Contributors:* Picture taken with my IXUS 800 IS *Original artist:* Liné1
- File:Cedrus_wood.jpg *Source:* https://upload.wikimedia.org/wikipedia/commons/d/da/Cedrus_wood.jpg *License:* CC BY-SA 3.0 *Contributors:* No machine-readable source provided. Own work assumed (based on copyright claims). *Original artist:* No machine-readable author provided. Brodo assumed (based on copyright claims).
- File:Celtis-caucasica-fruit.JPG *Source:* https://upload.wikimedia.org/wikipedia/commons/3/3c/Celtis-caucasica-fruit.JPG *License:* CC-BY-SA-3.0 *Contributors:* own work by Sten Porse *Original artist:* Sten Porse
- File:Celtis_aetnensis.jpg *Source:* https://upload.wikimedia.org/wikipedia/commons/a/a7/Celtis_aetnensis.jpg *License:* CC-BY-SA-3.0 *Contributors:* http://web.tiscali.it/florasicula/ authorization *Original artist:* Girolamo Giardina
    uploaded by Esculapio
- File:Celtis_africana,_blomme,_Manie_van_der_Schijff_BT,_a.jpg *Source:* https://upload.wikimedia.org/wikipedia/commons/f/fc/Celtis_africana%2C_blomme%2C_Manie_van_der_Schijff_BT%2C_a.jpg *License:* CC BY-SA 3.0 *Contributors:* Own work *Original artist:* JMK
- File:Celtis_australis-StSauveur-4925~{}2015_10_31.JPG *Source:* https://upload.wikimedia.org/wikipedia/commons/6/65/Celtis_australis-StSauveur-4925~{}2015_10_31.JPG *License:* CC BY-SA 4.0 *Contributors:* Own work *Original artist:* **This picture is a work by Emmanuel Douzery**.
- File:Celtis_integrifolia.jpg *Source:* https://upload.wikimedia.org/wikipedia/commons/3/3b/Celtis_integrifolia.jpg *License:* Public domain *Contributors:* ? *Original artist:* ?
- File:Celtis_occidentalis_leaf.png *Source:* https://upload.wikimedia.org/wikipedia/commons/3/35/Celtis_occidentalis_leaf.png *License:* CC BY-SA 3.0 *Contributors:* Own work *Original artist:* Sapphosyne
- File:Celtis_sinensis=Chinese_Hackberry.jpg *Source:* https://upload.wikimedia.org/wikipedia/commons/a/a6/Celtis_sinensis%3DChinese_Hackberry.jpg *License:* CC BY 3.0 *Contributors:* Own work by the original uploader *Original artist:* Geographer (talk)
- File:CerejeirasEstufaJBCuritiba.JPG *Source:* https://upload.wikimedia.org/wikipedia/commons/4/49/CerejeirasEstufaJBCuritiba.JPG *License:* CC BY 3.0 *Contributors:* Own work *Original artist:* SamirNosteb
- File:ChaenomelesFruit02floweringquince02.jpg *Source:* https://upload.wikimedia.org/wikipedia/commons/f/fd/ChaenomelesFruit02floweringquince02.jpg *License:* CC-BY-SA-3.0 *Contributors:* No machine-readable source provided. Own work assumed (based on copyright claims). *Original artist:* No machine-readable author provided. Meika assumed (based on copyright claims).
- File:Chaenomeles_japonica1.jpg *Source:* https://upload.wikimedia.org/wikipedia/commons/d/d3/Chaenomeles_japonica1.jpg *License:* CC BY-SA 2.5 *Contributors:* self-made (Nikon D40) *Original artist:* Daniel78
- File:Chamaecyparis_Obtusa_bonsai.JPG *Source:* https://upload.wikimedia.org/wikipedia/commons/9/9e/Chamaecyparis_Obtusa_bonsai.JPG *License:* CC BY-SA 3.0 *Contributors:* Own work *Original artist:* Jeffrey O. Gustafson
- File:Chamaecyparis_Pisifera_bonsai.JPG *Source:* https://upload.wikimedia.org/wikipedia/commons/c/cf/Chamaecyparis_Pisifera_bonsai.JPG *License:* CC BY-SA 3.0 *Contributors:* Own work *Original artist:* Jeffrey O. Gustafson

4.2. IMAGES

- **File:Chamaecyparis_obtusa2.jpg** *Source:* https://upload.wikimedia.org/wikipedia/commons/7/7c/Chamaecyparis_obtusa2.jpg *License:* CC-BY-SA-3.0 *Contributors:* Hamachidori *Original artist:* Hamachidori
- **File:Chamaecyparis_obtusa5.jpg** *Source:* https://upload.wikimedia.org/wikipedia/commons/4/40/Chamaecyparis_obtusa5.jpg *License:* CC-BY-SA-3.0 *Contributors:* KENPEI's photo *Original artist:* KENPEI
- **File:Chamaecyparis_obtusa_'Nana_gracilis'{}.jpg** *Source:* https://upload.wikimedia.org/wikipedia/commons/0/00/Chamaecyparis_obtusa_%27Nana_gracilis%27.jpg *License:* Public domain *Contributors:* Transferred from en.wikipedia to Commons by Sreejithk2000 using CommonsHelper. *Original artist:* HelloMojo at English Wikipedia
- **File:Chamaecyparis_obtusa_01.jpg** *Source:* https://upload.wikimedia.org/wikipedia/commons/6/6e/Chamaecyparis_obtusa_01.jpg *License:* CC BY 3.0 *Contributors:* Own work *Original artist:* Σ64
- **File:Chamaecyparis_pisifera_golden_charm_sawara_cypress_MN_2007.JPG** *Source:* https://upload.wikimedia.org/wikipedia/commons/9/90/Chamaecyparis_pisifera_golden_charm_sawara_cypress_MN_2007.JPG *License:* CC-BY-SA-3.0 *Contributors:* Own work *Original artist:* SEWilco
- **File:CheckmateProper.jpg** *Source:* https://upload.wikimedia.org/wikipedia/commons/c/c4/CheckmateProper.jpg *License:* CC-BY-SA-3.0 *Contributors:* Transferred from en.wikipedia to Commons. *Original artist:* Bubba73 at English Wikipedia
- **File:Cherry_Blossoms_Owensboro_Public_Library_4-6-15.JPG** *Source:* https://upload.wikimedia.org/wikipedia/commons/1/14/Cherry_Blossoms_Owensboro_Public_Library_4-6-15.JPG *License:* CC BY-SA 4.0 *Contributors:* Own work *Original artist:* KentuckyKevin
- **File:Cherry_blossoms_at_POSTECH.jpeg** *Source:* https://upload.wikimedia.org/wikipedia/commons/2/22/Cherry_blossoms_at_POSTECH.jpeg *License:* Public domain *Contributors:* Personal picture *Original artist:* user:Stegano
- **File:Cherry_blossoms_in_Vancouver_3_crop.jpg** *Source:* https://upload.wikimedia.org/wikipedia/commons/1/11/Cherry_blossoms_in_Vancouver_3_crop.jpg *License:* CC BY-SA 3.0 *Contributors:* This file was derived from Cherry blossoms in Vancouver 3.JPG: <a href='//commons.wikimedia.org/wiki/File:Cherry_blossoms_in_Vancouver_3.JPG' class='image'><img alt='Cherry blossoms in Vancouver 3.JPG' src='https://upload.wikimedia.org/wikipedia/commons/thumb/2/24/Cherry_blossoms_in_Vancouver_3.JPG/50px-Cherry_blossoms_in_Vancouver_3.JPG' width='50' height='33' srcset='https://upload.wikimedia.org/wikipedia/commons/thumb/2/24/Cherry_blossoms_in_Vancouver_3.JPG/75px-Cherry_blossoms_in_Vancouver_3.JPG 1.5x, https://upload.wikimedia.org/wikipedia/commons/thumb/2/24/Cherry_blossoms_in_Vancouver_3.JPG/100px-Cherry_blossoms_in_Vancouver_3.JPG 2x' data-file-width='4288' data-file-height='2848' /></a>

    Original artist: Cherry_blossoms_in_Vancouver_3.JPG: Eviatar Bach
- **File:Cherryblossomtree.jpg** *Source:* https://upload.wikimedia.org/wikipedia/en/e/ed/Cherryblossomtree.jpg *License:* Fair use *Contributors:*
    Original publication: March 2015, Portland, OR

    Immediate source: Computer

    Original artist: Myself (Michael Farrington)
- **File:Chess_tile.png** *Source:* https://upload.wikimedia.org/wikipedia/commons/a/a2/Chess_tile.png *License:* Public domain *Contributors:* ? *Original artist:* ?
- **File:Chidorigafuchi_sakura.JPG** *Source:* https://upload.wikimedia.org/wikipedia/commons/f/f9/Chidorigafuchi_sakura.JPG *License:* Public domain *Contributors:* "Tyoron2's file" *Original artist:* "Tyoron2"
- **File:China_Schanghai_Jade_Buddah_Temple_5176519.jpg** *Source:* https://upload.wikimedia.org/wikipedia/commons/c/c0/China_Schanghai_Jade_Buddah_Temple_5176519.jpg *License:* CC BY-SA 3.0 *Contributors:* Own work *Original artist:* ermell
- **File:Chinese_Elm,_Ulmus_Parvifolia.jpg** *Source:* https://upload.wikimedia.org/wikipedia/commons/1/1c/Chinese_Elm%2C_Ulmus_Parvifolia.jpg *License:* CC BY-SA 3.0 *Contributors:* Taken in my house on my Vivitar 7340 *Original artist:* Captain rimmer
- **File:Citrus_aurantiifolia_in_Kadavoor.jpg** *Source:* https://upload.wikimedia.org/wikipedia/commons/5/55/Citrus_aurantiifolia_in_Kadavoor.jpg *License:* CC BY-SA 4.0 *Contributors:* Own work *Original artist:* **Jeevan Jose, Kerala, India**
- **File:Citrus_australasica_red_whole.jpg** *Source:* https://upload.wikimedia.org/wikipedia/commons/f/f9/Citrus_australasica_red_whole.jpg *License:* Public domain *Contributors:* Transferred from en.wikipedia to Commons by Sreejithk2000 using CommonsHelper. *Original artist:* Rjk at English Wikipedia
- **File:Citrus_canker_on_fruit.jpg** *Source:* https://upload.wikimedia.org/wikipedia/commons/2/25/Citrus_canker_on_fruit.jpg *License:* Public domain *Contributors:* ? *Original artist:* ?
- **File:Citrus_fruits.jpg** *Source:* https://upload.wikimedia.org/wikipedia/commons/e/e0/Citrus_fruits.jpg *License:* Public domain *Contributors:* This image was released by the Agricultural Research Service, the research agency of the United States Department of Agriculture, with the ID K7226-29 <a class='external text' href='//commons.wikimedia.org/w/index.php?title=Category:Media_created_by_the_United_States_Agricultural_Research_Service_with_known_IDs,<span>&,</span>,filefrom=K7226-29#mw-category-media'>(next)</a>. *Original artist:* Scott Bauer, USDA
- **File:Citrus_leaf.JPG** *Source:* https://upload.wikimedia.org/wikipedia/commons/e/e9/Citrus_leaf.JPG *License:* CC BY-SA 3.0 *Contributors:* Own work *Original artist:* ZooFari
- **File:Citrus_unshiu-unshu_mikan-2.jpg** *Source:* https://upload.wikimedia.org/wikipedia/commons/1/1e/Citrus_unshiu-unshu_mikan-2.jpg *License:* CC BY 2.5 *Contributors:* This is the creation of Tomomarusan *Original artist:* Tomomarusan
- **File:Clementinepeeled.jpg** *Source:* https://upload.wikimedia.org/wikipedia/commons/4/49/Clementinepeeled.jpg *License:* CC-BY-SA-3.0 *Contributors:* Originally uploaded to wikipedia by w:User:Tokugawapants on 20:22, 25 February 2006 *Original artist:* w:User:Tokugawapants
- **File:Commons-logo.svg** *Source:* https://upload.wikimedia.org/wikipedia/en/4/4a/Commons-logo.svg *License:* PD *Contributors:* ? *Original artist:* ?

- **File:Cornus-canadensis2.JPG** *Source:* https://upload.wikimedia.org/wikipedia/commons/a/a9/Cornus-canadensis2.JPG *License:* CC-BY-SA-3.0 *Contributors:* own work by Sten Porse *Original artist:* Sten Porse
- **File:Cornus_drummondii1.jpg** *Source:* https://upload.wikimedia.org/wikipedia/commons/2/20/Cornus_drummondii1.jpg *License:* Public domain *Contributors:* From en wiki *Original artist:* photo by John Knouse
- **File:Cornus_mas_F.jpg** *Source:* https://upload.wikimedia.org/wikipedia/commons/8/88/Cornus_mas_F.jpg *License:* Public domain *Contributors:* Own work *Original artist:* Wouter Hagens
- **File:Cornus_unalaschkensis_8561f.JPG** *Source:* https://upload.wikimedia.org/wikipedia/commons/f/f3/Cornus_unalaschkensis_8561f.JPG *License:* CC BY-SA 3.0 *Contributors:* Own work *Original artist:* Walter Siegmund (talk)
- **File:Corylus_avellana.jpg** *Source:* https://upload.wikimedia.org/wikipedia/commons/6/60/Corylus_avellana.jpg *License:* CC-BY-SA-3.0 *Contributors:* ? *Original artist:* ?
- **File:Crab_apples_by_the_roadside_-_geograph.org.uk_-_978786.jpg** *Source:* https://upload.wikimedia.org/wikipedia/commons/0/01/Crab_apples_by_the_roadside_-_geograph.org.uk_-_978786.jpg *License:* CC BY-SA 2.0 *Contributors:* From geograph.org.uk *Original artist:* Jonathan Billinger
- **File:Crabapple_bonsai_-_late_summer_photo.JPG** *Source:* https://upload.wikimedia.org/wikipedia/commons/b/b6/Crabapple_bonsai_-_late_summer_photo.JPG *License:* CC BY-SA 4.0 *Contributors:* Own work *Original artist:* Jeremy norbury
- **File:Crabapples.jpg** *Source:* https://upload.wikimedia.org/wikipedia/commons/2/29/Crabapples.jpg *License:* CC BY-SA 3.0 *Contributors:* Own work *Original artist:* Wehha
- **File:Cristoforo_munari-bodegon.JPG** *Source:* https://upload.wikimedia.org/wikipedia/commons/2/20/Cristoforo_munari-bodegon.JPG *License:* Public domain *Contributors:* http://ceres.mcu.es/pages/Viewer?accion=41&Museo=&AMuseo=MCM&Ninv=03876&txt_id_imagen=1&txt_rotar=0&txt_contraste=0&txt_zoom=10&cabecera=N&viewName=visorZoom *Original artist:* Cristoforo Munari
- **File:Crop-forecast.png** *Source:* https://upload.wikimedia.org/wikipedia/commons/1/10/Crop-forecast.png *License:* CC BY-SA 4.0 *Contributors:* Own work *Original artist:* J. Oteros
- **File:Cultivated_Fucshias_at_BBC_Gardeners'{}_World.jpg** *Source:* https://upload.wikimedia.org/wikipedia/commons/5/52/Cultivated_Fucshias_at_BBC_Gardeners%27_World.jpg *License:* CC BY-SA 3.0 *Contributors:* Own work *Original artist:* Andy Mabbett
- **File:Custura_Bucurei.jpg** *Source:* https://upload.wikimedia.org/wikipedia/commons/6/63/Custura_Bucurei.jpg *License:* CC BY 3.0 *Contributors:* Own work *Original artist:* Dezidor
- **File:Cyca-revoluta.jpg** *Source:* https://upload.wikimedia.org/wikipedia/commons/7/71/Cyca-revoluta.jpg *License:* CC-BY-SA-3.0 *Contributors:* ? *Original artist:* ?
- **File:CycadKingSago.jpg** *Source:* https://upload.wikimedia.org/wikipedia/commons/7/7f/CycadKingSago.jpg *License:* CC-BY-SA-3.0 *Contributors:* ? *Original artist:* ?
- **File:Cycas_Sago.palm.arp.750pix.jpg** *Source:* https://upload.wikimedia.org/wikipedia/commons/0/08/Cycas_Sago.palm.arp.750pix.jpg *License:* Public domain *Contributors:* ? *Original artist:* ?
- **File:Cycas_revoluta.Düsseldorf.jpg** *Source:* https://upload.wikimedia.org/wikipedia/commons/a/ae/Cycas_revoluta.D%C3%BCsseldorf.jpg *License:* CC BY 3.0 *Contributors:* Own work *Original artist:* Holek
- **File:Cycas_revoluta004.jpg** *Source:* https://upload.wikimedia.org/wikipedia/commons/4/4c/Cycas_revoluta004.jpg *License:* CC BY-SA 2.5 *Contributors:* ? *Original artist:* ?
- **File:Cycas_revoluta01.jpg** *Source:* https://upload.wikimedia.org/wikipedia/commons/d/d5/Cycas_revoluta01.jpg *License:* CC-BY-SA-3.0 *Contributors:* ? *Original artist:* ?
- **File:Cycas_revoluta02.jpg** *Source:* https://upload.wikimedia.org/wikipedia/commons/b/b9/Cycas_revoluta02.jpg *License:* CC-BY-SA-3.0 *Contributors:* ? *Original artist:* ?
- **File:Cycas_revoluta1328A.JPG** *Source:* https://upload.wikimedia.org/wikipedia/commons/4/45/Cycas_revoluta1328A.JPG *License:* CC BY-SA 2.5 *Contributors:* Own work (personal work) *Original artist:* Esculapio
- **File:Cycas_revoluta_female_cone01.jpg** *Source:* https://upload.wikimedia.org/wikipedia/commons/a/a4/Cycas_revoluta_female_cone01.jpg *License:* CC BY 2.5 *Contributors:* ? *Original artist:* ?
- **File:Cycas_revoluta_new_leafs.JPG** *Source:* https://upload.wikimedia.org/wikipedia/en/3/36/Cycas_revoluta_new_leafs.JPG *License:* Cc-by-sa-3.0 *Contributors:* ? *Original artist:* ?
- **File:Cycas_revoluta_seedling.jpg** *Source:* https://upload.wikimedia.org/wikipedia/en/3/30/Cycas_revoluta_seedling.jpg *License:* CC-BY-SA-2.5 *Contributors:* ? *Original artist:* ?
- **File:Cycas_revoluta_seeds.jpg** *Source:* https://upload.wikimedia.org/wikipedia/commons/a/a1/Cycas_revoluta_seeds.jpg *License:* CC-BY-SA-3.0 *Contributors:* Own work (personal work) *Original artist:* Esculapio
- **File:Cydonia.jpg** *Source:* https://upload.wikimedia.org/wikipedia/commons/d/d6/Cydonia.jpg *License:* CC-BY-SA-3.0 *Contributors:* ? *Original artist:* ?
- **File:Cydonia_oblonga_-_Köhler–s_Medizinal-Pflanzen-049.jpg** *Source:* https://upload.wikimedia.org/wikipedia/commons/f/fd/Cydonia_oblonga_-_K%C3%B6hler%E2%80%93s_Medizinal-Pflanzen-049.jpg *License:* Public domain *Contributors:* List of Koehler Images (original upload), http://caliban.mpiz-koeln.mpg.de/koehler1/high/DSC_2642.html (first resolution increase) *Original artist:* Franz Eugen Köhler, *Köhler's Medizinal-Pflanzen*
- **File:Cypress_8001.JPG** *Source:* https://upload.wikimedia.org/wikipedia/commons/c/c5/Cypress_8001.JPG *License:* CC-BY-SA-3.0 *Contributors:* Transferred from en.wikipedia by SreeBot *Original artist:* Pollinator at en.wikipedia

4.2. IMAGES

- **File:Des_cerisiers_en_fleur_au_Parc_de_Sceaux.JPG** *Source:* https://upload.wikimedia.org/wikipedia/commons/6/62/Des_cerisiers_en_fleur_au_Parc_de_Sceaux.JPG *License:* CC BY-SA 4.0 *Contributors:* Own work *Original artist:* Ethel Mannin
- **File:Dogwood_blossom.jpg** *Source:* https://upload.wikimedia.org/wikipedia/commons/7/73/Dogwood_blossom.jpg *License:* CC BY-SA 3.0 *Contributors:* Own work *Original artist:* Dennis Brown
- **File:DosenmoorBirken1.jpg** *Source:* https://upload.wikimedia.org/wikipedia/commons/1/1b/DosenmoorBirken1.jpg *License:* CC BY-SA 2.0 de *Contributors:* Original: de.wikipedia.org *12:20, 2008-06-29 . . 3.872×2.592 (6 MB) . . Wilde Natur* *Original artist:* Wilde Natur
- **File:Dulce_de_Membrillo.jpg** *Source:* https://upload.wikimedia.org/wikipedia/commons/d/db/Dulce_de_Membrillo.jpg *License:* CC BY 2.0 *Contributors:* Dulce de Membrillo *Original artist:* Javier Lastras from España/Spain
- **File:Dwarf_Japanese_Juniper,_1975-2007.jpg** *Source:* https://upload.wikimedia.org/wikipedia/commons/2/2d/Dwarf_Japanese_Juniper%2C_1975-2007.jpg *License:* CC-BY-SA-3.0 *Contributors:* Own work *Original artist:* Ragesoss
- **File:Eastern_Bluebird-27527.jpg** *Source:* https://upload.wikimedia.org/wikipedia/commons/f/f7/Eastern_Bluebird-27527.jpg *License:* Public domain *Contributors:* KenThomas.us
  Original artist: Ken Thomas
- **File:Eastern_Redcedar_Juniperus_virginiana_'Corcorcor'_Berries_1800px.jpg** *Source:* https://upload.wikimedia.org/wikipedia/commons/5/53/Eastern_Redcedar_Juniperus_virginiana_%27Corcorcor%27_Berries_1800px.jpg *License:* GFDL 1.2 *Contributors:* Self-photographed *Original artist:* Photo (c)2007 Derek Ramsey (Ram-Man)
- **File:Eastern_White_Pine_Pinus_strobus_Bark_Vertical.JPG** *Source:* https://upload.wikimedia.org/wikipedia/commons/f/f4/Eastern_White_Pine_Pinus_strobus_Bark_Vertical.JPG *License:* CC BY-SA 4.0 *Contributors:* Self-photographed *Original artist:* Photo by and (c)2016 Derek Ramsey (Ram-Man)
- **File:Edit-clear.svg** *Source:* https://upload.wikimedia.org/wikipedia/en/f/f2/Edit-clear.svg *License:* Public domain *Contributors:* The *Tango! Desktop Project.* *Original artist:*

  The people from the Tango! project. And according to the meta-data in the file, specifically: "Andreas Nilsson, and Jakub Steiner (although minimally)."
- **File:English_Yew_600.jpg** *Source:* https://upload.wikimedia.org/wikipedia/commons/d/d6/English_Yew_600.jpg *License:* CC-BY-SA-3.0 *Contributors:* Transferred from en.wikipedia to Commons by Sfan00_IMG using CommonsHelper. *Original artist:* The original uploader was Sannse at English Wikipedia
- **File:English_Yew_close_250.jpg** *Source:* https://upload.wikimedia.org/wikipedia/commons/3/35/English_Yew_close_250.jpg *License:* CC-BY-SA-3.0 *Contributors:* Transferred from en.wikipedia to Commons. *Original artist:* Sannse at English Wikipedia
- **File:Entzia_-_Acer_Campestre_02.jpg** *Source:* https://upload.wikimedia.org/wikipedia/commons/0/0e/Entzia_-_Acer_Campestre_02.jpg *License:* CC BY-SA 4.0 *Contributors:* Own work *Original artist:* Basotxerri
- **File:Erethia_theezans_(bonsaï).jpg** *Source:* https://upload.wikimedia.org/wikipedia/commons/1/13/Erethia_theezans_%28bonsa%C3%AF%29.jpg *License:* Public domain *Contributors:* Own work *Original artist:* Richieman
- **File:Eriophyes_inangulis_N_on_upper_surface.JPG** *Source:* https://upload.wikimedia.org/wikipedia/commons/d/d1/Eriophyes_inangulis_N_on_upper_surface.JPG *License:* CC BY-SA 3.0 *Contributors:* Own work *Original artist:* Rosser1954
- **File:Eurya,_1970-2007.jpg** *Source:* https://upload.wikimedia.org/wikipedia/commons/4/4b/Eurya%2C_1970-2007.jpg *License:* CC-BY-SA-3.0 *Contributors:* Own work *Original artist:* Ragesoss
- **File:Fasciated_Lilac.JPG** *Source:* https://upload.wikimedia.org/wikipedia/commons/6/69/Fasciated_Lilac.JPG *License:* CC BY-SA 3.0 *Contributors:* Own work *Original artist:* Limulus
- **File:FeldahornBlatt.jpg** *Source:* https://upload.wikimedia.org/wikipedia/commons/a/a0/FeldahornBlatt.jpg *License:* CC-BY-SA-3.0 *Contributors:* ? *Original artist:* ?
- **File:Felifera_Aurea_leaves_201601_JAPAN.jpg** *Source:* https://upload.wikimedia.org/wikipedia/commons/6/6a/Felifera_Aurea_leaves_201601_JAPAN.jpg *License:* CC BY-SA 4.0 *Contributors:* Own work *Original artist:* メルビル
- **File:Ficus_aurea.JPG** *Source:* https://upload.wikimedia.org/wikipedia/commons/a/aa/Ficus_aurea.JPG *License:* CC-BY-SA-3.0 *Contributors:* From author *Original artist:* D. Walker
- **File:Ficus_aurea01.jpg** *Source:* https://upload.wikimedia.org/wikipedia/commons/1/1a/Ficus_aurea01.jpg *License:* CC BY-SA 3.0 *Contributors:* http://www.hear.org/starr/hiplants/images/600max/html/starr_031108_2144_ficus_aurea.htm *Original artist:* Forest Starr and Kim Starr
- **File:Ficus_benjamina_(Weeping_Fig)_in_Hyderabad_W_IMG_8308.jpg** *Source:* https://upload.wikimedia.org/wikipedia/commons/5/58/Ficus_benjamina_%28Weeping_Fig%29_in_Hyderabad_W_IMG_8308.jpg *License:* CC BY 3.0 *Contributors:* Own work *Original artist:* J.M.Garg
- **File:Ficus_benjamina_(Weeping_Fig)_in_Hyderabad_W_IMG_8313.jpg** *Source:* https://upload.wikimedia.org/wikipedia/commons/e/e0/Ficus_benjamina_%28Weeping_Fig%29_in_Hyderabad_W_IMG_8313.jpg *License:* CC BY 3.0 *Contributors:* Own work *Original artist:* J.M.Garg
- **File:Ficus_benjamina_(Weeping_Fig)_in_Hyderabad_W_IMG_8314.jpg** *Source:* https://upload.wikimedia.org/wikipedia/commons/9/99/Ficus_benjamina_%28Weeping_Fig%29_in_Hyderabad_W_IMG_8314.jpg *License:* CC BY 3.0 *Contributors:* Own work *Original artist:* J.M.Garg
- **File:Ficus_benjamina_(Weeping_Fig)_trunk_in_Hyderabad_W_IMG_8310.jpg** *Source:* https://upload.wikimedia.org/wikipedia/commons/8/8c/Ficus_benjamina_%28Weeping_Fig%29_trunk_in_Hyderabad_W_IMG_8310.jpg *License:* CC BY 3.0 *Contributors:* Own work *Original artist:* J.M.Garg

- **File:Ficus_microcarpa1.jpg** *Source:* https://upload.wikimedia.org/wikipedia/commons/9/91/Ficus_microcarpa1.jpg *License:* CC-BY-SA-3.0 *Contributors:* KENPEI's photo *Original artist:* KENPEI
- **File:Ficus_neriifolia_bonsai.jpg** *Source:* https://upload.wikimedia.org/wikipedia/commons/8/89/Ficus_neriifolia_bonsai.jpg *License:* CC0 *Contributors:* Own work *Original artist:* Tortie tude
- **File:Ficus_obliqua_Kirsova_PG_Glebe_sml.jpg** *Source:* https://upload.wikimedia.org/wikipedia/commons/8/82/Ficus_obliqua_PG_Glebe_sml.jpg *License:* Public domain *Contributors:* Own work *Original artist:* Casliber
- **File:Ficus_obliqua_Kirsova_PG_Glebe_yngfruit_sml.jpg** *Source:* https://upload.wikimedia.org/wikipedia/commons/a/a8/Ficus_obliqua_Kirsova_PG_Glebe_yngfruit_sml.jpg *License:* Public domain *Contributors:* Own work *Original artist:* Casliber
- **File:Ficus_obliqua_Watagans_National_Park.jpg** *Source:* https://upload.wikimedia.org/wikipedia/commons/b/b0/Ficus_obliqua_Watagans_National_Park.jpg *License:* Public domain *Contributors:* Own work *Original artist:* Poyt448 Peter Woodard
- **File:Ficus_obliqua_trunk.jpg** *Source:* https://upload.wikimedia.org/wikipedia/commons/c/cf/Ficus_obliqua_trunk.jpg *License:* CC BY 2.0 *Contributors:* http://www.flickr.com/photos/kounelli/2303010065/ *Original artist:* http://www.flickr.com/photos/kounelli/
- **File:Ficus_platypoda_fruit.jpg** *Source:* https://upload.wikimedia.org/wikipedia/commons/e/e4/Ficus_platypoda_fruit.jpg *License:* CC BY-SA 3.0 *Contributors:* Own work *Original artist:* Mark Marathon
- **File:Ficus_rubiginosa_at_Barrenjoey.JPG** *Source:* https://upload.wikimedia.org/wikipedia/commons/e/eb/Ficus_rubiginosa_at_Barrenjoey.JPG *License:* CC0 *Contributors:* Own work *Original artist:* Poyt448 Peter Woodard
- **File:Ficus_rubiginosa_'Variegata',_Allan_Gardens.jpg** *Source:* https://upload.wikimedia.org/wikipedia/commons/1/1e/Ficus_rubiginosa_%E2%80%98Variegata%E2%80%99%2C_Allan_Gardens.jpg *License:* CC BY-SA 4.0 *Contributors:* Own work *Original artist:* Nadiatalent
- **File:Ficusindicamaxima.jpg** *Source:* https://upload.wikimedia.org/wikipedia/commons/0/04/Ficusindicamaxima.jpg *License:* Public domain *Contributors:* http://www.botanicus.org/page/188734 *Original artist:* Hans Sloane
- **File:Field_maple.JPG** *Source:* https://upload.wikimedia.org/wikipedia/commons/6/61/Field_maple.JPG *License:* Public domain *Contributors:* Transferred from en.wikipedia to Commons. *Original artist:* Jackaranga at English Wikipedia
- **File:Filet_Olive_de_Nice.jpg** *Source:* https://upload.wikimedia.org/wikipedia/commons/f/f4/Filet_Olive_de_Nice.jpg *License:* CC BY-SA 3.0 *Contributors:* Own work *Original artist:* Myrabella
- **File:Filifera_aurea.jpg** *Source:* https://upload.wikimedia.org/wikipedia/commons/4/4d/Filifera_aurea.jpg *License:* CC BY-SA 4.0 *Contributors:* Own work *Original artist:* メルビル
- **File:Flag_of_Algeria.svg** *Source:* https://upload.wikimedia.org/wikipedia/commons/7/77/Flag_of_Algeria.svg *License:* Public domain *Contributors:* SVG implementation of the 63-145 Algerian law "*on Characteristics of the Algerian national emblem*" ("Caractéristiques du Drapeau Algérien", in English). *Original artist:* This graphic was originaly drawn by User:SKopp.
- **File:Flag_of_Argentina.svg** *Source:* https://upload.wikimedia.org/wikipedia/commons/1/1a/Flag_of_Argentina.svg *License:* Public domain *Contributors:* Here, based on: http://manuelbelgrano.gov.ar/bandera/creacion-de-la-bandera-nacional/ *Original artist:* Government of Argentina
- **File:Flag_of_Azerbaijan.svg** *Source:* https://upload.wikimedia.org/wikipedia/commons/d/dd/Flag_of_Azerbaijan.svg *License:* Public domain *Contributors:* http://www.elibrary.az/docs/remz/pdf/remz_bayraq.pdf and http://www.meclis.gov.az/?/az/topcontent/21 *Original artist:* SKopp and others
- **File:Flag_of_Egypt.svg** *Source:* https://upload.wikimedia.org/wikipedia/commons/f/fe/Flag_of_Egypt.svg *License:* CC0 *Contributors:* From the Open Clip Art website. *Original artist:* Open Clip Art
- **File:Flag_of_Greece.svg** *Source:* https://upload.wikimedia.org/wikipedia/commons/5/5c/Flag_of_Greece.svg *License:* Public domain *Contributors:* own code *Original artist:* (of code) cs:User:-xfi- (talk)
- **File:Flag_of_Iran.svg** *Source:* https://upload.wikimedia.org/wikipedia/commons/c/ca/Flag_of_Iran.svg *License:* Public domain *Contributors:* URL http://www.isiri.org/portal/files/std/1.htm and an English translation / interpretation at URL http://flagspot.net/flags/ir'.html *Original artist:* Various
- **File:Flag_of_Italy.svg** *Source:* https://upload.wikimedia.org/wikipedia/en/0/03/Flag_of_Italy.svg *License:* PD *Contributors:* ? *Original artist:* ?
- **File:Flag_of_Japan.svg** *Source:* https://upload.wikimedia.org/wikipedia/en/9/9e/Flag_of_Japan.svg *License:* PD *Contributors:* ? *Original artist:* ?
- **File:Flag_of_Lebanon.svg** *Source:* https://upload.wikimedia.org/wikipedia/commons/5/59/Flag_of_Lebanon.svg *License:* Public domain *Contributors:* ? *Original artist:* Traced based on the CIA World Factbook with some modification done to the colours based on information at Vexilla mundi.
- **File:Flag_of_Morocco.svg** *Source:* https://upload.wikimedia.org/wikipedia/commons/2/2c/Flag_of_Morocco.svg *License:* Public domain *Contributors:* Flag of the Kingdom of Morocco

    <a data-x-rel='nofollow' class='external text' href='http://81.192.52.100/BO/AR/1915/BO_135_ar.PDF'>Moroccan royal decree (17 November 1915), BO-135-ar *page 6*</a>

    Original artist: Denelson83, Zscout370
- **File:Flag_of_Portugal.svg** *Source:* https://upload.wikimedia.org/wikipedia/commons/5/5c/Flag_of_Portugal.svg *License:* Public domain *Contributors:* http://jorgesampaio.arquivo.presidencia.pt/pt/republica/simbolos/bandeiras/index.html#imgs *Original artist:* Columbano Bordalo Pinheiro (1910; generic design); Vítor Luís Rodrigues; António Martins-Tuválkin (2004; this specific vector set: see sources)

4.2. IMAGES

- **File:Flag_of_Serbia.svg** *Source:* https://upload.wikimedia.org/wikipedia/commons/f/ff/Flag_of_Serbia.svg *License:* Public domain *Contributors:* From http://www.parlament.gov.rs/content/cir/o_skupstini/simboli/simboli.asp. *Original artist:* sodipodi.com
- **File:Flag_of_Spain.svg** *Source:* https://upload.wikimedia.org/wikipedia/en/9/9a/Flag_of_Spain.svg *License:* PD *Contributors:* ? *Original artist:* ?
- **File:Flag_of_Syria.svg** *Source:* https://upload.wikimedia.org/wikipedia/commons/5/53/Flag_of_Syria.svg *License:* Public domain *Contributors:* see below *Original artist:* see below
- **File:Flag_of_Tunisia.svg** *Source:* https://upload.wikimedia.org/wikipedia/commons/c/ce/Flag_of_Tunisia.svg *License:* Public domain *Contributors:* http://www.w3.org/ *Original artist:* entraîneur: BEN KHALIFA WISSAM
- **File:Flag_of_Turkey.svg** *Source:* https://upload.wikimedia.org/wikipedia/commons/b/b4/Flag_of_Turkey.svg *License:* Public domain *Contributors:* Turkish Flag Law (Türk Bayrağı Kanunu), Law nr. 2893 of 22 September 1983. Text (in Turkish) at the website of the Turkish Historical Society (Türk Tarih Kurumu) *Original artist:* David Benbennick (original author)
- **File:Flag_of_Uzbekistan.svg** *Source:* https://upload.wikimedia.org/wikipedia/commons/8/84/Flag_of_Uzbekistan.svg *License:* Public domain *Contributors:* Own work *Original artist:* Oʻzbekiston Respublikasining Davlat bayrogʻi. The officially defined colours are Pantone 313C for blue and 361C for green (source: [1], [2]). Drawn by User:Zscout370.
- **File:Flag_of_the_People'{}s_Republic_of_China.svg** *Source:* https://upload.wikimedia.org/wikipedia/commons/f/fa/Flag_of_the_People%27s_Republic_of_China.svg *License:* Public domain *Contributors:* Own work, http://www.protocol.gov.hk/flags/eng/n_flag/design.html *Original artist:* Drawn by User:SKopp, redrawn by User:Denelson83 and User:Zscout370
- **File:Flowering_crabapple_in_Washington_DC.jpg** *Source:* https://upload.wikimedia.org/wikipedia/commons/8/82/Flowering_crabapple_in_Washington_DC.jpg *License:* CC BY-SA 3.0 *Contributors:* Own work *Original artist:* Kilo22
- **File:Folder_Hexagonal_Icon.svg** *Source:* https://upload.wikimedia.org/wikipedia/en/4/48/Folder_Hexagonal_Icon.svg *License:* Cc-by-sa-3.0 *Contributors:* ? *Original artist:* ?
- **File:Foodlogo2.svg** *Source:* https://upload.wikimedia.org/wikipedia/commons/d/d6/Foodlogo2.svg *License:* CC-BY-SA-3.0 *Contributors:* Original *Original artist:* Seahen
- **File:Forsythia.x.intermedia03.jpg** *Source:* https://upload.wikimedia.org/wikipedia/commons/a/a2/Forsythia.x.intermedia03.jpg *License:* CC-BY-SA-3.0 *Contributors:* ? *Original artist:* ?
- **File:Forsythia_50years.jpg** *Source:* https://upload.wikimedia.org/wikipedia/commons/d/df/Forsythia_50years.jpg *License:* Attribution *Contributors:* Transferred from en.wikipedia to Commons.; Transfer was made by User:JGHowes. *Original artist:* The original uploader was JGHowes at English Wikipedia
- **File:Forsythia_flower_1r.jpg** *Source:* https://upload.wikimedia.org/wikipedia/commons/2/2a/Forsythia_flower_1r.jpg *License:* CC BY 2.0 *Contributors:* http://www.flickr.com/photos/calliope/10248626/in/photostream/ *Original artist:* Muffet
- **File:Forsythia_flower_cut.JPG** *Source:* https://upload.wikimedia.org/wikipedia/commons/5/57/Forsythia_flower_cut.JPG *License:* CC BY-SA 3.0 *Contributors:* Own work *Original artist:* Seha bs
- **File:Forsythia_suspensa_4090392_レンギョウ(連翹).JPG** *Source:* https://upload.wikimedia.org/wikipedia/commons/0/0c/Forsythia_suspensa_4090392_%E3%83%AC%E3%83%B3%E3%82%AE%E3%83%A7%E3%82%A6%EF%BC%88%E9%80%A3%E7%BF%B9%EF%BC%89.JPG *License:* CC BY-SA 3.0 *Contributors:* 松岡明芳 *Original artist:* 松岡明芳
- **File:Fossil_Plant_Ginkgo.jpg** *Source:* https://upload.wikimedia.org/wikipedia/commons/b/b5/Fossil_Plant_Ginkgo.jpg *License:* CC-BY-SA-3.0 *Contributors:* ? *Original artist:* ?
- **File:Frankie_winn_camellia.jpg** *Source:* https://upload.wikimedia.org/wikipedia/commons/3/37/Frankie_winn_camellia.jpg *License:* GFDL *Contributors:* Own work *Original artist:* J Burghardt
- **File:Frutto_pompia.jpg** *Source:* https://upload.wikimedia.org/wikipedia/commons/a/a3/Frutto_pompia.jpg *License:* CC BY-SA 3.0 *Contributors:* Own work *Original artist:* Isolacomputer
- **File:Fuchsia_2008.jpg** *Source:* https://upload.wikimedia.org/wikipedia/commons/f/f2/Fuchsia_2008.jpg *License:* CC BY-SA 3.0 *Contributors:* Own work *Original artist:* User:O'Dea
- **File:Fuchsia_boliviana_3.jpg** *Source:* https://upload.wikimedia.org/wikipedia/commons/8/85/Fuchsia_boliviana_3.jpg *License:* CC BY-SA 3.0 *Contributors:* Own work *Original artist:* Stan Shebs
- **File:Fuchsia_flowerフクシアの花7137619.jpg** *Source:* https://upload.wikimedia.org/wikipedia/commons/3/31/Fuchsia_flower%E3%83%95%E3%82%AF%E3%82%B7%E3%82%A2%E3%81%AE%E8%8A%B17137619.jpg *License:* CC BY-SA 3.0 *Contributors:* 松岡明芳 *Original artist:* 松岡明芳
- **File:Fuchsia_hybrida_-_flower_view_01.jpg** *Source:* https://upload.wikimedia.org/wikipedia/commons/4/4e/Fuchsia_hybrida_-_flower_view_01.jpg *License:* CC BY-SA 4.0 *Contributors:* Own workhttp://www.flowersview.com/Fuchsia%20hybrida/02-IMG_6309-1.jpg.html *Original artist:* Fan Wen
- **File:Fuchsia_regia_-_blossom_(aka).jpg** *Source:* https://upload.wikimedia.org/wikipedia/commons/b/bc/Fuchsia_regia_-_blossom_%28aka%29.jpg *License:* CC BY-SA 2.5 *Contributors:* Own work *Original artist:* André Karwath aka Aka
- **File:Funchal,_Monte_-_Cycas_revoluta_IMG_1907.JPG** *Source:* https://upload.wikimedia.org/wikipedia/commons/7/73/Funchal%2C_Monte_-_Cycas_revoluta_IMG_1907.JPG *License:* CC BY-SA 3.0 *Contributors:* Own work *Original artist:* Hedwig Storch
- **File:Funchal,_Monte_-_Cycas_revoluta_IMG_1970.JPG** *Source:* https://upload.wikimedia.org/wikipedia/commons/5/52/Funchal%2C_Monte_-_Cycas_revoluta_IMG_1970.JPG *License:* CC BY-SA 3.0 *Contributors:* Own work *Original artist:* Hedwig Storch

- **File:Funchal_Botanical_garden_-_Cycas_revoluta.JPG** *Source:* https://upload.wikimedia.org/wikipedia/commons/9/99/Funchal_Botanical_garden_-_Cycas_revoluta.JPG *License:* CC BY-SA 3.0 *Contributors:* Own work *Original artist:* Hedwig Storch
- **File:George_Taber_azalea.jpg** *Source:* https://upload.wikimedia.org/wikipedia/commons/8/8f/George_Taber_azalea.jpg *License:* CC BY-SA 3.0 *Contributors:* Own work by the original uploader *Original artist:* Jud McCranie, aka Bubba73
- **File:GingkoFruitingTwigSpring.jpg** *Source:* https://upload.wikimedia.org/wikipedia/commons/6/60/GingkoFruitingTwigSpring.jpg *License:* CC BY-SA 3.0 *Contributors:* Transferred from en.wikipedia by Ronhjones *Original artist:* Imc at en.wikipedia
- **File:Gingko_biloba_JPG2b.jpg** *Source:* https://upload.wikimedia.org/wikipedia/commons/9/99/Gingko_biloba_JPG2b.jpg *License:* CC BY 3.0 *Contributors:*
  - travail personnel

  Original artist: Jean-Pol GRANDMONT
- **File:Gingko_fg01.jpg** *Source:* https://upload.wikimedia.org/wikipedia/commons/5/51/Gingko_fg01.jpg *License:* CC BY-SA 2.5 *Contributors:* Own work *Original artist:* Fritz Geller-Grimm
- **File:Ginkgo-biloba-male.JPG** *Source:* https://upload.wikimedia.org/wikipedia/commons/f/f2/Ginkgo-biloba-male.JPG *License:* CC-BY-SA-3.0 *Contributors:* ? *Original artist:* ?
- **File:Ginkgo-penjing-montreal-botanical-gardens.jpg** *Source:* https://upload.wikimedia.org/wikipedia/commons/2/22/Ginkgo-penjing-montreal-botanical-gardens.jpg *License:* Public domain *Contributors:* No machine-readable source provided. Own work assumed (based on copyright claims). *Original artist:* No machine-readable author provided. Nordelch assumed (based on copyright claims).
- **File:Ginkgo-reborn-2.jpg** *Source:* https://upload.wikimedia.org/wikipedia/commons/4/48/Ginkgo-reborn-2.jpg *License:* Public domain *Contributors:* Own work *Original artist:* Urashimataro
- **File:GinkgoLeaves.jpg** *Source:* https://upload.wikimedia.org/wikipedia/commons/7/78/GinkgoLeaves.jpg *License:* CC BY-SA 3.0 *Contributors:* Own work *Original artist:* Joe Schneid, Louisville, Kentucky
- **File:GinkgoSaplings.jpg** *Source:* https://upload.wikimedia.org/wikipedia/commons/c/c7/GinkgoSaplings.jpg *License:* Public domain *Contributors:* Own work *Original artist:* Douglas W. Jones
- **File:Ginkgo_Biloba_Leaves_-_Black_Background.jpg** *Source:* https://upload.wikimedia.org/wikipedia/commons/f/f5/Ginkgo_Biloba_Leaves_-_Black_Background.jpg *License:* CC BY-SA 3.0 *Contributors:* Own work *Original artist:* James Field (Jame)
- **File:Ginkgo_Seed.JPG** *Source:* https://upload.wikimedia.org/wikipedia/commons/2/28/Ginkgo_Seed.JPG *License:* CC-BY-SA-3.0 *Contributors:* Sony Cyber-shot DSC-H3 *Original artist:* Aomorikuma
- **File:Ginkgo_Tree_Ginkgo_biloba_Trunk_Bark_2000px.jpg** *Source:* https://upload.wikimedia.org/wikipedia/commons/d/d2/Ginkgo_Tree_Ginkgo_biloba_Trunk_Bark_2000px.jpg *License:* GFDL 1.2 *Contributors:* Self-photographed *Original artist:* Photo (c)2007 Derek Ramsey (Ram-Man)
- **File:Ginkgo_adiantoides_-_G._cranii.jpg** *Source:* https://upload.wikimedia.org/wikipedia/commons/a/a1/Ginkgo_adiantoides_-_G._cranii.jpg *License:* CC BY-SA 3.0 *Contributors:* Own work *Original artist:* Ginkgob
- **File:Ginkgo_and_coconut_dessert.jpg** *Source:* https://upload.wikimedia.org/wikipedia/commons/b/b0/Ginkgo_and_coconut_dessert.jpg *License:* GFDL *Contributors:* self-made: photo of Bangkok restaurant dessert. *Original artist:* David Richfield
- **File:Ginkgo_apodes.jpg** *Source:* https://upload.wikimedia.org/wikipedia/commons/a/a7/Ginkgo_apodes.jpg *License:* CC BY-SA 3.0 *Contributors:* Own work *Original artist:* Ginkgob
- **File:Ginkgo_biloba0.jpg** *Source:* https://upload.wikimedia.org/wikipedia/commons/a/a3/Ginkgo_biloba0.jpg *License:* CC-BY-SA-3.0 *Contributors:* caliban.mpiz-koeln.mpg.de/mavica/index.html part of www.biolib.de *Original artist:* Kurt Stüber [1]
- **File:Ginkgo_biloba_(new_form).jpg** *Source:* https://upload.wikimedia.org/wikipedia/commons/b/b0/Ginkgo_biloba_%28new_form%29.jpg *License:* CC BY-SA 3.0 *Contributors:* Own work *Original artist:* Ginkgob
- **File:Ginkgo_biloba_JPG1a.jpg** *Source:* https://upload.wikimedia.org/wikipedia/commons/4/45/Ginkgo_biloba_JPG1a.jpg *License:* CC BY 3.0 *Contributors:*
  - Own work

  Original artist: Jean-Pol GRANDMONT
- **File:Ginkgo_biloba_MHNT.BOT.2010.13.1.jpg** *Source:* https://upload.wikimedia.org/wikipedia/commons/1/19/Ginkgo_biloba_MHNT.BOT.2010.13.1.jpg *License:* CC BY-SA 3.0 *Contributors:* Own work *Original artist:* Jean-Pierre Chéreau & Roger Culos
- **File:Ginkgo_biloba_MacAbee_BC.jpg** *Source:* https://upload.wikimedia.org/wikipedia/commons/c/c5/Ginkgo_biloba_MacAbee_BC.jpg *License:* CC-BY-SA-3.0 *Contributors:* English Wikipedia *Original artist:* User:SNP(upload to en:wikipedia) ; User:tangopaso (transfer to Commons)
- **File:Ginkgo_biloba_female_flower.jpg** *Source:* https://upload.wikimedia.org/wikipedia/commons/e/ec/Ginkgo_biloba_female_flower.jpg *License:* CC BY-SA 3.0 *Contributors:* Own work *Original artist:* Ginkgob
- **File:Ginkgo_biloba_male_flower.jpg** *Source:* https://upload.wikimedia.org/wikipedia/commons/e/e3/Ginkgo_biloba_male_flower.jpg *License:* CC BY-SA 3.0 *Contributors:* Own work *Original artist:* Ginkgob
- **File:Ginkgo_embryo_and_gametophyte.jpg** *Source:* https://upload.wikimedia.org/wikipedia/commons/0/03/Ginkgo_embryo_and_gametophyte.jpg *License:* CC BY-SA 2.5 *Contributors:* Photography by Curtis Clark *Original artist:* Copyright by Curtis Clark, licensed as noted

4.2. IMAGES

- **File:Ginkgo_yimaensis.jpg** *Source:* https://upload.wikimedia.org/wikipedia/commons/3/3f/Ginkgo_yimaensis.jpg *License:* CC BY-SA 3.0 *Contributors:* Own work *Original artist:* Ginkgob
- **File:Ginko_bud.jpg** *Source:* https://upload.wikimedia.org/wikipedia/commons/d/dd/Ginko_bud.jpg *License:* CC BY-SA 4.0 *Contributors:* Own work *Original artist:* (jubi-net)
- **File:Girl_with_a_pomegranate,_by_William_Bouguereau.jpg** *Source:* https://upload.wikimedia.org/wikipedia/commons/1/1d/Girl_with_a_pomegranate%2C_by_William_Bouguereau.jpg *License:* Public domain *Contributors:* Sotheby's *Original artist:* William-Adolphe Bouguereau
- **File:Goshin,_September_15,_2007.jpg** *Source:* https://upload.wikimedia.org/wikipedia/commons/c/c5/Goshin%2C_September_15%2C_2007.jpg *License:* CC BY 2.0 *Contributors:* Flickr *Original artist:* Joanna
- **File:GraberOliveHouseVatRoom.JPG** *Source:* https://upload.wikimedia.org/wikipedia/commons/a/ae/GraberOliveHouseVatRoom.JPG *License:* Public domain *Contributors:* Own work *Original artist:* Uzma Gamal
- **File:Granatapfelblüte_3.jpg** *Source:* https://upload.wikimedia.org/wikipedia/commons/4/47/Granatapfelbl%C3%BCte_3.jpg *License:* CC BY 3.0 *Contributors:* Own work *Original artist:* Uwe Barghaan
- **File:Grove_of_Sawara_Cypress,_Upton_State_Forest,_MA.jpeg** *Source:* https://upload.wikimedia.org/wikipedia/en/1/13/Grove_of_Sawara_Cypress%2C_Upton_State_Forest%2C_MA.jpeg *License:* CC0 *Contributors:* ? *Original artist:* ?
- **File:Grüne_Oliven.jpg** *Source:* https://upload.wikimedia.org/wikipedia/commons/6/62/Gr%C3%BCne_Oliven.jpg *License:* CC BY-SA 3.0 *Contributors:* Own work *Original artist:* Marco Almbauer
- **File:Haeckel_Coniferae_Chamaecyparis_obtusa.jpg** *Source:* https://upload.wikimedia.org/wikipedia/commons/4/4d/Haeckel_Coniferae_Chamaecyparis_obtusa.jpg *License:* Public domain *Contributors:* ? *Original artist:* ?
- **File:Half_Peeled_Pomegranate_BNC.jpg** *Source:* https://upload.wikimedia.org/wikipedia/commons/8/8f/Half_Peeled_Pomegranate_BNC.jpg *License:* GFDL 1.2 *Contributors:* Own work *Original artist:* **Prathyush Thomas**
- **File:Halleria_lucida00.jpg** *Source:* https://upload.wikimedia.org/wikipedia/commons/f/f9/Halleria_lucida00.jpg *License:* CC BY-SA 3.0 *Contributors:* Own work *Original artist:* Paul venter
- **File:Halleria_lucida01.jpg** *Source:* https://upload.wikimedia.org/wikipedia/commons/d/d2/Halleria_lucida01.jpg *License:* CC BY-SA 3.0 *Contributors:* Own work *Original artist:* Paul venter
- **File:Halleria_lucida02.jpg** *Source:* https://upload.wikimedia.org/wikipedia/commons/f/f6/Halleria_lucida02.jpg *License:* CC BY-SA 3.0 *Contributors:* Own work *Original artist:* Paul venter
- **File:Halleria_lucida_-_foliage_3.JPG** *Source:* https://upload.wikimedia.org/wikipedia/commons/b/b6/Halleria_lucida_-_foliage_3.JPG *License:* Public domain *Contributors:* Abu Shawka (talk) *Original artist:* Abu Shawka (talk)
- **File:Halleria_lucida_-_fruits_6.JPG** *Source:* https://upload.wikimedia.org/wikipedia/commons/6/62/Halleria_lucida_-_fruits_6.JPG *License:* Public domain *Contributors:* Own work *Original artist:* Abu Shawka
- **File:Halleria_lucida_TreeFuchsia_flowers_3.JPG** *Source:* https://upload.wikimedia.org/wikipedia/commons/3/38/Halleria_lucida_TreeFuchsia_flowers_3.JPG *License:* Public domain *Contributors:* Own work *Original artist:* Abu Shawka
- **File:Halleria_lucida_TreeFuschia_flowers_4.JPG** *Source:* https://upload.wikimedia.org/wikipedia/commons/0/0a/Halleria_lucida_TreeFuschia_flowers_4.JPG *License:* Public domain *Contributors:* Own work *Original artist:* Abu Shawka
- **File:Halleria_lucida_tree_-_Cape_Town_4.jpg** *Source:* https://upload.wikimedia.org/wikipedia/commons/5/54/Halleria_lucida_tree_-_Cape_Town_4.jpg *License:* Public domain *Contributors:* Own work *Original artist:* Abu Shawka
- **File:Hankasalmi_stream.jpg** *Source:* https://upload.wikimedia.org/wikipedia/commons/9/9b/Hankasalmi_stream.jpg *License:* CC BY-SA 3.0 *Contributors:* Own work *Original artist:* Tiia Monto
- **File:Hauptanbaugebiete-Zitrusfrüchte.svg** *Source:* https://upload.wikimedia.org/wikipedia/commons/4/41/Hauptanbaugebiete-Zitrusfr%C3%BCchte.svg *License:* Public domain *Contributors:* Own work according to data from M. Weltenburger (ed.): *Wissen*. Zweiburgen Verlag. Munich, 1987. *Original artist:* chris 論
- **File:Hikarugenji_trevarez.jpg** *Source:* https://upload.wikimedia.org/wikipedia/commons/4/4c/Hikarugenji_trevarez.jpg *License:* Public domain *Contributors:* Own work *Original artist:* Trévarez
- **File:Hiroshige,_36_Views_of_Mount_Fuji_Series_7.jpg** *Source:* https://upload.wikimedia.org/wikipedia/commons/8/80/Hiroshige%2C_36_Views_of_Mount_Fuji_Series_7.jpg *License:* Public domain *Contributors:* http://visipix.com/search/search.php?q=Hiroshige&Submit=Search&u=2&userid=1616934267&l=en&searchtype=word&searchmethod=keyword&jump_to= *Original artist:* Utagawa Hiroshige (歌川広重)
- **File:Horse-chestnut_800.jpg** *Source:* https://upload.wikimedia.org/wikipedia/commons/f/f7/Horse-chestnut_800.jpg *License:* CC-BY-SA-3.0 *Contributors:* Transferred from en.wikipedia to Commons. *Original artist:* Sannse at English Wikipedia
- **File:IMG_1527Dogwood.JPG** *Source:* https://upload.wikimedia.org/wikipedia/commons/7/7e/IMG_1527Dogwood.JPG *License:* Public domain *Contributors:* No machine-readable source provided. Own work assumed (based on copyright claims). *Original artist:* No machine-readable author provided. Mickaw~commonswiki assumed (based on copyright claims).
- **File:If_Estry.jpg** *Source:* https://upload.wikimedia.org/wikipedia/commons/9/9f/If_Estry.jpg *License:* CC BY-SA 3.0 *Contributors:* Own work *Original artist:* Roi.dagobert
- **File:If_cincentenaire_49.JPG** *Source:* https://upload.wikimedia.org/wikipedia/commons/6/65/If_cincentenaire_49.JPG *License:* CC BY-SA 3.0 *Contributors:* Own work *Original artist:* Lamiot

- **File:Ilex_mitis_-_Cape_Holly_-_foliage.JPG** *Source:* https://upload.wikimedia.org/wikipedia/commons/d/da/Ilex_mitis_-_Cape_Holly_-_foliage.JPG *License:* Public domain *Contributors:* Abu Shawka (talk). Completely own work. *Original artist:* Abu Shawka (talk)
- **File:Ilex_mitis_-_Cape_Town.JPG** *Source:* https://upload.wikimedia.org/wikipedia/commons/a/af/Ilex_mitis_-_Cape_Town.JPG *License:* Public domain *Contributors:* Transferred from en.wikipedia *Original artist:* {{subst:usernameexpand:Abu Shawka}}
- **File:Ilex_mitis_-_blossoms_-_2.jpg** *Source:* https://upload.wikimedia.org/wikipedia/commons/5/52/Ilex_mitis_-_blossoms_-_2.jpg *License:* Public domain *Contributors:* Own work *Original artist:* Abu Shawka
- **File:Ilex_mitis_tree_-_Cape_Town_3.JPG** *Source:* https://upload.wikimedia.org/wikipedia/commons/a/a5/Ilex_mitis_tree_-_Cape_Town_3.JPG *License:* Public domain *Contributors:* Abu Shawka (talk). Completely own work. *Original artist:* Abu Shawka (talk)
- **File:Illustration_Punica_granatum2.jpg** *Source:* https://upload.wikimedia.org/wikipedia/commons/d/db/Illustration_Punica_granatum2.jpg *License:* Public domain *Contributors:* ? *Original artist:* ?
- **File:Imperial_Seal_of_Japan.svg** *Source:* https://upload.wikimedia.org/wikipedia/commons/3/37/Imperial_Seal_of_Japan.svg *License:* Public domain *Contributors:* Inspired by File:Japan coa kiku.png *Original artist:* User:Philip Nilsson
- **File:Indian_Hawthorn,_India_Hawthorn_(Rhaphiolepis_indica)_at_a_distance.jpg** *Source:* https://upload.wikimedia.org/wikipedia/commons/7/7a/Indian_Hawthorn%2C_India_Hawthorn_%28Rhaphiolepis_indica%29_at_a_distance.jpg *License:* CC-BY-SA-3.0 *Contributors:* at All Things Plants. *Original artist:* This photo was taken by Dave Whitinger
- **File:InsectsAffectingWhitePine.jpg** *Source:* https://upload.wikimedia.org/wikipedia/en/9/9d/InsectsAffectingWhitePine.jpg *License:* PD-US *Contributors:*

  Seventh Report of the Forest, Fish and Game Commission of the State of New York

  Original artist:

  L. H. Joutel
- **File:Invasive_weeds_in_the_adelaide_hills.jpg** *Source:* https://upload.wikimedia.org/wikipedia/commons/7/73/Invasive_weeds_in_the_adelaide_hills.jpg *License:* CC BY-SA 3.0 *Contributors:* Own work *Original artist:* Peripitus
- **File:Ipomoea_tricolor-1.jpg** *Source:* https://upload.wikimedia.org/wikipedia/commons/1/14/Ipomoea_tricolor-1.jpg *License:* CC-BY-SA-3.0 *Contributors:* http://en.wikipedia.org/wiki/Image:Ipomoea_violacea.jpg *Original artist:* Russell E (Photograph of Ipomoea violacea, taken by rkundalini.)
- **File:ItalAlderFruit.jpg** *Source:* https://upload.wikimedia.org/wikipedia/commons/8/8f/ItalAlderFruit.jpg *License:* CC-BY-SA-3.0 *Contributors:* Transferred from en.wikipedia to Commons by Quadell using CommonsHelper. *Original artist:* The original uploader was MPF at English Wikipedia
- **File:Jabuticaba_(1).jpg** *Source:* https://upload.wikimedia.org/wikipedia/commons/6/62/Jabuticaba_%281%29.jpg *License:* Public domain *Contributors:* Own work (Original text: *I created this work entirely by myself.*) *Original artist:* Adamantiaf
- **File:Jap_blk_pine.jpg** *Source:* https://upload.wikimedia.org/wikipedia/en/4/4b/Jap_blk_pine.jpg *License:* PD *Contributors:* ? *Original artist:* ?
- **File:Japan_1961_Camellia.jpg** *Source:* https://upload.wikimedia.org/wikipedia/commons/3/3d/Japan_1961_Camellia.jpg *License:* Public domain *Contributors:* Own collection *Original artist:* Japan Post
- **File:Japanese_Black_Pine,_1936-2007.jpg** *Source:* https://upload.wikimedia.org/wikipedia/commons/2/22/Japanese_Black_Pine%2C_1936-2007.jpg *License:* GFDL *Contributors:* Own work *Original artist:* Ragesoss
- **File:Japanese_Black_Pine.JPG** *Source:* https://upload.wikimedia.org/wikipedia/en/4/49/Japanese_Black_Pine.JPG *License:* CC-BY-SA-3.0 *Contributors:*

  I created this work entirely by myself.

  Original artist:

  Marfoir (talk)
- **File:Japanese_Black_Pine_in_Ichikawa_Chiba.jpg** *Source:* https://upload.wikimedia.org/wikipedia/commons/4/45/Japanese_Black_Pine_in_Ichikawa_Chiba.jpg *License:* CC BY-SA 3.0 *Contributors:* Self shot *Original artist:* Namazu-tron
- **File:Japanese_Camellia_bonsai_55,_December_24,_2008.jpg** *Source:* https://upload.wikimedia.org/wikipedia/commons/9/9b/Japanese_Camellia_bonsai_55%2C_December_24%2C_2008.jpg *License:* CC-BY-SA-3.0 *Contributors:* Own work *Original artist:* Sage Ross
- **File:Japanese_White_Pine,_unknown-2007.jpg** *Source:* https://upload.wikimedia.org/wikipedia/commons/6/6e/Japanese_White_Pine%2C_unknown-2007.jpg *License:* CC BY-SA 3.0 *Contributors:* Own work *Original artist:* Ragesoss
- **File:Japanese_White_Pine_at_National_Bonsai_&_Penjing_Museum,_May_29_2011_-_Stierch.jpg** *Source:* https://upload.wikimedia.org/wikipedia/commons/d/d6/Japanese_White_Pine_at_National_Bonsai_%26_Penjing_Museum%2C_May_29_2011_-_Stierch.jpg *License:* CC BY 4.0 *Contributors:* Own work *Original artist:* Sarah Stierch
- **File:Japanese_Yew_Taxus_cuspidata_Bark_3008px.jpg** *Source:* https://upload.wikimedia.org/wikipedia/commons/8/84/Japanese_Yew_Taxus_cuspidata_Bark_3008px.jpg *License:* GFDL 1.2 *Contributors:* Self-photographed *Original artist:* Photo (c)2007 Derek Ramsey (Ram-Man)
- **File:Japanese_Yew_Taxus_cuspidata_Leaf_Closeup_3008px.jpg** *Source:* https://upload.wikimedia.org/wikipedia/commons/3/34/Japanese_Yew_Taxus_cuspidata_Leaf_Closeup_3008px.jpg *License:* GFDL 1.2 *Contributors:* Self-photographed *Original artist:* Photo (c)2007 Derek Ramsey (Ram-Man)

4.2. IMAGES

- **File:Japanese_Zelkova,_1895-2007.jpg** *Source:* https://upload.wikimedia.org/wikipedia/commons/9/94/Japanese_Zelkova%2C_1895-2007.jpg *License:* CC BY-SA 3.0 *Contributors:* Own work *Original artist:* Ragesoss
- **File:Japanese_cypress_woods_C032473.jpg** *Source:* https://upload.wikimedia.org/wikipedia/commons/7/72/Japanese_cypress_woods_C032473.jpg *License:* CC BY-SA 3.0 *Contributors:* Own work *Original artist:* 陳炬燵
- **File:Japanese_karin_fruits.JPG** *Source:* https://upload.wikimedia.org/wikipedia/commons/d/d2/Japanese_karin_fruits.JPG *License:* CC BY-SA 3.0 *Contributors:* Own work *Original artist:* Alexander Mirochnik
- **File:Jun_chin_shoot.jpg** *Source:* https://upload.wikimedia.org/wikipedia/commons/2/27/Jun_chin_shoot.jpg *License:* CC BY-SA 3.0 *Contributors:* Transferred from en.wikipedia to Commons. *Original artist:* MPF at English Wikipedia
- **File:Junge_Zapfen.jpg** *Source:* https://upload.wikimedia.org/wikipedia/commons/6/62/Junge_Zapfen.jpg *License:* CC-BY-SA-3.0 *Contributors:* Own work *Original artist:* Queryzo
- **File:JuniperLogs.jpg** *Source:* https://upload.wikimedia.org/wikipedia/commons/7/79/JuniperLogs.jpg *License:* Public domain *Contributors:* Own work (Original text: *self-made*) *Original artist:* Disputantum (talk)
- **File:Juniper_berries_q.jpg** *Source:* https://upload.wikimedia.org/wikipedia/commons/e/eb/Juniper_berries_q.jpg *License:* CC-BY-SA-3.0 *Contributors:* Transferred from en.wikipedia to Commons. *Original artist:* Quadell at English Wikipedia
- **File:JuniperusChinensis.jpg** *Source:* https://upload.wikimedia.org/wikipedia/commons/2/25/JuniperusChinensis.jpg *License:* Public domain *Contributors:* Own work (Original text: *I created this work entirely by myself.*) *Original artist:* Chhe (talk)
- **File:Juniperus_californica_00090.JPG** *Source:* https://upload.wikimedia.org/wikipedia/commons/4/44/Juniperus_californica_00090.JPG *License:* CC BY 2.5 *Contributors:* Own work *Original artist:* Walter Siegmund
- **File:Juniperus_chinensis_01.JPG** *Source:* https://upload.wikimedia.org/wikipedia/commons/6/6f/Juniperus_chinensis_01.JPG *License:* CC BY-SA 3.0 *Contributors:* Own work *Original artist:* Pescov
- **File:Juniperus_chinensis_bonsai.jpg** *Source:* https://upload.wikimedia.org/wikipedia/commons/6/67/Juniperus_chinensis_bonsai.jpg *License:* CC0 *Contributors:* Own work *Original artist:* Peter coxhead
- **File:Juniperus_chinensis_'Expamsa_Variegata'.jpg** *Source:* https://upload.wikimedia.org/wikipedia/commons/4/46/Juniperus_chinensis_%E2%80%98Expamsa_Variegata%E2%80%99.jpg *License:* CC BY-SA 4.0 *Contributors:* Own work *Original artist:* メルビル
- **File:Juniperus_pfitzeriana___xunadd_text_character:nN\{\textquotedbl\}\{"\}\{\}Old_Gold".jpg** *Source:* https://upload.wikimedia.org/wikipedia/commons/8/8d/Juniperus_pfitzeriana_%22Old_Gold%22.jpg *License:* CC BY-SA 4.0 *Contributors:* Own work *Original artist:* メルビル
- **File:Juniperus_procumbens_nana_MN_2007.JPG** *Source:* https://upload.wikimedia.org/wikipedia/commons/b/bb/Juniperus_procumbens_nana_MN_2007.JPG *License:* CC-BY-SA-3.0 *Contributors:* Own work *Original artist:* SEWilco
- **File:Juniperus_squamata0.jpg** *Source:* https://upload.wikimedia.org/wikipedia/commons/b/b6/Juniperus_squamata0.jpg *License:* CC BY 2.5 *Contributors:* Own work *Original artist:* MPF
- **File:Juniperus_virginiana_near_Oxford,_Ohio.jpg** *Source:* https://upload.wikimedia.org/wikipedia/commons/2/20/Juniperus_virginiana_near_Oxford%2C_Ohio.jpg *License:* CC BY-SA 3.0 *Contributors:* Own work *Original artist:* Greg Hume
- **File:KG_Cycas_revoluta.jpg** *Source:* https://upload.wikimedia.org/wikipedia/commons/2/2d/KG_Cycas_revoluta.jpg *License:* CC BY-SA 3.0 *Contributors:* Own work *Original artist:* Jared Preston
- **File:Kamelie_Knospe.JPG** *Source:* https://upload.wikimedia.org/wikipedia/commons/1/1c/Kamelie_Knospe.JPG *License:* Public domain *Contributors:* Own work *Original artist:* Please report references to marco.almbauer<img alt='-at-' src='https://upload.wikimedia.org/wikipedia/commons/thumb/b/b6/At_char.svg/11px-At_char.svg.png' title='-at-' width='11' height='11' srcset='https://upload.wikimedia.org/wikipedia/commons/thumb/b/b6/At_char.svg/17px-At_char.svg.png 1.5x, https://upload.wikimedia.org/wikipedia/commons/thumb/b/b6/At_char.svg/22px-At_char.svg.png 2x' data-file-width='10' data-file-height='10' />gmail.com.
- **File:Kamelie_in_Pirna_23.JPG** *Source:* https://upload.wikimedia.org/wikipedia/commons/5/5a/Kamelie_in_Pirna_23.JPG *License:* CC0 *Contributors:* Own work *Original artist:* Brücke-Osteuropa
- **File:Kamelien-Königsbrück-Rotblüte.jpg** *Source:* https://upload.wikimedia.org/wikipedia/commons/3/3c/Kamelien-K%C3%B6nigsbr%C3%BCck-Rotbl%C3%BCte.jpg *License:* CC BY-SA 3.0 *Contributors:* Own work *Original artist:* DynaMoToR
- **File:Kaštan_1.jpg** *Source:* https://upload.wikimedia.org/wikipedia/commons/2/2a/Ka%C5%A1tan_1.jpg *License:* Public domain *Contributors:* No machine-readable source provided. Own work assumed (based on copyright claims). *Original artist:* No machine-readable author provided. Karelj assumed (based on copyright claims).
- **File:Kiefernzapfen_P4202406.jpg** *Source:* https://upload.wikimedia.org/wikipedia/commons/e/ea/Kiefernzapfen_P4202406.jpg *License:* Public domain *Contributors:* Own work *Original artist:* Roman Köhler
- **File:Klimopblad_Hedera_helix.jpg** *Source:* https://upload.wikimedia.org/wikipedia/commons/8/80/Klimopblad_Hedera_helix.jpg *License:* CC-BY-SA-3.0 *Contributors:* Own work *Original artist:* (nl: Klimopblad)
- **File:Koeh-258.jpg** *Source:* https://upload.wikimedia.org/wikipedia/commons/0/00/Rosmarinus_officinalis_-_K%C3%B6hler%E2%80%93s_Medizinal-Pflanzen-258.jpg *License:* Public domain *Contributors:* List of Koehler Images *Original artist:* Franz Eugen Köhler, *Köhler's Medizinal-Pflanzen*
- **File:Kyoto_Toji_Hiwadabuki_C0990.jpg** *Source:* https://upload.wikimedia.org/wikipedia/commons/7/7a/Kyoto_Toji_Hiwadabuki_C0990.jpg *License:* Public domain *Contributors:* No machine-readable source provided. Own work assumed (based on copyright claims). *Original artist:* No machine-readable author provided. Fg2 assumed (based on copyright claims).
- **File:LaHayeDeRoutotIf1.JPG** *Source:* https://upload.wikimedia.org/wikipedia/commons/0/03/LaHayeDeRoutotIf1.JPG *License:* CC BY 3.0 *Contributors:* Own work *Original artist:* Gérard Janot

- **File:Lee-Russell-Farm-Security-Administration-1939-Crab-Apples.jpg** *Source:* https://upload.wikimedia.org/wikipedia/commons/0/03/Lee-Russell-Farm-Security-Administration-1939-Crab-Apples.jpg *License:* Public domain *Contributors:* This image is available from the United States Library of Congress's Prints and Photographs division under the digital ID fsa.8a27278. This tag does not indicate the copyright status of the attached work. A normal copyright tag is still required. See Commons:Licensing for more information. *Original artist:* Russell Lee

- **File:Lemon_on_a_Wood_Table.jpg** *Source:* https://upload.wikimedia.org/wikipedia/commons/b/bd/Lemon_on_a_Wood_Table.jpg *License:* CC BY-SA 4.0 *Contributors:* Own work *Original artist:* Karl Thomas Moore

- **File:Libanonzeder.jpg** *Source:* https://upload.wikimedia.org/wikipedia/commons/2/25/Libanonzeder.jpg *License:* CC-BY-SA-3.0 *Contributors:* ? *Original artist:* ?

- **File:Libythea_celtis1.jpg** *Source:* https://upload.wikimedia.org/wikipedia/commons/7/77/Libythea_celtis1.jpg *License:* CC-BY-SA-3.0 *Contributors:* KENPEI's photo *Original artist:* KENPEI

- **File:Limes.jpg** *Source:* https://upload.wikimedia.org/wikipedia/commons/f/f2/Limes.jpg *License:* CC BY-SA 2.5 *Contributors:* ? *Original artist:* ?

- **File:Lock-green.svg** *Source:* https://upload.wikimedia.org/wikipedia/commons/6/65/Lock-green.svg *License:* CC0 *Contributors:* en:File:Free-to-read_lock_75.svg *Original artist:* User:Trappist the monk

- **File:Locust-railing.jpg** *Source:* https://upload.wikimedia.org/wikipedia/commons/7/75/Locust-railing.jpg *License:* CC BY-SA 3.0 *Contributors:* Wood Railing http://awoodrailing.com *Original artist:* Jimmypader

- **File:Loudspeaker.svg** *Source:* https://upload.wikimedia.org/wikipedia/commons/8/8a/Loudspeaker.svg *License:* Public domain *Contributors:* New version of Image:Loudspeaker.png, by AzaToth and compressed by Hautala *Original artist:* Nethac DIU, waves corrected by Zoid

- **File:Male_cone_of_Cedar_of_Lebanon.JPG** *Source:* https://upload.wikimedia.org/wikipedia/commons/e/ee/Male_cone_of_Cedar_of_Lebanon.JPG *License:* Public domain *Contributors:* Own work *Original artist:* Rosser1954 Roger Griffith

- **File:Malecones.jpg** *Source:* https://upload.wikimedia.org/wikipedia/commons/3/3f/Malecones.jpg *License:* CC BY-SA 4.0 *Contributors:* Own work *Original artist:* DigbyDalton

- **File:Mandariner_Citrus_deliciosa.jpg** *Source:* https://upload.wikimedia.org/wikipedia/commons/5/51/Mandariner_Citrus_deliciosa.jpg *License:* CC BY-SA 3.0 *Contributors:* Own work *Original artist:* Paucabot

- **File:Maple_syrup.jpg** *Source:* https://upload.wikimedia.org/wikipedia/commons/1/18/Maple_syrup.jpg *License:* Public domain *Contributors:* Own work *Original artist:* User:Miguel Andrade

- **File:Maplekeys.jpg** *Source:* https://upload.wikimedia.org/wikipedia/commons/6/6d/Maplekeys.jpg *License:* CC-BY-SA-3.0 *Contributors:* ? *Original artist:* ?

- **File:Maslina_Kastela_0807_2.jpg** *Source:* https://upload.wikimedia.org/wikipedia/commons/8/8f/Maslina_Kastela_0807_2.jpg *License:* CC BY-SA 3.0 *Contributors:* Own work *Original artist:* Roberta F.

- **File:Miharu_Miharu-Takizakura_Front_1.jpg** *Source:* https://upload.wikimedia.org/wikipedia/commons/8/8f/Miharu_Miharu-Takizakura_Front_1.jpg *License:* CC BY-SA 3.0 *Contributors:* The uploader photographed it *Original artist:* 京浜にけ

- **File:Ming-Imperial-Court.jpg** *Source:* https://upload.wikimedia.org/wikipedia/commons/1/12/Ming-Imperial-Court.jpg *License:* Public domain *Contributors:* Unknown *Original artist:* unknow court artist

- **File:MonarchButterfly-5635.jpg** *Source:* https://upload.wikimedia.org/wikipedia/commons/8/83/MonarchButterfly-5635.jpg *License:* CC BY-SA 3.0 *Contributors:* Own work *Original artist:* Loadmaster (David R. Tribble)

- **File:Morus_alba_fruits_and_leaves.jpg** *Source:* https://upload.wikimedia.org/wikipedia/commons/b/bf/Morus_alba_fruits_and_leaves.jpg *License:* CC BY-SA 2.5 *Contributors:* Own work *Original artist:* Andre Abrahami

- **File:Mustard_Seed_Garden_1st_set1.JPG** *Source:* https://upload.wikimedia.org/wikipedia/commons/4/42/Mustard_Seed_Garden_1st_set1.JPG *License:* CC BY-SA 3.0 *Contributors:* Own work *Original artist:* ReijiYamashina

- **File:Myrciaria_cauliflora.jpg** *Source:* https://upload.wikimedia.org/wikipedia/commons/c/cf/Myrciaria_cauliflora.jpg *License:* CC BY-SA 3.0 *Contributors:* Own work *Original artist:* Bruno.karklis

- **File:Myrciaria_cauliflora_leaves.jpg** *Source:* https://upload.wikimedia.org/wikipedia/commons/5/57/Myrciaria_cauliflora_leaves.jpg *License:* Public domain *Contributors:* Own work *Original artist:* Ben Cody

- **File:NCArboretum_Bonsai-27527-1.jpg** *Source:* https://upload.wikimedia.org/wikipedia/commons/c/c6/NCArboretum_Bonsai-27527-1.jpg *License:* Public domain *Contributors:* KenThomas.us *Original artist:* Ken Thomas

- **File:NCArboretum_Bonsai-27527-3.jpg** *Source:* https://upload.wikimedia.org/wikipedia/commons/6/6e/NCArboretum_Bonsai-27527-3.jpg *License:* Public domain *Contributors:* KenThomas.us *Original artist:* Ken Thomas

- **File:NIH_citrus.jpg** *Source:* https://upload.wikimedia.org/wikipedia/commons/9/9d/NIH_citrus.jpg *License:* Public domain *Contributors:* ? *Original artist:* ?

- **File:Newark_cherry_blossoms.jpg** *Source:* https://upload.wikimedia.org/wikipedia/commons/3/3c/Newark_cherry_blossoms.jpg *License:* CC BY 3.0 *Contributors:* Own work *Original artist:* Cjbvii

- **File:Odichukuthi_lime_crossection.JPG** *Source:* https://upload.wikimedia.org/wikipedia/commons/f/f2/Odichukuthi_lime_crossection.JPG *License:* CC BY-SA 3.0 *Contributors:* Transferred from ml.wikipedia to Commons by Sreejithk2000 using CommonsHelper. *Original artist:* Noblevmy at Malayalam Wikipedia

4.2. IMAGES

- **File:Odichukuthi_naranga.JPG** *Source:* https://upload.wikimedia.org/wikipedia/commons/f/f9/Odichukuthi_naranga.JPG *License:* CC BY-SA 3.0 *Contributors:* Transferred from ml.wikipedia to Commons by Sreejithk2000 using CommonsHelper. *Original artist:* Noblevmy at Malayalam Wikipedia
- **File:Old_olive.jpg** *Source:* https://upload.wikimedia.org/wikipedia/commons/b/b0/Old_olive.jpg *License:* CC BY-SA 4.0 *Contributors:* Own work *Original artist:* Sergeagle
- **File:Olea_europaea_-_Köhler–s_Medizinal-Pflanzen-229.jpg** *Source:* https://upload.wikimedia.org/wikipedia/commons/1/16/Olea_europaea_-_K%C3%B6hler%E2%80%93s_Medizinal-Pflanzen-229.jpg *License:* Public domain *Contributors:* List of Koehler Images *Original artist:* Franz Eugen Köhler, *Köhler's Medizinal-Pflanzen*
- **File:Olea_europaea_young_plant01.jpg** *Source:* https://upload.wikimedia.org/wikipedia/commons/d/d4/Olea_europaea_young_plant01.jpg *License:* CC BY 2.5 *Contributors:* No machine-readable source provided. Own work assumed (based on copyright claims). *Original artist:* No machine-readable author provided. Rickjpelleg assumed (based on copyright claims).
- **File:Olivares_de_la_campiña_estepeña.jpg** *Source:* https://upload.wikimedia.org/wikipedia/commons/8/89/Olivares_de_la_campi%C3%B1a_estepe%C3%B1a.jpg *License:* GFDL *Contributors:* Own work *Original artist:* Frobles
- **File:Olive-tree-trunk-0.jpg** *Source:* https://upload.wikimedia.org/wikipedia/commons/1/1a/Olive-tree-trunk-0.jpg *License:* CC-BY-SA-3.0 *Contributors:* English Wikipedia *Original artist:* Rnbc
- **File:Olive_Phenology.png** *Source:* https://upload.wikimedia.org/wikipedia/commons/0/0f/Olive_Phenology.png *License:* CC BY-SA 4.0 *Contributors:* Own work *Original artist:* J. Oteros
- **File:Olive_blossoms.jpg** *Source:* https://upload.wikimedia.org/wikipedia/commons/c/c0/Olive_blossoms.jpg *License:* CC-BY-SA-3.0 *Contributors:* Transferred from en.wikipedia to Commons. *Original artist:* Sputnikcccp at English Wikipedia
- **File:Olive_niche.jpg** *Source:* https://upload.wikimedia.org/wikipedia/commons/a/ab/Olive_niche.jpg *License:* CC BY-SA 4.0 *Contributors:* Own work *Original artist:* J. Oteros
- **File:Olive_tree_Karystos2.jpg** *Source:* https://upload.wikimedia.org/wikipedia/commons/d/d8/Olive_tree_Karystos2.jpg *License:* Public domain *Contributors:* No machine-readable source provided. Own work assumed (based on copyright claims). *Original artist:* No machine-readable author provided. Tbc assumed (based on copyright claims).
- **File:Olive_trees_on_Thassos.JPG** *Source:* https://upload.wikimedia.org/wikipedia/commons/b/b2/Olive_trees_on_Thassos.JPG *License:* CC BY-SA 2.5 *Contributors:* Own work *Original artist:* Petr Pakandl
- **File:Olives_au_marche_de_Toulon_p1040238.jpg** *Source:* https://upload.wikimedia.org/wikipedia/commons/0/09/Olives_au_marche_de_Toulon_p1040238.jpg *License:* CC-BY-SA-3.0 *Contributors:* Own work *Original artist:* David Monniaux
- **File:Olives_vertes.JPG** *Source:* https://upload.wikimedia.org/wikipedia/commons/1/16/Olives_vertes.JPG *License:* CC-BY-SA-3.0 *Contributors:* ? *Original artist:* ?
- **File:Olives_à_l'apéritif.jpg** *Source:* https://upload.wikimedia.org/wikipedia/commons/d/d3/Olives_%C3%A0_l%27ap%C3%A9ritif.jpg *License:* CC BY-SA 3.0 *Contributors:* Own work *Original artist:* K'm
- **File:Orangerie_Kruidtuin_Leuven.jpg** *Source:* https://upload.wikimedia.org/wikipedia/commons/0/05/Orangerie_Kruidtuin_Leuven.jpg *License:* CC-BY-SA-3.0 *Contributors:* Own work *Original artist:* Athenchen
- **File:Outeniqua_Yellowwood.JPG** *Source:* https://upload.wikimedia.org/wikipedia/commons/a/ad/Outeniqua_Yellowwood.JPG *License:* Public domain *Contributors:* Transferred from en.wikipedia *Original artist:* Abu Shawka at en.wikipedia
- **File:Peeled_Pomegranate.jpg** *Source:* https://upload.wikimedia.org/wikipedia/commons/e/e5/Peeled_Pomegranate.jpg *License:* CC BY-SA 4.0 *Contributors:* Own work *Original artist:* Umais Bin Sajjad
- **File:Pemphis_acidula.jpg** *Source:* https://upload.wikimedia.org/wikipedia/commons/1/16/Pemphis_acidula.jpg *License:* CC-BY-SA-3.0 *Contributors:* Own work *Original artist:* Tau'olunga
- **File:Pemphis_acidula_(7374295704).jpg** *Source:* https://upload.wikimedia.org/wikipedia/commons/9/99/Pemphis_acidula_%287374295704%29.jpg *License:* CC BY 2.0 *Contributors:* Pemphis acidula *Original artist:* Akos Kokai
- **File:Pemphis_acidula_bushes02.JPG** *Source:* https://upload.wikimedia.org/wikipedia/commons/2/28/Pemphis_acidula_bushes02.JPG *License:* CC-BY-SA-3.0 *Contributors:* Own work *Original artist:* B.navez
- **File:Penjing.JPG** *Source:* https://upload.wikimedia.org/wikipedia/commons/1/16/Penjing.JPG *License:* CC BY-SA 3.0 *Contributors:* Own work *Original artist:* Pascal3012
- **File:Penjing_img_2257.jpg** *Source:* https://upload.wikimedia.org/wikipedia/commons/e/e8/Penjing_img_2257.jpg *License:* GPL *Contributors:* ? *Original artist:* ?
- **File:People_icon.svg** *Source:* https://upload.wikimedia.org/wikipedia/commons/3/37/People_icon.svg *License:* CC0 *Contributors:* OpenClipart *Original artist:* OpenClipart
- **File:Pillnitz_Castle._Camellia_japonica_001.jpg** *Source:* https://upload.wikimedia.org/wikipedia/commons/7/75/Pillnitz_Castle._Camellia_japonica_001.jpg *License:* CC BY 3.0 *Contributors:* Own work *Original artist:* JoJan
- **File:Pinus-parviflora-close.JPG** *Source:* https://upload.wikimedia.org/wikipedia/commons/3/37/Pinus-parviflora-close.JPG *License:* CC-BY-SA-3.0 *Contributors:* ? *Original artist:* ?
- **File:PinusStrobusBoard.jpg** *Source:* https://upload.wikimedia.org/wikipedia/en/f/f2/PinusStrobusBoard.jpg *License:* PD *Contributors:* self-made

    Original artist:

    Disputantum (talk)

- **File:Pinus_clausa.jpg** *Source:* https://upload.wikimedia.org/wikipedia/commons/2/2e/Pinus_clausa.jpg *License:* Public domain *Contributors:* Own work *Original artist:* Mason Brock (Masebrock)
- **File:Pinus_clausa_range_map_1.png** *Source:* https://upload.wikimedia.org/wikipedia/commons/f/f7/Pinus_clausa_range_map_1.png *License:* Public domain *Contributors:* USGS Geosciences and Environmental Change Science Center: Digital Representations of Tree Species Range Maps from "Atlas of United States Trees" by Elbert L. Little, Jr. (and other publications) *Original artist:* Elbert L. Little, Jr., of the U.S. Department of Agriculture, Forest Service, and others
- **File:Pinus_mugo_Blüten.jpg** *Source:* https://upload.wikimedia.org/wikipedia/commons/2/23/Pinus_mugo_Bl%C3%BCten.jpg *License:* CC BY-SA 4.0 *Contributors:* Own work *Original artist:* Geo-Science-International
- **File:Pinus_mugo_Rila_1.jpg** *Source:* https://upload.wikimedia.org/wikipedia/commons/9/9f/Pinus_mugo_Rila_1.jpg *License:* CC BY 2.0 *Contributors:* IMG_1894 *Original artist:* jason_hockman
- **File:Pinus_mugo_bonsai_at_the_BBG,_August_2,_2008.jpg** *Source:* https://upload.wikimedia.org/wikipedia/commons/5/5f/Pinus_mugo_bonsai_at_the_BBG%2C_August_2%2C_2008.jpg *License:* CC BY-SA 3.0 *Contributors:* Own work *Original artist:* Ragesoss
- **File:Pinus_mugo_uncinata_trees.jpg** *Source:* https://upload.wikimedia.org/wikipedia/commons/d/d5/Pinus_mugo_uncinata_trees.jpg *License:* CC BY-SA 2.0 *Contributors:* Flickr *Original artist:* Pastilletes at Flickr
- **File:Pinus_nigra_cone.jpg** *Source:* https://upload.wikimedia.org/wikipedia/commons/f/f3/Pinus_nigra_cone.jpg *License:* CC-BY-SA-3.0 *Contributors:* Originally uploaded to English Wikipedia as en:Image:Pine cones, mature female.jpg by Menchi (10:48, 14 May 2004): "camcorder'ed myself" *Original artist:* Menchi
- **File:Pinus_ponderosa_scopulorum_Custer_State_Park_SD.jpg** *Source:* https://upload.wikimedia.org/wikipedia/commons/7/76/Pinus_ponderosa_scopulorum_Custer_State_Park_SD.jpg *License:* CC BY 2.0 *Contributors:* Custer State Park, Pahá Sápa (Black Hills), South Dakota *Original artist:* Jason Sturner
- **File:Pinus_rigida_cone_Poland.jpg** *Source:* https://upload.wikimedia.org/wikipedia/commons/8/80/Pinus_rigida_cone_Poland.jpg *License:* CC BY 3.0 *Contributors:* Own work *Original artist:* Crusier
- **File:Pinus_strobus_Cone.jpg** *Source:* https://upload.wikimedia.org/wikipedia/commons/8/8d/Pinus_strobus_Cone.jpg *License:* CC BY 3.0 us *Contributors:* This image is Image Number 5350005 at Forestry Images, a source for forest health, natural resources and silviculture images operated by The Bugwood Network at the University of Georgia and the USDA Forest Service. *Original artist:* Keith Kanoti, Maine Forest Service, USA
- **File:Pinus_strobus_JPG1b.jpg** *Source:* https://upload.wikimedia.org/wikipedia/commons/9/9f/Pinus_strobus_JPG1b.jpg *License:* CC BY 3.0 *Contributors:* Own work *Original artist:* Jean-Pol GRANDMONT
- **File:Pinus_strobus_Syvania.jpg** *Source:* https://upload.wikimedia.org/wikipedia/commons/3/30/Pinus_strobus_Syvania.jpg *License:* CC BY 3.0 us *Contributors:* This image is Image Number 1397002 at Forestry Images, a source for forest health, natural resources and silviculture images operated by The Bugwood Network at the University of Georgia and the USDA Forest Service. *Original artist:* Joseph O'Brien, USDA Forest Service
- **File:Pinus_strobus_needles3.jpg** *Source:* https://upload.wikimedia.org/wikipedia/commons/a/af/Pinus_strobus_needles3.jpg *License:* Public domain *Contributors:* Own work *Original artist:* Hardyplants at English Wikipedia
- **File:Pinus_strobus_range_map_1.png** *Source:* https://upload.wikimedia.org/wikipedia/commons/c/c7/Pinus_strobus_range_map_1.png *License:* Public domain *Contributors:* USGS Geosciences and Environmental Change Science Center: Digital Representations of Tree Species Range Maps from "Atlas of United States Trees" by Elbert L. Little, Jr. (and other publications) *Original artist:* Elbert L. Little, Jr., U.S. Department of Agriculture, Forest Service, and others
- **File:Pinus_thunbergii_Bonsai.JPG** *Source:* https://upload.wikimedia.org/wikipedia/en/5/53/Pinus_thunbergii_Bonsai.JPG *License:* PD *Contributors:*

self-made

Original artist:

1000Faces (talk)
- **File:Pinus_virginiana_Scrub_Pine_Branch_3200px.jpg** *Source:* https://upload.wikimedia.org/wikipedia/commons/9/9f/Pinus_virginiana_Scrub_Pine_Branch_3200px.jpg *License:* GFDL 1.2 *Contributors:* Self-photographed *Original artist:* Photo (c)2007 Derek Ramsey (Ram-Man)
- **File:Pjfigbonsai.jpg** *Source:* https://upload.wikimedia.org/wikipedia/commons/d/d9/Pjfigbonsai.jpg *License:* Public domain *Contributors:* Own work *Original artist:* Casliber
- **File:Podocarpus_costalis_area.JPG** *Source:* https://upload.wikimedia.org/wikipedia/commons/6/6d/Podocarpus_costalis_area.JPG *License:* CC BY-SA 3.0 *Contributors:* Own work *Original artist:* Pc1878
- **File:Podocarpus_latifolius_-_Cape_Town_-_1.JPG** *Source:* https://upload.wikimedia.org/wikipedia/commons/a/a3/Podocarpus_latifolius_-_Cape_Town_-_1.JPG *License:* Public domain *Contributors:* Own work *Original artist:* Abu Shawka
- **File:Podocarpus_latifolius_-_Cape_Town_-_2.JPG** *Source:* https://upload.wikimedia.org/wikipedia/commons/1/19/Podocarpus_latifolius_-_Cape_Town_-_2.JPG *License:* Public domain *Contributors:* Own work *Original artist:* Abu Shawka
- **File:Podocarpus_latifolius_-_Cape_Town_-_3.JPG** *Source:* https://upload.wikimedia.org/wikipedia/commons/0/09/Podocarpus_latifolius_-_Cape_Town_-_3.JPG *License:* Public domain *Contributors:* Transferred from en.wikipedia *Original artist:* Abu Shawka
- **File:Pomegranate02_edit.jpg** *Source:* https://upload.wikimedia.org/wikipedia/commons/9/9b/Pomegranate02_edit.jpg *License:* GFDL 1.2 *Contributors:* Own work *Original artist:* Fir0002
- **File:PomegranateChina.jpg** *Source:* https://upload.wikimedia.org/wikipedia/commons/4/48/PomegranateChina.jpg *License:* CC BY-SA 3.0 *Contributors:* Own work *Original artist:* Philg88

4.2. IMAGES

- **File:Pomegranate_LACMA_M.81.61.5.jpg** *Source:* https://upload.wikimedia.org/wikipedia/commons/2/22/Pomegranate_LACMA_M.81.61.5.jpg *License:* Public domain *Contributors:*
- Image: http://collections.lacma.org/sites/default/files/remote_images/piction/ma-31788694-O3.jpg *Original artist:* ?
- **File:Pomegranate_Seeds_BNC.jpg** *Source:* https://upload.wikimedia.org/wikipedia/commons/6/69/Pomegranate_Seeds_BNC.jpg *License:* GFDL 1.2 *Contributors:* Own work *Original artist:* **Prathyush Thomas**
- **File:Pomegranate_fruit.jpg** *Source:* https://upload.wikimedia.org/wikipedia/commons/6/6b/Pomegranate_fruit.jpg *License:* GFDL 1.2 *Contributors:* Own work *Original artist:*
fir0002 | flagstaffotos.com.au
- **File:PonderosaPinebarkidaho.JPG** *Source:* https://upload.wikimedia.org/wikipedia/commons/e/ea/PonderosaPinebarkidaho.JPG *License:* Public domain *Contributors:* http://www.flickr.com/photos/74281168@N00/191429570/ *Original artist:* Jami Dwyer (talk · contribs)
- **File:PonderosaRangeMap.png** *Source:* https://upload.wikimedia.org/wikipedia/commons/2/29/PonderosaRangeMap.png *License:* Public domain *Contributors:* Pinus ponderosa: A Taxonomic Review With Five Subspecies in the United States, Pacific Southwest Research Station Research Paper PSW-RP-264, p. 2 *Original artist:* Robert Z. Callaham (talk · contribs)
- **File:Ponderosa_Identification.jpg** *Source:* https://upload.wikimedia.org/wikipedia/commons/b/b9/Ponderosa_Identification.jpg *License:* CC BY 3.0 *Contributors:* Own work *Original artist:* Clyde frogg
- **File:Porducción_de_olivas.PNG** *Source:* https://upload.wikimedia.org/wikipedia/commons/a/a9/Porducci%C3%B3n_de_olivas.PNG *License:* CC BY-SA 4.0 *Contributors:* Own work *Original artist:* Fobos92
- **File:Port_Jackson_fig_fruit_(3392277172).jpg** *Source:* https://upload.wikimedia.org/wikipedia/commons/2/25/Port_Jackson_fig_fruit_%283392277172%29.jpg *License:* CC BY 2.0 *Contributors:* Port Jackson fig fruit *Original artist:* John Tann from Sydney, Australia
- **File:Portulacaria_afra_2.jpg** *Source:* https://upload.wikimedia.org/wikipedia/commons/5/53/Portulacaria_afra_2.jpg *License:* CC BY-SA 2.0 *Contributors:* Elephant Bush *Original artist:* Claire H. from New York City, USA
- **File:PrefSymbol-Tokyo.svg** *Source:* https://upload.wikimedia.org/wikipedia/commons/c/cb/PrefSymbol-Tokyo.svg *License:* Public domain *Contributors:* Own work *Original artist:* User:Pmx
- **File:PrunusSerrulataBark.jpg** *Source:* https://upload.wikimedia.org/wikipedia/commons/8/83/PrunusSerrulataBark.jpg *License:* Public domain *Contributors:* Own work (Original text: *I created this work entirely by myself.*) *Original artist:* Chhe (talk)
- **File:PrunusSerrulataLeaf.jpg** *Source:* https://upload.wikimedia.org/wikipedia/commons/0/08/PrunusSerrulataLeaf.jpg *License:* Public domain *Contributors:* Own work (Original text: *I created this work entirely by myself.*) *Original artist:* Chhe at English Wikipedia
- **File:Prunus_serrulata1.jpg** *Source:* https://upload.wikimedia.org/wikipedia/commons/2/28/Prunus_serrulata1.jpg *License:* CC-BY-SA-3.0 *Contributors:* Own work *Original artist:* M.Minderhoud
- **File:Prunus_serrulata_'Kanzan'_03.JPG** *Source:* https://upload.wikimedia.org/wikipedia/commons/d/d3/Prunus_serrulata_%27Kanzan%27_03.JPG *License:* CC BY-SA 3.0 *Contributors:* Own work *Original artist:* Captain-tucker
- **File:Prunus_serrulata_-_flowers_close-up.jpg** *Source:* https://upload.wikimedia.org/wikipedia/commons/e/e4/Prunus_serrulata_-_flowers_close-up.jpg *License:* GFDL *Contributors:* Own work *Original artist:* Dodek
- **File:Prunus_serrulata_2005_spring_018.jpg** *Source:* https://upload.wikimedia.org/wikipedia/commons/2/29/Prunus_serrulata_2005_spring_018.jpg *License:* CC-BY-SA-3.0 *Contributors:* photo taken by Kropsoq *Original artist:* Kropsoq
- **File:Punica.granatum(01).jpg** *Source:* https://upload.wikimedia.org/wikipedia/commons/b/b3/Punica.granatum%2801%29.jpg *License:* CC-BY-SA-3.0 *Contributors:* ? *Original artist:* ?
- **File:Question_book-new.svg** *Source:* https://upload.wikimedia.org/wikipedia/en/9/99/Question_book-new.svg *License:* Cc-by-sa-3.0 *Contributors:*
Created from scratch in Adobe Illustrator. Based on Image:Question book.png created by User:Equazcion *Original artist:*
Tkgd2007
- **File:Quince_flowers.jpg** *Source:* https://upload.wikimedia.org/wikipedia/commons/2/2c/Quince_flowers.jpg *License:* CC-BY-SA-3.0 *Contributors:* Transferred from en.wikipedia to Commons by Syp using CommonsHelper. *Original artist:* Fir0002 at English Wikipedia
- **File:Quinces_skin_closeup.JPG** *Source:* https://upload.wikimedia.org/wikipedia/commons/2/29/Quinces_skin_closeup.JPG *License:* CC BY-SA 4.0 *Contributors:* Own work *Original artist:* Wuerzele
- **File:RN_Ulmus_parvifolia_bark.JPG** *Source:* https://upload.wikimedia.org/wikipedia/commons/a/a9/RN_Ulmus_parvifolia_bark.JPG *License:* CC0 *Contributors:* Nijboer collection *Original artist:* Ronnie Nijboer
- **File:RN_Ulmus_parvifolia_leaves_and_seeds.JPG** *Source:* https://upload.wikimedia.org/wikipedia/commons/2/23/RN_Ulmus_parvifolia_leaves_and_seeds.JPG *License:* CC0 *Contributors:* Nijboer collection *Original artist:* Ronnie Nijboer
- **File:Rapanea_melanophloeos01.jpg** *Source:* https://upload.wikimedia.org/wikipedia/commons/6/66/Rapanea_melanophloeos01.jpg *License:* CC BY-SA 3.0 *Contributors:* Own work *Original artist:* Paul venter
- **File:Rapanea_melanophloeos02.jpg** *Source:* https://upload.wikimedia.org/wikipedia/commons/8/83/Rapanea_melanophloeos02.jpg *License:* CC BY-SA 3.0 *Contributors:* Own work *Original artist:* Paul venter
- **File:Rapanea_melanophloeos_-_cape_town_1.jpg** *Source:* https://upload.wikimedia.org/wikipedia/commons/e/ec/Rapanea_melanophloeos_-_cape_town_1.jpg *License:* CC BY-SA 3.0 *Contributors:* Own work *Original artist:* Abu Shawka

- **File:Rapanea_melanophloeos_tree_-_Harold_Porter_garden_South_Africa_2.jpg** *Source:* https://upload.wikimedia.org/wikipedia/commons/8/8c/Rapanea_melanophloeos_tree_-_Harold_Porter_garden_South_Africa_2.jpg *License:* CC BY-SA 3.0 *Contributors:* Own work *Original artist:* Abu Shawka
- **File:Red_Pencil_Icon.png** *Source:* https://upload.wikimedia.org/wikipedia/commons/7/74/Red_Pencil_Icon.png *License:* CC0 *Contributors:* Own work *Original artist:* Peter coxhead
- **File:Redmaplefoliage.jpg** *Source:* https://upload.wikimedia.org/wikipedia/commons/1/14/Redmaplefoliage.jpg *License:* CC BY-SA 4.0 *Contributors:* Own work *Original artist:* DigbyDalton
- **File:Renaissance_C14_Füllmaurer_Leonhart_Fuchs.jpg** *Source:* https://upload.wikimedia.org/wikipedia/commons/4/40/Renaissance_C14_F%C3%BCllmaurer_Leonhart_Fuchs.jpg *License:* Public domain *Contributors:* Württembergisches Landesmuseu, Stuttgart *Original artist:* Heinrich Füllmaurer (tätig um 1530/40)
- **File:Rhaphiolepis_indica_Hong_Kong.jpg** *Source:* https://upload.wikimedia.org/wikipedia/commons/5/57/Rhaphiolepis_indica_Hong_Kong.jpg *License:* CC BY-SA 3.0 *Contributors:* Own work *Original artist:* Geographer
- **File:Robinia_pseudacacia00.jpg** *Source:* https://upload.wikimedia.org/wikipedia/commons/d/d6/Robinia_pseudacacia00.jpg *License:* Public domain *Contributors:* Own work *Original artist:* Androstachys
- **File:Robinia_pseudacacia02.jpg** *Source:* https://upload.wikimedia.org/wikipedia/commons/9/9e/Robinia_pseudacacia02.jpg *License:* Public domain *Contributors:* Own work *Original artist:* Androstachys
- **File:Robinia_pseudoacacia_'Frisia'.jpg** *Source:* https://upload.wikimedia.org/wikipedia/commons/f/f5/Robinia_pseudoacacia_%27Frisia%27.jpg *License:* CC BY-SA 3.0 *Contributors:* Own work *Original artist:* Colin
- **File:Robinia_pseudoacacia_004.JPG** *Source:* https://upload.wikimedia.org/wikipedia/commons/d/d3/Robinia_pseudoacacia_004.JPG *License:* CC BY-SA 3.0 *Contributors:* Own work *Original artist:* H. Zell
- **File:Robinia_pseudoacacia_seeds.jpg** *Source:* https://upload.wikimedia.org/wikipedia/commons/4/4b/Robinia_pseudoacacia_seeds.jpg *License:* CC BY-SA 3.0 *Contributors:* Own work *Original artist:* Simon A. Eugster
- **File:Robinia_spines_kz.jpg** *Source:* https://upload.wikimedia.org/wikipedia/commons/6/6f/Robinia_spines_kz.jpg *License:* CC BY-SA 3.0 *Contributors:* Own work *Original artist:* Kenraiz
- **File:Rose_Amber_Flush_20070601.jpg** *Source:* https://upload.wikimedia.org/wikipedia/commons/3/37/Rose_Amber_Flush_20070601.jpg *License:* CC BY-SA 3.0 *Contributors:* Own work *Original artist:* Georges Seguin (Okki)
- **File:Rosemary,_ca_1500.jpg** *Source:* https://upload.wikimedia.org/wikipedia/commons/2/24/Rosemary%2C_ca_1500.jpg *License:* Public domain *Contributors:* http://digital2.library.ucla.edu/viewItem.do?ark=21198/zz0000zzrs *Original artist:* Unknown artist from Italy
- **File:RosemaryEssentialOil.png** *Source:* https://upload.wikimedia.org/wikipedia/commons/4/44/RosemaryEssentialOil.png *License:* Public domain *Contributors:* Own work *Original artist:* Itineranttrader
- **File:Rosemary_(▯▯▯▯▯▯).JPG** *Source:* https://upload.wikimedia.org/wikipedia/commons/e/e6/Rosemary_%28%E0%A6%B0%E0%A7%8B%E0%A6%9C%E0%A6%AE%E0%A7%87%E0%A6%B0%E0%A7%80%29.JPG *License:* CC BY-SA 4.0 *Contributors:* Own work *Original artist:* Atudu
- **File:Rosemary_in_bloom.JPG** *Source:* https://upload.wikimedia.org/wikipedia/commons/a/a3/Rosemary_in_bloom.JPG *License:* CC BY-SA 4.0 *Contributors:* Own work *Original artist:* Margalob
- **File:Rosmarinus_officinalis_MHNT.BOT.2008.1.19.jpg** *Source:* https://upload.wikimedia.org/wikipedia/commons/0/09/Rosmarinus_officinalis_MHNT.BOT.2008.1.19.jpg *License:* CC BY-SA 3.0 *Contributors:* Own work *Original artist:* Roger Culos
- **File:Rosmarinus_officinalis_prostratus.jpg** *Source:* https://upload.wikimedia.org/wikipedia/commons/d/d9/Rosmarinus_officinalis_prostratus.jpg *License:* CC BY-SA 3.0 *Contributors:* Own work *Original artist:* Petar43
- **File:Rubber,_or_Banyan_Tree,_on_Banana_River,_Florida.jpg** *Source:* https://upload.wikimedia.org/wikipedia/commons/a/a9/Rubber%2C_or_Banyan_Tree%2C_on_Banana_River%2C_Florida.jpg *License:* Public domain *Contributors:* Reproduced from an original duotone print from *America's Wonderlands,* Historical Publishing Company, Philadelphia, Pennsylvania *Original artist:* James W. Buel
- **File:S12863-014-0152-1-3.gif** *Source:* https://upload.wikimedia.org/wikipedia/commons/0/00/S12863-014-0152-1-3.gif *License:* CC BY 4.0 *Contributors:* http://www.biomedcentral.com/1471-2156/15/152/figure/F3 *Original artist:* Franck Curk, Gema Ancillo, Andres Garcia-Lor, François Luro, Xavier Perrier, Jean-Pierre Jacquemoud-Collet, Luis Navarro and Patrick Ollitrault
- **File:Sago_Palm.jpg** *Source:* https://upload.wikimedia.org/wikipedia/commons/2/2d/Sago_Palm.jpg *License:* CC BY 2.0 *Contributors:* Flickr *Original artist:* Nadia Prigoda from Toronto, Canada
- **File:Sakura_Tree_Blossom_-_Turkey,_Ankara,_Dikmen_Vâdisi_-_Spring,_2015.jpg** *Source:* https://upload.wikimedia.org/wikipedia/commons/0/07/Sakura_Tree_Blossom_-_Turkey%2C_Ankara%2C_Dikmen_V%C3%A2disi_-_Spring%2C_2015.jpg *License:* CC BY-SA 4.0 *Contributors:* Own work *Original artist:* AhmedHan
- **File:Sakura_and_Moss_Pink_-_▯(▯▯▯)▯▯▯(▯▯▯▯▯).jpg** *Source:* https://upload.wikimedia.org/wikipedia/commons/9/96/Sakura_and_Moss_Pink_-_%E6%A1%9C%28%E3%81%95%E3%81%8F%E3%82%89%29%E3%81%A8%E8%8A%9D%E6%A1%9C%28%E3%81%97%E3%81%B0%E3%81%96%E3%81%8F%E3%82%89%29.jpg *License:* CC BY 2.0 *Contributors:* Sakura and Moss Pink / 桜 (さくら) と芝桜 (しばざくら) *Original artist:* TANAKA Juuyoh (田中十洋)
- **File:Sakura_yu.jpg** *Source:* https://upload.wikimedia.org/wikipedia/commons/6/67/Sakura_yu.jpg *License:* CC-BY-SA-3.0 *Contributors:* Own work *Original artist:* Suguri F
- **File:Sakura_yu2.jpg** *Source:* https://upload.wikimedia.org/wikipedia/commons/6/6e/Sakura_yu2.jpg *License:* CC BY-SA 2.5 *Contributors:* Own work *Original artist:* Suguri F

4.2. IMAGES

- **File:Sargent_Juniper,_1905-2007.jpg** *Source:* https://upload.wikimedia.org/wikipedia/commons/6/6e/Sargent_Juniper%2C_1905-2007.jpg *License:* CC-BY-SA-3.0 *Contributors:* Own work *Original artist:* Ragesoss
- **File:Sawara_Falsecypress_Chamaecyparis_pisifera_Bark_2000px.jpg** *Source:* https://upload.wikimedia.org/wikipedia/commons/a/a2/Sawara_Falsecypress_Chamaecyparis_pisifera_Bark_2000px.jpg *License:* GFDL 1.2 *Contributors:* Own work (Own Picture) *Original artist:* Photo by and (c)2007 Derek Ramsey (Ram-Man)
- **File:Sawara_Falsecypress_Chamaecyparis_pisifera_Sprig_3008px.jpg** *Source:* https://upload.wikimedia.org/wikipedia/commons/5/5c/Sawara_Falsecypress_Chamaecyparis_pisifera_Sprig_3008px.jpg *License:* GFDL 1.2 *Contributors:* Own work (Own Picture) *Original artist:* Photo by and (c)2007 Derek Ramsey (Ram-Man)
- **File:Sawara_Falsecypress_Chamaecyparis_pisifera_Tree_2000px.jpg** *Source:* https://upload.wikimedia.org/wikipedia/commons/d/d1/Sawara_Falsecypress_Chamaecyparis_pisifera_Tree_2000px.jpg *License:* GFDL 1.2 *Contributors:* Self-photographed *Original artist:* Photo by and (c)2007 Derek Ramsey (Ram-Man)
- **File:Schefflera_gabriellae_MHNT.BOT.2010.6.60.jpg** *Source:* https://upload.wikimedia.org/wikipedia/commons/8/8b/Schefflera_gabriellae_MHNT.BOT.2010.6.60.jpg *License:* CC BY-SA 3.0 *Contributors:* Own work *Original artist:* Jean-Pierre Chéreau & Roger Culos
- **File:Schefflera_venulosa_20a.JPG** *Source:* https://upload.wikimedia.org/wikipedia/commons/6/62/Schefflera_venulosa_20a.JPG *License:* CC BY-SA 3.0 *Contributors:* Own work *Original artist:* Vinayaraj
- **File:Schwarze_Oliven.jpg** *Source:* https://upload.wikimedia.org/wikipedia/commons/0/01/Schwarze_Oliven.jpg *License:* CC BY-SA 4.0 *Contributors:* Own work *Original artist:* Marco Almbauer
- **File:Scrub_Pine_Pinus_virginiana_3264px.jpg** *Source:* https://upload.wikimedia.org/wikipedia/commons/5/5f/Scrub_Pine_Pinus_virginiana_3264px.jpg *License:* GFDL 1.2 *Contributors:* Self-photographed *Original artist:* Photo (c)2007 Derek Ramsey (Ram-Man)
- **File:Scrub_Pine_Pinus_virginiana_Cone_Closeup_2000px.jpg** *Source:* https://upload.wikimedia.org/wikipedia/commons/9/97/Scrub_Pine_Pinus_virginiana_Cone_Closeup_2000px.jpg *License:* GFDL 1.2 *Contributors:* Own work (Own Picture) *Original artist:* Photo (c)2007 Derek Ramsey (Ram-Man)
- **File:Scrub_Pine_Pinus_virginiana_Trunk_Bark_2000px.jpg** *Source:* https://upload.wikimedia.org/wikipedia/commons/e/e2/Scrub_Pine_Pinus_virginiana_Trunk_Bark_2000px.jpg *License:* GFDL 1.2 *Contributors:* Self-photographed *Original artist:* Photo (c)2007 Derek Ramsey (Ram-Man)
- **File:Sendai_Tansu.jpg** *Source:* https://upload.wikimedia.org/wikipedia/commons/a/a5/Sendai_Tansu.jpg *License:* CC BY-SA 3.0 *Contributors:* Transferred from en.wikipedia to Commons. *Original artist:* The original uploader was Kunchan at English Wikipedia
- **File:Shodoshima_Olive_Park_Shodo_Island_Japan23bs34.jpg** *Source:* https://upload.wikimedia.org/wikipedia/commons/b/b7/Shodoshima_Olive_Park_Shodo_Island_Japan23bs34.jpg *License:* CC BY 2.5 *Contributors:* Own work *Original artist:* 663highland
- **File:Shoku.JPG** *Source:* https://upload.wikimedia.org/wikipedia/commons/f/f7/Shoku.JPG *License:* CC BY-SA 3.0 *Contributors:* Own work *Original artist:* Diako1971
- **File:Sierra_Madre_Wistaria_Festival_2016_01.jpg** *Source:* https://upload.wikimedia.org/wikipedia/commons/3/3f/Sierra_Madre_Wistaria_Festival_2016_01.jpg *License:* CC BY-SA 4.0 *Contributors:* Own work *Original artist:* Patrick Pelletier
- **File:Silver-back,_GSBF-CN_247,_September_12,_2008.jpg** *Source:* https://upload.wikimedia.org/wikipedia/commons/b/b8/Silver-back%2C_GSBF-CN_247%2C_September_12%2C_2008.jpg *License:* CC-BY-SA-3.0 *Contributors:* Own work *Original artist:* Sage Ross
- **File:Small-leaved_Elm_Ulmus_minor_bonsai_257,_December_24,_2008.jpg** *Source:* https://upload.wikimedia.org/wikipedia/commons/6/62/Small-leaved_Elm_Ulmus_minor_bonsai_257%2C_December_24%2C_2008.jpg *License:* CC BY-SA 3.0 *Contributors:* Own work *Original artist:* Sage Ross
- **File:Snow_on_Cycas_revoluta.jpg** *Source:* https://upload.wikimedia.org/wikipedia/commons/c/c7/Snow_on_Cycas_revoluta.jpg *License:* CC BY-SA 3.0 *Contributors:* Own work by the original uploader *Original artist:* Umais Bin Sajjad
- **File:Southafrica430yellowwood.jpg** *Source:* https://upload.wikimedia.org/wikipedia/commons/0/0f/Southafrica430yellowwood.jpg *License:* CC-BY-SA-3.0 *Contributors:* Transferred from en.wikipedia to Commons by Innotata using CommonsHelper. *Original artist:* Jimfbleak at English Wikipedia
- **File:Stand_of_birch_trees.jpg** *Source:* https://upload.wikimedia.org/wikipedia/en/c/cf/Stand_of_birch_trees.jpg *License:* CC-BY-3.0 *Contributors:* ? *Original artist:* ?
- **File:Starr_010820-0009_Carissa_macrocarpa.jpg** *Source:* https://upload.wikimedia.org/wikipedia/commons/1/17/Starr_010820-0009_Carissa_macrocarpa.jpg *License:* CC BY 3.0 *Contributors:* Plants of Hawaii, Image 010820-0009 from http://www.hear.org/starr/plants/images/image/?q=010820-0009 *Original artist:* Forest & Kim Starr
- **File:Starr_040514-0204_Ficus_microcarpa.jpg** *Source:* https://upload.wikimedia.org/wikipedia/commons/f/f4/Starr_040514-0204_Ficus_microcarpa.jpg *License:* CC BY 3.0 *Contributors:* Plants of Hawaii, Image 040514-0204 from http://www.hear.org/starr/plants/images/image/?q=040514-0204 *Original artist:* Forest & Kim Starr
- **File:Starr_080601-5190_Ficus_microcarpa.jpg** *Source:* https://upload.wikimedia.org/wikipedia/commons/7/78/Starr_080601-5190_Ficus_microcarpa.jpg *License:* CC BY 3.0 *Contributors:* Plants of Hawaii, Image 080601-5190 from http://www.hear.org/starr/plants/images/image/?q=080601-5190 *Original artist:* Forest & Kim Starr
- **File:Stickling2.jpg** *Source:* https://upload.wikimedia.org/wikipedia/commons/8/8c/Stickling2.jpg *License:* CC-BY-SA-3.0 *Contributors:* ? *Original artist:* User Chrizz on sv.wikipedia
- **File:Sweetie_(Citrus).jpg** *Source:* https://upload.wikimedia.org/wikipedia/commons/8/8c/Sweetie_%28Citrus%29.jpg *License:* CC-BY-SA-3.0 *Contributors:* Own work *Original artist:* Yot (he:משתמש)

- **File:Swiss_National_Park_007.JPG** *Source:* https://upload.wikimedia.org/wikipedia/commons/7/74/Swiss_National_Park_007.JPG *License:* CC BY-SA 3.0 *Contributors:* Own work: Hansueli Krapf (User Simisa (talk · contribs)) *Original artist:* Hansueli Krapf
- **File:Symbol_book_class2.svg** *Source:* https://upload.wikimedia.org/wikipedia/commons/8/89/Symbol_book_class2.svg *License:* CC BY-SA 2.5 *Contributors:* Mad by Lokal_Profil by combining: *Original artist:* Lokal_Profil
- **File:Syr.vulg.Charles_Joly.jpg** *Source:* https://upload.wikimedia.org/wikipedia/commons/8/86/Syr.vulg.Charles_Joly.jpg *License:* CC-BY-SA-3.0 *Contributors:* ? *Original artist:* ?
- **File:Syringa.vulgaris(01).jpg** *Source:* https://upload.wikimedia.org/wikipedia/commons/a/ac/Syringa.vulgaris%2801%29.jpg *License:* CC-BY-SA-3.0 *Contributors:* ? *Original artist:* ?
- **File:SyringaVulgarisCorondel1a.UME.jpg** *Source:* https://upload.wikimedia.org/wikipedia/commons/b/b7/SyringaVulgarisCorondel1a.UME.jpg *License:* CC BY 2.5 *Contributors:* Own work *Original artist:* Ulf Eliasson
- **File:SyringaVulgarisEtna2b.UME.jpg** *Source:* https://upload.wikimedia.org/wikipedia/commons/8/84/SyringaVulgarisEtna2b.UME.jpg *License:* CC BY 2.5 *Contributors:* Own work *Original artist:* Ulf Eliasson
- **File:SyringaVulgarisMarechalFock1a.UME.jpg** *Source:* https://upload.wikimedia.org/wikipedia/commons/3/35/SyringaVulgarisMarechalFock1a.UME.jpg *License:* CC BY 2.5 *Contributors:* Own work *Original artist:* Ulf Eliasson
- **File:SyringaVulgarisMmeFrancisqueMorel1UME.jpg** *Source:* https://upload.wikimedia.org/wikipedia/commons/5/53/SyringaVulgarisMmeFrancisqueMorel1UME.jpg *License:* CC BY 2.5 *Contributors:* Own work *Original artist:* Ulf Eliasson
- **File:Syringa_vulgaris_wood_1.jpg** *Source:* https://upload.wikimedia.org/wikipedia/commons/1/13/Syringa_vulgaris_wood_1.jpg *License:* CC BY-SA 3.0 *Contributors:* Own work *Original artist:* Dominik Matus
- **File:Sügise_märgid.jpg** *Source:* https://upload.wikimedia.org/wikipedia/commons/5/59/S%C3%BCgise_m%C3%A4rgid.jpg *License:* CC BY-SA 4.0 *Contributors:* Own work *Original artist:* Aleksander Kaasik
- **File:Tang_dynasty_penzai.JPG** *Source:* https://upload.wikimedia.org/wikipedia/commons/d/df/Tang_dynasty_penzai.JPG *License:* Public domain *Contributors:* mybook *Original artist:* anon
- **File:Taphrina_amentorum_gall.JPG** *Source:* https://upload.wikimedia.org/wikipedia/commons/a/a4/Taphrina_amentorum_gall.JPG *License:* Public domain *Contributors:* Own work *Original artist:* Rosser1954 Roger Griffith
- **File:Taphrina_amentorum_tongue_gall.JPG** *Source:* https://upload.wikimedia.org/wikipedia/commons/8/8e/Taphrina_amentorum_tongue_gall.JPG *License:* Public domain *Contributors:* Own work *Original artist:* Rosser1954 Roger Griffith
- **File:Taxodium_ascendens.jpg** *Source:* https://upload.wikimedia.org/wikipedia/commons/4/4d/Taxodium_ascendens.jpg *License:* Public domain *Contributors:* ? *Original artist:* ?
- **File:Taxodium_ascendens_in_the_Black_Water,_Okefenokee.jpg** *Source:* https://upload.wikimedia.org/wikipedia/commons/d/d9/Taxodium_ascendens_in_the_Black_Water%2C_Okefenokee.jpg *License:* CC BY 2.0 *Contributors:* Mangroves in the Black Water *Original artist:* Clinton Steeds from Los Angeles, USA
- **File:Taxodium_distichum02.jpg** *Source:* https://upload.wikimedia.org/wikipedia/commons/e/eb/Taxodium_distichum02.jpg *License:* Public domain *Contributors:* Own work *Original artist:* Androstachys
- **File:Taxus_baccata_MHNT.jpg** *Source:* https://upload.wikimedia.org/wikipedia/commons/3/31/Taxus_baccata_MHNT.jpg *License:* CC BY-SA 4.0 *Contributors:* Own work *Original artist:* Didier Descouens
- **File:Taxus_baccata_MHNT_seed.jpg** *Source:* https://upload.wikimedia.org/wikipedia/commons/d/d6/Taxus_baccata_MHNT_seed.jpg *License:* CC BY-SA 4.0 *Contributors:* Own work *Original artist:* Didier Descouens
- **File:Taxus_cuspidata_fruits.JPG** *Source:* https://upload.wikimedia.org/wikipedia/commons/f/f3/Taxus_cuspidata_fruits.JPG *License:* CC BY-SA 3.0 *Contributors:* Own work *Original artist:* Alpsdake
- **File:Taxus_media.JPG** *Source:* https://upload.wikimedia.org/wikipedia/commons/2/21/Taxus_media.JPG *License:* CC0 *Contributors:* Own work *Original artist:* Anand Kulanthaivel
- **File:Tetraclinis_articulata.JPG** *Source:* https://upload.wikimedia.org/wikipedia/commons/0/04/Tetraclinis_articulata.JPG *License:* CC BY-SA 3.0 *Contributors:* Own work *Original artist:* Cs california
- **File:Tetraclinis_articulata8.jpg** *Source:* https://upload.wikimedia.org/wikipedia/commons/3/3b/Tetraclinis_articulata8.jpg *License:* Public domain *Contributors:* Own work *Original artist:* Nanosanchez
- **File:Tetraclinis_articulata_-_Köhler–s_Medizinal-Pflanzen-270.jpg** *Source:* https://upload.wikimedia.org/wikipedia/commons/0/02/Tetraclinis_articulata_-_K%C3%B6hler%E2%80%93s_Medizinal-Pflanzen-270.jpg *License:* Public domain *Contributors:* List of Koehler Images *Original artist:* Franz Eugen Köhler, *Köhler's Medizinal-Pflanzen*
- **File:Tetraclinis_articulata_MHNT.BOT.2007.52.39.jpg** *Source:* https://upload.wikimedia.org/wikipedia/commons/6/66/Tetraclinis_articulata_MHNT.BOT.2007.52.39.jpg *License:* CC BY-SA 3.0 *Contributors:* Own work *Original artist:* Roger Culos
- **File:TexasEbony.JPG** *Source:* https://upload.wikimedia.org/wikipedia/commons/c/ca/TexasEbony.JPG *License:* CC BY-SA 4.0 *Contributors:* Own work *Original artist:* Mpinedag
- **File:Text_document_with_red_question_mark.svg** *Source:* https://upload.wikimedia.org/wikipedia/commons/a/a4/Text_document_with_red_question_mark.svg *License:* Public domain *Contributors:* Created by bdesham with Inkscape; based upon Text-x-generic.svg from the Tango project. *Original artist:* Benjamin D. Esham (bdesham)
- **File:The_Llangernyw_yew.jpg** *Source:* https://upload.wikimedia.org/wikipedia/commons/0/03/The_Llangernyw_yew.jpg *License:* CC BY-SA 3.0 *Contributors:* Own work *Original artist:* Emgaol

4.2. IMAGES

- **File:Thunderhead_Japanese_Black_Pine.JPG** *Source:* https://upload.wikimedia.org/wikipedia/commons/2/27/Thunderhead_Japanese_Black_Pine.JPG *License:* CC BY-SA 4.0 *Contributors:* Own work *Original artist:* Greg Hume
- **File:Tokyo_Imperial_Palace_pic_08.jpg** *Source:* https://upload.wikimedia.org/wikipedia/commons/0/08/Tokyo_Imperial_Palace_pic_08.jpg *License:* Public domain *Contributors:* [1] *Original artist:* Ukiyo-e artist
- **File:Tree_dsc00856.jpg** *Source:* https://upload.wikimedia.org/wikipedia/commons/3/36/Tree_dsc00856.jpg *License:* CC-BY-SA-3.0 *Contributors:* ? *Original artist:* ?
- **File:Tree_template.svg** *Source:* https://upload.wikimedia.org/wikipedia/commons/9/98/Tree_template.svg *License:* CC BY-SA 3.0 *Contributors:*

  - File:Tango icon nature.svg
  - File:Blank_template.svg

  Original artist:

  - DarKobra
  - Urutseg
  - Ain92

- **File:Treestub.jpg** *Source:* https://upload.wikimedia.org/wikipedia/commons/1/1b/Treestub.jpg *License:* CC-BY-SA-3.0 *Contributors:* Transferred from en.wikipedia to Commons by Rockfang. *Original artist:* The original uploader was MPF at English Wikipedia
- **File:Trident_Maple_Acer_buegerianum_Bark_Horizontal.JPG** *Source:* https://upload.wikimedia.org/wikipedia/commons/a/a2/Trident_Maple_Acer_buegerianum_Bark_Horizontal.JPG *License:* CC BY-SA 4.0 *Contributors:* Self-photographed *Original artist:* Photo by and (c)2016 Derek Ramsey (Ram-Man)
- **File:Trident_Maple_bonsai_202,_October_10,_2008.jpg** *Source:* https://upload.wikimedia.org/wikipedia/commons/d/db/Trident_Maple_bonsai_202%2C_October_10%2C_2008.jpg *License:* CC-BY-SA-3.0 *Contributors:* Own work *Original artist:* Sage Ross
- **File:Tsubo-en_Wisteria_seasons-356x267-Opt.gif** *Source:* https://upload.wikimedia.org/wikipedia/commons/9/9e/Tsubo-en_Wisteria_seasons-356x267-Opt.gif *License:* GFDL *Contributors:* Own work *Original artist:* http://www.zen-garden.org Karesansui Petrus M Patings
- **File:USA-Cherry_Blossom0.jpg** *Source:* https://upload.wikimedia.org/wikipedia/commons/8/8e/USA-Cherry_Blossom0.jpg *License:* CC BY-SA 3.0 *Contributors:* Own work *Original artist:* Ingfbruno
- **File:Ukon.JPG** *Source:* https://upload.wikimedia.org/wikipedia/commons/4/47/Ukon.JPG *License:* CC-BY-SA-3.0 *Contributors:* ? *Original artist:* ?
- **File:Ulivone.jpg** *Source:* https://upload.wikimedia.org/wikipedia/commons/b/b5/Ulivone.jpg *License:* Public domain *Contributors:* Own work *Original artist:* Emanuele.tommasino
- **File:Ulmus-leave_20040126_part1.jpg** *Source:* https://upload.wikimedia.org/wikipedia/commons/7/74/Ulmus-leave_20040126_part1.jpg *License:* CC-BY-SA-3.0 *Contributors:* ? *Original artist:* ?
- **File:Ulmus_Parvifolia.JPG** *Source:* https://upload.wikimedia.org/wikipedia/commons/3/32/Ulmus_Parvifolia.JPG *License:* Public domain *Contributors:* Own work *Original artist:* 1000Faces
- **File:Ulmus_crassifolia_(USDA).jpg** *Source:* https://upload.wikimedia.org/wikipedia/commons/2/26/Ulmus_crassifolia_%28USDA%29.jpg *License:* Public domain *Contributors:* ? *Original artist:* ?
- **File:Ulmus_parvifolia,_juvenile.jpg** *Source:* https://upload.wikimedia.org/wikipedia/commons/2/25/Ulmus_parvifolia%2C_juvenile.jpg *License:* Public domain *Contributors:* Transferred from en.wikipedia *Original artist:* HelloMojo at en.wikipedia
- **File:Unknown_Ulmus._Calton_Hill_Park,_Edinburgh_(3).jpg** *Source:* https://upload.wikimedia.org/wikipedia/commons/4/43/Unknown_Ulmus._Calton_Hill_Park%2C_Edinburgh_%283%29.jpg *License:* CC BY-SA 4.0 *Contributors:* Own work *Original artist:* Tom elm
- **File:Unripened_pomegranate.jpg** *Source:* https://upload.wikimedia.org/wikipedia/commons/e/e9/Unripened_pomegranate.jpg *License:* CC BY-SA 3.0 *Contributors:* Own work *Original artist:* HitroMilanese
- **File:Unterspreewald-Gross-Wasserburger-Spree-01.jpg** *Source:* https://upload.wikimedia.org/wikipedia/commons/a/a0/Unterspreewald-Gross-Wasserburger-Spree-01.jpg *License:* CC-BY-SA-3.0 *Contributors:* Photo of myself (19.12.2006). - selbst fotografiert (own work) *Original artist:* Botaurus-stellaris
- **File:Uprooted_bonsai.jpg** *Source:* https://upload.wikimedia.org/wikipedia/commons/6/61/Uprooted_bonsai.jpg *License:* CC BY-SA 2.0 *Contributors:* This image was originally posted to **Flickr** as Uprooted bonsai (just a bit cropped) *Original artist:* ericskiff/Glitch010101
- **File:View_from_the_Barouk_Forest_1.JPG** *Source:* https://upload.wikimedia.org/wikipedia/commons/e/ed/View_from_the_Barouk_Forest_1.JPG *License:* Public domain *Contributors:* Transferred from en.wikipedia to Commons by SreeBot. *Original artist:* Yhabbouche at en.wikipedia
- **File:VulgarisAlba1bbUME.jpg** *Source:* https://upload.wikimedia.org/wikipedia/commons/6/61/VulgarisAlba1bbUME.jpg *License:* CC BY 2.5 *Contributors:* Own work *Original artist:* Ulf Eliasson
- **File:Washington_C_D.C._Tidal_Basin_cherry_trees.jpg** *Source:* https://upload.wikimedia.org/wikipedia/commons/5/56/Washington_C_D.C._Tidal_Basin_cherry_trees.jpg *License:* Public domain *Contributors:* United States Department of Agriculture *Original artist:* USDA photo by Scott Bauer

- **File:Weeping-fig_Ficus-benjamina.jpg** *Source:* https://upload.wikimedia.org/wikipedia/commons/0/04/Weeping-fig_Ficus-benjamina.jpg *License:* CC-BY-SA-3.0 *Contributors:* ? *Original artist:* ?
- **File:Weeping_Fig_(Ficus_benjamina)_in_Hyderabad,_AP_W_IMG_7645.jpg** *Source:* https://upload.wikimedia.org/wikipedia/commons/5/5c/Weeping_Fig_%28Ficus_benjamina%29_in_Hyderabad%2C_AP_W_IMG_7645.jpg *License:* GFDL *Contributors:* Own work *Original artist:* J.M.Garg
- **File:White_Sakura_Cherry_Blossoms.jpg** *Source:* https://upload.wikimedia.org/wikipedia/commons/9/9b/White_Sakura_Cherry_Blossoms.jpg *License:* CC BY-SA 3.0 *Contributors:* Photograph *Original artist:* HRae
- **File:White_pine_shedding_old_foliage_in_autumn.jpg** *Source:* https://upload.wikimedia.org/wikipedia/commons/2/24/White_pine_shedding_old_foliage_in_autumn.jpg *License:* CC BY-SA 3.0 *Contributors:* Own work *Original artist:* DigbyDalton
- **File:Wikibooks-logo-en-noslogan.svg** *Source:* https://upload.wikimedia.org/wikipedia/commons/d/df/Wikibooks-logo-en-noslogan.svg *License:* CC BY-SA 3.0 *Contributors:* Own work *Original artist:* User:Bastique, User:Ramac et al.
- **File:Wikibooks-logo.svg** *Source:* https://upload.wikimedia.org/wikipedia/commons/f/fa/Wikibooks-logo.svg *License:* CC BY-SA 3.0 *Contributors:* Own work *Original artist:* User:Bastique, User:Ramac et al.
- **File:Wikidata-logo.svg** *Source:* https://upload.wikimedia.org/wikipedia/commons/f/ff/Wikidata-logo.svg *License:* Public domain *Contributors:* Own work *Original artist:* User:Planemad
- **File:Wikinews-logo.svg** *Source:* https://upload.wikimedia.org/wikipedia/commons/2/24/Wikinews-logo.svg *License:* CC BY-SA 3.0 *Contributors:* This is a cropped version of Image:Wikinews-logo-en.png. *Original artist:* Vectorized by Simon 01:05, 2 August 2006 (UTC) Updated by Time3000 17 April 2007 to use official Wikinews colours and appear correctly on dark backgrounds. Originally uploaded by Simon.
- **File:Wikiquote-logo.svg** *Source:* https://upload.wikimedia.org/wikipedia/commons/f/fa/Wikiquote-logo.svg *License:* Public domain *Contributors:* Own work *Original artist:* Rei-artur
- **File:Wikisource-logo.svg** *Source:* https://upload.wikimedia.org/wikipedia/commons/4/4c/Wikisource-logo.svg *License:* CC BY-SA 3.0 *Contributors:* Rei-artur *Original artist:* Nicholas Moreau
- **File:Wikispecies-logo.svg** *Source:* https://upload.wikimedia.org/wikipedia/commons/d/df/Wikispecies-logo.svg *License:* CC BY-SA 3.0 *Contributors:* Image:Wikispecies-logo.jpg *Original artist:* (of code) cs:User:-xfi-
- **File:Wikiversity-logo-Snorky.svg** *Source:* https://upload.wikimedia.org/wikipedia/commons/1/1b/Wikiversity-logo-en.svg *License:* CC BY-SA 3.0 *Contributors:* Own work *Original artist:* Snorky
- **File:Wiktionary-logo-v2.svg** *Source:* https://upload.wikimedia.org/wikipedia/commons/0/06/Wiktionary-logo-v2.svg *License:* CC BY-SA 4.0 *Contributors:* Own work *Original artist:* Dan Polansky based on work currently attributed to Wikimedia Foundation but originally created by Smurrayinchester
- **File:Winged_Elm_Ulmus_alata_2009-05-10.jpg** *Source:* https://upload.wikimedia.org/wikipedia/commons/d/da/Winged_Elm_Ulmus_alata_2009-05-10.jpg *License:* CC BY-SA 3.0 *Contributors:* Own work *Original artist:* Gaberlunzi (Richard Murphy)
- **File:Wisteria_floribunda5.jpg** *Source:* https://upload.wikimedia.org/wikipedia/commons/d/da/Wisteria_floribunda5.jpg *License:* CC-BY-SA-3.0 *Contributors:* ? *Original artist:* ?
- **File:Wisteria_floribunda_MHNT.BOT.2008.1.38.jpg** *Source:* https://upload.wikimedia.org/wikipedia/commons/d/d5/Wisteria_floribunda_MHNT.BOT.2008.1.38.jpg *License:* CC BY-SA 3.0 *Contributors:* Own work *Original artist:* Roger Culos
- **File:Wisteria_sinensis_weed.jpg** *Source:* https://upload.wikimedia.org/wikipedia/commons/8/87/Wisteria_sinensis_weed.jpg *License:* Public domain *Contributors:* Own work *Original artist:* Nadiatalent
- **File:WuhanPenjing1.jpg** *Source:* https://upload.wikimedia.org/wikipedia/commons/0/0b/WuhanPenjing1.jpg *License:* CC SA 1.0 *Contributors:* ? *Original artist:* ?
- **File:Yaiza_La_Hoya_-_LZ-2-LZ-703_-_Portulacaria_afra_02_ies.jpg** *Source:* https://upload.wikimedia.org/wikipedia/commons/d/d5/Yaiza_La_Hoya_-_LZ-2-LZ-703_-_Portulacaria_afra_02_ies.jpg *License:* CC BY-SA 3.0 *Contributors:* Own work *Original artist:* Frank Vincentz
- **File:Yemenite.jpg** *Source:* https://upload.wikimedia.org/wikipedia/commons/9/91/Yemenite.jpg *License:* Public domain *Contributors:* Own work *Original artist:* BlackDot
- **File:Yoshitoshi_The_Spirit_of_the_Komachi_Cherry_Tree.jpg** *Source:* https://upload.wikimedia.org/wikipedia/commons/8/8c/Yoshitoshi_The_Spirit_of_the_Komachi_Cherry_Tree.jpg *License:* Public domain *Contributors:* ? *Original artist:* ?
- **File:Zelkova_serrata5.jpg** *Source:* https://upload.wikimedia.org/wikipedia/commons/b/bb/Zelkova_serrata5.jpg *License:* CC-BY-SA-3.0 *Contributors:* KENPEI's photo *Original artist:* KENPEI
- **File:Zelkova_serrata_entire.jpg** *Source:* https://upload.wikimedia.org/wikipedia/commons/1/19/Zelkova_serrata_entire.jpg *License:* CC BY-SA 2.5 *Contributors:* Own work http://www.cirrusimage.com/tree_Japanese_zelkova.htm *Original artist:* Bruce Marlin
- **File:Zelkova_serrata_in_Oasa_HigashimachiPark_Ebetsu,_Hokkaido_2.jpg** *Source:* https://upload.wikimedia.org/wikipedia/commons/f/f0/Zelkova_serrata_in_Oasa_HigashimachiPark_Ebetsu%2C_Hokkaido_2.jpg *License:* CC BY-SA 3.0 *Contributors:* Own work *Original artist:* タクナワン
- **File:Zelkova_serrata_japan-2006.jpg** *Source:* https://upload.wikimedia.org/wikipedia/commons/d/df/Zelkova_serrata_japan-2006.jpg *License:* Public domain *Contributors:* No machine-readable source provided. Own work assumed (based on copyright claims). *Original artist:* No machine-readable author provided. Kici assumed (based on copyright claims).
- **File:Zelkova_serrata_ケヤキ(欅)_DSCF2794.jpg** *Source:* https://upload.wikimedia.org/wikipedia/commons/7/7b/Zelkova_serrata_%E3%82%B1%E3%83%A4%E3%82%AD%EF%BC%88%E6%AC%85%29_DSCF2794.jpg *License:* CC BY-SA 3.0 *Contributors:* Own work *Original artist:* 松岡明芳

- **File:Zosterops_palpebrosus_2.jpg** *Source:* https://upload.wikimedia.org/wikipedia/commons/1/1e/Zosterops_palpebrosus_2.jpg *License:* CC BY-SA 2.0 *Contributors:* Oriental White-eye (Zosterops palpebrosus) *Original artist:* Lip Kee Yap from Singapore, Republic of Singapore
- **File:Zwiesel_2014_-_5_044.JPG** *Source:* https://upload.wikimedia.org/wikipedia/commons/4/43/Zwiesel_2014_-_5_044.JPG *License:* CC BY-SA 3.0 *Contributors:* Own work *Original artist:* Rosa-Maria Rinkl
- **File:Бор_кривул_01.JPG** *Source:* https://upload.wikimedia.org/wikipedia/commons/f/fd/%D0%91%D0%BE%D1%80_%D0%BA%D1%80%D0%B8%D0%B2%D1%83%D0%BB_01.JPG *License:* CC BY-SA 4.0 *Contributors:* Own work *Original artist:* Македонец

4.3 Content license

- Creative Commons Attribution-Share Alike 3.0

Printed in Poland
by Amazon Fulfillment
Poland Sp. z o.o., Wrocław